[incr Tcl/Tk]
from the Ground Up

Chad Smith

D1601872

Osborne/**McGraw-Hill**

Berkeley   New York   St. Louis   San Francisco
Auckland   Bogotá   Hamburg   London   Madrid
Mexico City   Milan   Montreal   New Delhi   Panama City
Paris   São Paulo   Singapore   Sydney
Tokyo   Toronto

Osborne/**McGraw-Hill**
2600 Tenth Street
Berkeley, California 94710
U.S.A.

For information on translations or book distributors outside the U.S.A., or to arrange bulk purchase discounts for sales promotions, premiums, or fund-raisers, please contact Osborne/**McGraw-Hill** at the above address.

[incr Tcl/Tk] from the Ground Up

1234567890 AGM AGM 019876543210

ISBN 0-07-212106-8

Publisher
Brandon A. Nordin

Associate Publisher and Editor-in-Chief
Scott Rogers

Acquisitions Editor
Wendy Rinaldi

Project Editor
Cynthia Douglas

Acquisitions Coordinator
Monika Faltiss

Technical Editor
Peter Loveman

Copy Editor
Dennis Weaver

Proofreader
Doug Robert

Indexer
Rebecca Plunkett

Computer Designers
Gary Corrigan
Elizabeth Jang
Liz Pauw
Dick Schwartz

Illustrators
Beth Young
Robert Hansen
Brian Wells

Series Design
Peter Hancik

This book is dedicated to my granddad, Allen Smith, a.k.a. Papaw. He has been a role model for me as long as I can remember and has taught me countless lessons throughout my life. He is largely responsible for instilling in me a never quit attitude, encouraging me to work hard from start to finish no matter how long it takes and never settle for mediocrity. Many years ago he taught me something that I have never forgotten: A job worth doing is worth doing well. I have always tried to follow this in everything I do, and this book is no exception.

About the Author ...

Chad Smith is a software engineer at ADC Telecommunications in Richardson, Texas, where he writes mostly [incr Tcl] code for the front end to ADC's Cellworx™ product. Chad works in a network management group (NMIC) and has designed much of the graphical interface to Cellworx™, which is an ATM (Asynchronous Transfer Mode) network ring management system. He uses [incr Tcl] with other members of the NMIC group as the front end to a C++ application core to provide quick and convenient access for customers to configure, manage, and measure the performance of their networks. Chad has been programming in [incr Tcl] for four years.

Outside of work, Chad is a professional clarinetist with 16 years of playing experience and performs with various groups in the greater Dallas area. He enjoys music and teaching; he spent four years teaching music in public schools before venturing into the software and telecommunications industry. Chad also enjoys golf, woodworking, traveling, the outdoors, and spending time with his wife and family.

Contents

Foreword

Today, as I begin this foreword, I enter a new phase of my relationship with Tcl.

My first recollections relating to Tcl are of frustrations. I was a member of a Tcl mailing list that was pretty active. Fellow list members and I found ourselves hungry for more information on Tcl. This was in the days before John Ousterhout's book—before magazine coverage or Web pages of information. After asking, then later answering and watching others answer, the same questions a number of times, I began putting the bits of questions and answers, along with other items of interest into a FAQ. When the newsgroup began, more people discovered Tcl—and more questions arose. John's book came out, and still the questions came—different ones, but still more. I spent my time as a Tcl user rather than as a programmer. I also tried to act as an advocate. As new extensions were announced, I built them, read the doc, and recommended them.

Then three years ago I attended my first Tcl conference. What a blast to put faces to names! More books were being announced, and one of the themes I heard from other attendees was a need for more documentation!

Things have matured from that point. In the past few years, publishers post to the comp.lang.tcl newsgroup, as well as sending e-mail to some of us asking whether we knew of any people interested in writing books on Tcl. I would investigate and try to help make connections when I could.

In the summer of 1998, I scheduled a Scriptics class in [incr Tcl] to be given in the late fall. I wanted to extend my experience a bit and add a useful tool to my toolset. I had been signed up on the [incr Tcl] mailing list for some time, and noticed that there were lots of questions. I began asking on the mailing list for pointers to reference materials. In the fall of 1998, I attended another Tcl conference. During all the excitement of meeting various people, I made the acquaintance of Chad Smith. I was pleased to meet Chad, because his name was among the list of the [incr Tcl] mailing list members who consistently answered questions cheerfully, enthusiastically, and accurately— and provided fixes and so forth.

Just a few weeks after I returned from the conference, I attended the [incr Tcl] classes. I realized that as useful as [incr Tcl] was, to make the power available to the staff I support, I needed something more than man pages as reference. The next time a publisher contacted me looking for ideas about Tcl related books, I suggested a book centered around writing software using [incr Tcl]. When I was asked who would be best to write, I started asking around. Chad was one of the first people I contacted. He was busy, but apparently the idea caught his attention, because here we are, about to embark on an interesting adventure!

While reading this book as it has developed over the past year, I have been struck again and again with the impression that the choice for author of this book was one of the best that could have been made. Chad's style, thoroughness, and thoughtfulness has taught me much. I hope that you, too, find this book as useful as I have.

Larry W. Virden

Maintainer of the Tcl FAQ

www.purl.org/NET/Tcl-FAQ/

November 30, 1999

Acknowledgments

Thanks first and foremost to God above, without whom none of this would have been possible. The ease with which this book came together—from start to finish was a little more than eight months—can only be attributed to Him.

Thanks to my wonderful wife, Chris, who has put up with my writing every night and weekend for most of this year, while household chores and quality time often fell by the wayside. She's been nothing but patient and supportive throughout this project, and I couldn't have done it without her.

I have no doubt that I have the best and most supportive family and friends in the world. My parents and stepparents, sisters, grandparents, aunts, uncles, and cousins have been wonderfully supportive this year, as I often had to stay home and write instead of traveling to visit. I promise I'll be visiting more often now! The support and prayers of my family and friends will be forever appreciated.

Thanks to Larry Virden. Osborne contacted me on Larry's recommendation, so he is largely responsible for my writing this book. Not only that, but he also agreed at the onset to read each chapter as I completed it and give me feedback. Larry really went above and beyond and provided me with great insights and suggestions throughout the project. His numerous "what if you tried this" and "why don't you think about this" ideas helped me to make several chapters more solid and robust.

Thanks to Michael McLennan. Michael was instrumental in helping me lay out this book's chapters. He gave me great feedback on my original outline, which really helped me get the first few chapters completed. His detailed suggestions were extremely helpful, and his willingness to provide technical assistance when necessary and his supportive attitude were greatly appreciated. Michael also graciously took time out of his schedule to read more than half the chapters in the book just to give me a front cover quote. And of course, if it weren't for Michael, there would be no [incr Tcl]! Thanks a lot, Michael!

Thanks to Peter Loveman, technical editor extraordinaire. Peter patiently waded through all 750 pages of the book and was a great help to me in pointing out problems as they arose, checking all the code, and making several useful suggestions along the way.

Thanks to the wonderful folks I worked with at Osborne. Thanks to Wendy Rinaldi for giving me the chance to write this book. From our first conversation last December, she has been very supportive and has had nothing but kind words to say throughout the project. She didn't know me from Adam but had faith in me to write a solid, successful piece of work. Thanks for the opportunity, Wendy. Thanks to Monika Faltiss for being well organized and working with me throughout the year to keep the schedule on track. Thanks to Cynthia Douglas for keeping the project sailing smoothly. Cynthia was a great coordinator for copy edits and page proofs and really helped keep the last stages of the book on schedule. Thanks to Dennis "Eagle Eye" Weaver for his tireless copy editing. Dennis read through 750 pages of a technical book on a language he didn't know, which is a daunting task to say the least. He was a tremendous help to me in finalizing each chapter. Also many thanks to each of the folks behind the scenes at Osborne whom I didn't work with directly but helped to make this book possible: composition technicians Gary Corrigan, Elizabeth Jang, Liz Pauw, and Dick Schwartz; illustrators Beth Young, Robert Hansen, and Brian Wells; proofreader Doug Robert; and indexer Rebecca Plunkett.

Thanks to my employer, ADC Telecommunications. Thanks in particular to my manager, Michael Cooper, and the NMIC group. Michael was extremely supportive of me this year as I juggled my tasks at work with writing my book. Sometimes late nights of writing interfered with work, and I owe Michael a sincere thanks for his support and understanding. If everyone had a manager like Michael Cooper, attrition would be a thing of the past. Thanks also to Cuong Nguyen for "various consults as needed." I modeled the tracing classes in Chapters 5 and 7 after one of Cuong's designs. Cuong is an OO guru and has provided me with design skills that I used in the book. And thanks to Uma Gavani for the cool idea for the multiple inheritance example in Chapter 8.

Introduction

[incr Tcl] (pronounced ink-er tickle) is the object-oriented extension to Tcl and was created by Michael McLennan in 1993. Michael modeled [incr Tcl] after C++, even its name. C++ is the increment of C, and [incr Tcl] is how you write the increment of Tcl. This language is extremely powerful and yet is extremely easy to use. It has grown by leaps and bounds and has a tremendous following today, especially after it became a dynamically loadable extension to Tcl with the introduction of namespaces into the Tcl core in version 8.0.

So why did I write a book on [incr Tcl]? Well, the short answer is because I was given the opportunity to do so. I was contacted by Wendy Rinaldi from Osborne in December of last year and was asked if I'd be interested in writing a complete reference on Tcl. I told her I didn't feel technically proficient enough to write such a book, not to mention the fact that authors such as Brent Welch, John Ousterhout, and Cliff Flynt already have that market more than covered. I mentioned a popular and growing extension to Tcl, [incr Tcl], and that there were zero books devoted to it. We both did research and discovered that such a book would likely do quite well and was very much needed. That's how this book was born.

I began writing early this year after settling on a chapter outline. The approach I decided to take was one of teaching. As a result, this book fits well into Osborne's "from the Ground Up" series as opposed to the "Complete Reference" series. It's actually a mixture of both, because I view this book as a complete reference, but I approach it from the ground up. I spent several years teaching in public schools and rely on that background experience when I explain things to others. I try to be clear and concise and yet provide enough detail to cover all the bases. I also try to avoid the foo bar examples and implement ones that are useful and practical. Sometimes the foo bar types are used just to get a quick point across, but generally I try to make the examples fun and interesting.

Learning a new language shouldn't be a chore. It should be something you want to do and enjoy doing. This is how I approach teaching [incr Tcl] to others, and I hope that if you are brand new to this language you will enjoy learning it. On the other hand, if you are an [incr Tcl] expert, I promise you'll also learn from this book. I cover a wide variety of advanced topics in addition to all the language fundamentals. I think the reference chapter on the [incr Widgets] will be of particular interest to beginners and advanced programmers alike.

This book is organized like layers of an onion—each chapter generally builds on the next. I frequently reference previous chapters assuming you've read them, but you should be able to skip around and find topics of interest if you're already fairly comfortable with the language. The book is organized into three parts: [incr Tcl], [incr Tk], and [incr Widgets]. The following bullets provide a brief outline for each chapter.

Part I: [incr Tcl]

◆ **Chapter 1, "Getting Started"** This chapter provides a quick tour of [incr Tcl] fundamentals as well as a brief discussion of object-oriented programming in general.

◆ **Chapter 2, "Methods"** This chapter discusses everything you ever wanted to know about [incr Tcl] class methods.

◆ **Chapter 3, "Data Members"** Like Chapter 2's discussion on methods, this chapter discusses everything you ever wanted to know about [incr Tcl] class data members.

◆ **Chapter 4, "Construction and Destruction"** This is an "under the hood" chapter because it goes into great detail to describe what happens behind the scenes for the class definition and object construction/destruction processes.

◆ **Chapter 5, "Debugging"** If you're at all familiar with Tcl then the first part of the chapter will likely be nothing new to you, but the Trace class at the end of the chapter should be useful for you. Note that an alternative (and perhaps better) implementation of this class is provided in Chapter 7. The end of this chapter shows you how to add facilities in your applications for dynamic debugging.

◆ **Chapter 6, "Tying it all Together with Sockets"** I added this chapter because I really wanted to have a chapter that provided a larger scale example to integrate much of the information provided in the previous five chapters. You are walked through each phase of development from analysis to testing as a new client/server framework is designed and implemented.

◆ **Chapter 7, "Using Composition"** A debugging utility is provided at the beginning of the chapter that you should find quite useful in your applications, and a chat room model is implemented in the rest of the chapter as an example of how to take advantage of code reuse through composition.

◆ **Chapter 8, "Advanced Inheritance"** Simple inheritance hierarchies are provided in examples throughout the first several chapters. This chapter is devoted to more advanced topics such as virtual methods, abstract base classes, overloading, and multiple inheritance.

◆ **Chapter 9, "Integrating [incr Tcl] with C/C++"** This is the only chapter that isn't devoted to scripting. Most of the code is in C/C++, so you may have problems following along if you don't know either of these languages. If you ever wanted to know how to integrate [incr Tcl] with C or how to access C++ objects from [incr Tcl], this chapter is for you.

◆ **Chapter 10, "Namespaces and Packages"** Namespaces and packages are actually not specific to [incr Tcl]; rather, they're Tcl topics that are covered in other Tcl books. But I think you'll find this chapter useful and interesting even if you already know about namespaces and packages because I approach these topics with an [incr Tcl] slant.

Part II: [incr Tk]

◆ **Chapter 11, "Mega-Widget Basics"** What is a mega-widget? The answer to this question as well as a detailed discussion of the [incr Tk] base class hierarchy is provided in this chapter.

◆ **Chapter 12, "Configuration Options"** This chapter provides a detailed discussion of how to manage the composite option list when creating new mega-widgets.

Part III: [incr Widgets]

◆ **Chapter 13, "Introduction and Childsites"** This chapter provides a brief introduction to the Iwidgets package as well as a class hierarchy of the [incr Tk] and [incr Widget] framework. Childsites, which are an integral part of many of the [incr Widgets], are also discussed in this chapter.

◆ **Chapter 14, "Reference"** This is more of a reference section than a chapter. Each of the 50 [incr Widgets] is discussed in great detail in alphabetical order similar to man pages. You can use this chapter as a handy [incr Widgets] reference, or you can use it to quickly look through screen snapshots to find [incr Widgets] that can be used in your applications. This chapter should prove very useful to both beginning and advanced users.

What Version of [incr Tcl] Do You Need?

I used itcl3.0.1 (with iwidgets3.0.0 for chapters that use the Iwidgets package) built against tcl8.0.5 for all examples in this book. Version 8.1 of Tcl came out while I was writing, but I wanted to remain consistent and therefore stuck with 8.0.5. [incr Tcl] version 3.1.0 became available at the very end of the book, so I have not yet tested any code with this version. The latest version of Tcl, 8.2, will not work with itcl3.0.1, so if you are using this version of Tcl, make sure to use version 3.1.0 of [incr Tcl].

For those of you who are porting from pre-itcl3.x releases to itcl3.x, make sure to give yourself plenty of time, especially if you made extensive use of iwidgets2.2.0. The latest release of the [incr Widgets] includes numerous changes such as component widgets that no longer exist or have changed names, configuration options that no longer exist, inheritance structures that have changed, and so on. Refer to the [incr Widgets] reference section in Chapter 14 for help. I covered all of the [incr Widgets] in great detail, in part to help with porting efforts. Occasionally, I mention some potential pitfalls you can avoid or things that have changed between versions, but most examples assume you are using version 3.x only.

Conventions

Throughout the book there are several different formatting conventions that are consistently used. These are outlined as follows:

◆ Class names begin with an uppercase letter.

◆ All class methods are in *italics* when referenced in the text.

◆ All class data members have a leading underscore.

◆ Both static class methods and static data members are in all caps.

◆ All commands are shown in **bold** when referenced outside of code. This includes built-in Tcl and [incr Tcl] commands as well as class instance names.

◆ Method and procedure arguments have a trailing underscore.

◆ `All code is shown in this font.`

Errors

As with any large-scale project, this book is subject to the occasional typographical error. Several people have read and reread each chapter, and I personally took great pains to meticulously look for errors. But undoubtedly some mistakes have slipped through. Feel free to report any errors to me at csmith@adc.com or itclguy@yahoo.com.

PART I

[incr Tcl]

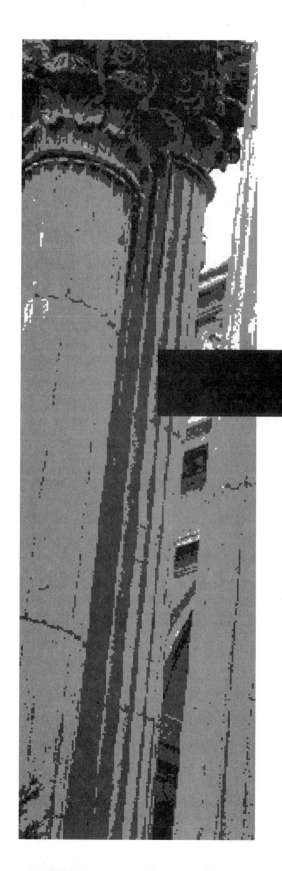

CHAPTER 1

Getting Started

This chapter presents a quick-start tutorial on the fundamentals of [incr Tcl]. It provides you with the means necessary to quickly begin designing and implementing [incr Tcl] applications. You start by learning about classes and objects, the most fundamental components of [incr Tcl], followed by detailed instructions on how to define classes in the Tk and [incr Tk] shells, **wish** and **itkwish**. You then learn how to create and use objects with a working dialog window example. Creating more robust designs is then discussed through an object-oriented concept called *inheritance*, and you learn how to expand the dialog window example into a class hierarchy and take advantage of software reuse. Finally, once you have a basic understanding of the building blocks of [incr Tcl], the fundamentals of object-oriented programming in general are discussed, and you learn how to approach an object-oriented design and how to establish early habits to aid your development as an [incr Tcl] designer and programmer.

Classes and Objects

The most fundamental component of any object-oriented programming language is the class. A class is a self-contained data structure that defines attributes, components, and actions for some object. This object may be tangible like a clock, or it may be intangible like the communication process between a computer and a printer. To fully grasp the concept of the object-oriented paradigm, you must first begin thinking in terms of objects. To the user, an object should be like a black box. The internal components of the object should be hidden from the outside world. The user doesn't know and doesn't need to know how the object operates internally in order for the object to operate properly. When you look at a clock, you notice the time and perhaps the second hand moving around the face. You probably don't know how all the internal mechanical parts work together to keep accurate time, and it isn't necessary for you to know this in order to use the clock. The clock designer creates an object with built-in attributes and behaviors and provides a user-friendly interface to that object, the clock face. The important thing to realize is that the clock is a black box to the user. The manufacturer and repairperson are the only ones who must understand the clock's internal structure.

Consider your home or office computer. You may be unfamiliar with its internal components and not know exactly what happens, for example, when you press the power button. Again, it is not necessary for you to understand exactly what series of events occurs internally for the computer to initialize itself, establish communication with peripheral devices, etc. This behavior is built into the computer, which is a black box to the outside world. It is not

1

necessary for you to see inside the black box for it to operate as expected. This concept is called *abstraction* and is an important goal of the object designer. The designer creates a level of abstraction between the user and the object by encapsulating all necessary attributes and behaviors inside the object and by providing simple interface mechanisms for the user. Understanding this concept is one of the keys needed to understand object-oriented programming (OOP) and to become a good software designer.

NOTE: There are numerous books devoted solely to OOP and object-oriented design, such as *Object-Oriented Modeling and Design* (Prentice Hall, 1991), by James Rumbaugh et al., and *Object-Oriented Analysis and Design with Applications*, Addison-Wesley, 1994), by Grady Booch. The purpose of this chapter is not to present an in-depth study of OOP, but to provide a high-level view of concepts you should understand in order to write well-designed [incr Tcl] projects.

Now let's move on to your first example, none other than "Hello world!" Suppose your software application needs to display informational dialog windows to the user. You need to define an object whose job it will be to provide a user-friendly interface for displaying a message and closing its window. Remember, the internal details of the class are known only to you, the designer. The user of the class only needs to know how to make the dialog window display itself with the desired message. To create a class definition in [incr Tcl], you use the **class** command. It must be preceded by a namespace qualifier, the mechanism used to tell the interpreter where a command is defined. The fully qualified command name for **class** is **::itcl::class**. Namespace qualifiers are discussed further in the following section. The **class** command in its simplest form is

```
::itcl::class DialogWindow {}
```

The name of the class follows the **class** command, which is then followed by the class definition enclosed in braces. Class names should begin with an uppercase. The interpreter will not complain if you use lowercase, but using an uppercase makes it easy to distinguish between class names and other Tcl/Tk commands. This is the first of many habits you should develop as you begin coding. In this example, DialogWindow has an empty class definition. You could actually create an object of type DialogWindow, but you would not be able to do anything with it because a class without any attributes or behaviors is just an empty shell.

To fill in the braces for the class definition and create a working DialogWindow object, you need to think about what a dialog window should look like and what behaviors it has. At a minimum, it should have a top-level window, a text message, and an OK button, and it should know how to display itself onscreen. Consider the following example:

Example 1-1
Completing the
class definition
for a dialog
window

```
::itcl::class DialogWindow {
    # Class constructor and destructor
    constructor {message_} {
        set _toplevelWindow [toplevel .top]
        wm withdraw $_toplevelWindow
        set _textMessage [label $_toplevelWindow.txt -text $message_]
        set _okButton [button $_toplevelWindow.ok -text OK]
    }
    destructor {destroy .top}

    # Class Methods
    method draw {} {
        pack $_textMessage -pady 8
        pack $_okButton -pady 8 -ipadx 8
        wm deiconify $_toplevelWindow
    }

    # Class Data Members
    variable _toplevelWindow
    variable _textMessage
    variable _okButton
}
```

This example is grouped into three sections. The first section defines the class *constructor* and *destructor*. The *constructor* is a special function that is called automatically when you create an instance of the class. It typically initializes each of the class data members and does other initialization tasks as necessary to construct the object. The *destructor* is also a special function that is called automatically. It is the opposite of the *constructor*; whereas the *constructor* is called when you create an object to create components and allocate memory, the *destructor* is called when you delete an object to destroy components and free memory. Class construction and destruction is discussed in detail in Chapter 4. The second section defines class methods. Methods are functions that can be used by the class itself or by outside sources to tell the object to perform some task. DialogWindow has a single method called *draw*, which is used to tell a DialogWindow object to display itself onscreen. Class methods are discussed in detail in Chapter 2. The third section uses the **variable** keyword to define class attributes and components. DialogWindow has three components: a top-level window, _toplevelWindow; a text message, _textMessage; and an OK button, _okButton. These components are called *data members*, which are discussed in Chapter 3. As a convention in this book, data members are preceded with an underscore to distinguish them from local variables and method arguments. These three sections are presented in this order to provide logical groupings inside the class definition. The following definition of DialogWindow is logically equivalent to the previous definition as far as the interpreter is concerned.

Example 1-2
Rearranging the class definition works, but is hard to read and maintain

```
::itcl::class DialogWindow {
   variable _textMessage
   destructor {destroy .top}
   method draw {} {
      pack $_textMessage -pady 8
      pack $_okButton -pady 8 -ipadx 8
      wm deiconify $_toplevelWindow
   }
   variable _toplevelWindow
   constructor {message_} {
      set _toplevelWindow [toplevel .top]
      wm withdraw $_toplevelWindow
      set _textMessage [label $_toplevelWindow.txt -text $message_]
      set _okButton [button $_toplevelWindow.ok -text OK]
   }
   variable _okButton
}
```

However, the first definition is much easier to read and maintain. Get into an early habit of grouping class variables and class methods together in separate sections of the class definition. Future maintainers of your code will thank you.

Now recall briefly the definition of a class: a self-contained data structure that *defines* attributes, components, and behaviors for some object. A class is not an object. It is just the definition of an object. This may be a difficult concept to understand, so take a look at the following illustration:

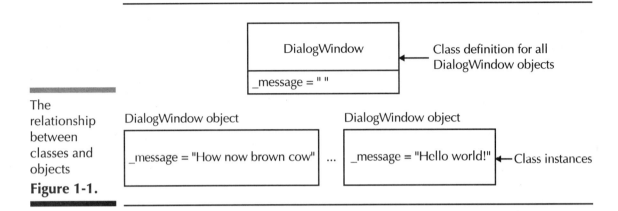

The
relationship
between
classes and
objects
Figure 1-1.

The DialogWindow class is represented by the uppermost box and defines the characteristics of all dialog window objects, which are represented by the boxes below the class. Each object is independent of other objects and has its own allocated space in memory and its own copy of internal data. The text message on one DialogWindow object might read, "How now brown cow," while the text message of another DialogWindow object might read, "Hello world!" Each of the objects shown in this illustration has its own copy of the class definition's components. This is how different DialogWindow objects can have different text messages. Any number of objects may exist simultaneously, as long as an object does not try to create a widget or window with a Tk window pathname that already exists. This is discussed further in the section, "Creating Objects," later in this chapter. Now that you have the class definition on paper, let's walk through the procedure of defining the class in a Tk or [incr Tk] shell.

Defining a Class in the Shell

Once a class is defined, the class name is recognized by the Tcl interpreter as a new command, which is used to instantiate the class. The first step, then, is to define the class in the interpreter. DialogWindow's *constructor* creates Tk widgets, so either the Tk shell (**wish**) or the [incr Tk] shell (**itkwish**) must be used.

Class Definition with wish

The **class** command does not exist in Tcl/Tk, so before using it to define DialogWindow, the [incr Tcl] package must be loaded. To do this, start the **wish** shell and use the **package** command:

```
% package require Itcl
3.0
```

The text "3.0" is printed on the line following the **package** command to indicate that itcl3.0 is loaded. After this, **class** is available for use, and DialogWindow can be defined directly on the command line.

Command-line Class Definition with *wish*

Type the DialogWindow class definition into a **wish** shell, as shown in Figure 1-2 (note that this code is available online). Notice that before the class is defined, "info commands DialogWindow" returns an empty string, which simply means that a command called DialogWindow does not exist. After the class is defined, however, notice the same command returns a nonempty string, which means DialogWindow is now a valid Tcl command and can be used to create an object. Since **class** only exists in the [incr Tcl] package, it's necessary to tell the interpreter exactly where this command is defined by preceding **class** with the namespace qualifier mentioned earlier, ::itcl::. This namespace resolution tells the interpreter that the **class** command is defined in the itcl library. Note that the leading double-colon is optional. Using this command without its appropriate namespace qualifier results in an "invalid command name" Tcl error. This is discussed in more detail in Chapter 10.

NOTE: Note that the leading double-colon to the namespace qualifier ::itcl:: is optional. It simply means that the following command or variable is defined in the global namespace, which is actually the default behavior. As a result, using a leading double-colon is redundant, but it is still used throughout most of this book just to be explicit. In most real-world applications, it is deleted.

Sourcing a Class Definition from a File

Now you know how to define a class at the command line, but as you can probably imagine, this usually isn't very practical. If adjustments need to be made like changing the packing options, the class name has to be deleted from the interpreter, and the definition has to be retyped—an awful lot of work for such a minor change. To avoid this unnecessary rework, the class definition can be saved in a file, which can then be sourced from the command line, as shown in Figure 1-3. Then, each time the file is modified as the designer fine-tunes the window layout, **wish** can be restarted, and the updated file can be sourced and retested quickly. Save the DialogWindow class definition in a file, and name it DialogWindow.itcl. You should name

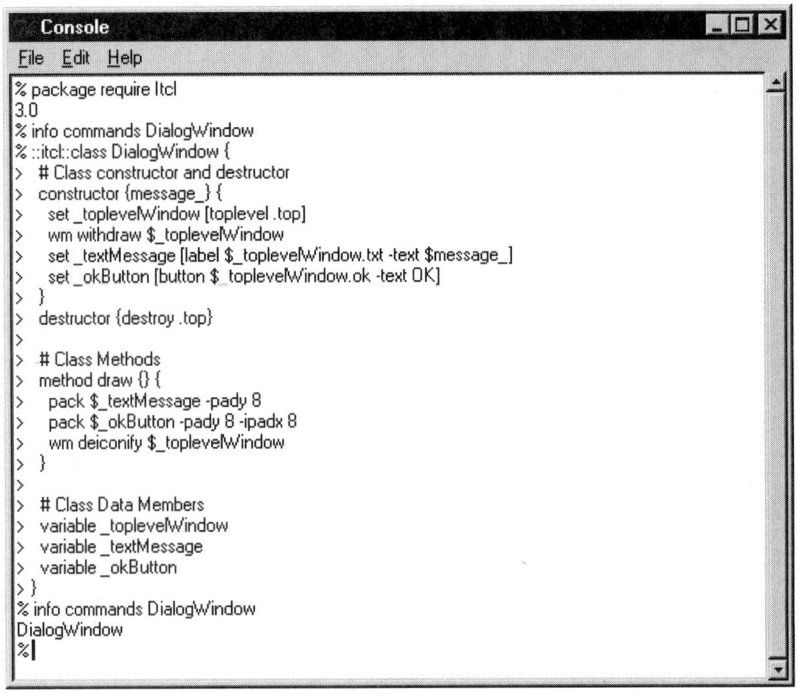

```
Console                                          _ □ ×
File  Edit  Help
% package require Itcl
3.0
% info commands DialogWindow
% ::itcl::class DialogWindow {
>   # Class constructor and destructor
>   constructor {message_} {
>     set _toplevelWindow [toplevel .top]
>     wm withdraw $_toplevelWindow
>     set _textMessage [label $_toplevelWindow.txt -text $message_]
>     set _okButton [button $_toplevelWindow.ok -text OK]
>   }
>   destructor {destroy .top}
>
>   # Class Methods
>   method draw {} {
>     pack $_textMessage -pady 8
>     pack $_okButton -pady 8 -ipadx 8
>     wm deiconify $_toplevelWindow
>   }
>
>   # Class Data Members
>   variable _toplevelWindow
>   variable _textMessage
>   variable _okButton
> }
% info commands DialogWindow
DialogWindow
%|
```

DialogWindow
is a valid
command after
entering the
class definition

Figure 1-2.

the file with the same name as the class so that you know immediately
what class is defined in the file. Use the extension ".itcl" for filenames
that define [incr Tcl] classes. You will then quickly know, for example,
that DialogWindow.itcl defines an [incr Tcl] class called DialogWindow,
as opposed to an [incr Tk] class.

Sourcing a Class Definition Using the auto_path
The previous approach works best when working with a single class. Your
application will undoubtedly contain more than one class definition,
however, so you should build tclIndex files and add the corresponding
directories to your *auto_path* variable. Start a new **wish** shell and type the
following commands to create a tclIndex file:

```
% package require Itcl
3.0
% auto_mkindex . *.itcl
% lappend auto_path .
```

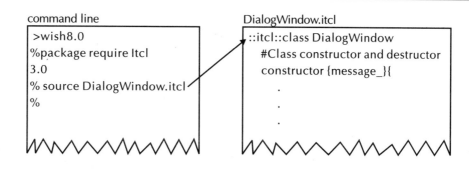

Define
DialogWindow
in a separate
file and source
from the
command line
Figure 1-3.

NOTE: A tclIndex file is a special file used by Tcl's autoloading facility when the interpreter encounters a command it doesn't understand. When the interpreter sees the command, DialogWindow, the first action it takes is to invoke a built-in Tcl procedure called **unknown** with the unrecognized command and its arguments. This procedure first checks to see if the autoloading mechanism can locate the command in a Tcl script file. To do this, it parses the tclIndex files located in one or more of the directories outlined by your *auto_path* variable until it finds a source file containing the definition for the command.

If you have executed **auto_mkindex** as previously shown and have named your file DialogWindow.itcl as previously discussed, an entry in the resulting tclIndex file will look something like this:

```
set auto_index(DialogWindow) [list source [file join $dir \
DialogWindow.itcl]]
```

When this line is parsed during auto-loading, DialogWindow.itcl is sourced, which loads the class definition for DialogWindow and resolves the unrecognized command. If the interpreter fails to locate a source file containing the definition for the unrecognized command, several other steps are taken including globbing, history substitution, and auto-execution. These are beyond the scope of this book, however.

REMEMBER: When using **wish**, make sure you remember to load the [incr Tcl] package before you build your tclIndex file. It will be empty if you forget, and you'll probably wonder why things don't work later when you try to create an object.

Class Definition with itkwish

When you start the [incr Tk] shell, you don't need to load the [incr Tcl] package because it's built into the shell. Starting **itkwish**, therefore, is equivalent to loading the Itcl package in a **wish** shell. You should continue to use the appropriate namespace qualifiers for package-specific commands like **class**, however, as a good programming habit. With this in mind, you can define DialogWindow in **itkwish** exactly as you did in **wish**. Now that you know how to define a class in the shell of your choice, it's time to create an object!

Creating Objects

A class's "power button" is its *constructor*. When you press the power button on your computer, it goes through a series of predefined, built-in events to initialize itself. Similarly, when the class *constructor* is called, the object goes through a series of predefined, built-in events to initialize itself. This is called *instantiation*. To instantiate a class simply means to create an object of that class type. An object is a usable instance of the class. To instantiate DialogWindow and create a dialog window object that displays the text "Hello world!", start a **wish** shell and enter the following commands:

```
% package require Itcl
3.0
% source DialogWindow.itcl
% DialogWindow dw "Hello world!"
dw
```

You use the class name, DialogWindow, as a command to instantiate an object called **dw**. The text string "Hello world!" is automatically passed to the *constructor* as its message_ parameter. The *constructor*'s parameter list as shown in the class definition expects exactly one argument, so you must provide an argument following the object name. Failure to do so will result in a "wrong # args" error message, just like passing the wrong number of arguments to a Tcl **proc**. The *constructor* then initializes its internal components by creating a top-level window and the appropriate Tk widgets to display the message. You will notice after typing this command that nothing happens visually. The dialog window is not displayed, and you might think the command didn't work. Actually, it did exactly what it was supposed to do. It created an object called **dw**, which gets printed as a result of the command on the following line. To make **dw** display itself onscreen, you have to tell it to do so. It does not know it's supposed to display itself because the only code interpreted so far other than the class definition is the body of the *constructor*. The *constructor* creates a top-level window and then withdraws it while it builds the internal widgets behind the scenes. A common practice is to create all widgets while the window is withdrawn and to display the window only after it's fully constructed. It's usually desirable to do this rather than have the window construct itself in front of the user's eyes. To tell **dw** to display itself, use its *draw* method:

```
% dw draw
```

It's as simple as that! The resulting dialog window object is shown next.

Notice that the sole purpose of this example is to create a top-level window with some embedded Tk widgets used to form a dialog window. DialogWindow, then, *has* a top-level window with embedded widgets. This relationship is actually not the best choice. The better choice would be for DialogWindow to actually *be* a top-level window. This is accomplished by making DialogWindow an [incr Tk] class instead of an [incr Tcl] class and setting up something called a class hierarchy through inheritance. The differences between [incr Tcl] and [incr Tk] and when you should use one as opposed to the other are discussed in detail in Chapter 11. For now, let's keep things simple and stick with the original approach.

You have seen how simple it is to create an instance of DialogWindow once the class is defined. Now you will see how simple it is to modify the class definition and add components to the dialog window. For example, you may

want to add an info bitmap to the left of the text message and a separator bar
between the text and the button. The following example adds these new
components, showing changes and additions in boldface:

Example 1-3
Adding new
components
to the class
definition

```
::itcl::class DialogWindow {
  # Class constructor and destructor
  constructor {message_} {
    set _toplevelWindow [toplevel .top]
    wm withdraw $_toplevelWindow
    set _bitmap [label $_toplevelWindow.bmap -bitmap info -fg blue]
    set _textMessage [label $_toplevelWindow.txt -text $message_]
    set _separator \
      [frame $_toplevelWindow.sep -height 4 -bd 2 -relief sunken]
    set _okButton [button $_toplevelWindow.ok -text OK]
  }
  destructor {
    destroy $_toplevelWindow
  }

  # Class Methods
  method draw {} {
    grid $_bitmap -padx 16 -sticky w
    grid $_textMessage -sticky w -row 0 -column 1
    grid $_separator -sticky ew -columnspan 2 -pady 12
    grid $_okButton -columnspan 2 -ipadx 8 -pady 4
    grid columnconfigure $_toplevelWindow 0 -weight 1
    grid columnconfigure $_toplevelWindow 1 -weight 1
    wm deiconify $_toplevelWindow
  }

  # Class Data Members
  variable _toplevelWindow
  variable _bitmap
  variable _textMessage
  variable _separator
  variable _okButton
}
```

First notice the two new components, _bitmap and _separator. Each is
initialized in the *constructor* to the appropriate widget type. The *draw*
method is then modified to pack the new widgets into the window. You
may have noticed that *draw* now uses **grid** instead of **pack**. This is done
to illustrate that it does not matter how *draw* accomplishes its task, because
the user is only concerned with the final result. You can use **pack**, **grid**, or

place, or you can create windows in a canvas. That is up to you, the designer. As long as the final result is the expected dialog window drawn onscreen, and the interface to the public method *draw* does not change, you can implement in any number of ways. After saving the class definition in a file, you can invoke a new **wish** shell and type the following commands to create the revised dialog window shown in the screen snapshot below.

```
% package require Itcl
3.0
% source DialogWindow.itcl
% DialogWindow dw "Hello world, take 2!"
dw
% dw draw
```

Naming Conflicts

As mentioned earlier, any number of DialogWindow objects can be created at a time, as long as no naming conflicts occur. Invoke a new **wish** shell, and try to create two objects as follows:

```
% package require Itcl
3.0
% source DialogWindow.itcl
% DialogWindow dw [list Hello world, #1.]
dw
% DialogWindow dw2 [list Hello world, #2.]
window name "top" already exists in parent
```

As you can see, the interpreter didn't like the second attempt very much. What caused this error? The first line of the *constructor* in the class definition creates a top-level window called .top. When you instantiate a class, the class definition is interpreted the same way every time. During construction of object **dw**, a top-level window called .top is created. During construction of object **dw2**, Tk attempts to create another top-level window called .top. This is because each instance interprets the same code. Remember, there is only one class definition. Multiple instances of the class can exist, but each instance has the same class definition. As a result, you can only create one instance of DialogWindow at a time. As a general rule of thumb, you should avoid hardcoding Tk window pathnames to avoid potential naming conflicts. You'll see how to do this effectively in Chapter 4. For now, Example 1-4 provides one possible solution to this problem (only changes to the class definition are shown).

Example 1-4
Avoiding Tk
window
pathname
conflicts

```
::itcl::class DialogWindow {
  constructor {message_} {
    set foundOne 0
    for {set x 1} {$x <= $_maxObjects} {incr x} {
      if {[winfo exists .top$x]} {
        puts ".top$x exists!  Checking .top[expr $x + 1]..."
      } else {
        set foundOne 1
        break
      }
    }
    if {$foundOne} {
      set _toplevelWindow [toplevel .top$x]
    } else {
      puts "Error: Maximum # of objects already created."
      return
    }
    ...
  }
  ...
  variable _maxObjects 3
}
```

A new data member, _maxObjects, stores the maximum number of objects that will be allowed to exist at one time. The constructor loops from 1 to this maximum value, 3, checking to see if the Tk window pathname .top$x exists, for 1<=$x$<=3. It prints a message informing you of naming conflicts and sets a local Boolean, foundOne, to True if an unused pathname is found. If one is found, a new top-level window is created with a controlled name by embedding a count into the window name. Otherwise, an error message is printed indicating that the maximum number of DialogWindow objects has already been created. The following screen snapshot shows what happens when the maximum number of DialogWindow objects is exceeded:

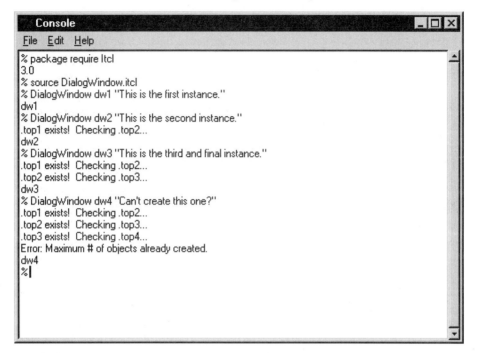

```
% package require Itcl
3.0
% source DialogWindow.itcl
% DialogWindow dw1 "This is the first instance."
dw1
% DialogWindow dw2 "This is the second instance."
.top1 exists!  Checking .top2...
dw2
% DialogWindow dw3 "This is the third and final instance."
.top1 exists!  Checking .top2...
.top2 exists!  Checking .top3...
dw3
% DialogWindow dw4 "Can't create this one?"
.top1 exists!  Checking .top2...
.top2 exists!  Checking .top3...
.top3 exists!  Checking .top4...
Error: Maximum # of objects already created.
dw4
%
```

Take note of two important items shown in this illustration: **dw4** and unique object names. Notice after the error message informing you that the maximum number of objects has already been created that the text "dw4" appears on the following line. You should recognize this as being the result of the previous command, which instantiates DialogWindow. The *constructor* fails to create a top-level window, but it does *not* fail to create the object. This is an important concept to understand. Notice the *constructor* returns once it discovers it can't create a top-level window that does not already exist. Returning from a *constructor* in this way does not mean the object is not constructed! You will learn how to handle this scenario in Chapter 4 by either returning an error code and letting the calling function handle destruction of the object or by destructing the object inside the *constructor*.

Next, notice that a different object name is used with each class instantiation. Since creating an object creates a new Tcl command, you must use unique object names:

```
% class Foo {}
% Foo f
f
% Foo f
command "f" already exists in namespace "::"
```

The interpreter will complain if you try and create an object when another object of the same name already exists. In this case, the second object **f** is not created. The interpreter halts execution of the command before the *constructor* is ever entered.

Using an Object

In the previous section, you displayed the DialogWindow object by using its *draw* method. That was your first example on how to use an object. An object is idle until you tell it to do something. The class definition provides interface mechanisms for the "outside world" called public methods. Methods are public by default, which means they can be invoked from outside the class definition (i.e., the command line). There are three access levels for methods: public, protected, and private. Each level has a certain set of restrictions regarding who can invoke the associated method. Protected and private methods are discussed further in the "Inheritance" section later in this chapter and in detail in Chapter 2.

In order to determine what public methods to provide in your class definition, ask yourself the question, "What does this object need to be able to do?" A dialog window should be able to display itself. Maybe it should also be able to hide itself. Then the next time it's drawn, it can display a new message if instructed to do so. To add this new behavior, you can simply add a new public method in the methods "section" of the class definition. The new method definition may look like this:

```
public method hide {} {
  wm withdraw $_toplevelWindow
}
```

This method couldn't be any simpler! Notice the new **public** keyword used here. Since all methods are public by default, you don't have to specify the access level for public methods, but you should continue to do so until you're used to each of the access levels. Once data member access levels are introduced, it's easy to forget what the default levels are because data members default to being protected, not public. By specifying **public** with the method declaration, you can rest assured that the method is indeed public.

Now instead of exiting the shell each time you want to get rid of a dialog window, you can simply tell it to hide itself. Its *hide* method is used, which instructs the object's top-level window to withdraw itself. Use this method just like the *draw* method:

```
% DialogWindow dw "Hello world!"
dw
% dw draw
% dw hide
```

Now let's modify the *draw* method so that when you tell the object to draw itself again, you can tell it what message to display. This way, you can avoid creating a new DialogWindow object for each message you display to the user. Instead, you can keep a single object around at all times, hidden from the user when it doesn't need to display a message:

```
public method draw {{newMessage_ ""}} {
  if {[string length $newMessage_]} {
    $_textMessage configure -text $newMessage_
  }
  wm deiconify $_toplevelWindow
}
```

By adding a default argument to *draw*'s argument list, you keep the existing interface the same as before. This is extremely important! If you modify *draw* such that its interface changes and it requires an argument, you will encounter a lot of grief from all the users of your class who are used to using *draw* without any arguments. Granted, in this case, you don't have any users of DialogWindow other than yourself. But the important thing to remember is to never change the interface definition for class methods without carefully examining any potential repercussions beforehand.

Now notice the syntax used to declare a default argument. If you already know Tcl, you'll recognize this as the same syntax for default **proc** arguments. To give an argument a default value, place braces around the argument and its default value. In this case, the default value for newMessage_ is the empty string. In the method body, the length of the string is checked, and if non-Null, the new message is displayed by changing the text message widget's –text configuration option. Also notice the trailing underscore in the method argument. Just as a leading underscore is used throughout this book as a convention to easily identify class data members, so is a trailing underscore used to easily identify method arguments. The only exception to this will be public data members, which are discussed in Chapter 3.

Consider the following example. You create two objects, **dw1** and **dw2**, and instruct each to display itself. Using the new *draw* method, what happens when you tell **dw1** to draw itself and display a different message? Since an argument is passed to *draw*, the text message will be modified. But what about **dw2**? It's also a DialogWindow object, so would it not also be updated with the new text message? The answer, of course, is absolutely not. Remember that an object is independent of other objects, each with its *own* copy of the class definition's internal data. Instructing one object to modify its data *does not* affect any other objects of that class type. The only exception would be for static data (discussed in Chapter 3), which is class-level data as opposed to object-level data. As far as you are concerned right now, modifying one object never affects other objects. Try the following lines of code:

```
% DialogWindow dw1 "The quick brown fox"
dw1
% DialogWindow dw2 "the lazy dog."
dw2
% dw1 draw; dw2 draw
% dw1 draw "jumps over"
```

You will notice that "The quick brown fox" becomes "jumps over" in DialogWindow object dw1, and dw2's "the lazy dog" is unaffected by the change.

Deleting Objects

Now that you know how to create an object and use its public methods, you need to know how to delete an object. To create an object, you know to use the class name, the new command created by the class definition. Deleting an object is accomplished with the **delete** command. As with the **class** command, you must precede **delete** with its namespace qualifier.

```
% ::itcl::delete object dw1
```

This will not only delete instance **dw1** of DialogWindow but also remove it as a command from the interpreter. Recall that during object construction, the *constructor* is automatically invoked with the command-line arguments. Conversely, during object destruction, the *destructor* is automatically invoked with no arguments. The purpose of the *destructor* is to do housekeeping, plain and simple. It destroys windows, deletes objects, closes files, and destroys images that your object creates during its lifetime. There should be a one-to-one correspondence between deallocation tasks in the *destructor* and allocated resources in the class, *if those resources have not already been deallocated*. The *destructor* does not *always* have to deallocate memory. If you delete objects, close files, etc., elsewhere in the class, then the *destructor* should not also deallocate these resources. Use the *destructor* to handle housekeeping tasks that are not handled elsewhere in the class. The following illustration provides an example of how the *constructor* and *destructor* could work together to preserve memory:

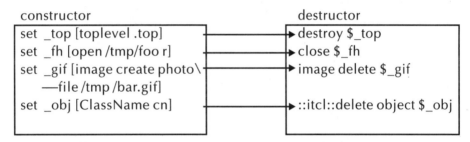

```
constructor                              destructor
set _top [toplevel .top]                 destroy $_top
set _fh [open /tmp/foo r]                close $_fh
set _gif [image create photo\            image delete $_gif
   —file /tmp /bar.gif]
set _obj [ClassName cn]                  ::itcl::delete object $_obj
```

Memory management in [incr Tcl] is like C++. It is handled explicitly by the programmer. If you know C++, you already know that for every "new" there should be a "delete". Otherwise, you'll leak memory, and if you have ever had the pleasure of tracking down memory leaks in projects with hundreds of thousands of lines of code, you never forget this rule. The same rule applies in [incr Tcl]. You can create class instances within class definitions. For each instance created, you must remember to delete it in the *destructor*. Otherwise, you'll jeopardize the resources of your system by potentially chewing up large quantities of memory. An exception to this rule is creating class instances using the **local** command, which creates an object that is treated like a local variable. It exists only while within the body of the method in which it is created. This is discussed further in Chapter 7.

NOTE: It is a common misconception that the *destructor* must also unset data members. The lifetime of a class data member is only as long as the lifetime of its object. [incr Tcl] automatically unsets all class data members when an object is deleted, just as Tk automatically destroys embedded widgets when a top-level window is destroyed.

DialogWindow creates a top-level window in its *constructor*. Following the rule of the housekeeping *destructor*, notice that its *destructor* explicitly destroys the top-level window. If the *destructor* does not do this, then when you delete the object, its window will still be visible onscreen. At that point, you would have to manually destroy the top-level window, assuming your OK button didn't do this for you. This is bad programming practice because an object should take care of cleaning up after itself when it is deleted. You might think of an object as being polite, because when it's gone, it shouldn't leave a mess behind. The –command configuration option associated with the DialogWindow's OK button may be configured to execute the **delete** command to delete the object when pressed:

```
...
set _okButton [button $_toplevelWindow.ok -text OK \
  -command "::itcl::delete object $this"]
...
```

A new variable, **this**, is introduced in the –command code fragment. This variable is used as a self-reference mechanism in [incr Tcl]. The **this** variable is a built-in variable and is discussed further in Chapter 3. Changing the OK button's –command configuration option as shown will result in the associated object's being deleted when the OK button is pressed, which follows the good programming practice of "polite objects" previously discussed.

Inheritance

Now that you know how to define a class, create objects, use objects, and delete objects, you're well on your way to becoming an [incr Tcl] programmer! These are the building blocks of the language. From now on, this book will build on the concepts you have learned so far. Let's jump right in and begin with a new concept called *inheritance*. For an advanced discussion on inheritance, you can refer to Chapter 8. This section provides a brief overview and example.

The concept of inheritance is shown in Figure 1-4. The box at the top of the diagram represents the definition of a class named Tool. Follow the line that connects Tool to the triangle below. This triangle means each of the classes below it *inherits* from Tool. You can think of the triangle as a multiplexer. A single line enters from the top, and multiple lines can branch underneath. So this figure shows you that Hammer, Saw, and Wrench inherit from Tool, and SledgeHammer and ClawHammer inherit from Hammer *and* Tool. Tool is called a base class, and each of the other classes is referred to as a derived class. Inheritance is a powerful construct of object-oriented languages because it allows multiple classes to use the same code. Since Hammer inherits from Tool, all designated methods and data members in Tool are also available for Hammer to use. Likewise, all designated methods and data members in Hammer are available for ClawHammer to use. As a result, ClawHammer and SledgeHammer get to use code from Hammer and Tool. This reuse of code is the key strength of inheritance.

Now consider the dialog window example. Currently, it displays an info bitmap and a message. To make this more robust, you can create a base class that defines characteristics common to all dialog windows. For example, all dialog windows have a message, a bitmap, and a top-level window. These are

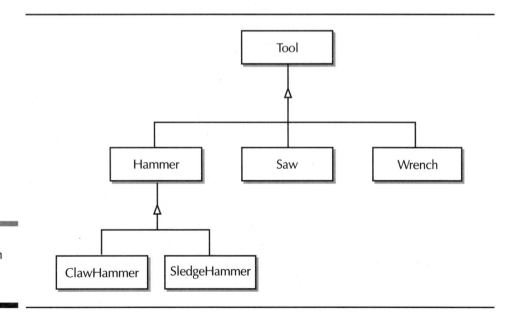

Inheritance
tree diagram
for Tool

Figure 1-4.

good base class components because whether a dialog window asks a question, displays a warning, or sounds an alarm, it contains these components. On the other hand, not all dialog windows have an OK button, so button creation should be left up to the derived class. For a simple inheritance example, refer to Figure 1-5. The diagram shows two new classes that inherit from DialogWindow: ErrorDialog and InfoDialog. Since each of these classes has access to designated code inside DialogWindow, its class definition should change to be completely generic, only defining characteristics that are common to all types of dialog windows. This "designated code" refers to code in the base class that can be seen by the derived class. Methods and data members in the base class that need to be visible to its derived classes should be defined with the **protected** access level. Being protected means that the code is encapsulated within the class definition and available to its derived classes while remaining hidden from the outside world.

This is a lot of information for you to absorb at once, so let's slow down a minute and think about the base class, DialogWindow. It should still have a top-level window, a bitmap, a text message, and a separator bar because all types of dialog windows have these components. The bitmap, however, should not be created in the base class *constructor* because the base class does not know what kind of bitmap to display. It doesn't know whether it should be an info bitmap or an error bitmap. That depends on what type of message is being displayed and should be taken care of by the derived class.

ErrorDialog
and InfoDialog
inherit from
DialogWindow

Figure 1-5.

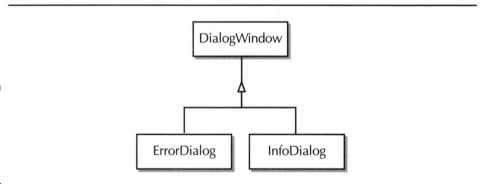

The following example provides the new definition for DialogWindow as a base class:

Example 1-5
Rewriting
DialogWindow as
a base class

```
::itcl::class DialogWindow {
  # Class constructor and destructor
  constructor {message_} {
    set _toplevelWindow [toplevel .top]
    wm withdraw $_toplevelWindow
    set _textFrame [frame $_toplevelWindow.txtFrame]
    set _textMessage [label $_textFrame.txt -text $message_]
    set _separator \
      [frame $_toplevelWindow.sep -height 3 -bd 2 -relief sunken]
  }
  destructor {
    destroy $_toplevelWindow
  }

  # Class Methods
  protected method draw {} {
    pack $_textMessage -side right -expand 1
    pack $_textFrame -fill both -pady 8 -padx 12
    pack $_separator -fill both -pady 12
  }

  # Class Data Members
  protected variable _toplevelWindow
  protected variable _textFrame
  protected variable _bitmap
  protected variable _textMessage
  protected variable _separator
}
```

The code to detect a maximum number of objects has been removed to make the class definition as simple as possible. Next, notice that access levels are now being explicitly stated. Recall that the default access level for methods is public, and the default for data members is protected. Protected variables, then, do not need to use the **protected** keyword, just as public methods do not need to use the **public** keyword. However, remember it's always a good idea to use explicit access levels not only for your sake, but also for the sake of future maintainers of your code who might not remember the defaults.

The OK button has been removed because derived classes might not need an OK button. Remember to think generically. The base class has no way of knowing what kind of button should be displayed, much less how many buttons should be displayed, so this must be left up to the derived class.

The next change is to the *draw* method, which is now protected instead of public. To explain the reason for this, you need a bit of background first. Base classes not meant to be instantiated are called abstract base classes. DialogWindow as defined here should be an abstract base class because instantiating it won't do you a bit of good since you can't do anything with the object. As a result, there is no reason to have any public methods defined in DialogWindow. Instead, make *draw* protected so that it can be accessed by derived classes, and provide a public method *draw* in each derived class that performs derived-class-specific tasks. The purpose of an abstract base class is to provide common data members and methods that derived classes can inherit. In C++, you define an abstract base class by making one or more of the class' virtual functions pure virtual. Doing this disallows you from ever instantiating the class, because the compiler won't let you. To *force* a class to become abstract in [incr Tcl], you must add code in its *constructor* to keep it from being instantiated. You can see how to do this in Chapter 8.

Another change in the *draw* method is a missing line of code. It no longer deiconifies the top-level window. The detailed reasoning behind this will become clear to you in Chapter 4, but for now just accept that if you deiconify the window in the base class, any widgets added by the derived class' *draw* method, such as buttons, may be constructed while the window is visible. Recall that a good protocol to follow is to finish all graphical processing prior to displaying the window.

Defining the base class is the hardest part. You have to think about what belongs in the base class definition and what belongs in the derived class definition. This insight just comes with time and practice. Now that the base class is defined, Example 1-6 provides the definition for the derived class, ErrorDialog:

Example 1-6
Creating a derived class from DialogWindow

```
::itcl::class ErrorDialog {
    # Inheritance
    inherit DialogWindow

    # Class constructor and destructor
    constructor {message_} {DialogWindow::constructor $message_} {
        set _bitmap [label $_textFrame.bmap -bitmap error -fg red]
        set _buttonFrame [frame $_toplevelWindow.bbox]
        set _okButton [button $_buttonFrame.ok -text OK \
```

```
      -command "::itcl::delete object $this"]
    set _detailsButton \
      [button $_buttonFrame.details -text "Details >>"]
  }
  destructor {}

  # Class Methods
  public method draw {} {
    DialogWindow::draw
    pack $_bitmap -side left -expand 1
    pack $_okButton $_detailsButton -side left -expand 1
    pack $_buttonFrame -fill both -pady 8
    wm deiconify $_toplevelWindow
  }

  # Class Data Members
  private variable _buttonFrame
  private variable _okButton
  private variable _detailsButton
}
```

The first thing you should notice is the new section in the class definition
for inheritance. The **inherit** command is used to establish the inheritance
structure between ErrorDialog and DialogWindow as shown in Figure 1-6.
ErrorDialog *inherits from* DialogWindow. Next, the *constructor* is shown with a
new syntax, which is used for passing arguments to the base class *constructor*.
This is discussed in detail in Chapter 4. The responsibility of the derived class
constructor is to create derived-class-specific components: an error bitmap,
an OK button, and a "details" button used for giving more details about the
error message. This button is just an example to illustrate why the base class
cannot create any buttons. It could not have known to create a button for
giving details about an error message. Specific widgets such as this should
always be created in derived classes. Then, notice that the *destructor* body is
empty. Since the base class *destructor*, which is called when you delete a
derived class object, takes care of destroying the top-level window, then you
do not need to do anything further in the derived class *destructor*. Next, a new
means of access, DialogWindow::draw, is introduced in the *draw* public
method. This syntax is discussed further in Chapter 8. It is used here to
explicitly call DialogWindow's *draw* method so that base class functionality
can be invoked prior to derived class functionality. And finally, the OK
button is initialized as a private data member. No outside source ever needs
to manipulate the OK button, so it should be declared as private, which
means that it's only visible within the ErrorDialog class definition.

Now to create and display an instance of the new ErrorDialog class, create a tclIndex file as described previously and type the following commands in an **itkwish** shell:

```
% lappend auto_path .
% ErrorDialog dw "Error: Alarm threshold exceeded!"
% dw draw
```

The resulting window is shown next.

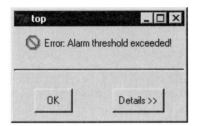

Once the end user is prompted with this error message, the OK button provides an exit route, and the "details" button provides an intuitive means for the user to determine the possible source of the error.

An important thing to note is the existence of a *draw* method in both the base class and the derived class. The derived class method always overrides the base class method, even if the base class method is public and the derived class method is private. In order to access the base class method, you have to explicitly call it with the syntax,

```
BaseClassName::baseClassMethod
```

which is shown previously with DialogWindow::draw. There is a command you can use to automatically search the class hierarchy for a method of the same name and avoid using an explicit call. This command, **chain**, is discussed in Chapter 8. The purpose of overriding methods is to keep common functionality in the base class and more specific functionality in the derived class. In this example, DialogWindow provides the functionality of packing the widgets common to all dialog window types. ErrorDialog, then, takes care of packing widgets found only in dialog windows that display error messages. This is a key concept in understanding inheritance. Just remember to use the base class for generic characteristics and the derived class for specifics. Unless the behavior or component is common to all types, it should be defined in a derived class.

The Object-Oriented Paradigm

You have discovered in this chapter how to define classes, create and use objects, and set up a simple class hierarchy through inheritance, each of which is a fundamental concept of OOP. You have probably also discovered that you must understand object-oriented design (OOD) in order to understand [incr Tcl]. With this in mind, this section discusses how to approach an object-oriented design and briefly outlines some key features of OOP.

1

Approaching OOP

Approaching a new problem domain for the first time can be a little intimidating. A good way to begin is to think of what components comprise the domain and what characteristics each component has. You should try and establish early in the process a separation of concerns, delegating specific tasks to each component. Don't worry at first how the tasks are to be implemented. Instead, decide *what* needs to be done and *what component* needs to do it. Suppose your problem domain is to design a way to read statistical data from a file and display the data in a bar chart. You might have several immediate concerns. What kind of statistical data is provided? What is the format of the file? How large can the file be? How in the world do you draw a bar chart? Don't let yourself get caught up in the details when you first begin the design process. Instead of reading statistical data from a file and displaying a bar chart, just concern yourself with reading *stuff* from a file and *displaying* it. Step back from the details and take a high-level view at the problem. Treat the problem like a black box. You don't know yet *how* it accomplishes its task, but you do know *what* tasks it needs to accomplish.

CRC Cards

A standard OOD method is called the CRC approach. (For more information, you can refer to *An Introduction to Object-Oriented Programming* (Addison-Wesley, 1997) by Timothy Budd.) Use index cards, referred to as CRC cards, to represent potential classes as you brainstorm your design. Each card is divided into three sections: the *class* name, *responsibilities* of the class, and *collaborators* of the class, as shown in Figure 1-6. For the data display problem, what tasks need to be accomplished? You need to read data from a file, format it, and display it. Your first potential class, then, might be a data retriever. Its responsibility would be to check for the file's existence, make sure the file is readable, perhaps make a backup copy of the file, open the file, and read and store the data. Another class might be a data formatter, which accepts data retrieved from the file by the data retriever and formats it in such a way that it can be understood by another class used for displaying the data, the display manager. Finally, the display manager decides how the data is to be displayed. In this case, it should be displayed in a bar chart, so the display manager collaborates with a bar chart class to display the end result, a bar chart graph of the original data.

Class names for this design might be DataRetriever, DataFormatter, DisplayManager, and BarChart. Now try creating a CRC card for each of these classes on your own. Think about what each class should be responsible for and how each class may interact or collaborate with other classes. Remember to create a separation of concerns in your design. Each class should have a specific set of tasks that only it knows how to manage. Then refer to Figure 1-7. OOD is not an exact science, so don't be surprised if you provide characteristics or behaviors not shown. Likewise, more information may be provided than what you have written on your CRC cards. If you think designing in such a manner as this is a waste of time, you will soon come to appreciate ample time spent up front designing your system as your customers eventually begin to request changes and features down the road. For example, consider the role of the display manager. This class is added to the design not because it is needed to tell a bar chart class to draw itself, but for future robustness. What if a customer requests data to be shown in a tabular format or a pie chart instead of a bar chart? All you would have to do, then, is create a sister class to BarChart, such as PieChart or Table, and add the appropriate hooks in the display manager. As you create and implement designs, you will learn to think about future possibilities like this up front, and your designs will become much more robust and portable.

Class name	Collaborators
Responsibilities	

CRC cards outline the responsibilities and collaborators for each class

Figure 1-6.

DataRetriever	Collaborators	DataFormatter	Collaborators
-Check for file existence -Verify file permissions -Open file -Create backup copy of file -Read data from file -Store data	DisplayManager DataFormatter	-Format data to be used by a display class	Data Retriever

DisplayManager	Collaborators	BarChart	Collaborators
-Decide how to display data -Create specific type of display class	Data Retriever BarChart	-Create a graphical bar chart from giving data	Display Manager

Example set of CRC cards for the data display task

Figure 1-7.

OOP Versus Function-Oriented

Why, you might ask yourself, should you consider OOP in the first place? Why not stick with a function-oriented approach? After all, you may have been coding in C for the last 20 years, or you may be a seasoned Tcl programmer who is perfectly happy using **namespace**s and **proc**s. Several advantages for OOP are outlined in the following sections, including encapsulation, inheritance, maintainability, and code reuse. The main disadvantage of OOP, arguably, is performance. An object-oriented application will run slower than its function-oriented counterpart because OOD adds an extra layer of abstraction on top, which naturally adds some processing overhead. What you lose is some processing time. What you gain is a system that is easier to understand and maintain. You have to choose what approach works best for your particular problem domain. Don't use OOP just because it's the latest industry buzz word, but don't rule it out just because you are proficient in a function-oriented language.

Maintainability and Code Reuse

A major benefit of OOP is the ability to reuse software modules across multiple projects. If defined properly, a module can be plugged into another project with minimal overhead and reused as is. As an example, consider the BarChart class from the previous section. The class doesn't care if the data to be displayed is the number of CDs you buy per month or the price fluctuation of your favorite stock over the last few weeks. It is generic enough to accept *data* and display it. As a result, the same class can be used in different applications.

If you are the maintainer of this class, you can do your job without impacting the rest of the application. Since internal components and behaviors are not seen outside the class, it follows that internal modifications do not affect other classes. The only contact with other classes is through well-defined, carefully controlled interfaces called public methods. As long as the interface definition itself is not changed, any maintenance done inside the class definition is not seen by others. This is ideal for development because once the interfaces are defined (the Collaborators section of your CRC card), *how* methods are implemented is unimportant. Remember the *draw* method of the first dialog window example. It is unimportant whether *draw* uses **grid**, **pack**, or **place**. As long as it does what it is supposed to do, it does not matter how it goes about doing it. Of course, you have to take into consideration performance issues and readability (creating windows in a canvas would be too slow, and it's easier to use **grid** with a listbox and horizontal and vertical scrollbars than **pack**), but the concept is the same. You can change the code without changing the interface and thus without affecting other parts of the system.

When problems occurs within your application, tracking down the location of the problem code is simplified because each class is designed to manage a certain set of tasks. If a file format changes, the DataReader class, for instance, can be changed to read the new file format without affecting any of the other classes in the system. If a bug in the bar chart is noticed, it's easy to determine where this bug will probably be found, the BarChart class. In general, maintaining large software systems can be quite difficult when all functionality is divided into partitions of the global namespace. OOP, on the other hand, subdivides the global namespace into multiple classes, each of which is responsible for a precise section of the problem domain, making ease of maintenance a key advantage of object-oriented languages.

Encapsulation

Another strength of OOP is encapsulation. This refers to the characteristic of a class to hide data from the outside world. Encapsulation is often referred to as data hiding. The key is to design a class that is self-contained. It knows what it needs to know, and it knows how to do what it needs to do. The behaviors and responsibilities are built into the class definition and outside sources can't see inside the class definition. Recall the black box from the beginning of the chapter. The user doesn't need to see inside the black box for it to work properly. If an outside source does need to access its data, the source must ask for it. The class, then, must provide an interface for this request. For instance, a class may be responsible for displaying a login window and accepting a password before allowing a user access to a system. A manager class may ask the login class how many times the user's login attempt fails due to an invalid password or login name. The login class would provide a public method that would return a private internal data member that stores failed login attempts. No other class needs to know login failures except the class responsible for validating the user's login. When you design an object-oriented system, one of your main goals should be establishing who needs to do what. A login class validates logins. A table display class builds a table and displays data in it. A data reader class reads a file and stores data. A class definition encapsulates its characteristics, providing public access only as necessary.

Inheritance and Composition

You already have a basic understanding of how inheritance works in OOP. Inheritance provides a mechanism for defining a software module in generic terms and allowing multiple other modules to inherit the characteristics from it and define further, more specific characteristics of their own. Inheritance is often referred to as an *is-a* relationship. From the example given in Figure 1-5, a Saw *is-a* Tool, and a ClawHammer *is-a* Hammer. Another relationship in OOP is called *composition*. This is often referred to as a *has-a* relationship. Objects can actually contain other objects. Think of a top-level window and the widgets built into it. The top-level window *has* some number of widgets. This is what makes [incr Tk] so powerful. A top-level window consisting of multiple Tk widgets as well as other objects, instances of [incr Tk] classes, can itself be treated like a Tk widget. This is discussed in detail beginning in Chapter 11.

In summary, you now have the tools you need to begin designing your own [incr Tcl] projects! The remainder of Part I now focuses on programming. Language constructs are dissected and explained. Sections from Chapter 1 are further elaborated, and you will learn in detail how to write [incr Tcl] code, from the simple use of member functions to the advanced integration of [incr Tcl] and C/C++.

CHAPTER 2

Methods

The purpose of this chapter is to cover [incr Tcl] methods. You will learn how to interface with methods through a detailed discussion of arguments and parameters, how to organize your code by separating method prototypes from implementation, how to use the auto-loader to automatically load method definitions at run time, and how to optimize your development and testing time with some interactive debugging techniques. Additionally, you will learn about namespace qualifiers, protection levels, and methods that are built into objects. At the end of the chapter, you will have the tools needed to design classes with well thought out interfaces and behaviors, you will know the syntax needed to declare and use methods, and you will know how and when to use methods with appropriate parameters and protection levels.

Introduction

Methods are used to describe the behaviors of an object: how it interfaces with other objects as well as how it behaves internally. Methods are the [incr Tcl] equivalent of C++ member functions in their purpose and use. Defining object behaviors is part of the class definition process. When designing a Timer class, for example, you first ask, "What do timers do?" That's simple—they time things. When approaching the design for this class, you should model the class definition after a real-world object such as a stopwatch. A stopwatch has an interface for starting, stopping, and resetting itself. It follows that the Timer class would also have interface methods called *start*, *stop*, and *reset*. Once you have modeled your class definition after some real-world object, you can begin to think about other requirements this class may have in your particular problem domain. For example, it may also require a *notify* method used to notify other objects when it reaches some predefined upper limit, or it may require a *repeat* method used to count down an interval multiple times.

To make your class definition more extensible, try to think of all the possible behaviors the object can have. Plenty of design time spent up front brainstorming behaviors like this pays for itself in the long run when users of your class ask for new behaviors. If you have done your homework, you may have already included the requested behaviors in the class definition, and instead of having to write code from scratch to add the new behaviors, you simply have to explain how to interface with your class to access behaviors that already exist. Maybe you have written graphical applications in the past, either in Tcl/Tk or some other language, and thought, "Gosh, if only this widget knew how to do this, I'd be set," and then you read the man page (see following "Note:") and the behavior you wanted was already built into the widget. If so, then you already understand first-hand the importance of up-front design time for future extensibility. If not, you soon will.

NOTE: If you are only familiar with the Windows environment, you may be unfamiliar with the term "man page." Man pages are online reference materials, short for **man**ual pages, in UNIX. UNIX users can use the **man** command for displaying reference material on any Tcl/Tk or [incr Tcl/Tk] command. Windows users should select the "Tcl Help" or "[incr Tcl] Help Topics" in your Tcl Desktop folder to display these pages.

2

It is not the purpose of this chapter to present a how-to on object-oriented design. The remainder of the chapter, rather, focuses on object behavior and the syntax used to define and use the various types of [incr Tcl] methods. It is important, however, that you understand how the methods get into the definition in the first place, by modeling the class after a real-world object and then brainstorming other possibilities for class robustness and extensibility.

Arguments and Parameters

A method often requires input in order to perform its task. This input is called an *argument list*. An argument list consists of one or more *arguments*, which are passed into a method. Methods have placeholders for arguments called *parameters*. Parameters are declared within braces immediately following the declaration of the method name. The number of parameters and the number of arguments are usually, but not always, the same. You may require the user to specify zero or more arguments, or you may provide a way for the user to specify optional arguments or even a variable number of arguments. Figure 2-1 provides an overview of the syntax for each of these cases, and the following sections elaborate on each.

```
::itcl::class  Args  {
    public method none                  { }←Empty parameter list requires no arguments.
    public method singleRequired        {required}←Single parameter requires one argument.
    public method multipleRequired      {required_ required2_ required3_}←n parameters require n arguments.
    public method singleOptional        {{optional_ "default value"}}←Single optional parameter defaulted to "default value".
    public method multipleWithOptional  {required_ required2_ {optional_ default}}←Multiple parameters with an optional
                                                                                   parameter. The optional one must be last.
    public method variableLength        {args}←Variable-length argument list allowed by args parameter.
    public method multipleWithVariable  {required_ required2_ args}←Multiple parameters with args, args must
                                                                    be last in the parameter list.
}
```

Specifying different kinds of parameters in the class definition

Figure 2-1.

Empty Argument Lists

A class method may know how to accomplish its task without any input. Consider the *draw* method for the dialog window in Chapter 1. A dialog window knows how to draw itself without your giving it any more information than it already has since that knowledge is built into the *draw* method itself. It knows to pack its internal widgets and display its top-level window. If a method can be self-contained like this, then you should not require any arguments. The only exception may be the need to allow an optional argument, which is discussed in an upcoming section. Now consider Example 2-1. A Timer object can be told to start, stop, or reset itself. Each of these methods will manipulate internal data members to accomplish its task and therefore does not need any input. (The code is provided later in the chapter. For now, only method prototypes are given.)

Example 2-1
Timer objects should not require input to start, stop, or reset themselves

```
::itcl::class Timer {
   public method start {} {
      # Code here to initiate a recursive timer loop.
   }
   public method stop {} {
      # Code here to cancel the timer event.
   }
   public method reset {} {
      # Code here to reinitialize internal counter to zero.
   }
}
```

The three public methods provide an intuitive interface for the user of the class to use a Timer object. The methods are designed with a stopwatch in mind. When you press the start button on a stopwatch, for example, you don't have to provide any extra information for the stopwatch to do what you expect it to do. Similarly, to make a Timer object start running, just tell it to start. It should not require any arguments, because *how* it accomplishes starting itself should be built into the object. The same analogy can be applied to the *stop* and *reset* methods.

REMEMBER: [incr Tcl] methods are public by default. You don't have to specify the **public** keyword to declare a public method, but you should do so for clarity.

2

Multiple Arguments

Sometimes it is necessary to provide one or more pieces of information in order for a method to complete its task. This is commonly found in the *constructor*. Remember the *constructor's* job is to initialize an object. Where does the *constructor* get the data used to initialize the object? It's either hardcoded in the class definition through data member initialization, hardcoded in the *constructor* body itself, or passed into the *constructor's* parameter list during class instantiation. If the data is not dependent on user input, then initialize it in the data members section of the class definition or in the *constructor* body. If, on the other hand, you want to provide options for the user during object creation, then you need to declare parameters in the *constructor's* parameter list. You may need to provide an upper limit, for example, to Timer's *constructor*. When the Timer object reaches this upper limit, it performs some predefined task, like beeping or displaying an alarm. You may also consider adding another parameter, action_, to tell the object what to do when it reaches its upper limit. Neither the upper limit nor the action should be hardcoded into the class definition because a generic Timer object does not know what its upper limit should be, much less what it should do when that limit is reached. In this case, you would declare two parameters in the *constructor's* parameter list, which forces the user to pass two arguments on the command line during instantiation.

Example 2-2
Declaring
parameters in
the *constructor*

```
::itcl::class Timer {
   # Class constructor
   constructor {upperLimit_ action_} {
      set _upperLimit $upperLimit_
      set _action $action_
   }

   # Class Methods
   public method start {}
   public method stop {}
   public method reset {}

   # Class Data Members
   private variable _upperLimit
   private variable _action
}
```

Private variables, _upperLimit and _action, are declared to store the upper limit value and the associated action, respectively, in each object. To create an instance of Timer, save the class definition in a file named Timer.itcl, and type the following commands at an **itkwish** prompt:

```
% source Timer.itcl
% Timer t 20 beep
```

This will create an object called **t** and initialize its upper limit to 20 and its action to "beep," as shown in Figure 2-2. Once the object is created, you can't change these values unless you provide special interface methods for doing so. Such methods are called accessor methods and are discussed later in this chapter.

Optional Arguments

You may specify default values for parameters to allow the user the option of keeping the default values or overriding them with optional arguments. You use default values when you want to provide multiple possible values for a single parameter. To declare an optional parameter, enclose its name and default value in braces:

```
public method foo {{optionalText_ "hello world"} {optionalNum_ 7}}
```

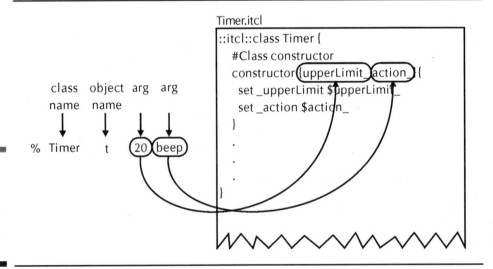

Passing arguments to the *constructor*'s parameter list.

Figure 2-2.

This method declaration contains two optional parameters: optionalText_ is defaulted to, you guessed it, "hello world," and optionalNum_ is defaulted to 7. Notice the quotes around the text string. When a default value contains whitespace, you must enclose it in quotes or braces. It isn't necessary to place quotes or braces around the 7.

So, how do you determine when to require arguments and when to make them optional? Basically, you just have to think about what makes the most sense. Take the Timer class as an example. You probably wouldn't want to hardcode the upper limit because that would force all Timer objects to have the same upper limit. This would be like buying a kitchen timer that could only be set to 12 minutes. It might work for some things, but for most it would be practically worthless. You should therefore require the user to specify an upper limit for each object, which means you need to declare a parameter for the upper limit argument in the *constructor*. Just as you have to turn the dial on a kitchen timer to tell it how long to run, so do you need to tell a Timer object how long it's supposed to run. One Timer object might run for three minutes while another Timer object might run for three seconds. That needs to be up to the user.

Now consider the action_ parameter, and again think about a kitchen timer. What does it do when it reaches zero? It lets you know by ringing a bell. Similarly, you can make action_ an optional argument that defaults to "ringing a bell." Simply change the *constructor's* prototype as follows:

```
constructor {upperLimit_ {action_ beep}}
```

Now the user does not need to specify "beep" to get this behavior. All Timer objects will default their action to beep when the upper limit is reached. The user may override this value simply by specifying another action, like "exit."

```
% Timer t 300 exit
```

In this case, the "exit" argument is passed in as action_ in the *constructor's* parameter list and replaces "beep." Creating an object in this way may tell it to exit once it has counted for the specified five minutes, instead of beeping.

In addition to the *constructor*, you may decide to allow the user to pass an optional argument to the *start* method for instructing the Timer object to wait some number of seconds before it starts. The default value could be to start immediately, like pressing the start button on a stopwatch, or the user could override the default value by specifying some other number. The method declaration would look like this:

```
public method start {{when_ 0}}
```

Now, the user can call *start* without any arguments, and the Timer object will start immediately, or a single argument may be specified that would override the parameter, when_, to start the countdown at some point in the future.

Notice that in the *constructor*, a single parameter is declared followed by an optional parameter, and in *start*, a single optional parameter is declared. You can declare as many optional parameters as you want, but they must always be declared *after* any required parameters. Consider Example 2-3. The *constructor* defaults the first parameter and requires a second one.

Example 2-3
Always declare optional parameters *after* required parameters

```
::itcl::class Example {
    constructor {{doesntMakeSense_ default} requiredArg_} {
        puts "optional arg: $doesntMakeSense_"
        puts "required arg: $requiredArg_"
    }
}
```

If you think about this example, you'll realize it doesn't make any sense. If you specify a single argument when you instantiate Example, it will override the first, optional parameter. This basically means you can't specify a single argument because no value would be given for the required second parameter, thus defeating the purpose of allowing the optional argument in the first place. In order to instantiate this class, you have to pass two arguments into the *constructor*'s parameter list:

```
% Example e arg1
wrong # args: should be "::Example e ?doesntMakeSense_? requiredArg_"
% Example e arg1 arg2
optional arg: arg1  ← arg1 ends up being required, not optional.
required arg: arg2  ← You must specify the "optional" argument first.
e
```

As you can see, Example cannot be instantiated unless the "optional" argument is specified, which means the argument isn't optional. Simply reverse the order of parameters in this example to achieve the desired results.

Optional arguments are useful not only when designing the class to give the user the ability to override default behavior but also for future maintenance. Consider the following scenario. Your design does not declare an optional parameter in *start*, and after you release your class for others to use in their own applications, you get a request to allow users to specify start times for Timer objects. By this time, there could be hundreds of references to *start* across multiple applications. You now have four choices:

1. Add a parameter to *start* and modify all calls to *start* to specify a start time.
2. Tell all users of your class that if they want to be able to specify a start time when they use *start*, they will have to implement a timer of their own.
3. Allow an optional argument to *start*, defaulting the parameter value to behave the same way the method behaved previously.
4. Define a new method similar to *start* to implement this new behavior.

The answer is option 3. If you try to implement option 1, you will soon get a phone call asking why the interface to *start* has changed and that you have broken someone's application. Option 2 is not a good choice because the customer request in this case is actually a good, useful idea and will make your design more robust. You will undoubtedly receive requests at times to add features that are unreasonable or involve too much overhead to implement, and you should handle these on a case-by-case basis. In this case, however, it makes sense to be able to specify a start time, so rule out option 2. Option 4 would work well, except there is no reason to introduce a new method in the class definition that would basically do the same thing as another method. You *could* implement another method that creates a timer event that would invoke *start* at the designated future time, but this could just as easily be implemented in *start* itself.

NOTE: You should combine like methods rather than using multiple, trivial methods because this greatly hinders performance in [incr Tcl].

Option 3, then, is your best choice. It allows all current users the ability to take advantage of this new feature without affecting legacy code. As a rule of thumb, *never* change the interface to a method without guaranteeing that all users are aware of the change. The best option is to implement a solution that satisfies the customer request and doesn't affect other customers. This isn't always possible, of course, but the majority of the time, you will be able to use techniques such as optional arguments to meet requests with minimal or no impact to existing implementation.

Variable-Length Argument Lists

A method may be self-contained and need no arguments, it may require one or more arguments, or it could be a mixture of both. By using the **args** keyword, you allow the user to specify zero or more arguments. Example 2-4 illustrates how **args** is treated by the interpreter.

Example 2-4
The **args** parameter is treated like a Tcl list

```
% ::itcl::class ArgsExample {
    constructor {args} {
        puts "Number of args: [llength $args]"
        puts "First: [lindex $args 0]"
        puts "Last: [lindex $args end]"
        puts "Sorted: [lsort -integer $args]"
    }
}
% ArgsExample ae 96 9 21
Number of args: 3
First: 96
Last: 21
Sorted: 9 21 96
ae
```

Another example can be illustrated with a simple Tk widget. Think about a button, for instance. When you create a button, you specify zero or more configuration options to initialize it. You probably do specify a –text option to add text to the button's face, and you probably specify a –command option to tell the button what to do when it is pressed. Think of these two configuration options and their associated values as a variable number of arguments passed into the button's *constructor*. Tk doesn't know beforehand whether you are going to specify zero configuration options or all 31 of them.

To simulate a Tk button in [incr Tcl], use **args** to store all command-line arguments and the *configure* method to initialize each argument, as shown in Example 2-5. Public variables text, fg, and bg are provided as example configuration options. The *constructor* declares **args** to capture all command-line arguments, and each of the public variables, or configuration options, are overridden if specified during object creation.

2

Example 2-5
Allowing a
variable number
of arguments
with **args**

```
::itcl::class Button {
  # Configuration Options
  public variable text "Default Text"
  public variable fg black
  public variable bg #d9d9d9

  # Class constructor/destructor
  constructor {args} {
    eval configure $args
    pack [button .b -text $text -fg $fg -bg $bg]
  }
  destructor {destroy .b}
}
```

You may notice a few confusing things in this example. First, the keyword **public** is used to specify public access for each of the three data members, and they are declared in a new section, "Configuration Options," in the class definition. Further, the data members are declared without leading underscores, as is the protocol defined in Chapter 1 for all class data members. Each of these issues is thoroughly discussed in the next chapter, but briefly, public variables in [incr Tcl] are used as configuration options similar to Tk widget configuration options. As such, they are treated a little differently than protected or private data members and should be placed in their own section in the class definition. Next, recall from Chapter 1 that the convention of this book is to use trailing underscores on all method parameters to be able to quickly differentiate them from local variables and class data members within the method body. You may notice that the *constructor*'s **args** parameter does not have a trailing underscore. This is because **args** is a Tcl keyword and must be declared exactly as shown. Now, to create an instance of Button, save the class definition in Button.itcl and type the following at the command prompt:

```
% source Button.itcl
% Button b -text "Hello world"
```

Assuming you don't have any other widget or top-level window named .b, a button will appear in the root window. The default text is overridden with "Hello world," and the button's colors are defaulted to black letters on a light gray background. To create a button that reads "Yikes!" with yellow letters on a red background, use the following instead:

```
% Button b -text "Yikes!" -fg yellow -bg red
```

The order of configuration option arguments does not matter. Notice that "eval configure $args" is executed before the widget is packed, so each of the configuration options is initialized before the widget is displayed. The *configure* method is built into the object. This is explained thoroughly in the next chapter, but for now, just understand that its purpose is to initialize public data members.

You now know how to allow users to specify variable-length argument lists with **args** as the sole parameter. It may be necessary, though, to force the user to specify one or more values for a method and then provide a mechanism for capturing the rest of the command-line arguments. In this case, you should declare the required arguments as usual and then place **args** at the end of the parameter list. If you want to force the user of the Button class to specify a text string and still allow the foreground and background colors to be overridden, you could modify the class definition as shown in Example 2-6. A new parameter is added to the *constructor*, and a private data member is added to store the argument's value until it's needed by the *draw* method.

Example 2-6
Declare **args** at the end of the parameter list

```
::itcl::class Button {
  # Configuration Options
  public variable fg black
  public variable bg #d9d9d9

  # Class constructor/destructor
  constructor {text_ args} {
    set _text $text_
    eval configure $args
  }
  destructor {catch {destroy .b}}

  # Class Methods
  public method draw {} {
```

```
    pack [button .b -text $_text -fg $fg -bg $bg]
  }

  # Class Data Members
  private variable _text
}
```

REMEMBER: The **args** parameter must always be declared at the end of the parameter list. Since **args** refers to a variable-length number of arguments, it serves as a container for all remaining arguments. If you specify any parameters following **args**, any calls to the associated method will result in a Tcl error.

With this new definition, you must tell the Button object to display itself by using its *draw* method. As a result, notice that the *destructor* places a catch around the command fragment to destroy the Tk button widget. Since the *constructor* in this case does not create the widget, it does not exist until the *draw* method is called, so if you instantiate Button, you will be unable to delete the object without the catch in the *destructor*. You will learn how to handle *destructor* errors in Chapter 4, but for now, the catch will allow you to safely delete Button objects that haven't been drawn.

After this last example, you might wonder when it is appropriate to create Tk widgets in a class that provides a graphical interface—in the *constructor*, in a *draw* method, or elsewhere. The dialog window of Chapter 1 creates its widgets in the *constructor*, and Example 2-5 creates its Tk button in *draw*. There is no right answer, unfortunately. Take comfort in the fact that object-oriented design is not an exact science. You learn by doing and gain experience by iteration. Fred Brooks asserts in *The Mythical Man-Month* (Addison-Wesley, 1995), "Plan to throw one away; you will, anyhow." In other words, don't be discouraged if you're just beginning to learn OOD. Even seasoned programmers and designers rarely do things the same the second time around. The first pass is usually a learning experience that gets the job done, but usually not optimally. The truth of the matter is it doesn't matter where the widgets are created. In some applications, it may make sense to create them in the *constructor* since the *constructor's* job is to initialize the object. In other cases, the widgets may not be needed until later, so it may be better to avoid the extra overhead during construction and create them only when needed. The previous example and the dialog window are implemented as shown to illustrate that you have many options when it comes to implementation. The *design* of the system is the most important step. You can usually implement the system any number of ways, but remember to strive for ease of maintenance.

Passing Arguments by Reference

Each example you have seen so far uses arguments that are passed by value. To pass an argument by reference, send the *name* of the argument to the method, and use the **upvar** command to obtain a local reference to that argument. The following class definition provides two examples of how **upvar** is used to modify variables that exist outside the current method.

Example 2-7
Using **upvar** to
pass arguments
by reference

```
::itcl::class Example {
  # Constructor
  constructor {blit_} {
    # Get a reference to blit_
    upvar $blit_ reference

    # Make sure the argument is a variable.
    if {![info exists reference]} {
      return -code error "Variable $blit_ doesn't exist!"
    }

    # Make sure the value is an integer.
    if {![regexp {^[1-9]*[0-9]$} $reference]} {
      return -code error "Usage: Example objName \#"
    }

    # Increment the argument.
    puts "$blit_: $reference"
    incr reference 10

    # The argument is modified!
    puts "$blit_ after \"incr 10\": $reference"

    # Modify it further.
    decr $blit_
    puts "$blit_ after decr:    $reference"
  }

  # Class Methods
  private method decr {val_} {
```

```
      upvar 2 $val_ num
      incr num -1
   }
}
```

The *constructor* declares a single parameter, so you must specify an argument in order to instantiate this class. The first order of business during class instantiation is to get a reference to the command-line argument. **upvar** is used to assign a local variable, *reference*, to the same memory address as the argument. When *reference* is modified, if it occupies the same space in memory as the argument, then it follows that the argument is also modified. Think of **upvar** as a command used to walk down the calling stack to grab a reference to some variable that exists outside the current scope. The default number of steps taken by **upvar** is one, so the first call is equivalent to

```
upvar 1 $blit_ reference
```

The *constructor* then calls a private method, *decr*, which uses **upvar** to go two steps down the stack to gain access to the original command-line argument. (The variable, *reference*, would probably be passed to *decr* under normal circumstances, but the value of blit_ is passed instead to illustrate how to access variables multiple levels down the stack.) Now save the class definition in Example.itcl and type the following commands at an **itkwish** prompt:

```
% source Example.itcl
% set var 10
10
% Example e var
var: 10
var after "incr 10": 20
var after decr:      19
e
% set var
19
```

Notice that the value of *var* after instantiation of object **e** equals 19. Its name is passed into the *constructor*, which sets up a reference to it and adds 10 to the reference. A private method, *decr*, is then called which also sets up a reference, this time decrementing the reference by one. Figure 2-3 shows visually how **upvar** is used in this example.

The **upvar** command is used to gain access to variables outside the current scope

Figure 2-3.

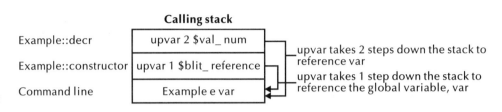

Separating Interface from Implementation

More than likely, one or more methods within your [incr Tcl] applications will consist of several more lines of code than the examples given so far. If you define a class with five methods, for instance, each of which consists of 15 lines of code, then your class definition may be nearly 100 lines long. You can imagine how cluttered the class definition can become as more and more functionality is added and how difficult it could be to maintain. For this reason, a common practice is to implement class methods containing multiple lines of code *outside* the class definition. This enables you to quickly examine the class definition and determine what methods are available, their access levels, what data members are defined, what parameters are required by each method, etc. The class definition is much more readable and maintainable when implemented in this way. If a method only contains a single line of code, and its purpose is obvious, then you should go ahead and implement it in the class definition. This is called *inlining*, and is most commonly used with accessor methods, which are discussed later in this chapter.

Using the body **Command**

To implement a method outside the class definition, you use the **body** command. As an example, the code for Timer's methods is given. First, let's revisit the class definition:

```
::itcl::class Timer {
  # Class constructor
  constructor {upperLimit_ {action_ beep}} {
    set _upperLimit $upperLimit_
    if {$action_ == "beep"} {
      set _action bell
```

```
      } else {
        set _action $action_
      }
  }

  # Class Methods
  public method start {{when_ 0}}
  public method stop {}
  public method reset {} {set _elapsedTime 0}
  private method count {}

  # Class Data Members
  private variable _upperLimit
  private variable _action
  private variable _elapsedTime 0
  private variable _afterId
}
```

A new private method, *count*, is declared as well as new data members—
_elapsedTime, for tracking elapsed time, and _afterId, for storing the
identifier returned by **after**. The methods *start*, *stop*, and *count* each will
have multiple lines of code and should be implemented outside the class
definition. The *reset* method is inlined since it consists of a single line of
code. Now you might wonder why *count* is declared as private. If you think
about how a timer should operate, the user tells the timer to start, stop,
or reset. Interface methods are defined for each of these events, and these
interfaces are all you need to operate a timer. If you make *count* public, then
the user has the ability to call it just like any other interface method, and
you should never allow public access to a class method unless it is meant to
serve as a public interface. Since the interface to Timer is already defined, any
other methods should be declared as private or protected. Example 2-8 now
provides the implementation for methods *start*, *stop*, and *count*. (Note that an
error is intentionally introduced in this example and is addressed in the next
section on interactive debugging.)

Example 2-8
Use the **body**
command to
implement
methods outside
the class definition

```
::itcl::body Timer::start {{when_ 0}} {
  if {$_elapsedTime > $_upperLimit} {
    puts "Please reset the timer before restarting."
    return
  }
  if {$when_} {
    puts "Waiting $when_ seconds before starting..."
  }
```

```
    set _afterId [after [expr 1000 * $when_] count]
}

::itcl::body Timer::stop {} {
  puts "Stopping timer!"
  after cancel $_afterId
}

::itcl::body Timer::count {} {
  if {$_elapsedTime == $_upperLimit} {
    incr _elapsedTime
    puts "Done!"
    eval $_action
  } else {
    incr _elapsedTime
    puts " $_elapsedTime"
    set _afterId [after 1000 count]
  }
}
```

The syntax of the **body** command is very similar to a **proc**. The first argument must be the fully qualified method name, which means the method name must be preceded by its namespace qualifier. The next argument is the method's parameter list enclosed in braces, followed by the method's body, also enclosed in braces. Now enter the method implementations given in Example 2-7 directly below the class definition in Timer.itcl. The interface to Timer is then defined at the top of the file, with the methods implemented below. Take note of the order of method implementation as well. The methods are implemented in the order in which they are declared in the class definition. The more methods you declare, the more you'll appreciate having done this for convenience during future debugging and maintenance.

Now consider how these methods work together. The *start* method serves as the public interface for the user to tell a Timer object to start counting. As far as the user is concerned, *start* handles the countdown. The user doesn't care how the Timer keeps track of elapsed time, only that it functions properly. Remember the black box concept from Chapter 1. The Timer is a black box with a few well-defined interfaces that allow access into its internal components. If *start* detects that the upper limit has already been reached, it instructs the user to reset the object first, via the *reset* method. The actual countdown is done in the private class method, *count*, which is invoked from *start*. This method establishes a recursive loop that runs until the object's upper limit is reached, at which time the given action is invoked. If the Timer object was told to beep, then the Tk **bell** command is used to produce an audible beep. Finally, the *stop* method stops the countdown by simply canceling the identifier returned by the **after** command from *start* or *count*. At an **itkwish** prompt (you must use either **wish** or **itkwish** because **after** and **bell** are Tk commands), type the following commands to create a Timer object:

```
% source Timer.itcl
% Timer t 20
t
% t start
```

If you have typed these commands, then you know by now that the code doesn't work. The interpreter complains about an invalid command name, *count*. The stack trace shows you that this happens during the **after** callback. Welcome to your first debugging session!

Interactive Debugging

When you are designing and testing a new class, you typically spend some time debugging and fine-tuning your code (unless your code always runs correctly the first time, in which case you should consider publishing your techniques). When you encounter a bug like the problem with the **after** callback in the previous section, you might first decide to exit your shell and edit your class definition to make the fix. If you do this, you could end up exiting and restarting the shell many times before you figure out the solution. Instead, all you need to do is tell the interpreter to forget that it ever knew about the class definition in question and then re-source the file containing the class definition. This way, you can use the same shell throughout your testing and debug interactively.

Using *delete* and *source* to Debug Interactively

One way to avoid exiting and restarting your interpreter multiple times for testing code changes is to use the **delete** command with the **class** option to delete the class definition from the interpreter and the **source** command to reintroduce it:

```
% ::itcl::delete class Timer
% source Timer.itcl
```

Then, you simply reinstantiate Timer to test your code changes. With Tcl's C-shell-like support, you can also use history and command-line substitution to optimize your debugging efforts even further. After you delete your class from the interpreter, you may need to reedit your code and make another fix or add another line of debug. Instead of typing out the full command to source the class again, you just need to type **!s** to repeat the last command that started with an "s." The following few lines illustrate:

```
% source Timer.itcl
% Timer t 2
t
% t start
Error occurs, so you edit Timer.itcl and add necessary debug code.
% ::itcl::delete class Timer
% !s  ← replaced with "source Timer.itcl"
% Timer t 2
t
% t start
Error occurs again. Edit file again and add more debug.
% ::itcl::delete class Timer
% $!s
```

You just need to be careful when you use history replacement like this that you double check your history beforehand. If you don't, you could easily end up invoking a command you didn't mean to invoke.

NOTE: Windows users may be unfamiliar with the term, "C-shell." A shell is a program that runs under UNIX and provides a command prompt to accept system commands. It is similar to the DOS prompt, which you can think of as a "shell" in which you type system commands like *move* or *del*. The C-shell is one particular type of shell that pioneered the particular style of history interaction and I/O redirection that Tcl models.

Using Cut and Paste to Debug Interactively

Another debugging technique you can use is to cut and paste updated method bodies (or retype them) directly to the command prompt. You don't need to delete class methods from the interpreter, because they aren't registered like class names. Methods are sourced each time they are invoked, so you can modify them dynamically. Consider the following simple example.

Example 2-9
Updating
class methods
dynamically

```
% ::itcl::class ToughGuy {
    method fight {} {
        puts "Pow!  Blam!  Zot!  Bonk!"
    }
}
% ToughGuy tg
tg
% tg fight
Pow!  Blam!  Zot!  Bonk!
% ::itcl::body ToughGuy::fight {} {    ← rewrite fight to be
friendlier
    puts "Be civil. Let's talk about this first."
}
% tg fight
Be civil. Let's talk about this first.
```

2

As you can see, the *fight* method is rewritten and reused without having to create a new object. You can use techniques like these to considerably decrease the amount of time it takes you to debug your code.

Now before getting to the original Timer bug and how to fix it, you must first understand a concept called *scope*. A simple analogy to illustrate this concept is your office environment. Consider the picture of your spouse or family member you may have sitting on your desk. This picture can probably only be seen from within your own office or cubicle. Your coworker down the hall must enter your office in order to see the pictures on your desk, and, likewise, you must enter your coworker's office to see the pictures on his or her desk. The visibility of items within the offices is called the *scope* of the offices. Similarly, when you talk to your coworker in your office, the conversation exists only within the scope of your office. On the other hand, if you are paged over the intercom, that page is heard not only in your office but in all other offices as well. Think of this event as having *global scope*. Global scope is a scope in which all items within it are globally visible. Whereas the conversations you have in your own office cannot be heard on the other end of the building, the pages you make over the intercom can be heard throughout the building. This is analogous of local scope (inside the office) versus global scope (inside the building). The local scope of your office is defined by its physical walls or partitions. The local scope of an [incr Tcl] class is defined by the opening and closing braces surrounding the class definition and method bodies. Variables and classes defined at the command line exist only at the global scope, but variables and methods defined within class definitions exist only within the scope of the associated class.

With this new concept of scope in mind, understand that the **after** command always invokes the given code fragment at the global scope. Within Timer's class definition or any of its method bodies, *count* is a valid command since it is the name of a class method. Once outside the scope of the class, however, like at the command-line prompt, *count* does not exist. It only makes sense from within the namespace of the Timer class. In order to access *count* from outside the class, you can make it a public method and call it the same way you call *start*:

```
set _afterId [after [expr 1000 * $when_] "t count"]
```

If you make *count* a public method, then this command will work, but remember, you don't want to make it public, because it is not an interface method. The user should only tell a Timer object to start. Timer's *start* method should take care of initiating the countdown. So, your problem really is how to access private class methods from the global scope.

T IP: To access private class methods from outside the class scope, use the **::itcl::code** command to wrap the command fragments in the proper namespace context.

Now edit Timer.itcl and modify both **after** events as follows:

```
set _afterId [after [expr 1000 * $when_] [::itcl::code $this count]]
...
set _afterId [after 1000 [::itcl::code $this count]]
```

The *count* method is now called in the proper namespace context because the **::itcl::code** command captures the current namespace information so that the given command fragment can be executed from within *any* namespace, not just at the global scope. For more information on namespaces, refer to Chapter 10.

You can now create a functional Timer object that counts to a specified value and beeps at you by default when it's done. You can always override the default action by specifying any other desired action. For example, you may have a Login class that displays a login prompt to allow privileged access to a certain application. This class could provide a *notify* method that would display an error dialog window letting the user know when the login time expires. The instance of this class could create an instance of Timer, passing to its *constructor* a string such as "loginObject notify" (*notify* must be public) to notify the Login object when the timer expires. Clicking OK on the error dialog window, then, might exit the application. This is the whole point of creating a generic Timer class and the beauty of OOD, so that you can use Timer objects in many different ways and in many different applications.

If you've already tried creating multiple Timer objects in the same shell, you've probably noticed that the first object works fine, but that any other objects behave strangely. This is because the *start* and *count* methods both hardcode the object name, **t**, in the **after** callbacks. As a result, any Timer object you tell to start will call **t count**, and if an object named **t** has not been instantiated, you will get a stack trace. You should never hardcode object names within class definitions or source code. This restricts the user from creating multiple objects and forces the user to use a particular object name. You will find out in the next chapter how an object can reference itself generically from within its own namespace.

Header and Source Files

You now know to use the **body** command to separate the class definition from the implementation of class methods. You can do this in a single file such as Timer.itcl, or you can take another approach and enter the class definition in one file and the method implementations in another. This is commonly done in C++, where programmers place the class definition, or header, in a header file and the member function source code in a separate file called the source file. In C++, each source file then uses the *#include* preprocessor directive to obtain function prototypes from the associated header file. In [incr Tcl], you can follow the same protocol and then use **auto_mkindex** and the *auto_path* to auto-load class and method names at run time.

As an example, let's split the Timer.itcl file you created in the previous section. Rename this file to Timer.def, edit the file, and cut out the method implementations. Then, paste them into a new file, Timer.src. You will then have a class definition file used to prototype each class method as well as a source file used to implement each method. Once you've done this, type the following commands at a **tclsh** prompt:

```
% package require Itcl
3.0
% auto_mkindex . *.def *.src
```

This creates a tclIndex file from all filenames with .def and .src extensions in the current working directory. The tclIndex file should contain one entry for the class name and one entry for each of the three methods in the source file, with directions instructing the interpreter where to go to find definitions for unknown commands like "Timer." Your tclIndex file should contain the following entries:

```
set auto_index(Timer) [list source [file join $dir Timer.def]]
set auto_index(::Timer::start) [list source [file join $dir Timer.src]]
set auto_index(::Timer::stop) [list source [file join $dir Timer.src]]
set auto_index(::Timer::count) [list source [file join $dir Timer.src]]
```

Now you can create Timer objects just by appending the directory containing this tclIndex file to your *auto_path*. The interpreter handles sourcing the files as needed through its auto-load mechanism. If you have several classes in your application, each with a separate source file, then you'll quickly gain an appreciation for auto-loading when you realize you have to source so many files manually to test minor code changes. The following illustration uses auto-loading and shows the output generated from creating and using a Timer object.

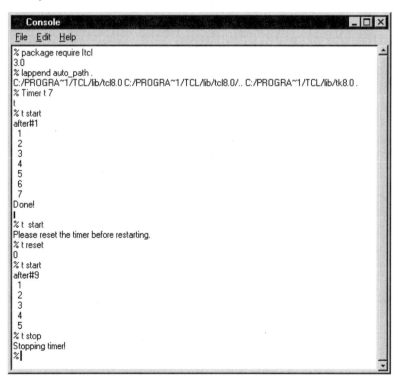

Accessor Methods

When working with objects, you often need to access an object's nonpublic data. If you initialize a Timer object to count for 10 minutes, for example, it's reasonable that you might want to intermittently ask it how much time is left. Since the associated data member, _elapsedTime, is private, you have no way of retrieving it unless you provide a special method for doing so. Public methods that get or set an object's nonpublic data are referred to as accessor methods, or accessors, because they provide *access* to otherwise inaccessible data. Public data is already accessible to outside resources via the built-in *cget* and *configure* methods, which are discussed in the next chapter. Protected and private data, on the other hand, are not publicly available and must have associated accessor methods for retrieving or modifying them. A get accessor allows you to retrieve the value of an object's nonpublic data, and a set accessor allows you to modify an object's nonpublic data. In your class definition for data members you should only provide accessor methods that you want to allow the user to modify or retrieve. Rarely is there a one-to-one correspondence between the number of data members and the number of accessors. If you don't want the upper limit to ever change once a Timer object is created, for example, then don't provide an accessor for setting it. You might want to ask Timer objects how much time is left before they reach their upper limits, however, so you should provide an accessor for retrieving this data. (Currently, the code prints the elapsed time each second, so this would only be useful if you remove this output.) Example 2-10 modifies Timer's class definition and provides appropriate accessors.

Example 2-10
Declare accessors
for data members
that need to be
publicly available

```
::itcl::class Timer {
    ...
    # Accessor Methods
    public method elapsedTime {} {return $_elapsedTime}
    public method changeAction {newAction_} {set _action $newAction_}
    public method reset {} {set _elapsedTime 0}
    ...
}
```

Notice the new "Accessor Methods" section in the class definition. Just as you learned to separate methods and data members in Chapter 1, so should you also separate accessor methods into their own section. Grouping accessors together provides you as well as future maintainers of your code with the ability to quickly determine what accessors are defined for your class. You should notice that the *reset* method has been moved into this new section since its sole purpose is to reset a Timer object's elapsed time to zero.

REMEMBER: The interpreter is unaware of any methods called "accessor methods." To the interpreter, accessor methods are just public methods. This nomenclature is used to partition public methods into different types. Public methods whose sole responsibility is to get or set a class's nonpublic internal data are referred to as accessor methods.

In C++, both get and set accessors are commonly named the same name as the data member, only differentiated by the parameter list. This is because C++ supports function overloading. The compiler knows which function to invoke based on the arguments provided, if multiple functions exist with the same name. In [incr Tcl], however, all class method names must be unique within the same class. You can declare ten methods named *abort* in your application as long as you place each one in a different class. This way, the interpreter views each method as unique since the namespace qualifier for each is different. You'll see in the next chapter how to simulate function overloading by using the **args** parameter.

Namespace Qualifiers

You just learned that you can declare methods with the same name in your application as long as each method is defined in a different class or namespace. What happens, though, when you have identical method names within the same inheritance hierarchy? Since the derived class inherits all public and protected behaviors from the base class, what happens when the derived class tries to call a base class method with a name that's already defined in the derived class? The following example illustrates this problem.

Example 2-11
Identical method names in an inheritance tree

```
::itcl::class Parent {
  # Class Methods
  protected method baseMethod {} {print "A virtual example."}
  protected method print {string_} {puts "Parent::print - $string_"}
}

::itcl::class Child {
  inherit Parent

  # Class Methods
  public method go {} {baseMethod}
  private method print {string_} {puts "Child::print - $string_"}
}
```

If you instantiate Child and call its *go* method, the base class method *baseMethod* is called, but which *print* is called, Child::print or Parent::print?

You might guess that the base class *print* is called since it is invoked from another base class method. However, the short answer is that Child::print is called because all methods in [incr Tcl] are virtual. For the long answer and a detailed explanation of what "virtual" means, refer to Chapter 8. Enter the class definitions on the command line and type the following to see:

```
% Child c
c
% c go
Child::print - A virtual example.
```

The problem then becomes, if you don't want to call the derived class method, how do you force the interpreter to call the base class method? To do this, you have to use a namespace qualifier. Unqualified names are interpreted relative to the class context in which they are used. You might think that the class context in which *print* is called in this example *is* the base class, and it does look that way since the invocation is actually inside the base class method, *baseMethod*. But you have to think in terms of the object, not the class. By instantiating Child, not Parent, any methods called by the object, regardless of their location in the inheritance hierarchy, will always be interpreted relative to Child's namespace. To force the base class *print* method to be called, simply prepend Parent's namespace qualifier to *print* like this:

```
::Parent::print "hello world"
```

This explicit namespace qualification tells the interpreter to call Parent's *print* method. Note, however, that you can only do this from within the scope of the class hierarchy. The command, "::Parent::print," does not exist outside the scopes of Parent and Child. To make a method visible in other scopes, you have to make the method static, which is discussed in the next section.

A similar example is when a *derived* class method invokes a method defined in both the derived and base classes:

```
::itcl::class Parent {
  # Class Methods
  protected method print {string_} {puts "Parent::print - $string_"}
}

::itcl::class Child {
  inherit Parent

  # Class Methods
  public method go {} {print "hello world"}
  private method print {string_} {puts "Child::print - $string_"}
}
```

Now the call to *print* is actually done from within the derived class definition instead of the base class definition. In this case, Child::print will still be called since *print* is unqualified. In inheritance structures like this, it is usually necessary to call the base class method prior to calling the derived class method. The base class method typically does some initial generic setup, and the derived class method then fills in the holes. Modify Child::print as follows, and remember that you can type this new method definition directly on the command line.

```
% ::itcl::body Child::print {string_} {
    ::Parent::print "Explicitly calling the base class method first."
    puts "Child::print - $string_"
  }
```

Now any time a Child object calls *print*, the base class *print* is invoked first. This is very common when using inheritance, and a special command called **chain** exists just for this purpose, which is discussed further in Chapter 8. After these modifications, the new code behaves as follows:

```
% Child c2
c2
% c2 go
Parent::print - Explicitly calling the base class method first.
Child::print - A virtual example.
```

Static Methods

Static methods exist independent of any class instances and are useful for bundling related procedures within a class definition. To create static methods within an [incr Tcl] class, simply use **proc** in place of **method**. Procedures within class definitions behave just like static C++ member functions. Consider the following example for bundling related procedures within a class:

Example 2-12
Use **proc** to declare static, class-level methods

```
::itcl::class Color {
   proc RGB {color_}
}

::itcl::body Color::RGB {color_} {
   switch -- $color_ {
      red      {set val "255   0    0"}
      orange   {set val "255 165    0"}
```

```
     yellow  {set val "255 255   0"}
     green   {set val "0   255   0"}
     blue    {set val "0     0 255"}
     indigo  {set val "138  43 226"}
     violet  {set val "238 130 238"}
     default {set val " 0   0   0"}
  }
  return $val
}
```

You don't have to create an instance of Color in order to use *RGB*:

```
% Color::RGB violet
238 130 238
```

However, what happens if you do create an instance of Color? Since the only method defined in Color is a static method, any class instances will be unable to access this method because static methods are class-level methods, not instance-level methods:

```
% Color col
col
% col RGB
bad option "RGB": should be one of...
  c cget -option
  c configure ?-option? ?value -option value...?
  c isa className
```

Notice also that Color does not declare any data members. Since static methods exist independent of class instances, they cannot access object-specific data, only class-specific data. This makes static methods useful for returning constant data, like the values outlined in Color. Color declares the static method *RGB* to serve as a conversion utility for returning the RGB value associated with the given text string. A similar static method could be implemented to convert an RGB value to a text string. Static methods are mostly used in conjunction with static data members, so other useful examples are covered in the next chapter when static data members are introduced.

Access Levels

Methods may be declared as **public**, **protected**, or **private**. This is how you restrict as well as provide access to class methods. Public methods are accessible from outside the class scope, which means any object from any namespace can access them. You typically only want to declare a method as public if it will serve as an interface or an accessor to your class. If a method is neither an interface method nor an accessor, then don't make it public. Protected methods add a layer of restriction on top of public methods. They are only accessible within a class inheritance hierarchy, meaning that protected base class methods may be called from derived classes. The order of this is important because the reverse is not true; base class methods *cannot* call protected derived class methods. Protected methods are only visible "up" the inheritance tree. Last but not least, private methods add yet another layer of restriction. They are only accessible within the class scope in which they are declared.

You can think about these three access levels as stacked layers. The bottom layer, public, has no restrictions; anyone can access public methods. The middle layer, protected, adds a restriction to the public layer; only derived classes can access protected methods outside the class scope. And the top layer, private, further restricts access by disallowing even derived class access. Table 2-1 outlines access level information for class methods.

Now let's get to a simple code example. A base class, Dog, declares one public method, *sit*, which means any object can instantiate Dog and tell it to sit, including Dog itself. It also declares three protected methods. Only Dog and any of its derived classes have access to these methods. A derived class, ScottishTerrier, provides two public methods, *speak* and *doTricks*, so any object can instantiate this class and tell the object to speak or do tricks. The

Access Level	Restrictions
Private	Restricted to use within the class scope in which the method is declared
Protected	Can be used within the class scope in which the method is declared as well as within any derived class scope
Public	Can be used from within any class scope as well as the global scope

Access Levels and Their Associated Restrictions

Table 2-1.

derived class also declares a private method, *feedme*, which is only accessible from within the scope of ScottishTerrier.

Example 2-12
Public,
protected, and
private method
access levels

```
::itcl::class Dog {
  # Class Methods
  public method sit {} {
    puts "Sitting!"
  }
  protected method bark {} {
    puts "Woof!"
  }
  protected method rollover {} {
    puts "Rolling over!"
  }
  protected method scratch {} {
    puts "I need a flea collar!"
  }
}

::itcl::class ScottishTerrier  {
  inherit Dog

  # Class Methods
  public method speak {} {
    bark
  }
  public method doTricks {} {
    sit
    rollover
    feedme
  }
  private method feedme {} {
    puts -nonewline "OK, where's my treat?   "
    bark
  }
}
```

Save Dog in a file called Dog.itcl and ScottishTerrier in a filed called ScottishTerrier.itcl, as you learned previously in this chapter. Then, create a tclIndex file and type the following commands at the shell prompt:

```
% lappend auto_path .
% ScottishTerrier coco
coco
% coco sit    ← The sit method is available through inheritance.
Sitting!
% coco speak
Woof!   ← speak calls the protected method, bark, in the base class.
% coco doTricks
Sitting!
Rolling over!
OK, where's my treat?  Woof!
% coco scratch
bad option "scratch": should be one of...
  coco cget -option
  coco configure ?-option? ?value -option value...?
  coco doTricks
  ...
```

Notice that the public methods are available for use on the command line, which is outside the namespace of the class. That's appropriate because that's exactly what public methods are meant for—to interface with the object. The first call is to the *sit* method. This method is defined in the Dog class, but inheritance allows a ScottishTerrier object to call it. A derived class inherits all protected *and* public base class methods. Next, you tell **coco** to speak, and the protected base class method *bark* is called, also made available through inheritance. Then you tell **coco** to do some tricks. The *doTricks* public method then calls the public base class method, *sit*; the protected base class method, *rollover*; and the private derived class method *feedme*. Only ScottishTerrier methods are allowed to call *feedme* since it's a private method. Finally, notice what happens when you try to tell **coco** to scratch. The interpreter complains because *scratch* is not a public method. Only methods *within* Dog or ScottishTerrier have access to *scratch* since it's declared as protected.

Built-In Methods

In the previous example, notice that the interpreter tells you the available methods associated with the object when you try to access a nonpublic method. You probably expect to see *doTricks* and *sit* as available methods, but there are additional methods that are not declared in either Dog or ScottishTerrier. This is because all objects have a few built-in methods that exist independent of class methods: *configure, cget, info,* and *isa.* The first two are used in conjunction with public data members and are discussed in the next chapter. The next two are discussed in the following sections.

The *info* Method

The *info* method is a little known built-in method that can be useful for debugging and introspection. The syntax for this method is

```
objectName info option ?arg arg ...?
```

and the following table outlines the various options associated with it. (Note that question marks surrounding an argument denote the argument is optional.)

Option	Argument(s)	Description
args	methodName	Returns the specified method's parameter list.
body	methodName	Returns the body of the specified method.
class	--	Returns the object's associated class name.
function	--	Returns a complete list of all class method names, all inherited method names, and all built-in commands. Each name is prepended with the respective fully qualified class name.
	?methodName?	Returns all information on the given method name, including the access level, method type, fully qualified method name, parameter list, and method body.
	methodName ?-protection?	Returns the access level (also referred to as the protection level) for the given method.
	methodName ?-type?	Returns the type of method (regular class method or static, "method" or "proc").
	methodName ?-name?	Returns the fully qualified method name.

Option	Argument(s)	Description
	methodName ?-args?	Returns the specified method's parameter list.
	methodName ?-body?	Returns the specified method's body.
heritage	--	Returns a list of class names outlining the class inheritance hierarchy, starting with the specified object.
inherit	--	Returns a list of class names from which the object inherits.
variable	--	Returns a list of all class variable names, all variable names in base classes, and the *this* variable. Each variable is prepended with the fully qualified class name.
	?variableName?	Returns all information on the given variable name, including the access level, variable type, fully qualified variable name, default value, current value, and configuration body.
	variableName ?-protection?	Returns the access level (also referred to as the protection level) for the given variable.
	variableName ?-type?	Returns the type of variable (regular class variable or static, "variable" or "common").
	variableName ?-init?	Returns the value of the variable if it is initialized in the class definition; otherwise, returns "<undefined>."
	variableName ?-value?	Returns the current value of the variable. If empty, returns "<undefined>."
	variableName ?-config?	Used with public variables. Returns the associated configuration body. If empty, returns "<undefined>."

As you can see, *info* gives you the ability to quickly find a wealth of information about an object. You can use this as a debugging tool. If you wanted to know all accessible methods for a given object, for instance, and place the data into a listbox, you can type the few lines of code given in Example 2-13 in an **itkwish** shell. The resulting window is shown after the example.

Example 2-13
*Using info
to display
class method
information*

```
% pack [listbox .l] -fill both -expand 1
.l
% lappend auto_path .
% ScottishTerrier mcDuff
mcDuff
% set num 1
% foreach method [mcDuff info function] {
    .l insert end "$num) \
      [mcDuff info function $method -protection -type -name -args]"
    incr num
  }
```

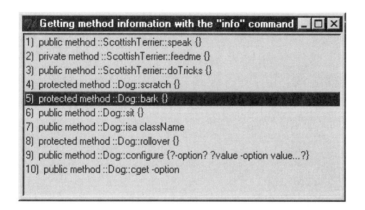

```
Getting method information with the "info" command  _ □ ✕
1) public method ::ScottishTerrier::speak {}
2) private method ::ScottishTerrier::feedme {}
3) public method ::ScottishTerrier::doTricks {}
4) protected method ::Dog::scratch {}
5) protected method ::Dog::bark {}
6) public method ::Dog::sit {}
7) public method ::Dog::isa className
8) protected method ::Dog::rollover {}
9) public method ::Dog::configure {?-option? ?value -option value...?}
10) public method ::Dog::cget -option
```

You can modify this example to find out class inheritance information, to print out the complete method bodies, or to list information on class data members. This command is a helpful debugging tool you can use during the course of development and testing. In production code, however, you should not use *info* as shown here, as that would violate OOD. Instead, declare appropriate accessor methods as needed.

The *isa* Method

In C++, base class pointers can point to objects of the base class or any derived class objects as well. As a result, it is not always possible for functions to know what kind of object the base class pointer is pointing to in advance. This is a problem called *run-time type identification* (RTTI). In [incr Tcl], a similar problem exists. Methods and procedures have no way of enforcing a particular object type to be passed into their parameter lists. A procedure might expect an argument to be an object of a particular class type, but it can't guarantee the object is the right kind until it asks it. To do this, you can use the *isa* method. This method is used for type safety, verifying that an object *is a* particular class type before proceeding. It accepts one argument, the class type, and returns a Boolean result. Example 2-14 illustrates this.

Example 2-14
Using *isa* for RTTI

```
% ::itcl::class Foo {}
% ::itcl::class Bar {}
% proc checkitout {object_} {
      if {[catch {$object_ isa Foo} rc]} {
        error "Invalid argument: $object_"
      }
      if {!$rc} {
        puts "Please pass an instance of Foo to this procedure."
        return
      } else {
        puts "OK!"
      }
  }
% Foo f
f
% Bar b
b
% checkitout b
Please pass an instance of Foo to this procedure.
% checkitout f
OK!
```

The checkitout procedure is able to determine at run time if it is passed the correct kind of object by using *isa* to determine if the object is an instance of the expected class type, Foo. Using *isa* like this can help you avoid unexpected results caused by accessing the wrong object type. Another example is when a base class method takes a particular action depending on the type of derived class being used. The base class method can ask a special variable called **this** which kind of derived class it is before it proceeds. You will learn more about this in the next chapter when the **this** variable is introduced. It is an extremely useful built-in variable that provides a generic way for objects to refer to themselves.

CHAPTER 3

Data Members

This chapter provides a thorough discussion of how data members are declared, accessed, and used in [incr Tcl]. First, you learn about the three access levels available for data member declaration and what restrictions are associated with each level. Next, the indispensable **this** variable is discussed in detail with several working examples, including drag-and-drop and a ticker tape. You will then learn about the different kinds of data members such as instance arrays and static scalars—when you should declare each and how you initialize each in the class definition. At the end of this chapter, you will be better equipped to optimize your applications and make them more robust and maintainable through a better understanding of [incr Tcl] data members.

Introduction

Data members are used to describe the characteristics of an object. They typically serve two main purposes: defining composition and maintaining state information. Think of composition as what an object *has*. A dialog window object, for example, *has* a button and a text message. These two components along with other data members define the composition of this object. Think of state information as what an object *knows*. A light switch object *knows* whether it's on or off, and a socket object *knows* whether it's readable or writable.

Whether used for composition or state information, data members determine the interface characteristics as well as the internal characteristics of objects. They may be public and used like Tk widget configuration options, they may be protected and encapsulated in a class hierarchy, or they may be private and used strictly for internal purposes. In any case, the name of the data member should always be intuitive enough to reflect its purpose. For example, you may define a Socket class that declares a data member used to determine whether the Socket object is writable. A good choice for the variable's name might be _writable. This variable could act as a Boolean with 1 meaning the object is writable and 0 meaning it's read-only. You could abbreviate this name to _w, but it isn't clear that "w" stands for writable. The other extreme would be to name it something like _aBooleanToStoreWhetherTheObjectIsWritable. Sure, it's obvious what a variable with this name is used to store, but long names like this are overkill and will greatly hinder your application's performance. For readability and maintainability, use concise, intuitive names.

Access Levels

Before you learn how to use data members, you must first understand the three different access, or protection, levels. Like class methods, data members may be declared as **public**, **protected**, or **private**. As Table 3-1 illustrates, the same access restrictions apply to data members that apply to methods.

Access Level	Restrictions
private	Restricted to use within the class scope in which the data member is declared.
protected	Like private data members, but can also be accessed in derived classes.
public	Can be accessed from within any scope.

3

Private Access

Access to private data members is just what you expect it to be—private. This is the most restricted access level. Private variables are visible only inside the class in which they are declared. The only way to access a private data member from outside the class is for the class to provide an accessor method, which is a controlled mechanism for getting or setting nonpublic class data (refer to the "Accessor Methods" section in Chapter 2 for more details). Most of the data members you declare should be private. The majority of the time, a data member does not need to be accessible outside its class scope, and if it does not *need* to be accessible, then encapsulate it by making it private. Example 3-1 shows how private variables are declared and accessed.

Example 3-1
Private data members are visible inside their class scope only

```
::itcl::class Opaque {
  # Accessor Methods
  public method info1 {args} {
    if {[llength $args]} {
      set _info1 $args
    } else {
      return $_info1
    }
  }

  # Class Methods
  private method doSomething {} {
    set _info2 val
    if {[string length $_info3]} {
      # do something
    }
  }

  # Class Data Members
  private variable _info1 5
  private variable _info2 ""
  private variable _info3 "hello world"
}
```

The name of this class reflects the visibility of its data members. You can only see them inside of the class itself. Method *doSomething* can freely access the class's private data members because class methods have privileged access to each of the protection levels. The only way to access them from outside the class, though, is to provide accessors like *info1*. Notice that the name of the accessor in this example is the same name as the data member, without the leading underscore. This is a common programming feature. The method body shows you how you can use accessor methods to service both get and set requests for class data members. This is a programming technique you can use to give the accessor method the ability to service both get and set requests for the data member.

Protected Access

Protected data members can be accessed by their associated class just like private data members. In addition, they can be accessed by derived classes. The protected access level is the "middle" level. It has fewer restrictions than private access but more than public access. This level is useful for defining in one location characteristics and components that can be shared by multiple classes. All dialog window objects, for example, have bitmaps, text messages, separator bars, and buttons, as discussed in Chapter 1. There may be different kinds of dialog windows, like informational dialogs or error dialogs that differ only in appearance. A base class can define protected data members to store the components that are common to all dialog window objects, and any specific kind of dialog window can access these components through inheritance. This way, each dialog window can share common component definitions and doesn't have to redefine components that may otherwise already be defined by sibling classes. Make sure to note the direction of inheritance. A derived class inherits protected base class functionality and can thus access protected base class data members. A base class *cannot* access protected derived class data members. This type of access is a one-way street. Examples that take advantage of the protected access level through inheritance can be found in Chapter 6.

Public Access

Public data members are often referred to as configuration options because they are used to configure objects. In Tk, you can change a label's foreground color or a frame's relief using Tk's **configure** command. [incr Tcl] provides similar functionality with two built-in methods, *configure* and *cget*. Each is used in conjunction with public data members. The *configure* method is used for modification, though it can also be used for retrieval, and the *cget* method is used for retrieval only. If you want to define an adjustable parameter, you can always provide accessor methods for getting and setting its value, but it's much easier to declare the variable as public instead. This way, the user can use *configure* to modify the variable and *cget* to retrieve it. The following sections explain how public data is declared and how to use these built-in methods.

3

Public Data Member Initialization

Declare public data members just as you do other access levels, but place them in a separate location in the class definition and always initialize them as shown in the following example.

Example 3-2
Initialize public
data members in
the "Configura-
tion Options"
section

```
::itcl::class Chord {
  # Configuration Options
  public variable root C
  public variable inversion root
  public variable octave 3
  public variable seventh none

  # Class constructor
  constructor {args} {
    eval configure $args
  }
}
```

A new section in the class definition called "Configuration Options" is shown for grouping public data members. Note that each one is initialized as it is declared. You should always initialize public data members as you declare them because even though *your* code may not access them until a particular method is called (as may be the case with a private variable), you have no control over when *other* code may access these data members since they are publicly available. To avoid potential stack traces resulting from this, simply provide default values as soon as you declare public variables.

Next, notice the use of the *configure* method in the *constructor*. Its purpose is to initialize any configuration options that may be specified during object creation. You may overwrite any default values specified in the variable declaration section when you instantiate the class by passing command-line arguments to the *constructor*. Now save the class definition in a file called Chord.itcl and type the following commands:

```
% source Chord.itcl
% Chord dmajor -root D -inversion first
dmajor
```

When the *constructor* is entered, each of the public data members is already initialized with its specified default value. The *configure* method then takes the **args** argument as input to overwrite these default values for the given configuration options. The -root configuration option is initialized to "D," and the -inversion configuration option is initialized to "first." The order of command-line configuration options does not matter, but each one must be followed by a single initialization value. As a result, you should always have an even number of **args** arguments.

NOTE: The dash in front of each configuration option is required. When parsing the command, the interpreter uses the dash to determine which argument is a configuration option and which one is the value. The dash is only used with the *configure* and *cget* methods. It is not part of the data member name in the class definition.

What happens, though, if you do *not* specify pairs of configuration options and their respective values, sending extra arguments into the **args** parameter? Perhaps you'd like the first two arguments to be used for initializing some private data and the rest of the arguments to be used for configuring public data. Doing this requires the effort of extracting from the **args** list which part of the list is configuration options and which part is other data, like this:

```
set _privateData1 [lindex $args 0]
set _privateData2 [lindex $args 1]
eval configure [lrange $args 2 end]
```

You should never do this because you have no way of enforcing how the user is going to specify *constructor* arguments. You could always return an error condition from the *constructor* and explain that a certain order of arguments is expected, but this would be a poor design because the **args** argument is used for passing in any number of arguments in any order. When you enforce a certain order with **args**, you defeat the purpose of using **args**. Instead, you should explicitly declare extra parameters in the parameter list. The user would then specify the two required arguments and then have the freedom to specify zero or more configuration options. The following *constructor* definition would satisfy this requirement:

```
constructor {arg1_ arg2_ args} {
  set _privateData1 $arg1_
  set _privateData2 $arg2_
  eval configure $args
}
```

Using configure *and* cget *for Public Data Member Access*

Use the *configure* method to modify individual or multiple configuration options or to list all available configuration options like this:

```
% dmajor configure
{-root C D} {-seventh none none} {-inversion root first} {-octave 3 3}
```

Notice that there are four available configuration options corresponding to the four public variables in the class definition. Each option is shown with three components: the name of the configuration option, its default value, and its current value. As an example, consider the first option, -root. It is defaulted to "C" in the class definition, shown by the second value in the list, but its current value is "D," shown by the last value. Neither –seventh nor –octave were specified during object creation, so notice that their current and default values are equal. To ask the object for the current value of one of its configuration options, use the *cget* method.

```
% dmajor cget -seventh
none
% dmajor cget -inversion
first
```

This built-in method provides quick access for retrieving configuration options' current values. If you specify a configuration option following the *configure* method on the other hand, then the interpreter returns the name of the option plus its default and current values like this:

```
% dmajor configure -inversion
-inversion root first
```

Technically, you could extract the current value from this list, but doing it this way takes about 34 percent longer than using *cget*, so if you just need to find out the current value of a public variable, use the *cget* method. Use *configure* for option modifications or for determining default values.

Controlling Public Data Member Values with Config Code

The declaration of a public data member has a special syntax that allows you to add code directly in the class definition for controlling configuration option values. You can use this code to do inline error checking for validation purposes. Modify the Chord class as follows to add error checking for the -root configuration option:

```
::itcl::class Chord {
  # Configuration Options
  public variable root C {
    puts "Validating specified value: \"$root\"..."
    if {![regexp {[A-G]} $root]} {
      # Returning from config code keeps the variable from changing!
      error "Invalid value!  Usage: configure -root \[A-G\]"
    } else {
      puts "Success!"
    }
  }
  . . .
}
```

After the public variable's default value, you can optionally add an opening brace followed by any number of lines of code and a closing brace. This is called *config code*. To invoke this code, use the *configure* method to attempt to modify the option's value.

```
% Chord fminor
fminor
% fminor configure -root "this text should not pass validation."
Validating specified value: "this text should not pass
validation."...
Invalid value!  Usage: configure -root [A-G]
% fminor cget -root
C  ← Note that the variable has not been modified.
% fminor configure -root F
Validating specified value: "F"...
Success!
% fminor cget -root
F  ← The "F" passed validation, so -root is successfully modified.
```

Specifying Config Code Outside the Class Definition with *configbody*

As you might imagine, the class definition can become very cluttered if you have multiple public data members, each with multiple lines of config code for error checking. Just as you can implement method bodies outside the class definition using the **body** command, you can also implement config code outside the class definition using a command called **configbody**. After moving the code for validating the -root option outside the class definition, your Chord.itcl file should look like this:

```
::itcl::class Chord {
  # Configuration Options
  public variable root C
  public variable inversion root
  public variable octave 3
  public variable seventh none

  # Class constructor
  constructor {args} {
    eval configure $args
  }
}

::itcl::configbody Chord::root {
  puts "Validating specified value: \"$root\"..."
  if {![regexp {[A-G]} $root]} {
    # Returning from config code keeps the variable from changing!
    error "Invalid value!  Usage: configure -root \[A-G\]"
  } else {
    puts "Success!"
  }
}
```

Notice that the syntax of **configbody** does not allow for any arguments. The argument is actually the configuration option itself, which is built into the config code. As soon as the config code is entered, the value of the configuration option becomes the value specified on the command line. Error checking follows, and if it is determined that the value is invalid, then the config code returns. Using the **error** command in the config code causes the configuration option to be reset to its original value. The configuration option is only modified if execution reaches the closing brace of the config code.

The this **Variable**

Recall from Chapter 2 that [incr Tcl] provides several built-in methods, like *isa* and *configure*. [incr Tcl] also provides a single built-in data member, **this**. Its purpose is to act as a "pointer" to the object. It contains the fully qualified name of the object itself, so you can use it in place of the object name as a generic way for self-reference.

The **this** variable models the variable of the same name in C++, and you will use it extensively in your [incr Tcl] projects. In order to configure user-initiated events (such as pressing a button) to invoke methods in your class, you have to use **this**. In order to register an object with another object for a future callback, you have to use **this**. In order for an object to invoke one of its own methods during an **after** event, you have to use **this**. You could also use the actual name of the object in each of these cases, but as a designer, you never know what object names the user is going to use. As a result, objects should have a generic way of referencing themselves, which is exactly what **this** provides. To summarize, any event that occurs outside the scope of a class that needs to invoke a method in that class must use **this**. The following simple example shows you the actual value of the **this** variable:

Example 3-3
The **this** variable
contains the
name of the
object

```
% ::itcl::class GolfClub {
    constructor {} {
        puts "I'm a $this!"
    }
}
% GolfClub 3wood
I'm a ::3wood!
3wood
% GolfClub sandWedge
I'm a ::sandWedge!
sandWedge
```

You might wonder why a "::" is printed in front of each object name. This is the global namespace identifier, and the **this** variable adds full namespace resolution to the object name. Since object **3wood** is created on the command line, the global namespace identifier is prepended to the object name. Remember that objects created on the command line are created in the global namespace. If you instantiate GolfClub from within some other namespace, *its* identifier is prepended in addition to the global identifier:

Example 3-4
Namespace
qualification and
the **this** variable

```
% ::itcl::class Golfer {
    constructor {} {
        puts "Creating GolfClub objects..."
        GolfClub 9iron
        GolfClub driver
    }
}
% Golfer me
Creating GolfClub objects...
I'm a ::Golfer::9iron!
I'm a ::Golfer::driver!
me
```

3

Since **9iron** and **driver** are both created from within the namespace of class Golfer, the **this** variable for each object contains the fully qualified namespace identifier, "::Golfer::." Now, what happens if you try to use **9iron** from the command line without its namespace identifier? You know that an object called **9iron** has been created, so you might try to use its built-in *isa* method, for instance, to ask it if it is a GolfClub object:

```
% 9iron isa GolfClub
invalid command name "9iron"
```

Why does the interpreter complain about this? You probably have already guessed correctly that the object name **9iron** only exists within the namespace context in which it was created, Golfer. In order to access it, then, you must use proper namespace resolution:

```
% ::Golfer::9iron isa GolfClub
1
```

REMEMBER: In order to use an object, you must specify its fully qualified name. Full namespace resolution is automatically built into the **this** variable.

Using *this For Binding User-Initiated Callbacks*

User-initiated callbacks can result from events such as pressing a button, clicking in a listbox, pressing a key, or moving the mouse. It is often necessary to capture such events using **bind** to call methods within your class. One example of this is dragging an object within a canvas, a utility that is commonly needed for graphical applications. Example 3-5 provides the drag-and-drop code for canvas items. (Before running this example, refer to step 5 following the code for comments regarding the drag-and-drop item.)

Example 3-5
Dragging and
dropping items
on a canvas—
user-initiated
callbacks

```
::itcl::class DragAndDrop {
  # Class constructor/destructor
  constructor {} {
    # Create and hide a new toplevel window.
    set _top [toplevel .[namespace tail $this] -relief ridge -bd 4]
    wm withdraw $_top

    # Create and pack internal tk components.
    set _canvas [canvas $_top.c -bg grey]
    set separator [frame $_top.sep -height 4 -relief sunken -bd 2]
    set b [button $_top.b -text Close \
      -command "::itcl::delete object $this"]
    pack $_canvas -fill both -expand 1
    pack $separator -fill x
    pack $b -ipadx 8 -ipady 4 -pady 8

    # Create canvas image.
    set itclman [label $_canvas.image -image [image create photo \
      -file ./iman2.gif]]
    $_canvas create window 200 125 -window $itclman -tags $_tag

    # Set up internal bindings on canvas tag.
    bind $itclman <1> [::itcl::code $this mark %X %Y]
    bind $itclman <B1-Motion> [::itcl::code $this drag %X %Y]
  }
  destructor {
    destroy $_top
  }

  # Class Methods
  public method draw {} {wm deiconify $_top}
  private method mark {oldx_ oldy_}
```

```
private method drag {currentx_ currenty_}

# Class Data Members
private {
  variable _oldx
  variable _oldy
  variable _tag icon
  variable _top
  variable _canvas
}
}

::itcl::body DragAndDrop::mark {newx_ newy_} {
  set _oldx $newx_
  set _oldy $newy_
}

::itcl::body DragAndDrop::drag {currentx_ currenty_} {
  set x [expr $currentx_ - $_oldx]
  set y [expr $currenty_ - $_oldy]
  $_canvas move $_tag $x $y
  mark $currentx_ $currenty_
}
```

Save the class definition in a file called DragAndDrop.def and the method bodies in a file called DragAndDrop.src, following the protocol discussed in Chapter 2. Note that all code in this chapter is available online. Then, type the following commands to create a tclIndex file and an instance of the class. The resulting window is shown in Figure 3-1.

```
% auto_mkindex . DragAndDrop.*
% lappend auto_path .
% DragAndDrop obj
obj
% obj draw
```

NOTE: Each time you invoke the **auto_mkindex** command as shown, your tclIndex file in the current working directory is overwritten. Be aware of this as you proceed with the examples.

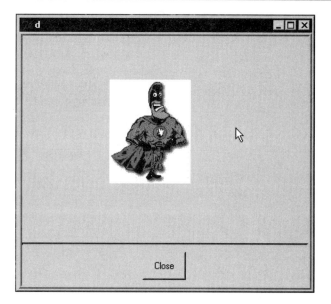

You can now drag and drop the image around the canvas. Let's walk through the code to understand exactly what happens (actions you should take are specified in italics):

1. `DragAndDrop obj`   The *constructor* is entered upon instantiation of the object, and it immediately creates a new top-level window.

2. `namespace tail $this`   This is one way that you can usually guarantee a unique top-level window name. The **namespace tail** command extracts the name of the object from its fully qualified name. For example, it returns "e" for objects named "::A::B::C::D::e" and "::e." Since objects of the same name can exist in different namespaces, this isn't bulletproof, but it is one way to help you choose top-level window names without having to think of new ones each time.

3. `wm withdraw $_window`   Once the top-level window is created, it is withdrawn. Recall from Chapter 1 that it is a common practice to withdraw windows so that the user doesn't see them until they are finished being constructed.

4. Canvas and button widgets are created and packed into the window. The canvas widget is saved as a private data member because it needs to be accessed by the class later during user-initiated callbacks. The frame (separator) and button widgets are not needed, so local variables are used instead. The **this** variable is used with the button's –command configuration option to delete the object when the button is pressed. In Chapter 1, you learned that you can use the **delete** command to delete objects. It follows that you can specify "$this" with the **delete** command since it is a container for the current object name.

3

5. `set itclman [label ...`   The **image** command provides input to the label's –image configuration option. You can either replace the path to the GIF image to point to another image of your choice, or you can download the image as shown in Figure 3-1 from http://www.tcltk.com/itcl/heroes.html. The label is then created inside the canvas widget, similar to placing a button inside of a frame. Note that the GIF image must be placed in the same directory in which you run the example because of the relative pathname.

6. `$_canvas create window ...`   A window is created inside the canvas at the specified coordinates to display the image, and it is tagged with the private data member, _tag, which is used later for moving the image across the canvas.

7. `bind $itclman ...`   Two bindings are tied to the image, the left button press event and the left button motion event. Recall from Chapter 2 that the **::itcl::code** command allows private method access from outside the scope of the class. User-initiated events happen at the global scope, so you must use this command fragment in order to access the *mark* and *drag* methods. The x and y coordinates of the mouse click relative to the top-level window are passed into each method.

8. `obj draw`   The object is fully constructed now, and you tell it to draw itself. The top-level window is simply de-iconified at this point.

9. *Click the left mouse button at any point in the image.* The *mark* method is called, which "marks" the point on the canvas corresponding to the button press event by storing the x and y coordinates in the private data members, _oldx and _oldy. These coordinates are needed for calculating the number of pixels to move the image during the "B1-Motion" callback.

10. *While holding the left mouse button down, move the mouse.* The *drag* method is called repeatedly to move the image across the canvas. The number of pixels to move the image is calculated by subtracting the old coordinates from the current coordinates. The old coordinates are then updated with the current values.

11. *Release the left mouse button.* The image is dropped at the most recent coordinates from the motion event. No callbacks have been tied to this mouse event, though you could easily do so by binding to the <ButtonRelease-1> option. A common drag-and-drop utility is to take some action that is invoked after release of the item. You may want to do this to control where you allow the user to drop the image. You could automatically redraw the image inside the viewable area, for example, if it is released outside the top-level window's boundaries.

Before moving on to the next example, you have probably noticed that the keyword, **private**, does not precede each variable name. Rather, it is specified once followed by an open brace, several variables, and a close brace. This is just an alternative way you can group variables and methods of the same protection level. So instead of doing this:

```
private variable _oldx
private variable _oldy
private variable _tag shape
private variable _window
private variable _canvas
```

you can do this:

```
private {
    variable _oldx
    variable _oldy
    variable _tag shape
    variable _window
    variable _canvas
}
```

Each method of declaration is equivalent, and you can use either method in your own applications. It is recommended that you use the first method so that it is crystal clear which protection level is associated with each variable/method since the level is specified on the same line as the variable or method name.

Using *this* *to Register Objects with Other Objects*

The Timer example from Chapter 2 mentions that you can use Timer objects to notify other objects when they expire. This would be useful so that an object can remain idle and wait for notification from the Timer when to proceed. You can use this facility to automatically exit your application after a certain amount of idle time. The application creates an instance of the Timer class and passes to its *constructor* a notification command, using "$this", that handles application shutdown. The following example shows one way to detect user idle time. You need to define the Timer class as given in Chapter 2 before you can run this example.

Example 3-6
Tracking idle users—registering objects for future callbacks

```
::itcl::class Watchdog {
  # Class constructor/destructor
  constructor {idleTime_} {
    # Create a timer and start it.
    set _timer [Timer t $idleTime_ [::itcl::code $this shutdown]]
    $_timer start

    # Set up watchdog mechanisms.
    foreach mouseButton {1 2 3} {
      bind . <$mouseButton> [::itcl::code $_timer reset]
      bind . <B$mouseButton-Motion> [::itcl::code $_timer reset]
      bind . <ButtonRelease-$mouseButton> \
        [namespace code "$_timer reset"]
    }
    foreach event {KeyPress Enter Leave} {
      bind . <$event> [::itcl::code $_timer reset]
    }
  }

  # Class Methods
  private method shutdown {} {
    puts "IDLE TIME EXCEEDED.  APPLICATION SHUT DOWN!"
    # Exit the program here, display a dialog window, etc.
  }
}
```

Save this class definition in a file called Watchdog.itcl in the same directory as Timer.def and Timer.src (as defined in Chapter 2) and type the following commands to run the Watchdog:

```
% auto_mkindex . Timer.* Watchdog.itcl
% lappend auto_path .
% Watchdog cujo 7
cujo
```

You will notice immediately that the Timer object begins counting. Again, let's walk through the code to understand how the two classes work together to create the working example (actions you should take are specified in italics):

1. `Watchdog cujo` The *constructor* is entered upon instantiation of the object and immediately instantiates the Timer class, passing to its *constructor* a threshold value and a command fragment. You should notice that this is the first time a class creates an instance of another class and stores the object in a data member. This is called *composition* and is discussed further in Chapter 7. The threshold is deliberately set to a small value in this example. You could set it to five minutes or five seconds, depending on your application. The **this** variable is used to register the *shutdown* method with the Timer object. When the Timer object reaches the specified threshold, it evaluates the given code fragment. Note the use of double quotes around the fragment. The interpreter replaces "$this" with the name of the Watchdog object before sending the string to Timer's *constructor*. If you use braces instead of quotes, "$this" won't be interpreted until the timer expires, and you will get an error since a variable of this name does not exist at the global scope.

2. `$_timer start` The Timer object is started and begins counting.

3. The core of the Watchdog class is its binding mechanisms. Several mouse bindings and a keypress binding are tied to the root window. When the mouse enters or leaves the root window or any of its internal components, or when any key is pressed or mouse button is clicked, the Timer object is instructed to reset itself. Once again, note the use of the **namespace code** command to wrap the proper namespace context around the object name, $_timer. This is needed because the Timer object only exists relative to Watchdog's namespace. Any use of the object name as a command outside the scope of this namespace must be preceded by its fully qualified namespace identifier like this, ::Watchdog::t.

4. `private method shutdown ...` Take note of the relationship between Timer and Watchdog resulting from the use of this method. A Timer object calls *shutdown*, which is a private method inside Watchdog's namespace. How can this be? In C++, the friend keyword allows objects the ability to access class's nonpublic member functions. The **namespace code** command is used for this purpose in [incr Tcl]. When the call to *shutdown* is sent to Timer's *constructor*, the call itself is actually wrapped with the proper namespace context and stored that way inside Timer's data member, _action.

5. *Experiment with events.* Try clicking in the root window, entering and leaving the window, etc. Each event should reset the Timer's _elapsedTime data member to 1.

6. Once the Timer object reaches the 7-second threshold, the command "::cujo shutdown" is invoked. The *shutdown* message is then printed in the window in which your interpreter was started. You can make *shutdown* do any number of things, from literally exiting the application to logging the user's name to a file to displaying a warning dialog box. The skeleton is provided, and you can implement the method body as your design dictates.

NOTE: You should be careful when implementing a utility like this to consider change detection. For example, you might consider saving the state of the application before shutting it down when the timer expires and then reinitializing that state when the user restarts the application.

3

Using *this* **for Self-Reference during** *after* **Callbacks**

In the previous example, the timer object uses the **after** command to access its *count* method once every second. This is a good example of how objects use **this** for self-reference during **after** callbacks. A graphical example can be illustrated with a class that scrolls text across the screen similar to a ticker tape. Consider the following class definition.

Example 3-7
A ticker tape uses **this** during **after** callbacks for scrolling

```
::itcl::class TickerTape {
  # Class constructor/destructor
  constructor {msg_} {
    set _canvas [canvas .c -bg grey40 -relief ridge -bd 4 \
      -width 400 -height 30]
    $_canvas create text [expr [winfo reqwidth .c] + \
      [expr [winfo reqwidth [label ._tmp_ -text $msg_]] / 2]] 20 \
      -text $msg_ -tag $_tag -fill green
    destroy ._tmp_
    pack $_canvas
  }

  # Class Methods
  public method scroll {} {
    $_canvas move $_tag -1 0
    if {[lindex [$_canvas bbox $_tag] 2] < 0} {
      return
    }
    after 5 [::itcl::code $this scroll]
  }

  # Class Data Members
  private variable _canvas
  private variable _tag txt
}
```

Save this class definition in a file and create an object as you have done in previous examples. This time, a blank screen appears, but note that nothing will happen until you tell the object to begin scrolling. Type the following lines of code to start the ticker tape. Figure 3-2 provides three snapshots of the same window as the text is scrolling. The text enters from the right side of the screen, scrolls to the left, and exits the left side of the screen.

```
% source TickerTape.itcl
% TickerTape tape \
    "True genius is the simple expression of complex ideas."
tape
% tape scroll
```

The implementation in this example is more complicated than previous examples, so let's once again walk through the code to see exactly how the text gets scrolled across the screen.

1. `TickerTape tape`   The *constructor* is entered upon instantiation of the object (note the required parameter, msg_) and immediately creates a canvas widget with a specific width and height.

Scrollable text on a canvas simulates a ticker tape

Figure 3-2.

3

2. `$_canvas create text …`   The canvas widget's "create" command is used with its –text option to create a text string on the canvas. The text should initially appear offscreen, so coordinates are calculated such that the leftmost character in the text will be just to the right of the canvas's viewable area. To do this, the text must be placed at an x coordinate equal to the width of the canvas plus half the width of the text. This is because the x coordinate passed to a canvas's "coords" command to position text is interpreted relative to the *center* of the text string in pixels. Since you can't ask a text string how many pixels it will take up on screen (that depends on the font used), a temporary label widget is created with the text string, its requested width is retrieved, and it is destroyed. A name for the label widget, "_tmp_" is chosen to minimize the chances of naming conflicts under the root window. The vertical center of the text (the y coordinate) is just hardcoded at 20 pixels from the top. The canvas is then packed, and the interpreter waits for further input.

3. `tape scroll`   The public *scroll* method is used to begin scrolling the text. The canvas moves the text via its canvas tag one pixel to the left every 5 milliseconds. An **after** event is created and uses this to recursively call *scroll*. With each iteration, the bounding box of the text is retrieved, and once the rightmost point in the text (the third entry in the list returned by the canvas's "bbox" command) is less than zero, *scroll* returns before creating another **after** event. This means that when the text disappears off the left edge of the screen, it stops scrolling.

Instance Variables

By now, you are probably familiar with instance variables because each variable in each example so far has been this type. An instance variable is an object-specific variable. Each class instance has its own copy of the variable, so when one object modifies its copy, any other objects of the same class type are unaffected. The majority of the variables you declare will be instance variables because it makes sense in most cases for variables to be associated with individual objects. Instance variables may be subdivided into two types: scalars and arrays.

Scalar Instance Variables

Scalar variables are one-dimensional. In other words, a scalar variable is only ever associated with one value. This value may be "5," "hello world," or "$this count." Not only has each of the variables you have seen so far been an instance variable, each one has been a scalar instance variable. They are usually initialized in the variable declaration section of the class definition or in the *constructor*, but they can also be initialized in any method body. Example 3-8 illustrates.

Example 3-8
Initialize scalar instance variables in the class definition, in the *constructor*, or in a method body

```
::itcl::class ScalarInstanceVars {
    # Class constructor
    constructor {} {
        set _sum [expr $_x + $_y]
    }

    # Class Methods
    public method product {i_ j_} {
        set _product [expr $i_ * $j_]
    }

    # Class Data Members
    private {
        variable _x 5
        variable _y 10
        variable _sum
        variable _product
    }
}
```

In this example, _x and _y are initialized in the variable declaration section. The variable _sum depends on the values of _x and _y, so it is initialized in the *constructor*. And the variable _product is not needed until the user calls the *product* method, so it is initialized in that method body. As this example illustrates, there are three ways you can initialize scalar instance variables. When trying to decide which of these ways to choose for initialization, consider the following suggestions:

◆ *Initialize the variable when it is declared*. It's safest to initialize the variable here to eliminate the possibility of potential errors caused by accessing the variable before it gets set. Assign an empty string if necessary just to give the variable a value. Sometimes, however, initialization in the variable declaration section is not practical.

◆ *Initialize the variable in the constructor*. If the value of the variable depends on the result of a command, like the creation of a widget or the instantiation of a class, then use the *constructor* to initialize it. Remember that the *constructor's* purpose is to *construct* the object, which includes the task of data member initialization.

◆ *Initialize the variable in a method body*. Most of the time, the variable should already have been initialized in the declaration section or in the *constructor*, but your particular application may guarantee that the variable will not be accessed until a particular method is called, so you can initialize the variable in the method body itself.

Array Instance Variables

Whereas scalar variables may contain only one value, arrays may be two-dimensional, containing several different values corresponding to different indices in the array. Array instance variable initialization is slightly different than scalars because you can't initialize them in the variable declaration section. They *must* be initialized in the *constructor* or in a method body. Consider the following example, which illustrates a common mistake.

Example 3-9
Once initialized, a variable name cannot be treated like an array

```
::itcl::class Equations {
   # Class constructor
   constructor {} {
      set _formulas(relativity) "E=mc^2"; #This causes an error.
   }

   # Class Data Members
   private variable _formulas ""; #This is a scalar variable now!
}
```

Before the *constructor* is entered during instantiation, the variable _formulas is initialized to an empty string, which means that this variable is now a *scalar instance* variable. Treating _formulas like an array any time after this results in an error. If you try to instantiate class Equations, the *constructor* error will disallow the object from being created. Notice that the following **info** command returns an empty string, which means that object **eq** does not get created.

```
% Equations eq
can't set "_formulas(relativity)": variable isn't array
% info commands eq
%
```

Once a variable is initialized in the variable declaration section, it becomes a scalar. You can change a scalar into an array by replacing the *constructor* from the Equations class with the following:

```
constructor {} {
   catch {unset _formulas}
   set _formulas(relativity) "E=mc^2"
}
```

The *constructor* now blindly unsets _formulas so that it can then be made into an array. Even though this works, it's impractical. If _formulas is meant to be an array, then don't initialize it in the variable declaration section. Instead, use the original *constructor* and remove the empty string initialization value. After it is properly initialized, you can add and remove entries from the array dynamically as shown in the following example:

Example 3-10
Like scalars, arrays can be modified at run time

```
::itcl::class Equations {
   # Class constructor
   constructor {} {
      array set _formulas [list circle-area pi*r^2 \
         circle-circumference 2*pi*r]
   }

   # Class Methods
   public method print {} {parray _formulas}
   public method add3dFormulas {} {
      set _formulas(sphere-volume) (4pi*r^3)/3
      set _formulas(box-volume) lwh
   }
   public method remove3dFormulas {} {
      unset _formulas(sphere-volume) _formulas(box-volume)
   }

   # Class Data Members
   private variable _formulas; #This fixes the error.
}
```

This example illustrates some of the versatility of instance arrays. Items are added to the _formulas array in the *constructor*, and the user can dynamically modify the array through a couple of interface methods. The following lines of code illustrate:

```
% Equations eq
eq
% eq print
_formulas(circle-area)          = pi*r^2
_formulas(circle-circumference) = 2*pi*r
% eq add3dFormulas
% eq print
_formulas(box-volume)           = lwh
_formulas(circle-area)          = pi*r^2
_formulas(circle-circumference) = 2*pi*r
_formulas(sphere-volume)        = (4pi*r^3)/3
```

```
% eq remove3dFormulas
% eq print
_formulas(circle-area)          = pi*r^2
_formulas(circle-circumference) = 2*pi*r
```

Static Variables

In the previous section, you learned that instance variables are object-specific. Each object maintains its own copy of instance data, and when that data is modified, other objects are unaffected. Static variables, on the other hand, are shared by all class instances and are class-level variables as opposed to object-level variables. When a static variable is modified, all class instances immediately see the new value because there is a 1:*n* correspondence between static data and any class instances, just like there is a 1:*n* correspondence between a class definition and any class instances. Any number of like objects may exist at the same time, but there is only one class definition for those objects. Similarly, there is only one copy of a static variable that all of the objects see. This is helpful for maintaining class-level data to avoid the overhead of storing the same data in each object. Static variables may be subdivided like instance variables into two types: scalars and arrays.

Scalar Static Variables

Scalar static variables are one-dimensional, containing a single value at any one time, just like scalar instance variables. Their accessibility is similar to global variables because you can typically access them from any namespace using the proper namespace resolution. Consider the following example that uses a static variable to keep track of the number of class instances.

Example 3-11
Use static variables to count the number of class instances

```
::itcl::class Coin {
  # Class constructor
  constructor {} {
    incr _INSTANCES
  }

  # Class Methods
  public method numberOfCoins {} {
    puts "$this: $_INSTANCES objects created"
  }

  # Class Data Members
  public common _INSTANCES 0
}
```

By replacing the **variable** keyword with **common**, class Coin declares a single static variable. Note that it is in all-caps to easily differentiate it from an instance variable. This protocol is followed throughout the rest of this book. As soon as the class is defined, the static variable exists and is initialized to zero. To access it outside the scope of the class, simply prepend the class's namespace identifier, "::Coin::." Now save the class definition in the file Coin.itcl and type the following commands:

```
% source Coin.itcl
% set ::Coin::_INSTANCES
0
```

As you can see, the static variable exists independently of any class instances since there *are* no class instances yet. As each object is created, the static variable is incremented to keep track of the number of objects.

```
% Coin schilling
schilling
% Coin pound
pound
% Coin dime
dime
% set ::Coin::_INSTANCES
3
```

In addition to accessing _INSTANCES from the command line, each object can see the variable without any namespace resolution, as shown in the *numberOfCoins* method:

```
% schilling numberOfCoins
::schilling: 3 objects created
% dime numberOfCoins
::dime: 3 objects created
```

Notice that the value of $_INSTANCES is the same for both objects. Remember, all objects *share* static data. Further, notice that the *numberOfCoins* method is nonstatic. As a result, you must create an instance of Coin in order to call *numberOfCoins*. This defeats the purpose of declaring a method to retrieve the static data in the first place since static data exists independently of class instances. You shouldn't force the user to instantiate a class to access data that is not dependent on instantiation. Instead, make *numberOfCoins* static. Then it can return the contents of the static variables whether or not Coin objects exist.

Notice that the static variable is declared as public. What happens if you declare it as private instead? This is a good question you might ask. Do static variables follow the same access rules as instance variables? The answer is yes and no. Change the access level for Coin::_INSTANCES to private, and then type the following commands to see:

3

```
% set ::Coin::_INSTANCES
0
% set ::Coin::_INSTANCES 5
5
% Coin penny
penny
% set ::Coin::_INSTANCES
6
```

No, this isn't a typographical error. Even though the variable is declared as private, you can still modify its value! This being the case, you might wonder why you would ever declare a private static variable in the first place. In [incr Tcl], access rules only pertain to static variables in inheritance. A derived class cannot access a base class's private static variable without proper namespace resolution. With proper namespace resolution, however, static variables, regardless of their access level, can be accessed from within *any* namespace.

 NOTE: In itcl3.0.x, access levels do not protect a class's static data. With proper namespace resolution, you can modify static data, regardless of the access level, from within any namespace. This may change in a future release.

Indeed, this violates encapsulation, but you should still select appropriate access levels for static variables just as you do for instance variables because this is likely to change in a future release of [incr Tcl]. Declare public static methods (static methods *do* follow access level rules) to access nonpublic static variables, and advertise the methods, not the variables, when outlining your class's interface for your customers.

Next, notice that the _INSTANCES variable is initialized in the variable declaration section of the class definition. Recall from the previous section that instance variables are typically initialized in the variable declaration section or in the *constructor* body. What happens if scalar static initialization is done in the *constructor* body? Modify the class definition as shown and then create class instances as you did earlier.

```
% ::itcl::class Coin {
    # Class constructor
    constructor {} {
      set _INSTANCES 0   ← Never initialize static data here!
      incr _INSTANCES
    }

    # Class Data Members
    public common _INSTANCES
  }
% set ::Coin::_INSTANCES
can't read "::Coin::_INSTANCES": no such variable
% Coin quarter
quarter
% Coin looney
looney
% Coin lyra
lyra
% set ::Coin::_INSTANCES
1
```

The first problem is that accessing the static variable before the class is instantiated causes a "no such variable" error. This is because it doesn't get initialized until the *constructor* is called. Forcing the user to instantiate a class in order to assign a value to a static data member defeats the purpose of declaring the data member static in the first place. Next, why is _INSTANCES equal to 1 after creating three objects? It gets incremented with each new class instance, so shouldn't it equal 3? As usual, the code is doing exactly what the programmer has told it to do, and alas, the programmer is at fault, not the code. Each time you create a new object, the static variable gets reinitialized to 0 again and overwrites the previous value. This brings up a rule of thumb you should always follow for static data initialization:

REMEMBER: Never initialize static data in the class *constructor* because each time you instantiate the class, the data will be reinitialized again, overwriting the previous value. Instead, always initialize static data in the variable declaration section of the class definition.

Static Array Variables

Static arrays may be two-dimensional just like instance arrays, and they are similar to global arrays just like static instance variables are similar to global variables. The main difference between static arrays and instance arrays is the initialization process. You cannot initialize instance arrays in the class definition, and you *should* initialize static arrays in the class definition, immediately following the array declaration.

Example 3-12
Initialize static
arrays in the
class definition

```
% ::itcl::class Example {
    # Class constructor
    constructor {} {
        # Don't do this! This overwrites indices a, b, c, and d each
        # time you create a new object!
        array set STATIC_ARRAY "a 10 b 20 c 30 d 40"
    }

    # Class Data Members
    public common STATIC_ARRAY
    array set STATIC_ARRAY "a 1 b 2 c 3 d 4"#; Initialize array here.
}
% parray ::Example::STATIC_ARRAY
Example::STATIC_ARRAY(a) = 1
Example::STATIC_ARRAY(b) = 2
Example::STATIC_ARRAY(c) = 3
Example::STATIC_ARRAY(d) = 4
% Example e
e
% !p   ← Replaced with "parray ::Example::STATIC_ARRAY"
Example::STATIC_ARRAY(a) = 10
Example::STATIC_ARRAY(b) = 20
Example::STATIC_ARRAY(c) = 30
Example::STATIC_ARRAY(d) = 40
```

3

The same rule that applies to static scalar variables also applies to static arrays, that you never initialize them in the class *constructor*. If so, each instantiation will overwrite any previous modifications to the values corresponding to those array indices, as shown in the example.

Now that you are familiar with each type of [incr Tcl] variable, you can use the following table as a quick future reference to determine when to initialize them.

Variable Type	Where to Initialize
scalar instance	(1) Variable declaration section (2) Constructor (3) Method body
array instance	(1) Constructor (2) Method body
scalar static	Variable declaration section
array static	Variable declaration section

Scoping

Class data members only have direct visibility within their class namespace. This means that direct access to data members is restricted to the class scope in which they are declared. Indirect access is provided for public data members via the *configure* and *cget* methods, as you learned earlier in this chapter. Sometimes, however, it's also necessary to gain access to nonpublic data members from outside the class scope. Recall from Chapter 2 that you must use the **::itcl::code** command to gain access to nonpublic methods. Similarly, [incr Tcl] provides the **scope** command to gain access to nonpublic data members. This is typically needed only in conjunction with widgets that maintain state information such as radiobuttons or checkbuttons. To illustrate, try the following example in a **wish** shell.

Example 3-13 Using **scope** to access nonpublic data members from the global scope

```
% package require Itcl
3.0
% ::itcl::class Toggle {
    constructor {} {
        checkbutton .cb -text Enable -onvalue 1 \
            -variable [::itcl::scope _state] \
            -command [::itcl::code $this toggle]
```

```
        frame .sep -height 4 -relief sunken -bd 2
        set _button [button .b -text OK]
        pack .cb
        pack .sep -pady 8 -fill x
        pack .b -pady 4
    }
    private method toggle {} {
        if {$_state} {
            $_button configure -state normal
        } else {
            $_button configure -state disabled
        }
    }
    private variable _button
    private variable _state 1
}
% Toggle t
t
```

3

The resulting window is shown on the left:

A checkbutton is used to toggle the state of the OK button. When the checkbutton is selected, the button is enabled (as shown on the left), and when the checkbutton is deselected, the button is disabled (as shown on the right). This is only possible because of the **scope** command, which wraps the proper namespace context around the private data member, _state, so that it can be modified when the user clicks the checkbutton. Remember that user-initiated events such as clicking a checkbutton occur at the global scope, so any variable modifications or method invocations also occur at the global scope and must therefore be wrapped with proper namespace resolution as necessary. Without the **scope** command, then, _state would be treated as a global variable, and the toggling of the button's state wouldn't work.

PORTABILITY TIP: In versions of [incr Tcl] prior to 3.x, you could use the **scope** command with variables that didn't exist. In version 3.x, however, the variable must exist. If it does not exist, you will get an error message similar to the following: *variable "_varname" not found in class "::MyClass".*

To see how the **scope** command works, you can simply print its return value as follows:

```
% ::itcl::class ScopeContent {
    constructor {} {
      puts "\[scope _varname\] == \"[::itcl::scope _varname]\""
    }
    private variable _varname 0; # Initialized prior to using scope!
  }
% ScopeContent sc
[scope _varname] == "@itcl ::sc ::ScopeContent::_varname"
sc
```

The interpreter recognizes this string as an instance variable belonging to object **sc**. By wrapping the namespace context around the variable name, a global event such as clicking a check button can modify an object's nonpublic instance variables. To the interpreter, the string returned from the **scope** command is equivalent to directly accessing the variable from within the class context.

Take note of two important items in this example. First, _varname is initialized in the variable declaration section. If you don't initialize the variable here or in the *constructor* prior to the use of **scope**, you'll get an error message as described in the portability tip. Next, _varname is the name of a variable. This may seem obvious, but unless the argument to **scope** is a variable name (either instance, static, or global), then **scope** returns an error.

The string returned by **scope** depends on the type of variable passed to it. Instance variables are treated as shown in the previous example. If the variable name is not an instance variable, then it must either be static or global. In both cases, the fully qualified name of the variable is returned. Rewrite ScopeContent as follows to illustrate:

```
% ::itcl::delete class ScopeContent
% ::itcl::class ScopeContent {
    public proc printScopedVar {} {
       puts "\[scope _VARNAME\] == \"[::itcl::scope _VARNAME]\""
    }
    public common _VARNAME default
  }
% ::ScopeContent::printScopedVar
[scope _VARNAME] == "::ScopeContent::_VARNAME"
```

3

Since _VARNAME is a static variable, **scope** works properly and returns the fully qualified variable name.

This concludes the discussion on [incr Tcl] data members. You now have the fundamentals necessary to design, implement, and use [incr Tcl] classes based on the information provided in this chapter as well as the previous chapter's discussion of methods. The next chapter digs into the process of construction and destruction. You will learn exactly what happens when you define a class and when you create an object, along with several other aspects of the construction and destruction processes.

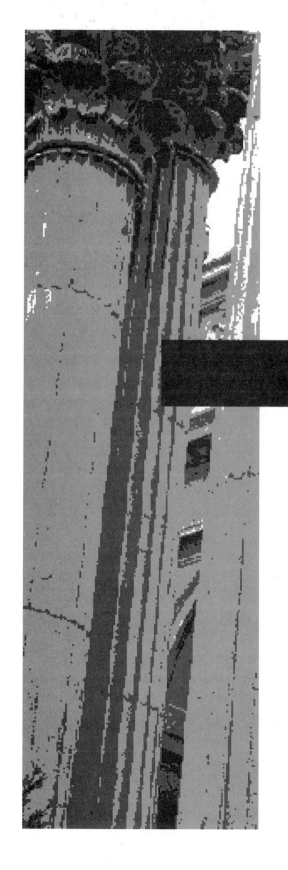

CHAPTER 4

Construction and Destruction

This chapter is entirely devoted to *constructors* and *destructors*. If you've ever wondered exactly what happens under the hood when you source a class definition or when you create an object, then all your questions should be answered in the first section, "The Construction Process." A detailed view of the class definition process, followed by the object creation process, is thoroughly discussed. Once you understand how classes are defined and objects are created, you will then learn several different aspects of construction and destruction, including the order of construction and destruction in a class hierarchy and how to pass arguments from a derived class across multiple levels of inheritance to a base class. You will also learn how to successfully handle errors encountered during construction and destruction, and even how to simulate overloaded *constructors* and copy *constructors* in [incr Tcl].

The Construction Process

Understanding the construction process is perhaps the most important part of learning [incr Tcl]. Before you can create an [incr Tcl] application, you must be able to create objects, and before you can create objects, you must be able to define classes. The first step, then, to understanding the construction process as a whole begins with class definition. The following sections outline what happens under the hood when you define and instantiate a class.

Defining the Class

As you learned in Chapter 1, you can define a class either by entering the definition directly on the command line or by saving it in a file and then sourcing it into the interpreter via the **source** command. After the class is defined, its name is registered with the interpreter as a new command that is used to create instances of that class. The following list outlines the internal steps taken to accomplish this:

1. Verify that the given class name doesn't already exist in the current namespace context.
2. Verify that a command with the given class name does not exist.
3. Verify that the class name doesn't contain reserved characters.
4. Allocate memory for a new [incr Tcl] class structure and initialize it.
5. Create a namespace to represent the given class.
6. Add the **this** variable to the list of class data members.

7. Create a command in the current namespace with the class name.

8. Parse the class definition.

9. Add built-in class methods.

10. Build namespace resolution tables for class methods and variables.

These steps represent the series of events that occur when you invoke the **source** command to read the class definition from a file or when you hit the carriage return key after the closing brace for a class definition on the command line. Each step is discussed in detail for the remainder of this section.

Step 1: Verify that the given class name doesn't already exist in the current namespace context

The first step is to ensure that there are no naming conflicts with the class name. In Tk, if you try to create two widgets with the same window pathname in the same interpreter, you will get an error message and the interpreter will fail to create the second widget. Similarly, if you try to define two classes with the same name in the same namespace, you will get the following error message:

```
% ::itcl::class A {}
% ::itcl::class A {}
class "A" already exists
```

Since both definitions are done in the global namespace, an error results. If you are familiar with the concept of namespaces, then you can skip to step 2. Otherwise, for a quick analogy, invoke a **wish** interpreter and type the following command:

```
% pack [button .b -text "Hello world" -command {puts ".b"}]
```

Simple enough—a button is packed into the root window and prints its name when you click it. Now type the same command again:

```
% pack [button .b -text "Hello world" -command {puts ".b"}]
window name "b" already exists in parent
```

As expected, you get an error message because you can't create two buttons with the same name in the same interpreter.

Now invoke another **wish** interpreter and type the same command in it. Notice that this interpreter does *not* complain about a naming conflict. This is because the two interpreters are independent, and each has its own copy of a root window. This is analogous to namespaces. Class names defined in one namespace do not conflict with class names in other namespaces, just as widget names defined in one interpreter do not conflict with widget names in other interpreters. For a more detailed discussion on namespaces, refer to Chapter 10.

Step 2: Verify that a command with the given class name does not exist

After determining that the class name is unique, [incr Tcl] then makes sure that you don't overwrite existing commands such as object names, procedures, or shell-specific built-in commands. Unexpected errors from naming ambiguities could easily result from overwriting commands like this. For example, suppose you define a **proc** called AlarmHandler that you use to handle generic error situations in your particular subsystem. You eventually integrate your code with another subsystem that may be responsible for application-level alarm and trap handling. Unknown to you, one of the classes in this subsystem is named AlarmHandler. If both the procedure and the class are defined in the same namespace, then you'll get unexpected results, depending on which AlarmHandler is sourced first—the procedure or the class. If the procedure is sourced first, then the class is unusable, as shown in the following lines of code:

```
% proc AlarmHandler {args} {
    puts "proc \"AlarmHandler\" called with arguments \"$args\"."
  }
% ::itcl::class AlarmHandler {}
command "AlarmHandler" already exists in namespace "::"
```

As soon as you type the first line, AlarmHandler is registered with the interpreter as a valid command in the global namespace. On the next line, you attempt to define a class with the same name. According to step 2 of the class definition process, an error is generated since AlarmHandler already exists as a command in the same namespace. Now exit and restart the shell and reverse the order of definition.

```
% ::itcl::class AlarmHandler {}
% proc AlarmHandler {args} {
    puts "proc \"AlarmHandler\" called with arguments \"$args\"."
  }
```

```
% AlarmHandler alarmHandlerObject
proc "AlarmHandler" called with arguments "alarmHandlerObject".
```

You expect to create an instance of the AlarmHandler class, but as you can see, if the class is defined before the procedure, then the class definition will be overwritten by the procedure definition! Be aware of this potential pitfall in your applications. In this example, it's easy to quickly spot the problem since the procedure and class are defined one right after the other on the command line. As you can imagine, though, this could be a difficult problem to debug if your application consists of thousands of lines of code and possibly hundreds of classes and procedures.

4

[incr Tcl] prevents you from overwriting shell-specific built-in commands in addition to user-defined commands such as procedure names. In an **itkwish** shell, for example, you cannot define a class named wm or winfo because each of these is a built-in Tk command. Imagine the chaos if [incr Tcl] allowed you to define a class called ::itcl::class in an [incr Tcl] shell! As the following line of code illustrates, the interpreter does not allow you to shoot yourself in the foot by overwriting basic shell commands.

```
%::itcl::class ::itcl::class {}
command "::itcl::class" already exists
```

Step 3: Verify that the class name doesn't contain reserved characters

In [incr Tcl], the "." character is reserved for internal use, so you can't embed a dot inside a class name. You can expect the following error message if you try to do so:

```
% ::itcl::class Embedd.edDot {}
bad class name "Embedd.edDot"
```

The dot is the only reserved character, so [incr Tcl] won't keep you from using other nonalpha characters and naming a class like this:

```
% ::itcl::class (*#@#$^@% {
    constructor {} {
      puts "Object name: $this"
      puts "Class type: [info heritage]"
    }
  }
% (*#@#$^@% garbage
```

```
Object name: ::garbage
Class type: {::(*#@#$^@%}
garbage
```

Needless to say, don't name classes like this. Use intuitive names, because any future maintainers of your code will have no idea what this class is supposed to do by its name. It's clear that a class named AlarmHandler probably handles alarms, and that a class named DialogWindow probably displays a dialog window. But if you name a class (*#@#$^@%, there is no way of determining its purpose without reading the code.

Step 4: Allocate memory for a new [incr Tcl] class structure and initialize it
After determining that there are no naming conflicts and that the class name is syntactically valid, memory is then allocated for the internal structure that contains all class definition data. The structure's data is initialized to null in this step and filled with data as the class definition is parsed in step 8. The class's heritage information is also initialized in this step with the class name.

Step 5: Create a namespace to represent the given class
The next step is to create a namespace reserved for use by the given class name. Each class defined in [incr Tcl] represents its own namespace. Again, think of a namespace as a "new interpreter." All methods and variables defined within this new namespace must be unique, but the same names can be used across multiple namespaces.

Step 6: Add the *this* variable to the list of class data members
This is where the **this** variable is "born." It is added to a hash table of class data members in the [incr Tcl] class structure allocated in step 4 and its access level is set to **protected**. Later during object creation, its value is initialized to the fully qualified object name.

Step 7: Create a command in the current namespace with the class name
This step registers the class name as a new command with the interpreter. As mentioned at the beginning of this section, the class name can then be used to create class instances. Note that the command is created in the *current* namespace. This refers to the namespace in which the class is defined. For example, if you enter a class definition directly on the command line, the class name becomes a command in the global namespace. This is also true for

each of the class definitions up to this point that are sourced from files. In Chapter 10, you will learn how to create new namespaces with embedded classes. For now, however, all examples will remain in the global namespace to keep from introducing another level of complexity.

Step 8: Parse the class definition

Once the class name becomes a new command, the class definition itself is parsed to make sure its syntax follows all [incr Tcl] class definition rules. As the parser goes through the class definition, each line is checked to make sure it adheres to the rules outlined in Table 4-1. [incr Tcl] keywords are shown in boldface, and optional items are surrounded by question marks.

4

As an example, take a look at the syntax for declaring public variables. The **public** keyword is followed by the **variable** keyword, a variable name, an optional initialization value, and an optional configuration body (refer to Chapter 3 for an example of the configuration body). Notice that braces are

Keyword	Syntax
inherit	**inherit** baseClassName ?baseClassName baseClassName ...?
constructor	**constructor** {?parameterList?} ?{init code}? {?body?}
destructor	**destructor** {?body?}
public	?**public**? **proc|method** methodName {?parameterList?} ?{body}?
	public variable variableName ?initValue? ?{body}?
	public common variableName ?initValue?
protected	**protected proc|method** methodName {?parameterList?} ?{body}?
	?**protected**? **common|variable** variableName ?initValue?
private	**private proc|method** methodName {?parameterList?} ?{body}?
	private common|variable variableName ?initValue?

Class Definition Syntax Rules

Table 4-1.

sometimes shown inside the pair of question marks and sometimes outside. Consider the *constructor*. The *constructor* keyword is followed by an open brace, an optional list of parameters, a close brace, optional init code enclosed in braces, another open brace, an optional body, and a close brace. (Note that the init code together with the braces are optional. This is discussed later in this chapter.)

As each item in the class definition is successfully parsed, new entries are added to the hash tables in the [incr Tcl] class structure discussed in step 4 to register all data members, methods, inheritance information, etc. But what happens if the item is *not* successfully parsed? If a syntax error is encountered during parsing of the class definition, then any allocated memory is freed, and the interpreter generates an error message. Common mistakes include forgetting one of the pairs of braces in the *constructor* prototype, incorrectly embedding comments, or adding a pair of braces in the *destructor* prototype. Each mistake is outlined in the following example.

Example 4-1
Common syntax errors made in the class definition

```
% ::itcl::class SyntaxError {
    constructor {}
  }
wrong # args: should be "constructor args ?init? body"
%
% ::itcl::class SyntaxError {
    private variable _foo  # Comment here describing foo's use.
  }
wrong # args: should be "variable name ?init?"
%
% ::itcl::class SyntaxError {
    destructor {} {
      # Housekeeping tasks done in here
    }
  }
wrong # args: should be "destructor body"
```

For the first error, review the rules for a *constructor*'s syntax from Table 4-1, and you'll see that its prototype must include two pairs of braces. The reason for this is discussed later in this chapter. Note that the *constructor* is the *only* class method that requires two sets of braces. For the second error, remember that in order to embed comments in the class definition, you must mark the end of the previous command with a semicolon, so in this case, a semicolon must come between _foo and the pound sign. The last example needs a little more discussion. *Inside* the class definition, the *destructor* must be followed by exactly one pair of braces, which contain an optional body. *Outside* the class definition, however, the rules for the **body** command prevail, and you must include a pair of braces that normally are used for method parameters. The syntax for the *destructor* when implementing it outside the class definition is

```
::itcl::body Classname::destructor {} {
  # destructor body goes here
}
```

REMEMBER: When implementing the *destructor* outside the class definition, you must include a pair of braces between the *destructor* keyword and its body because of the syntax required by the **body** command.

4

Step 9: Add built-in class methods

By this point, the class definition has been successfully parsed, and the built-in methods *cget*, *configure*, and *isa* are added. However, these methods are only added if you haven't explicitly overwritten them with methods of the same name elsewhere in the class hierarchy. Be careful when naming class methods, because [incr Tcl] allows you to overwrite built-in methods and commands. Consider the following example.

Example 4-2
Be careful when overwriting built-in methods and commands in the class definition

```
% ::itcl::class Overwrite {
    public {
       variable publicVar "default value"
       method update {parameter_} {puts "Overwrite::update called!"}
       method cget {} {puts "Overwrite::cget called!"}
       method go {} {
          update idletasks
          set data [cget -publicVar]
       }
    }
}
% Overwrite obj
obj
% obj go
Overwrite::update called!
wrong # args: should be "obj cget"
```

This example shows you how overwriting built-in command and methods can be dangerous. When you invoke the Overwrite object's *go* method, the programmer may think that the Tk **update** command is being called with the idletasks argument to refresh the screen, but as you can see, the class definition has declared its own *update* method, which takes precedence over

Tk's **update** command. Further, Overwrite also declares a *cget* method, which overwrites the built-in *cget* method that is normally added in step 9 of the class definition process. The method in this example does not declare any parameters, so when the publicVar data member is accessed via *cget*, as would normally be the case, an error occurs. Just be aware that unexpected results can happen if you're not careful when using class methods that override built-in commands. The best practice is to avoid doing this altogether.

Step 10: Build namespace resolution tables for class methods and variables

This final step in the class definition process sets up virtual namespace resolution tables for all class data members and methods, which allow you to access them internally and across class hierarchies without having to use full namespace resolution. In the following example, the Child class can access Parent's *print* method without having to specify a namespace qualifier.

Example 4-3
Common syntax errors made in the class definition

```
% ::itcl::class Parent {
    # Class Methods
    protected method print {} {puts "Parent::print"}
    private method restricted {} {
        # Only instances of Parent can access this method.
    }
}

% ::itcl::class Child {
    inherit Parent
    constructor {} {print}; # "::Parent::print" is not needed here.
    public method access {} {::Parent::restricted}
}
% Child c
Parent::print
c
```

Additionally, this step prevents you from accessing a class's private methods from outside its namespace, regardless of whether you use namespace resolution, as shown when the Child object tries to call Parent's *restricted* method.

```
% c access
invalid command name "::Parent::restricted"
```

Object Creation

The next step of the construction process is to create an object. Like the class definition process, object creation involves several steps before the resulting object name is returned as a new command. The following list outlines the internal steps taken to accomplish this:

1. Automatically generate the object name if necessary.
2. Verify that a command with the given object name does not exist in the current namespace context.
3. Allocate memory for a new [incr Tcl] object structure and initialize it.
4. Create a command in the current namespace with the object name.
5. Allocate and initialize instance variables, most specific class first.
6. Invoke class *constructors*, most specific class first.
7. Add the object name to the list of known objects.

These steps represent the series of events that occur when you instantiate a class. Several of them are similar to steps from the class definition process, and you will be referred back to these steps accordingly.

Step 1: Automatically generate the object name if necessary

If the specified object name contains the string "#auto," then that part of the object name is replaced with a uniquely generated string based on the class name. This allows you to avoid any possible naming conflicts by relying on [incr Tcl] to generate the object name for you. The generated name is guaranteed to be unique. If "#auto" is specified, then the resulting generated name is used for the remainder of the object creation process. Auto-generated object names are discussed in more detail later in this chapter.

Step 2: Verify that a command with the given object name does not exist in the current namespace context

In step 2 of the class definition process, you learned that you can't overwrite procedure names or built-in shell commands. Similarly, the second step of the object creation process prevents you from declaring object names that conflict with existing commands in the current namespace. For example, you can't create an object called "puts" or "format" since each of these strings is actually a built-in Tcl command. Likewise, you can't create two objects of the same name. The generated error for illegal names in this step is the same as the error in step 2 of the class definition process.

Step 3: Allocate memory for a new [incr Tcl] object structure and initialize it

This step is similar to step 4 of the class definition process. Space is allocated for a new [incr Tcl] object structure, and it is initialized to null. The structure is filled with data later in the object creation process.

Step 4: Create a command in the current namespace with the object name

Similar to step 7 in the class definition process, this step registers the object name as a new command in the interpreter. Once the object creation process completes, you can use the object name to access class methods and data members.

Step 5: Allocate and initialize instance variables, most specific class first

This is the step referred to in step 6 of the class definition process. The list containing the data member information is now used for allocating and initializing each of the class's instance variables. By initializing them prior to *constructor* invocation, you are able to access instance variables immediately in the *constructor* body. For example, you can set the default value of a filename in the variable declaration section and then access the data member for opening the file in the *constructor* as shown in the example below.

Example 4-4
Data members initialized in the variable declaration section are accessible in the constructor

```
::itcl::class File {
   constructor {} {
      if {[file exists $_filename]} {
         set fid [open $_filename r]
         ...
      }
   }
   private variable _filename "/foo/bar/baz"
}
```

Now notice that instance variables are allocated and initialized "most specific class first." This means that if the class is part of an inheritance tree, then the instance variables of the class being instantiated are initialized first, followed by the class's immediate base class, and continuing up the inheritance ladder until the instance variables in the least specific class are initialized. This allows derived classes the ability to override public and protected data members in base classes with the same name. Consider the following simple class hierarchy:

```
::itcl::class Mode {
  public variable tonic
  protected variable _mode
  protected variable _notes
}
::itcl::class Ionian {
  inherit Mode
  protected variable _fourth major
}
::itcl::class Lydian {
  inherit Ionian
  private variable _fourth augmented
}
```

4

If you instantiate Lydian, then *its* instance variable, _fourth, is initialized first. Ionian's instance variables are next in order for initialization, but since _fourth is already in the chain of data members, it is skipped, overwritten by Lydian's _fourth. As a result, any reference to _fourth in Lydian's namespace will refer to *its* data member, not the one in its base class. Finally, the three instance variables in Mode are initialized.

Step 6: Invoke class constructors, most specific class first

Once instance variables are allocated and initialized, each *constructor* in the class hierarchy is invoked, starting with the most specific class. Don't be confused by this, because the actual order in which the *constructor* bodies are *interpreted* begins with the least specific class! It's the order of *invocation* that begins with the most specific class. Here's how this happens. The most specific class's *constructor* is invoked first, but before the body of the *constructor* is actually executed, the class's inheritance is examined. If the class inherits from another class, then *that* class's *constructor* is invoked. Similarly, if the base class inherits from another class, then *that* class's *constructor* is invoked. This chain reaction continues until the top of the inheritance tree is reached, at which time the interpreting of the *constructor* bodies begins, traversing the order of *constructor* invocations in the reverse order.

NOTE: The order of *constructor* invocation begins with the most specific class, but the order of the actual *constructor* body execution begins with the *least* specific class. As a result, class hierarchies are constructed in order from the least specific class to the most specific class.

Notice from the example in step 5 that Mode, Ionian, and Lydian each lack a *constructor* definition. The order of *constructor* invocations and executions does not change, however, just because there are no *constructor*s defined. Recall from Chapter 1 that it isn't necessary to declare a *constructor* in order to create an object. [incr Tcl] provides a default *constructor* that is invoked for any class that does not explicitly define one. So the default *constructor* for Lydian is invoked first. The interpreter determines its inheritance information from the table set up by step 5 of the class definition process and invokes Ionian's *constructor* as a result. Likewise, the interpreter determines Ionian's base class and invokes Mode's *constructor*. Mode's inheritance information is queried, and when it is determined that Mode does not inherit from any class, each *constructor* body in the class hierarchy is executed, Mode first, followed by Ionian and Lydian.

This is a lot of information to absorb, so consider the following example, which adds *constructor*s with **puts** statements to each of the class definitions to visually show the order of construction.

Example 4-5
Classes are constructed "top-down"

```
% ::itcl::class Mode {
    public variable tonic
    constructor {} {
      puts "Mode::constructor"
    }
    protected variable _mode
    protected variable _notes
  }
% ::itcl::class Ionian {
    inherit Mode
    constructor {} {
      puts "Ionian::constructor"
      puts " - _fourth: $_fourth"
    }
    protected variable _fourth major
  }
% ::itcl::class Lydian {
    inherit Ionian
    constructor {} {
      puts "Lydian::constructor"
      puts " - _fourth: $_fourth"
    }
    private variable _fourth augmented
  }
% Lydian g
Mode::constructor
```

```
Ionian::constructor
 - _fourth: major
Lydian::constructor
 - _fourth: augmented
g
```

Don't worry if you don't understand what the terminology in these classes means. If you do, you're probably a musician. It is more important for you to understand the *concepts* involved. First, the order of *constructor* body execution is "top-down," meaning that the *constructor* body in the topmost class of the hierarchy, Mode, is interpreted first, traveling down the inheritance tree to the bottommost class, Lydian. How is it determined that Mode is the topmost class in the tree? This is done by invoking each *constructor*, starting with the bottommost class and querying inheritance information until the top of the tree is reached. Next, notice that both Lydian and its immediate base class, Ionian, contain the same **puts** statement for printing the value of _fourth. As you can see from the output, when Ionian's *constructor* is executed, it prints "major" for the value of _fourth since as far as Ionian knows, the only _fourth in existence is its own. Then when Lydian's *constructor* is executed, *its* _fourth overwrites Ionian's, so "augmented" is printed.

Step 7: Add the object name to the list of known objects
By this point, the object is fully constructed, and the last step is to add the object name to an internal list of all known objects of this class type. This step allows you the ability to query the interpreter for instances of this class via the **find** command. This is a handy tool you can use throughout your application if you're not sure if objects of a particular class type exist, or if you need to know the names of those objects. In the following example, the **find** command locates instances of Keys that you may have "lost" in your application.

Example 4-6
Use the **find** command to locate instances of a class

```
% ::itcl::class Keys {
   }
% Keys car
car
% Keys house
house
% Keys fileCabinet
fileCabinet
% ::itcl::find objects -class Keys
car fileCabinet house
```

After completion of step 7, the object creation process is finished and the object is ready for use! Now when you define a class and create an object, you know exactly what happens under the hood to set things up for you. Don't be concerned if you think the previous sections are a bit overwhelming. A lot of reference details have been provided, and you don't need to understand every detail of the construction process in order to use [incr Tcl] and design well-organized programs. The construction process can be summarized by the following key steps:

1. Source the class definition.
   a) Class name is registered as a command used to create objects.
2. Instantiate the class.
   a) Instance variables are allocated and initialized.
   b) If *constructors* are defined, they are executed, least specific class first.
   c) Any *constructor* errors prevent object creation (discussed later in this chapter).
   d) The object name is registered as a command used to access class methods and variables.

Auto-Generated Object Names

In step 1 of the object creation process, you learned that [incr Tcl] can automatically generate unique object names for you. If you embed the text "#auto" in the object name, this text is replaced with a uniquely generated string based on the class name. You should take advantage of this mechanism whenever possible to avoid any namespace conflicts. Since the resulting object name is always unique, you don't have to worry about explicitly checking for the existence of the object with the specified name prior to instantiation. Type the following commands in a **tclsh** shell to experiment.

Example 4-7
Use #auto to generate unique object names

```
% package require Itcl
3.0
% ::itcl::class Unique {}
% Unique #auto
unique0
% Unique #auto
unique1
% ::itcl::find objects -class Unique
unique0 unique1
```

The name of the class and a trailing number replace the text string, "#auto." The trailing number is based on the current number of objects that exist in the current namespace—in this case, the global namespace. Since no Unique objects exist at first, a zero is appended to the object name. The next instantiation results in a one being appended to the object name since only one object exists at that time.

The most common use of "#auto" is just by itself, as shown in the previous example. You can embed this text anywhere in the object name, however, and that part of the name is replaced with a uniquely generated string. Continue the example by creating the following objects.

4

```
% Unique inThe#autoMiddle
inTheunique2Middle
% Unique #autoInFront
unique3InFront
% Unique atTheEnd#auto
atTheEndunique4
% ::itcl::find objects -class Unique
unique0 unique1 inTheunique2Middle atTheEndunique4 unique3InFront
```

As you can see, "#auto" can be embedded in the middle of the object name, it can be the first part of the name, or it can be at the end of the name. In each case in this example, it is replaced with "unique" and a number based on the current number of objects. For the remainder of this book, the "#auto" mechanism is used for all objects created in working application code, such as the socket programming framework in Chapter 6.

Default Constructors/Destructors

The construction process implies that the *constructor* declaration in the class definition is not required, stating in certain steps that *if* you declare a *constructor*, then some corresponding action will be invoked. Indeed, neither the *constructor* nor the *destructor* is needed in order for you to create, use, and delete objects. [incr Tcl] provides default methods for you.

The *constructor* is used for object initialization. If you can initialize class data members in the variable declaration section or in other method bodies, and you don't need to manage any other initialization tasks during object creation, then you may not need a *constructor*. Conversely, the *destructor* is used to deallocate any open resources when the object is deleted. If you have any open files, or if the object has created any images or other objects, then these resources must be freed in the *destructor* if they are not freed elsewhere.

You would define a *destructor* to close the open files and delete the images and other objects. If the object does not open files or allocate any other resources, then you may not need a *destructor*.

Knowing when to declare *constructor*s and *destructor*s depends on the task at hand. If you want to maintain control over the construction and destruction process, then you need to define your own methods. For example, you may not need to handle any initialization or deallocation tasks, but you may want to verify that certain conditions exist before allowing the object to be created or deleted. You would have to define a *constructor* and/or *destructor* to handle such tasks. If you are learning [incr Tcl], then you should develop a habit of always declaring both methods. Once you become familiar with programming and developing [incr Tcl] applications, you will know when you should declare each and when you should use the defaults.

Initializing Configuration Options

If you declare any configuration options in your class definition, then you need to include the **args** parameter in the *constructor*'s parameter list. (Recall from Chapter 2 that the **args** keyword is used to pass a variable number of arguments to a method.) Then, at some point in the *constructor* body, typically at the end, you should use the built-in *configure* method to initialize any configuration options that may have been specified during instantiation. To do this, use the **eval** command to properly bundle the list of options in **args** as arguments to *configure* like this:

```
eval configure $args
```

As you learned earlier in this chapter (step 10 of the class definition process), you don't have to specify any namespace resolution or use the **this** variable to invoke *configure*. You typically specify this line of code as the last line in the *constructor*'s body. Sometimes it may be necessary to access updated configuration option values in the *constructor*, however, so you can specify this line of code earlier if needed.

When invoked, the *configure* method expects optional pairs of configuration options and their corresponding values as arguments.

```
configure ?-option value -option value ...?
```

These pairs are optional because **args** may be empty. Notice that each option is preceded by a dash. This is required for accessing and modifying configuration options. Even though the dash is not physically part of the variable name in the class definition, it must precede the name when accessing it with *configure*. Another rule that must be followed is declaration of the proper access level. Configuration options must be declared as public in the class definition. This is probably obvious because the definition of a configuration option states that it is a public data member. If either one of these rules is broken, the interpreter will generate an error message as shown in the following example.

Example 4-8
Configuration options must be public and preceded by a dash when using the *configure* method

```
% ::itcl::class Example {
    public variable var1 "default value"
    variable var2
    constructor {args} {
      eval configure $args
    }
  }
% Example e -var2 0
unknown option "-var2"    ← var2 is protected, not public!
% Example e var1 0
unknown option "var1"     ← option must be preceded by a dash!
% Example e -var3 0
unknown option "-var3"    ← option is not defined in Example!
% Example e -var1 0
e
% e cget -var1
0
```

4

As you can see, the same error is generated when either a nonpublic access level is declared (remember that data members are protected by default) or when the first character is not a dash. The error also occurs, of course, when the option really doesn't exist, as the attempt to use –var3 illustrates. When you encounter this error message as you program and debug your applications, it will be the result of one of the conditions shown in this example.

Passing Arguments to Base Class Constructors

One of the most common mistakes made when creating an inheritance hierarchy occurs when the programmer forgets to specify arguments for base class *constructors*. Earlier in this chapter, you learned that when you instantiate a derived class, [incr Tcl] automatically executes each of the base class *constructors*, from least specific to most specific. But what happens if they require arguments? How does the interpreter know what arguments to pass when it executes the base class *constructors*? Recall the syntax for the *constructor* prototype:

```
constructor {?parameterList?} ?{initCode}? {?body?}
```

The init code portion of the prototype is used for this purpose. When the base class *constructor* is invoked, the init code is used, if it exists, to specify the required arguments.

Before showing you the proper syntax for doing this, take a look at what happens when you do *not* specify required arguments.

Example 4-9
You must
specify init code
for base class
constructors that
require
arguments
```
% ::itcl::class Phone {
    constructor {manufacturer_} {
        set _manufacturer $manufacturer_
    }
    protected variable _manufacturer
}
% ::itcl::class Cellular {
    inherit Phone
}
% Cellular cellphone
wrong # args: should be "::Cellular cellphone manufacturer_"
```

According to the error message, it looks like you are supposed to pass an argument into Cellular's *constructor*. If you were debugging this error message in your application, you would probably first review the Cellular class definition to track down the problem. You would then notice that Cellular does not even declare a *constructor*, so you wonder why you're supposed to pass an argument to a *constructor* that doesn't even exist! (Note that even if Cellular *does* declare a *constructor* that requires an argument, the same error message results.) You might then go ahead and try specifying an argument like the error message states and reinstantiate to see what happens.

```
% Cellular cellphone companyXYZ
wrong # args: should be "::Cellular cellphone manufacturer_"
```

You get the same error message again, so at this point you become thoroughly confused before finally realizing that the problem is not with the derived class *constructor* after all. Rather, the *base* class *constructor* is the one that requires the manufacturer_ argument.

If this scenario sounds familiar, then the following explanation should clarify the problem and how to fix it. If you do not tell the interpreter what to pass the base class *constructor* via the derived class *constructor*'s init code, then it will invoke the base class *constructor* with *no* arguments, generating the error message shown in this example. Remember, the interpreter invokes *all constructor*s in a class hierarchy, so even though you're not instantiating the base class, passing arguments to its *constructor* directly on the command line, its *constructor* still gets invoked. You *must* use the init code to specify arguments for *any* base class *constructor* that requires arguments.

REMEMBER: If a base class *constructor* requires arguments, then you **4** *must* include the init code portion of the derived class *constructor* prototype to specify the required arguments.

Now that you are familiar with the error message and how you might encounter it, the syntax for the init code is

```
BaseClass::constructor arg ?arg arg ...?
```

Within the braces immediately following the *constructor*'s parameter list, specify the fully qualified base class *constructor* name and any necessary arguments. Now you can delete Cellular's class definition from the interpreter and rewrite it as follows to fix the problem:

```
% ::itcl::delete class Cellular
% ::itcl::class Cellular {
    inherit Phone
    constructor {} {Phone::constructor companyXYZ} {}
  }
% Cellular cellphone
cellphone
```

Since Cellular's *constructor* now provides the required argument in its init code for Phone's *constructor*, the object is successfully created. Most of the time, argument values cannot be hardcoded into the init code as this example does, because the value isn't known until run time. In this case, you should either require an argument in the derived class *constructor* or just declare an optional argument like the following:

```
::itcl::class Cellular {
  inherit Phone
  constructor {{manufacturer_ "companyXYZ"}} \
    {Phone::constructor $manufacturer_} {}
}
```

This allows the user to specify the base class *constructor* argument when instantiating the derived class, and since the parameter has a default value, instantiating the derived class still does not require an argument.

Now that you are comfortable with a single level of inheritance, consider the following class hierarchy that creates a scrollable listbox through multiple levels of inheritance. (Note that this does not refer to the concept of *multiple inheritance*, which is discussed in Chapter 8.)

Example 4-10
Passing *constructor* arguments up multiple levels of inheritance

```
::itcl::class BaseWidget {
  constructor {type_} {
    set _type $type_
    lappend _WIDGETS $this
  }
  public proc WIDGETS {} {return $_WIDGETS}
  protected variable _type
  private common _WIDGETS
}

::itcl::class Listbox {
  inherit BaseWidget
  constructor {{type_ "listbox"}} {BaseWidget::constructor $type_} {
    set _listbox [listbox .[namespace tail $this]]
  }
  protected variable _listbox
}

::itcl::class ScrollableListbox {
  inherit Listbox
  constructor {} {Listbox::constructor scrollable} {
    # Create the scrollbars and glue them together with the listbox.
    set _vsb [scrollbar .vsb -command "$_listbox yview"]
    set _hsb [scrollbar .hsb -command "$_listbox xview" \
      -orient horizontal]
    $_listbox configure -xscrollcommand "$_hsb set" \
```

```
            -yscrollcommand "$_vsb set"

        # Pack the widgets into the screen and add text to the listbox.
        grid $_listbox $_vsb -sticky nsew
        grid $_hsb -column 0 -sticky ew
        grid columnconfigure . 0 -weight 1
        grid rowconfigure . 0 -weight 1
        foreach word "This example shows you how to pass arguments up\
          multiple levels of inheritance in a class hierarchy." {
          $_listbox insert end $word
        }
    }
}
```

4

Let's start with the *constructor* in the least specific class, BaseWidget, since it gets interpreted first. Since it requires an argument, it's up to Listbox's *constructor* to supply the init code to specify this argument. Listbox's *constructor* does this by specifying the value of its optional parameter. Since the parameter is optional, ScrollableListbox's *constructor* is not required to declare any init code. It does, however, in order to override type_'s default value with "scrollable."

When you instantiate ScrollableListbox, then, BaseWidget's *constructor* is invoked first with the same argument value passed to ScrollableListbox's *constructor*. BaseWidget then appends the object name to a static list of objects so that it can keep track of all derived class instances. Next, Listbox's *constructor* is executed, and it creates a listbox widget. Finally, ScrollableListbox's *constructor* adds scrollbars to the listbox and packs everything in the window. The resulting window is shown in Figure 4-1.

In a nutshell, in order to pass arguments up multiple levels of an inheritance hierarchy, you simply need to specify init code at each level, regardless of whether the *constructor*s of the classes in the middle of the hierarchy need any arguments. If the base class requires arguments, the derived class must provide them.

Constructor/Destructor Errors

Error conditions are like death and taxes. They are unavoidable. The following sections explain what happens when an error condition occurs during the construction and destruction processes.

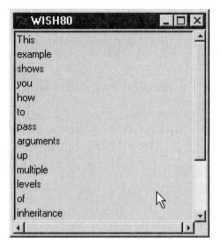

Scrollable
listbox created
through
multiple levels
of inheritance

Figure 4-1.

When Construction Fails

Anytime the construction process fails, any allocated memory is freed and the object is *not* created. Errors in the *constructor* prevent instantiation. Sometimes *constructor* errors are accidental syntax or logic errors in the code, and sometimes *constructor*s return errors deliberately. The following example illustrates a common Tcl syntax error and what happens when it is encountered.

Example 4-11
Syntax errors in
the *constructor*
prevent
instantiation

```
% ::itcl::class Geography {
    constructor {} {
      # Handle several lines of initialization tasks here, and then
      # initialize a list, forgetting the closing bracket.
      set _cities [list "Dallas TX" "Huntsville AL" "Brookhaven MS"
    }
    destructor {puts "Deleting object!"}
    private variable _cities
  }
% Geography g
Deleting object!
missing close-bracket or close-brace
```

The first thing you should notice is that the *destructor* is invoked automatically when the *constructor* error is encountered, so the object is automatically deleted before the end of the *constructor* body is reached. This is an important point to remember. Recall from the object creation process that by the time the constructor(s) is invoked, the [incr Tcl] object structure is fully initialized. When a *constructor* error occurs, invocation of the class *destructor* causes this structure to be deleted.

REMEMBER: If the *constructor* returns an error during class instantiation, the *destructor* is executed, halting the object creation process and deleting the object.

4

Sometimes, however, it's necessary to force the construction process to fail. For example, if you need to validate *constructor* parameter values, you can use the **error** command to return from the *constructor* if the validation fails so that the object won't get created. Consider the following class definition that defines a new data type.

Example 4-12
Explicitly return
an error code in
the *constructor*
to prevent
instantiation

```
::itcl::class Int {
  constructor {value_} {
    # Validate the parameter.
    if {[catch {validate $value_} err]} {
      error $err
    }
    set _int $value_
  }

  # Accessor Methods
  public method int {} {return $_int}

  # Class Methods
  public method + {val_} {return [expr $_int + [validate $val_]]}
  private method validate {value_} {}
  private method isaInt {value_} {}

  # Class Data Members
  private variable _int
}

::itcl::body Int::validate {value_} {
  # Check length.
  if {[string length $value_] > 5} {
```

```
      error "String too long: \"$value_\""
   }
   # Make sure it's a number > 0.
   if {![regexp {^[1-9][0-9]*} $value_]} {
     error "Bad value: \"$value_\" Enter a number."
   }
   # Let's just go with 2^15.
   if {$value_ > [expr pow(2,15)]} {
     error "Number too large. Must be 0 < num < 32768."
   }
   return $value_
}

::itcl::body Int::isaInt {value_} {
   if {![catch {$value_ isa Int} result]} {
     return $result
   } else {
     return 0
   }
}

::itcl::body Int::+ {value_} {
   if [isaInt $value_] {
     return {[expr $_int + [$value_ int]]}
   } else {
     return [expr $_int + [validate $value_]]
   }
}
```

In this example, the goal is to create an object that represents a number between 0 and 32768. The *constructor*, then, must verify that the command-line argument meets these criteria. If parameter validation fails, then the **error** command is used to deliberately cause the *constructor* to fail. This is a common programming practice used to prevent the creation of an object. As you just learned, this automatically invokes the *destructor* and deletes the object. Now save the class definition in a file, Int.itcl, and type the following commands to experiment with different *constructor* arguments:

```
% source Int.itcl
% Int x abcdefg
String too long: "abcdefg"
% Int x abcd
Bad value: "abcd" Enter a number.
```

```
% Int x 123456
String too long: "123456"
% Int x 40000
Number too large. Must be 0 < num < 32768.
% Int x 5
x
% Int y 10
y
% x + y
15
% x + 50
55
% y + foo
Bad value: "foo" Enter a number.
```

4

After successful instantiation, Int objects can then be used to simulate numbers and can even be added together as illustrated by the public method, "+". This method accepts a value that can either be an Int object or a number that successfully passes Int's *validate* method.

There are several possible situations that would warrant your deliberately causing object creation to fail. You could check a static variable to keep the user from creating some maximum number of objects. You could enforce a naming convention for objects of a certain class type by checking the value of the **this** variable. You could do error checking for such things as the existence of a file, an open socket, or a global variable. You could even define new data types like integers, floats, or characters if you wanted to, as shown in the previous example. The ability to control the construction process is a powerful tool you can take advantage of in many different areas.

When Destruction Fails

When the construction process fails, you can delete the class definition from the interpreter, edit the *constructor* to correct any problems, and re-source the class definition back into the interpreter. Recovering from *destructor* errors is a little different. Consider the following class example.

Example 4-13
Destructor errors prevent object deletion

```
% ::itcl::class FileMgr {
    constructor {} {}
    destructor {
      puts "Closing file descriptor and deleting object..."
      closeFile
    }
    private method closeFile {} {
```

```
        close $_fd
      }
      private variable _fd
    }
% FileMgr mgr
mgr
% ::itcl::delete object mgr
Closing file descriptor and deleting object...
can't read "_fd": no such variable
% ::itcl::find objects -class FileMgr
mgr
```

FileMgr's *destructor* calls the *closeFile* method to close the file descriptor of an open file. This is one of the jobs a class *destructor* is supposed to do, but in this example, the file descriptor has not been created at the time of destruction. Once the interpreter encounters this error, it does what it normally does when it reaches an error condition—it bails out. This is a unique situation, however, because the *destructor* error prevents you from deleting the object. You might try to delete the entire class from the interpreter instead of just the object, like this:

```
% ::itcl::delete class FileMgr
Closing file descriptor and deleting object...
can't read "_fd": no such variable
```

As you can see, the same error message results because deleting the class invokes the *destructor* as well. So now it looks like the only way to get rid of the object is to kill the interpreter. That would certainly do it, but this may be a last resort. Killing the interpreter could potentially undo a lot of work that has already been done up to this point in your application.

As you probably imagined, there are a few tricks you can use in situations like this. First, recall from earlier in the chapter that a procedure with the same name as a class will overwrite the class access command (the name of the class) if the procedure is defined in the interpreter *after* the class definition. The same is true for object names as well. You can delete the object by overwriting its access command with an empty procedure. Type the following line of code to delete the "undeletable" object, **mgr**:

```
% proc mgr {} {}
Closing file descriptor and deleting object...
% ::itcl::find objects -class FileMgr
%
```

As soon as you overwrite the object name with a procedure of the same name, the *destructor* is automatically invoked, and the object is deleted regardless of *destructor* errors! Another way to delete the object is to delete its access command with **rename**. Simply use the following command:

```
% rename mgr {}
Closing file descriptor and deleting object...
```

Lastly, you can use a method you are already familiar with, reimplementing a method body on the command line with the **body** command. You can simply overwrite the *destructor's* definition like this:

```
% ::itcl::body FileMgr::destructor {} {
    catch {close $_fd}
  }
```

By adding the **catch** command, the object can be deleted without generating an error. You can do this instead of overwriting the object name. One important thing you should notice, however, is the pair of braces immediately following the *destructor* keyword. Recall that a *destructor* cannot accept any arguments, but the **body** command requires these braces.

You now know how to handle both construction and destruction errors. The remainder of this chapter shows you how to simulate overloaded *constructors* and copy *constructors*.

Constructor Overloading

If you are familiar with C++, then you know how to overload a *constructor* by declaring it multiple times with different parameter lists. In [incr Tcl], you can't declare methods multiple times, but there is a way you can simulate this behavior. Example 4-14 shows you how to do this by using the **args** parameter.

Example 4-14
Use **args** to simulate constructor overloading

```
% ::itcl::class Date {
    constructor {args} {
      if ![llength $args] {
        set _date [clock format [clock seconds]]
      } elseif {[llength $args] == 1} {
        if {$args == "now" || $args == "current"} {
          set _date [clock format [clock seconds]]
        } elseif {$args == "tomorrow"} {
          set currtime [clock seconds]
```

4

```
            set _date \
               [clock format [expr $currtime + $_ONEDAY] -format "%D"]
         } elseif [regexp {^[1-9]*$} $args] {
            set _date [clock format $args]
         } else {
            # Error condition. Throw an error to auto-delete the object
            error "Invalid date specification: \"$args\""
         }
      } elseif {$args == "2 days ago"} {
         set currtime [clock seconds]
         set _date [clock format \
            [expr $currtime - [expr $_ONEDAY * 2]] -format "%D"]
      } else {
         # Error condition. Throw an error to auto-delete the object.
         error "Invalid date specification: \"$args\""
      }
   }
   public method date {} {return $_date}
   private common _ONEDAY [expr 3600*24]
   private variable _date
}
% Date d
d
% d date
Tue May 04 22:18:32 Central Daylight Time 1999
% Date d2 tomorrow
d2
% d2 date
05/05/99
% Date d3 2 days ago
d3
% d3 date
05/02/99
% Date d4 next week
Invalid date specification: "next week"
```

By declaring **args** in the *constructor*'s parameter list, you are able to specify
any number of arguments during instantiation. The *constructor* can then parse
over the list and take different actions depending on the values it finds. This
allows you to initialize the Date object with the current time, tomorrow's
date, the date two days ago, or any other specification you care to check for
in the *constructor*. The number of possibilities is up to you.

Copy Constructors

A copy *constructor* is another term used in C++. A copy *constructor*'s purpose is to create a copy of an object of the same class type. It is a type of overloaded *constructor* where the argument you pass into the parameter list is an instance of that class type, which is then used to create a new instance with the same values. Since a copy *constructor* is an overloaded *constructor*, you simulate one the same way you learned in the previous section, with **args**. The *constructor* must first determine whether the command-line argument is an instance of that class type. If so, then it should initialize each of its data members with the corresponding values of the given object's data members. The following example shows one way you can implement a copy *constructor* in [incr Tcl].

4

Example 4-15
Copy *constructors*
create copies of
objects

```
% ::itcl::class Radio {
    constructor {args} {
      if ![catch {$args isa Radio}] {
        # The parameter is a Radio object. Copy it.
        copy $args
        return
      }
      eval configure $args
    }
    private method copy {object_}
    public variable volume 15dB
    public variable station 88.1
    public variable band fm
    public variable stereo 1
  }
% ::itcl::body Radio::copy {object_} {
    puts "Copying data from $object_ to $this..."
    foreach dataMember "volume station band stereo" {
      puts " - $dataMember"
      configure -$dataMember [$object_ cget -$dataMember]
    }
  }
% Radio r1 -station 94.1
r1
% r1 configure
{-volume 15dB 15dB} {-band fm fm} {-stereo 1 1} {-station 88.1 94.1}
% Radio r2 r1
Copying data from r1 to ::r2...
 - volume
 - station
 - band
 - stereo
r2
% r2 configure
{-volume 15dB 15dB} {-band fm fm} {-stereo 1 1} {-station 88.1 94.1}
```

A Radio object named **r1** is created. It is then passed into the *constructor* when **r2** is instantiated. The *constructor* determines that the argument is an instance of the class and makes a copy of the instance. The result is that **r2** becomes an exact copy of **r1**.

This is accomplished via the *copy* method. For each data member defined in the class, *copy* uses the data member's value to initialize the new object's corresponding data member. In this example, each of the data members is public, which makes the copying a bit easier since you can use the object's built-in *cget* method. For nonpublic data members, you must set up appropriate accessors for retrieving their values. You wouldn't need to declare one accessor per data member, though. You could provide a single public method that returns a list of each of the nonpublic data member values. The *copy* method could then copy from the list in the same order in which the list was created.

This completes the discussion on *constructor*s and *destructor*s. You should now know everything necessary to construct and destruct objects under normal circumstances as well as how to handle error conditions. The end of this chapter also marks the completion of the fundamental components in [incr Tcl]. You learned how to use objects from Chapter 2's discussion on methods, how to describe objects from Chapter 3's discussion on data members, and how to create and destroy objects in this chapter. It's now time to begin tying all this information together into a larger example that makes use of many of the things you have learned thus far. The next chapter serves as final preparation for such an example. You will learn about several debugging techniques you can use as you implement and test your code. Then, in Chapter 6, you'll see how to "tie it all together" with a fully functional client-server framework example that uses sockets for user authentication.

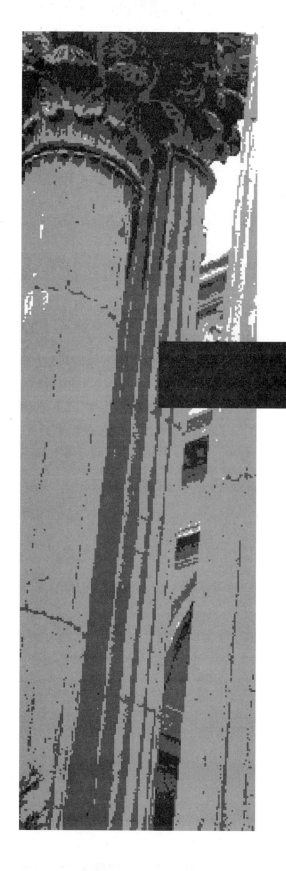

CHAPTER 5

Debugging

This chapter presents a variety of techniques you can use to debug your [incr Tcl] applications. Its purpose is not to discuss various debugging tools that you can download from the Internet. Several such tools are mentioned as possibilities for you to use, but the discussion focuses on facilities that are built into the language. First, several built-in commands are discussed and how you can use each to find certain types of errors. Then, a new [incr Tcl] class is implemented that you can use to "watch" your code at run time by seeing the order of execution of each method and procedure as it gets invoked. Finally, an advanced debugging topic shows you how to use this new class to *dynamically* turn debugging on and off through a simple socket interface.

Introduction

Debugging is more of an art form than an engineering technique. There are no set rules and guidelines you have to follow, and there is no documentation that says you have to use debugging tool x as opposed to debugging tool y for locating certain error types. Good debugging techniques simply come with time spent getting your hands dirty in the code. While a solid familiarity with the language is helpful, it is not a necessity for tracking down bugs. You don't have to be an expert in [incr Tcl] to add a few well-placed **puts** statements in the code to find an error.

Debugging may be black and white in terms of having a bug that you need to fix. It certainly isn't black and white, however, in terms of how you go about finding the bug and fixing it. There are typically many different approaches you can take and available tools you can use while debugging and testing. There are interactive source-level debuggers such as Tuba and Scriptics' TclPro Debugger, there are static code analyzers such as TclParse and Scriptics' TclPro Checker, there are regression testing and playback utilities such as TkReplay, and there is a wealth of other helpful extensions and introspection utilities such as Tkinspect. The possibilities and combinations are really endless. You just have to find through trial and error what tools suit your own needs and applications. The goal of debugging is to minimize the amount of time it takes you to find and resolve problems, regardless of what tools or techniques you use.

So, when does debugging start in the software development life cycle? In short, it's when you come across that first stack dump or error message during implementation. Debugging is an ongoing process throughout the development cycle. It doesn't fall into its own slice of development like analysis, design, and implementation. As you write code, you test it along the way, finding and resolving problems as you go. Then, as you test your code upon completion of the implementation, you also find and fix bugs. And finally, as bugs are fixed during testing or as new features are added, you debug as you find problems during regression testing.

One thing you can count on as a developer is that you *will* debug your code eventually because programs almost inevitably behave in an unexpected manner. Within the first iteration of testing or customer use, you can pretty much count on the user's initiating some sequence of events you'd never thought of handling. The question then becomes what technique to use to isolate a problem once it's reported. This is where no one technique is always correct. It usually depends on the developer. If it takes 15 minutes to walk through the code step by step in a source-level debugger to locate a problem or 5 minutes to add a few **puts** to locate the same problem, you probably choose the latter even though both have the same end result. Remember, your goal should be to minimize debugging time.

5

Basic Debugging: Built-In Commands

There are several built-in debugging facilities available for you to use to locate errors in your code. While graphical debugging tools may be attractive, you may not be able to beat the convenience of quick editing and using one or more of the built-in commands presented in this section, depending on your particular problem. Note that the error situations presented here are purposely simple. Rather than present complex code or multipage examples with subtle error conditions, it may be easier for you to learn and grasp the concepts presented in these simple examples and then take that knowledge and apply it to your own applications.

Using *errorInfo* to Locate Errors

Tcl has a built-in global variable called *errorInfo* that always contains the stack trace of the most recent error. By printing the contents of *errorInfo*, you can usually determine the source of the error you're trying to find. Save the following class definition in a file named Debug.itcl:

```
::itcl::class Debug {
  constructor {} {
    first
    second
    third
    fourth
  }
```

```
private method first {} {}
private method second {} {}
private method third {} {
  # Error is introduced here
  set x
}
private method fourth {} {}
}
```

The *constructor* in this class invokes several methods. The *third* method
produces an error because the variable *x* does not exist. Try to create an
instance of Debug by typing the following commands in a **wish** shell:

```
% package require Itcl
3.0
% source Debug.itcl
% Debug d
can't read "x": no such variable
```

As you can see, an error is generated when you try to create the object. (It's
also important to note that as a result of this error during construction, the
object is not created.) In this case, it's quite easy to track down the source of
the error because there's only one place where variable *x* is accessed. But
imagine if the file containing the method bodies is several thousand lines
long with multiple references to the variable. By printing the value of
errorInfo, you can see exactly which method generates the error message. To
do this, you can simply use the **set** command as follows:

```
% set errorInfo
can't read "x": no such variable
    while executing
"set x"
    (object "::d" method "::Debug::third" body line 1)
    invoked from within
"third"
    while constructing object "::d" in ::Debug::constructor (body line 4)
    invoked from within
"Debug d"
```

The third line of the stack trace tells you that the error occurs while trying
to execute the command, set x, and the fourth line tells you that this
command is in the method called *third*. It's that simple, but if only it was

that easy all the time. Sometimes, you can't rely on *errorInfo* to help you. To illustrate, modify Debug's *constructor* by adding the following line of code as the first line:

```
after 1000 {catch {set y}}
```

Then, type the following commands to create another instance of Debug:

```
% ::itcl::delete class Debug
% source Debug.itcl
% Debug d
can't read "x": no such variable
% set errorInfo
can't read "y": no such variable
    while executing
"set y"
```

As you can see, the error message stored in *errorInfo* is not what you might have expected when trying to locate the source of an error concerning a variable named *x*. In some applications, the interpreter may encounter errors while invoking code fragments *after* encountering other errors in the main thread of execution. This can be caused by an **after** event as shown here, a trap or alarm-handling mechanism, or by handling a message received over a socket. In this example, the interpreter reaches the error condition in *third* and halts the object construction process at that point. Then, an external event causes the interpreter to invoke another command fragment, set y, which also causes an error. Remember, *errorInfo* always contains the stack trace of the *most recent error*, so even though the error message concerning variable *x* is printed on the command line, the last error concerning variable *y* is stored in *errorInfo*. As a result, the stack trace you could otherwise have used to locate the source of the first error is overwritten.

Situations like this can be very difficult to debug. The tracing mechanism presented later in this chapter is ideal for such error conditions. Another approach you might take, however, is to try and resolve the error reported by *errorInfo*, rerun the code, and try checking *errorInfo* again. This could work, but externally generated errors are sometimes unavoidable, or perhaps even intentional or acceptable under certain conditions or depending on the current state of your application. And regardless of the intent of the error, *errorInfo* will still always contain the most recent stack trace. In situations like this, it's best to resort to a different debugging tactic such as one of the other built-in commands shown in the following sections.

Using catch **to Locate Errors**

Similar to *errorInfo*, you can use the **catch** command to locate syntax errors.
Whereas you cannot always rely on *errorInfo* since its contents can be
overwritten by other errors as shown in the previous example, you can
always rely on **catch** to pinpoint syntax errors. The first step is to determine
where to place the **catch** statements. Since the error in the Debug class
occurs during construction, the logical starting point is in the class
constructor. A divide-and-conquer approach is one method you can use if you
have no idea from where the error originates. To use this approach, divide
the number of possible error locations, such as method invocations, in half,
and then wrap a **catch** around each half. Remove the **after** command you
added to Debug's *constructor* during the previous section's discussion and add
catch statements as follows:

Example 5-1
Using a divide-
and-conquer
approach to
locate syntax
errors with **catch**

```
::itcl::body Debug::constructor {} {
  if {[catch {
    first
    second
  } err]} {
    error "Error invoking first or second: $err"
  }
  if {[catch {
    third
    fourth
  } err]} {
    error "Error invoking third or fourth: $err"
  }
}
```

Then delete the class, re-source the file, and reinstantiate as follows:

```
% ::itcl::delete class Debug
% source Debug.itcl
% Debug d
Error invoking third or fourth: can't read "x": no such variable
```

The error is now narrowed down to either *third* or *fourth*. You can continue
using this technique until you pinpoint the offending code fragment. Once
again, modify the *constructor*, and use the previous run's result to determine
where the next **catch** statements should be placed.

```
::itcl::body Debug::constructor {} {
  first
  second
  if {[catch {third} err]} {
    error "It's third!"
  }
  if {[catch {fourth} err]} {
    error "It's fourth!"
  }
}
% ::itcl::delete class Debug
% source Debug.itcl
% Debug d
It's third!
```

5

You might think you're done, but this only tells you that the location of the error is either in *third* or a method or procedure invoked by *third*. If you determine that the latter is the case, then you can use the same approach in *third* as you used in the *constructor*.

As with the *errorInfo* section, locating this particular error is easily done by inspection. The concept, however, of using a divide-and-conquer approach to narrow down the error location can be quite helpful in large-scale applications.

The key strength of using **catch** like this is that you *will* ultimately find the error. On the other hand, a con is the amount of time it may take. Depending on the size of the code and the number of embedded function calls, it may take considerable time to add enough **catch** statements to find and fix a problem. Much of the time, you need a faster way to accomplish the same task. This can usually be done with some simple **puts** statements, as shown in the next section.

T IP: Error conditions are often trapped and handled with **catch** statements in production code. Make sure that the generated error report, whether it is logged to a file or displayed in an error dialog window, has enough useful information in it that a developer can easily determine the location of the error as well as the context in which it occurred.

Using puts **to Locate Errors**

The **puts** command is probably the single most commonly used facility for debugging Tcl applications as well as any of its extensions, including [incr Tcl]. Since Tcl and its extensions are interpreted, adding **puts** statements throughout the code for locating errors is quick and easy. All you have to do is edit the file(s), add a few well-placed **puts**, save the changes, and re-source the code in an interpreter. Once again, modify the *constructor* body as follows, and then reinstantiate the object.

```
::itcl::body Debug::constructor {} {
  puts "Calling first..."
  first
  puts "Calling second..."
  second
  puts "Calling third..."
  third
  puts "Calling fourth..."
  fourth
}
% ::itcl::delete class Debug
% source Debug.itcl
% Debug d
Calling first...
Calling second...
Calling third...
can't read "x": no such variable
```

A **puts** statement is added before the call to each method. Each statement is concise, and the amount of time it takes to add each one is minimal. Note that adding **catch** statements for debugging requires either modifying the line containing the method invocation itself or adding multiple lines of code. Using **puts**, however, you can simply add single independent lines to the *constructor* that are easily removed once the error is located.

By wrapping **puts** statements around method invocations like this, you can continually narrow down the source of the error by determining between which two statements the error occurs. Since the error message occurs before "Calling fourth..." is printed, you know that the error is either in *third* or a method invoked by *third*. And as you learned in the previous section, if you determine that the error occurs in a method or procedure invoked by *third*, you can continue adding **puts** statements throughout the method body, wrapping method invocations as you did in the *constructor*.

Using **puts** is fast and simple. To make debugging with **puts** even faster, you can choose not to use descriptive debug strings like "Calling second." On the contrary, you can just as easily track down problems by using shorter strings, even single numbers or letters. You can use "1" instead of "Calling first," "2" instead of "Calling second," etc. You want to find and fix the problem as quickly as possible, so don't spend a lot of time with unnecessarily long and descriptive debug statements.

Using trace **to Locate Errors**

The **trace** command is used to monitor a variable throughout the lifetime of your application. By placing a **trace** on a variable name, the interpreter automatically invokes a designated command fragment when the variable is modified. As a result, you can use **trace** to track down logic errors related to invalid settings of class data members or even local variables. Consider the following class definition:

5

```
% ::itcl::class Traceit {
    constructor {} {}
    public method run {} {
      add 5
      subtract 10
      method1
      method2
    }
    private method method1 {} {
      add 12
      subtract 9
    }
    private method method2 {} {
      subtract 10
    }
    private method add {val_} {incr _var $val_}
    private method subtract {val_} {incr _var -$val_}
    private variable _var 0
  }
```

Suppose Traceit's private variable _var needs to alternate between positive and negative numbers. You determine that a customer bug report is due to the fact that _var gets set to successive negative values. Suppose this class is too large to trace through the code manually, and using **puts** would take too long due to the code size and the number of references to _var. Further, this error is not a syntax error, so you can't use *errorInfo* to view a stack trace or **catch** to trap the error. Ideally, you need a way you can monitor _var and have the interpreter print a message each time _var is modified, informing you in which method the modification occurs. You guessed it. This can be done with the **trace** command.

Setting Up the Trace

Implement the *constructor* as follows, and add a procedure to print useful debugging information when _var is modified. Then, create an instance of Traceit and invoke its *run* method to test the tracing mechanism.

Example 5-2
Adding a trace to
a class data
member

```
% ::itcl::body Traceit::constructor {} {
    trace variable _var w debug
  }
% proc debug {varname_ index_ ops_} {
    upvar $varname_ localCopy
    set command [info level [expr [info level] - 1]]
    puts "Command: \"$command\"\n  New Value for $varname_:\
      \"$localCopy\""
  }
% Traceit t
t
% t run
Command: "add 5"
  New Value for _var: "5"
Command: "subtract 10"
  New Value for _var: "-5"
Command: "add 12"
  New Value for _var: "7"
Command: "subtract 9"
  New Value for _var: "-2"
Command: "subtract 10"
  New Value for _var: "-12"
```

As you can see, the trace is successful. _var is modified several times when you invoke *run*, and *debug* is automatically invoked for each modification. Notice that the final call to *subtract* results in the error since the resulting negative value follows a previous negative result. Notice also, however, that there are two calls to *subtract* with the same argument, 10. If there are multiple identical method invocations, the output from *debug* may not be very helpful because you won't be able to search for a unique string in the code. By making *debug* a little smarter, you can not only see which method modifies the variable, but you can walk up the calling stack to see the order of method invocations. Modify the procedure as follows, and invoke the *run* method again.

```
% proc debug {varname_ index_ ops_} {
    upvar $varname_ localCopy
    set indent ""
    set bottom [expr [info level] - 1]
    for {set curr 1} {$curr <= $bottom} {incr curr 1} {
      puts "${indent}-- Command: \"[info level $curr]\""
      set indent "  $indent"
    }
    puts "New Value for $varname_: \"$localCopy\""
    puts "=============="
  }
% t run
-- Command: "run"
  -- Command: "add 5"
New Value for _var: "5"
==============
-- Command: "run"
  -- Command: "subtract 10"
New Value for _var: "-5"
==============
-- Command: "run"
  -- Command: "method1"
    -- Command: "add 12"
New Value for _var: "7"
==============
-- Command: "run"
  -- Command: "method1"
    -- Command: "subtract 9"
New Value for _var: "-2"
==============
-- Command: "run"
  -- Command: "method2"
    -- Command: "subtract 10"
New Value for _var: "-12"
==============
```

5

Now you can see the calling stack and find out exactly which methods are invoked prior to the invalid modification of _var. This makes isolation of the offending line of code much easier, and this concept is the basis for the design of the tracing tool implemented later in this chapter.

How It Works

So how does the tracing mechanism work? To find out, first take a look at the syntax for the **trace** command, which is directly followed by the **trace** command fragment from the *constructor*.

```
trace variable name ops command
trace variable _var  w    debug
```

The *name* argument (_var) is the variable name. The *ops* argument (w) is one or more of the letters w, r, and u, which are used for tracing on writes, reads, and unsets, respectively. The final argument, *command* (debug), is the method or procedure to be invoked when the variable is written to, read, or unset, according to the *ops* argument. In this example, a trace is set up to automatically invoke the *debug* procedure when Traceit's private variable _var is modified.

Next, notice that *debug* declares three parameters, but no arguments are specified for *debug* when the trace is initialized. This is because **trace** automatically invokes the specified method or procedure with three arguments in addition to any that you may specify. The first parameter, varname_, is the name of the variable being traced. The second parameter, index_, is only used for array variables. If varname_ is an array, then index_ is the index into the array. Otherwise, if varname_ is a scalar, then index_ is an empty string. The last parameter, ops_, corresponds to the *ops* argument to **trace,** as shown previously in the command's syntax. In this case, ops_ contains the letter w.

Now take a closer look at the body of the procedure. Notice that varname_ is passed by reference (via the use of **upvar**) so that you can see the value of the variable as it gets modified in Traceit. The **info** command is then used to walk up the calling stack, and each method name in the stack is printed along with its arguments. From the output, you can quickly determine that the error occurs after the following order of execution: *run→method2→subtract 10*. After locating the error, you can modify the code appropriately and simply remove the **trace** command fragment from the *constructor*.

Choosing an Approach

Now that you're familiar with several built-in techniques for debugging your code, how do you decide which one to use? Unfortunately, there is no correct answer. You can use any of the techniques presented in this chapter, or you can use a combination of them. Just remember that the key is to strive for speed of resolution. Don't spend 30 minutes adding **catch** commands throughout your code when you can possibly spend half that time using **puts** instead. And don't spend 15 minutes tracking down a logic error using **puts** when you can possibly spend half that time using **trace** instead. Sometimes it's clear which technique you should use, and other times you can take your pick. As with anything else, this comes with practice.

Now, what if you could track down errors in your code without having to spend time adding any **puts** or **catch** statements or without having to set up a trace or use *errorInfo*? What if you could locate most errors by integrating a built-in tracing mechanism during implementation that could be turned on and off by setting a single variable? You can! The following section outlines a class that uses techniques similar to the **debug** procedure presented earlier for printing a code trace that follows the execution of your code as well as printing a variety of debug messages.

5

A New Debugging Tool

All built-in Tcl debugging facilities have two things in common. You have to spend time adding the debug code to your application after it's been implemented, and you have to remove or comment out the debug statements once you're done. You can avoid a lot of this overhead by defining an [incr Tcl] class that can be used to toggle the printing of debug statements on separate runs of the code. Later in the chapter, you'll see how you can toggle the debug statements dynamically. By integrating the debug code during implementation, you can simply tell the class to activate itself if you want to turn on debugging and deactivate itself to turn off debugging.

Definition and Implementation

The new class will be named Trace since its main purpose will be to trace through execution of your code. The class definition looks like this (note that this code is available online):

```
::itcl::class Trace {
  # Static Methods
  public proc ACTIVATE {flags_} {SET_FLAGS $flags_ 1}
```

```
public proc DEACTIVATE {flags_} {SET_FLAGS $flags_ 0}
public proc EXE {where_}
public proc ERR {string_}
public proc WARN {string_}
public proc COMM {string_}
private proc SET_FLAGS {flags_ val_}

# Static Data Members
private common _ON
  array set _ON "x 0 e 0 w 0 c 0"
private common _CHARS
  array set _CHARS "e * w ! c #"
private common _INDENT ""
private common _LEVEL 1
private common _PAD "  "
}
```

The purpose of this class is to provide a quick and efficient means to print a variety of debugging statements that allow you to trace through the code at run time without having to manually edit the code and add debug statements after implementation. Several public static methods are defined as interfaces to the class. First, take a look at the three methods ERR, WARN, and COMM.

```
::itcl::body Trace::ERR {string_} {
  if {$_ON(e)} {
    puts "${_INDENT}$_CHARS(e)$_CHARS(e) ERROR: $string_"
  }
}

::itcl::body Trace::WARN {string_} {
  if {$_ON(w)} {
    puts "${_INDENT}$_CHARS(w)$_CHARS(w) WARNING: $string_"
  }
}

::itcl::body Trace::COMM {string_} {
  if {$_ON(c)} {
    puts "${_INDENT}$_CHARS(c)$_CHARS(c) COMMENT: $string_"
  }
}
```

These methods are used to print error, warning, and comment messages, respectively. Each method checks a corresponding indexed value in the static array, _ON. ERR checks index e, WARN checks w, and COMM checks c. The value corresponding to each index in the array is a Boolean used to determine whether Trace is configured to print that type of message. If error messaging is turned on, for example, then _ON(e) is set to 1, and likewise for warnings and comments. Another static array, _CHARS, is used to associate certain characters with each message type. Asterisks are associated with errors, exclamation points with warnings, and hashes with comments or informational messages. You can easily adjust the formatting schemes by modifying the contents of this array.

The static array, _ON, is manipulated by the two methods ACTIVATE and DEACTIVATE. Each of these methods invokes a private static method, SET_FLAGS, whose job it is to configure the array, enabling or disabling the various types of debug messages. The SET_FLAGS method is implemented as follows:

5

```
::itcl::body Trace::SET_FLAGS {flags_ val_} {
  if {$flags_ == "all"} {
    foreach type "x e w c" {
      set _ON($type) $val_
    }
  } else {
    foreach type "x e w c" {
      if {[string first $type $flags_] != -1} {
        set _ON($type) $val_
      }
    }
  }
}
```

This method expects two arguments. The first parameter, flags_, may be set to "all" or a combination of the following letters:

◆ **x:** Print the order of execution

◆ **e:** Print error messages

◆ **w:** Print warning messages

◆ **c:** Print comments or informational messages

The second parameter, val_, is either a 1 or 0, which represents turning the type of debug specified in flags_ on or off, respectively. The ACTIVATE method, for example, can be used to enable warning and error messages by executing the following command:

```
::Trace::ACTIVATE we
```

Likewise, the DEACTIVATE method can be used to disable comment messages by executing the following command:

```
::Trace::DEACTIVATE c
```

In each case, SET_FLAGS sets the appropriate flags in _ON to True or False. (Note that by default, all debug output is disabled.)

The last method to discuss is EXE. This is the most useful method, as its job is to print the order of execution of each method and procedure in your application. Most of the time, you can locate error conditions in your code by seeing the order of method invocations. An indenting scheme is used to create a stair-step effect in the output to make the invocation order of embedded methods and procedures easy to follow. Instead of jumping around in the code to manually trace through the order of execution, you can view the formatted trace printed by EXE. The method body is implemented as follows:

```
::itcl::body Trace::EXE {where_} {
  set callingMethod [lindex [info level [expr [info level] - 1]] 0]
  set commandName [uplevel [list namespace which $callingMethod]]
  if {$_ON(x)} {
    if {$where_ == "begin"} {
      puts "${_INDENT}$commandName"
      puts "$_INDENT\{"
      set _INDENT "$_INDENT$_PAD"
    } elseif {$where_ == "end"} {
      set _INDENT [string range $_INDENT 2 end]
      puts "$_INDENT\}"
    }
  }
}
```

The scheme is very simple. EXE expects a single argument containing one of two values, "begin" or "end." By specifying "begin," you inform EXE that a new method is being invoked. The fully qualified method name is printed on one line along with an opening brace on the next line. Likewise, specifying "end" results in a closing brace's being printed to match the corresponding opening brace. In the next section, you'll see how useful these braces can be. The where_ parameter is the key to maintaining the output's two-space indentation scheme. (In Chapter 7, you'll see how to accomplish the same output with one line of code per method and without having to specify "begin" or "end.")

Using the New Tool

That's it! Now all you need to do is add the hooks into your application. Let's begin with a simple example. Save the Trace class definition and method bodies in a file, Trace.itcl, and type the following commands in an **itclsh** shell. (You should also save class TraceTest in a file, TraceTest.itcl, for use later in the chapter.)

5

Example 5-3
Integrating Trace
methods in an
application

```
% source Trace.itcl
% ::Trace::ACTIVATE x
% ::itcl::class TraceTest {
    constructor {} {
        ::Trace::EXE begin
        method1
        method2
        ::Trace::COMM "Wow, this is easy!"
        method3
        ::Trace::EXE end
    }
    public method method1 {} {
        ::Trace::EXE begin
        ::Trace::ERR "This is an example of an error message."
        method3
        ::Trace::EXE end
    }
    private method method2 {} {
        ::Trace::EXE begin
        ::Trace::EXE end
    }
    private method method3 {} {
        ::Trace::EXE begin
        ::Trace::WARN "This is a warning message."
        ::Trace::EXE end
    }
}
```

Each method contains two calls to EXE, and one of each of the other types of debug messages is also integrated for illustration. The letter x is passed to ACTIVATE, so the first instantiation results in the execution order's being printed. Now create an instance of TraceTest to try things out.

```
% TraceTest herewego
::TraceTest::constructor
{
   ::TraceTest::method1
   {
     ::TraceTest::method3
     {
     }
   }
   ::TraceTest::method2
   {
   }
   ::TraceTest::method3
   {
   }
}
herewego
```

The result is a neatly formatted stair-step effect that you can follow quickly to trace the order of execution resulting from object construction. You can use this in your own applications to isolate performance slowdowns and other problems such as unnecessary method calls within a loop. Now turn on all debug output and create another object.

```
% ::Trace::ACTIVATE all
% TraceTest herewegoAgain
::TraceTest::constructor
{
   ::TraceTest::method1
   {
     ** ERROR: This is an example of an error message.
     ::TraceTest::method3
     {
        !! WARNING: This is a warning message.
     }
   }
   ::TraceTest::method2
   {
   }
```

```
## COMMENT: Wow, this is easy!
::TraceTest::method3
{
  !! WARNING: This is a warning message.
}
}
herewegoAgain
```

After activating all debug output, you can see the different kinds of formatting that Trace adds to the various debug message types. Once full debugging is enabled, don't be surprised when your application runs slower. You can expect performance slowdowns of up to ten times. But the purpose of this debugging utility is clearly not to optimize performance. Rather, its purpose is to optimize error location and resolution. When you are satisfied with your code's stability, you should remove or comment out all calls to Trace methods. (It may be better to just comment them out so that you can uncomment them if future errors arise that necessitate turning the tracing back on again.) The reason for this is that even though you may disable all debug output, the Trace methods are still invoked. Recall that the _ON array is checked at the beginning of each method. So even though output may be disabled, this check is still executed and adds some extra processing overhead.

5

T IP: Many editors such as vi and emacs support brace matching. This means you can save the trace output to a file, place the cursor over an open or close brace, and use an editor-specific key sequence to move the cursor to its matching close or open brace, respectively. This allows you to quickly isolate a single stack level from the output and can be extremely useful when you're debugging large amounts of trace code that contain several nested function calls.

You can probably see how useful the tracing mechanism can be, but the drawback is that you must exit your application and rerun it in order to change the type of debug messages that are printed. In the following section, you'll see how you can send a message to your application *while it is running* to modify debug output dynamically.

Advanced Debugging: Modifying Debug Output Dynamically

Imagine how much time you could save from having to reconfigure your environment to reproduce reported problems with your code if you could dynamically enable debug output as soon as the problem is found during application development and testing. Most of the time, it is much easier and convenient to reproduce the problem while the application is already in a problematic state than to have to reproduce it on your own from scratch. You can create a back door to your application to send in messages over a socket interface that will turn on the tracing mechanism implemented in the previous section. To see how this works, take a look at the following illustration.

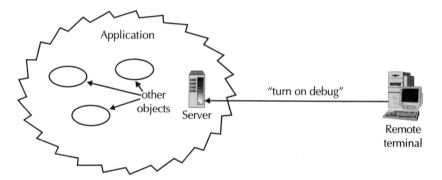

The application is depicted on the left, with multiple objects in existence along with a single server object that can be connected to from a remote terminal, shown on the right. The remote terminal can open a back door to the server, send a message across the communication link like "turn on debug" as shown in the illustration, and dynamically modify the debug output of the application. As a result, you can potentially debug a problem by enabling debug output as soon as the problem is encountered and then repeating the error condition without having to exit and restart the application. Setting up this link between the server and the remote terminal is the key to this design.

Creating the Debug Server

To set up this backdoor mechanism, you first need to create a server whose purpose it is to continually monitor some designated port for incoming

5

requests to modify debug output. You can do this with a simple [incr Tcl] class as follows:

```
::itcl::class DebugServer {
  # Class constructor/destructor
  constructor {port_} {}
  destructor {catch {close $_socket}}

  # Class Methods
  private method connect {sd_ address_ port_}
  private method processRequest {sd_}

  # Class Data Members
  private variable _socket
}

::itcl::body DebugServer::constructor {port_} {
  # Create the server socket
  if {[catch {
    socket -server [::itcl::code $this connect] $port_
  } _socket]} {
    return -code error
  }
}

::itcl::body DebugServer::connect {sd_ address_ port_} {
  fconfigure $sd_ -buffering line
  fileevent $sd_ readable [::itcl::code $this processRequest $sd_]
  puts "New connection accepted from client on $address_, port
$port_"
}

::itcl::body DebugServer::processRequest {sd_} {
  if {[catch {gets $sd_ data} rc]} {
    close $sd_
    puts "Unable to process client request: $rc"
    return
  }
  if {$rc > 0} {
    set type [lindex $data 0]
    set flags [lindex $data end]
    if {$type == "activate"} {
      if {[catch {Trace::ACTIVATE $flags} err]} {
        puts "Unable to activate debug output: $err"
```

```
      } else {
        puts "Successfully turned on Trace flags: $flags"
      }
    } elseif {$type == "deactivate"} {
      if {[catch {Trace::DEACTIVATE $flags} err]} {
        puts "Unable to deactivate debug output: $err"
      } else {
        puts "Successfully disabled Trace flags: $flags"
      }
    }
  } else {
    puts "Lost client connection."
    close $sd_
  }
}
```

Don't worry about the implementation details for now. The next chapter thoroughly discusses socket handling. With the server now defined, you need to integrate it into your application by instantiating the class when the application starts. To create a DebugServer object, you must specify a port number on which the object should listen for client requests. Later, when you create the client side, you then have to specify the same port number so the communication link is established successfully. After instantiation, the DebugServer object will wait patiently for client connections from the back door, and your application will be unaffected by its existence.

Creating the Back Door

Once the server is defined and ready to use, you have to have a way of connecting to it and communicating with it. You can do this with a simple class as follows:

```
::itcl::class Backdoor {
  # Class constructor/destructor
  constructor {port_ {host_ localhost}} {}
  destructor {catch {close $_socket}}

  # Class Methods
  public method write {msg_} {puts $_socket $msg_}

  # Class Data Members
  private variable _socket
}
```

```
::itcl::body Backdoor::constructor {port_ {host_ localhost}} {
  # Connect with the server.
  if {[catch {socket $host_ $port_} _socket]} {
    puts "Unable to connect with server."
    return -code error
  }
  fconfigure $_socket -buffering line
}
```

The *constructor* opens a socket to the server according to the specified host
and port number. You have to make sure that the host_ parameter is the
hostname of the machine where the server is running. Further, the port
number must match the DebugServer object's port number, specified during
DebugServer instantiation. For testing purposes, the hostname defaults to
localhost, which means you can communicate with a DebugServer object
from Backdoor objects running in separate interpreters on the same machine.
Now let's try out this new mechanism with the same TraceTest class defined
earlier.

Communicating with the Debug Server

Start two **wish** interpreters. (You must use a Tk-based shell for proper event
loop handling. More information is given on this in the next chapter.) One
will be for the server side (interpreter S), and the other will be for the client
side (interpreter C). In interpreter S, type the following commands to create a
DebugServer object and a TraceTest object:

```
% package require Itcl
3.0
% source DebugServer.itcl
% source TraceTest.itcl
% source Trace.itcl
% DebugServer ds 51195
ds
% TraceTest t1
t1
% t1 method1
%
```

Recall from earlier in the chapter that TraceTest contains several Trace method
invocations, and notice that no debug output is printed either during object

creation or calling *method1*. This is because Trace::ACTIVATE hasn't been invoked yet. Now type the following commands in interpreter C to open a back door to the application running in interpreter S.

```
% package require Itcl
3.0
% source Backdoor.itcl
% Backdoor stealth 51195
stealth
```

After creation of Backdoor object **stealth**, you now have a communication pipe opened to interpreter S through which you can send messages via Backdoor's *write* method. Turn on full tracing by sending the following message:

```
% stealth write "activate all"
```

When the DebugServer object receives this message, it invokes Trace::ACTIVATE (refer to DebugServer's *processRequest* method) with the argument, all. You'll notice a message in interpreter S that reads, "Successfully turned on Trace flags: all." Now invoke *method1* again in interpreter S, and you'll notice that debug output is now printed! Screen snapshots of the two interpreters are shown in Figure 5-1.

With the debugging techniques you learned in this chapter and the fundamentals of [incr Tcl] you learned throughout Chapters 1–4, you're now ready for a larger-scale example. The next chapter is devoted to such an example, providing the design and implementation of an object-oriented client/server framework using sockets similar to the implementation provided in the previous section. Then, Chapter 7 builds on the client/server framework by creating a chat room to show you how to update multiple graphical displays on separate hosts from a central server using an object-oriented technique called *composition*.

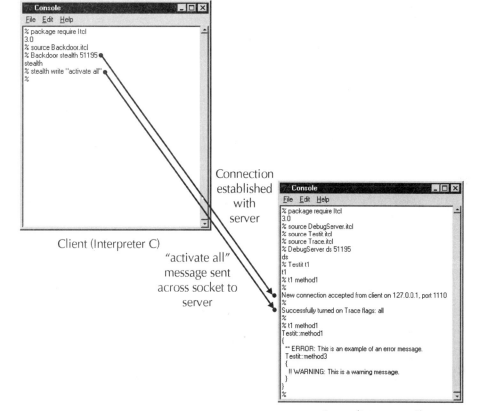

Client (Interpreter C)

Connection established with server

"activate all" message sent across socket to server

Server (Interpreter S)

Dynamically enabling debug output over a socket interface.

Figure 5-1.

5

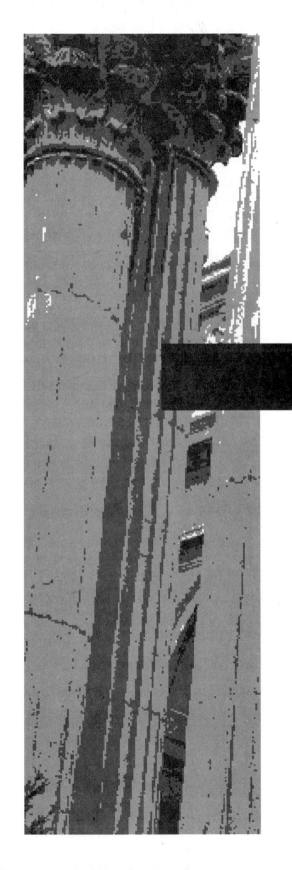

CHAPTER 6

Tying It All Together with Sockets

This chapter walks you through the analysis, design, implementation, and testing of a new object-oriented model that uses sockets to communicate between clients and servers. If you are new to object-oriented programming, then the first few sections will help you to get your feet wet; you'll see the thought processes typically involved in architecting a new OO model from inception. If you're an OO veteran, on the other hand, then feel free to skip to the implementation section of the client/server example. This chapter first shows you how to analyze the problem domain by brainstorming ideas and grouping them together for outlining potential classes. Next, you learn how CRC cards and scenario diagrams help you to solidify your design prior to implementation. Then, you learn how to use the analysis and design for implementing the class definitions and method bodies. Finally, you learn how to thoroughly test your code before releasing it to a customer for public use. Following this procedure, a simple user authentication example is provided to show you how you can use the new model for managing socket communication between a login manager and a graphical interface client for validating usernames and passwords prior to allowing the user access to your application. At the end of this chapter, you'll not only have a better understanding of how clients and servers can use sockets for communicating across a network, but you'll also have a fully functional, self-contained object-oriented model that you can reuse in any application for sending any type of data between clients and servers.

Analysis and Design

The goal of this chapter is to create a generic object-oriented model that uses sockets to communicate between clients and servers. Instead of immediately providing the implementation for this model and then discussing how it is used, it may be more beneficial for you to learn the details involved in designing the model prior to its actual implementation, especially if you are new to object-oriented programming. With this in mind, the remainder of this section leads you through the development life cycle of analyzing and designing this model.

Analyzing the Problem Domain

The first step in the development cycle is to analyze the problem at hand. What is it that you need to accomplish? From the goal just mentioned, you want to design a model that can be used by any [incr Tcl] application for sending data across sockets between clients and servers. Once you realize *what* needs to be done, you just need to figure out *how* to begin. Analysis typically begins with a process you may already be familiar with, brainstorming. The goal of brainstorming is to generate ideas. You begin by writing down the first thing that comes to mind about the given topic. This generally results in a chain reaction of additional ideas and questions, and before you realize it, you have a long list of bullets for summarizing the problem domain.

The best way to learn a new concept is to gain the experience of doing it, so go ahead and get a clean sheet of paper for brainstorming. Then, start writing down any ideas you have about the given topic as well as any questions that may arise. You should write concise phrases, and don't worry about their logical order or their level of complexity. It doesn't matter if an idea is high-level, like "server listens for client connections," or low-level, like "default server port." Try to write down at least five ideas, and when you're finished, take a look at the following bullets:

◆ Handling communication between a server and a client

◆ Server waits for client requests to connect

◆ Number of clients allowed

◆ Opening the physical socket

◆ Where to invoke the server

◆ Reading data from the sockets

Your list may include several more items than this, or it may contain fewer, depending on your level of understanding of a client/server framework. But this gives you an idea of what you should be thinking about.

One of the first things that might come to mind when brainstorming the concept of socket programming, for example, might be how a physical socket gets created. You might note this idea as "opening the physical socket," as shown in the bulleted items. This idea might lead to others such as what port to use or how to handle socket errors. As previously mentioned, ideas build on one another, and the more ideas you have, the better equipped you'll be later to create a robust and well-organized design. Try not to worry about code-specific issues such as what classes open sockets, what parameters any *constructor*s might accept, what variables should be used for configuration options, or any other implementation details such as these. Just write down each idea and worry about the code later.

A common problem software designers and programmers face during analysis is thinking too far ahead. They may avoid writing down an idea because they don't know how to implement it, or they may write down certain ideas based on how they think the implementation might develop. Try not to fall into this trap. This isn't the implementation phase, so don't let implementation details affect your analysis. Worry about *how* you'll implement your design once the design is complete. The analysis phase should be used strictly for analyzing the problem domain and generating ideas.

Designing the Model

Once you have completed the list of bullets from your analysis, you should sort the items into like groups. You might wonder how you know when the list is complete. Unfortunately, this is a gray area at best. Odds are that no matter how much time you spend analyzing the problem domain, you will think of other issues when you begin designing the model. Further, you will probably think of even more issues when you begin implementation. So there really is no definitive point after which you can claim full completion of your analysis. You just need to spend enough time analyzing the problem and consulting others until you're satisfied with the amount of available information before proceeding with the design.

Sorting your list into like groups is the first step taken towards designing the model. Each group is used to outline potential classes. For this example, you should be able to place every item in your list into one of two categories: clients or servers. Some items, like "opening the physical socket," might go in both categories. After this, you'll have an outline for two classes: one for handling the client side of the connection, and the other for handling the server side. The class for the client category might be named ClientSocket, and the class for the server category might be named ServerSocket.

Establishing Class Relationships with CRC Cards

After deciding on the two class names, your next step is to establish the relationships between these classes. A common approach is to use CRC cards. Recall from Chapter 1 that CRC cards list the responsibilities and collaborators of each class (refer to the "CRC Cards" section in Chapter 1 for more details). Review the bullets you have outlined for each class, and enter the appropriate items in the "Responsibilities" section of each respective CRC card. Since you only have two classes, the "Collaborators" section is obvious; ClientSocket collaborates with ServerSocket and vice versa. As you enter class responsibilities from your lists, you'll notice that several items involve both classes. For example, a ServerSocket item might read "handle client disconnect," and a ClientSocket item might read "register with server." Items like these lay the foundation for how classes interact with one another and provide a natural means for determining class relationships. Example CRC cards for the two classes are shown in Figure 6-1.

ClientSocket	ServerSocket
- connect to server - process server data - register with server - handle loss of communication with server - forward client requests to server - handle invalid data from server - close socket on destruction - open the physical socket	

ServerSocket	ClientSocket
- handle client connections - create the physical socket - maintain list of active clients - handle loss of communication with client - request registration from clients - verify activated state before accepting client connections - close all client sockets on destruction	

Example CRC
cards for
ClientSocket
and
ServerSocket

Figure 6-1.

6

Outlining Class Interactions with Scenarios

Once you have created CRC cards, you should be familiar with each class's
responsibilities as well as how each class interacts with the other. The next
step during the design phase is typically the creation of timeline diagrams
called *scenarios*. Scenarios are used to show the sequence of events in a
particular interaction between multiple classes. The "register with server"
item listed under ClientSocket's responsibilities is an example of such an
event. A scenario outlines the steps taken to accomplish this registration.
Thick vertical lines in a scenario represent classes, and horizontal arrows
between the lines represent data flow. You read the data flow top-down,
meaning that the topmost arrow is the first step in the scenario, and the
bottommost arrow is the last step. The following sections outline three
simple scenarios that could occur during the connection process between
a ClientSocket object and a ServerSocket object.

Client Attempts to Connect to Server When you create a ClientSocket object, it should try and establish a link across a physical socket with the ServerSocket object. Without worrying about exactly how this process might be implemented, think about the general order of events and refer to the scenario diagram shown in the following illustration.

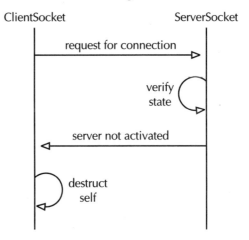

The first step is for the ClientSocket object (client) to send a request to the ServerSocket object (server) for connection. The server then checks to see if it is currently accepting client connections. It may have a maximum number of client connections already, or it may not be properly initialized yet. If it isn't activated, then it sends an appropriate message back to the client. The client, being unable to establish a connection, then destructs itself.

NOTE: The default behavior of the client is self-destruction following a connection error during initialization. Depending on your application, you may choose to log an error message in a file, display an error dialog window, or implement a retry mechanism so that the client tries to reconnect some predetermined number of times before handling the error.

Client Registers with Server Once the connection is established between the two physical sockets, another scenario might outline the process by which the client registers itself with the server. Consider the following illustration.

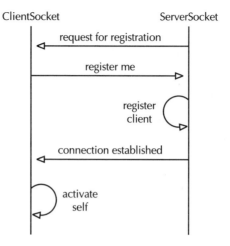

The server sends a request to the client for registration to verify that the client understands a predetermined protocol. In other words, the server verifies that the client speaks the same language (the next section discusses this in more detail). The client reads this message and understands that it must send a certain message back to the server in order to establish a successful communication link for passing data. The client sends the appropriate message back to the server, which registers the client and then sends a final message back to the client saying the registration succeeded. After this, the client activates itself to allow outside resources the ability to write to the client and send data to the server.

6

Server Disconnects Client on Error   Another example scenario would be handling the error condition of an unexpected client disconnect. The following scenario outlines the steps taken to handle this situation.

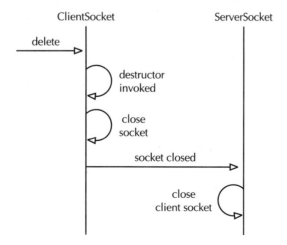

First, the client's *destructor* is invoked. This can result from an outside source's deleting the object or from an internal detection of a corrupt state causing the object to delete itself. Either way, the client's physical socket is closed, which sends an error condition across the physical socket to the server. The server then determines that the client side of the connection has been closed and closes its end of the connection. You will see the importance of handling this error condition later in this chapter.

There are several other possible interactions between ClientSocket and ServerSocket objects. You should try to create at least one more scenario diagram before proceeding to the next section. The three previous scenarios should serve as adequate examples. Additional scenarios include losing connection with the server or handling server responses to client requests.

Establishing a Protocol

One of the previous scenarios mentions that the server sends a message to the client requesting proper registration to verify that the client and server "speak the same language." This language is called a *protocol*. A protocol is simply a set of rules that allow devices that may normally be incompatible to effectively communicate with one another. Protocols are often referred to as *handshaking*. A message is sent from device A to device B. If B understands this message, it acknowledges it by sending a properly formatted message back to A. If A understands B, then the handshaking is complete, and a link is established for communication flow.

Figure 6-2 illustrates the concept of handshaking. Terminal A informs terminal B that it needs to transfer some data. B doesn't understand, so A asks it if it speaks English. Still, B doesn't understand. After a few more rounds, B finally understands A's question, and the two terminals are able to settle on a language that each understands. This process is analogous to two pieces of hardware that are manufactured by different companies but are able to communicate because each piece understands the same protocol.

In the ClientSocket/ServerSocket model, a protocol needs to be established so that each object understands what the other is trying to communicate. When the server sends a "request for registration" message to the client, the client needs to know that the server is asking it to register. In order for the client to understand the server's message, you must decide on a protocol prior to implementation. For example, the client might interpret the message "you need to register" as a request for registering itself with the server. The server would have to know to send this message when it wants the client to register, and the client would have to know to reply with some sort of registration

Protocols break
the language
barrier

Figure 6-2.

request when it receives this message from the server. The client response
might be, "please register me." When the server sees this message on the
socket, it knows that the client understood its original request for registration
and then proceeds to register the client in its list of active clients. This is an
example of a protocol that you could establish between ClientSocket and
ServerSocket objects. By enforcing the use of a certain protocol, you ensure
the integrity of the connection. This way, only ClientSocket objects can
connect to a ServerSocket object's port for passing data.

The following section provides and discusses the implementation of the
ClientSocket and ServerSocket classes. You should notice the use of certain

messages that are sent across the physical socket during the initialization process. These messages are part of the protocol that allows the objects to communicate, as you learned in this section.

Implementing the Design

At this point, you have class names from grouping your brainstorming ideas in the analysis phase, you know the responsibilities of each class from the CRC cards, and you know the sequence of events for class interactions from the scenario diagrams. You're now ready to begin implementing the design.

NOTE: As mentioned in Chapter 5, Trace methods are integrated in both ServerSocket and ClientSocket methods during implementation to aid in later testing. Recall that the Trace class allows you to dynamically enable or disable various types of debugging messages. Full debugging will be enabled to aid in the testing process following implementation. You should review the Trace class as necessary. This class is available in the file Trace.itcl.

The ServerSocket class is provided first since a server must be running before a client can connect.

The ServerSocket Class

The ServerSocket class definition outlines methods and data members corresponding to the issues discussed during analysis and design. Each method is discussed individually in sections following the class definition.

```
::itcl::class ServerSocket {
  # Class constructor/destructor
  constructor {{port_ 20002}} {}
  destructor {
    catch {close $_socket}
    foreach clientSocket $_activeClients {
      catch {close $clientSocket}
    }
  }

  # Class Methods
  public method activate {command_}
```

```
public method write {sd_ data_}
public method broadcast {data_}
private method accept {sd_ address_ port_}
private method handleClientInput {sd_}
private method disconnect {sd_}

# Class Data Members
private variable _socket
private variable _activeClients
private variable _serverFunction
private variable _active 0
}
```

Constructing ServerSocket Objects

First, consider the *constructor*. The only task a ServerSocket object needs to do during construction is to create the physical socket. The *constructor* body then looks like this:

6

```
::itcl::body ServerSocket::constructor {{port_ 20002}} {
  Trace::EXE begin
  # Open the physical socket.
  if {[catch {
    socket -server [::itcl::code $this accept] $port_
  } _socket]} {
    Trace::ERR "Could not create socket: $_socket"
    Trace::EXE end
    return -code error
  }
  Trace::EXE end
}
```

The **socket** command is used to open a server socket to the specified port number. Note that the user is allowed, but not required, to specify this port number. By default, ServerSocket objects open port 20002 on the local host.

NOTE: There is no special significance to this particular port number. You can usually specify any number between 2^{10} and 2^{16}, depending on your system. Numbers less than 1024 (2^{10}) are typically reserved for internal use, and 65536 (2^{16}) is typically the upper limit. Port 20002 is arbitrarily chosen for this example.

This port is monitored for client connections, and when a client attempts to connect, the *accept* method is called. This method is registered with the interpreter by specifying it immediately following the –server option of the **socket** command. The **code** command is used to provide proper namespace resolution for this private method to be called from outside the class scope. If an error occurs during creation of the physical socket, the **return** command is used with "-code error" to report the error and halt the construction process. The object does not get created in this situation. If no errors occur, then the result of the **socket** command, the socket descriptor, will be stored in the _socket data member.

NOTE: The physical socket opened by the ServerSocket object is neither readable nor writable by the object. The sole purpose of this server socket is for accepting client connections. It is managed by the interpreter, and you will get an error if you try to write to or read from this socket.

Handling New Client Connections

Next, you need to implement the *accept* method. This method is automatically invoked by the interpreter each time a client attempts to connect to the ServerSocket object's port. The interpreter invokes the method with three arguments: the client's socket descriptor, the client's address, and the client's port number. The method body is implemented as follows:

```
::itcl::body ServerSocket::accept {sd_ address_ port_} {
  Trace::EXE begin
  # Close the socket if the server's not activated yet. This causes
  # the ClientSocket object to delete itself.
  if {!$_active} {
    Trace::ERR "Server not activated, closing client socket $sd_..."
    close $sd_
    Trace::EXE end
    return
  }

  # Configure the socket to automatically flush when newline
  # characters are detected and set up a callback method to be
  # invoked when the socket becomes readable.
  fconfigure $sd_ -buffering line
  fileevent $sd_ readable [::itcl::code $this handleClientInput $sd_]
```

```
Trace::COMM \
  "Accepted new client connection from $address_, port $port_"
Trace::COMM "Asking client to register..."
puts $sd_ "registration requested"
Trace::EXE end
}
```

First, the ServerSocket object checks its _active flag to determine whether or not to accept the client's request for connection. (Note that internally, the physical connection actually already exists at this point.) As discussed earlier, this is one way for the server to manage the number of client connections. If the ServerSocket object has not been activated, then it closes its end of the socket connection. Otherwise, the object uses the **fconfigure** command to modify its end of the connection, setting the –buffering option to "line." This means that the socket will automatically be flushed each time a newline character is written to it, which will avoid any unwanted buffering on the server's side of the connection. As a result, you can use the **puts** command to immediately send a message to the client since **puts** automatically appends a newline character to its argument (assuming the –nonewline option is not specified).

6

NOTE: The **fconfigure** command can be used to control many different aspects of the socket connection. Refer to its man page for more details.

Next, the ServerSocket object uses the **fileevent** command to set up a "watch" on the socket. Similar to Tcl's **trace** command, **fileevent** can be used to tell the interpreter to automatically invoke a command when a channel becomes readable or writable. In this case, the *handleClientInput* method is invoked with the client's socket descriptor when the socket becomes readable. This means that each time a client writes to the socket, *handleClientInput* is invoked on the server side to process the client request.

The last task that *accept* needs to complete is instructing the client to properly register itself with the server. This is accomplished by sending the message "registration requested" across the physical socket to the client. This message is part of the predefined protocol discussed earlier. The server assumes that the client has also set up a "watch" via the **fileevent** command to automatically receive and process data written to the server end of the socket connection. When the client detects this message on the socket, it proceeds accordingly. You will learn the steps taken on the client side when the ClientSocket class is implemented in the next section.

The fundamental concepts of a client/server framework have been covered in the previous couple of sections. Before proceeding to the next ServerSocket method, let's take a moment to review. If you're not lost right now, then the rest of this chapter will be easy for you. Otherwise, the following summary of the steps taken so far should help to clarify the order of events.

1. ServerSocket's *constructor* is invoked on instantiation.
2. The physical server socket is created.
3. ServerSocket's *accept* method is registered with the interpreter to be automatically invoked when a client attempts to connect to the server's port.
4. The client attempts to connect, and the server accepts/denies access based on its _active flag. (Steps end here if the server denies access.)
5. Buffering is turned off on the server side of the connection.
6. ServerSocket's *handleClientInput* method is registered with the interpreter to be automatically invoked when the physical socket becomes readable.
7. The server instructs the client to properly register itself by writing "registration requested" to the socket.

Activating the ServerSocket Object

In the previous section, you learned that the ServerSocket object will not accept client connections until it is activated. To do this, the user must invoke its *activate* method. The responsibility of this method is to activate the object and store the argument passed into the command_ parameter in a private data member for later use. This argument should be the properly scoped name of a procedure or method that the ServerSocket object can invoke to process specific client requests. If the designated procedure is defined at the global scope, then you don't have to specify any namespace resolution because it will be invoked at the global scope, but if you pass in a non-public class method to *activate*, you have to specify proper scoping. You'll see an example of this later in the chapter. The method body looks like this:

```
::itcl::body ServerSocket::activate {command_} {
  Trace::EXE begin
  set _serverFunction $command_
  set _active 1
  Trace::COMM \
    "Server is activated and ready to accept client messages."
  Trace::EXE end
}
```

As you can see, activating the ServerSocket object is as simple as setting the _active flag to True. After this method is called, the conditional will pass in the *accept* method, and client connections will be accepted.

Processing Client Requests

Once the connection between the ServerSocket object and the ClientSocket object is fully established, the ServerSocket object needs a way to forward specific client requests to an outside source for processing. Remember that the goal for this model is to create a *generic* communication backbone that is used for sending data between clients and servers. The *type* of data being passed should not affect the implementation of the model. As a result, appropriate hooks must be established in each end of the connection to forward and receive outside messages. One such hook is ServerSocket's *write* method, and another occurs in ServerSocket's *handleClientInput* method. These methods are closely associated, so they are both implemented and discussed together as follows:

6

```
::itcl::body ServerSocket::handleClientInput {sd_} {
  Trace::EXE begin
  Trace::COMM \
    "Servicing new client message detected on socket $sd_..."
  if {[catch {gets $sd_ data} rc]} {
    disconnect $sd_
      Trace::EXE end
    return
  }
  if {$rc > 0} {
    if {$data == "register me"} {
      Trace::COMM "Client is requesting registration."
      puts $sd_ "connection established"
      lappend _activeClients $sd_
    } else {
      # Make sure this client is already registered.
      if {[lsearch $_activeClients $sd_] == -1} {
        Trace::ERR "This client is not registered! Closing socket!"
        close $sd_
      } else {
        # Send the request to the server function.
        Trace::COMM "Forwarding client request for processing..."
        eval $_serverFunction [list $data] $sd_
      }
    }
  } else {
    # Client end of socket has been closed. Close this side
```

```
        # and remove the client from the active list.
        Trace::WARN \
          "Loss of connection detected on $sd_. Closing socket..."
        disconnect $sd_
      }
      Trace::EXE end
    }

::itcl::body ServerSocket::write {sd_ data_} {
    Trace::EXE begin
    if {[catch {puts $sd_ $data_} err]} {
      Trace::ERR "Failed to forward message to client: --> $err"
      Trace::EXE end
      error $err
    }
    Trace::EXE end
  }
```

The *handleClientInput* method first verifies that there is valid data in the socket by checking the result of the **gets** command. If the result is positive, then the value of the data is compared against a phrase that is part of the known protocol defined between ServerSocket and ClientSocket objects. If the data does not match any known protocol string, then the server first verifies that this message is from a client that has already registered itself with the server. This is done to ensure that the handshaking process has been properly completed. If this message is from a client that has not properly registered, then the server closes its end of the connection. Otherwise, *handleClientInput* evaluates the command that was passed into its *activate* method, sending the associated procedure or method the client's request and the client's socket descriptor as arguments. This procedure or method is then expected to service the client's request and notify the client of the results if necessary by sending a response back to the client via ServerSocket's *write* method.

Think of the ServerSocket object as a kind of information router, as depicted in Figure 6-3. Data flows across the socket from a client requesting some service (1), the ServerSocket object forwards the request to some outside source for processing by evaluating its _serverFunction data member (2), and the outside source handles the client request and then notifies the client (4) of the result via ServerSocket's *write* method (3). This is exactly what the design should have accomplished, defining a model generic enough to forward any type of data between client and server objects. The only requirement is for the user of the ServerSocket class to declare two parameters in the procedure or method that is registered with ServerSocket's *activate* method. From the *handleClientInput* method, note that the reason for this is that the designated command (_serverFunction) is invoked with two arguments, the client request and the socket descriptor. The procedure or method must therefore declare two parameters to accept these two arguments.

Now that you understand the information flow, take a look at the "else" condition at the end of *handleClientInput*. If the client side of the connection is closed, this method is automatically called because a channel is considered readable if an end-of-file or error condition is present on the socket. (Recall that this method is automatically invoked each time the socket becomes readable.) It's extremely important to handle this condition on each side of the connection. Failure to do so could result in an infinite loop where *handleClientInput* reads no data, returns, and is immediately invoked again if the client side of the connection is lost. This is the purpose of checking the result of the **gets** command and closing the socket descriptor if the result is less than or equal to zero.

6

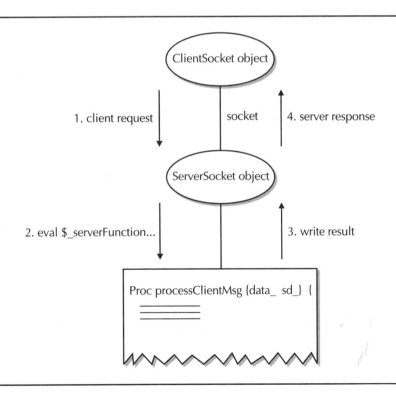

The ServerSocket object routes messages between the client and the proc/method

Figure 6-3.

Handling Error Conditions

There are two error conditions that require the server to close its end of the socket connection and remove the corresponding client from its list of active clients, each of which occurs in *handleClientInput*. First, the socket descriptor may be corrupted, causing the interpreter to be unable to read data from it, and next, the client side of the socket may have been closed. The *disconnect* method to handle these cases is implemented as follows:

```
::itcl::body ServerSocket::disconnect {sd_} {
  Trace::EXE begin
  # This is a hook to notify any attached servers that this
  # socket descriptor is corrupted or has been closed.
  eval $_serverFunction disconnectingSocket $sd_

  Trace::COMM "Disconnecting socket $sd_..."
  set index [lsearch $_activeClients $sd_]
  set _activeClients [lreplace $_activeClients $index $index]
  close $sd_
  Trace::EXE end
}
```

Notice the line containing the **eval** command. This line is used to attempt to notify any other kinds of application servers that may be using the ServerSocket class that one of the client socket descriptors is corrupted or has been closed on the client end of the connection. You'll see an example of the need for this in the next chapter.

Broadcasting

Broadcasting is a facility built into the ServerSocket to allow the user to broadcast messages, or to send messages to all clients at once. This method will prove to be invaluable in the next chapter when a chat room model is implemented. The idea is simply to iterate over the list of active clients (stored in the _activeClients data member) and write the designated message to each client socket descriptor. This method is implemented as follows:

```
::itcl::body ServerSocket::broadcast {data_} {
  Trace::EXE begin
  foreach client $_activeClients {
    if {[catch {puts $client $data_} err]} {
      error $err
    }
  }
  Trace::EXE end
}
```

The ClientSocket Class

You now have a fully functional ServerSocket class, but it is useless without the ClientSocket counterpart. The purpose of this class is to forward client requests to the ServerSocket object for processing. The class definition follows and each method is discussed separately, similar to the ServerSocket methods:

```
::itcl::class ClientSocket {
  # Class constructor/destructor
  constructor {{host_ localhost} {port_ 20002}} {}
  destructor {close $_socket}

  # Class Methods
  public method write {data_}
  public method register {command_} {set _clientFunction $command_}
  private method handleServerInput {}

  # Class Data Members
  private variable _socket
  private variable _activated 0
  private variable _clientFunction ""
}
```

The class definition includes a *constructor* and *destructor*, two interface methods, a private method for handling responses from the server, and three private data members similar to the ones declared in ServerSocket.

Constructing ClientSocket Objects

As mentioned earlier, when you create a ClientSocket object, it should try to connect with the physical socket opened by the ServerSocket object. With this in mind, consider the *constructor* body.

```
::itcl::body ClientSocket::constructor \
{{host_ localhost} {port_ 20002}} {
  Trace::EXE begin
  # Connect with the socket opened by the ServerSocket object.
  if {[catch {socket $host_ $port_} _socket]} {
    Trace::ERR "Failed to connect to server: $_socket"
    Trace::EXE end
    return -code error
  }

  # When the server writes to the socket, handle its input.
  fconfigure $_socket -buffering line
  fileevent $_socket readable [::itcl::code $this handleServerInput]
  Trace::EXE end
}
```

6

The ClientSocket *constructor* has two main functions: opening a physical socket to the server and setting up a callback method to handle input from the server's side of the connection. For the first function, the **socket** command is used to open a physical socket to the specified host and port number. The host should be the name or IP address of the computer where the server is running, and the port number should be the same as the port number opened by the ServerSocket object. The default host and port number are the same for both ClientSocket and ServerSocket. So if you create the ServerSocket object on a machine in your network other than the local host, or if you specify a server port other than 20002, then you must pass the appropriate arguments into ClientSocket's *constructor*.

For the second function, the socket is configured to automatically flush when newline characters are detected, and the *handleServerInput* method is registered with the interpreter to be invoked when the socket becomes readable. If creation of the physical socket fails, then ClientSocket behaves the same way as ServerSocket; an error is generated, and the object is not created.

Processing Server Messages

You learned in the implementation of ServerSocket that the *handleClientInput* method is automatically invoked to process client requests. A method must also be implemented on the client side for processing messages coming from the server. This is the responsibility of the *handleServerInput* method.

```
::itcl::body ClientSocket::handleServerInput {} {
  Trace::EXE begin
  Trace::COMM "Processing new data from the server..."
  if {[gets $_socket data] < 0} {
    Trace::ERR "Server has closed socket.  Deleting self..."
    ::itcl::delete object $this
  } elseif {$data == "registration requested"} {
    Trace::COMM "Registering with the server..."
    puts $_socket "register me"
  } elseif {$data == "connection established"} {
    Trace::COMM "Connection is established.  Activating..."
    set _activated 1
    uplevel #0 {set CONNECTION_ESTABLISHED 1}
  } else {
    Trace::COMM "Received message: \"$data\""
    if {[llength $_clientFunction]} {
      Trace::COMM \
        " - Forwarding to client function for processing..."
      $_clientFunction $data
    } else {
      Trace::WARN "  - Don't know what to do with it.  Returning..."
    }
  }
  Trace::EXE end
}
```

As you can see, this method is very similar to the server counterpart. If valid data is on the socket, then it is compared to phrases outlined by the protocol. If the server has requested registration, then the client writes "register me" to the socket. If the server informs the client that the connection has been successfully established, then the client activates itself so that the user can send specific client requests to the server for processing. (Don't worry about the global flag, *CONNECTION_ESTABLISHED*. You'll see what this is needed for in the next chapter.) Finally, if the data does not match any known protocol messages, then the client executes its _clientFunction data member if it has been specified.

The _clientFunction data member is analogous to ServerSocket's _serverFunction data member. It stores the name of a properly scoped procedure or method registered by an outside source, via the *register* method, for handling specific server messages. The data from the socket is passed to this procedure or method for processing. If _clientFunction has not been specified, then *handleServerInput* prints a message informing you that it doesn't know what to do with the data.

6

Sending Requests to the Server
Once the connection between client and server is fully established, the client must have a way to forward requests to the server for processing. This is accomplished with the *write* method, implemented as follows:

```
::itcl::body ClientSocket::write {data_} {
  Trace::EXE begin
  # If not activated, return an error.
  if {!$_activated} {
    Trace::ERR \
      "Cannot write to socket.  Connection not yet established."
    Trace::EXE end
    return -code error
  }
  puts $_socket $data_
  Trace::EXE end
}
```

This method is responsible for sending data across the physical socket to the server. First, it verifies that the ClientSocket object is activated. This keeps users of the class from sending data to the server until the connection is established. Recall that the connection is only established after it is determined that both ClientSocket and ServerSocket objects understand the same protocol. If the ClientSocket object is activated, then the specified data is written to the physical socket for processing by the server. Otherwise, the

return command is used in conjunction with "-code error" to generate an error condition. This means the calling function should place a **catch** around the call to *write*. An example might look like this:

```
if {[catch {$clientSocketObject write "some message"} err]} {
    Trace::ERR "Failed to send data to the server:\n  --> \"$err\""
}
```

If the **catch** command is not used to trap the possible error condition, a stack trace will occur. And as you probably know, delivering code that produces stack traces does not lend itself to positive customer relations.

This concludes the implementation for the ClientSocket class. Now that both ClientSocket and ServerSocket are defined and implemented, it's time to test the code. The following section takes you through the steps to make sure the classes work together as expected. (If you wondered why all the Trace debug statements are scattered about the class methods, you'll find out during testing.)

Testing the Code

The most important step prior to customer delivery is thorough testing of your code. You should try each and every condition to make sure all paths are executed and behave as expected. You can do this with the ClientSocket and ServerSocket classes directly on the command line, or you can create simple driver scripts. This section shows you how to test the code from the command line.

You will first need to save the class definitions in appropriate files, ServerSocket.itcl and ClientSocket.itcl. Additionally, you need access to the Trace class, so it must also be saved in a file, Trace.itcl. Then invoke two **wish** interpreters. One will handle the server side (interpreter S), and the other will handle the client side (interpreter C). You could perform the same test in a single interpreter, but two will help you to better visualize a separation of concerns between a server and a client.

NOTE: You must use Tk-based interpreters in order to test the code interactively (i.e., on the command line in the same interpreter session). The reason for this is that Tcl-based shells do not automatically enter the event loop. You must use the **vwait** command to do this, and doing so disallows your interacting with the application dynamically during your debug session. See the **vwait** man page for further details.

Now type the following commands in interpreter S to create a ServerSocket object. (All output printed by Trace is shown in italics.)

```
% package require Itcl
3.0
% source ServerSocket.itcl
% source Trace.itcl
% Trace::ACTIVATE all
% ServerSocket s
::ServerSocket::constructor
{
}
s
```

A ServerSocket object is created, opening a physical socket to the default port, 20002, on the local host. Since no error message was printed, you know instantiation succeeded. Trace's EXE method prints the output shown. The socket is now being monitored for client connections, and when a client attempts to connect, the server's *accept* method will automatically be invoked.

6

Now create a ClientSocket object in interpreter C with the following commands before you activate the server. As soon as you hit ENTER, notice the output that gets printed in interpreter S (shown in boldface).

```
% package require Itcl
3.0
% source ClientSocket.itcl
% source Trace.itcl
% Trace::ACTIVATE all
% ClientSocket c
c
::ServerSocket::accept
{
   ** ERROR: Server not activated, closing client socket sock5...
}
::ClientSocket::handleServerInput
{
   ## COMMENT: Processing new data from the server...
   ** ERROR: Server has closed socket.  Deleting self...
}
```

This tests the case when the ServerSocket object is not yet activated. As you can see, the ServerSocket object's *accept* method is invoked, prints an error message, and closes the server end of the physical socket connection. This results in destruction of the ClientSocket object, shown by the Trace messages printed in *handleServerInput*.

The next step is to activate the server and try creating the ClientSocket object again. First you need to define a procedure that will be invoked after the connection has been established. Then, pass the procedure name into ServerSocket's *activate* method to activate the server. Type the following code in interpreter S:

```
% proc processClientMsg {data_ sd_} {
    Trace::EXE begin
    Trace::COMM "Received data \"$data_\" from socket $sd_"
    Trace::EXE end
  }
% s activate processClientMsg
::ServerSocket::activate
{
    ## COMMENT: Server is activated and ready to accept client messages.
}
```

Now that the server is activated, try and create the ClientSocket object again in interpreter C. If all goes well, then the server and client will go through the handshaking process, and the connection will be successfully established. The server's output as printed in interpreter S is again shown in boldface.

```
% ClientSocket c
c
::ClientSocket::constructor
{
}
::ServerSocket::accept
{
    ## COMMENT: Accepted new client connection from 127.0.0.1 port 34611
    ## COMMENT: Asking client to register...
}
::ClientSocket::handleServerInput
{
    ## COMMENT: Processing new data from the server...
    ## COMMENT: Registering with the server...
}
::ServerSocket::handleClientInput
{
    ## COMMENT: Servicing new client message detected on socket sock5...
    ## COMMENT: Client is requesting registration.
}
::ClientSocket::handleServerInput
{
    ## COMMENT: Processing new data from the server...
    ## COMMENT: Connection is established.  Activating...
}
```

From this output, it looks like the code works as expected. Both objects determined that they could communicate with one another, and a connection is established for passing data back and forth between the client and server.

In Depth

You should take a minute now to review what just happened in the previous step. From the user's perspective, if no Trace debug messages had been printed, the only thing that happened was the creation of a ClientSocket object. This is the beauty of abstraction. The interface that is exposed to the user is very simple to use. The complexity of the internal behavior of the system is appropriately hidden behind the scenes.

When you hit ENTER after typing **ClientSocket c**, interpreter C sent a message to port 20002 on the ServerSocket object's host. (Note that the server's host could be the same computer as the client, a separate computer in the same network, or a machine in another country thousands of miles away connected via the Internet! As long as there is physical connectivity, the ServerSocket object can be in an interpreter running on a computer anywhere.) Interpreter S monitors that port for connection attempts. When it detects the request coming from interpreter C, it invokes the ServerSocket object's *accept* method. This method writes a message back into the socket to start the handshaking process. Interpreter C detects this message and invokes the ClientSocket object's *handleServerInput* method to process it.

Recall that the interpreter can do this automatically because the **fileevent** command had been used to register the method to be invoked when the socket becomes readable. The ClientSocket object reads the data from the socket, determines that the server is asking it to register, and sends an appropriate response back into the socket. The server detects this new message, reads the data from the socket, registers the client, and sends another message saying the connection is established. Finally, the client once again detects a new message coming from the server, reads the data from the socket, interprets the message as a protocol message that means the connection has successfully been established, and configures itself to allow public write access to the socket.

All this happens just by typing, **ClientSocket c**! You can see the ease with which [incr Tcl] allows you to get two objects created in two different interpreters on two different machines to successfully communicate with one another via the built-in socket mechanism provided by Tcl.

Now that the connection has been established, you need to test the path from the ClientSocket object across the physical socket connection to the ServerSocket object. This is done simply by invoking the ClientSocket object's *write* method. Type the following command in interpreter C. Output from Trace methods is shown immediately following this command.

```
% c write "hello world"
::ClientSocket::write
{
}
::ServerSocket::handleClientInput
{
## COMMENT: Servicing new client message detected on socket sock5...
## COMMENT: Forwarding client request for processing...
  ::processClientMsg
  {
    ## COMMENT: Received data "hello world" from socket sock5
  }
}
```

This test is successful as well. The message sent through the client was received by the server and forwarded to the **processClientMsg** procedure for processing.

The same test should now be done in the reverse direction. In order to do this, you must modify the **processClientMsg** procedure to send a response to the ClientSocket object. Rewrite the procedure in interpreter S as follows:

```
% proc processClientMsg {data_ sd_} {
    Trace::EXE begin
    Trace::COMM "Received data \"$data_\" from socket $sd_"
    Trace::COMM "  --> sending response..."
    ::s write $sd_ "What do I look like, a genie?"
    Trace::EXE end
  }
```

After making this modification on the server side, send another request to the ServerSocket object in interpreter C like this:

```
% c write "I want 3 wishes."
::ClientSocket::write
{
}
::ServerSocket::handleClientInput
{
```

```
## COMMENT: Servicing new client message detected on socket sock5...
## COMMENT: Forwarding client request for processing...
::processClientMsg
{
  ## COMMENT: Received data "I want 3 wishes." from socket sock5
  ## COMMENT:   --> sending response...
  ServerSocket::write
  {
  }
}
}
::ClientSocket::handleServerInput
{
  ## COMMENT: Processing new data from the server...
  ## COMMENT: Received message: "What do I look like, a genie?"
  !! WARNING:   - Don't know what to do with it.  Returning...
}
```

6

Perfect. The ServerSocket object received the request from the client and forwarded it to the **processClientMsg** procedure, which instructed the ServerSocket object to send a message back to its socket. The ClientSocket object receives this message, doesn't know how to interpret it, and prints an appropriate warning message via Trace::WARN.

Next, you need to register a procedure with the ClientSocket object to make sure the message forwarding mechanism works correctly on that side. Type the following code in interpreter C to do this:

```
% proc processServerMsg {data_} {
    Trace::EXE begin
    Trace::COMM "Received data \"$data_\""
    Trace::EXE end
  }
% c register processServerMsg
% c write "How about 1 wish?"
::ClientSocket::write
{
}
::ServerSocket::handleClientInput
{
  ## COMMENT: Servicing new client message detected on socket sock5...
  ## COMMENT: Forwarding client request for processing...
  ::processClientMsg
  {
```

```
      ## COMMENT: Received data "How about 1 wish?" from socket sock5
      ## COMMENT:    --> sending response...
      ::ServerSocket::write
      {
      }
    }
  }
}
::ClientSocket::handleServerInput
{
  ## COMMENT: Processing new data from the server...
  ## COMMENT: Received message: "What do I look likc, a genie?"
  ## COMMENT:    - Forwarding to client function for processing...
  ::processServerMsg
  {
    ## COMMENT: Received data "What do I look like, a genie?"
  }
}
```

As you can see, messages printed by Trace's static methods are extremely helpful in watching the order of execution. It looks like this last external hook also works as expected. The ClientSocket object correctly forwarded the server response to the **processServerMsg** procedure for processing.

Now that you have tested the functionality of the model, try deleting the ClientSocket object to make sure the server side handles the closing of the socket appropriately. Type the following command in interpreter C:

```
% ::itcl::delete object c
::ServerSocket::handleClientInput
{
  ## COMMENT: Servicing new client message detected on socket sock5...
  !! WARNING: Loss of connection detected on sock5. Closing socket...
  ::ServerSocket::disconnect
  {
    ::processClientMsg
    {
      ## COMMENT:Received data "disconnectingSocket" from socket sock5
      ## COMMENT:    --> sending response...
      ::ServerSocket::write
      {
      }
    }
    ## COMMENT: Disconnecting socket sock28...
  }
}
```

As expected, the ServerSocket object detects the loss of communication with the client and closes its end of the socket connection. You now have one final test to check. You need to make sure that the client handles loss of communication with the server. In order to do this, you need to create another ClientSocket object and then delete the ServerSocket object. Type the following commands in interpreter C. Since you know that construction works, you can disable debug output with Trace::DEACTIVATE. (Both client and server debug messages are deactivated in the following output).

```
% Trace::DEACTIVATE all
% ClientSocket newClient
newClient
```

Now reenable debug output on both sides and then delete the ServerSocket object by typing the following commands in interpreter S:

```
% Trace::ACTIVATE all
% ::itcl::delete object s
::ClientSocket::handleServerInput
 {
   ## COMMENT: Processing new data from the server...
   ** ERROR: Server has closed socket.  Deleting self...
}
```

6

As soon as you type this command, the text shown in boldface is printed in interpreter C (note that this is the client side this time instead of the server side). The ClientSocket object successfully detects the closing of the server end of the socket and destructs itself. You may want to modify the behavior of ClientSocket objects so that they don't destruct themselves after losing connection with the server, but instead display an error message or dialog window. This depends on your own application.

With this last test completed, you can pat yourself on the back because you have now completed analysis, design, full implementation, and testing of the original model from the beginning of this chapter. Let's use the model in a useful example now. The next section shows you how to implement a simple login manager that verifies usernames and passwords before allowing access to an application.

Tying It All Together: User Authentication

To implement a simple system that authenticates usernames and passwords, you can use the model you just developed for the communication backbone and create two new classes to interface with the model. One of the classes should be a login manager that performs the actual authentication process, and the other class should act as a client, forwarding the username and password to the login manager. Let's begin with the server side again. The following section walks through the implementation of the LoginMgr class.

Implementing the Server Side

```
::itcl::class LoginMgr {
  constructor {} {}

  # Class Methods
  protected method authenticate {data_ sd_}

  # Class Data Members
  protected variable _serverSocket
  protected variable _validIds
}
```

The class definition declares a *constructor*, a protected method, and two protected data members. The content and purpose of each method is discussed in the following sections. You'll see the reason why each method and data member is declared as protected in Chapter 8 on using inheritance.

Creating the Server Socket

The responsibility of a LoginMgr object is to make sure that the username and password supplied to it are valid. In order to do this, the *constructor* must create a socket for accepting messages for authentication from clients requesting login service. Additionally, the *constructor* needs to initialize a list of valid user identifiers. This list could also be stored in an encrypted file, but for simplicity's sake, the identifiers are hardcoded into the *constructor* body, implemented as follows:

```
::itcl::body LoginMgr::constructor {} {
  Trace::EXE begin
  if {[catch {ServerSocket #auto 20002} _serverSocket]} {
    Trace::ERR "Unable to create socket: $_serverSocket"
    Trace::EXE end
    return -code error
  }
```

```
set _validIds(lyle_stavast) mr.admin
set _validIds(don_hurd) toolsguy
$_serverSocket activate [::itcl::code [$this authenticate]
Trace::EXE end
}
```

If creation of the ServerSocket object succeeds, then valid user identifiers are initialized, and the ServerSocket object is activated. In the previous section, you activated the object from the command line, specifying a procedure name. In this case, you need to specify proper namespace resolution because the method being registered is private. If you want to allow automatic invocation of this method when clients attempt to connect to the server's port, then you have to provide privileged access by using **code** command as shown.

Performing the Authentication

After construction completes, the interpreter monitors port 20002 on the server's host to watch for client connections as discussed earlier. When a client attempts to connect, the *authenticate* method is invoked. This method looks like this:

```
::itcl::body LoginMgr::authenticate {data_ sd_} {
  Trace::EXE begin
  set request [lindex $data_ 0]
  if {$request == "login" && [llength $data_] == 3} {
    set username [lindex $data_ 1]
    set password [lindex $data_ 2]
    if {[info exists _validIds($username)]} {
      if {$_validIds($username) == $password} {
        $_serverSocket write $sd_ "access granted"
      } else {
        $_serverSocket write $sd_ "access denied - bad password"
      }
    } else {
      $_serverSocket write $sd_ "access denied - bad username"
    }
  } else {
    Trace::ERR "BAD DATA: $data_"
  }
  Trace::EXE end
}
```

The *authenticate* method is the key to the entire design. It reads data from the socket, makes sure it matches the protocol of specifying "login" as the first word in a login request, validates the username and password, and instructs the ServerSocket object to write the appropriate response to its socket to inform the client of the authentication result.

NOTE: For illustration purposes, this example code informs the user of the reason for any login failures. Under normal conditions, you should just deny the login without giving a reason.

Implementing the Client Side

Now that the server side is implemented, you need to develop the client side. The definition for the LoginClient class is as follows:

```
::itcl::class LoginClient {
  # Class constructor/destructor
  constructor {} {}
  destructor {
    catch {
      destroy $_toplevel
      ::itcl::delete object $_clientSocket
    }
  }

  # Class Methods
  public method draw {} {wm deiconify $_toplevel}
  protected method process {data_}
  private method createClientSocket {}
  private method createMainScreen {}
  private method requestLogin {}

  # Class Data Members
  private variable _toplevel
  private variable _clientSocket
  private variable _password ""
  private variable _username ""
}
```

As you can see, this class definition is more involved than LoginMgr. This is mainly because the client side is responsible for displaying a graphical interface, prompting the user to enter a username and password and then click an OK button.

Connecting the Client and Server Sockets

The LoginClient *constructor*'s first task should be creating an information conduit for passing data to the server. This conduit is a ClientSocket object. After the handshaking process is complete and the connection is established, the main screen should be created. The *constructor* and *createClientSocket* methods are implemented as follows:

```
::itcl::body LoginClient::constructor {} {
  Trace::EXE begin
  # Create the socket for sending login request to server.
  if {[catch {createClientSocket} err]} {
    Trace::ERR "Failed to create client socket: - $err"
    Trace::EXE end
    return -code error
  }
  # Socket creation succeeded.  Create login screen.
  createMainScreen
  Trace::EXE end
}

::itcl::body LoginClient::createClientSocket {} {
  Trace::EXE begin
  Trace::COMM "Creating client socket..."
  if {[catch {ClientSocket #auto} _clientSocket]} {
    Trace::ERR "Failed to open client socket: $_clientSocket"
    Trace::EXE end
    return -code error
  }
  Trace::COMM "Succeeded. Registering processing method..."
  # Register a method for handling server responses.
  $_clientSocket register [::itcl::code [$this process]
  Trace::EXE end
}
```

After construction of the ClientSocket object, the connection is established between the client and server. The next step is to register a method to process server responses to client requests. This is the purpose of the *process* method. When the socket between the client and server becomes readable, *process* is invoked to process the data written to the socket. This data should be a response from the server corresponding to a previous client request.

Processing Server Responses to Client Requests

The *process* method is the gateway to the rest of your application. It processes the response from the server to determine whether to allow the user access to the application beyond the login screen. Note that this is a protected method. As with ServerSocket's protected items, you'll see how to extend this class through inheritance in Chapter 8. The implementation for this method is straightforward as follows:

```
::itcl::body LoginClient::process {data_} {
  Trace::EXE begin
  if {$data_ == "access granted"} {
    Trace::COMM "Login is successful!"
    # Place code here to continue with the application.
  } else {
    Trace::WARN "Login failed!"
  }
  Trace::EXE end
}
```

Once again, a protocol has been established such that the client side and server side both know what "access granted" means. If this text is read from the socket, then the client knows that the username and password are valid. A message is printed for both success and failure cases. On successful authentication, code may be added to provide access to the rest of the application. You'll see an example of this for logging into a chat room in the next chapter.

Creating the Main Login Screen

As mentioned earlier, one of the responsibilities of the client side is to provide a graphical interface for user authentication. This is the purpose of the *createMainScreen* method, implemented as follows:

```
::itcl::body LoginClient::createMainScreen {} {
  Trace::EXE begin
  set _toplevel [toplevel .[namespace tail $this]]
  wm withdraw $_toplevel
  wm resizable $_toplevel 0 0

  label $_toplevel.name -text "User Name:"
  entry $_toplevel.nametxt -width 12 \
    -textvariable [::itcl::scope _username]

  label $_toplevel.pswd -text "Password:"
  entry $_toplevel.pswdtxt -show * -width 12 \
    -textvariable [::itcl::scope _password]
```

```
frame $_toplevel.sep -height 4 -relief sunken -bd 2
button $_toplevel.ok -text OK \
  -command [::itcl::code $this requestLogin]
button $_toplevel.cancel -text Cancel \
  -command "::itcl::delete object $this"

grid $_toplevel.name $_toplevel.nametxt -pady 4
grid $_toplevel.pswd $_toplevel.pswdtxt
grid configure $_toplevel.pswd -sticky w
grid $_toplevel.sep -sticky ew -pady 12 -columnspan 2
grid $_toplevel.ok $_toplevel.cancel -pady 4
Trace::EXE end
}
```

This method simply creates and packs widgets in a new top-level window to present an intuitive screen to the user for entering the username and password. Notice the use of the **scope** command with the –textvariable configuration option. Recall from Chapter 3 that you must use **scope** so that the variable is updated properly from the global scope.

Sending the Authentication Request

When the user presses the OK button, the username and password as entered on the screen must be sent to the server for authentication. To do this, the *requestLogin* method is tied to the button via its –command configuration option. This method is implemented as follows:

```
::itcl::body LoginClient::requestLogin {} {
  Trace::EXE begin
  # Return if nothing is entered.
  if {$_username == "" || $_password == ""} {
    Trace::COMM "Username and password must be entered."
    Trace::EXE end
    return
  }
  # Send the request.
  $_clientSocket write "login $_username $_password"
  Trace::EXE end
}
```

6

If the user has not entered a name and/or password, then a corresponding message is printed, and the method returns. Otherwise, the ClientSocket object is instructed to send the data across the socket to the server. Once the server validates the data, it writes back to the socket, at which time the *process* method is called to process server input.

Testing the Model

Now that you understand how the classes are tied together, it's time to see if things work. Invoke two **wish** interpreters as you did in the previous example. Once again, one will handle the server side (interpreter S), and the other will handle the client side (interpreter C). If you have not done so already, download the code available online from Osborne's web site and extract and place the files LoginMgr.itcl, LoginClient.itcl, ServerSocket.itcl, ClientSocket.itcl, and Trace.itcl into a common directory. Then cd into that directory and type the following commands in interpreter S to create a LoginMgr object:

```
% package require Itcl
3.0
% auto_mkindex . *.itcl
% lappend auto_path .
% Trace::ACTIVATE all
% LoginMgr mgr
::LoginMgr::constructor
{
  ::ServerSocket::constructor
  {
  }
  ::ServerSocket::activate
  {
    ## COMMENT: Server is activated and ready to accept client messages.
  }
}
mgr
```

Now from the same directory in which you just created the tclIndex file, type the following commands in interpreter C to create the graphical login screen. You'll notice quite a few messages that get printed in each intepreter before

the object name is returned. As previously, server output (interpreter S) is
shown in boldface.

```
% package require Itcl
3.0
% lappend auto_path .
% Trace::ACTIVATE all
% LoginClient client
::LoginClient::constructor
{
  ::LoginClient::createClientSocket
  {
    ## COMMENT: Creating client socket...
    ::ClientSocket::constructor
    {
::ServerSocket::accept
{
  ## COMMENT: Accepted new client connection from 127.0.0.1, port 1028
  ## COMMENT: Asking client to register...
}
    }
    ## COMMENT: Succeeded. Registering processing method...
  }
  ::LoginClient::createMainScreen
  {
  }
}
::ClientSocket::handleServerInput
{
  ## COMMENT: Processing new data from the server...
  ## COMMENT: Registering with the server...
}
::ServerSocket::handleClientInput
{
  ## COMMENT: Servicing new client message detected on socket sock5...
  ## COMMENT: Client is requesting registration.
}
::ClientSocket::handleServerInput
{
  ## COMMENT: Processing new data from the server...
  ## COMMENT: Connection is established.  Activating...
}
client
% client draw
```

6

At this point, the screen is drawn, and you can enter text in the username and password fields. The login screen is shown in Figure 6-4 with various login attempts and the resulting actions. Try typing **lyle_stavast** as the username and **abc** as the password. The following messages are printed when you click the OK button (server side in boldface).

```
::LoginClient::requestLogin
{
  ::ClientSocket::write
  {
  }
}
::ServerSocket::handleClientInput
{
  ## COMMENT: Servicing new client message detected on socket sock5...
  ## COMMENT: Forwarding client request for processing...
  ::LoginMgr::authenticate
  {
    ::ServerSocket::write
    {
    }
  }
}
::ClientSocket::handleServerInput
{
  ## COMMENT: Processing new data from the server...
  ## COMMENT: Received message: "access denied - bad password"
  ## COMMENT:     - Forwarding to client function for processing...
  ::LoginClient::process
  {
    !! WARNING: Login failed!
  }
}
```

The login screen prompts the user for a username and password

Figure 6-4.

As expected, the login attempt fails because the specified password, "abc," does not match the valid password, "mr.admin," as defined in LoginMgr's *constructor*. Now enter the valid password and notice the messages that are printed.

```
::LoginClient::requestLogin
{
  ::ClientSocket::write
  {
  }
}
::ServerSocket::handleClientInput
{
  ## COMMENT: Servicing new client message detected on socket sock5...
  ## COMMENT: Forwarding client request for processing...
  ::LoginMgr::authenticate
  {
    ::ServerSocket::write
    {
    }
  }
}
::ClientSocket::handleServerInput
{
  ## COMMENT: Processing new data from the server...
  ## COMMENT: Received message: "access granted"
  ## COMMENT:   - Forwarding to client function for processing...
  ::LoginClient::process
  {
    ## COMMENT: Login is successful!
  }
}
```

6

Success! All you need to do now is implement the code to handle login attempts as your application requires. This code is stubbed out in the example to just show you the concepts involved. You can add code to allow only a certain number of invalid login attempts—for example, by storing each attempt in a static array data member—or you could display an error dialog box for invalid login attempts. You can do other things as well, like enforcing a certain password format such as requiring that at least one special character be embedded in the password, or you can enforce a minimum or maximum username or password length.

There are numerous ways to make this model more robust and useful. You can modify the LoginMgr and LoginClient classes as desired and add more classes and functionality to the design. The strength of this design is the reusability of the ClientSocket and ServerSocket classes, which perform all socket management for you. All you have to do is instantiate each of these classes and provide the appropriate external hooks as discussed for interfacing. Creation of the socket, management of the socket's lifetime, monitoring of the socket, and sending data across the socket are all managed by instances of these two classes. You have seen how simple it is to create a user authentication model. The same ClientSocket and ServerSocket classes are used in the next chapter for providing the communication backbone for a chat room application.

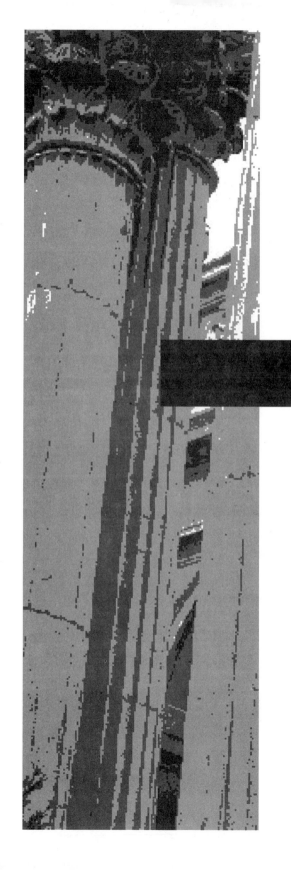

CHAPTER 7

Using
Composition

This chapter is the first of two chapters that show you how to take advantage of code reuse through object-oriented utilities. In this chapter, you'll learn how to significantly shorten your development time by using composition. Most of the chapter is devoted to the development of a large-scale example, a multiuser chat room controlled by a central server. By designing classes in the previous chapter generically, you'll see firsthand the strength of code reuse through composition, as two-thirds of the classes needed to create the chat room model have already been defined. By the end of this chapter, you'll not only know how to create a chat room, but you'll also have a greater appreciation for code reuse through composition as well as a clearer understanding of the importance of the design process, which lays the foundation for future code reuse.

Introduction

Most software programmers are intimately familiar with the term, "reinventing the wheel." It is quite common for programmers to rewrite code in a new project that had already been written in a previous or parallel project. There are several reasons for this. Sometimes code is rewritten simply because the programmer is unaware of its existence. Other times, code is rewritten because it becomes a maintenance nightmare due to a poor original design, or it becomes cost-prohibitive to take the time to learn how it works due to its complexity. In any case, the inability to reuse code is unfortunate, not to mention expensive.

As an object-oriented software designer, one of your design goals should be to strive for as much reusability of your classes as possible. Designs meant to handle specific tasks for a specific project may have limited reuse, but in most cases, you can plan ahead and make your design robust enough so that you can reuse some if not all of the code in future applications. Once you experience code reuse firsthand for the first time, your design philosophy will forever be altered to strive for the convenience of reusability.

[incr Tcl] provides two ways to reuse classes: *composition* and *inheritance*. Composition refers to a type of relationship between objects where one object contains another. (Inheritance is discussed in the next chapter.) It is often referred to as a "has-a" relationship—an object *has* other objects, or an object is *composed of* other objects. This is possible by using class data members to serve as containers for objects. By instantiating a class and saving the object in another class's data member, you have the ability to reuse existing code in a new design.

Object Lifetime

Object lifetime is an important consideration for memory management purposes when using composition. It is a common misconception that deleting the containing object also deletes any objects created within its namespace. This is untrue. By default, objects remain in the namespace in which you create them until you explicitly delete them.

Forgetting to do this results in memory leaks that could eventually crash your application. Type the following lines of code in an **itclsh** shell to illustrate.

Example 7-1
Forgetting to manually delete objects results in memory leaks

```
% ::itcl::class Floor {}
% ::itcl::class Building {
    constructor {} {
      set _floor [Floor #auto]
    }
    destructor {}
    private variable _floor ""
  }
% Building #auto
building0
% ::itcl::find objects -class Floor
::Building::floor0
% ::itcl::delete object building0
% ::itcl::find objects -class Floor
::Building::floor0   ← The Floor object still exists!
```

As you can see from the **find** command, deleting the Building object did not result in the destruction of its contained Floor object. This is a memory leak in the Building class. For each Building object destroyed, the amount of memory needed for allocating a Floor object is lost. If the Building has a hundred floors instead of one, and your application creates and destroys multiple Building objects, you can imagine the potential memory problems. The situation is worse when one of your customers reports that your application can't run for more than 24 hours without crashing, which can easily happen with memory leaks.

So how do you avoid this problem? Luckily, it's very simple. Just follow the same rule followed in C++: for every "new," make sure you have a "delete."

7

In [incr Tcl], for every class instantiation, make sure that the object is deleted before its containing object gets deleted. The best and easiest way to accomplish this is to delete the objects in the *destructor*. Complete Building's *destructor* body, and then reinstantiate as follows:

```
% ::itcl::body Building::destructor {} {
    if {$_floor !=""} {
        ::ital::delete object $_floor
    }
}
% Building #auto
building1
% ::itcl::find objects -class Floor
::Building::floor0 ::Building::floor1
% ::itcl::delete object building1
% ::itcl::find objects -class Floor
::Building::floor0
```

Notice that the original object, **floor0**, still exists, but the new object, **floor1**, has been deleted after the addition of the **delete** command in the *destructor*. As a result, the memory leak is plugged.

Now consider how the *destructor* determines whether or not to delete the Floor object. Since _floor is initialized to the empty string, the *destructor* only invokes the delete command if _floor is non-empty. You could also use the **catch** command and just ignore any deletion errors, but using the conditional as shown is a cleaner approach.

Creating Temporary Objects

Most of the time when you use composition, you declare class data members to store objects, and you delete the objects in the class *destructor* as previously discussed for proper memory management. This is because the default lifetime of an object is the lifetime of the interpreter shell, not the lifetime of the containing object. Sometimes, however, you don't want the object to hang around indefinitely. You may only want a temporary object that exists only within the method body in which it is created and then gets automatically deleted when the method terminates. To do this, you can use the **local** command. Type the following lines of code in a **tclsh** shell to illustrate.

Example 7-2
Creating
temporary
objects with the
local command

```
% package require Itcl
3.0
% ::itcl::class Dictionary {}
% ::itcl::class Student {
    public method proofread {text_} {
       set localObject [::itcl::local Dictionary #auto]
       # Remainder of method...
    }
}
% set junior [Student #auto]
student0
% $junior proofread "separate"
% ::itcl::find objects -class Dictionary
%
```

In this example, the Student object is instructed to verify a commonly misspelled word via its *proofread* method. The object then creates a temporary Dictionary object that it may use to verify the correct spelling. By using the **local** command, the Dictionary object is created local to the scope of *proofread*, just like a local variable. When an object is only needed in a single method like this, then it's not necessary to store the object in an instance variable, especially if the method is rarely invoked. Instead, you can use **local** to create a temporary object that automatically gets deleted when the method terminates. In this example, maybe the only time Student objects ever need access to a Dictionary object is in the *proofread* method. If *proofread* is only invoked a few times, then it makes sense to create a temporary Dictionary object for *proofread* to use. Then, after *proofread* finishes, the Dictionary object is no longer needed and is automatically deleted. It probably would not make sense, on the other hand, to use **local** if *proofread* were embedded in a loop and invoked multiple successive times. In that case, you should store a Dictionary object in a private class data member to avoid the overhead of re-creating the object each time the method is invoked.

You might wonder why you should use the **local** command in the first place when you can just as easily delete the object yourself when you're done with it. While this is acceptable, you might as well let [incr Tcl] manage object deletion for you if you're not going to store it in an instance variable. Since this built-in facility is available for use, you should take advantage of it when applicable.

7

An Alternative Implementation for Trace Using local

In Chapter 5, a class named Trace is defined as a debugging tool for use during development and testing. Trace makes extensive use of static methods to print debug messages at run time. Recall that Trace::EXE is used to print the order in which methods and procedures are invoked in the application. The method name and an open brace are printed when the method is invoked, and a close brace is printed when the method terminates. The design requires that EXE be invoked twice to do this, once at the beginning of the method and once just before the method returns. As a result, you must invoke EXE before each **return** statement. Failure to do this results in a missing close brace in the output. So, a method could potentially be strewn with calls to EXE, depending on the number of **return** statements. It would be a cleaner design to only require the user to have one line of code that accomplishes the same task. As you probably guessed, this can be done with the **local** command. Consider the following alternative class definition for Trace (The class is renamed Trace2 for differentiation):

```
::itcl::class Trace2 {
  # Class constructor/destructor
  constructor {} {print EXE}
  destructor {print EXE "" 1}

  # Class Methods
  public method print {type_ {string_ ""} {destructing_ 0}}

  # Static Methods
  public proc ACTIVATE {flags_} {SET_FLAGS $flags_ 1}
  public proc DEACTIVATE {flags_} {SET_FLAGS $flags_ 0}
  private proc SET_FLAGS {flags_ val_}

  # Static Data Members
  private common _ON
    array set _ON "x 0 e 0 w 0 c 0"
  private common _INDENT ""
  private common _PAD "   "
  private common _CHARS
    array set _CHARS "e * w ! c #"
}
```

Each of the class data members remains the same, and the methods ACTIVATE, DEACTIVATE, and SET_FLAGS also remain the same. Refer to Chapter 5 for information on these methods. The mechanism for printing debug messages, however, is completely different. Instead of declaring individual static methods for printing various types of messages, all debug methods are now combined into a single public method, *print*, which declares a parameter used to determine the kind of message to print. The new *print* method is implemented as follows:

```
::itcl::body Trace2::print {type_ {string_ ""} {destructing_ 0}} {
  switch -- $type_ {
    EXE {
      if {$_ON(x)} {
        if {$destructing_} {
          set _INDENT [string range $_INDENT 2 end]
          puts "$_INDENT\}"
        } else {
          # Grab the invoking method name 2 levels down the stack.
          set methodName \
            [lindex [info level [expr [info level] - 2]] 0]
          set fullyQualifiedName \
            [uplevel 2 [list namespace which $methodName]]
          puts "${_INDENT}$fullyQualifiedName"
          puts "$_INDENT\{"
          set _INDENT "$_INDENT$_PAD"
        }
      }
      return
    }
    ERR     {if ($_ON{e)} {set char e} else {return}}
    WARN    {if ($_ON{w)} {set char w} else {return}}
    COMM    {if ($_ON{c)} {set char c} else {return}}
    default {set char c}
  }
  puts "${_INDENT}$_CHARS($char)$_CHARS($char) $type_: $string_"
}
```

With this new printing scheme, the type of printed message depends on the string passed into the type_ parameter. Notice that these values are the same as the original static method names. An optional parameter, destructing_, is used to determine when to print the final closing brace during object destruction, which automatically occurs when the calling method returns because of the **local** command. The fact that there is an object to destruct in the first place is the main difference between the two implementations. In the original design, all output was printed by invoking static methods. As a result, there was no need for objects since data members and methods were all at the class level. In this new design, a *constructor* and *destructor* are declared to implement the code execution tracing part of the debug tool. When a Trace2 object is created, the *constructor* invokes the public method, *print*, to print the calling method's name and an open brace, which is the equivalent of the command fragment,

```
Trace::EXE begin
```

Then as a result of the **local** command, the *destructor* is automatically invoked when the calling method finishes, which in turn also invokes *print* to print a close brace to match the open brace printed during construction. This eliminates the need for the command,

```
Trace::EXE end
```

which was needed at the end of the method as well as prior to each **return** statement in the original design. The new tracing scheme is accomplished with the following single line of code:

```
::itcl::local Trace2 #auto
```

Now take a look at how the name of the method that creates each Trace2 object is determined. This is done with the following two lines of code:

```
set methodName [lindex [info level [expr [info level] - 2]] 0]
set fullyQualifiedName [uplevel 2 [list namespace which $methodName]]
```

The difference you need to note here is the explicit 2 used in both lines. In Trace::EXE, a 1 is used, so why is Trace2 different? The reason is that *print* is now directly invoked by Trace2's *constructor* and *destructor*, so the calling method, or the method one level down the call stack, is always the *constructor* or *destructor* when the type_ parameter equals the string, EXE. As a result, the method that creates/destroys the Trace2 object needs to be determined instead, and this is done by skipping the first level on the call stack and querying information from the next one.

Suppose you want to print comments or warning or error messages in addition to tracing. To do this, simply save the result of the instantiation and use the object as follows:

```
::itcl::body MyClass::myMethod {
  set t [::itcl::local Trace2 #auto]
  $t print COMM "This is a comment."
  $t print WARN "This is a warning message."
  $t print ERR "This is an error message."
}
```

Now let's test the new tracing code by defining a class similar to TraceTest from Chapter 5. You can type the following code into a **tclsh** shell (the code is also available online), or you can just follow along.

```
% package require Itcl
3.0
% ::itcl::class TraceTest2 {
    constructor {} {
      set t [::itcl::local Trace2 #auto]
      method1
      method2
      $t print COMM "Wow, this is easy!"
      method3
    }
    public method method1 {} {
      set t [::itcl::local Trace2 #auto]
      $t print ERR "This is an example of an error message."
      method3
    }
    private method method2 {} {
      ::itcl::local Trace2 #auto
    }
    private method method3 {} {
      set t [::itcl::local Trace2 #auto]
      $t print WARN "This is a warning message."
    }
  }
% source Trace2.itcl
% Trace2::ACTIVATE all
% TraceTest2 #auto
::TraceTest2::constructor
{
  ::TraceTest2::method1
  {
```

7

```
      ** ERR: This is an example of an error message.
      ::TraceTest2::method3
      {
        !! WARN: This is a warning message.
      }
    }
    ::TraceTest2::method2
    {
    }
    ## COMM: Wow, this is easy!
    ::TraceTest2::method3
    {
      !! WARN: This is a warning message.
    }
  }
traceTest20
```

Just a few lines of code in TraceTest2 generate this debug output. Now instead of having to remember to call Trace::EXE once at the beginning of each method and once at the end of each method as well as prior to each **return** statement, you can simply instantiate Trace2 at the beginning of the method and let [incr Tcl] handle the rest for you. This is a very convenient and powerful utility that you should find quite useful.

Since this new design calls for object creation instead of static method invocation, you might have a concern about performance. Indeed, creating a new instance of Trace2 for each debug tracing output is much slower than invoking Trace::EXE. But again, as discussed in Chapter 5, performance of the application isn't the issue when tracking down bugs. It's not the purpose of Trace or Trace2 to boost performance. The issue, rather, is to minimize the amount of time it takes to locate and fix bugs. By designing an intuitive, easy-to-integrate debugging tool such as Trace or Trace2, you can significantly cut down the amount of time you spend debugging your code.

Using Composition to Design a Chat Room

Suppose you are contracted to design and implement a multiuser chat room, where you can log in to the chat room and participate in conference-type discussions with other chat room users. Each chat room instance should be monitored by a common central server whose responsibility it will be to broadcast messages to all chat room users or to establish private chat sessions between pairs of chat room users. As you brainstorm the design, you realize that you need some sort of communication backbone for sending messages across a network to multiple clients. If this sounds familiar, then you have already read Chapter 6, which provides a generic client/server framework with the ServerSocket and ClientSocket classes for message handling over sockets. You also realize that you need some sort of user authentication mechanism for providing login access to the chat room. This has also already been done in Chapter 6 with the LoginMgr and LoginClient classes. By now, you should begin to see the strength of using composition for code reuse! To gain a better appreciation for this, take a look at the following object model diagram.

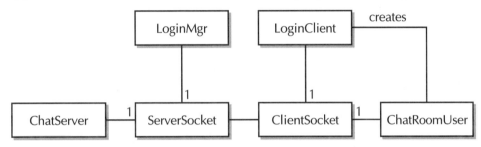

This diagram provides a high-level view of the classes needed to create the chat room application. Each box represents a class, and the lines between them represent relationships, some of which are composition. The 1 above the ServerSocket class, for example, means that LoginMgr *has* one ServerSocket. By reusing code through composition, notice that two-thirds of the implementation is already done! This greatly reduces your development time because the only classes you need to write are ChatRoomUser and ChatServer. The ChatRoomUser class will be responsible for creating the graphical chat session display and for sending chat postings to the server, and the ChatServer class will be responsible for broadcasting messages to each of the ChatRoomUser objects as well as monitoring the chat sessions. The initial user authentication mechanism is already done, and the communication mechanism between the LoginMgr and LoginClient and the ChatServer and ChatRoomUser is already done as well. By originally designing these classes generically, you are able to reuse them in their entirety in the chat room example!

NOTE: Typically, you should not need to modify classes that you reuse in composition. In the case of the LoginMgr, however, you need to add appropriate usernames and passwords for logins. A better design is to create a new class that inherits from LoginMgr and that defines chat room–specific login information. You'll see how to do this in the next chapter.

Speaking the Same Language

Before discussing the chat room server, you first need to understand the protocol that ChatServer and ChatRoomUser objects use to communicate. Understanding this protocol will help you to understand the code when the classes are implemented later in the chapter. There are several protocol messages that ChatRoomUser and ChatServer objects must understand. These strings are outlined in Table 7-1. The string in the first column is sent across a socket to the class instance in the second column, from the class instance in the third column. The fourth column provides a brief explanation of the events surrounding the communication of the message.

Each of these protocol messages is discussed further in upcoming sections. For now, you can use this table as a reference.

Creating the Back End: The Chat Room Server

The ChatServer's main responsibility is to broadcast chat messages from individual ChatRoomUser objects to all other ChatRoomUser objects. To do this, the ChatServer can use the ServerSocket/ClientSocket framework developed in Chapter 6. In order to broadcast messages to all ChatRoomUser objects, the ChatServer must maintain a list of active ChatRoomUsers. When a ChatRoomUser object is created, it registers with the server, and when it is deleted, its entry is removed from the server's list. The ChatServer can also act as a sort of parental monitor. When it receives a chat message, it can filter the message before broadcasting it. Another responsibility of the ChatServer is to service specific ChatRoomUser requests, such as whispering, which is discussed later in this section. The class is defined as follows:

```
::itcl::class ChatServer {
  # Class constructor/destructor
  constructor {{port_ 21112}} {}
  destructor {catch {::itcl::delete object $_socket}}

  # Class Methods
  private method filter {msg_}
  private method processClientInput {data_ sd_}
  private method serverMessage {msg_ sd_}

  # Class Data Members
  private variable _serverSocket    ; # ServerSocket object
  private variable _currentChatters; # array of active chat rooms
  private variable _whispering      ; # array of whispering chatters
  private variable _maxMsgLen 70    ; # maximum message length
  private variable _reasonDenied "";# reason for denial to post
}
```

Protocol Message	Receiving Object	Sending Object	Definition
"new chatter"	ChatServer	ChatRoomUser	A new ChatRoomUser object has been created and is registering itself with the server.
"whisper on"	ChatServer	ChatRoomUser	A ChatRoomUser object requests a private chat session with another ChatRoomUser object.
"whisper off"	ChatServer	ChatRoomUser	A ChatRoomUser object terminates a private chat session.
"disconnectingSocket"	ChatServer	ServerSocket	The ServerSocket object notifies the ChatServer object if the physical socket is lost.
"current chatters"	ChatRoomUser	ChatServer	The ChatServer object broadcasts the list of current chatters to all ChatRoomUser objects.

7

Defining the Protocol Between ChatServer and ChatRoomUser Objects

Table 7-1.

Protocol Message	Receiving Object	Sending Object	Definition
"new chatter"	ChatRoomUser	ChatServer	The ChatServer object broadcasts a new chatter's name to all ChatRoomUser objects.
"server: remove"	ChatRoomUser	ChatServer	A ChatRoomUser object has been deleted, and the ChatServer object instructs all ChatRoomUser objects to remove the corresponding name.

Defining the
Protocol
Between
ChatServer and
ChatRoomUser
Objects
(continued)

Table 7-1.

Creating the Object

Before a new user can log in to the chat room, a ChatServer object must be "running" somewhere, listening for chat room login requests on a socket. To accomplish this, all the ChatServer must do when it is instantiated is create an instance of ServerSocket and activate it. With this in mind, the *constructor* is implemented as follows:

```
::itcl::body ChatServer::constructor {{port_ 21112}} {
  # Create the ServerSocket object. This is an example of composition.
  if {[catch {ServerSocket #auto $port_} _serverSocket]} {
    error $_serverSocket
  }
  $_serverSocket activate [::itcl::code $this processClientInput]
}
```

An optional port number may be specified during construction, but if the default port is overridden, then the same port number must be specified for ChatRoomUser objects because they also use port 21112 as the default for their ClientSocket objects.

Servicing Requests

Once a ChatServer object is created, it remains idle until a new request comes across the socket link to the SocketServer, which then forwards the request to the ChatServer object for handling. From Table 7-1, you can see that the ChatServer understands four different protocol messages. First, when a new ChatRoomUser object is created, it instructs its ClientSocket object to send the protocol message, "new chatter," to the server. When the ChatServer object receives this message, it sends a list of all current chatters back to the requesting ChatRoomUser object and then broadcasts the new object's name to all other ChatRoomUser objects. This way, ChatRoomUsers are able to maintain an updated list of current chatters.

Figure 7-1 provides a visual representation of this process. A new ChatRoomUser object with username "bill" registers with the server by sending {"new chatter" bill} through its ClientSocket object to the server. The chat server then sends back {"current chatters" "susie tobie"} to bill so that it can update its screen with the names of the other chatters in the chat room. The server then broadcasts a message, {"new chatter" bill}, to all ChatRoomUser objects for similar display updates. Each chat room user then knows that usernames bill, susie, and tobie are all in the chat room.

The next two messages, "whisper on" and "whisper off," refer to establishing and terminating a private chat session between two ChatRoomUser objects. This feature is discussed when the ChatRoomUser class is implemented in the next section. The fourth message, "disconnectingSocket," is generated by the ChatServer's ServerSocket object in cases where the physical socket has been destroyed. This could happen, for instance, if you exit the interpreter in which a ChatRoomUser object exists before deleting the object. The *processClientInput* method is implemented to handle each of these protocol messages as follows:

```
::itcl::body ChatServer::processClientInput {data_ sd_} {
  set protocolString [lindex $data_ 0]
  switch -- $protocolString {
    "new chatter" {
      # A new chat room session has started and is requesting a list
      # of current chatters. Return the list and tell all the other
      # ChatRoomUser objects that a new chatter has entered the room.
```

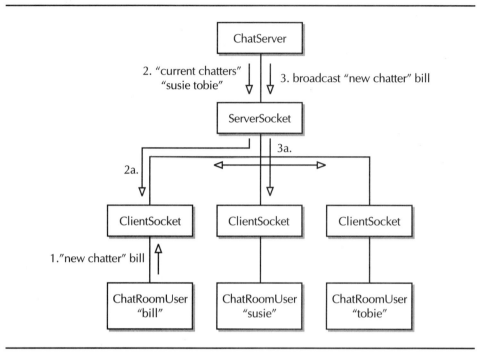

Order of events
when a new
ChatRoomUser
object is
created

Figure 7-1.

```
if {[array exists _currentChatters]} {
  foreach sd [array names _currentChatters] {
    lappend names $_currentChatters($sd)
  }
  $_serverSocket write $sd_ [list "current chatters" $names]
}
set _currentChatters($sd_) [lindex $data_ end]
$_serverSocket broadcast \
  [list "new chatter" $_currentChatters($sd_)]
}

"whisper on" {
  # A user is requesting a private chat session with another
  # user. Save the requestor's socket descriptor, and notify
  # the other user of the chat request.
  set _whispering($sd_) [lindex $data_ end]
  foreach sd [array names _currentChatters] {
    if {$_currentChatters($sd) == [lindex $data_ end]} {
```

```
            serverMessage "$_currentChatters($sd_) WANTS TO \
              WHISPER SOMETHING TO YOU" $sd
        }
      }
    }


    "whisper off" {
      # A user has terminated the private chat session. Unset the
      # corresponding index in the array and notify the other user
      # of the chat termination.
      unset _whispering($sd_)
      foreach sd [array names _currentChatters] {
        if {$_currentChatters($sd) == [lindex $data_ end]} {
          serverMessage "$_currentChatters($sd_) HAS \
            STOPPED WHISPERING" $sd
        }
      }
    }


    "disconnectingSocket" {
      # The physical socket connection has been corrupted or
      # closed. Broadcast this information to all other chatters.
      $_serverSocket broadcast \
        [list "server: remove" $_currentChatters($sd_)]
      catch {unset _currentChatters($sd_)}
      if {[array names _currentChatters] == ""} {
        unset _currentChatters
      }
    }


    default {
      # A user is requesting to post a new message to the chat room.
      # Filter it. If filtering fails, then only post the message if
      # the user is in a private chat session. If filtering succeeds,
      # post accordingly.
      if {![filter $data_]} {
        if {![info exists _whispering($sd_)]} {
          serverMessage \
            "The server refuses to post this message!" $sd_
          return
        }
      }
      if {[info exists _whispering($sd_)]} {
        foreach sd [array names _currentChatters] {
          if {$_currentChatters($sd) == $_whispering($sd_)} {
            $_serverSocket write $sd_ \
```

7

```
        "<$_currentChatters($sd_) (whisper)> $data_"
          $_serverSocket write $sd \
            "<$_currentChatters($sd_) (whisper)> $data_"
        }
      }
    } else {
      $_serverSocket broadcast "<$_currentChatters($sd_)> $data_"
    }
  }
 }
}
```

Filtering Chat Messages

The chat server has the feature of being able to filter messages that are sent by chat room users. Each message received by the ChatServer object is validated to make sure it doesn't exceed a predefined maximum character length. You can add a number of additional filtering utilities in the *filter* method to keep certain words or phrases from being posted to the chat room or even to disconnect a chat session if a user violates filtering rules multiple times. You can add this type of filtering following the message length comparison if desired. The *filter* method is implemented as follows:

```
::itcl::body ChatServer::filter {msg_} {
  set len [string length $msg_]
  if {$len > $_maxMsgLen} {
    set _reasonDenied "Message too long ($len chars). Maximum\
      message length is $_maxMsgLen characters."
    return 0
  }

  # Add optional additional filtering here.
  return 1
}
```

Messages from the Server

Sometimes it is necessary for the server to send a specific message to a specific chat room user. The message should be formatted in such a way that it can't be mistaken for another chat room user's posting. It should be clear that the message is from the server. Examples include notifying a user that another user wants to open a private chat session or notifying a user that the requested chat message cannot be posted. In the case of the latter, the reason for the failure to post is printed, and the private data member, _reasonDenied, is reset to the empty string. The *serverMessage* method is implemented as follows to handle specific server messages:

```
::itcl::body ChatServer::serverMessage {msg_ sd_} {
   $_serverSocket write $sd_ "---------------"
   $_serverSocket write $sd_ "  ** MESSAGE FROM CHAT SERVER"
   $_serverSocket write $sd_ "  ** $msg_"
   if {$_reasonDenied != ""} {
      $_serverSocket write $sd_ "      --> $_reasonDenied"
      set _reasonDenied ""
   }
   $_serverSocket write $sd_ "---------------"
}
```

With the implementation of *serverMessage*, the back end of the chat room application is now complete. Let's continue now with the client side of the application.

Controlling Access

7

When the chat room application is initially started, the user needs to provide a username and password in order to log in to the chat room. This access control is provided by LoginMgr and LoginClient. A LoginClient object displays the window requesting the username and password, and a LoginMgr object validates the login request. ServerSocket and ClientSocket objects handle the communication between LoginMgr and LoginClient. This login process is summarized in the following scenario. (Refer to Chapter 6 for a more detailed discussion.)

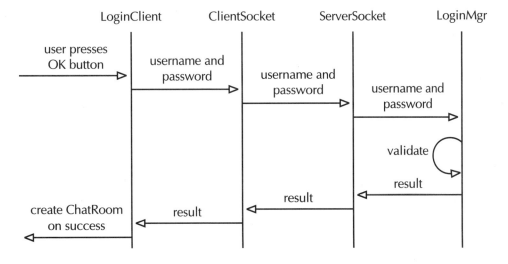

When the user presses the OK button on the login screen, the LoginClient object tells its ClientSocket object to send the specified username and password across the physical socket link to the ServerSocket object, which then forwards the data to the LoginMgr object for authentication. A message indicating success or failure is then sent back across the connection to the LoginClient object. If the authentication is successful, then the LoginClient object should create an instance of ChatRoomUser.

Recall from the previous chapter that LoginClient's *process* method contains a comment informing you where to place continuation code. The comment states, "Place code here to continue with the application." This is similar to ChatServer's *filter* method, where you are instructed to add code as necessary. It's at this point in the *process* method that you should add code to create the ChatRoomUser object. This method should be modified as follows (note that the Trace messages from the original implementation are removed):

```
::itcl::body LoginClient::process {data_} {
  if {$data_ == "access granted"} {
    if {[catch {ChatRoomUser #auto $_username} chatRoomUser]} {
      # Display error message as desired.
    } else {
      $chatRoomUser activate
      ::itcl::delete object $this
    }
  }
}
```

NOTE: Similar to LoginMgr, a better design is to create a class that inherits from LoginClient to handle chat room–specific events. You'll see how to do this in the next chapter.

The ChatRoomUser object is created, and its *activate* method is invoked if construction is successful. You can handle *constructor* errors with a **puts** statement, an error dialog window, a Trace message, or some other notification mechanism. Once the ChatRoomUser object is activated, the LoginClient object is deleted since its job is complete at that point. Control is then passed to ChatRoomUser, which is discussed in the following section.

Creating the Front End: The Chat Room Client

The purpose of the ChatRoomUser class is to create the user interface for accepting and displaying chat messages and for forwarding messages and requests to ChatServer. Since there is a graphical user interface (GUI) involved, the class definition is much longer than the ChatServer. It is defined as follows:

```
::itcl::class ChatRoomUser {
  # Class constructor/destructor
  constructor {name_ {host_ localhost} {port_ 21112}} {}
  destructor {
    catch {
      ::itcl::delete object $_socket
      destroy $_top
    }
  }

  # Class Methods
  public method activate {}
  private method processServerInput {data_}
  private method insertNewMsg {data_}
  private method post {}
  private method pause {}
  private method whisper {}
  private method buildScreen {}

  # Class Data Members
  private variable _socket       ; # ClientSocket object
  private variable _top          ; # toplevel window
  private variable _widgets      ; # array of widgets
  private variable _name         ; # user name from LoginClient
  private variable _paused 0     ; # boolean to pause chat session
  private variable _whispering  0 ; # boolean to whisper to someone
  private variable _whisperPartner; # user name of whisper partner
  private variable _activated   0 ; # boolean for session activation
}
```

7

Creating the Object

When a ChatRoomUser object is created, its first task should be to establish a link with the server by creating an instance of ClientSocket. Just as ChatServer

uses composition to store an instance of ServerSocket, so does ChatRoomUser
by storing an instance of ClientSocket. Once the connection is established,
a method is registered with the ClientSocket object to be invoked when the
physical socket becomes readable (as discussed in Chapter 6), and then the
main screen is built. ChatRoomUser's *constructor* looks like this:

```
::itcl::body ChatRoomUser::constructor {name_ {host_ localhost} \
{port_ 21112}} {
  # If ClientSocket can't be instantiated, return immediately.
  if {[catch {ClientSocket #auto $host_ $port_} _socket]} {
    return -code error "Unable to open socket connection: $_socket"
  }
  set _name $name_
  $_socket register [::itcl::code $this processServerInput]
  if {[catch {buildScreen} err]} {
    return -code error $err
  }
  focus $_widgets(entry)

  # Wait until handshaking is complete before returning.
  tkwait variable CONNECTION_ESTABLISHED
}
```

The *constructor* requires one argument and declares two optional parameters.
You must specify a username when instantiating ChatRoomUser (retrieved
from the login screen), and you have the option of specifying the hostname
where the server is running as well as the port number. Note that defaults
match those of the server, so if you override them, you must also override
ChatServer's defaults.

Now recall from Chapter 6 that the global variable, *CONNECTION_*
ESTABLISHED, gets set at the end of ClientSocket's *constructor*. This is done
to ensure that the handshaking process between the ClientSocket and
ServerSocket objects is complete. If you were to try and write to the physical
socket during the handshaking process, you will get unexpected results or
errors. You need to wait until communication is finished before sending any
messages to the server. This is the purpose of the **tkwait variable** command
in ChatRoomUser's *constructor*. It is only needed because ChatRoomUser's
activate method, discussed later in this chapter, writes to the socket to register
with the ChatServer object. So, if the *activate* method is invoked immediately
following ChatRoomUser instantiation, the registration request sent to the
server from *activate* may arrive before the handshaking process initiated by

the *constructor* is completed. By using **tkwait variable**, the interpreter halts execution of the code until *CONNECTION_ESTABLISHED* is modified. This ensures that handshaking is completed before you can activate a ChatRoomUser object.

Building the GUI

From the user's perspective, the most important part of this application may very well be the GUI. If the GUI is not attractive and easy to use and interact with, then the user most likely will find another chat room to use. The GUI must be well designed, intuitive, and user-friendly. Other than the login window, this is the only screen the user sees. It's built entirely in Tk and takes about 65 lines of code. In Chapter 15, you'll learn about [incr Widgets] that allow you to create this same screen in less than half this amount of code.

Now take a look at the final product before going through the code. Figure 7-2 shows a snapshot of the chat room screen as it appears when it is first drawn. In this snapshot, four other users are already logged in to the chat room when the new chat session is initiated. On the left side of the screen, a listbox titled, "Current Chatters," lists all users who are currently logged in to the chat room. A total count is displayed directly beneath this listbox. The large white area to its right is the message output area. Messages from all chatters are displayed here. The server prepends each message with the username enclosed in angle brackets so that each user can see who posts each message. Directly beneath both listboxes is a dark gray entry field where you insert new chat messages to be posted to the chat room. When you press ENTER or click the Post button, the string specified in this entry field is sent to the server as discussed previously for posting. Several buttons on the bottom of the screen provide a variety of features that are discussed in upcoming sections. The code to build this screen is as follows.

```
::itcl::body ChatRoomUser::buildScreen {} {
  # Create the toplevel window. If this window name already
  # exists, return an error.
  set _top .[namespace tail $this]
  if {[winfo exists $_top]} {
    error "Failed to create toplevel window.\
      Window name \"$_top\" exists."
  }
  toplevel $_top
  wm title $_top "Welcome to the Chat Room!"
  wm withdraw $_top
  wm minsize $_top 500 150
```

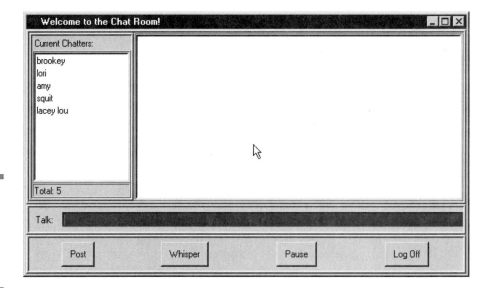

The graphical chat room window as it initially appears

Figure 7-2.

```
# ----------------------------------------
# Create the buttons (bb = "button box") and pack them first.
# ----------------------------------------
set bb [frame $_top.bottom -relief ridge -bd 4]
set b1 [button $bb.b1 -text Post -command [::itcl::code $this post]]
set _widgets(whisper) [button $bb.b2 -text Whisper \
  -command [::itcl::code $this whisper]]
set _widgets(pause) [button $bb.b3 -text Pause \
  -command [::itcl::code $this pause]]
set b4 [button $bb.b4 -text "Log Off" \
  -command "::itcl::delete object $this"]
pack $b1 $_widgets(whisper) $_widgets(pause) $b4 \
  -ipadx 4 -ipady 2 -side left -expand 1
pack $bb -ipady 5 -fill both -side bottom


# ----------------------------------------
# Create the entry field for talking (tf = "talk frame").
# ----------------------------------------
set mid    [frame $_top.middle -relief ridge -bd 4]
set tf     [frame $mid.f]
set tfLabel [label $tf.talk -text "Talk: "]
set _widgets(entry) [entry $tf.e -bg grey40 -fg green \
  -insertbackground green]
```

```
bind $_widgets(entry) <Return> [::itcl::code $this post]
pack $tfLabel          -side left -anchor w -padx 6
pack $_widgets(entry) -side left -fill x -expand 1 -pady 6
pack $tf $mid          -fill both -side bottom


# ---------------------------------------
# Create the current chatters listbox area
# (cc = "current chatters").
# ---------------------------------------
set topFrame           [frame $_top.top -relief ridge -bd 4]
set ccFrame            [frame $topFrame.left -relief ridge -bd 4]
set ccLabel            [label $ccFrame.l -text "Current Chatters:"]
set ccLboxFrame        [frame $ccFrame.f -relief ridge -bd 2]
set _widgets(ccLbox) [listbox $ccLboxFrame.lbox -bg ghostwhite \
   -width 20 -selectmode single -exportselection 0]
set _widgets(total)  [label $ccFrame.total -relief ridge \
   -bd 2 -anchor w]
pack $ccLabel                         -anchor w
grid $_widgets(ccLbox)                -sticky nsew
pack $ccLboxFrame                     -fill both -expand 1
pack $_widgets(total)                 -anchor w -fill x
pack $ccFrame                         -fill both -expand 1 -side left
grid columnconfigure $ccLboxFrame 0 -weight 1
grid rowconfigure $ccLboxFrame 0    -weight 1
grid columnconfigure $_widgets(ccLbox) 0 -weight 1
grid rowconfigure $_widgets(ccLbox)    0 -weight 1


# ---------------------------------------
# Create the listbox area to display the chat session
# (cs = "chat session").
# ---------------------------------------
set csLboxFrame        [frame $topFrame.right -relief ridge -bd 2]
set _widgets(csLbox) [listbox $csLboxFrame.lbox -bg ghostwhite \
   -width 70]
grid $_widgets(csLbox)                -sticky nsew
pack $csLboxFrame                     -side left -fill both -expand 1
pack $topFrame                        -fill both -expand 1
grid columnconfigure $csLboxFrame 0 -weight 1
grid rowconfigure $csLboxFrame 0    -weight 1
}
```

7

If you're already familiar with Tk, then this method should be straightforward. The screen is built with a few frames, a couple of listboxes, and some other rudimentary widgets. You don't need to understand how this screen is built, but the code is provided for your reference.

Activating the Chat Room

Once construction succeeds, the ChatRoomUser object must be activated. You could activate the object from within the *constructor*, but it's common to separate construction and activation into two separate tasks. The *activate* method looks like this:

```
::itcl::body ChatRoomUser::activate {} {
  set _activated 1
  $_socket write [list "new chatter" $_name]
  $_widgets(ccLbox) insert 0 $_name
  $_widgets(total) configure -text "Total: 1"
  wm deiconify $_top
}
```

An internal flag is marked so that the object knows it's activated. This flag is used later when processing server input. Then a protocol message, "new chatter," is sent to the server. As you learned in the ChatServer implementation, the server receives this message and updates the ChatRoomUser object with the names of other users logged in to the chat room and then broadcasts the new object's name to all other ChatRoomUser objects. The listbox containing the current chatters is then initialized along with the total chatter count. Finally, the screen is displayed for the first time. Before the screen appears, the ChatRoomUser object will have already received the current chatters list from the server and updated its listbox and total chatters count, so the screen will appear as if each of the names was already in the list.

Posting Messages

After the main screen is drawn, you relinquish control of the application as the developer and pass it to the chat room user. By this point, you should have covered all possible user interface events such as key presses and button clicks. If you didn't, you're sure to hear about it from your customers soon.

The first thing you might do as a new chat room user is introduce yourself. To do this, enter text into the Talk entry field and press ENTER or click the Post button. Each event invokes ChatRoomUser's *post* method, the purpose of which is simply to notify the server of a new message request. If the text string is empty, the request is ignored. If the text string passes ChatServer's *filter* method, then it is posted to the chat room. The *post* method is implemented as follows:

```
::itcl::body ChatRoomUser::post {} {
  set data [$_widgets(entry) get]
  if {$data == ""} {
    return
  }
  $_socket write $data
  $_widgets(entry) delete 0 end
}
```

Processing Input from the Server

After you submit a message to the server via the *post* method, the message is broadcast to all active ChatRoomUser objects. To do this, the server sends the message to each object for displaying. When a ChatRoomUser object receives any input from the server, it first checks to see if it matches a known protocol message for which it must perform some task. There are three different protocol messages understood by ChatRoomUser objects, as previously defined in Table 7-1. If the server sends "current chatters," then the ChatRoomUser object knows to insert each name from the specified list into the corresponding listbox. If the server sends "new chatter," then this means a new user has logged in to the chat room, and each current ChatRoomUser object should update its listbox with the new user's name. Conversely, if the server sends "server: remove," then a chat room user has logged off or has been disconnected, and each current ChatRoomUser object should update its listbox to remove the old user's name. If the message does not match any of these strings, then it is posted to the message window. The *processServerInput* method is implemented to handle each of these cases as follows:

```
::itcl::body ChatRoomUser::processServerInput {data_} {
  if {!$_activated} {
    return
  }
  set protocolString [lindex $data_ 0]
  switch -- $protocolString {
    "current chatters" {
      # This ChatRoomUser object has just been activated and has
      # requested to register with the server. The server has in
      # response sent a list of all current chat room users.
```

```
    foreach name [lindex $data_ end] {
      $_widgets(ccLbox) insert end $name
    }
    $_widgets(total) configure \
      -text "Total: [expr [llength [lindex $data_ end]]+ 1]"
  }

  "new chatter" {
    # A new user has logged into the chat room. Since this data
    # is broadcast, only insert the name if it doesn't match _name.
    if {[lindex $data_ end] !- $_name} {
      $_widgets(ccLbox) insert end [lindex $data_ end]
      set currTotal [lindex [$_widgets(total) cget -text] end]
      $_widgets(total) configure \
        -text "Total: [expr $currTotal + 1]"
    }
  }

  "server: remove" {
    # A user has logged off of the chat room. Remove the name from
    # the "Current Chatters" listbox.
    set size [$_widgets(ccLbox) size]
    for {set index 0} {$index < $size} {incr index} {
      if {[$_widgets(ccLbox) get $index] == [lindex $data_ end]} {
        $_widgets(ccLbox) delete $index
        set currTotal [lindex [$_widgets(total) cget -text] end]
        $_widgets(total) configure \
          -text "Total: [expr $currTotal - 1]"
      }
    }
  }

  default {
    # This is either a new posting or a message from the server
    # directed to this instance. Put it in the message window
    # if not currently paused.
    if {!$_paused} {
      insertNewMsg $data_
    }
  }
  }
}
```

Displaying Messages

As shown in the previous section, if the server sends anything other than a protocol message to a ChatRoomUser object, then the message gets posted to the message listbox. This is handled by the *insertNewMsg* method, whose sole responsibility is to accept a text string and insert it into the chat message listbox. This simple method looks like this:

```
::itcl::body ChatRoomUser::insertNewMsg {data_} {
  $_widgets(csLbox) insert end $data_
  $_widgets(csLbox) see end
}
```

The message is added to the bottom of the listbox, and the listbox is then told to adjust all entries so that the bottommost entry is viewable. This is the simplest approach to use, but may not be the best. Scroll bars could be added, but would add to the complexity of the code, so for simplicity's sake, the Tk listbox widget's **see** command is used instead. In the [incr Tk] section of this book, you'll learn about an [incr Widget] called the scrolledlistbox. This is the widget that should be used in ChatRoomUser. You can tell this widget to add scroll bars only when necessary via special configuration options. To do the same thing with Tk would take too many lines of code and make the code too complicated to present here. The window can be resized if the user wants to see more messages than what appears in the default window size.

7

Pausing Output

The user may want to temporarily pause the output from being displayed in the message window. If there are several users logged in to the chat room, and several messages are being continuously posted, a user may want to pause the output to catch up on reading previous posts. This is the responsibility of the *pause* method, which is invoked by pressing the Pause button. When this button is pressed, a message is posted to the user's message window saying that the chat session is paused. The button's text is also changed to read Resume. When pressed again, the text is changed back to Pause, and another message is printed to the message window that the chat session has been resumed. The *pause* method is implemented as follows:

```
::itcl::body ChatRoomUser::pause {} {
  set _paused [expr $_paused == 0]
  if {$_paused} {
    insertNewMsg "  -- CHAT SESSION PAUSED --"
    $_widgets(pause) configure -text Resume
  } else {
    insertNewMsg "  -- CHAT SESSION RESUMED --"
    $_widgets(pause) configure -text Pause
  }
}
```

Whispering

Whispering is a special feature added to the chat room that allows two users to establish a private chat session with one another. This is like a dedicated connection between two ChatRoomUser objects. In order to initiate this session, a user can highlight the desired name in the current chatters listbox and press the Whisper button. The button's text then changes to Broadcast, and a protocol message, "whisper on," is sent to the server along with the highlighted name. The server then notifies the ChatRoomUser object corresponding to the designated username about the private chat request. Once this user also presses the Whisper button, the dedicated connection is set up, and a private chat session is established. Messages posted by either user are then only seen by each other. To stop whispering, the user presses the Broadcast button. This event sends another protocol message, "whisper off," to the server, which notifies the ChatRoomUser object on the other end of the connection that the private chat session is terminated. Messages posted by this user are then broadcast to all chat room users as usual. Note that both users must press Broadcast in order to terminate the session fully. The whisper method is implemented as follows:

```
::itcl::body ChatRoomUser::whisper {} {
  # If currently whispering, return to broadcast mode.
  if {$_whispering} {
    set _whispering 0
    $_socket write [list "whisper off" $_whisperPartner]
    insertNewMsg "  -- WHISPER MODE TERMINATED --"
    $_widgets(whisper) configure -text Whisper
    return
  }

  # Ignore if no user name is highlighted.
  set index [$_widgets(ccLbox) curselection]
  if {$index == ""} {
    insertNewMsg "  -- PLEASE SELECT A CHATTER FIRST --"
    return
  }

  # Ignore if highlighted name is self.
  set _whisperPartner [$_widgets(ccLbox) get $index]
  if {$_whisperPartner == $_name} {
    insertNewMsg "  -- YOU CAN'T WHISPER TO YOURSELF --"
    return
  }

  set _whispering [expr $_whispering == 0]
  if {$_whispering} {
    $_socket write [list "whisper on" $_whisperPartner]
    insertNewMsg \
      "  -- WHISPER MODE ESTABLISHED WITH $_whisperPartner --"
    $_widgets(whisper) configure -text Broadcast
  } else {
    $_socket write [list "whisper off" $_whisperPartner]
```

```
     insertNewMsg "  -- WHISPER MODE TERMINATED --"
     $_widgets(whisper) configure -text Whisper
  }
}
```

Refer to Figure 7-3 for an illustration of the communication that occurs between ChatRoomUser objects and the server to establish a private chat session. Users A, B, and C are each logged into the chat room and connected to the server. User A requests a private session with user C by pressing Whisper (1). The server sends the appropriate message to user C (2), who then replies by also pressing Whisper (3). User A is then notified (4), and the dedicated connection is established. The screen snapshots show what each user sees in his or her view of the chat room. Messages submitted from user A are only seen by user C and vice versa, so in this case, user B can't see any messages but his or her own. Messages submitted by user B are seen by all three users.

Logging into the Chat Room

Now that the design is fully implemented, you need to know how to tie everything together and log in to the chat room. The process to do this is given for both Windows and Unix platforms. One part is common, though: creating the tclIndex file. So, regardless of your operating system, the first thing you should do is download the code available online and extract and place the following six files in a common directory: LoginMgr.itcl, LoginClient.itcl, ServerSocket.itcl, ClientSocket.itcl, ChatServer.itcl, and ChatRoomUser.itcl. Then start an **itclsh** shell, cd to this directory, and type the following command to create a tclIndex file (refer to Chapter 1 for more information on this file):

```
% auto_mkindex . *.itcl
```

After this, the procedure is a little different depending on your platform. The following sections outline how to run the code in both Windows and Unix.

Getting Started in Windows

First create a new text file named "server" with your favorite editor and insert the following lines. Use the directory name where you saved the source files in place of C:/Program Files/Tcl/src.

```
wm withdraw .
lappend auto_path "C:/Program Files/Tcl/src"
package require Itcl
LoginMgr #auto
ChatServer #auto
```

7

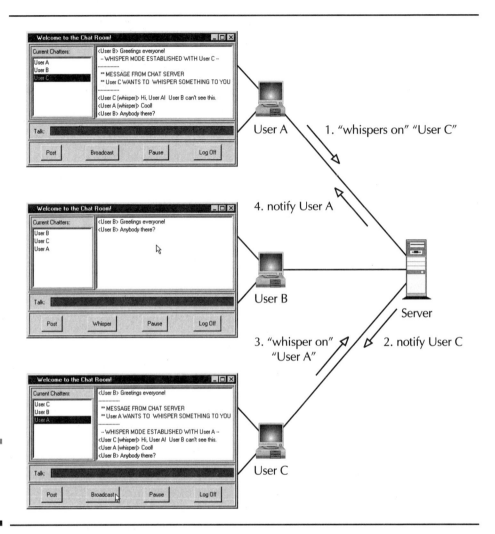

Setting up a
private chat
session

Figure 7-3.

Next, start a **wish** interpreter and source this new file with the
following command:

```
% source server
loginMgr0
```

A LoginMgr object is created to continually watch port 20002 for login
requests from LoginClient objects, and a ChatServer object is created to

continually watch port 21112 for registration requests from new ChatRoomUser objects.

Now to create the chat room window, create another file named "chat" with the following lines:

```
wm withdraw .
lappend auto_path "C:/Program Files/Tcl/src"
package require Itcl
LoginClient client
client draw
```

Then invoke another **wish** shell and source the new file as before. The user authentication window from Chapter 6 will appear. Enter a username and password (don't forget you need to modify LoginMgr.itcl to add names and passwords) and press the OK button. The chat room window will then appear with the username you entered in the Current Chatters listbox. Now on successive runs, you'll see that with each new chat room display, the new username will appear in each of the previous displays. Figure 7-4 shows a snapshot of a chat room with four users.

Getting Started in Unix

The procedure for Unix is similar. First create a new text file named "server" and insert the following lines, replacing the auto_path pathname with the directory in which your source files reside. (You'll also need to modify the path to the **wish** binary as necessary.)

```
#!/bin/sh
# \
   exec /usr/local/bin/wish8.0 $0 $*
wm withdraw .
lappend auto_path /usr/local/tcl/src
package require Itcl
LoginMgr #auto
ChatServer #auto
```

Next, use **chmod** to make the file executable and then run it as follows:

```
> chmod +x server
> ./server &
```

A LoginMgr object is created to continually watch port 20002 for login requests from LoginClient objects, and a ChatServer object is created to

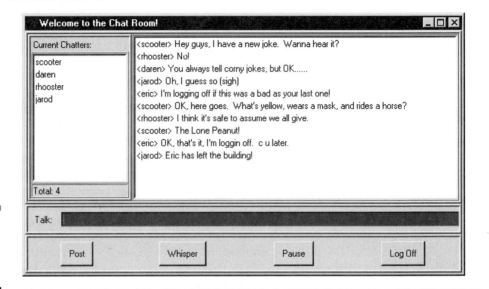

Figure 7-4.

continually watch port 21112 for registration requests from new ChatRoomUser objects.

Now to create a chat room, create another file with the following lines:

```
#!/bin/sh
# \
  exec /usr/local/bin/wish8.0 $0 $*
wm withdraw .
lappend auto_path /usr/local/tcl/src
package require Itcl
LoginClient client
client draw
```

Make the file executable as you did with "server," and run it. The user authentication window from Chapter 6 will appear. You can now enter a username and password (valid ones must be added to LoginMgr.itcl) to open the chat room window. Refer to Figure 7-4 for a sample chat room screen snapshot.

The Chat Room: A Network-Oriented Application
After you've run the previous code to create a chat room window, you'll probably quickly become bored chatting with yourself. A chat room is

supposed to be a network-oriented application. If you have access to a network, then the chat room will be more appropriate to use. If you don't have access to a network, then hopefully the design and code in this chapter will prove to be useful to you.

For network users, anyone in the network can log in to the chat room, but first you need to modify LoginClient's *process* and *createClientSocket* methods to specify the hostname on which the server is running. For example, if you start the server (the "server" file) on a workstation named myWorkstation, then each method should be implemented as follows:

```
::itcl::body LoginClient::process {data_} {
  if {$data_ == "access granted"} {
    if {[catch {
      ChatRoomUser #auto $_username myWorkstation
    } chatRoomUser]} {
      # Display error message as desired.
    } else {
      $chatRoomUser activate
      ::itcl::delete object $this
    }
  }
}

::itcl::body LoginClient::createClientSocket {} {
  if {[catch {ClientSocket #auto myWorkstation} _clientSocket]} {
    error "Failed to open client socket: $_clientSocket"
  }

  # Register a method for handling server response.
  $_clientSocket register [::itcl::code $this process]"
}
```

Then, as long as each machine in the network recognizes myWorkstation as a valid hostname, ChatRoomUser objects on multiple hosts can each communicate with the ChatServer object on myWorkstation for posting messages.

This concludes this chapter's discussion of code reuse through composition. As you saw with the chat room example, composition is a powerful feature that can greatly shorten your development time. In the next chapter, you'll learn another way to optimize development time through code reuse by taking advantage of another object-oriented utility, inheritance.

7

CHAPTER 8

Advanced Inheritance

Inheritance, like composition, describes a type of relationship between classes. Recall from the previous chapter that composition is referred to as a "has-a" relationship – objects may *have* or *be composed of* other objects. Inheritance, on the other hand, is referred to as an "is-a" relationship. Think of this kind of relationship as a parent-child relationship, where the child inherits attributes and behaviors defined in the parent. You are probably already familiar with the fundamentals of inheritance, which have been discussed in various sections and examples throughout Chapters 1–4. You learned how derived (child) classes inherit behaviors and attributes from base (parent) classes through privileged access levels. The purpose of this chapter is not to discuss such fundamental concepts. Rather, you'll learn about more advanced topics such as overloaded methods and data members, virtual methods, and multiple inheritance.

Overloading

When a derived class defines a method with the same name as a nonprivate base class method, the derived class is said to *overload* that method. Overloading simply means that the derived class provides its own definition for the method, overriding the base class definition. Overloading applies to data members as well, but the visibility is quite different than methods, as you'll see later in this section. Notice the assertion that overloading only applies to nonprivate base class methods or data members. The reason for this, according to the access rules outlined in Chapters 2 and 3, is that private methods and data members are only visible within the scope of the class in which they are defined. So, if a base class defines a private method named *init* and a derived class also defines a method named *init*, then the derived class does not overload that method because private methods are not inherited. The remainder of this section discusses how overloaded methods and data members are treated in [incr Tcl].

Methods

Methods are implicitly virtual, which is the opposite behavior of C++, where programmers must explicitly declare functions to be virtual. Being virtual means that [incr Tcl] methods are always interpreted relative to the scope of the object. In other words, if a derived class is instantiated and overloads a base class method, then the derived class method is interpreted regardless of the location of the method invocation, even if the method invocation is in a base class method. If you have no or relatively little object-oriented programming experience, then be sure to read this section carefully because dealing with virtual methods can be quite tricky if you're new to the subject.

Consider the following example to illustrate (you can type in the code as shown here in a **tclsh** shell or just follow along).

Example 8-1
A base class that
invokes a derived
class method

```
% package require Itcl
3.0
% ::itcl::class Parent {
    protected method greet {} {print "Hi there!"}
    protected method print {msg_} {
      puts "Parent::print - $msg_"
    }
  }
% ::itcl::class Child {
    inherit Parent
    constructor {} {greet}
    private method print {msg_} {
      puts "Child::print - $msg_"
    }
  }
```

Child overloads Parent's *print* method, so any calls to *print* from within a Child method refer to Child's version of *print*, as expected. Now notice what happens during object construction. When Child is instantiated, its *constructor* invokes *greet*, a protected method defined in the base class. Then *greet* invokes *print* to print a friendly message. Since *print* is invoked from within a base class method, you might think that the base class version of *print* would be interpreted. Let's find out.

```
% Child c
Child::print - Hi there!
c
```

You can see from the output that even though *print* is invoked from within a base class method, the derived class version of *print* is interpreted. This is because *print* is virtual. When the interpreter evaluates the command,

```
print "Hi there!"
```

it knows that the invoking object is of type Child. It then determines that Child has defined a method called *print* and invokes that method. Child's version of *print* takes priority over Parent's version because of the object type.

8

Remember, regardless of the location of the method invocation, methods are always interpreted relative to the scope of the object.

To get a clearer understanding of this, imagine the **this** variable in front of each method invocation. So think of the call to *print* from the *greet* method like this instead:

```
$this print "Hi there!"
```

Since **::c** is a Child object, and since Child defines a *print* method, you can see that Child's *print* would be invoked. This is because the **this** variable always contains the name of the object, even when it is referenced from within a base class. (For further information on using **this** for self-reference, refer to Chapter 3.) If you imagine the **this** variable in front of each method invocation like this, you can better determine which method will be invoked when there are multiple methods with the same name in a class hierarchy.

Now consider a more complex class hierarchy with several levels of inheritance. Think about an orchestral instrument, the clarinet, and how it might fit into an object-oriented class inheritance hierarchy as shown in Figure 8-1. (Note that this many levels of inheritance are actually impractical because the system would be too hard to understand and maintain. Typically, five levels or more defeats the purpose of using inheritance because the programmer is forced to learn and understand all of the base classes. This hierarchy is shown for example only.)

One behavior all musical instruments have in common is the ability to produce sound, so a method named *playPitch* may be defined in the base class, Instrument. The manner in which the sound is produced is different for Brass and Woodwind instruments, so each of these classes also defines a *playPitch* method. For Woodwind instruments, sound is produced one way for Reed instruments and another way for Flutes. Continuing down the inheritance tree, imagine that each class down to EflatClarinet defines its own version of *playPitch* to handle varying nuances in the way sound is produced for that part of the class hierarchy.

Now if EflatClarinet is instantiated and the *constructor* six levels up the inheritance hierarchy in class Instrument invokes *playPitch*, which *playPitch* is interpreted? You have seven choices: Instrument, Woodwind, Reed, SingleReed, Clarinet, SopranoClarinet, or EflatClarinet. If you don't understand the concept of virtual methods, this class hierarchy could certainly be confusing since each of the seven layers defines a method of the same name.

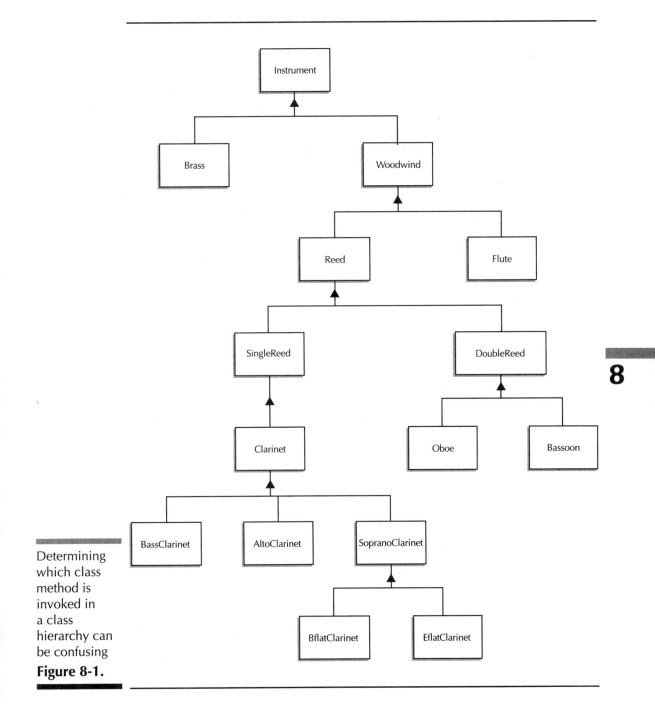

Determining which class method is invoked in a class hierarchy can be confusing

Figure 8-1.

But as you learned earlier in this section, think of the actual command fragment as

```
$this playPitch
```

and you'll realize that since the **this** variable contains the name of the EflatClarinet object, EflatClarinet's *playPitch* is interpreted when invoked by Instrument.

REMEMBER: All methods in [incr Tcl] are virtual. Methods are always interpreted relative to the type of class instance, not the class name in which they are invoked.

Accessing Overloaded Base Class Methods

As you learned in the previous section, if a derived class overloads a base class method, the derived class method takes priority when using a derived class instance. But what if you need to invoke the base class method? By default, it is not interpreted if it is overloaded, but it may perform certain tasks that need to be handled prior to invoking the derived class method. To access overloaded base class methods from a derived class, you have two options. You can use explicit namespace resolution, or you can use the **chain** command. (As previously, you can type these commands in a new **tclsh** shell or just follow along.)

Example 8-2
Using namespace resolution to access overloaded base class methods

```
% package require Itcl
3.0
% ::itcl::class Parent {
    protected method initialize {} {
       # Some necessary base class initialization tasks are typically
       # defined here.
       puts "  - ::Parent::initialize"
    }
  }
% ::itcl::class Child {
    inherit Parent
    constructor {} {
      initialize
    }
```

```
private method initialize {} {
  Parent::initialize; # Invoke the base class version first.
  # Now Child can handle derived class specific initialization
  # tasks as necessary.
  puts "  - ::Child::initialize"
}
}
```

Child overloads the base class method, *initialize*. It may be necessary, however, for Parent's *initialize* to be interpreted prior to Child's version. This may be the case, for example, if Parent needs to initialize some protected data members or needs to create common widgets or top-level windows, any of which may be referenced in Child's *initialize* method. This is commonly done in inheritance hierarchies. In order to accomplish this, the first line of code in Child's *initialize* method uses explicit namespace resolution to invoke the base class version. Then, when Child is instantiated, you can see in the following output that the order of method execution is as expected—base class followed by derived class:

```
% Child #auto
  - ::Parent::initialize
  - ::Child::initialize
child0
```

8

You can replace the first line of code in Child's *initialize* with a single word, **chain**, an [incr Tcl] command that searches through the inheritance hierarchy for the first instance of the overloaded method and invokes it.

```
% ::itcl::body Child::initialize {} {
    chain
    puts "  - ::Child::initialize"
}
% Child #auto
  - ::Parent::initialize
  - ::Child::initialize
child1
```

The output is exactly the same when using **chain** with one level of inheritance like this instead of using explicit namespace resolution. If you have multiple levels of inheritance with multiple definitions of a method, however, then **chain** may not work for you. Consider the following example.

Example 8-3
Using **chain** may
not accomplish
the desired order
of execution

```
% ::itcl::class A {
    protected method init {} {puts "  - ::A::init"}
}
% ::itcl::class B {
    inherit A
    protected method init {} {puts "  - ::B::init"}
}
% ::itcl::class C {
    inherit B
    protected method init {} {puts "  - ::C::init"}
}
% ::itcl::class D {
    inherit C
    constructor {} {init}
    private method init {} {
      chain
      puts "  - ::D::init"
    }
}
% D #auto
  - ::C::init
  - ::D::init
d0
```

As you can see from the output, **chain** only invokes the first instance of the overloaded method *init* that it finds in the inheritance tree. If you need to additionally invoke B's *init*, you would have to add the **chain** command to C's *init*; modifying base class methods like this is generally a bad idea because other programmers using the base classes may not want C's *init* to be modified. You should use namespace resolution in this case and rewrite D's *init* method as follows:

```
% ::itcl::body D::init {} {
    B::init
    C::init
    puts "  - ::D::init"
}
% D #auto
  - ::B::init
```

```
    - ::C::init
    - ::D::init
d1
```

Not only have you achieved the order of execution you wanted, but you have
also made the code easier to read. For this reason, you should typically avoid
using **chain**, which is just a shortcut to avoid using fully qualified base class
method calls. Using such fully qualified calls, however, is easier to read,
understand, and maintain, and the behavior of the code is more predictable.

Data Members

You have now seen how virtual methods are interpreted in a class hierarchy,
but what about data members? Since methods are virtual, you might think
that data members are also virtual. This is not true! Many programmers make
the mistake of overloading a data member in a derived class and are surprised
to find out that the base class can't see the derived class variable. To illustrate
this common mistake, take a look at the following example.

Example 8-4
Methods are
virtual, but data
members are not

```
% package require Itcl
3.0
% ::itcl::class Window {
    public method getSize {} {return $_size}
    public method getBaseClassSize {} {return $_size}
    protected variable _size 600x400
}
% ::itcl::class MsgWindow {
    inherit Window
    public method getSize {} {
      puts [Window::getSize]
      return $_size
    }
    public method getDerivedClassSize {} {return $_size}
    private variable _size 200x150
}
% MsgWindow mw
mw
% mw getBaseClassSize
600x400
% mw getDerivedClassSize
200x150
% mw getSize
600x400
200x150
```

8

MsgWindow overloads Window's _size data member, so MsgWindow has a copy of _size initialized to 200x150, and Window has its own independent copy of _size initialized to 600x400. When *getBaseClassSize* is invoked, the content of the base class's _size variable is returned. Likewise, when *getDerivedClassSize* is invoked, the content of the derived class's _size variable is returned. Now notice the overloaded method, *getSize*. Since *getSize* is virtual, the command

```
mw getSize
```

invokes MsgWindow's version of the method, which in turn first invokes the base class version before returning the derived class copy of _size.

REMEMBER: Methods are virtual, but data members are not. If a data member is overloaded in a derived class, the base class cannot see the derived class copy of the data member.

Taking Advantage of Virtual Methods

Now that you understand the rules of overloading and virtual methods, you might wonder why they're needed or how you might take advantage of them. The key strength of virtual methods is *extensibility*. Derived classes have the ability to extend the behavior of or completely rewrite nonprivate base class methods by overloading them. (Note that a derived class may implement a method of the same name as a private base class method, but this is not considered overloading or rewriting that method since private base class methods are not visible to derived classes.)

Recall the chat room model designed in the previous chapter. Since the concept of virtual methods had not yet been introduced, the design relied entirely on composition. Now, by using inheritance and taking advantage of virtual methods, you can make this design more robust and extensible through some very simple code relocation, allowing other applications the future ability to inherit from a generic base class framework. The object model diagram shown next describes the original chat room model from Chapter 7.

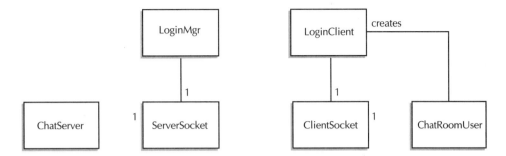

Recall that you had to modify LoginMgr and LoginClient to add code specific to the chat room application. Adding specialized code like this destroys the ability of a class to be used generically. This defeats the purpose of originally trying to make LoginMgr and LoginClient generic enough to be used for application-independent user authentication tasks. A better design is to add two more classes to the model, one inheriting from LoginMgr and the other inheriting from LoginClient. The purpose of each new class is to add the specialized code necessary for using the chat room application, extending the functionality of the base classes and maintaining their generic nature. The new model is shown in the diagram in Figure 8-2.

In this model, LoginMgr and LoginClient remain independent of the specific application at hand and are therefore able to be used in other applications instead of being tied to the chat room. ChatLoginClient now provides the chat room–specific mechanism of creating ChatRoomUser instances after the specified usernames and passwords are validated by the server. To see how this is implemented, first recall the modified version of LoginClient's *process* method as shown in Chapter 7 and repeated here:

8

```
::itcl::body LoginClient::process {data_} {
  if {$data_ == "access granted"} {
    if {[catch {ChatRoomUser #auto $_username} chatRoomUser]} {
      # Display error message as desired.
    } else {
      $chatRoomUser activate
      ::itcl::delete object $this
    }
  }
}
```

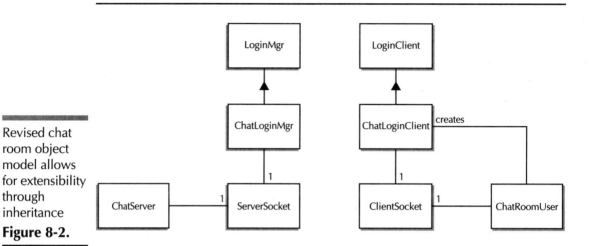

Figure 8-2.

Instead of implementing *process* in LoginClient, the design should instead
make LoginClient a base class and force a derived class to implement this
method since all login clients must be able to process input from the
login server. Pushing specialized code like this into a derived class allows
LoginClient to be generic enough to be used in other applications instead of
being tied to a specific one. The ChatLoginClient derived class is implemented
as follows:

```
::itcl::class ChatLoginClient {
  inherit LoginClient
  private method process {data_} {
    # Code for this method is moved from LoginClient::process.
  }
}
```

It's as simple as that! With the introduction of this class, *process* is overloaded
and automatically invoked when input is received from the server. This is
made possible because of virtual methods. Recall the initialization mechanism
from LoginClient's *createClientSocket* method, as shown here:

```
...
# Register a method for handling server response.
$_clientSocket register [::itcl::code $this process]
...
```

The **this** variable will contain the derived class instance, and as you learned earlier, even though *process* exists in both the base and derived classes, the derived class version is invoked since *process* is virtual.

Next, a similar bit of code relocation needs to happen on the server side. The _validIds array initialized in LoginMgr's *constructor* contains application-specific data and should therefore be initialized in ChatLoginMgr's *constructor* instead. The code is available online and isn't shown here, but the reason for moving this code is similar to the modification to LoginClient. Specialized code belongs in derived classes, and generic, common code belongs in base classes. By designing classes generically, you allow yourself the potential future opportunity of being able to take advantage of code reuse through inheritance. The LoginClient and LoginMgr classes can now be reused and extended in other applications that need a user-authentication mechanism.

Synthesizing Pure Virtual Methods

A pure virtual method is a method that is defined in a base class, called an abstract base class, and must be implemented in a derived class. In C++, abstract base classes will not compile unless all pure virtual methods are implemented in one or more derived classes. Since Tcl is interpreted, you can't stop a programmer from defining but not implementing a method and then trying to use the class without adding the code yourself to check for this. There is no built-in support for pure virtual methods in [incr Tcl], but they can be synthesized quite easily with the built-in command, **info**.

8

Pure virtual methods may be needed in cases like LoginClient's *process* method mentioned in the previous section. Since all LoginClient objects must define a *process* method to handle input from the server, and since the code to handle this input is dependent on the application, all classes that inherit from LoginClient should be forced to implement this method. The following example shows the syntax necessary to create an abstract base class with a pure virtual method. You can follow this template and modify LoginClient or other base classes in your own applications as necessary.

Example 8-5
Defining an
abstract
base class

```
% package require Itcl
3.0
% ::itcl::class Abstract {
    constructor {} {
        # Don't let the user create instances of Abstract.
        if {[namespace tail [$this info class]] == "Abstract"} {
            error "Can't instantiate an abstract base class!"
        }
```

```
      # Make sure the derived class has implemented the pv (pure
      # virtual) method.
      if {![string length [$this info function pv -body]]} {
        error "You must define method pv in order to\
           inherit from Abstract!"
      }
    }
    protected method pv {} {}
}
```

First, notice that you cannot instantiate this class. This is the appropriate behavior for a class that defines a pure virtual method because the class is incomplete without the implementation of this method. To disallow instantiation, you can use the **info** command with the class option to query the name of object's class name. (For detailed information on the built-in **info** command, refer to Chapter 2.) Recall from Chapter 4 that at the point this command is interpreted, the object exists internally. As a result, you can use the **this** variable to gather certain information from the object, such as its class name. The **namespace** command is used to strip the name of the class from the end of the string returned by the **info** command. If the object reports it's of type Abstract, then an error is generated and the object is not created.

Next, the *constructor* needs to verify that the derived class has implemented the designated pure virtual method, *pv*. You can use the **info** command again to determine this by using the function option. By asking the object if the body of *pv* exists, Abstract's *constructor* is able to determine if the method has been implemented in the derived class. If not, then an error is generated and the object is not created.

Multiple Inheritance

Each example that uses inheritance so far in this book inherits from a single base class. This type of inheritance is called *single inheritance*. When a class inherits from multiple base classes, you guessed it—it's called *multiple inheritance*. Multiple inheritance is a powerful utility that can be used to solve difficult classification problems, but using it can be troublesome and difficult to maintain. It's something you should know about but generally avoid.

Bjarne Stroustrup states in *The Design and Evolution of C++* (Addison-Wesley, 1994), "The original and fundamental reason for considering multiple inheritance was simply to allow two classes to be combined into one in such a way that objects of the resulting class would behave as objects of either base class." This is the main reason for supporting multiple inheritance in [incr Tcl] as well—to allow the designer to mix the attributes and behaviors of two independent classes into one. Most of the time, you can achieve the desired design by using single inheritance, but you may find at times that multiple inheritance becomes necessary. Grady Booch states in *Object-Oriented Analysis and Design with Applications* (Addison-Wesley, 1994) that multiple inheritance is "like a parachute: you don't always need it, but when you do, you're really happy to have it on hand." The remainder of this section shows you the basics of multiple inheritance as well as how to avoid some tricky ambiguity problems.

Construction/Destruction Order

Understanding the order of construction and destruction in multiple inheritance can be a little tricky, so first recall the syntax for *constructors* from Chapter 4, shown here:

```
constructor {?parameterList?} ?{initCode}? {?body?}
```

The second optional argument is used to pass arguments to base class *constructors* in both single and multiple inheritance. By default, the order in which base class *constructors* are invoked during construction involving multiple inheritance is the opposite order in which the base class names are listed in the derived class definition. If each base class requires arguments, on the other hand, then the order of base class construction in multiple inheritance is determined by the order in which you manually invoke each *constructor* in the init code portion of the *constructor* prototype. This is an important point to remember! If you want the base classes to be constructed in a certain order, then you have to specify their order in this init code section. If you do not specify their order (assuming they do not require arguments), then they will be constructed in the opposite order in which they are listed after the **inherit** command.

The **inherit** command accepts multiple arguments, so configuring a class to inherit from multiple base classes is as simple as adding another class name to the list. Consider the following example.

8

Example 8-6
The default order of construction for multiple inheritance is opposite of what you might expect

```
% package require Itcl
3.0
% ::itcl::class A {
    constructor {} {puts A}
    destructor {puts A}
```

```
    }
% ::itcl::class B {
    constructor {} {puts B}
    destructor {puts B}
}
% ::itcl::class C {
    inherit A B
    constructor {} {puts C}
    destructor {puts C}
}
% C #auto
B
A
C
c0
```

As you can see from the output, B is constructed before A, followed by the derived class C. Since neither base class in this example requires arguments, you don't have to specify any init code in C's *constructor*. If you want A to be constructed prior to B, however, you do have to specify the init code as follows:

```
% ::itcl::class D {
    inherit A B
    constructor {} {
      A::constructor
      B::constructor
    } {
      puts D
    }
    destructor {puts D}
}
% D #auto
A
B
D
d0
```

 REMEMBER: The default order of construction in multiple inheritance is the reverse order in which the base classes are listed in the derived class definition. Use the init code portion of the *constructor* prototype to specify construction order.

As you have seen, you can specify the order of construction in the
constructor's init code. The *destructor*, on the other hand, doesn't have an
init code argument. So to specify desctruction order, you have to add explicit
destructor calls inside the *destructor* body. First consider the default order
of destruction, which is the reverse of the default order of construction,
regardless of the *actual* construction order. The easiest way to see this is to
try it. Delete object c0 (recall that the order of construction was B→A→C).

```
%::itcl::delete object c0
C
A
B
```

Now delete object d0 (recall that the order of construction in this case was
A→B→D).

```
%::itcl:: delete object d0
D
A
B
```

The destruction order is the same in both cases because regardless of the
order of construction, the default order of destruction is always the reverse
of the default construction order.

8

Now suppose that for some reason you want to override the default behavior
and call B's *destructor* before D's *destructor*. To do this, simply modify D's
destructor as follows:

```
%::itcl::body D::destructor {} {
B::destructor
   puts A
  }
```

Then create another instance of D and delete it.

```
%D d1
A
B
D
d1
```

```
%::itcl::delete object d1
B
D
A
```

As you can see, the order of destruction is altered such that B is now destructed before D.

Combining Class Functionality with Multiple Inheritance

Multiple inheritance is commonly used in situations where you have two independent classes, perhaps purchased in packages by two different vendors, and you want to combine the attributes of each class into a common class to avoid rewriting code. For example, suppose you have a class that handles timed events—TimerHandler—and a class that handles client sockets—SocketHandler—and you want to combine these two classes so that you can do some socket manipulation with timers. Let's define the goal of this example as being able to automatically retry connecting to a server every ten seconds for one minute if a socket link is disconnected. The object model diagram for this class structure is shown in Figure 8-3. Class TimedSocket inherits all non-private attributes and behaviors defined in each base class.

Object model
diagram
showing a
derived class
inheriting from
two base
classes

Figure 8-3.

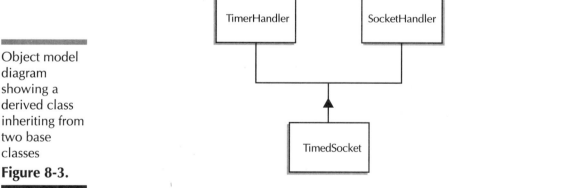

Base Class Definition

Odds are that if you encounter a situation in which multiple inheritance is warranted, the base classes involved will be much more complicated than the ones provided in this example. For simplicity's sake, each base class is conveniently stripped down to the bare essentials to make the example easy to follow and understand.

Similar to the Timer class provided in Chapter 2, TimerHandler is used to start and stop a timer, evaluating some event when a threshold is reached. This class is implemented as follows:

```
::itcl::class TimerHandler {
  # Class constructor
  constructor {upperLimit_} {set _upperLimit $upperLimit_}

  # Class Methods
  public method start {} {count}
  public method stop {} {after cancel $_afterId}
  protected method count {}

  # Class Data Members
  protected variable _upperLimit
  protected variable _action
  protected variable _afterId
  protected variable _elapsedTime 0
}
```

Two interface methods, *start* and *stop*, are defined to allow the user to start and stop the timer. A protected method, *count*, handles the countdown. This method will be overloaded in the derived class, so *start* will invoke the derived class version of *count* instead, as you'll see a little later. The base class version of *count* is therefore unimportant in this example and isn't shown here.

The SocketHandler class is also similar to a class you are familiar with from previous chapters, ClientSocket. SocketHandler is implemented as follows:

```
::itcl::class SocketHandler {
  # Class constructor/destructor
  constructor {sd_} {}
  destructor {catch {close $_sd}}

  # Class Methods
```

8

```
    protected method connect {host_ port_}
    protected method handleServerInput {}

    # Class Data Members
    protected variable _sd
}

::itcl::body SocketHandler::constructor {sd_} {
    set _sd $sd_
    fconfigure $_sd -buffering line
    fileevent $_sd readable [::itcl::code $this handleServerInput]
}

::itcl::body SocketHandler::connect {host_ port_} {
    if {[catch {socket $host_ $port_} _sd]} {
        puts "Failed to reconnect."
        return -code error
    } else {
        puts "Connection is re-established!"
        fconfigure $_sd -buffering line
        fileevent $_sd readable [::itcl::code $this handleServerInput]
    }
}
```

This class definition declares two protected methods and one protected data member. The data member stores the socket descriptor passed into the *constructor*.

Then, a file event is set up to automatically invoke *handleServerInput* when the designated socket becomes readable. Similar to TimerHandler's *count* method, *handleServerInput* is also overloaded by the derived class, so the file event will actually invoke the derived class version. The base class version implementation is therefore not provided.

The *connect* method is used to open a client socket to the designated host and port number. This method will be used by the derived class to attempt to reconnect to the server. If connection fails, then *connect* returns an error code and an appropriate message is printed. Otherwise, the socket descriptor is configured just as the original one passed into the *constructor*.

Derived Class Definition
Now that the base classes are defined, let's define the derived class. Your goal is to use multiple inheritance to combine the attributes and behaviors from each base class into a single class that accomplishes the desired task,

to automatically attempt to reconnect to the server after a disconnect is detected. The class definition for TimedSocket is as follows:

```
::itcl::class TimedSocket {
  inherit SocketHandler TimerHandler

  # Class constructor
  constructor {upperLimit_ sd_ {host_ localhost} {port_ 31213}} {
    SocketHandler::constructor $sd_
    TimerHandler::constructor $upperLimit_
  } {
    set _host $host_
    set _port $port_
  }

  # Class Methods
  private method handleServerInput {}
  private method count {}
  private method reconnect {}

  # Class Data Members
  private variable _host
  private variable _port
}
```

8

TimedSocket is configured to inherit from each base class via the **inherit** command, as previously discussed. Note the order in which the base classes are listed following **inherit**. Order can be very important, as you'll see a little later in the chapter. Each base class *constructor* in this case requires an argument, so you have to specify the init code portion of TimedSocket's *constructor* to invoke each base class *constructor* with the necessary argument. Optional parameters for the location of the server socket are declared in the *constructor*'s parameter list. These variables are used later when attempting to reconnect with the server. Finally, three private methods are defined. Two of these overload base class methods, each of which is invoked from a base class since [incr Tcl] methods are virtual. These three methods are implemented as follows:

```
::itcl::body TimedSocket::handleServerInput {} {
  if {[gets $_sd data] < 0} {
    # Connection is lost!
    puts "Lost connection with server! Attempting reconnect..."
    close $_sd
```

```
        start
      } else {
        # Handle server input here as necessary.
      }
  }

::itcl::body TimedSocket::count {} {
    if {$_elapsedTime >= $_upperLimit} {
      puts "Time has expired."
    } else {
      incr _elapsedTime 10
      set _afterId [after 10000 [::itcl::code $this count]]
      reconnect
    }
  }

::itcl::body TimedSocket::reconnect {} {
    if {![catch {connect $_host $_port}]} {
      stop
    }
  }
```

The *handleServerInput* method is automatically invoked by the interpreter when the socket becomes readable. This will happen, for example, if the server is destroyed. This method invokes the base class *start* method in such a condition, which in turn invokes *count* to start the timer and attempt to reconnect to the server. Remember, even though *count* is invoked from within the base class, the derived class *count* is actually interpreted. The **after** command is then used to set up the chain of timed events, and *reconnect* is then invoked. This method calls the base class *connect* method to try and create another client socket connection to the host and port number optionally specified during construction. If *connect* fails, then *reconnect* is called again ten seconds later via the **after** command. Otherwise, if reconnection is successful, the base class *stop* method is invoked to cancel the timer.

Testing the Code

With each class implemented, you can now test the multiple inheritance example. You first need to download the source code and extract and save the files TimerHandler.itcl, SocketHandler.itcl, and TimedSocket.itcl in a common directory. Then, invoke two **wish** interpreters, A and B, and type the following commands in interpreter A to create a server socket:

```
% proc accept {sock_ port_ addr_} {
    puts "Accepted new connection from $sock_, port $port_, $addr_"
}
% socket -server accept 31213
sock24
```

Then type the following commands in interpreter B to create a
TimedSocket instance:

```
% package require Itcl
3.0
% set testSocket [socket localhost 31213]
sock24
% source TimerHandler.itcl
% source SocketHandler.itcl
% source TimedSocket.itcl
% TimedSocket #auto 60 $testSocket
timedSocket0
```

NOTE: The actual socket name may vary on your system. Don't worry if
you type this example and see something other than "sock24" printed after
creating the client socket.

8

The client socket in interpreter B is now waiting idly for input from the
server socket in interpreter A. Type **exit** in interpreter A to destroy the socket
connection. An error condition exists on the socket at this point, and
TimedSocket's *handleServerInput* is automatically invoked. Reading from the
socket descriptor with **gets** will fail, so the TimedSocket object will then try
to reconnect to the server for the next 60 seconds. Every ten seconds, you'll
see "Failed to reconnect" printed in interpreter B. After the time expires,
"Time has expired" is printed to let you know that reconnection failed.

Now repeat this procedure, and after you exit interpreter A, start another
wish shell and re-create the server socket before the 60-second timer expires.
You'll see the message, "Connection is re-established!" in interpreter B on the
next iteration of the timer. The automatic reconnect works, and you have
successfully created a simple multiple inheritance hierarchy that combines
the functionality of two completely different classes into one to take
advantage of code reuse through inheritance.

Naming Ambiguities

With the previous example, you see the potential usefulness of multiple inheritance. This example intentionally didn't contain any problems commonly associated with multiple inheritance, though. In the real world, you'll likely come across a common problem—naming ambiguity. What happens if two or more base classes have a method named *setup*, and a derived class invokes this method? Consider the following example to illustrate.

Example 8-7
Ambiguous
method and data
member names

```
% package require Itcl
3.0
% ::itcl::class Base1 {
      protected method setup {} {puts Base1::setup}
      protected variable _x 10
  }
% ::itcl::class Base2 {
      protected method setup {} {puts Base2::setup}
      protected variable _x 20
  }
% ::itcl::class Base3 {
      protected method setup {} {puts Base3::setup}
      protected variable _x 30
  }
% ::itcl::class Derived {
      inherit Base2 Base1 Base3
      constructor {} {setup}
      method get {} {return $_x}
  }
```

Since all three base classes have a method named *setup*, the one that gets invoked from Derived's *constructor* may not be the one you intended to invoke. In cases like this, [incr Tcl] refers to the order of base class names listed after the **inherit** command. Since Base2 is listed first, Base2's version of *setup* will be invoked.

```
% Derived #auto
Base2::setup
derived0
```

For this reason, it's very important that you specify the order of base classes in their order of importance. In the TimedSocket example, for instance, a

TimedSocket is first a type of SocketHandler, then a type of TimerHandler. This is the reason why they are listed in this order in the **inherit** statement. Now invoke Derived's public *get* method to see if the same rule applies to data members.

```
% derived0 get
20
```

The same rule applies! Each of the base classes defines a protected data member, _x. When _x is referenced in Derived's *get* method, the interpreter doesn't know which _x to access so it uses the order of base class declaration as it does with method name ambiguities.

T IP: List base classes in their order of importance in the **inherit** statement. If base classes contain methods or data members with the same name, their order can adversely affect the behavior of the derived class. It's the listing order in the **inherit** statement that matters, not the order of construction specified in the *constructor*'s init code.

One Limitation

8

There is one intentional limitation built into [incr Tcl]'s support of multiple inheritance. You cannot define a class that has multiple paths through an inheritance hierarchy to the same base class. The simplest example of this is the diamond graph, in which four classes are related through inheritance in the shape of a diamond, as shown in Figure 8-4. Bottom inherits from Top through both Left and Right. Your first question might be "Why can't you define such a hierarchy?" One reason is because of construction ambiguities. Think about how Bottom would be instantiated. There are two paths to Top, so how would the interpreter decide which path to take to invoke Top's *constructor*? Similarly, if a Bottom object is deleted, how does the interpreter know which *destructor* to invoke next, Left or Right? After one of these classes is chosen, then Top's *destructor* is invoked according to the rules of destruction order, and you have a class in the middle of the hierarchy that hasn't yet been destructed. Ambiguities like these have resulted in the diamond graph's being disallowed in [incr Tcl]. If you try to define this hierarchy, the interpreter will generate an error at parse time, disallowing the definition of the derived class as shown in the following example.

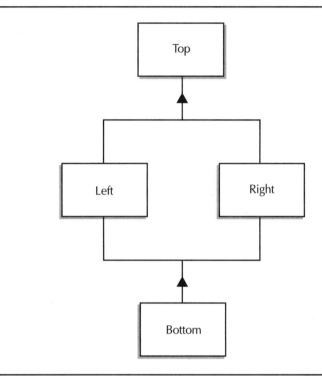

Defining this type of heritage is not possible in [incr Tcl]

Figure 8-4.

Example 8-8: The interpreter generates an error when parsing the diamond graph

```
% package require Itcl
3.0
% ::itcl::class Top {}
% ::itcl::class Left {inherit Top}
% ::itcl::class Right {inherit Top}
% ::itcl::class Bottom {inherit Left Right}
class "::Bottom" inherits base class "::Top" more than once:
  Bottom->Left->Top
  Bottom->Right->Top
% info command Bottom
%
```

Notice that the **info command** statement returns an empty string when asking about Bottom. This is because the interpreter halts the class definition process when it discovers that the same base class appears twice in Bottom's heritage. This problem is solved in C++ with the support of virtual inheritance, but for now this type of heritage is not supported in [incr Tcl]. This may change in a future release, but in the meantime you can work around the problem by using composition instead of inheritance for one or more of the inheritance relationships.

This concludes this chapter's discussion on inheritance. You should now be familiar with a variety of advanced topics such as abstract base classes, overloaded data members, virtual methods, and the diamond graph. Further, you have seen how you can use inheritance and virtual methods to take advantage of code reuse, similar to using composition as you learned in the previous chapter. The next chapter delves into the layer beneath [incr Tcl], the C application core. You will learn how you can optimize performance of particularly slow [incr Tcl] class methods by implementing them in C and referencing the C function directly in [incr Tcl] scripts.

8

CHAPTER 9

Integrating
[incr Tcl] with
C/C++

This chapter shows you how to integrate [incr Tcl] classes with C and C++. It is assumed that you have at least some C programming experience. If not, you may have a hard time understanding some of the C code examples. There are numerous references to Tcl C API functions in this chapter as well. Each of them is explained as it is used, but if you want to learn more about the Tcl library functions, you can refer to *Tcl and the Tk Toolkit* (Addison-Wesley, 1994) by John Ousterhout as well as the third edition of *Practical Programming in Tcl and Tk* (Prentice Hall, 1999) by Brent Welch, each of which has invaluable material on the Tcl C API.

In this chapter, you first learn how to rewrite [incr Tcl] class methods in C code. You can do this, for instance, to remove performance bottlenecks in the interpreter and move the code into the C layer. This is commonly done for mission-critical applications. Then, you learn how to access [incr Tcl] class data members from C code as well as how to invoke [incr Tcl] class methods from C. With the knowledge you get from these sections, you then learn how to access C++ objects from within an [incr Tcl] class as well as how to wrap an [incr Tcl] class around a C++ object. This chapter is the only chapter in this book that does not focus on [incr Tcl/Tk] code. It is mostly dedicated to the C API with which you can extend your [incr Tcl] code into underlying C/C++ layers.

Introduction

One of the key strengths of Tcl is that it provides a simple API that can be used to create new Tcl commands written in C, which can then be invoked from within Tcl scripts. You can interface with X libraries and define a new widget to add to Tk's basic widget set, you can create the hooks necessary to communicate with third-party or proprietary software such as a database package, or you can isolate performance bottlenecks in your scripts and rewrite sections of code in C to make your application run faster. In any case, Tcl's extensibility through its C API is a powerful feature you can take advantage of to write a wide variety of software applications. This API is the reason there are so many useful extensions to Tcl today.

[incr Tcl] interfaces with Tcl's C API to add object-oriented support to the Tcl core, creating new commands that allow [incr Tcl] developers to define classes and use object-oriented facilities such as inheritance and composition. [incr Tcl] also takes this one step further, allowing developers to write class methods or procedures in C, in effect creating new commands in the extension similar to what an extension does to create new commands in the Tcl core.

As a result, a single class can have some parts written in C and others written in Tcl. The following sections show you the steps you need to take to do this. It is important to note that the examples are developed and shown in a Unix environment.

Class Methods as C Functions

There are two approaches you can take to implement class methods in C. The first approach uses dynamic loading. You should verify that dynamic loading is available on your system before proceeding with the example because some systems do not support it. The second approach uses static linking where you create a specialized shell that has the new commands built into it.

Dynamic Loading

Dynamic loading is a powerful and popular alternative to static linking on systems that support it because it allows you to maintain a separation of concerns by creating shared libraries that can be loaded into an interpreter with the **load** command. It is also much less intrusive than static linking because you don't have to modify the binary executable. Instead, you create a shared library that is loaded dynamically as needed. There are three main steps you must take to do this, outlined by the following bullets. Each step is discussed and expanded in the next few sections.

◆ Write the [incr Tcl] class definition and decide which methods should be implemented in C.

◆ Write the C functions that correspond to the designated class methods.

◆ Register the new C functions with the interpreter.

9

The Class Definition
When you initially define new classes, you probably don't think about writing certain methods or procedures in C. This is usually decided after the fact when the need for better performance might become an issue, or if you don't have access to a Tcl compiler and want to hide part of your source code. In the case of the latter, suppose you need to write a class that handles encryption and decryption. You clearly would not want your customer to be able to read the source code and determine the encryption algorithm, and you need to be able to integrate this class into an existing [incr Tcl] application. One solution is to implement the encryption and

decryption portions of the class in C and just invoke the C functions from the Tcl code. The algorithms will be compiled into a shared library and therefore be hidden from your customers. Consider the following class definition:

```
::itcl::class Crypto {
  public method encrypt {string_} @encipher
  public method decrypt {string_} @decipher
}
```

You should immediately notice a new syntax in the class definition that you may not have seen before. The @ sign preceding encipher and decipher indicates that the bodies of *encrypt* and *decrypt* are actually implemented as C functions. When the interpreter parses through the class definition, it recognizes @encipher as a symbolic name for a C function that has been appropriately registered with the interpreter. Since these functions have not yet been written, if you try to define this class in a vanilla **itclsh** shell you'll get the following error message:

```
no registered C procedure with name "encipher"
```

So, before you can even define this class, you must first write the new C functions and register them with the interpreter.

Writing the C Function

When you download the [incr Tcl] distribution package from the Internet and install it, a top-level directory is created that contains several subdirectories. Once you have [incr Tcl] installed, change directories to .../itcl/generic, located directly beneath this top-level directory. This is the directory in which you'll create a new file to implement the C functions corresponding to the class methods, *encrypt* and *decrypt*. You can actually place the file anywhere, but it's more convenient to create it in this directory because this is where other itcl-specific files are located, and this non-graphical example will be used in a Tcl shell. If the example required a Tk interpreter, you would place the new file in .../itk/generic instead.

Now that you are in the correct directory, create a new file called encrypt.c. The remainder of this section provides the C source code, step by step, for the encryption function in this new file. The decryption function is very similar to encryption and is therefore not shown here. The source code for both functions is available online.

NOTE: This chapter is devoted to neither C programming nor cryptography. Though not required, it will help if you are familiar with C. If not, then you may be able to use the examples as templates for your own applications without having to understand exactly how they work.

Getting Started Before function implementation, you first need to include the [incr Tcl] header file. Then, you need a few global variables for the particular encryption algorithm that will be used in this example. The following lines are the first few lines of encrypt.c:

```
#include "itcl.h"

const int minAscii = 32;        /* Smallest valid ASCII value: ' ' */
const int maxAscii = 126;       /* Largest valid ASCII value : '~' */
const int maxLen   = 128;       /* Longest string length allowed   */
const char* key    = "j3o:h1n6"; /* Transposition key              */
```

Next, you need to decide what type of handler the C function will be. You can define an argument-style handler or an object-style handler. An argument-style handler declares argc and argv in the function parameter list. If you are familiar with C or C++, you'll recognize these two parameters as the number of arguments passed into the function and an array of argument strings, respectively. The function signature for an argument style handler looks like this:

9

Example 9-1
Signature for argument-style handler (used in conjunction with Itcl_RegisterC)

```
int YourNewCFunction(cdata, interp, argc, argv)
   ClientData cdata;        /* required but usually not used */
   Tcl_Interp *interp;      /* pointer to the interpreter    */
   int argc;                /* number of arguments           */
   char **argv;             /* array of argument strings     */
```

An object-style handler uses Tcl8 objects, which are used in the Tcl8.x core instead of strings to improve execution efficiency. This style handler declares objc and objv in the function parameter list. The first parameter is the same as argc, the number of function arguments. The second parameter, however, is an array of Tcl objects (Tcl_Obj structures) as opposed to character strings.

(For more information on Tcl objects, refer to the Object man page.)
The function signature for an object-style handler looks like this:

Example 9-2
Signature
for object-style
handler (used in
conjunction with
Itcl_RegisterObjC)

```
int YourNewCFunction(cdata, interp, objc, objv)
   ClientData cdata;       /* required but usually not used  */
   Tcl_Interp *interp;     /* pointer to the interpreter     */
   int objc;               /* number of arguments            */
   Tcl_Obj *CONST objv[]; /* array of Tcl Object structures */
```

For this example, an object-style handler will be used. (Note that you can use
different names for each parameter. The names shown are declared as such
for convention only.)

Function Prototype   Now you need to decide on a name for the C
functions. The @encipher string from the class definition is a symbolic name
that represents the real C function. For encryption, the name EncipherCmd
is chosen. Likewise, DecipherCmd is chosen for decryption. It's common to
insert a trailing "Cmd" like this when defining new Tcl commands or
implementing class methods in C.

Since this example uses the object-style handler, the function prototype is
identical to the previous example except for the function name. Add the
following lines below the global variable declarations in encrypt.c:

```
int EncipherCmd(cdata, interp, objc, objv)
   ClientData cdata;       /* required but usually not used  */
   Tcl_Interp *interp;     /* pointer to the interpreter     */
   int objc;               /* number of arguments            */
   Tcl_Obj *CONST objv[];  /* array of Tcl Object structures */
{
```

Note that this function must return an integer value. You should always
return either TCL_OK or TCL_ERROR (0 or 1) from these functions. This
allows you to use the **catch** command to properly handle error conditions.

Validating Arguments   Your first task in the actual function body is to
specify some local variables and then do some argument validation. You need
to make sure the correct number of arguments is specified, and you need to

check the length of the string to be encrypted. For this example, the user may not specify more than 128 characters according to the maxLen constant defined at the top of the file:

```
int index;           /* Index into the plaintext                 */
int keyIndex = 0;    /* Index into the key                        */
char* ciphertext;    /* Encrypted string buffer                   */
char* stringToEncrypt; /* User-designated string to be encrypted */

/*
 * Make sure the correct number of arguments is specified.
 * Syntax = <objectName methodName "string to be encrypted">
 */
if (objc != 2)
{
  Tcl_WrongNumArgs(interp, 1, objv, "string-to-encrypt");
  return TCL_ERROR;
}

/*
 * Extract the user-designated string to be encrypted from the
 * Tcl_Obj array.
 */
stringToEncrypt = Tcl_GetStringFromObj(objv[1], (int*)NULL);

/*
 * Return if the length of the string to be encrypted is greater
 * than the maximum allowed # of characters or if it's zero length.
 */
if (strlen(stringToEncrypt) > maxLen)
{
  char buf[5];
  sprintf(buf,"%d",maxLen);
  Tcl_AppendResult(interp, "specified string is too long: ",
    "must not exceed ", buf, " characters", (char *)NULL);
  return TCL_ERROR;
}
else if (strlen(stringToEncrypt) == 0)
{
  Tcl_AppendResult(interp, "specified string is zero length",
    (char *)NULL);
  return TCL_ERROR;
}
```

9

For the first failure condition, an invalid number of arguments, the Tcl_WrongNumArgs function is used to report the error. You can use this function only when using the object-style handler since it requires objv as one of its arguments. It prints the same generic message you would get, for example, if you typed **lindex** without any arguments. The next two error conditions are handled by Tcl_AppendResult, which is used to save an error message into the result buffer. Each error condition is followed by a command to return TCL_ERROR, which will cause *encrypt* to fail and the specified error message to get printed.

Implementing the Task at Hand   Once error handling is done, you're ready to get to the meat of the function body. First you need to allocate some memory to store the encrypted text string. Tcl_Alloc and Tcl_Free are used here for memory allocation instead of alloc and free. These functions are defined by Tcl to provide platform- and compiler-independent mechanisms for heap manipulation. Refer to the Alloc man page for more details.

Next is the actual encryption algorithm. Don't be concerned with exactly how this algorithm works. There are countless ways to encrypt a text string. The approach chosen for this example is a simple kind of transposition cipher in which the integral value of a character is added to the integral value of a corresponding character in a known key to calculate a new character. This concept is taken from a cipher known as the Vigenere cipher. A bit of extra manipulation is done here to ensure that the new character is within the ASCII character set so that you can see the result. Otherwise, the character may be unprintable, such as a control character.

```
ciphertext = Tcl_Alloc(maxLen+1);
for (index=0; index < strlen(stringToEncrypt); index++)
{
  /* Convert the string one character at a time. */
  ciphertext[index] =
    (char)((((int)key[keyIndex] + (int)stringToEncrypt[index]) %
            (maxAscii-minAscii+1)) + minAscii);

  /* When the end of the key is reached, wrap back to the front. */
  if (keyIndex==strlen(key)-1)
    keyIndex=0;
  else
    keyIndex++;
}

/* Null terminate the encrypted string. */
ciphertext[index]='\0';
```

Once the string is encrypted and stored in the character string, ciphertext, the string is null terminated and you're ready to return from the function.

Returning from the Function   The last step is to copy the encrypted text string into the result buffer with Tcl_AppendResult and then free the heap space. The encrypted text is printed to standard output, so you can capture the result of the function call in a script just like a regular command fragment enclosed in brackets. The final few lines of EncipherCmd are as follows:

```
Tcl_AppendResult(interp, ciphertext, (char *)NULL);
Tcl_Free(ciphertext);
return TCL_OK;
}
```

Implementing the Initialization Procedure

Once function implementation is complete, you're ready for the next step—registering them with the interpreter so that when *encrypt* or *decrypt* is invoked, the interpreter knows to actually invoke EncipherCmd or DecipherCmd, respectively. This is the responsibility of a special function called the initialization procedure. Its name is determined by the Tcl_LoadCmd function and is derived from the name of the shared library. For a shared library named encrypt.so, the function name is Encrypt_Init. The first letter must be capitalized, and the .so is replaced with the string, _Init. This rule applies to all shared libraries you build, so if you build one named helloWorld.so, then you must implement a function named Helloworld_Init.

9

In this example, since encrypt.c is the only filename, encrypt.so is chosen for the shared library name. You must therefore implement a new function called Encrypt_Init. Place this new function at the bottom of encrypt.c. It should return an integer (TCL_OK or TCL_ERROR), and it must accept a single argument, a pointer to the current interpreter. Remember, its purpose is to register the new commands with the interpreter, so you may recognize the code in the function body, which is implemented as follows:

```
int Encrypt_Init(interp)
  Tcl_Interp* interp;
{
  if (Itcl_RegisterObjC(interp,
        "encipher", (Tcl_ObjCmdProc*)EncipherCmd,
        (ClientData)NULL, (Tcl_CmdDeleteProc*)NULL) != TCL_OK ||
```

```
    Itcl_RegisterObjC(interp,
        "decipher", (Tcl_ObjCmdProc*)DecipherCmd,
        (ClientData)NULL, (Tcl_CmdDeleteProc*)NULL) != TCL_OK)
  {
    return TCL_ERROR;
  }
  return TCL_OK;
}
```

When you use the **load** command to load the shared library, the Tcl_LoadCmd function is invoked to load the library as well as to invoke this initialization procedure to register the new commands with the interpreter. This registration is the responsibility of the Itcl_RegisterObjC function when using the object-style handler. When using the argument style handler, you need to use Itcl_RegisterC instead. Recall that you won't be able to use useful functions such as Tcl_WrongNumArgs if you use the latter.

In either case, the first argument is the pointer to the current interpreter, the second argument is the text string without the @ sign from the [incr Tcl] class definition, and the third argument is the name of the C function to be invoked for the designated class method. Note that you'll need to cast this argument appropriately depending on the chosen style. For object-style handlers, cast the function name to a Tcl_ObjCmdProc pointer. For argument-style handlers, cast it to a Tcl_CmdProc pointer. There are two more arguments, but these last two are unused here and are just cast to NULL. You'll see how to take advantage of these arguments in the C++ section of this chapter. Now, the only step left for you to do is build the shared library.

Building the Shared Library
You must have object files in order to build a shared library, so the next task at hand is to compile encrypt.c. Compiler flags vary widely across systems, but you may be able to compile with a command similar to the following:

```
gcc -fPIC -I${TCL_DIR} -I. -o encrypt.o -c encrypt.c
```

The variable, TCL_DIR, is the directory in which the Tcl header file is located, typically the generic directory underneath Tcl's top-level installation directory. Once you've compiled encrypt.c and created the object file, you need to create the shared library. Again, flags may differ on your system, but you may be able to use something similar to the following:

```
gcc -shared -o encrypt.so encrypt.o
```

This creates a shared library, encrypt.so, from the object file, encrypt.o. Now you're ready to load the library in an interpreter!

Loading and Using the Shared Library

Loading the library is as simple as using the **load** command. Change directories to the location of the new shared library (the generic directory), start a vanilla **tclsh** shell, and type the following commands. (Remember that the decryption function was not provided. You must retrieve it from the online site for the following code to work. The filename is encrypt-dl.c.)

```
% package require Itcl
3.0
% ::itcl::class CryptoTest {
    method encrypt {string_} @encipher
    method decrypt {string_} @decipher
}
no registered C procedure with name "encipher"
```

As expected, EncipherCmd has not yet been registered with the interpreter, so an error is generated. Now, use the **load** command to perform the necessary registration.

```
% load ./encrypt.so
% ::itcl::class CryptoTest {
    method encrypt {string_} @encipher
    method decrypt {string_} @decipher
}
% CryptoTest ct
ct
% set garbage \
    [ct encrypt "This is a test of the emergency broadcast system."]
 \:nI[Cv-sE`=f0f2sEc/q5d1f8`8Uiv.f@\.U1j@sDt=f5dy
```

So far so good! The encrypted text is printed as expected and captured in the variable, garbage. It certainly appears that the designated string is encrypted

9

beyond recognition. Now the true test comes when you try to decrypt the resulting string.

```
% ct decrypt $garbage
This is a test of the emergency broadcast system.
```

The decryption is successful! Now you have an independent library that you can load to access the new encrypting/decrypting functions whenever you need them. The library is only integrated with the interpreter when you load it. (Note that once you load the library, however, you cannot unload it.) Until then, the interpreter is completely unaffected by your new code.

T IP: You must load the Itcl package before loading the shared library! If you attempt to load the shared library first, you will get an error similar to the following example.

Example 9-3
The Itcl package must be loaded prior to loading the shared library

```
% load ./encrypt.so
couldn't load file "./encrypt.so": ld.so.1:
/usr/local/bin/tclsh8.0:
fatal relocation error: file ./encrypt.so: symbol
Itcl_RegisterObjC:
referenced symbol not found
```

The error occurs because the loader cannot resolve the reference to the Itcl_RegisterObjC function, which is defined in the [incr Tcl] library. Unless you are using a shell which has this library built into it, such as the **itclsh** or **itkwish** shells, you have to manually load the Itcl package first. As a general rule of thumb, you must always preload any libraries that are required for your new shared libraries to work properly.

Dynamic loading can prove to be a very useful utility that can help you avoid the possible high-risk maintenance of a shell that has multiple unrelated functions added. Instead, you can define multiple shared libraries, separating them into sets of related functionality. For example, you can create the encryption library as you did in this section, and you could create another shared library that defines different database utility functions. The two libraries would be independent of one another and could be loaded into an interpreter separately only as needed.

Static Linking

Static linking is much more intrusive than dynamic loading because it involves actually modifying the binary executable shell. Most of the time, you should avoid using static linking and build shared libraries to encapsulate your extensions or extra command utilities. But it may be necessary for you to include new commands directly into the shell, so the following sections show you how to do this. The steps begin with the assumption that you have already implemented each of the C functions. The first step in the following sections corresponds to the step to implement the initialization procedure in the previous section.

Registering the New Functions with the Interpreter

If you read the previous section on dynamic loading, you know that new command registration is handled by a special function called the initialization procedure. For static linking, the initialization procedure is already implemented for you. It's called Tcl_AppInit and is located in the tclAppInit.c file in the …/itcl/unix directory. Each Tcl shell type (**tclsh**, **itclsh**, etc.) for each Tcl extension has its own version of Tcl_AppInit. It is generically responsible for extension-specific initialization and is automatically invoked each time you start a new interpreter session.

The version of Tcl_AppInit in this particular directory is responsible for implementing the hooks necessary for **itclsh** shell initialization. It also defines a few other itcl-specific tasks as well. For example, when you develop in an **itclsh** shell, you do not have to use fully qualified names for [incr Tcl] commands. You can instead use simple command names without namespace resolution such as **class** and **delete** instead of **::itcl::class** and **::itcl::delete**. This is because the version of Tcl_AppInit for an **itclsh** shell automatically imports all [incr Tcl] specific commands from the itcl namespace. You'll learn more about how this works and why you shouldn't do it in the next chapter.

Now edit tclAppInit.c to add a few lines of code for the registration process. You should make a backup copy of this file first in case you want to undo your modifications later. You'll be referencing both EncipherCmd and

9

DecipherCmd in this file, so you first need to use the extern command to let the compiler know these functions are defined elsewhere.

```
extern int EncipherCmd();
extern int DecipherCmd();
```

Add these two lines of code at the top of the file after the #include preprocessor directives and prior to the implementation of the main function.

Next, go to the Tcl_AppInit function. Near the bottom you'll see a comment about creating application-specific commands. This comment is shown along with the lines of code that you need to add directly following it.

```
/*
 * Call Tcl_CreateCommand for application-specific commands,
 * if they weren't already created by the init procedures
 * called above.
 */
if (Itcl_RegisterObjC(interp,
        "encipher", (Tcl_ObjCmdProc*)EncipherCmd,
        (ClientData)NULL, (Tcl_CmdDeleteProc*)NULL) != TCL_OK ||

    Itcl_RegisterObjC(interp,
        "decipher", (Tcl_ObjCmdProc*)DecipherCmd,
        (ClientData)NULL, (Tcl_CmdDeleteProc*)NULL) != TCL_OK)
{
  return TCL_ERROR;
}
```

The Itcl_RegisterObjC function is used to perform the registration process with the interpreter when using the object-style handler. When using the argument-style handler, you need to use Itcl_RegisterC instead. Note that you won't be able to use such functions as Tcl_WrongNumArgs if you use the latter.

In either case, the first argument is the pointer to the current interpreter, the second argument is the text string without the @ sign from the [incr Tcl] class definition, and the third argument is the name of the C function to be invoked for the designated class method. Note that you'll need to cast this argument appropriately depending on the chosen style. For object-style handlers, cast the function name to a Tcl_ObjCmdProc pointer. For argument-style handlers, cast it to a Tcl_CmdProc pointer. There are two more arguments, but the last two are unused here and are just cast to NULL. You'll see how to take advantage of these arguments later in the C++ section of this chapter. Now, the only step left for you to do is to build a new shell.

Building the New Shell

You have a couple of options to choose from when building the new **itclsh** shell, the easiest of which is to simply modify the Makefile and add the lines necessary to handle the compilation of the new file, encrypt.c. This way, all you need to do is type **make** to compile the new file and link it into the **itclsh** executable. Your other option is to manually compile encrypt.c and link the resulting object file into the **itclsh** executable.

To use the Makefile approach, you need to modify four sections of the file. First, add an entry to the SRCS variable definition as follows (note that all modifications to the Makefile are shown in boldface):

```
SRCS =  $(GENERIC_DIR)/itcl_bicmds.c \
        $(GENERIC_DIR)/itcl_class.c \
        $(GENERIC_DIR)/itcl_cmds.c \
        $(GENERIC_DIR)/itcl_ensemble.c \
        $(GENERIC_DIR)/itcl_linkage.c \
        $(GENERIC_DIR)/itcl_methods.c \
        $(GENERIC_DIR)/itcl_migrate.c \
        $(GENERIC_DIR)/itcl_objects.c \
        $(GENERIC_DIR)/itcl_obsolete.c \
        $(GENERIC_DIR)/itcl_parse.c \
        $(GENERIC_DIR)/itcl_util.c \
        $(GENERIC_DIR)/encrypt.c \
        $(GENERIC_DIR)/tclAppInit.c
```

Next, append the object file name to the OBJS variable definition.

9

```
OBJS =  itcl_bicmds.o itcl_class.o itcl_cmds.o itcl_ensemble.o \
        itcl_linkage.o itcl_methods.o itcl_migrate.o itcl_objects.o \
        itcl_obsolete.o itcl_parse.o itcl_util.o encrypt.o
```

Then, define a new rule for creating the object file by adding the following two lines near the bottom of the file:

```
encrypt.o: $(GENERIC_DIR)/encrypt.c
        $(CC) -c $(CC_SWITCHES) $(GENERIC_DIR)/encrypt.c
```

Finally, add the object filename to the rule for building the **itclsh** executable (Note that the pathname will likely vary on your own system).

```
itclsh: tclAppInit.o $(ITCL_LIB_FILE)
        $(CC) encrypt.o tclAppInit.o \
        -L/usr/lib/tcl/itcl3.0.1/itcl/unix -litcl3.0 \
        $(LIBS) $(LD_SEARCH_FLAGS) -o itclsh
```

Once you've made these four modifications to the Makefile, all you need to do is type **make** in the unix directory, and a new **itclsh** shell will be built and placed in the directory. (Remember that the decryption function was not provided. You must retrieve it from the online site for the code to compile. The filename is encrypt-static1.c.) It's as simple as that!

Testing the Code

At this point, you have defined the [incr Tcl] class, using the @ sign to tell the interpreter that the bodies of *encrypt* and *decrypt* are actually implemented in C; you have written the C functions EncipherCmd and DecipherCmd and have registered each function appropriately with the interpreter; and you have built a new **itclsh** shell with which to test the new code. Invoke the new shell and type the following commands:

```
% class CryptoTest {
    public method encrypt {string_} @encipher
    public method decrypt {string_} @decipher
  }
% CryptoTest ct
ct
% set goldenRule \
    [ct encrypt "Do unto others as you would have them do unto you."]
ocPp8f?v;h9`<eOX?sJj?qGfA`5z2SF\Kh9`7q4fKi?o9qIfA"
% ct decrypt $goldenRule
Do unto others as you would have them do unto you.
```

There you have it. You now have a specialized shell with the new encryption and decryption functions built directly into it. Note that you can use the new shell with your existing scripts as well. It behaves exactly the same as a vanilla shell, only with the added behavior defined by the two new functions. As long as classes do not specify @encipher or @decipher as method bodies in a class definition, this new **itclsh** shell will behave as if the new functions were never added.

Accessing Class Data Members from C Functions

In the previous section, you learned how to implement a C function that gets invoked in place of a class method. As you are aware, class methods often need to access data members. It follows then that if you have the ability to implement methods in C, you should also have the ability to access data members from C. It wouldn't be nearly as useful if the C function was totally independent of the class from which it gets invoked. Tcl provides hooks for you to both get and set class data members. This can be done via the Tcl_GetVar and Tcl_SetVar functions, outlined in the following two sections.

Retrieving Data Members

The two functions you implemented in the previous section each share a constant variable, maxLen. What if your customer wanted to allow greater length strings to be encrypted or wanted to lessen this value instead? The only option would be to modify encrypt.c and rebuild another **itclsh** executable or shared library. This involves modification of application source code, which is a bad idea. Instead, the maximum length of the encrypted string should be stored in the [incr Tcl] class definition. Then EncipherCmd and DecipherCmd can use Tcl_GetVar to retrieve the value of this scalar class data member. For arrays, you would use Tcl_GetVar2 instead. (Note that you can use the Tcl_ObjGetVar2 function to retrieve both scalar and array data members. This example does not use this function to avoid adding any extra complexity.) The new class definition might look like this:

```
class Crypto {
  public method encrypt {string_} @encipher
  public method decrypt {string_} @decipher
  private variable _maxLen 10
}
```

9

To access _maxLen from C, you need to make a few modifications to encrypt.c. (Note that all modifications for this example are available online in the filename encrypt-static2.c. This section walks you through the modifications you need to make to encrypt.c, assuming you've created this file earlier in this chapter.) First, remove the following line from the variable declaration section at the top of the file. You will not need the global constant, maxLen, anymore. You'll instead declare local variables initialized to values retrieved from the [incr Tcl] class.

```
const int maxLen = 128;        /* Delete this line of code */
```

Next, you need to declare three additional local variables: one to store the name of the [incr Tcl] class data member, one to store the character string returned by Tcl_GetVar, and another to store the integer value of this character string. Since Tcl_GetVar returns a string, you must convert it to an integer value with a function called Tcl_GetInt. These variables should be placed immediately following the other local variables in the EncipherCmd function body. They are defined as follows:

```
char* name = "_maxLen"; /* Name of class data member          */
char* varRef;           /* Local reference to data member      */
int maxLen = 0;         /* Integer equivalent of data member   */
```

In the original implementation, you added code to verify the number of arguments, followed by code to validate the length of the designated string to be encrypted. Now the maxLen local variable is initialized to zero, so you need to determine its true value before validating the string length by retrieving it from the class definition. Immediately following verification of the number of arguments, add the following lines of code to retrieve the value of the private class data member, _maxLen:

```
varRef = Tcl_GetVar(interp,name,TCL_NAMESPACE_ONLY);
if (varRef)
{
  Tcl_GetInt(interp,varRef,&maxLen);
  if (!maxLen)
  {
    return TCL_ERROR;
  }
}
else
{
  Tcl_AppendResult(interp, "invalid variable access: _maxLen ",
    "does not exist or is not initialized", (char *)NULL);
  return TCL_ERROR;
}
```

First, notice that the variable varRef is assigned to the return value of Tcl_GetVar, which returns a pointer to a character string. If Tcl_GetVar fails to retrieve the value of the designated data member, _maxLen, then it returns NULL. The arguments to Tcl_GetVar are a pointer to the interpreter, the name of the class data member, and a set of flags that are logically OR'ed together to form a bit mask (See the SetVar man page for more details). The flag, TCL_NAMESPACE_ONLY, is used to tell the interpreter to search for the designated data member in the namespace of the calling context only, as opposed to the default behavior of also looking in the global namespace.

If the value returned by Tcl_GetVar is NULL, then you know that the designated variable name either does not exist in the class definition or has not been initialized. In such a case, you should make sure that the variable name is present and visible in the calling context. Private base class data members, for instance, are not visible in a derived class context. You can, however, access nonprivate base class data members from a C function invoked in a derived class context.

If the value returned by Tcl_GetVar is nonzero on the other hand, you must convert the resulting character string into an integer for later comparisons. To do this, you can use Tcl_GetInt. This function expects a pointer to the interpreter, the name of the character string to convert, and an integer pointer. The final argument is passed by reference so that it will contain the integer value when Tcl_GetInt returns. If Tcl_GetInt fails, the argument will not be modified. As a result, the content of this argument, maxLen, is checked following the call to Tcl_GetInt. If nonzero, then you know that the data retrieval was successful.

NOTE: You should try to make the same code modifications to DecipherCmd before downloading the online code. Manually modifying these functions like this will help you to better learn the concepts presented as well as the Tcl C API.

If you followed the static linking approach from the previous section, all you have to do is type **make** after finishing modifications to DecipherCmd. A new version of **itclsh** will be built, and you can now use it to test the new code as follows:

9

```
% itcl::class Crypto {
    public method encrypt {string_} @encipher
    public method decrypt {string_} @decipher
    public method setLength {val_} {set _maxLen $val_}
    private variable _maxLen 10
  }
% Crypto #auto
crypto0
% crypto0 encrypt "hello world"
specified string is too long: must not exceed 10 characters
% set result [crypto0 encrypt "hi world"]
4]Pr9d<[
% crypto0 decrypt $result
hi world
```

Then, if you want to change the maximum allowable string length, all you need to do is use the accessor method to modify the class data member—no compilation necessary.

```
% crypto0 setLength 100
% crypto0 encrypt "This is certainly longer than the original."
 \:nI[Cv/Yco+[>cEs=j8Y5iKh9\8qD_1s@m3Y9e`^
```

As you can see, a quick modification of _maxLen allows you to easily change the behavior of the C functions without having to worry about recompilation. The only restriction for using these new encrypting/decrypting functions is that the [incr Tcl] class must define a data member named _maxLen. If you forget to define this data member, or if you forget to initialize it, the interpreter will generate an error message as follows:

```
% itcl::class Broken {
    public method encrypt {string_} @encipher
 }
% Broken b
b
% b encrypt "this won't work"
invalid variable access: _maxLen does not exist or is not initialized
```

You learned how the Tcl_GetVar function allows you to retrieve the current value of [incr Tcl] data members. In the next section, you'll see how to modify the value of a data member with a counterpart function to Tcl_GetVar.

Modifying Data Members

Modifying data members from C functions can be done with the Tcl_SetVar function for scalars and the Tcl_SetVar2 function for arrays, the counterparts to Tcl_GetVar and Tcl_GetVar2. (Note that similar to Tcl_ObjGetVar2, you can use the Tcl_ObjSetVar2 function to modify both scalar and array data members. This example does not use this function to avoid adding extra complexity.) Since _maxLen is a scalar, Tcl_SetVar is used. It requires four arguments: a pointer to the interpreter, a character string representing the name of the class data member, a character string containing the new value, and flags as discussed in the previous section. Suppose you want to save the result of encryption into a class data member instead of printing it with Tcl_AppendResult. To do this, all you need to do is modify one line of code in EncipherCmd. (Note that the filename encrypt-static3.c is available online with this code change.) Change this line:

```
Tcl_AppendResult(interp, ciphertext, (char *)NULL);
```

to this instead:

```
Tcl_SetVar(interp, "_ciphertext", ciphertext, TCL_NAMESPACE_ONLY);
```

This command tells the interpreter to save the contents of ciphertext into a class data member called _ciphertext. Rebuild your **itclsh** shell after making this modification as you've done previously and try the following commands:

```
% class Test {
    public method encrypt {string_} @encipher
    public method get {} {return $_ciphertext}
    private variable _maxLen 50
    private variable _ciphertext ""
  }
% Test #auto
test0
% test0 encrypt "hello world"
% test0 get
4Y=g9qGf>`5
```

It's that easy! Now you know how to extend your [incr Tcl] classes by writing class methods in C and by accessing and modifying class data members from within C functions. The next logical functionality you may need during development is the ability to invoke [incr Tcl] class methods from C. This is discussed in the next section.

9

Invoking Class Methods from C Functions

If you can implement a class method in C and be able to access data members from the C function, it follows that you should be able to access other class methods from within the C function as well. A Tcl C API function called Tcl_Eval is available that allows you to do this. Instead of piling more code onto the encryption example, let's use a simple generic example instead. The following [incr Tcl] class definition should be placed in a file named Engineer.itcl, and the two C functions should be placed in work.c. (As with most examples, each file is already available online for you.) First, take a look at the class definition for Engineer.

```
itcl::class Engineer {
  public method work {} @work
  public method play {} {
    puts "All work and no play makes $this a dull boy!"
  }
}
```

You should recognize by now that the *work* method is actually implemented in C. The work.c file consists of two functions to support this example: the actual function that is invoked when *work* is called and the initialization procedure. These functions are implemented as follows:

```
#include "itcl.h"

int WorkCmd(cdata, interp, objc, objv)
  ClientData cdata;       /* required but usually not used */
  Tcl_Interp *interp;     /* pointer to the interpreter    */
  int objc;               /* number of arguments           */
  Tcl_Obj *CONST objv[];  /* array of argument strings      */
{
  if (Tcl_Eval(interp, "play") != TCL_OK)
  {
    interp->result = "Cannot play, must work!";
    return TCL_ERROR;
  }

  return TCL_OK;
}

int Work_Init(interp)
  Tcl_Interp* interp;
{
  if (Itcl_RegisterObjC(interp,
         "work", (Tcl_ObjCmdProc*)WorkCmd,
         (ClientData)NULL, (Tcl_CmdDeleteProc*)NULL) != TCL_OK)
  {
    return TCL_ERROR;
  }
  return TCL_OK;
}
```

These functions are very simple without any error handling. Now, build a shared library called work.so as you learned earlier in the chapter. Then start a **tclsh** shell and type the following commands:

Example 9-4
To work or
play, a difficult
decision for the
Engineer object
to make

```
% package require Itcl
3.0
% load ./work.so
% source Engineer.itcl
% Engineer wardrua
wardrua
% wardrua work
All work and no play makes ::wardrua a dull boy!
```

The [incr Tcl] class method *work* is invoked from the command line, but the text from the *play* method is actually printed! The Tcl_Eval function successfully invokes Engineer's *play* method. You can see how simple this is. Now that the playing is over, let's get back to work.

This concludes the section of the chapter devoted to C integration. Using the utilities you learned in the previous sections provides an excellent migration path that you can take advantage of to streamline your code as the need arises or to obfuscate certain functionality as you learned in the encryption example. The remainder of the chapter shows you how to integrate [incr Tcl] with C++. First you learn how to control C++ objects from within an [incr Tcl] class. Then, you build on this knowledge and learn how to wrap an [incr Tcl] class around a C++ object.

9

Using C++ Objects Within an [incr Tcl] Class

The key to manipulating a C++ object from within an [incr Tcl] class is to create a new Tcl command that maps to the C++ object. This new command then invokes a C wrapper function that in turn extracts the C++ object pointer from the argument list and invokes the designated function with that pointer. The following sections show you step by step how to accomplish this. The example is developed on Unix and uses dynamic loading. You can modify the online code to use static linking if your system does not support dynamic loading.

Implementing the C++ Class

Suppose your project is mission critical and you determine that the interpreter is just too slow to handle certain processing in your application. Your underlying code is in C++, so a natural migration path is to move some of the [incr Tcl] code to C++ as well. You narrow down a performance bottleneck to the maintenance of stack data structures you are emulating with an [incr Tcl] class. The first step to solve this problem is to reimplement the [incr Tcl] class functionality in C++. Let's define a simple Stack class as follows. (Note that for simplicity's sake all error handling is removed, so Stack objects in this example can be error prone.)

```
#ifndef STACK_H
#define STACK_H
class Stack
{
  public:
    Stack() {_top = _data;}
    void push(int i_) {*++_top = i_;}
    int pop() {return *_top--;}
    int top() {return *_top;}
  private:
    int _data[10];
    int* _top;
};
#endif
```

Place this class definition in a header file named stack.h in the .../itcl/generic directory directly underneath the top-level [incr Tcl] distribution directory. All code in this section should be placed in this directory. With the implementation of the C++ class complete, you're ready to provide the interface code between the C++ layer and the [incr Tcl] layer. You'll do this in C as discussed in the next section.

Creating a New C++ Object

The C++ object is created in a C wrapper function that is registered with the interpreter as an [incr Tcl] class method body. You learned how to register C functions like this in the first part of the chapter, so the registration process is not discussed here. This function is named NewStackCmd, and its purpose is to instantiate a new C++ Stack object and set up the hooks you need to manipulate this object from your [incr Tcl] class. NewStackCmd is implemented as follows (note that each function in this section should be implemented in a file named stackinit.cc):

```
int NewStackCmd(
  ClientData cdata,
  Tcl_Interp* interp,
  int argc, char** argv)
{
  static unsigned int id = 0;
  Stack* newStackPtr = new Stack();

  /*
   * Create a unique string to use for the new Tcl command and
   * then register the new command with the interpreter.
   */
  sprintf(interp->result,"stack%u",id++);
  Tcl_CreateCommand(interp, interp->result,
    (Tcl_CmdProc*)StackCmd, (ClientData)newStackPtr,
    (Tcl_CmdDeleteProc*)DeleteStackCmd);

  return TCL_OK;
};
```

The key to NewStackCmd's success is the Tcl_CreateCommand function, which is used to create a new Tcl command from a unique character string representing the new C++ Stack object. A static integer is embedded in this string and incremented after the string is created so that the next time NewStackCmd is invoked, the string will still be unique. Tcl_CreateCommand requires five arguments. The first three are the current interpreter, the name of the Tcl command to create, and the C function to invoke when the interpreter evaluates this command. The fourth and fifth arguments are discussed in later sections. The next step is to implement the C function tied to this new Tcl command.

9

Implementing the Command Procedure

The command procedure is the C wrapper function that gets invoked when the C++ object is accessed in [incr Tcl]. A new Tcl command representing the C++ object has been created and registered with the interpreter, so when the interpreter evaluates this command it knows to invoke StackCmd. The purpose of StackCmd is to provide the interface between the string representation of the C++ object at the [incr Tcl] level and the actual C++ object pointer at the application level. StackCmd is implemented as follows:

```
int StackCmd(
  ClientData cdata,
  Tcl_Interp* interp,
  int argc, char** argv)
{
  Stack* stack = (Stack *)cdata;

  if (argc < 2)
  {
    interp->result = "wrong # args";
    return TCL_ERROR;
  }

  if (strcmp(argv[1], "push") == 0)
  {
    int val;
    if (Tcl_GetInt(interp,argv[2],&val) != TCL_OK)
    {
      interp->result = "Error converting arg to integer.";
      return TCL_ERROR;
    }
    stack->push(val);
    interp->result = "Successfully pushed value onto C++ stack.";
  }
  else if (strcmp(argv[1], "pop") == 0)
  {
    stack->pop();
    interp->result = "Successfully popped value off of C++ stack.";
  }
  else if (strcmp(argv[1], "top") == 0)
  {
    int top = stack->top();
    sprintf(interp->result,"%d",top);
  }

  return TCL_OK;
};
```

The first line of code is extremely important, so take special note of this explanation! This is how you are able pass C++ object pointers to

C functions from [incr Tcl] scripts. The ClientData argument from the Tcl_CreateCommand function in NewStackCmd is registered with the interpreter as the address of the new C++ Stack object. Then, when the new Tcl command corresponding to this object is evaluated within the [incr Tcl] class, the interpreter passes the pointer through ClientData to the command procedure. The command procedure can then extract the C++ Stack object pointer by casting the ClientData argument to a Stack pointer. This is an extremely useful utility and makes C++ integration like this possible.

The remainder of StackCmd provides the interface to the C++ Stack functions, depending on the content of the argv array. Remember, this function is invoked when the new Tcl command representing the C++ object is evaluated in your [incr Tcl] class, so the argv array should contain the name of the C++ Stack function to be invoked. Valid function names are *push*, *pop*, and *top*. Invalid names and other error conditions are not handled in StackCmd to eliminate further complexity. Results of each function invocation are written directly to the interpreter's current result field. You can also use Tcl_AppendResult, but it's quicker to just write directly to the result field since there are no messages to be strung together in this case.

Destroying the C++ Object

You now have a way to create a new C++ object directly from [incr Tcl] via NewStackCmd, so you also need a way to delete the object. This is the purpose of the Tcl_CmdDeleteProc pointer argument to Tcl_CreateCommand. The C function specified as this argument, DeleteStackCmd, is automatically invoked when the new Tcl command representing the C++ object is removed from the interpreter. You'll see how to do this when the [incr Tcl] class is implemented later. DeleteStackCmd's only purpose is to delete the object, so it consists of a single line of code as follows (take note of the parameter list, which differs from parameter lists for most other functions registered with the interpreter):

9

```
int DeleteStackCmd(ClientData cdata)
{
  delete (Stack *)cdata;
};
```

You learned in the previous section about how ClientData is used to pass C++ object pointers to C functions from [incr Tcl]. DeleteStackCmd is another example of the usefulness of this. The ClientData argument is simply cast to a Stack pointer and deleted.

Implementing the Initialization Procedure

Recall from earlier in the chapter that the initialization procedure is just a C function used to register new commands with the interpreter at startup. The only function that needs to be registered in this case is NewStackCmd, so the initialization procedure is very simple and implemented as follows:

```
int Stack_Init(Tcl_Interp* interp)
{
  if (Itcl_RegisterC(interp,
        "createNewStack", (Tcl_CmdProc*)NewStackCmd,
        (ClientData)NULL, (Tcl_CmdDeleteProc*)NULL) != TCL_OK)
  {
    return TCL_ERROR;
  }

  return TCL_OK;
};
```

Avoiding Loader Problems

Now you're almost done. You've implemented four functions: NewStackCmd, StackCmd, DeleteStackCmd, and Stack_Init. Each of these functions has been referred to as a C function throughout these sections. Each of them, however, should be placed in a file with a C++ extension, .C or .cc, since the C++ Stack class is referenced throughout. As a result of this, you have to declare each function as extern "C" to avoid loader problems with C++ name mangling. If you don't tell the compiler explicitly that these functions are C functions, it will create names in the symbol table that don't match up with the actual names of the functions. You don't necessarily need to understand why or how this works. You just need to be aware of possible problems like this.

At the top of the stackinit.cc file, #include the header files for itcl and the Stack class and then add the extern "C" declarations for each of the four functions as follows. Each of the four function bodies should then follow these lines. Once you do this, you're ready to compile the code.

```
#include "itcl.h"
#include "stack.h"

extern "C" {
  int NewStackCmd(ClientData, Tcl_Interp*, int, char**);
  int DeleteStackCmd(ClientData);
  int StackCmd(ClientData, Tcl_Interp*, int, char**);
  int Stack_Init(Tcl_Interp*);
};
```

Building the Shared Library

As stated earlier, compiler flags may vary on your system, but you may be able to use commands similar to the following for compiling stack.cc and creating a shared library:

```
gcc -fPIC -I${TCL_DIR} -I. -o stackinit.o -c stackinit.cc
gcc -shared -o stack.so stackinit.o
```

Defining the [incr Tcl] Front End

With creation of the shared library complete, you're now ready to define the front end to the C++ Stack class with an [incr Tcl] class. Consider the following class definition:

```
::itcl::class ItclStack {
  constructor {} {set _stackObject [new]}
  destructor {destroy}

  # Class Methods
  public method push {val_} {$_stackObject push $val_}
  public method pop {} {$_stackObject pop}
  public method top {} {$_stackObject top}
  public method destroy {} {rename $_stackObject {}}
  private method new {} @createNewStack

  # Class Data Members
  private variable _stackObject
}
```

9

The *constructor* initializes the _stackObject data member to the return value of *new*. Notice that *new*'s body is implemented in C (the NewStackCmd function). Recall that the return value from this function is the unique character string name representing the C++ Stack object, which was made into a new Tcl command via Tcl_CreateCommand. This new command is then used in *push*, *pop*, and *top* to manipulate the C++ object.

Now recall the DeleteStackCmd function, which gets automatically invoked when the Tcl command stored in _stackObject is removed from the interpreter. This is the purpose of *destroy*. It uses the **rename** command to rename the content of _stackObject to the null string, causing DeleteStackCmd to be invoked because of the registration done in Tcl_CreateCommand. If you're familiar with Tcl's C API, then you should know that the **rename** command used like this is equivalent to using Tcl_DeleteCommand to remove the command from the interpreter.

A Test Run

All implementation is now done, and you're set to test the code. The ItclStack class should be in a file named ItclStack.itcl. For convenience, place this file in the same directory in which you created stack.h and stackinit.cc. Change directories to this directory and then type the following lines of code in an **itclsh** shell to see how things work:

```
% load ./stack.so
% source ItclStack.itcl
% ItclStack stack
stack
% stack push 2
Successfully pushed value onto C++ stack.
% stack push 4
Successfully pushed value onto C++ stack.
% stack push 6
Successfully pushed value onto C++ stack.
% stack top
6
% stack pop
Successfully popped value off of C++ stack.
% stack pop
Successfully popped value off of C++ stack.
% stack top
2
```

Success! The [incr Tcl] object, **stack**, is actually modifying a C++ Stack object through the C wrapper functions you implemented earlier. Now let's test destroying the C++ object.

```
% stack destroy
% stack push 8
invalid command name "stack0"
```

As you can see from the error message, the *destroy* method successfully deletes the C++ Stack object and removes the corresponding Tcl command from the interpreter.

You could extend the code in this section to create multiple C++ Stack objects and perhaps store their associated names in a list of objects in an [incr Tcl] StackManager class. Whereas this example is extensible in such a manner, the following section shows you how to create a one-to-one mapping between an [incr Tcl] object and an associated C++ object, in essence wrapping the C++ object as an [incr Tcl] class. The approach is a little different, but most of the concepts should be familiar to you after studying previous sections.

Wrapping C++ Objects As an [incr Tcl] Class

You now know how to create a new Tcl command representing a C++ object that can be used from within an [incr Tcl] class to manipulate that C++ object. Instead of creating new Tcl commands this time, you'll use the [incr Tcl] object itself to manipulate the C++ object by implementing a C wrapper function for each C++ class function and then by implementing an [incr Tcl] interface method for each of the C wrapper functions. This may seem a little complicated or overkill since you have to implement three different layers to accomplish the task. But the concepts provided in this example should prove to be very helpful to you. You will learn how to store C++ object pointers in a Tcl hash table and find the pointer associated with a particular [incr Tcl] object to then manipulate the C++ object. Similar to the previous section, the remainder of this section walks you through this process step by step so that you should become familiar enough with the information provided to be able to do this in your own applications.

Implementing the [incr Tcl] Wrapper Class

Instead of starting at the C or C++ layer this time, let's begin with the [incr Tcl] class definition. This way, you can refer back to the definition when you define the underlying C/C++ code. The same data structure, the stack, is used from the previous section. The C++ class will be unchanged, but the front end is very different. ItclStackWrapper is implemented as follows:

9

```
::itcl::class ItclStackWrapper {
  constructor {} {new}
  destructor {destroy}

  # Class Methods
  public method push {val_} @push
  public method pop {} @pop
  public method top {} @top
  private method new {} @createNewStack
  private method destroy {} @deleteStack

  # Class Data Members
  private variable _key
}
```

As you can see, each of the functions in the class is actually implemented in C. Take particular note that this includes the *constructor* and *destructor*. The bodies of these methods are not implemented in C, but they call *new* and *destroy*, respectively, whose bodies are both in C. You can probably tell why the class is named ItclStackWrapper now since it has no functionality at the [incr Tcl] layer. Its sole purpose is to serve as an interface to the C layer in order to gain access to the C++ layer beneath that.

Creating the C Wrapper Functions

The next step in the process is to define C wrappers for each of the C++ functions in Stack. There are five such functions corresponding to the five methods in ItclStackWrapper. The following sections discuss three of these functions: creating a new C++ object, pushing values onto the stack, and destroying the C++ object. The C wrapper functions for *pop* and *top* are implemented very similar to *push*, so they are not shown here. Each of the functions is available online from the filename wrappers.cc, or better yet, you can implement the other two functions yourself after studying the wrapper function for *push*.

Creating a New C++ Object

When ItclStackWrapper is instantiated, it follows that the C++ Stack class should also be instantiated. This is the purpose of the NewStackCmd C wrapper function. It's quite different from the function of the same name you created in the previous section. A line-by-line discussion follows the function implementation.

```
int NewStackCmd(
  ClientData cdata,
  Tcl_Interp* interp,
  int argc, char** argv)
{
  /*
   * This static variable is used to create unique keys for hash
   * table entries.  Each key will be the string "stack" with this
   * static variable appended to it.
   */
  static unsigned int id = 1;

  int returnVal;            /* Return value for Tcl_CreateHashEntry */
  Tcl_HashEntry* entryPtr;  /* New entry pointer in the hash table   */
  Stack* newStackPtr;       /* Pointer to a new C++ Stack object     */
```

```
   /*
    * Generate a unique key.  Post-increment the id so that the next
    * key will be different.
    */
   sprintf(interp->result,"stack%u",id++);

   /*
    * Create a new entry in the hash table with the unique key name.
    */
   entryPtr =
     Tcl_CreateHashEntry(&objects, interp->result, &returnVal);

   if (!returnVal)
   {
     Tcl_AppendResult(interp,
       "Failed to create hash entry.", (char*)NULL);
     return TCL_ERROR;
   }

   /* Create the new Stack object and store it in the hash table. */
   newStackPtr = new Stack();
   Tcl_SetHashValue(entryPtr,newStackPtr);

   /*
    * This is the mechanism used to determine which C++ Stack object
    * maps to which [incr Tcl] Stack object.  By storing the key in
    * a class data member, Stack methods are able to operate on the
    * correct Stack by searching through the hash table for an entry
    * that matches the key from the current [incr Tcl] object.
    */
   Tcl_SetVar(interp, "_key", interp->result, TCL_NAMESPACE_ONLY);

   return TCL_OK;
};
```

9

First, you should recognize the static integer from the previous section. This time, however, it's used in the creation of a unique key value for storing C++ Stack object pointers in a Tcl hash table. A few lines later, Tcl_CreateHashEntry is used to create a new entry in a global Tcl hash table named *objects* with this unique key. Then a new C++ Stack object is created, and its address is stored in the hash table via Tcl_SetHashValue. So, now a new entry has been created in the hash table, and it has been initialized to the address of the new C++ Stack object.

The next step is very important. It saves the key into the [incr Tcl] object with Tcl_SetVar, which you learned how to do earlier in the chapter. You'll see why this is necessary in the next section.

Pushing New Values onto the Stack

The ItclStackWrapper *push* method maps to the C wrapper function, PushCmd, which in turn pushes the designated value onto the stack represented by the C++ Stack object. This function is implemented as follows:

```
int PushCmd(
  ClientData cdata,
  Tcl_Interp* interp,
  int argc, char** argv)
{
  /*
   * Make sure the number of arguments is correct first.
   */
  if (argc != 2)
  {
    Tcl_AppendResult(interp, "wrong * args: should be \"push #\"",
      (char *)NULL);
    return TCL_ERROR;
  }

  /*
   * Get the string representing the C++ object name from the
   * [incr Tcl] class data member, _key.  This string is the key
   * used to search in the hash table.
   */
  char* name = Tcl_GetVar(interp,"_key",TCL_NAMESPACE_ONLY);
  if (!name)
  {
    Tcl_AppendResult(interp, "Failed to get contents of variable,",
      " _key.", (char *)NULL);
    return TCL_ERROR;
  }

  /*
   * Find the hash table entry corresponding to the object name.
   */
  Stack* stack = getStackPointer(interp,name);
  if (stack)
```

```
  {
    /*
     * Found the entry.  Now convert the argument to an integer.
     */
    int num;
    Tcl_GetInt(interp,argv[1],&num);
    if (!num)
    {
      Tcl_AppendResult(interp, "Failed to convert the specified ",
        "argument, ", argv[1], " to an integer value.", (char *)NULL);
      return TCL_ERROR;
    }

    /*
     * Use the C++ object pointer to push the designated number
     * onto the stack.
     */
    stack->push(num);
    Tcl_AppendResult(interp, "C++ object successfully updated.",
      (char *)NULL);
    return TCL_OK;
  }
  else
  {
    Tcl_AppendResult(interp, "Failed to get C++ object from the ",
      "hash table.", (char *)NULL);
    return TCL_ERROR;
  }
};
```

9

After checking the number of arguments, the key to the hash table is retrieved from the invoking [incr Tcl] object. As you learned earlier in the chapter, you can use Tcl_GetVar to retrieve [incr Tcl] class data members. The hash table key is stored in the [incr Tcl] class data member, _key, so once this key is retrieved, you can use it to search through the hash table and find the entry, a pointer to a C++ Stack object, associated with the key. You'll see how to search through the hash table later in this section. Once the C++ object is located, you're set. Just tell it to push the designated value onto the stack. The same concepts apply to PopCmd and TopCmd, the C wrapper functions for ItclStackWrapper's *pop* and *top* methods. You should try to implement these functions yourself as an exercise. The best way to learn a new concept is to actually do it.

Destroying the C++ Object

The last wrapper function to be provided in this section is DeleteStackCmd. This function is invoked by the interpreter when the ItclStackWrapper *destroy* method is invoked. DeleteStackCmd is implemented as follows:

```
int DeleteStackCmd(
  ClientData cdata,
  Tcl_Interp* interp,
  int argc, char** argv)
{
  /*
   * Get the C++ object name from the [incr Tcl] class data
   * member, _key.  The C++ object name is the key used
   * to search in the hash table.
   */
  char* name = Tcl_GetVar(interp,"_key",TCL_NAMESPACE_ONLY);
  if (!name)
  {
    Tcl_AppendResult(interp, "Failed to get contents of variable,",
      " _key.", (char *)NULL);
    return TCL_ERROR;
  }

  /*
   * Find the hash table entry corresponding to the object name.
   */
  Stack* stack = getStackPointer(interp,name);
  if (stack)
  {
    delete(stack);
    Tcl_AppendResult(interp, "C++ object successfully deleted.",
      (char *)NULL);
    return TCL_OK;
  }
  else
  {
    Tcl_AppendResult(interp, "Failed to get C++ object from the ",
      "hash table.", (char *)NULL);
    return TCL_ERROR;
  }
};
```

The purpose of this function is simply to locate the C++ object corresponding to the string stored in the [incr Tcl] object's _key data member and delete it. Locating the C++ object is a task handled by a specialized function called getStackPointer. This function is discussed in the next section.

Searching for C++ Objects in the Hash Table

You need to be able to locate a C++ object in the hash table given a key retrieved from the invoking [incr Tcl] object. This is the purpose of the getStackPointer function, a general-purpose function that is used by each of the C wrapper functions. This function is implemented as follows:

```
Stack* getStackPointer(Tcl_Interp* interp, char *key)
{
  /*
   * Locate the entry in the hash table corresponding to the
   * designated key.  This key is stored in the [incr Tcl] object.
   */
  Tcl_HashEntry* entryPtr;
  entryPtr = Tcl_FindHashEntry(&objects, key);
  if (entryPtr == NULL)
  {
    Tcl_AppendResult(interp, "Failed to locate C++ object",
      (char *)NULL);
    return (Stack *)TCL_ERROR;
  }

  return (Stack *)Tcl_GetHashValue(entryPtr);
};
```

The Tcl_FindHashEntry function is used to locate the entry in the hash table corresponding to the designated key, and Tcl_GetHashValue is then used to extract the contents of this entry in the table. Remember C++ Stack object addresses are stored in the hash table, so the return value of Tcl_GetHashValue (ClientData) is cast to a Stack pointer. The invoking wrapper function can then use the pointer as needed.

Implementing the Initialization Procedure

The last function to implement is the initialization procedure. You must register each of the five wrapper functions with the interpreter at application

9

startup. This function must also create a new hash table in which to store the C++ object pointers. Stack_Init is implemented as follows:

```
int Stack_Init(Tcl_Interp* interp)
{
  if (Itcl_RegisterC(interp,
        "createNewStack", (Tcl_CmdProc*)NewStackCmd,
        (ClientData)NULL, (Tcl_CmdDeleteProc*)NULL) != TCL_OK ||

      Itcl_RegisterC(interp,
        "deleteStack", (Tcl_CmdProc*)DeleteStackCmd,
        (ClientData)NULL, (Tcl_CmdDeleteProc*)NULL) != TCL_OK ||

      Itcl_RegisterC(interp,
        "push", (Tcl_CmdProc*)PushCmd,
        (ClientData)NULL, (Tcl_CmdDeleteProc*)NULL) != TCL_OK ||

      Itcl_RegisterC(interp,
        "pop", (Tcl_CmdProc*)PopCmd,
        (ClientData)NULL, (Tcl_CmdDeleteProc*)NULL) != TCL_OK ||

      Itcl_RegisterC(interp,
        "top", (Tcl_CmdProc*)TopCmd,
        (ClientData)NULL, (Tcl_CmdDeleteProc*)NULL) != TCL_OK)
  {
    return TCL_ERROR;
  }

  /*
   * Create a new hash table, storing information about the table
   * at the address of the Tcl_HashTable pointer, objects.
   */
  Tcl_InitHashTable(&objects,TCL_STRING_KEYS);
  return TCL_OK;
};
```

Wrapping Things Up

The last steps prior to compilation are to declare each function as extern "C" (recall from earlier that you must do this to avoid C++ name-mangling problems with the loader) and to create a Tcl hash table pointer. Insert the following lines at the top of the file, wrappers.cc, after which each of the C functions should be implemented:

```
#include "itcl.h"
#include "stack.h"

extern "C" {
  int NewStackCmd(ClientData, Tcl_Interp*, int, char**);
  int DeleteStackCmd(ClientData, Tcl_Interp*, int, char**);
  int PushCmd(ClientData, Tcl_Interp*, int, char**);
  int PopCmd(ClientData, Tcl_Interp*, int, char**);
  int TopCmd(ClientData, Tcl_Interp*, int, char**);
  Stack* getStackPointer(Tcl_Interp*, char*);
  int Stack_Init(Tcl_Interp*);
};

static Tcl_HashTable objects;
```

A Test Run

Before you can test the code, you need to compile wrappers.cc and build the shared library. Refer to previous sections in the chapter on how to do this. After you build the shared library, type the following lines in an **itclsh** shell to test the code:

```
% load ./stack.so
% source ItclStackWrapper.itcl
% ItclStackWrapper #auto
itclStackWrapper0
% ItclStackWrapper #auto
itclStackWrapper1
%
% itclStackWrapper0 push 1
C++ object successfully updated.
% itclStackWrapper0 push 11
C++ object successfully updated.
% itclStackWrapper0 push 111
C++ object successfully updated.
%
% itclStackWrapper1 push 2
C++ object successfully updated.
```

9

```
% itclStackWrapper1 push 22
C++ object successfully updated.
% itclStackWrapper1 push 222
C++ object successfully updated.
%
% itclStackWrapper0 pop
C++ object successfully updated.
% itclStackWrapper0 top
11
%
% itclStackWrapper1 pop
C++ object successfully updated.
% itclStackWrapper1 pop
C++ object successfully updated.
% itclStackWrapper1 top
2
% delete object itclStackWrapper0 itclStackWrapper1
```

The test is successful! From the output you can see that two ItclStackWrappers are created that result in the creation of two independent C++ Stack objects. You now have an [incr Tcl] class that actually wraps an underlying C++ object.

NOTE: There are a variety of real-world tools and applications that integrate Tcl with C++. You can refer to David Beazley's Simplified Wrapper and Interface Generator (SWIG) at http://www.swig.org. SWIG is an interface compiler that you can use to connect programs written in C++ with scripting languages such as Tcl or [incr Tcl]. You can also refer to the Modeling and Animation Machine/Virtual Rendering System (MAM/VRS) 3-D graphics library at http://wwwmath.uni-muenster.de/informatik/u/mam. This library is a good example of wrapping a Tcl front end around a C++ application core.

This concludes this chapter's discussion of C/C++ integration with [incr Tcl]. You have now learned how to implement [incr Tcl] class methods in C, how to retrieve and modify [incr Tcl] class data members from C, how to invoke [incr Tcl] class methods from C, how to access C++ objects from [incr Tcl], and how to wrap an [incr Tcl] class around a C++ object. You should be able to use what you learned in this chapter to extend your own [incr Tcl] projects into the C/C++ layer. Once you do this for the first time, you'll gain a great appreciation for the built-in Tcl C API hooks and for the ease with which you interface with them.

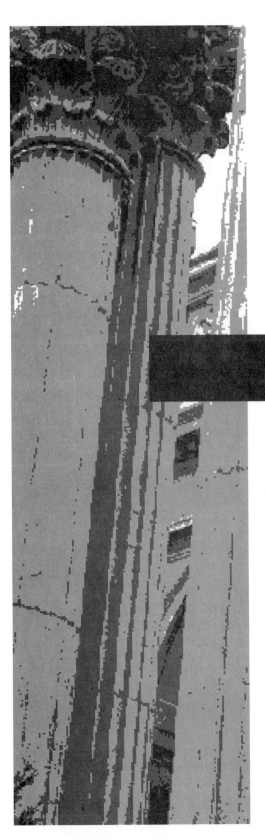

CHAPTER 10

Namespaces and Packages

This chapter shows you how to integrate [incr Tcl] classes with the new Tcl namespace facility and how to use namespaces to build portable packages. An overview of namespaces is provided first, outlining some of the key components of the **namespace** command. You will learn the similarities and differences between a namespace and an [incr Tcl] class. A section is then provided that covers some scoping problems when moving from one namespace to another. You'll see how to use certain commands to properly wrap object and variable names so that they can be accessed in multiple namespaces, thus avoiding some common pitfalls. Then, you will see how to create and install a package from a namespace. This process is outlined step by step, and at the end of this chapter you will know how to wrap up [incr Tcl] classes into a common namespace and use that namespace to build a portable package.

What Is a Namespace?

Before providing an overview of namespaces, you might first be interested in how they came to be. Namespaces are actually nothing new to [incr Tcl]. They are indispensable, in fact, because they provide the means necessary for defining classes and creating objects. This is why prior to version 3.0 [incr Tcl] included its own distribution of Tcl/Tk, modified to provide namespace support. This caused a lot of confusion for some because you could have multiple copies of Tcl/Tk libraries and binaries sitting around, which also consumed considerable disk space. At the time, however, this was necessary. Michael McLennan, creator of [incr Tcl], proposed that namespaces be added to the Tcl core. This was done in Tcl8.0. Version 3.0 of [incr Tcl] overhauled version 2.2 to integrate the new Tcl namespace facility, and with the release of this version [incr Tcl] became an extension to Tcl for the first time. This means it can now be dynamically loaded like other extensions such as Expect, BLT, and Scotty.

This gives you a little history, but you still might not have any idea what a namespace is. For an in-depth discussion, you can refer to the third edition of Brent Welch's *Practical Programming in Tcl and Tk* (Prentice Hall, 1999). Since **namespace** is a Tcl command, not an [incr Tcl] command, it is not discussed in great detail in this chapter. Brent provides an excellent discussion of **namespace** and each of its command-line options. The following sections, however, do provide a brief overview of namespaces—but with an [incr Tcl] slant. Namespaces are similar to a structure with which you are already quite familiar: the class. In fact, you may be surprised to find out that a class actually *is* a namespace under the hood! This is discussed further a little later in the chapter. Namespaces and classes are compared and contrasted in the following sections to give you an introduction to this new facility.

Usage

Classes are generally used for defining a set of behaviors and attributes that class instances, or objects, can manipulate. Each object fits into the class mold but contains its own independent set of instance data, or object-level data. Static data, or class-level data, is independent of the number of objects. You may recall from Chapter 3 that all objects of a given class type are affected when a static data member is modified and that its value exists prior to the creation of any objects.

Think of a namespace as a bucket or container. You can dump miscellaneous variables, procedures, and even classes into the bucket. A namespace is used to group such data into a common repository, encapsulating it and setting it apart from other namespaces. Namespaces are similar to the static portions of a class because their internal variables and commands can be accessed with fully qualified names. There is no concept of an object, though, in Tcl—namespaces cannot be instantiated like a class. They are merely data holders. The following example shows you how to create a namespace in a **tclsh** shell.

Example 10-1
Use **namespace eval** to group related procedures into a common location

```
% namespace eval SortingFunctions {
    proc heapSort {} {
       # Heapsort algorithm here.
    }
    proc quickSort {} {
       # Quicksort algorithm here.
    }
    proc bubbleSort {} {
       # Bubblesort algorithm here.
    }
}
```

10

As you can see, there is nothing special that must be done to create a namespace. The **namespace eval** command is built directly into the Tcl shell. This example groups three related procedures together in a single namespace called SortingFunctions. An equivalent [incr Tcl] class might be implemented as follows:

```
% package require Itcl
3.0
% ::itcl::class ItclVersion {
    public proc HEAP_SORT {} {}
    public proc QUICK_SORT {} {}
    public proc BUBBLE_SORT {} {}
}
```

It doesn't make as much sense, though, to group these kinds of functions in an [incr Tcl] class. A class is meant to be more autonomous, defining attributes and behaviors that are more specialized. Grouping different kinds of sorting algorithms or other related functions is best suited to a namespace. You can then use the namespace to create a package that can be delivered to your customers. You'll learn more about packages a little later in the chapter.

Encapsulation

Both namespaces and classes encapsulate information, ensuring that internal variable and command names do not clash with other namespace variables and commands. The following example illustrates.

Example 10-2
Declaring variables, procedures, and classes in a single namespace

```
% set quote "A job worth doing"
% namespace eval Misc {
    variable quote " is worth doing well."
    proc print {} {
      variable quote
      puts $quote
    }
  }
% package require Itcl
3.0
% ::itcl::class Misc2 {
    public common quote "is worth doing well."
    public proc print {} {puts "$::quote $quote"}
  }
% puts -nonewline $quote; ::Misc::print
A job worth doing is worth doing well.
% ::Misc2::print
A job worth doing is worth doing well.
```

Variables named quote are declared at the command line, in the Misc namespace, and in the Misc2 class. None of these variables clash with one another because they are all actually named differently. The global namespace is denoted by a double colon, so the name of the global variable is technically ::quote. (This is how Misc2's *print* method is able to access this variable without using the **global** command, which was required prior to version 3.0.) Similarly, Misc's quote variable is technically named ::Misc::quote. If this is new to you, try reading it from right to left as, "quote exists in the Misc namespace, which exists in the global namespace." This naming convention is similar to Tk window pathnames. Just as all Tk windows and widgets are created in a hierarchical manner "underneath" the root window, all new namespaces are created underneath the global namespace.

NOTE: The global namespace identifier, the leading double colon, is always optional unless explicitly required to avoid name clashes as in Misc2's *print* method. The names of all other namespaces, however, are always necessary unless the designated variables/commands within them are manually exported and imported. You'll learn more about this in the next section.

The two *print* procedures do not clash with one another for the same reason the three quote variables don't. The correct procedure is invoked depending on the preceding namespace name, Misc or Misc2. (Note that the **variable** command must be used in the *print* procedure to gain access to the namespace variable. This is similar to using **upvar**.) You might be wondering why Misc2 is referred to here as a namespace. Internally, each class actually has its own namespace that manages the class scope. When you define a new class, a new namespace is created via Tcl_CreateNamespace with the associated class definition data. This function is also invoked when you use the **namespace eval** command. So even though you refer to a class as a class, it is actually a carefully managed namespace under the covers. If you ever wondered, you can now see why namespaces are so important to [incr Tcl]!

Access Control

Classes and namespaces may have some similarities, but they have nothing in common when it comes to access control. Classes provide excellent access control via the **public**, **protected**, and **private** keywords. Namespaces, on the other hand, do not provide any real access control. Consider the following example to illustrate.

Example 10-3
Controlling access in a namespace

```
% package require Itcl
3.0
% namespace eval Restricted {
    variable password isaiah119
    proc fire {} {puts "Bombs away!"}
    ::itcl::class SecretWeapon {
      constructor {} {puts "Created SecretWeapon object, $this"}
    }
  }
```

This example creates a namespace called Restricted that contains a variable, a procedure, and a class. The name of this namespace certainly does not refer to a restricted level of access because as you learned in the previous section, you can always access namespace variables and commands with fully qualified names. Just precede the variable or command name with the namespace name and a double colon. As a result, namespaces have no concept of formal access control like classes. All data is in a sense public. This is proven with the following commands:

```
% Restricted::SecretWeapon #auto
Created SecretWeapon object, ::secretWeapon0
secretWeapon0
% Restricted::fire
Bombs away!
% set Restricted::password
isaiah119
```

You can manually control access to namespace variables with the **trace** command, but there is no simple way to restrict access to procedures or classes. Namespaces were obviously not designed to provide access control like classes, so you shouldn't be concerned with this. The purpose of a namespace is simply to organize, like shelves in a cabinet, for creating packages.

Namespaces do, however, provide a sort of access control via an import/export mechanism that simply removes the restriction of having to use fully qualified names to access internal commands. You make procedures or classes externally visible by using the **namespace export** command inside the namespace and outside any procedures, classes, or other nested namespaces within that namespace. (Note that you cannot export variable names, only valid commands such as the names of procedures and classes.) Users of the namespace can then import these designated commands with the **namespace import** command into their own namespaces to make access easier.

Namespaces are dynamic; you can add and remove commands and variables at any time with the **namespace eval** command. Restricted may be directly modified because of this to export its procedure and class name as illustrated in the following example.

Example 10-4
Dynamically
modifying a
namespace
to export
commands

```
% namespace eval Restricted {
     namespace export fire SecretWeapon
  }
% fire
invalid command name "fire"
% namespace import Restricted::fire
% fire
Bombs away!
```

Once **fire** is given visibility to the "outside world" via the **namespace export** command, you can invoke it from within any other namespace after you import it first. If you forget this important step, you'll get an error message as shown in the example.

If you want to gain access to all possible exported commands from within a namespace, you can use glob-style syntax, as the following example illustrates.

Example 10-5
Use glob-style syntax to import or export all namespace commands

```
% SecretWeapon #auto
invalid command name "SecretWeapon"   ← Hasn't yet been imported.
% namespace forget Restricted::fire   ← Forget since already imported.
% namespace import Restricted::*   ← Glob-style syntax imports all
% SecretWeapon #auto
Created SecretWeapon object, ::secretWeapon1
secretWeapon1
```

Since the **fire** procedure had already been imported, note that the **namespace forget** command is used in this example to remove it from the list of imported commands to avoid a "command already exists" error when using the glob-style syntax. Regardless of this import/export mechanism, remember that you can always use fully qualified command names instead. This mechanism is just a convenient way to avoid having to use potentially long access names.

Now notice the actual name of the SecretWeapon object you just created, **::secretWeapon1**. You might wonder why it isn't named **::Restricted::secretWeapon1** instead. This is because even though the class definition is inside a namespace, you instantiated the class on the command line, which is at the global scope. When an object is created, its access command is added to the current namespace context. Were you to instantiate the object inside Restricted instead, the resulting name would indeed be **::Restricted::secretWeapon1**. This can lead to some scoping problems that are discussed in the next section.

A good example of this export/import mechanism can be seen with the [incr Tcl] namespace. [incr Tcl] has one main namespace called ::itcl. To avoid having to precede each command defined within this namespace with ::itcl, you can import all exported commands into the global namespace as you just learned with the **namespace import** command.

Example 10-6
Import ::itcl commands to avoid using fully qualified command names

```
% package require Itcl
3.0
% class Widget {}
invalid command name "class"
% namespace import ::itcl::*
% class Widget {}
%
```

10

You can now use simple command names such as **class**, **delete**, and **scope** instead of having to use fully qualified names. This is not recommended, however. It's best to continue to use fully qualified names for readability and maintenance. Fully qualified names quickly clarify where a command is defined. Even though both **itclsh** and **itkwish** automatically import all package-specific commands into the global namespace, you should continue using fully qualified names for clarity and portability. If you deliver your [incr Tcl] code strewn with simple command names to a customer, for example, expecting the customer to continue using an [incr Tcl] shell, a **wish** shell may be used instead. The code would only work in such a case if the customer explicitly added the **namespace import** command as shown in the previous example, and it's not a good idea to place requirements like this on your code.

From One Namespace to Another

In the previous section, you learned that an object's access command is added to the namespace context in which it is created. This can cause problems when an object is created in one namespace and used in another. The following sections show you some pitfalls and how you can avoid them by using proper scoping techniques.

Object Visibility

Suppose you have two namespaces, FurnitureStore and Manufacturer. FurnitureStore preorders items from Manufacturer for a test trial run before agreeing to purchase them for resale to the general public. The FurnitureStore namespace is implemented as follows:

```
namespace eval FurnitureStore {
  proc preOrder {} {
    set lamp [Manufacturer::livingRoom lamp]
    if {[catch {$lamp turnOn} err]} {
      puts "Lamp test failed: $err"
    } else {
      puts "Lamp test passed!"
    }
  }
  proc buy {quantity_} {}
  proc sell {} {}
}
```

This namespace groups three related procedures: **preOrder**, **buy**, and **sell**. The body of **preOrder** is shown. The other two procedure bodies are unneeded for this example; they are prototyped as future possibilities. You can see that **preOrder** is interested in testing out a lamp. It contacts Manufacturer's living room department to preorder one. Then it tries to turn on the lamp as a simple test. Now take a look at the Manufacturer namespace (note that there is an intentional error present to show you a common problem to avoid).

```
namespace eval Manufacturer {
  package require Itcl

  itcl::class Lamp {
    public method turnOn  {} {puts "on"}
    public method turnOff {} {puts "off"}
  }
  itcl::class EndTable {}
  itcl::class Couch {}

  proc livingRoom {which_} {
    switch -- $which_ {
      lamp      {return [Lamp #auto]}
      endTable  {return [EndTable #auto]}
      couch     {return [Couch #auto]}
      default   {return "We don't sell that."}
    }
  }
}
```

This namespace bundles three [incr Tcl] classes and one procedure. It's very important to note the use of the **package require** command here. Since Manufacturer uses [incr Tcl] commands, it should load the Itcl package itself!

TIP: As a general rule of thumb, a namespace should always load any packages it needs. You should never require your customers to load a package that you could have loaded yourself. It's not good programming practice to deliver a product that doesn't work "out of the box."

Continuing with FurnitureStore, the **livingRoom** procedure expects a single argument to determine which piece of living room furniture is being ordered. Notice that each of the three cases returns the result of the corresponding class instantiation. Now let's test this code in a **tclsh** shell. Similar to the filenaming convention for classes, files containing namespaces will be the same name as the namespace plus the extension ns. You can place each namespace definition in an appropriately named file and type the following commands, or you can just follow along (note that the code is also available online):

```
% source FurnitureStore.ns
% source Manufacturer.ns
% ::FurnitureStore::preOrder
Lamp test failed: invalid command name "lamp0"
```

This failed because FurnitureStore is trying to use the simple name of an object created in another namespace. Now try using a fully qualified name instead of the simple one. You can modify FurnitureStore on the command line to try it (remember that namespaces can be modified dynamically).

Example 10-7
Use fully qualified names to access objects in other namespaces

```
% namespace eval FurnitureStore {
      proc preOrder {} {
         set lamp Manufacturer::[Manufacturer::livingRoom lamp]
         if {[catch {$lamp turnOn} err]} {
            puts "Lamp test failed: $err"
         } else {
            puts "Lamp test passed!"
         }
      }
   }
% ::FurnitureStore::preOrder
on
Lamp test passed!
```

Using the fully qualified name does work, but this is not the correct solution. You are not guaranteed that the object does indeed get created directly inside of Manufacturer. It could have been created inside another class or namespace nested in Manufacturer. So instead of forcing the user of the namespace to determine the fully qualified name, it would be better if the Manufacturer namespace itself wrapped the object name with the proper context before returning. This way the object is returned ready to use.

To accomplish this, simply use the **namespace current** command. This command returns the fully qualified name of the current namespace. Let's delete the FurnitureStore namespace to undo the **preOrder** modification and then add the **namespace current** command to Manufacturer's **livingRoom** procedure as follows:

```
% namespace delete FurnitureStore
% source FurnitureStore.ns
```

```
% namespace eval Manufacturer {
    proc livingRoom {which_} {
        switch -- $which_ {
            lamp     {return [namespace current]::[Lamp #auto]}
            endTable {return [namespace current]::[EndTable #auto]}
            couch    {return [namespace current]::[Couch #auto]}
            default  {return "We don't sell that."}
        }
    }
}
% ::FurnitureStore::preOrder
on
Lamp test passed!
```

As you can see, this method also works and is much cleaner than the first approach. You should always use the **namespace current** command when returning object names from a namespace.

If you're a seasoned [incr Tcl] programmer, you might have instead thought about using the **scope** command. Chapter 3 shows you how to use **scope** to wrap the proper namespace context around class data members so that they can be accessed outside the class scope. You might have thought about doing the same thing for the object name in this example. The key thing to remember about **scope** is that it is used for wrapping class data members or namespace variables. It is *not* intended to wrap object names. You can use it in this way, but the access code becomes very difficult to read and understand. Consider the following example to illustrate.

Example 10-8
Using **scope** to wrap object names leads to code that is difficult to read

```
% namespace eval Ns {
    package require Itcl
    variable obj
    ::itcl::class C {}
    proc go {} {
        variable obj
        set obj [C #auto]
        return [::itcl::scope obj]
    }
}
```

10

The first thing you have to remember is that the **scope** command requires the designated variable to be a valid namespace variable. In other words, you cannot do something like this:

```
return [itcl::code [C #auto]]
```

If you do this, you will get an error message complaining about the object name's not being found in the current namespace. As a result, you first have to save the object name in a valid namespace variable. In this example, the *obj* variable is used. Now try invoking the **go** procedure.

```
% set handle [::Ns::go]
::Ns::obj
% $handle isa C
invalid command name "::Ns::obj"
```

The **scope** command correctly wraps the proper namespace context around the variable name similar to the **namespace current** command; however, it's the variable name that gets wrapped, not the object name. Be aware of this possible pitfall. The variable is just a container for the real object name. In order to access the object name, you have to place a dollar sign in front of the fully qualified name and then fully qualify that name as well. But since this name is stored in the *handle* variable, accessing the object is even messier. The following two commands show you how to access the object name through the *handle* variable and then directly through the namespace.

```
% ::Ns::[set [set handle]] info heritage
::Ns::C
% ::Ns::$::Ns::obj info heritage
::Ns::C
```

Using **scope** may have seemed like a good idea at first, but as you can see, users of the Ns namespace will have a difficult time trying to extract the object name from the returned string.

REMEMBER: Use the **namespace current** command to wrap the proper context around an object name that is returned from a namespace.

Variable Visibility

You learned that you shouldn't use **scope** to access objects in the previous section. You *should* use **scope**, however, for variable access. Consider the following namespace used to display Tk radio button widgets.

Example 10-9
This namespace
uses **scope** to
update radio
button states
correctly

```
namespace eval Radiobox {
    package require Itcl

    variable value
    variable numButtons 0
    variable container
    variable separator

    proc selected {} {
        variable value
        return $value
    }

    proc add {text_} {
        variable value
        variable numButtons
        variable container
        variable separator

        incr numButtons
        pack [radiobutton $container.r$numButtons -text $text_ \
            -variable [itcl::scope value] -value $numButtons] \
            -before $separator
    }

    proc create {container_} {
        variable container
        variable separator

        set container $container_
        set outer [frame $container.rboxFrame]
        set separator \
            [frame $container.sep -height 4 -bd 2 -relief sunken]
        set ok [button $container.ok -text OK -width 8]
        set cancel [button $container.cancel -text Cancel -width 8]
        set space [frame $container.padding -height 10]
        pack $separator -fill x -pady 12
        pack $space -side bottom
        pack $ok $cancel -side left -expand 1 -ipadx 4 -ipady 4 -padx 12
    }
}
```

10

Notice the use of the **scope** command in Radiobox's **add** procedure. Without it, clicking on one of the radio buttons would actually modify a global variable instead of the namespace variable. The use of **scope** here is the same as its use in Chapter 2. Always use **scope** to wrap the proper namespace context around a class data member or a namespace variable that must be accessed outside the scope in which it is defined. With the definition saved in Radiobox.ns, you can create a Radiobox to test the code in a **wish** shell.

```
% source Radiobox.ns
% Radiobox::create .
% for {set choice 1} {$choice <= 4} {incr choice} {
    Radiobox::add "Choice #$choice"
  }
```

The resulting window is shown next.

Four radio buttons are added to the Radiobox namespace via its **add** procedure. In order to properly select the radio buttons, each one is configured with a different value for its –value configuration option. Additionally, each one is tied to the namespace variable, *value*, which gets updated with the corresponding radio button number when you select it. Go ahead and click on Choice #3 and then ask the namespace which button is selected as follows:

```
% Radiobox::selected
3
```

The correct value, 3, is returned. Now manually set Radiobox's *value* variable and see what happens.

```
% set Radiobox::value 1
1
```

The first radio button, Choice #1, is selected as expected. This is the key to how the Radiobox works. Each radio button is tied to a common namespace variable. Clicking a radio button modifies this variable, and modifying the variable likewise updates the radio buttons. If this sounds familiar to you, then you may already know about the radiobox [incr Widget]. All [incr Widgets] are discussed in detail in Part III, and mega-widgets in general are discussed thoroughly in the next few chapters. The concept behind making the Radiobox namespace and the radiobox [incr Widget] work correctly is the same.

Creating a Package

As mentioned earlier in the chapter, namespaces are used to bundle related variables, procedures, and classes to create packages. Packages can be loaded dynamically as needed in your application. The Itcl package is loaded in numerous examples throughout this book, so loading a package probably won't be new to you. This section focuses on package creation, starting with the implementation of a simple namespace.

Implementing the Namespace

Let's define a namespace to group different types of data structures. A linked list is provided for you. You can add other structures such as a stack or a circular queue as an exercise if desired. The implementation for this namespace is as follows:

```
namespace eval DataStructures {
  package require Itcl

  # Use this procedure to instantiate the corresponding class.
  proc create {what_} {
    switch -- $what_ {
      linkedlist    {
        return [namespace current]::[LinkedList #auto]
      }
      tree          {}
      circularqueue {}
      stack         {}
    }
  }

  # LinkedList Class Definition
  itcl::class LinkedList {
    public method add {data_}
    public method delete {data_}
```

10

```
    public method exists {data_}
    public method isEmpty {} {return [expr 0 == [llength $_nodes]]}
    public method print {}

    private variable _nodes ""
}

# Node Class Definition
itcl::class Node {
  constructor {data_} {set _data $data_}

  public method get {} {return $_data}
  public method next {} {return $_next}
  public method prev {} {return $_prev}
  public method hook {direction_ node_} {
    set _${direction_} $node_
  }

  private variable _data
  private variable _next 0
  private variable _prev 0
}

itcl::body LinkedList::add {data_} {
  set newLink [DataStructures::Node #auto $data_]
  if ![llength $_nodes] {
    lappend _nodes $newLink
    return
  }

  set tail [lindex $_nodes end]
  $tail hook next $newLink
  $newLink hook prev $tail
  lappend _nodes $newLink
  return
}

itcl::body LinkedList::delete {data_} {
  foreach node $_nodes {
    if {[$node get] == $data_} {
      set next [$node next]
      set prev [$node prev]
      if {$next != "0"} {
        $next hook prev $prev
      }
      if {$prev != "0"} {
```

```
            $prev hook next $next
         }
         itcl::delete object $node
         set index [lsearch $_nodes $node]
         set _nodes [lreplace $_nodes $index $index]
       }
     }
   }

   itcl::body LinkedList::exists {data_} {
     foreach node $_nodes {
       if {[$node get] == $data_} {
         return 1
       }
     }
     return 0
   }

   itcl::body LinkedList::print {} {
     foreach node $_nodes {
       puts -nonewline "[$node get] "
     }
     puts ""
   }
}
```

This namespace first loads the Itcl package as discussed earlier. Then, two classes are defined to create a linked list: LinkedList and Node. You're probably already quite familiar with this popular structure, so the implementation details won't be discussed here. The only difference between DataStructures and other namespace examples in this chapter is the implementation of class method bodies outside the class definition. This is perfectly acceptable, and is in fact recommended rather than inlining so much code inside the class definition. This code is available online, as shown here in the file DataStructures.ns. The following commands can be used to test this code:

10

```
% source DataStructures.ns
% set mylist [DataStructures::create linkedlist]
::DataStructures::linkedList0
% foreach letter "i n c r T c l" {
    $mylist add $letter
  }
% $mylist print
i n c r T c l
```

A diagram depicting the resulting data structure is shown in Figure 10-1. Seven Node objects are created—one for each of the designated letters. Each Node object contains a pointer to the next one in line as well as a pointer to the previous one. This type of structure is actually called a doubly linked list since it can be traversed in both directions. Two Node objects in the middle of the diagram are enlarged to provide greater detail. Now that the implementation of the namespace is complete, you're ready to continue with the next step in the package creation process.

Setting Up the Package

Once you have a namespace with which to create a package, setting up the package involves a few simple steps. Each step is outlined in the following sections.

Step 1: Create the Directory Structure

You first need to create a new directory structure to store the DataStructures namespace and related files. Use the name ds as an abbreviation for the namespace name and create a directory called ds1.0. The 1.0 will be the version number of the DataStructures package. If you add another type of

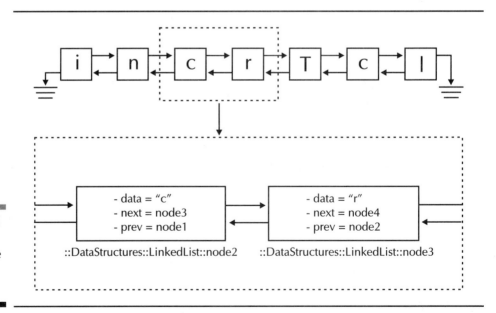

Doubly linked list consisting of seven Node objects

Figure 10-1.

data structure later, such as a circular queue, then you can increment the version number as desired. Underneath ds1.0, create a directory called src to contain the namespace source code. Now copy the file DataStructures.ns, which contains the source code, to the src directory. (Note that this is already done for you in the online code.) Then change directories to src and use the **auto_mkindex** command as follows to create a tclIndex file from DataStructures.ns (use an **itclsh** shell):

```
% auto_mkindex . DataStructures.ns
```

Later when you load the package, the directory containing the resulting tclIndex file will be appended to your *auto_path*. As a result, you will be able to use the DataStructures namespace name immediately because of the autoloading facility. You'll see how this works in the next section.

Step 2: Create Special Files

Next, you need to create two special-purpose files for package initialization. The first file must be called pkgIndex.tcl. Create a new file in the ds1.0 directory with this name. Both the name and location of this file are very important, as you'll see a little later. Now edit the file and add the following line:

```
package ifneeded DS 1.0 [list source [file join $dir ds.tcl]]
```

The **package ifneeded** command indicates in this example that a package named DS, version 1.0, is available to the interpreter if needed and that the interpreter may execute the designated command to load the package. Now let's investigate this designated command.

10

First, ds.tcl is the name of the other special file that you will create later in this section. Next, the *dir* variable following the **file join** command contains the directory name in which the pkgIndex.tcl file is located. This variable is automatically initialized by the interpreter according to the *auto_path* global variable. When you use the **package require** command to load a package, the interpreter searches each directory designated in the *auto_path* variable for files named pkgIndex.tcl. It then parses through each of these files until it finds an appropriate initialization line for the requested package name. In this case, the pkgIndex.tcl file is located in the ds1.0 directory, so the *dir* variable will contain this directory name. The **file join** command adds ds.tcl to this directory, passing the result to the **source** command. It follows that you must create a file called ds.tcl in the ds1.0 directory.

The purpose of ds.tcl is typically to set up autoloading for the commands in the package. It can also be used for dynamic loading of a shared library. You already created the tclIndex file, so all ds.tcl needs to do to set up autoloading is append the src directory to the *auto_path* variable. Edit this new file and add the following lines:

```
package provide DS 1.0
set dirname [file dirname [info script]]
lappend auto_path [file join $dirname src]
```

The **package provide** command tells the interpreter that version 1.0 of package DS is available. Notice that both the package name and the version number match the name and version from the corresponding **package ifneeded** command in the pkgIndex.tcl file. The **info script** command on the next line returns the name of the script currently being evaluated. In this case, it's the name of the current file, ds.tcl. The **file dirname** command is then used to determine the directory in which this file exists. Next, the **file join** command concatenates the src directory to this directory name. This is why you needed to create the src directory directly underneath the ds1.0 directory. And finally, the src directory is appended to the *auto_path* variable. Autoloading is now set up, so when the DS package is loaded, you can immediately create a linked list. The resulting directory structure is shown in Figure 10-2.

Step 3: Install the Package

The last step is to install the package directory so that it will be automatically located by the interpreter when you use the **package require** command to load it. This is done for convenience. You can actually install the package directory anywhere and append the containing directory to your *auto_path* variable. To determine a directory in which the interpreter will automatically search for a subdirectory containing a pkgIndex.tcl file, you have two choices. First, you can just check the default *auto_path* variable. On a Unix system, you can use the **file dirname** command to do this as illustrated in the following example.

Example 10-10
Using the
auto_path to
determine a
package installa-
tion directory

```
% foreach dir $auto_path {
      puts "Valid installation directory: [file dirname $dir]"
  }
Valid installation directory: /usr/lib
Valid installation directory: /usr
```

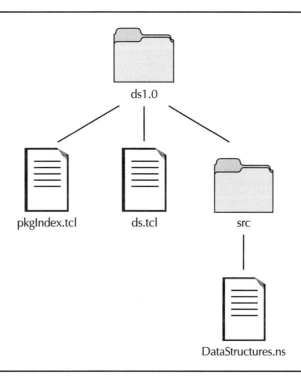

On a Windows system, you can use the **file attributes** command with the
–longname option to print the full pathname of the directories. Results may
be similar to the following:

```
% foreach dir $auto_path {
    puts "Valid installation directory: \
      [file attributes [file dirname $dir] -longname]"
  }
Valid installation directory: C:/Program Files/Tcl/lib
Valid installation directory: C:/Program Files/Tcl/lib/tcl8.0
Valid installation directory: C:/Program Files/Tcl/lib/tk8.0
```

The results indicate that there are two directories on the Unix platform and
three directories on the Windows platform in which the ds1.0 directory can
be copied to install the package.

Your second choice is to use the **info library** command, which returns the name of the directory in which standard Tcl scripts are stored. It is also part of the default *auto_path* variable. Possible locations for both Unix and Windows platforms are shown in the following example.

Example 10-11
Using **info library** to determine a package installation directory

```
% file dirname [info library]
/usr/lib

% file attributes [file dirname [info library]] -longname
C:/Program Files/Tcl/lib
```

Determine where to install your package directory based on one of these choices. (Note that it's easiest to install the package in a directory in which the interpreter will automatically look. Otherwise, you will have to manually modify your *auto_path*.) Then copy the ds1.0 directory to that selected installation directory. After you do this, you can load the DS package in a vanilla **tclsh** shell with the **package require** command as follows:

```
% package require DS
1.0
% set ll [::DataStructures::create linkedlist]
::DataStructures::linkedList0
% $ll add "It worked!"
% $ll print
It worked!
```

That's it! You've just successfully built and installed a portable package of [incr Tcl] classes. You should now be able to use this section as a template for wrapping your classes in a namespace and creating a portable package that can be delivered to your customers.

This chapter marks the end of Part I, the [incr Tcl] portion of this book. The next few chapters comprise Part II, which is devoted to [incr Tk]. In these chapters, you'll learn how to use [incr Tk] base classes to build complex widgets, called mega-widgets, that can be treated like regular Tk widgets.

PART II

[incr Tk]

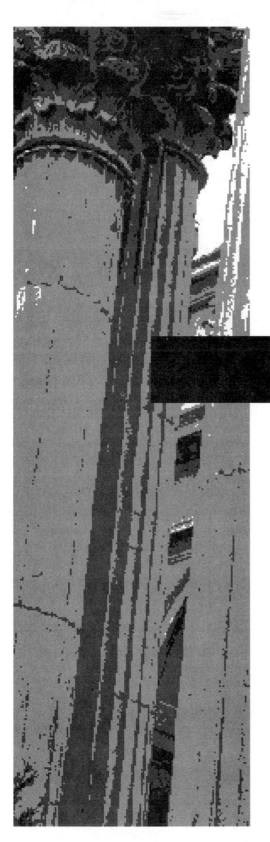

CHAPTER 11

Mega-Widget Basics

This chapter provides a high-level overview of [incr Tk] and mega-widgets. You will learn about the [incr Tk] base class hierarchy and all the available methods, data members, and configuration options you should be aware of when defining new mega-widgets. You will see how easy it is to create a new widget without having to do any C or X library programming. This will save you considerable development time by allowing you to create complex graphical applications in far fewer lines of code than straight Tcl/Tk. The resulting code is also much easier to maintain and troubleshoot. You'll also find out when you should use [incr Tk] to create new mega-widgets and when you should just use regular [incr Tcl] classes. By the end of this chapter, you will have the fundamentals necessary to define more complex mega-widgets and take advantage of the extensive configuration option utilities discussed in the next chapter.

Introduction

[incr Tcl] is an extension to Tcl that provides object-oriented facilities, allowing you to build large-scale applications that are easier to manage and maintain than equivalent applications written in straight Tcl. Tk is also an extension to Tcl, providing a convenient layer of abstraction between the programmer and low-level X library calls. Tk allows you to build graphical applications quickly and efficiently through a set of standard, easy-to-use widgets. As extensions, both Tk and [incr Tcl] cannot be used without Tcl.

[incr Tk] can be thought of as an extension to both [incr Tcl] and Tk. It uses the object-oriented facilities built into [incr Tcl] to further extend the Tk standard widget set, allowing you to create new widgets by gluing together multiple Tk widgets into a single class definition or class hierarchy. Refer to Figure 11-1 to see how [incr Tk] fits into the [incr Tcl] "protocol" stack. The Tcl C API is the bottom layer. Chapter 9 shows you how to use many of the API functions. Tcl sits on top of this layer, providing convenient access to C functions through a set of simple, intuitive scripting commands. [incr Tcl] and Tk are both specialized extensions that plug into the Tcl layer. [incr Tk] then plugs into both [incr Tcl] and Tk. And finally, the [incr Widgets] package, which is discussed later in the chapter and covered in-depth in Part III, sits on top of the stack, plugging into [incr Tk].

As previously mentioned, [incr Tk] allows you to glue multiple Tk widgets together to form new widgets. This unique ability is the key strength of [incr Tk] because it allows you to build new widgets completely at the scripting level. Therefore, you don't have to be a C programmer or understand any X library utilities. If you do have experience creating new widgets in C, you'll

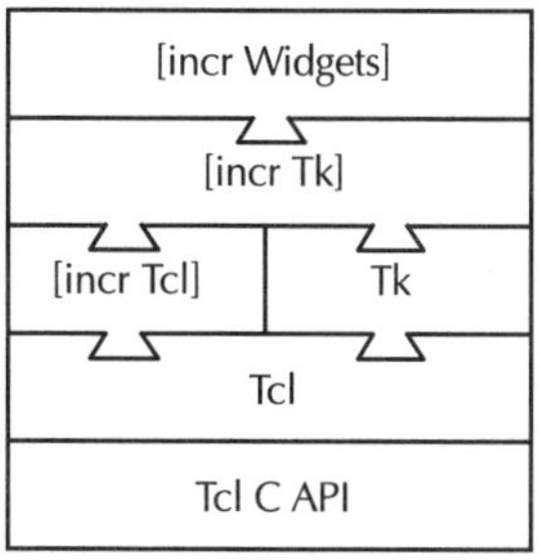

The [incr Tcl]
protocol stack
Figure 11-1.

develop an even greater appreciation for [incr Tk]. The only restriction is that these new widgets must be combinations of standard Tk widgets. You will find, however, that this restriction will not hinder your ability to take full advantage of [incr Tk] to make your graphical applications easier to build and easier to maintain. On the contrary, it is a great convenience. The following section discusses this further and provides a simple example to show you how useful [incr Tk] can be during development.

What Is a Mega-Widget?

A mega-widget is an [incr Tk] class that generally groups two or more widgets together to create a brand new widget. Mega-widgets may consist of standard Tk widgets only or a combination of Tk widgets and other mega-widgets. Despite their potential complexity, they can still be treated just like regular Tk widgets. This is what makes mega-widgets so attractive to developers. A developer familiar with Tk can use mega-widgets without having to know [incr Tcl/Tk] and with a minimal knowledge of object-oriented methodologies. Mega-widgets have configuration options just like Tk widgets, and they are usually placed into frames or windows with familiar geometry management commands like **pack** or **grid**. Since they are actually classes, they can further extend Tk by providing additional features and functionality through public methods, encapsulating any complexity under the hood. Furthermore, mega-widgets can be used in inheritance hierarchies. This means you can define a base class to provide a generic framework or structure that can be extended by derived classes. Several of the scrollable mega-widgets in the Iwidgets package use such an inheritance hierarchy.

Mega-widgets allow you to create complex graphical screens literally in minutes, instead of hours, by considerably decreasing the amount of code

11

you have to write. After a mega-widget is defined, it can be reused across multiple applications just like a Tk widget. This saves you from having to rewrite code to define groups of Tk widgets that aren't available in the standard Tk widget set. Let's begin with a simple example. How many times have you had to create your own scrollable listbox because Tk does not provide one? Scrollable listboxes are commonly used in today's graphical applications, and each time you need one in Tk, you have to create it yourself. The following example does this in a **wish** shell with standard Tk commands.

Example 11-1
Creating a
scrollable
listbox in Tk

```
% listbox .l -xscrollcommand {.hsb set} -yscrollcommand {.vsb set}
.l
% scrollbar .hsb -orient horizontal -command {.l xview}
.hsb
% scrollbar .vsb -command {.l yview}
.vsb
% grid .l .vsb -sticky nsew
% grid .hsb -column 0 -sticky ew
% grid columnconfigure . 0 -weight 1
% grid rowconfigure . 0 -weight 1
```

Using **grid** to place the widgets in the root window, it takes seven lines of code to create the scrollable listbox shown in Figure 11-2, not including the text that is displayed. You have to create the listbox and both scroll bars, and you probably have to spend some time looking up the syntax for tying them together. Then, you have to use a series of **grid** commands to properly pack the widgets into a window or frame. If you're a seasoned Tk programmer, you have probably written code similar to this many times. Wouldn't it be convenient if you never had to write it again? What if there were a scrollable listbox in the standard Tk widget set? You could then create this group of three widgets with a single command instead of seven. This is exactly what mega-widgets are intended to do, to provide the convenience of encapsulating multiple Tk widgets into a single interface that you can treat like a single widget.

You have probably already guessed that there *is* a standard scrollable listbox mega-widget. It's included in the Iwidgets package, which is part of the [incr Tcl] distribution. This package contains more than 50 standard mega-widgets, often referred to as [incr Widgets] or iwidgets. The scrollable listbox is defined in a class called Scrolledlistbox. To create an instance of this mega-widget, all you have to do is load the Iwidgets package and then type a *single* line of code. The following example shows you how to do this in a **wish** shell.

WISH80

This scrollable listbox is created in 7 lines of Tk code on the command line.

Creating a
scrollable
listbox in Tk
takes seven
lines of code

Figure 11-2.

Example 11-2
Creating a
scrollable listbox
using the
Iwidgets package

```
% package require Iwidgets
3.0.0
% pack [::iwidgets::Scrolledlistbox .sl -borderwidth 2] -fill both \
    -expand 1
```

First, note that the class name begins with an uppercase. This is nothing new
to you if you have read any of Part I. By convention, all [incr Tcl] and [incr
Tk] classes begin with an uppercase. However, since all Tk widgets begin with
a lowercase and since [incr Tk] models Tk in usage, you may also instantiate
each mega-widget in the Iwidgets package by specifying the class name with
an initial lowercase. Each of the [incr Widgets] includes a procedure that
allows you to do this. In the Scrolledlistbox class, for example, the following
procedure is provided:

```
proc ::iwidgets::scrolledlistbox {pathName args} {
    uplevel ::iwidgets::Scrolledlistbox $pathName $args
}
```

11

This procedure adds a new command in the iwidgets namespace that
allows you to instantiate Scrolledlistbox with an initial lowercase. For the
remainder of this book, all examples that instantiate mega-widgets will
follow this protocol.

Next, note that the first character of the specified object name begins with a dot. Just as you must begin all Tk widget names with a dot, you must also begin all mega-widget instance names with a dot. If you don't, you can expect an error message, as shown in the following example.

```
% ::iwidgets::scrolledlistbox nodot
bad window path name "nodot"
```

Since a scrolledlistbox is a widget, it must be preceded by a dot to follow the standard hierarchical Tk widget/window naming convention.

Now take a look at Figure 11-3, the result of the Scrolledlistbox instantiation from Example 11-2 with a bit of text added. As you can see, this figure looks very similar to Figure 11-2, the Tk example. Looks can be deceiving, though. On the outside, the scrolledlistbox appears to consist of a listbox and two scroll bars. It actually contains a label widget as well, plus several specialized configuration options and methods that provide a wide range of new functionality not present in its Tk counterpart from Example 11-1. Such specialized configuration options include –hscrollmode and –vscrollmode. These can be used to create a scrollable listbox that is smart enough to display its scrollbars only when they are needed. The following series of commands shows you how to do this. As with Tk configuration options, you can modify [incr Tk] configuration options dynamically with the built-in *configure* method as follows:

```
% .sl configure -hscrollmode dynamic -vscrollmode dynamic
```

Notice that both scroll bars disappear following this command. This is because they are currently not needed since there is no data being displayed. Now add some data with the following loop:

```
% for {set i 1} {$i <= 10} {incr i} {
    .sl insert end "Listbox entry #$i"
  }
```

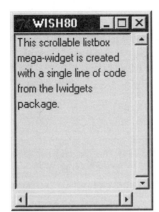

Creating a
scrollable
listbox in [incr
Tk] takes one
line of code

Figure 11-3.

The scroll bars are still not shown since all data can be fully displayed in
the default size of the window. If you add one more entry, however, watch
what happens:

```
% .sl insert 5 \
    "Both scrollbars are now drawn since this entry is so long!"
```

The data no longer fits into the viewable portion of the listbox after this last
entry is added. As a result, both scroll bars are drawn. (Note that if you
stretch the window so that all data is viewable, the scroll bars disappear
again.) Now type one more command as follows:

```
% .sl delete end
```

You'll notice this time that the vertical scroll bar disappears while the
horizontal one remains. Since you deleted the last entry, each of the other
entries can fit into the vertical viewable area, so the vertical scroll bar is no
longer needed. The long entry remains, so the horizontal scroll bar is still
needed. Figure 11-4 shows a succession of screen snapshots corresponding to
these previous commands.

11

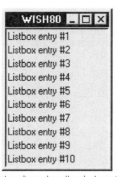 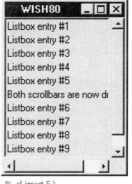 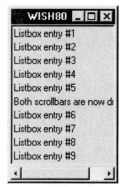

```
% .sl configure -hscrollmode dynamic \
    -vscrollmode dynamic
% for {set i 1  {$i <= 10} {incr i}{
    .sl insert end "Listbox entry #$i"
}
```

```
% .sl insert 5 \
  "Both scrollbars are now drawn
  since this entry is so long!"
```

```
% .sl delete end
```

Scroll bars that
come and go
as needed
Figure 11-4.

This is just one example of how you can use [incr Tk] to combine Tk widgets into useful and reusable new widgets to decrease development time and thus increase productivity. It's much easier to use a scrolledlistbox mega-widget than to build a scrollable listbox yourself. Further, the scrolledlistbox is much more powerful, providing several specialized configuration options, as shown in the previous example. Don't worry if you don't understand the details yet; this is just a high-level view. The remainder of this chapter goes into greater detail, starting with the following section on the [incr Tk] base classes.

Base Class Hierarchy

All [incr Tk] classes should inherit from one of two base classes, Toplevel or Widget. Each of these base classes in turn inherits from a common base class, Archetype. In order to understand how mega-widgets work and how to create new mega-widgets, you must be familiar with the available methods, data members, and configuration options defined in these base classes. The following sections provide this information, outlining each class.

Archetype

Archetype is the base class for all mega-widgets. Its main purpose is to provide the facilities necessary to maintain a list of composite configuration options. This is a list of configuration options that can be used to dynamically modify the mega-widget as a whole or one of its component widgets. Archetype also provides methods needed for mega-widget creation, as well as hooks for accessing internal widget components. Before discussing the details of this class, however, you may be interested in a bit of background first. In Chapter 9, you learned how to implement [incr Tcl] methods in C/C++ to make selected portions of your application run faster. Without the ability to do this, mega-widgets would not exist. Each of the eight methods defined in Archetype is actually implemented in C. Originally, they were implemented in [incr Tcl], but the resulting performance proved to be too much of a bottleneck to make [incr Tk] worthwhile. Michael McLennan then decided to move the code into C, and the speed improvement resulted in the [incr Tk] toolkit that is so widely used today.

Archetype provides three public interface methods as well as three protected methods that you can use when creating new mega-widgets. It also defines a configuration option common to all mega-widgets. This information is outlined in the following sections.

Public Methods
Archetype provides three public interface methods: *cget*, *configure*, and *component*. Each of these is outlined individually for the remainder of this section.

The cget Method   Archetype's *cget* method is very similar to the built-in method of the same name in [incr Tcl], which is used to retrieve the current values of public data members, also referred to as configuration options. Create an instance of Scrolledlistbox in a **wish** shell as follows and use *cget* to gather configuration option information:

```
% package require Iwidgets
3.0.0
% ::iwidgets::scrolledlistbox .sl -borderwidth 2
.sl
% pack .sl -fill both -expand 1
% .sl cget -hscrollmode
static
% .sl cget -visibleitems
20x10
```

11

With *cget*, you can quickly determine that the horizontal scroll bar mode (–hscrollmode) is static, which means it's always mapped, and the listbox is sized (–visibleitems) so that up to 10 entries, each up to 20 characters in length, are viewable without having to use scroll bars or resize the window.

The* configure *Method   This method is also similar to the built-in method of the same name in [incr Tcl]. It is used to query or modify configuration options. Without any arguments, *configure* returns a complete list of all mega-widget configuration options. Try the following commands to insert each scrolledlistbox option name and its current value into the listbox:

Example 11-4
Using ***configure***
to insert options
in the
scrolledlistbox

```
% set counter 1
1
% foreach option [.sl configure] {
    set name [lindex $option 0]
    set value [lindex $option end]
    .sl insert end "$counter) $name: \"$value\""
    incr counter
}
```

The resulting window is shown in Figure 11-5. (Note that this snapshot is taken on a Windows system. Some values will be different on Unix.) There are 38 scrolledlistbox configuration options, compared to 23 Tk listbox configuration options.

You may also pass a single argument to *configure*; it should be the name of a configuration option. A list of information is returned in the following format:

```
<option name> <resource name> <resource class> <def val> <curr val>
```

The <option name> is the actual name of the configuration option, which must begin with a – character. The <resource name> and <resource class> entries are discussed in the next chapter. The <def val> is the configuration option's default value, and the <curr val> is its current value. Type the following command to print information on the –borderwidth option:

```
% .sl configure –borderwidth
-borderwidth borderWidth BorderWidth 0 2
```

This tells you the widget's default borderwidth is zero pixels, and it is currently configured with a two-pixel border width. You should not use *configure* to obtain the widget's current value, even though it is part of the information available when you specify one argument like this. This method

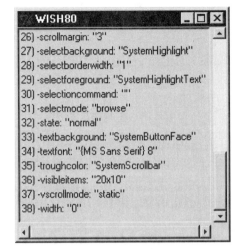

The scrolledlistbox mega-widget has 15 more configuration options than a Tk listbox

Figure 11-5.

is intended for option modification. Use *cget* to get the current option value; this is *cget*'s intended usage, and it is much faster than *configure*. If you need to determine other information such as the default option value, you should use *configure*.

The last usage of *configure* is when you specify multiple arguments, which should be pairs of configuration options and values, to dynamically modify a mega-widget. Type the following command to change the appearance of .sl:

```
% .sl configure -textbackground ghostwhite -cursor gumby \
    -textfont 9x15bold
```

The listbox component's background color is changed to ghostwhite, the mega-widget's cursor shape is changed to gumby, and the font of the text in the listbox is changed to 9x15bold.

11

The* component *Method   Unlike *cget* and *configure*, the *component* method does not resemble any built-in [incr Tcl] methods. The parameter list for *component* includes an optional parameter followed by **args**. The optional parameter is the symbolic name of an internal widget as registered with Archetype via the *itk_component* method. You'll see how this is done in the next section. The **args** parameter is used to accept a command fragment for modifying or querying an internal widget. Type the following command to determine the components of the scrolledlistbox:

```
% .sl component
label listbox horizsb hull vertsb
```

Without any arguments, *component* returns a list of all symbolic names for internal widget components. As expected, the scrolledlistbox has a label, a listbox, and two scroll bars (horizsb and versb). Additionally, it contains an outer frame (hull), which is common to all mega-widgets.

With a single argument, *component* returns the Tk window pathname of the argument, which should be the symbolic name of the component widget.

```
% .sl component horizsb
.sl.lwchildsite.horizsb
```

You can use *component* in this manner to determine the packing level of an internal widget. The horizontal scroll bar is embedded in a frame called .lwchildsite, which is in turn embedded in an outer frame called .sl.

Finally, you can use the *component* method to manipulate internal widgets without having to rely on Tk window pathnames. Suppose, for example, that you need to change the cursor shape of the listbox widget only. The scrolledlistbox has a top-level –cursor option, but it changes the cursor shape for the mega-widget as a whole, propagating the change to each of its internal component widgets. It does not have a configuration option that allows you to change the cursor shape of the listbox only, so you can pass a command fragment into *component*'s **args** parameter as follows:

```
% .sl component listbox configure –cursor clock
```

Now the cursor shape for the listbox component is modified without affecting the cursor shape for the rest of the mega-widget.

Usually, if you need to modify a mega-widget's appearance, top-level configuration options already exist for you. For instance, if you want to change the background color of the listbox, you can use the –textbackground configuration option. Sometimes, however, it's necessary to use the *component* method to manually modify individual internal widgets. If you're wondering why you can change the listbox's background color but not its cursor shape from the mega-widget level, this is a good question. The philosophy of determining new configuration options for mega-widgets is discussed in the next chapter.

Protected Methods

Archetype defines three protected methods for derived classes to use when implementing new mega-widgets: *itk_component*, *itk_option*, and *itk_initialize*. Each method is discussed similar to the public methods for the remainder of this section.

The itk_component *Method*   This method makes building mega-widgets possible. It allows you to piece them together by adding the individual components. The parameter list includes a single required argument followed by **args**. You can pass a variety of arguments into **args**, as shown by the following usage:

```
itk_component <add|delete> ?-protected|-private? ?--? <name> \
  <createCmds> ?<optionCmds>?
```

The first argument must be either add or delete. Use add to create component widgets and register them appropriately with Archetype. Use delete to deregister component widgets. Next, you may optionally specify either a protected or private access level. You can do this to hide component widgets from outside the class scope. These access levels are similar to the access levels associated with class data members. Hidden widgets like this may not be accessed publicly with the *component* method, as would normally be the case. If you specify the protected level, only the containing class and any derived classes have access to that component widget. Similarly, if you specify the private level, only the containing class has access to the widget.

Next, you may specify an optional double-dash. This is used to mark the end of the options. You would have to use this argument, for example, if the symbolic name of the widget specified by <name> begins with a dash. This is not recommended, however, and you will likely not need to use this argument. After the symbolic widget name, you must then specify one or more commands enclosed in braces for creating the component widget. Typically, you only need a single command to do this, but you can specify any number of commands as long as a valid Tk window pathname for the new widget is returned. The last argument is an optional set of commands that are used to describe how the widget's configuration options will be integrated into the composite configuration option list for the mega-widget.

11

The *itk_component* method is discussed in detail in the next chapter, but you can use Example 11-5 to answer any initial questions you may have about the method's usage.

Example 11-5
Using
itk_component
to add and
remove
component
widgets

```
(1) itk_component add -private -- secretLabel {
        label $itk_component(hull).secret
    }
(2) itk_component add -protected text {
        text $itk_component(outerFrame).text -background gray
    }
(3) itk_component add button {
        button $itk_component(buttonBox).b1 -text Apply \
            -command [code $this apply]
    }
(4) itk_component delete slider
```

The first example adds a private component widget with the symbolic name secretLabel to the mega-widget. The double-dash is optional and typically unused. The Tk window pathname of the label is the name of the mega-widget as stored in itk_component(hull) followed by .secret. (Don't be confused by the itk_component array. This array is a protected base class data member that happens to be named the same as the *itk_component* method. You'll learn more about this data member a little later in the chapter.) Once added, this component widget is only accessible inside the class in which it is created since the –private flag is specified.

The second example adds a protected component widget with the symbolic name text. Note that the symbolic name in this case is also a valid Tk keyword. It's common to use keywords for symbolic component widget names like this because it's intuitive to specify the type of widget with the *component* method when accessing the Tk window pathname of the component widget. This example creates a text widget with a gray background. Tk configuration options can be specified in the <createCmds> section of the *itk_component* invocation to initialize component widget attributes. Note that, similar to the secretLabel component in the first example, this widget is not publicly accessible. It can only be accessed within the class in which it is defined as well as within any derived class.

After the previous two examples, you should be able to understand the third on your own. It adds a new Tk button component widget to the mega-widget with the symbolic name button. The widget is created inside the containing widget (most likely a frame) stored in itk_component(buttonBox). The –text and –command configuration options are initialized in the <createCmds> section. Similar to both previous examples, the <optionCmds> section is unused. This section of the method prototype is discussed in detail in the next chapter.

The last example deregisters the component widget with the symbolic name slider from the mega-widget. The widget itself will actually still exist, but will no longer be accessible via the *component* method. Any configuration options associated with slider are also removed from the composite option list. To destroy component widgets, use the **destroy** command. This will deregister the widget *and* destroy it.

The* itk_initialize *Method   This method must be invoked in each class throughout a mega-widget's hierarchy. This is typically done in the *constructor*(s) and is already done for you in each of the [incr Tk] base class *constructor*s. The *itk_initialize* method is responsible for integrating all configuration options specified in the <optionCmds> section of the *itk_component* method invocation into the composite option list as well as setting all component options to initial values. You should invoke *itk_initialize* after all component widgets have been added. This is typically done near the end of the *constructor* body. Since this method handles configuration option management, you can learn more about it in the next chapter.

The* itk_option *Method   This method provides derived classes the ability to modify the composite option list. Use this method to manually add or remove configuration options to and from the composite option list or to create new specialized configuration options. Similar to *itk_initialize*, *itk_option* is also used for configuration option management and is therefore discussed further in the next chapter.

11

Protected Data Members
In addition to the six public and protected methods defined in Archetype, there are three protected data members that derived classes use when defining mega-widgets: itk_component, itk_interior, and itk_option. Notice

that itk_component and itk_option are named the same as Archetype methods you learned about in the previous section. To avoid confusion, method names are always italicized in this book. This convention should help you avoid any potential naming ambiguities.

The itk_component data member is an array indexed by the symbolic names you specify with the *itk_component* method when adding new component widgets. Each index in the array maps to the Tk window pathname of the component widget. Recall that you can retrieve this information by using the *component* method, but *component* is intended for use outside the scope of the class. Array access is much faster than a method invocation, so you should always use the itk_component array instead of the *component* method inside the class scope when accessing component widget Tk window pathnames.

The itk_interior data member stores the name of the Tk frame or top-level window that contains the component widgets. This is referred to as the mega-widget hull, which is created in the Widget and Toplevel classes. When you instantiate a mega-widget, the instance name is used as the pathname for the frame or top-level window. This is discussed further in upcoming sections on Widget and Toplevel.

The itk_option data member is also an array. It contains the current values for each of the mega-widget's configuration options. It is indexed by the configuration option name, including the preceding dash. Recall that you can use the *cget* method to get current configuration option values. Similar to *component*, *cget* is a public method and isn't intended to be used by derived classes. You should instead use the itk_option array when inside the class scope since array access is faster and more convenient to use than *cget*. The itk_option data member is discussed in more detail with other configuration option management methods and data members in the next chapter.

Configuration Options

Archetype adds a single configuration option called –clientdata to the composite option list. Since this option is defined in the bottommost base class, it is common to all mega-widgets. Though seldom used, –clientdata can be a convenient way to store bits of information in a mega-widget. If you are familiar with C or C++, think of this option as a void pointer—it can contain anything. This built-in facility can prove useful when you need to associate some data with a widget that cannot be stored in any other configuration option. Suppose, for example, that you have several scrolledlistbox mega-widgets that are identical except for the information saved in the listboxes themselves. To quickly and easily differentiate each scrolledlistbox instance, you can associate descriptive data by using the –clientdata configuration option. Consider the following example.

Example 11-6
Using –clientdata
to uniquely
identify identical
mega-widget
instances

```
% package require Iwidgets
3.0.0
% for {set i 1} {$i <= 5} {incr i} {
    ::iwidgets::scrolledlistbox .sl$i -clientdata "Listbox$i"
}
```

Five scrolledlistbox mega-widgets are created, and each one is identical except for the text saved in –clientdata. You could use this information to access a particular scrolledlistbox instead of relying on potentially long Tk window pathnames. When you define new mega-widgets, you could provide class data members that store information like this, but you should instead use the built-in –clientdata option since it's already available. When you use existing mega-widgets in the Iwidgets package, you don't have the option of defining class data members to store information that doesn't match existing configuration options since the classes are already defined. In this case, the –clientdata can be very useful to associate certain bits of information with each mega-widget instance.

Widget

The Widget class inherits from Archetype and creates a new Tk frame in its *constructor*. This frame is registered as a component widget called the hull. The *constructor* initializes Archetype's itk_interior data member to the Tk window pathname of the hull. The itk_interior data member and the hull component widget are one and the same. The only difference is accessibility. The itk_interior data member is protected, so it is only accessible by derived classes. The hull component is a part of the itk_component array, so it is publicly available via the *component* method. Derived classes can use itk_interior (or itk_component(hull)) to create specialized new mega-widgets by packing component widgets into the hull frame/window. Since Widget creates this outer container, mega-widgets that inherit from Widget can be packed into other frames or top-level windows. The Scrolledlistbox [incr Widget] from earlier in the chapter is an example of this.

11

Widget adds two configuration options to the composite option list maintained by Archetype: –background and –cursor. Any class that inherits from Widget automatically has these two options in addition to –clientdata from Archetype. Widget does not add any new methods or data members.

Toplevel

Whereas the Widget class is used to create mega-widgets that can be packed into frames and top-level windows, the Toplevel class is used to create mega-widgets that should remain independent from other windows, such as dialog boxes and other pop-up windows. Toplevel inherits from Archetype and creates a new top-level window in its *constructor* instead of a frame. Similar to Widget, this top-level window is registered as a component widget called the hull. The *constructor* initializes Archetype's itk_interior data member to the Tk window pathname of the hull. Derived classes can then create specialized top-level windows by packing component widgets into the hull.

Toplevel adds three configuration options to the composite option list maintained by Archetype: –cursor, –background, and –title. The first two options provide a way to modify the cursor shape or the background color for the mega-widget as a whole. The –title option is a widget-specific option used to modify the title of the window. This provides a convenient wrapper around the **wm title** command. Toplevel does not add any new methods or data members.

A Mega-Widget or Not a Mega-Widget?

That is the question. Programmers often wonder when you should create a new mega-widget and inherit from an [incr Tk] base class, and when you should just use a regular [incr Tcl] class. The simple answer is this: if a new class should be treated like a widget or a window and is generally generic enough to be application independent, then it should be an [incr Tk] mega-widget. The truth of the matter is that you can create any mega-widget without using [incr Tk]. This doesn't mean that you should, though. If you are going to create a dialog box hierarchy, for example, similar to the classes shown in Chapter 1, you could choose either [incr Tk] or [incr Tcl]. Since a dialog window is a top-level window that contains component widgets, it is a prime candidate for an [incr Tk] class that can take advantage of the many built-in facilities in the Itk package such as the composite configuration option list. Why reinvent the wheel and rewrite functionality that is already available in [incr Tk] base classes whose specific purpose it is to define methods and attributes for creating new mega-widgets? The answer, of course, is that you should take advantage of code that already exists when possible.

As with anything else, there are always exceptions. The [incr Tk] mega-widget framework provides a robust set of functionality for defining new mega-widgets. If you use [incr Tk], your application will run slower than if you use straight Tk in an [incr Tcl] framework. This is something that you must decide for yourself. If development time and future code maintenance aren't crucial, then [incr Tcl] and Tk may be your best option. For that matter, you could actually write the entire application in Tcl/Tk. However, the speed with which you can develop graphical applications by using [incr Tk], and in particular the Iwidgets package, is in itself a compelling argument for taking a bit of a performance hit. Furthermore, code size is much smaller and better organized with [incr Tk] than with Tk.

In general, [incr Tk] is an extremely useful package designed specifically for making it extremely easy to create complex graphical applications that are quickly developed and easily maintained. Moreover, [incr Tk] allows you to define self-contained widgets that are application independent. Just as you can use a Tk button in thousands of different applications, you can use a scrolledlistbox [incr Tk] mega-widget in just as many. As you read further in Part II, you'll understand this better, and as you study various [incr Widgets] in Part III, you'll most likely develop a great appreciation for [incr Tk].

Simple Example

Now that you're familiar with the [incr Tk] base classes, you should be ready to create a simple new mega-widget. An example might be a mega-widget that serves as the default button often used in dialog boxes and other pop-up windows. It would behave like a default button such that pressing the SPACEBAR or RETURN key anywhere in the window would be equivalent to clicking the button. Instead of having to worry about how to create the ring around the button or having to do this multiple times for multiple windows, users of this new mega-widget could simply instantiate it and pack it next to the other Tk buttons. Since this new class will be treated like a generic widget, it should be an [incr Tk] class instead of an [incr Tcl] class, as discussed in the previous section. Consider the following class definition for DefaultButton (This class is available online in the filename, DefaultButton.itk. Just as

11

[incr Tcl] classes use a .itcl filename extension, [incr Tk] classes use a .itk extension by convention.)

```
::itcl::class DefaultButton {
  inherit ::itk::Widget

  constructor {args} {}
  public method invoke {} {flash; $itk_component(button) invoke}
  private method flash {} {$itk_component(button) flash}
}

::itcl::body DefaultButton::constructor {args} {
  # Create the default ring around the button.
  itk_component add ring {
    frame $itk_interior.ring -relief sunken -bd 2
  }

  # Create the button inside the ring.
  itk_component add button {
    button $itk_component(ring).b
  } {
    # Add these options to the composite options list.
    keep -text -command
  }
  pack $itk_component(button) -ipadx 4 -ipady 2 -padx 4 -pady 3
  pack $itk_component(ring)

  # Invoke the button when the return key is pressed.
  bind [winfo toplevel $itk_interior] <Return> \
    "$itk_component(button) flash; $itk_component(button) invoke"

  # Always call itk_initialize after component widgets are added.
  eval itk_initialize $args
}
```

This class defines a new mega-widget that consists of two component widgets: a frame and a button. The frame is recessed, and the button is created inside of the frame. This synthesizes a ring around the button to signify the button as default. Notice that this class inherits from ::itk::Widget. The Widget class is defined in the itk namespace, so you need to specify Widget's fully qualified name when using it. By inheriting from Widget, you may pack DefaultButton instances into frames or top-level windows. It would not make any sense to inherit from Toplevel because a button is a widget, not a window. Now let's walk through the class *constructor* to see how component widgets are created.

Construction

Notice that the component widgets are created in a certain order, outermost widgets first. You must create the recessed frame before you can create the button, because the button must be placed inside the frame. The symbolic name for the frame is ring. You will be able to access the frame's Tk window pathname with the *component* method by specifying this symbolic name once an object is created, because no access level is specified. The frame is created inside itk_interior. Recall that the Widget class initializes this data member to a frame that it creates in its own *constructor*. So, DefaultButton is actually creating a frame inside a frame when it creates the ring component. You may wonder why you need to do this and why you can't just configure the hull component to look like the ring around the button. The reason is that the hull component only keeps the –cursor and –background configuration options of the frame. As a result, you can't configure the hull's –relief or –bd options, which are necessary for creating the ring, because these options are inaccessible. If you print out the available configuration options of the hull component, you will see a list of the following options:

```
{-background background Background SystemButtonFace SystemButtonFace}
{-clientdata clientData ClientData {} {}}
{-cursor cursor Cursor {} {}}
```

As you can see, there are only three options associated with the hull component, none of which include –relief or –bd.

Following creation of the ring, the button is created. Its symbolic name is simply button. As mentioned earlier, you can use keywords like this as symbolic names because these names are not used as commands; therefore, no naming conflicts can occur. Notice that the button is created inside the ring component by specifying the appropriate index of the itk_component array. Two of the button's configuration options are then added to the composite option list with the **keep** command. You'll learn more on how this works in the next chapter, but in a nutshell, this provides DefaultButton objects with –text and –command configuration options.

After component widget creation, a binding is set up such that pressing the RETURN key anywhere in the mega-widget's top-level window results in evaluation of the button component's –command configuration option. This option is defaulted to null, so if you don't initialize it, pressing the RETURN key will just cause the button to flash. Lastly, the *itk_initialize* method is invoked to properly initialize the composite option list. DefaultButton objects will have five configuration options: –clientdata from Archetype,

11

–background and –cursor from Widget, and –text and –command defined locally. Type the following commands in a **wish** shell to create an instance of DefaultButton (the code is available online):

```
% package require Itcl
3.0
% package require Itk
3.0
% source DefaultButton.itk
% DefaultButton .db -text "Press Me" -command {puts "Thanks!"}
.db
% pack .db
```

The DefaultButton object is constructed successfully and drawn in the root window, and the specified configuration options are initialized appropriately via the *itk_initialize* method. Use *cget* to verify that the options are correct as follows:

```
% .db cget -text
Press Me
% .db cget -command
puts "Thanks!"
```

Now you have a functional new mega-widget that was very simple to create. If you click the button or press the RETURN key anywhere in the root window, "Thanks!" is printed. You can change this behavior simply by changing the –command configuration option with the *configure* method as follows:

```
% .db configure -command {wm withdraw .}
```

Pressing the button or hitting the RETURN key now causes the root window to be withdrawn. You see how simple it is to modify the mega-widget once it's created. It's treated just like a regular Tk widget. If you also wanted the SPACEBAR to invoke the default button, you could use a widget operation as described in the next section.

Widget Operations

Widget operations are just ordinary method calls. DefaultButton defines one public method, *invoke*. This allows you to tell DefaultButton objects when to invoke themselves if, for instance, you wanted to use the SPACEBAR as the hot key instead of the RETURN key. When the *invoke* method is called, the button component's –command configuration option is evaluated. Type the following commands to illustrate:

```
% proc checkKeyPress {symbol_ key_} {
    if {$symbol_ == $key_} {
      return 1
    }
    return 0
  }
% bind . <KeyPress> {
    if [checkKeyPress %K space] {
      .db invoke
    }
  }
```

The **bind** command is used to create a new binding on the root window. Whenever a <KeyPress> event is detected, the **checkKeyPress** procedure is called to determine if the key that was pressed was the SPACEBAR. If so, the DefaultButton object's *invoke* method is executed.

As you can see, you can treat mega-widgets not only like regular Tk widgets but also like [incr Tcl] objects. The only difference on the outside between the object name and an [incr Tcl] object name is that mega-widgets must begin with a dot. Next, you need to understand mega-widget destruction.

Destruction

When a mega-widget's hull is destroyed, the corresponding object is deleted automatically. This is because both the Widget and Toplevel class *constructors* create a binding on the hull as follows:

```
bind itk-delete-$itk_hull <Destroy> "itcl::delete object $this"
```

11

The new binding tag, itk-delete-$itk_hull, is prepended to the bindtags list. This causes the specified command fragment to be executed when a <Destroy> event is detected, resulting in object destruction. The derived class *destructor* is invoked first, followed by Widget or Toplevel, followed by Archetype.

Since the hull is actually either a Tk frame or top-level window, all component widgets are also destroyed automatically. This makes cleanup very easy. All you have to do is use the **destroy** command, just like destroying a regular Tk widget.

```
% destroy .db
```

That's all there is to it! Figure 11-6 shows an informational dialog box that uses the DefaultButton. The code for this screen is available online. You now know the mega-widget basics: how to define a simple mega-widget and inherit from the appropriate [incr Tk] base class, how component widgets are created during object construction, how to use widget operations, and how mega-widget destruction works. This chapter gave you an overview of mega-widgets and the [incr Tk] base class hierarchy. The next chapter provides much more detailed information on mega-widget definition and implementation through a thorough discussion of configuration options.

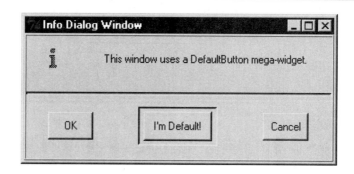

A message
dialog box
that uses a
DefaultButton
mega-widget

Figure 11-6.

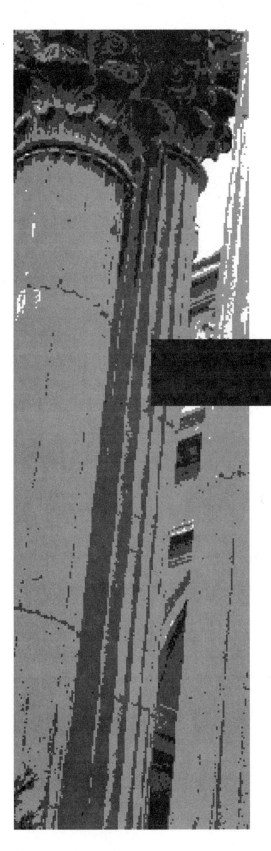

CHAPTER 12

Configuration
Options

This chapter focuses on mega-widget configuration. You first learn about the master list of mega-widget configuration options called the composite option list. Next, you learn how to control the content of this list by keeping, ignoring, and renaming component widget configuration options as each component is added to the mega-widget. You also learn how to define brand new configuration options and how to add and remove options to and from base class component widgets. Lastly, you learn how to set mega-widget default values with the options database. Simple examples help you to understand the concepts throughout the initial discussions, and a more robust example is provided near the end of the chapter. At the end of this chapter, you'll better understand how mega-widgets work and how you can take advantage of configuration options to group component widgets together as single units for better, more streamlined code.

The Composite Option List

All Tk widgets have a set of configuration options that can be used to modify their appearance, state, or behavior. Mega-widgets also have a set of configuration options called the composite option list. One difference between Tk configuration options and mega-widget configuration options is that Tk options are static; they're defined in the Tk core and cannot be changed. With mega-widgets, however, you can dynamically add and remove options from the composite option list, and you can even specify exactly what options get integrated into this list during mega-widget construction, as each component widget is added. Another difference is the relationship between the widget and the option. In Tk, configuration options have a one-to-one relationship with widgets. You know that configuring a button's –foreground option will change its foreground color only. It won't affect the foreground color of the button's containing frame or any other widget in the window. In [incr Tk], configuration options may have a one-to-many relationship with widgets. Configuring the –foreground option for a mega-widget may change a single component widget's foreground color, or it may change multiple component widgets' foreground colors. This depends on a special set of rules specified during component widget addition that you'll learn more about a little later in the chapter.

The composite option list is stored in an array called itk_option in the Archetype base class. Derived classes can access this list directly for component widget management, and it's publicly available through the built-in *configure* method. Just as you can use Tk's **configure** command to modify widgets or to list all their available configuration options, you can use [incr Tk]'s built-in *configure* method to modify mega-widgets or to print their composite option list, which represents all their available configuration options. Configuring an option in the composite option list results in the automatic propagation of the change to each appropriate component widget. This is a powerful feature of the Itk package because it enables you to modify multiple component widgets with a single configuration option. Therefore, you don't have to worry about making sure options like colors or fonts are synchronized for different component widgets since they can be treated as a single unit.

As mentioned previously, you can control what options are integrated into the composite option list. By default, however, the list represents the union of special component widget option sets called *usual* options. In order to understand how the composite option list is managed, you must first understand how usual options work, as discussed in the following section.

Usual Options

All component widgets must have a predefined set of configuration options called usual options. The Itk package defines usual options for each of the Tk widgets for you in a file named itk.tcl, which resides in the itk/library directory directly beneath the top-level installation directory. The Itk package also provides a command appropriately named **usual** for retrieving each widget's usual options. Without any arguments, **usual** lists all widget class types. (Note that this doesn't refer to an [incr Tcl] class; rather, it refers to the widget class type as returned by the **winfo class** command.) Type the following commands in a **wish** shell to print each of the Tk widget types:

```
% package require Itk
3.0
% ::itk::usual
Label Scale Menubutton Entry Frame Radiobutton Button Text Listbox
Checkbutton Toplevel Scrollbar Canvas Menu Message
```

To determine the usual options for a particular class type, you can pass the type as an argument to **usual** as follows:

12

```
% ::itk::usual Frame
    keep -background -cursor
```

This tells you that the –background and –cursor options are kept as usual options for frame widgets. A frame widget has 16 configuration options, but only two of them are kept as usual options. Typically, only a small subset of a widget's configuration options is kept in the usual option list in order to minimize the number of potential entries in the composite option list. If all options for all widgets were kept as usual options, mega-widgets could have huge configuration option lists. This would eventually affect their performance and perhaps render some unusable, depending on the number of component widgets.

When you add a component widget to a mega-widget, its usual options are added to the composite option list by default if they're not already there. It follows then that adding a frame widget should result in the –background and –cursor options' being added to the list. Recall from the previous chapter, however, that these two options *are* already there. The Widget base class adds a frame widget component and keeps its usual options, and the Toplevel base class adds a top-level window component and keeps its –background, –cursor, and –takefocus configuration options. Since a frame's usual options are already included in the composite option list by the time the derived class *constructor* is invoked, adding another frame component in a derived class does not affect the composite option list. Now retrieve the usual options for another widget type such as a button as follows:

```
% ::itk::usual Button
    keep -background -cursor -foreground -font
    keep -activebackground -activeforeground -disabledforeground
    keep -highlightcolor -highlightthickness
    rename -highlightbackground -background background Background
```

The usual options for a button are much more robust than those for a frame. When you add a button to a mega-widget, each of its nine usual options is integrated into the composite option list. Eight of the options are kept from the button's set of available configuration options, and one option, –highlightbackground, is renamed as –background. Don't worry about the **keep** and **rename** keywords for now. They're discussed in detail in the next section.

Now that you're somewhat familiar with the **usual** command and usual options, let's build a simple mega-widget and determine how the composite option list is created during component widget creation. Consider the following class definition that combines an entry widget and a label widget to create a labeled entry mega-widget. This class is available online as LabeledEntry.itk.

Example 12-1
Building the
composite option
list with usual
options

```
::itcl::class LabeledEntry {
   inherit ::itk::Widget

   constructor {args} {}
   private method printCurrentOptions {}
}

::itcl::body LabeledEntry::constructor {args} {
   puts "Configuration options before adding any component widgets:"
   printCurrentOptions

   itk_component add label {
      label $itk_interior.l
   }
   puts "Configuration options after adding the label widget:"
   printCurrentOptions

   itk_component add entry {
      entry $itk_interior.e
   }
   puts "Configuration options after adding the entry widget:"
   printCurrentOptions

   eval itk_initialize $args
}

::itcl::body LabeledEntry::printCurrentOptions {} {
   set count 1
   foreach option [configure] {
      puts "  $count) [lindex $option 0]"
      incr count
   }
   puts ""
}
```

LabeledEntry simply defines a *constructor* and a private method to print
the contents of the composite option list prior to the addition of each
component widget. Type the following commands to watch how the
composite option list is built during construction:

```
% package require Itcl
3.0
```

12

```
% package require Itk
3.0
% source LabeledEntry.itk
% LabeledEntry .le
Configuration options before adding any component widgets:
   1) -background
   2) -clientdata
   3) -cursor

Configuration options after adding the label widget:
   1) -background
   2) -clientdata
   3) -cursor
   4) -font
   5) -foreground
   6) -highlightcolor
   7) -highlightthickness

Configuration options after adding the entry widget:
   1) -background
   2) -clientdata
   3) -cursor
   4) -font
   5) -foreground
   6) -highlightcolor
   7) -highlightthickness
   8) -insertbackground
   9) -insertborderwidth
   10) -insertofftime
   11) -insertontime
   12) -insertwidth
   13) -selectbackground
   14) -selectborderwidth
   15) -selectforeground
```

NOTE: Notice that the Itcl package is loaded prior to the Itk package. This constraint will likely change in a future release, but you will need to load the packages in this order when using mega-widgets with itcl3.0 for proper initialization.

From the results, you can see that each component widget adds several new configuration options to the composite option list. As previously mentioned, the composite option list for classes that inherit from Widget already consists of three options prior to the addition of any component widgets. Adding the label widget results in the addition of four more options, and adding the entry widget results in the addition of eight more options. Each of these options is determined from the component widget's usual option list. If you print the usual options for the label and entry widgets, you will see that each option is integrated into LabeledEntry's composite option list.

Now, recall briefly the *itk_component* method usage from the previous chapter:

```
itk_component <add|delete> ?-protected|-private? ?--? <name> \
  <createCmds> ?<optionCmds>?
```

The <optionCmds> argument is an optional argument that is defaulted to the specified component widget's usual option set. The following command fragment is therefore functionally identical to the code in LabeledEntry's *constructor* that adds the label component:

```
itk_component add label {
  label $itk_interior.l
} {
  usual
}
```

The <optionCmds> argument is declared here to explicitly request that the label's usual options be integrated into the composite option list. Recall from earlier that the **usual** command returns a list of the specified widget's usual options, so this command fragment is equivalent to the following:

```
itk_component add label {
  label $itk_interior.l
} {
  keep -background -cursor -foreground -font
  keep -highlightcolor -highlightthickness
  rename -highlightbackground -background background Background
}
```

The **usual** command is automatically substituted with the specified component widget's usual options before the widget is created. Since the **usual** command is automatically invoked for each component widget by default, it isn't necessary to explicitly invoke it if you want to keep all of a component widget's usual options. You may want to do so for clarity, however. But what if you *don't* want a component widget's usual options?

12

What if you want to add options to the composite option list that aren't in a widget's usual options? [incr Tk] provides a robust set of functionality that enables you to carefully manage exactly how the composite option list is created as component widgets are added. The following section shows you how to do this.

Adding Component Widgets

When you add component widgets to a mega-widget, you have several choices regarding component widget configuration options. You can keep all the default usual options or you can pick and choose from the component widget's normal configuration options. You can keep selected options, you can ignore options, or you can rename options. You have to be careful when doing this, however, because you can inadvertently remove all a component widget's usual options from the composite option list. The following three sections show you how to control composite option list entries by keeping, ignoring, and renaming component widget configuration options.

Keeping Options

To add a component widget's configuration option to the mega-widget's composite option list, use the **keep** command. When keeping options, it's important to note that you're not restricted to selection from a widget's usual options. You can choose from the widget's basic set of configuration options, which typically includes many more options than the usual options.

When you keep a component widget option, configuring that option will configure the component widget as well as any other component widget that has kept the same option. This is how you can synchronize multiple component widgets to be treated as a single unit, configurable by top-level options in the composite option list. Before adding multiple component widgets though, let's first discuss a simple class definition with a single component as follows:

```
% package require Itcl
3.0
% package require Itk
3.0
% ::itcl::class MegaWidget {
    inherit ::itk::Widget
    constructor {args} {}
  }
```

```
% ::itcl::body MegaWidget::constructor {args} {
    itk_component add button {
      button $itk_interior.b -text "Hello World"
    }
    eval itk_initialize $args
  }
```

What will be in this mega-widget's composite option list? First, recall the three options that are added in the Widget base class: –background, –cursor, and –clientdata. Next, notice that a single component widget is added—a button. The <optionCmds> argument to *itk_component* is not specified, so all of the button's usual options are added to the list. To verify this, type the following commands:

```
% MegaWidget .mw
.mw
% foreach option [.mw configure] {
    puts "option: [lindex [lindex $option 0] 0]"
  }
option: -activebackground
option: -activeforeground
option: -background
option: -clientdata
option: -cursor
option: -disabledforeground
option: -font
option: -foreground
option: -highlightcolor
option: -highlightthickness
```

Notice that all of the button's usual options are indeed in the composite option list, in addition to the three options added in Widget's *constructor*. Now watch what happens if you specify only one option to keep. Modify the *constructor* body as follows:

```
% ::itcl::body MegaWidget::constructor {args} {
    itk_component add button {
      button $itk_interior.b -text "Hello World"
    } {
      keep -width
    }
    eval itk_initialize $args
  }
```

12

```
% MegaWidget .mw2
.mw2
% foreach option [.mw2 configure] {
    puts "option: [lindex [lindex $option 0] 0]"
  }
option: -background
option: -clientdata
option: -cursor
option: -width
```

This is an important point to remember! Anytime you specify the
<optionCmds> argument without specifying the **usual** command, you take
the composite option list into your own hands. The usual options are taken
out of the picture unless you explicitly request them. In this case, a single
keep command fragment is used to keep the –width option. The resulting
composite option list then consists of –width, as requested, in addition to
the three options added in Widget. None of the usual options are present.
If you want to keep –width *in addition to* the usual options, then you must
explicitly request them by using the **usual** command and then the **keep**
command as follows:

```
% ::itcl::body MegaWidget::constructor {args} {
    itk_component add button {
      button $itk_interior.b -text "Hello World"
    } {
      usual
      keep -width
    }
    eval itk_initialize $args
  }
% MegaWidget .mw3
.mw3
% foreach option [.mw3 configure] {
    puts "option: [lindex [lindex $option 0] 0]"
  }
```

You will notice in the output that the composite option list now consists of
all usual options and the three base class options as in the first iteration
of MegaWidget's *constructor* implementation, in addition to the requested
–width option.

Ignoring Options

In the previous section, you learned how to keep either all the usual options or none of them. Usual options shouldn't be an all or nothing choice, though. What if you would like to keep all usual options except for a couple? You wouldn't want to have to manually keep all desired options. Instead, you can use the **usual** command to pull in all usual options and then use the **ignore** command to remove selected options from the composite option list. Continuing with the same MegaWidget example from the previous section, reimplement the *constructor* again as follows:

```
% ::itcl::body MegaWidget::constructor {args} {
    itk_component add button {
      button $itk_interior.b -text "Hello World"
    } {
      usual
      keep -width
      ignore -highlightcolor -highlightthickness
    }
    eval itk_initialize $args
  }
```

This time all usual options are kept with the **usual** command, the –width option is added with the **keep** command, and the –highlightcolor and –highlightthickness options are removed from the composite option list with the **ignore** command. Create another instance of MegaWidget to test the new *constructor* as follows:

```
% MegaWidget .mw4
.mw4
% foreach option [.mw4 configure] {
    puts "option: [lindex [lindex $option 0] 0]"
  }
option: -activebackground
option: -activeforeground
option: -background
option: -clientdata
option: -cursor
option: -disabledforeground
option: -font
option: -foreground
option: -width
```

12

As you can see, entries in the composite option list can be manually controlled as component widgets are added. You might be wondering how this might affect other component widgets in the same mega-widget. Just like **keep**, using **ignore** is component widget specific. You can ignore options for one component and keep them for other components. Then, when you configure these options, the change is propagated to all component widgets that have kept the options. Component widgets that ignore the options will be unaffected by the configuration change.

Renaming Options

In addition to keeping and ignoring options, you even have the choice of renaming a component widget configuration option. For the MegaWidget example from the previous two sections, let's rename its –foreground option to –fg, a common abbreviation.

```
% ::itcl::body MegaWidget::constructor {args} {
    itk_component add button {
      button $itk_interior.b -text "Hello World"
    } {
      rename -foreground -fg foreground Foreground
    }
    eval itk_initialize $args
  }
% MegaWidget .mw5
.mw5
% foreach option [.mw5 configure] {
    puts "option: [lindex [lindex $option 0] 0]"
  }
option: -background
option: -clientdata
option: -cursor
option: -fg
```

Since the usual options are not explicitly requested, the composite option list only contains the three options added in Widget in addition to the newly renamed –fg option. The **rename** command has a different syntax than **keep** and **ignore**. Whereas the latter two accept variable-length arguments, **rename** has a more rigid syntax. You must declare exactly four arguments: the option you want to rename, the new name for the option (the leading dash is optional but helps clarify the argument list), the resource name, and the resource class. The latter two are used in conjunction with the options database, which is discussed a little later in the chapter.

Now that you're familiar with composite option list manipulation during component widget addition, you need to understand what happens to the list when component widgets are removed. This is discussed in the following section.

Removing Component Widgets

When a component widget is removed from a mega-widget, any options that are unique to that widget are automatically removed from the composite option list. Removing component widgets does not affect other component widgets, however, so if you remove a widget that has kept its –background option (for example), other widgets that have also kept –background will be unaffected. Consider the following simple class definition that creates a titled frame:

```
::itcl::class TitledFrame {
  inherit ::itk::Widget

  constructor {args} {}
  public method options {} {
    foreach option [configure] {
      puts "option: [lindex [lindex $option 0] 0]"
    }
  }
  public method remove {which_} {
    itk_component delete $which_
  }
}

::itcl::body TitledFrame::constructor {args} {
  itk_component add title {
    label $itk_interior.title
  } {
    keep -text
  }

  itk_component add frame {
    frame $itk_interior.f
  } {
    keep -relief -borderwidth
  }

  pack $itk_component(title) -anchor w
  pack $itk_component(frame) -fill both -expand 1
  eval itk_initialize $args
}
```

12

TitledFrame defines two component widgets: a frame and a label for the frame's title. Notice that the –text option is kept for the label so that you can modify the title at the mega-widget level. Similarly, you can configure TitledFrame objects' –relief and –borderwidth options to adjust the appearance of the frame component. For simplicity's sake, these are the only options that are kept for the mega-widget, so there will initially only be six options in the composite option list (remember that Widget adds three).

Two public methods are provided for demonstrating removal of component widgets. The *remove* method is used to remove a component from the mega-widget, and the *options* method is used to print the current composite option list. Retrieve this class definition from online or manually save it in a file called TitledFrame.itk. Then, type the following commands in a new **wish** shell to see how component widget removal affects the composite option list:

```
% package require Itcl
3.0
% package require Itk
3.0
% source TitledFrame.itk
% TitledFrame .tf
.tf
% .tf options
option: -background
option: -borderwidth
option: -clientdata
option: -cursor
option: -relief
option: -text
% .tf remove title
% .tf options
option: -background
option: -borderwidth
option: -clientdata
option: -cursor
option: -relief
```

After removal of the label component, notice that the –text option no longer exists in the composite option list. If you remove the frame component, then the –borderwidth and –relief options are also removed. This is useful for housekeeping purposes in the mega-widget so that configuration options for components that have been removed are also removed. Otherwise, you could get an error message if you try to configure an option for a component widget that doesn't exist.

NOTE: Only post-itcl3.0 releases correctly update the composite option list after component widget removal. You may want to be aware of this if you are using release 3.0.x.

Defining New Configuration Options

In addition to controlling the composite option list by keeping, ignoring, and renaming existing component widget configuration options, [incr Tk] allows you to define brand new configuration options. You can do this to add specialized behavior to your mega-widget instead of defining public methods since configuration options are a more natural means of widget modification than public methods. Consider the following modification to the TitledFrame class from the previous section to add a new –state option:

```
::itcl::class TitledFrame {
  inherit ::itk::Widget

  # Configuration Options
  itk_option define -state state State normal

  constructor {args} {}
}

::itcl::configbody TitledFrame::state {
  switch -- $itk_option(-state) {
    "normal" {
      $itk_component(title) configure -foreground black
      configure -cursor top_left_arrow
    }
    "disabled" {
      $itk_component(title) configure -foreground gray50
      configure -cursor X_cursor
    }
    default {
      error "Bad option: $itk_option(-state). Should be \"normal\"\
        or \"disabled\"."
    }
  }
}
```

12

The class definition is unchanged except for the addition of the new configuration option. The *itk_option* method from the Archetype class is used to define the option. When the first argument to this method is "define," the remaining arguments should be as follows: the name of the new option, its resource name, its resource class, and its default value. The resource name and resource class are discussed in the options database section later in the chapter.

Similar to [incr Tcl] public data members, you can use **configbody** to check configuration option values before allowing the option to be modified. Valid options for –state include normal and disabled. After modifying TitledFrame as shown, you can type the following commands in a **wish** shell to create a TitledFrame object (note that the new class definition is available online in TitledFrame2.itk):

```
% package require Itcl
3.0
% package require Itk
3.0
% source TitledFrame.itk
% TitledFrame .tf -relief ridge -borderwidth 3 -text "Hello world"
.tf
% pack .tf -fill both -expand 1
```

The resulting window will be in the normal state, the default value for –state. The cursor will be the default top_left_arrow shape, and the title's foreground will be black. Now modify the –state option as follows:

```
% .tf configure -state disabled
```

Now the cursor is in the shape of an X, and the title's foreground color is changed to a dark gray, which typically indicates a widget's being disabled. You can further extend the behavior of this option by disallowing input events such as key press or mouse events when the mega-widget is disabled.

What happens if you configure the object's –state option to an invalid value? Just as Tk widgets gracefully handle invalid configuration option values, you should also handle invalid values in the **configbody** implementation. Try the following lines to verify:

```
% .tf configure -state enabled
Bad option: enabled. Should be "normal" or "disabled".
% .tf cget -state
disabled
```

As you can see, the –state option retains its previous value. It's important to note that the **error** command is used here to return without the option's being modified. The **return** command will not work because the option will not be reverted to its previous value, even if you use the –code error flag. You need to use **error** to handle invalid configuration option values.

Adding new configuration options is as simple as that! Simply add the option definition in the body of the class definition (you cannot add configuration options within method bodies) and provide any configuration code as necessary. The following section shows you two more uses of the *itk_option* method: reinstating ignored base class options and removing base class options.

Manipulating Base Class Configuration Options

Sometimes base classes don't provide the options that you need in a derived class. Recall the DefaultButton class from the previous chapter. It defines two component widgets: a button and a frame to represent the ring around the button. Instead of creating a frame inside the outer hull frame created by the Widget class, you can pull in configuration options associated with the hull component that are not already in the composite option list and then modify the hull frame directly. In this case, you need the –borderwidth and –relief options in order to configure the hull as a sunken frame around the button of the original ring component. Consider the following alternative class definition for DefaultButton. The new use of *itk_option* is shown in boldface.

```
::itcl::class DefaultButton {
  inherit ::itk::Widget

  constructor {args} {}
  public method invoke {} {flash; $itk_component(button) invoke}
  private method flash {} {$itk_component(button) flash}
}

::itcl::body DefaultButton::constructor {args} {
  # Add these options to the composite option list since Widget
  # doesn't keep them.
  itk_option add hull.relief hull.borderwidth
  configure -relief sunken -borderwidth 3

  # Create the button inside the hull frame.
  itk_component add button {
```

12

```
    button $itk_interior.b
  } {
    # Add these options to the composite options list.
    keep -text -command -background -foreground
  }
  pack $itk_component(button) -ipadx 4 -ipady 2 -padx 3 -pady 3

  # Invoke the button when the return key is pressed.
  bind [winfo toplevel $itk_interior] <Return> \
    "$itk_component(button) flash; $itk_component(button) invoke"

  # Always call itk_initialize after component widgets are added.
  eval itk_initialize $args
}
```

Since the hull is created in the Widget base class, you can't modify how its options are integrated into the composite option list. You can, however, use *itk_option* as shown to keep extra options for the hull. The syntax for doing this depends on whether the options are for a component widget or are new options created with "*itk_option* define". For component widgets, use the symbolic name followed by a dot and the desired configuration option. This is the syntax as shown in DefaultButton since hull is a component widget. For new configuration options, the syntax is slightly different. Use the class name instead of a component widget name followed by a double colon and the desired configuration option. Note that in either case the option name does not include the leading dash.

In addition to adding base class component widget options to the composite option list, you can also remove them. For example, configuring a DefaultButton's –background option changes the background color for both the button and the ring around the button since both of these components keep this option. You can't modify the Widget base class to ignore this option, so [incr Tk] allows you to remove the option for specific component widgets. To do this, use the following command:

```
itk_option remove hull.background
```

This tells the interpreter that the hull component should be excluded when the –background option is configured. Note that the option is still in the composite option list but that the hull component is just unaffected when –background is configured. You can always use the *component* method to configure individual component widgets, so you still have the ability to modify hull's background color if desired.

Add this command immediately following the command to keep the hull component's –relief and –borderwidth options and then create a new instance of DefaultButton. The class is available online in DefaultButton.itk.

```
% package require Itcl
3.0
% package require Itk
3.0
% source DefaultButton.itk
% DefaultButton .db -text "Print Error" -background red \
    -foreground yellow
.db
% pack .db
```

As expected, the button will be configured yellow on red, but the ring around the button remains unaffected. One thing you should note is the placement of the code to add and remove base class component options. Always place this code before the call to *itk_initialize* because options you added or removed might exist in the *constructor*'s argument list. It's safest to just place this code at the beginning of the *constructor* body as shown.

A Working Example: The "Dual Listbox"

The basics of [incr Tk] have been covered, and you should have enough ammunition now to be able to define full-fledged, useful mega-widgets on your own. To help get you started, this section provides a robust example instead of the simple one- and two-component examples given in the chapter so far. This example is a mega-widget called a dual listbox. The idea is to provide two scrollable listboxes packed side by side with four buttons between them that are used to move data back and forth between the two listboxes. The class definition is as follows (all code is available online in DualListbox.itk):

```
::itcl::class DualListbox {
  inherit ::itk::Widget
  constructor {args} {}

  # Configuration Options
  itk_option define -state state State normal

  # Public Methods
  public method insert {side_ text_ {position_ "end"}}
  public method get {side_ {first_ "0"} {last_ "end"}}
  public method curselection {side_}
```

12

```
    # Private Methods
    private method move {where_ {howmany_ ""}}
    private method createComponentWidgets {}
    private method packComponentWidgets {}

    # Private Data Members
    private variable _cursor
}
```

When designing new mega-widgets, it's important to think as generically as possible. Sometimes a particular design may call for a highly specialized widget, but in most cases you should implement a new mega-widget such that it could be used independently of the application. The DualListbox class is designed like this. Public methods are available for actions you would expect to be able to perform on a listbox: inserting data, retrieving data, and determining what listbox entries are currently selected. A new configuration option, –state, is defined to enable and disable the button components. Since there are multiple component widgets, separate methods are defined for creating and packing them to make the *constructor* less cluttered. The *constructor* becomes much easier to read as a result, and is implemented as follows:

```
::itcl::body DualListbox::constructor {args} {
    set _cursor(normal) top_left_arrow
    set _cursor(disabled) X_cursor

    createComponentWidgets
    packComponentWidgets

    eval itk_initialize $args
}
```

A private data member is initialized to store the cursor shape, depending on the state of the mega-widget. Then, the component widgets are created and packed into the hull frame. Finally, *itk_initialize* is called to initialize the composite option list. Remember that you must always invoke this method in a mega-widget's *constructor*. The rest of the code is available online. The following commands show you how you could use a DualListbox:

```
% package require Itcl
3.0
% package require Itk
3.0
```

```
% source DualListbox.itk
% DualListbox .dl -textbackground ghostwhite -sbarwidth 14 \
  -lefttitle "Available Options:" -righttitle "Selected:" \
  -selectmode extended
.dl
% pack .dl -fill both -expand 1
% foreach option [list ABS "Air Conditioning" "CD Player" \
     "Leather Seats" "Standard Transmission" "Alarm System" \
     "Pin Stripes" "Mag Wheels" "Rear Spoiler" "Custom Paint"] {
   .dl insert left $option
}
```

The resulting window is shown in Figure 12-1 after selected options are moved to the right listbox. There are 16 individual component widgets in the screen, but [incr Tk] allows you to treat all 16 widgets like a single unit. You can change the background color of both listboxes with the –textbackground option, you can disable all four buttons and change their cursor shape with the –state option, and you can even change the widths of all four scrollbars with the –sbarwidth option. When you design new mega-widgets, try to think of what would be useful for users of your class. Don't go overboard on the number of configuration options you provide. Rather, try to determine a set that would cover typical requests. For example, the user will likely not want to change the foreground color of the buttons, so it isn't necessary to define a new option for doing this. If for some reason the user does want to change the buttons' foreground, the *component* method can be used to access each button widget individually to make the desired modification.

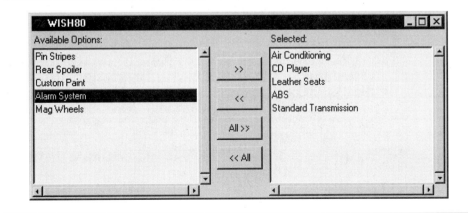

A DualListbox mega-widget instance

Figure 12-1.

12

Notice all the options that are specified on the command line to instantiate the DualListbox. It's common to provide default configuration option values through a mechanism called the options database so that you don't have to specify so many option/value pairs at creation. This is discussed further in the next section.

The Options Database

The options database is used to set default values for a mega-widget's configuration options. This is useful to avoid having to specify multiple configuration options when you instantiate a mega-widget. For example, you can make the listbox background color ghostwhite and the scroll bar widths 14 pixels with the following commands:

```
option add *DualListbox.textbackground ghostwhite widgetDefault
option add *DualListbox.sbarwidth 14 widgetDefault
```

The **option add** command should be invoked outside of the class definition and is typically done at the top of the file. It accepts three arguments: the class name preceded by an asterisk and followed by a dot and the resource name or resource class, the default value, and the priority. Let's briefly discuss each one of these arguments.

The *DualListbox portion of the first argument says that the designated values apply to all instances of DualListbox in the application. The .textbackground and .sbarwidth parts are resource names as specified by arguments to the **rename** command when the listbox and scroll bar component widgets are added. This means that any component widget option with this resource name will be defaulted to the specified values. DualListbox mega-widgets only have two component types that are affected by this: the listboxes and the scroll bars. You can specify a resource class instead of a resource name, which would typically affect many more component widgets. For instance, the resource class for –textbackground is Background, as is the resource class for –background. If you specified *DualListbox.Background instead, the result would be the same as configuring both the –background and –textbackground options to the specified default value. The last argument, widgetDefault, specifies the lowest priority level for the option, which basically means you can override the option later if desired. For more information on the different priority levels, refer to the option man page.

What happens if you don't use the **option add** command to specify mega-widget defaults? How does [incr Tk] determine what default values to give to each of the component widgets? It's actually very intuitive, because Tk makes the decision. All Tk widgets have default values for each of their configuration options. If you don't specify a default value for an option, the option is defaulted to the component widget that first kept the option. For example, if you don't specify a background color for the listbox widgets in the DualListbox mega-widget, then the default value will be a light gray color, which is the default for Tk listbox widgets. Oftentimes Tk widget default values are perfectly acceptable as mega-widget default values, but you can explicitly override them with **option add** as needed.

This marks the end of the two chapters on [incr Tk]. You should now have the knowledge base necessary to create your own portable mega-widgets. The following chapter discusses the [incr Widget] framework, which is built on top of [incr Tk]. You'll learn about a very important component of mega-widgets called the childsite that many of the [incr Widgets] use. The last chapter then provides a handy reference section that discusses each of the mega-widgets in the [incr Widgets] library in detail.

12

PART III

[incr Widgets]

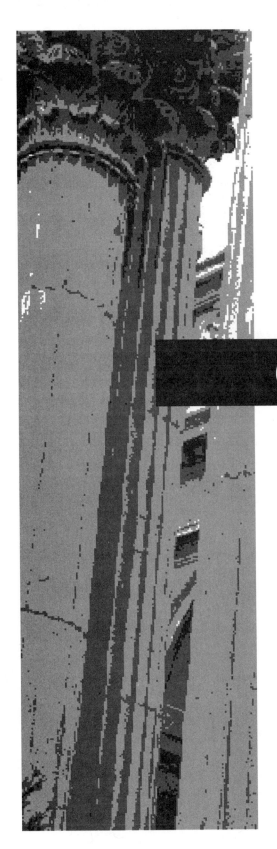

CHAPTER 13

Introduction and Childsites

This chapter provides a brief introduction to the Iwidgets package and discusses a very important component of many of the [incr Widgets], the childsite. You'll see firsthand how a complex graphical screen can be created using [incr Widgets] in just a few lines of code. Then you'll discover what a childsite is, how you access it, how you use it, and some pitfalls to avoid when dealing with it. If you have never used the Iwidgets package before, make sure you read this chapter first. A handy inheritance diagram of the class framework is provided, but most importantly, you need to understand childsites.

The Iwidgets Package

The Iwidgets package is included with the [incr Tcl/Tk] distribution that you download from the Internet. It consists of a robust class framework of over 50 ready-to-use mega-widgets. Refer to Figure 13-1 to see this framework in its entirety. The Archetype class is the bottommost base class. It has three derived classes: Widget, Toplevel, and Labeledframe. Widget and Toplevel are discussed in detail in Chapter 12. Labeledframe is specific to version 3.x of the Iwidgets package and serves as the base class for checkbox and radiobox [incr Widgets]. All others inherit from either Widget or Toplevel.

If you've never used the Iwidgets package before, you will be amazed at the variety of widgets and the ease with which you can create complex graphical screens in just a few lines of code. For example, consider Figure 13-2 and estimate how many lines of code you think it might take you to create this screen using straight Tk. Ten? Twenty? Using the Iwidgets package, the answer is one. You only have to write a *single* line of code after you load the package. Simply instantiate the Fileselectionbox class as follows:

```
% package require Iwidgets
3.0.0
% pack [::iwidgets::fileselectionbox .fs] -fill both -expand 1
.fs
```

NOTE: There are two items you should note in this code. First, in itcl3.0.1 you have to load the Itcl and Itk packages in that order *before* loading the Iwidgets package. In post-itcl3.0.1 releases, you can load the Iwidgets package by itself to gain access to the [incr Widgets]. Next, recall from Chaper 11 that each [incr Widget] provides a public procedure that allows you to instantiate the class with an initial lowercase. This is done to make [incr Widgets] appear more like regular Tk widgets than class instances.

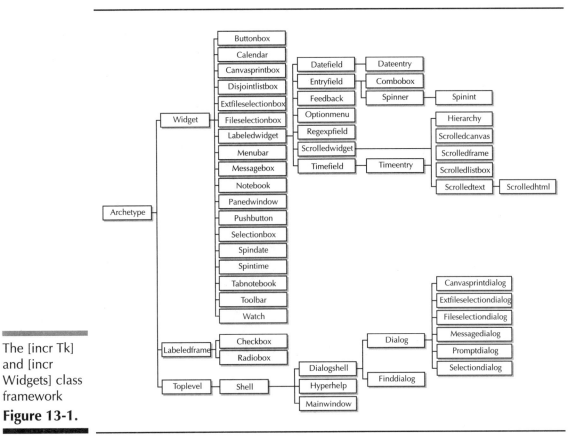

Now consider Figure 13-3 and make another estimate on the number of
lines of code you think it would take you to create *this* screen in straight Tk.
More than likely, your estimate will be in the 75+ range. However, using the
mainwindow and scrolledtext mega-widgets from the Iwidgets package,
you can create this screen in only 39 lines of code! The following example
provides this code for you (note that the code is also available online in the
file example13-1.tcl):

13

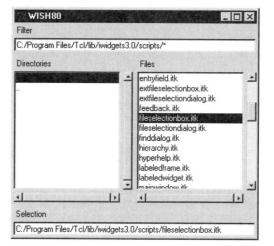

A file selection
screen that
takes one line
of code to
create

Figure 13-2.

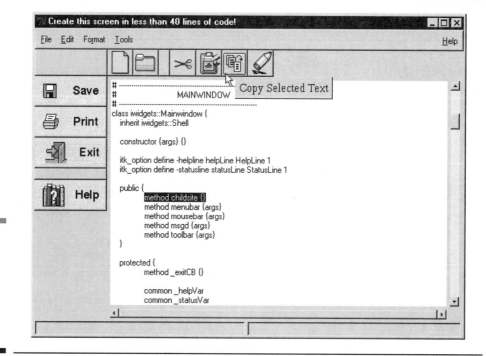

Using [incr
Widgets], this
screen takes
less than 40
lines of code
to create

Figure 13-3.

Example 13-1
Code for creating
the text editor
shown in
Figure 13-3

```
# Load the Iwidgets package and create an instance of the
# mainwindow [incr Widget].
package require Iwidgets
::iwidgets::mainwindow .mw -menubarfont {{MS Sans Serif} 8} \
    -title "Create this screen in less than 40 lines of code!"

# Add some toolbar buttons. The 107-pixel wide frame is used to
# move the toolbar over to the right the number of pixels equal
# to the width of the vertical toolbar. This number is the image
# width of the toolbar images plus a few extra pixels for the
# borderwidth.
set dir ${iwidgets::library}/demos/images
.mw toolbar add frame spacer1 -width 107 -relief raised -bd 2
.mw toolbar add button open -balloonstr "Create New File" \
    -image [image create photo -file $dir/open.gif]
.mw toolbar add button new -balloonstr "Open File" \
    -image [image create photo -file $dir/new.gif]
.mw toolbar add button close -balloonstr "Close File" \
    -image [image create photo -file $dir/close.gif]
.mw toolbar add frame spacer2 -width 16 -relief raised -bd 2
.mw toolbar add button cut -balloonstr "Cut Selected Text" \
    -image [image create photo -file $dir/cut.gif]
.mw toolbar add button paste -balloonstr "Paste Text From Clipboard" \
    -image [image create photo -file $dir/paste.gif]
.mw toolbar add button copy -balloonstr "Copy Selected Text" \
    -image [image create photo -file $dir/copy.gif]
.mw toolbar add button erase -balloonstr "Erase Selected Text" \
    -image [image create photo -file $dir/clear.gif]

# Add some mousebar buttons.
.mw mousebar add button save -balloonstr "Save File" \
    -image [image create photo -file $dir/save.gif]
.mw mousebar add button print -balloonstr "Print File" \
    -image [image create photo -file $dir/print.gif]
.mw mousebar add button exit -balloonstr "Close File and Exit" \
    -image [image create photo -file $dir/exit.gif]
.mw mousebar add frame spacer -width 107 -height 16 \
    -relief raised -bd 2
.mw mousebar add button help -balloonstr "Help me!" \
    -image [image create photo -file $dir/help.gif]

# Add the menu items.  Using -underline provides for convenient
# keyboard traversal of the menus.
```

13

```
.mw menubar add menubutton file -text File -underline 0
.mw menubar add menubutton edit -text Edit -underline 0
.mw ménubar add menubutton format -text Format -underline 2
.mw menubar add menubutton tools -text Tools -underline 0
.mw menubar add menubutton help -text Help -underline 0

# Create the scrolled text region and load the source code for
# the mainwindow [incr Widget].
set st [::iwidgets::scrolledtext [.mw childsite].st]
$st import $dir/../../scripts/mainwindow.itk
pack $st -fill both -expand 1

# Active the window.
.mw activate
```

First, a mainwindow [incr Widget] is created after the Iwidgets package is loaded. Then, several buttons are added to the built-in toolbar, which is actually another kind of [incr Widget]. Since [incr Tk] provides object-oriented functionality through its [incr Tcl] backbone, features such as composition and inheritance are available for developers to use. The mainwindow takes advantage of both composition and inheritance and contains several different [incr Widget] components (refer to Chapter 7 for more information on composition). One nice feature of the toolbar is that you can configure each component widget to display a pop-up balloon window when the cursor remains over the widget for a certain period of time. This can be handy to provide a brief description of the button's use. For example, the button with the pair of scissors on it has a balloon pop-up that says "Cut Selected Text." You can configure the balloon's foreground and background colors, font, and text to fit your application's needs.

Next, the mainwindow's mousebar component is initialized. The mousebar is the symbolic name for another toolbar that is oriented vertically instead of horizontally. It's common for an application's main screen to have both a horizontal toolbar at the top of the screen and a vertical toolbar on the left-hand side of the screen. In this example, buttons related to text editing such as cut and paste are added to the horizontal toolbar, and buttons related to file-level actions such as save and print are added to the vertical toolbar.

Following toolbar initialization, another type of [incr Widget] component is initialized, the menubar. Five menubuttons are added to the menubar, and each one has a unique underlined character that can be used for keyboard traversal to open the associated menus (there are no menus in this example). Lastly, a scrolledtext [incr Widget] is created, and its *import* method is used to load and display the source code for the mainwindow [incr Widget]. The important thing for you to notice here is how and where the scrolledtext gets added. A special mainwindow method called *childsite* is used to retrieve the Tk window pathname of the mainwindow's childsite area. Childsites are an integral part of the Iwidgets package and are discussed in the next section.

So, after 39 lines of code (comments and blank lines not counted), the screen is complete. Granted, it's just a shell; pressing a button or selecting a menu doesn't actually do anything. But just creating this screen without using the Iwidgets package would take many more lines of code and would most likely be much more cumbersome to maintain. As is, you don't have to worry about how new buttons are added to the toolbar or how new menubuttons are added to the menubar. You don't have to worry about how the balloon pop-up window knows when to display itself or when to destroy itself. There are several nontrivial characteristics of this screen that simply don't need to be understood by the developer in order to build the screen successfully.

The Iwidgets package has turned a fairly complicated screen into one that is very straightforward to create by hiding all the implementation details behind simple, intuitive interface methods and configuration options. As you continue to learn and use the Iwidgets package, you'll gain a great appreciation for its intuitiveness and simplicity, not to mention the time that you'll save during development.

Childsites

You can use many of the [incr Widgets] "right out of the box," regardless of your experience level. The scrolledlistbox, entryfield, spinner, calendar, and pushbutton are just a few examples that you can create even if you've never used the Iwidgets package before. Many of the [incr Widgets], however, necessitate your understanding a special internal component called the childsite. A childsite is the designated area in certain mega-widgets where you can pack other widgets. You should think of a childsite as a placeholder. In the previous example, a scrolledtext [incr Widget] is packed into the childsite of a mainwindow [incr Widget].

Under the hood, a childsite is usually a Tk frame component widget that is specifically created to act as a container for noncomponent widgets, meaning widgets that are created outside the scope of the [incr Widget] itself. In other words, childsites are typically empty until you explicitly pack widgets into them. Childsites are also nonpublic, so you can't access them via the *component* method like other component widgets. All [incr Widgets] that have a childsite provide an accessor for retrieving its Tk window pathname. This accessor is appropriately named *childsite*.

13

You most likely already know how to pack widgets into frames, so you won't have any problems packing widgets into childsites. So let's get started with a simple example. Start a **wish** shell and type the following commands:

```
% package require Iwidgets
3.0.0
% wm geometry . 250x200
% ::iwidgets::scrolledframe .sf -borderwidth 2
.sf
% pack .sf -fill both -expand 1
```

You should see a scrolledframe [incr Widget] packed into the root window. Now, suppose you need to pack a series of entryfields into the scrolledframe. (An entryfield is another [incr Widget] that combines a label widget and an entry widget.) If you're new to the Iwidgets package, you might try to pack the entryfields directly into the hull of the scrolledframe like this, which implies the scrolledframe is like a regular Tk frame:

```
% for {set num 1} {$num <= 15} {incr num} {
    ::iwidgets::entryfield .sf.ef$num -labeltext "Entry Number $num:"
    pack .sf.ef$num
  }
```

When you create Tk frames, you pack other widgets directly into them. A scrolledframe, however, is *not* a regular frame. It's a class instance with a specifically constructed component widget set. So, as you might imagine, this won't work.

The resulting screen is shown in Figure 13-4. Notice that the first entryfield doesn't quite fit inside the scrolledframe's border; it overlaps it slightly. More apparent, though, are the tenth and eleventh entryfields. These two completely overlap the horizontal scrollbar. If you try to scroll down with the vertical scrollbar, you'll find out it doesn't work, and if you stretch the window to see if the scrolledframe will expand and show the missing entryfields, you'll see that that doesn't work either. So what happened? In the case of a scrolledframe, the scrollable portion of the [incr Widget] is actually a canvas with an embedded frame that is resized as necessary when new widgets are added or the scrolledframe changes size. Packing widgets directly into the hull of a scrolledframe actually places them on top of the canvas component. Basically, this means you should never pack widgets directly into a scrolledframe. Always use the built-in childsite instead. This is true for *all* [incr Widgets] that have childsites. Now destroy the scrolledframe instance and try the following lines of code to fix the problem:

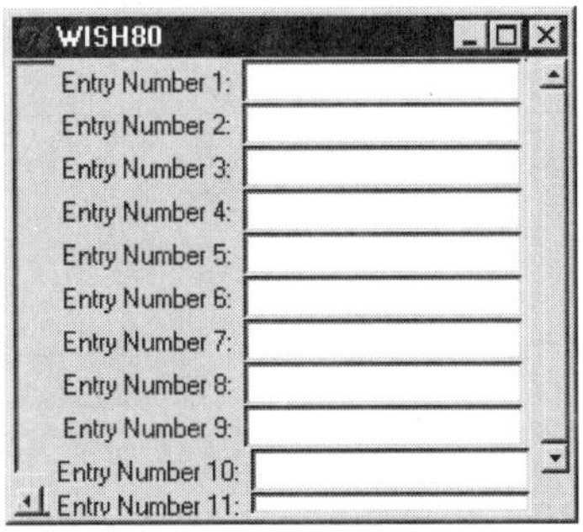

Unexpected
packing
problems
caused by
not using the
scrolledframe's
childsite

Figure 13-4.

```
% destroy .sf
% ::iwidgets::scrolledframe .sf -borderwidth 2
.sf
% wm geometry . 350x200
% pack .sf -fill both -expand 1
% set cs [.sf childsite]   ← Tk window pathname of childsite frame
% for {set num 0} {$num <= 15} {incr num} {
    ::iwidgets::entryfield $cs.ef$num \
      -labeltext "Entry Number $num:"
   pack $cs.ef$num
  }
```

The resulting screen is shown in Figure 13-5. You should notice that the entryfields are now appropriately packed inside the scrollable area of the scrolledframe and that the scroll bars behave as expected. Also notice that the window is wider this time. This is intentional so that you can see the empty space between the entryfields and the vertical scroll bar. This space is normal because the childsite frame only grows as wide as its widest contained widget. When you stretch the window horizontally, the entryfields won't stretch to fit because the childsite doesn't stretch to fit. You might be tempted to change the packing options of the childsite to fill in the horizontal space and then pack the entryfields to also fill in this space. After all, the childsite is just a frame, right? Try the following commands to see what happens:

13

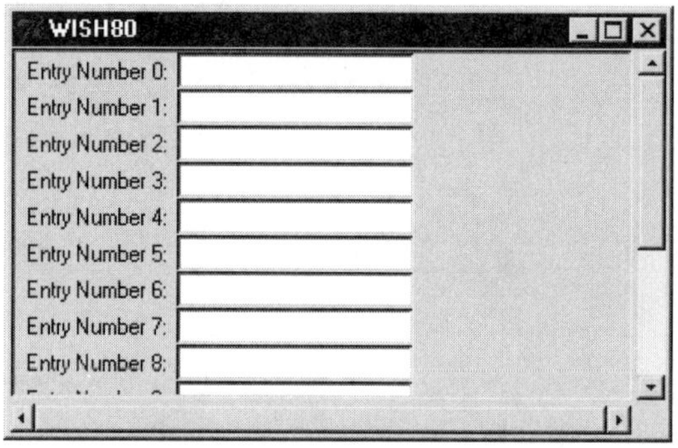

The space
between the
entryfields and
scroll bar is
normal for
scrolledframes

Figure 13-5.

```
% destroy .sf
% ::iwidgets::scrolledframe .sf -borderwidth 2
.sf
% pack .sf -fill both -expand 1
% set cs [.sf childsite]
% pack $cs -fill both
% for {set num 0} {$num <= 15} {incr num} {
    ::iwidgets::entryfield $cs.ef$num -labeltext "Entry Number $num:"
    pack $cs.ef$num -fill x
  }
```

The resulting window is shown in Figure 13-6. At first glance, it appears that you have achieved your goal, but when you try to use the scrollbars, you'll see that neither one works. This is because the geometry of the childsite is carefully controlled by the scrolledframe. Each time a new widget is added or the window changes size, the childsite is explicitly resized to fit the contained widgets. When you modify the childsite's geometry by packing it on the command line, it becomes out of sync with the scroll bars.

As a general rule of thumb, you should *never* modify a childsite's packing options. First, you don't know whether the childsite was packed into the window with **pack** or **grid**. Using one instead of the other could lead to some unusual side effects that you can't undo without destroying and re-creating the mega-widget. Second, the childsite is packed into the mega-widget in a certain expected manner, and the mega-widget expects the childsite to be in a certain state when it needs to be resized to fit around other widgets. If you override the default packing options of the childsite or if you manipulate its geometry in any other way, you will potentially destroy the mega-widget's ability to determine how to resize the childsite when you pack new widgets into it or when you resize the screen.

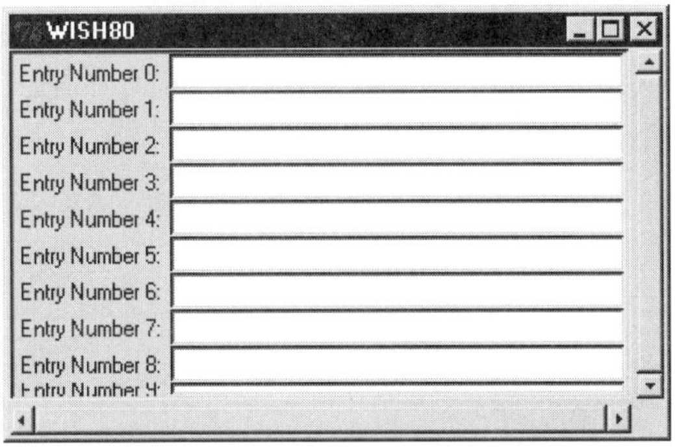

Modifying a
childsite's
packing
options is
generally a
bad idea

Figure 13-6.

[incr Widgets] such as the scrolledframe and mainwindow have childsites
that are specifically intended to be used. Without childsites, these [incr
Widgets] really wouldn't be very practical. Other [incr Widgets], on the other
hand, have childsites that aren't meant to be used externally because they're
reserved for internal use. The spinner [incr Widget], for example, inherits its
childsite from entryfield and packs the up and down arrows into it. Similarly,
the optionmenu [incr Widget] packs the selector into its childsite, which it
inherits from labeledwidget. As a general rule of thumb, you should avoid
using the childsite of any labeledwidget derived class because most of them
already use it for component widgets. Refer to Figure 13-1 to see the [incr
Widgets] inheritance structure. Packing additional widgets into childsites that
are already used will most likely result in overwriting the component widgets
that are already there. You would normally only use the childsite provided
by labeledwidget if you were creating a new mega-widget that inherits from
this base class.

One exception to this rule (there are others as well) is the spinner. From
Figure 13-1, you can see that this [incr Widget] inherits from entryfield, which
inherits from labeledwidget. The entryfield provides a childsite of its own, and
the spinner packs its up and down arrows into this childsite. The spinner does
not pack anything into the childsite provided by the labeledwidget, however,
so you can add text in *this* childsite to specify units—for example, for entry
input. You can see an example of this in the spinner section of Chapter 14.

13

In a nutshell, a childsite can be an extremely useful mega-widget component.
Remember to always use childsites when you want to pack widgets into a
mega-widget and to never change the packing options of a childsite. Follow
these two rules to take full advantage of [incr Widgets] that offer childsites.
Once you fully understand childsites after having experimented a bit, you

will be able to optimize your screens and decrease the amount of code you write by taking advantage of the childsite components when available.

The following chapter presents a handy reference manual for each of the [incr Widgets] in the Iwidgets package. They are presented in alphabetical order for quick and easy lookup. For each [incr Widget], you will be provided with the following information:

◆   A brief description

◆   A screen snapshot

◆   The code used to create the snapshot

◆   A class diagram that outlines inheritance and direct compositional relationships

◆   All [incr Widget] configuration options outlined as either standard, inherited, associated, or widget-specific

◆   All [incr Widget] public methods outlined as either associated, inherited, or widget-specific

◆   All of that [incr Widget]'s component widgets

Chapter 14 will likely be an extremely useful chapter that you will refer to time and time again to look up certain information for certain [incr Widgets], or to look through the screen snapshots for an [incr Widget] that looks like something you may need for your particular application.

CHAPTER 14

Reference

This chapter serves as an in-depth reference section for each of the [incr Widgets] in the Iwidgets package. Each [incr Widget] is discussed in alphabetical order according to the following template:

Description A brief description is provided that highlights some of the key features of the [incr Widget].

Snapshot and code A screen snapshot of the [incr Widget] is provided along with the code used to create it.

Class model An object-oriented class model shows you the inheritance hierarchy for the [incr Widget] as well as any direct compositional relationships that exist.

Configuration Options Each of the [incr Widget]'s configuration options is broken down into one of four types: standard, associated, inherited, or widget-specific. Standard options are fundamental Tk options that can be found in the options man page. Associated options are any options that the [incr Widget] provides that are associated directly with one or more of its components. Inherited options are those options that are inherited from a base class [incr Widget] or one of the [incr Tk] base classes. Widget-specific options are specific to the [incr Widget]. A widget-specific option is typically defined with *itk_option* define, but it may also be a standard option that is changed with the **rename** command. Standard, associated, and inherited options are displayed in tabular format. The widget-specific options are outlined in greater detail.

Public Methods Each of the [incr Widget]'s interface methods is broken down into one of three types: associated, inherited, or widget-specific. Associated methods are typically wrapper methods that are used to wrap a component widget method or command. Inherited methods are defined in a base class. Widget-specific methods are specific to the [incr Widget]. Similar to the configuration options, associated and inherited methods are presented in a tabular format, and widget-specific methods are outlined in greater detail.

Components Each component widget of the [incr Widget] is displayed in tabular format with its class type as returned by the **winfo class** command. The components that are shown are determined by the *component* method.

NOTE: If you are currently using Iwidgets2.2.0 and are intending to port your application to Iwidgets3.0.0, be aware that there are *numerous* differences in many of the [incr Widgets]. Plan for ample porting time.

buttonbox

The buttonbox [incr Widget] is used to arrange groups of buttons typically
found at the bottom of a window. All of the dialog windows in the [incr
Widgets] library, for example, use a buttonbox. The buttons in the buttonbox
are actually instances of the Pushbutton class, which is an [incr Widget] that
can be used to create a default button with a recessed ring. Pushbutton
instances must be manually added to a buttonbox via its *add* or *insert* methods.
Once added, they become components of the buttonbox and are then
accessible via a number of public methods. One nice feature of the buttonbox
is that all buttons are the same size. A button that reads "OK" will be the same
width as a button that reads "Press For More Details".

```
# Create the buttonbox.
iwidgets::buttonbox .bb -padx 8 -pady 8

# Add 5 pushbuttons.
.bb add prev -text "<< Prev"
.bb add apply -text Apply
.bb add clear -text Clear
.bb add close -text Close
.bb add next -text "Next >>"

# Make the Close pushbutton the default.
.bb default close

pack .bb -fill both -expand 1
```

Class Model

The buttonbox [incr Widget] inherits directly from itk::Widget, and it can
contain zero or more pushbutton [incr Widgets].

14

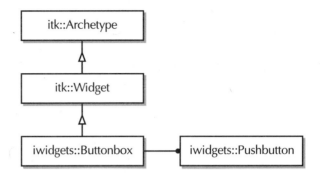

Configuration Options

Standard Options

Refer to the options man page for information on these standard options.

activebackground	activeforeground	background	borderwidth
cursor	disabledforeground	font	foreground
highlightcolor	highlightthickness	orient	padx
pady			

Associated Options
None

Inherited Options

Refer to Chapter 11 for information on this inherited option from the [incr Tk] Archetype base class.

Option Name	Inherited From
clientdata	itk::Archetype

Widget-Specific Options
None

Public Methods

Associated Methods
None

Inherited Methods

Refer to Chapter 11 for information on each of these inherited methods.

Method Name	Inherited From
cget	itk::Archetype
component	itk::Archetype
config	itk::Archetype
configure	itk::Archetype

Widget-Specific Methods

add

Usage: pathName *add* tag ?arg arg ...?
Description: Adds a new pushbutton to the buttonbox. The tag argument is the symbolic name to assign to the new pushbutton. This name can then be used with other methods such as *default* and *component* to access the pushbutton. You may optionally specify any valid pushbutton configuration option and a corresponding value following the tag argument to initialize the new pushbutton.

buttoncget

Usage: pathName *buttoncget* index option
Description: Retrieves the value of the specified configuration option for the specified pushbutton. The index argument can be either the symbolic name of the pushbutton specified when it was added or the numerical index of the pushbutton. For example, the leftmost pushbutton for a horizontally aligned buttonbox with four pushbuttons has a numerical index of 0, and the rightmost has a numerical index of 3. For vertically aligned buttonboxes, the topmost pushbutton is indexed as 0. The option argument is any valid pushbutton configuration option.

buttonconfigure

Usage: pathName *buttonconfigure* index ?arg arg ...?
Description: Use this method to modify a pushbutton's configuration option(s) or to print information about a single pushbutton option. See *buttoncget* for more information on the index argument. Following index, you may optionally specify a single configuration option or pairs of configuration options and values. If you only specify the index argument, then all of that

14

pushbutton's options are printed. If you specify a single option, then only that option's information is printed. If you specify one or more pairs of options and values, those options are configured with the designated values for the specified pushbutton.

default

Usage: pathName *default* index
Description: Configures the pushbutton specified by the index argument to be the default pushbutton in the buttonbox. This causes a recessed frame to be drawn around the pushbutton. See *buttoncget* for more information on the index argument. Note that there is no associated binding with a default pushbutton; you must set this up yourself.

delete

Usage: pathName *delete* index
Description: Deletes the pushbutton specified by the index argument. The pushbutton and its component widgets are destroyed, and the index values of the pushbuttons to the right of (horizontally aligned) or below (vertically aligned) the designated pushbutton are decremented by one. See *buttoncget* for more information on the index argument.

hide

Usage: pathName *hide* index
Description: This method uses the **place forget** command to withdraw the pushbutton specified by the index argument. See *buttoncget* for more information on this argument. You can use the *show* method to redraw the pushbutton in its original location.

index

Usage: pathName *index* index
Description: Returns the numerical index corresponding to the index argument. You can use this method to determine the numerical index corresponding to a pushbutton's symbolic name. See *buttoncget* for more information on the index argument.

insert

Usage: pathName *insert* index tag ?arg arg ...?
Description: Inserts a new pushbutton in the buttonbox just before the pushbutton specified by the index argument. See *buttoncget* for more

information on this argument. The tag argument is the symbolic name for the new pushbutton. You can then optionally specify any number of valid pushbutton configuration options with corresponding values to initialize the new pushbutton. This method is similar to *add* except you have control over where the new pushbutton is placed.

invoke

Usage: pathName *invoke* ?index?
Description: Use this method to evaluate the -command option of one of the pushbuttons in the buttonbox. If you don't specify the index argument, the default pushbutton is invoked. Otherwise, the argument is expected to be the numerical index or symbolic name of a pushbutton.

show

Usage: pathName *show* index
Description: This method is the counterpart to the *hide* method. It reinserts the pushbutton specified by the index argument back into the buttonbox. If the pushbutton is already displayed, nothing happens. For more information on the index argument, see *buttoncget*.

Components

When a buttonbox is first created, it only contains a hull component. As you add new pushbuttons to the buttonbox, each one becomes a new component widget.

Name	Class	Description
hull	Buttonbox	The frame around the pushbuttons

14

calendar

The calendar [incr Widget] allows you to create and manipulate a monthly calendar. One month is displayed at a time, but there are buttons that allow you to turn the pages of the calendar to different months. You can also use the public *show* method to show a particular month rather than paging with the buttons. The calendar can display dates up to December 2037 on most systems since most use a 32-bit time value. Some systems such as those running Solaris 2.7, however, can display dates beyond the year 2037.

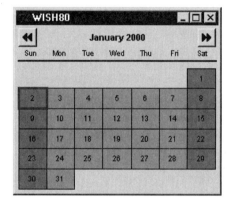

```
# Create the calendar
iwidgets::calendar .c -days "Sun Mon Tue Wed Thu Fri Sat" \
  -weekdaybackground grey68 -weekendbackground grey54 \
  -outline black -width 250 -height 200 -buttonforeground black
pack .c

# Show January 2000
.c show "3 months"; # If the current month is October 1999.

# Select a particular day on the calendar
.c select 1/2/00; # Note that 00 is interpreted as 2000.
```

Class Model

The calendar [incr Widget] inherits directly from itk::Widget. It does not interact with any other [incr Widget] outside of its inheritance tree.

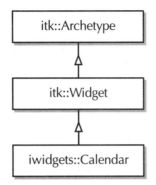

Configuration Options

Standard Options

Refer to the options man page for information on these standard options:

background	cursor

Associated Options

Refer to the associated Tk widget for information on each of these options:

Option Name	Associated With
height	Tk canvas widget
width	Tk canvas widget

Inherited Options

Refer to Chapter 11 for information on this inherited option from the [incr Tk] Archetype base class.

Option Name	Inherited From
clientdata	itk::Archetype

Widget-Specific Options

-backwardimage

Resource name: backwardImage
Resource class: Image

Description: The image used for the Backward button in the upper-left corner of the calendar. You can specify a bitmap or a photo. If you specify an empty string, then the default image, a double left arrow bitmap, is drawn.
Default value: {}

-buttonforeground

Resource name: buttonForeground
Resource class: Foreground
Description: The foreground color of the bitmap images on the Backward and Forward buttons. Note that you can only modify a bitmap's foreground color since -foreground is a valid bitmap option. You cannot modify a photo's foreground color, however, so if you use a photo instead of a bitmap, modifying this option will return an error.
Default value: blue

-command

Resource name: command
Resource class: Command
Description: Specifies a Tcl command to be evaluated when a day in the currently displayed month is selected with the left mouse button. The date is substituted in place of "%d" in the command fragment associated with this option. For example, -command {puts %d} will print the date each time a day of the month is clicked.
Default value: {}

-currentdatefont

Resource name: currentDateFont
Resource class: Font
Description: Specifies the font to be used for the current date. For example, if the current date is January 2nd, 2000, and the current month is displayed, then the font used to show the two (Sunday the 2nd) will be modified when you configure this option.
Default value: -*-helvetica-bold-r-normal-*-120-*

-datefont

Resource name: dateFont
Resource class: Font
Description: Specifies the font to be used for each day of the month. Note that modifying this option may override *-currentdatefont*.
Default value: -*-helvetica-bold-r-normal-*-120-*

-dayfont

Resource name: dayFont
Resource class: Font
Description: Specifies the font to be used for the days of the week at the top of the calendar. The text displayed for the days is stored in the -days option.
Default value: -*-helvetica-bold-r-normal-*-120-*

-days

Resource name: days
Resource class: Days
Description: The text used to show the days of the week at the top of the calendar.
Default value: "Su Mo Tu We Th Fr Sa"

-foreground

Resource name: foreground
Resource class: Foreground
Description: The foreground color of all text and the divider line. Modify the foreground color of the buttons with the -buttonforeground option.
Default value: black

-forwardimage

Resource name: forwardImage
Resource class: Image
Description: The image used for the Forward button in the upper-right corner of the calendar. You can specify a bitmap or a photo. If you specify an empty string then the default image, a double right arrow bitmap, is drawn.
Default value: {}

-outline

Resource name: outline
Resource class: Outline
Description: Use this option to give the calendar a grid-like appearance and draw a box around each day of the month.
Default value: #d9d9d9

-selectcolor

Resource name: selectColor
Resource class: Foreground

Description: When you click on a day of the month, a box is drawn around it. This option specifies the color of that box.
Default value: red

-selectthickness

Resource name: selectThickness
Resource class: SelectThickness
Description: When you click on a day of the month, a box is drawn around it. This option specifies the width in pixels of the outline of that box.
Default value: 3

-startday

Resource name: startDay
Resource class: Day
Description: Specifies the starting day of each week. By default, the leftmost column of days in the calendar contains Sundays. If you set -startday to Friday, for example, then the days of the month will be redrawn such that the leftmost column contains the Fridays of that month. Note that this does not alter the text at the top of the screen representing the days of the week, however, so you should probably modify -days if you modify -startday.
Default value: sunday

-titlefont

Resource name: titleFont
Resource class: Font
Description: Specifies the font to be used for the month and year at the top of the calendar.
Default value: -*-helvetica-bold-r-normal-*-140-*

-weekdaybackground

Resource name: weekdayBackground
Resource class: Background
Description: The background color for each weekday (Monday-Friday).
Default value: #d9d9d9

-weekendbackground

Resource name: weekendBackground
Resource class: Background
Description: The background color for each weekend day (Saturday and Sunday).
Default value: #d9d9d9

Public Methods

Associated Methods
None

Inherited Methods
Refer to Chapter 11 for information on each of these inherited methods.

Method Name	Inherited From
cget	itk::Archetype
component	itk::Archetype
config	itk::Archetype
configure	itk::Archetype

Widget-Specific Methods

get

Usage: pathName *get* ?format?
Description: Retrieves the currently selected date in one of two formats specified by the optional format argument. The default value for this argument is -string, which returns the selected date in the format, mm/dd/yyyy. You may also specify -clicks, which returns the date as the number of seconds since the epoch. You can then format this value in a number of ways with the **clock** command. See the clock man page for more details.

select

Usage: pathName *select* ?date?
Description: Changes the currently selected date to the value specified by the optional date argument. This argument may be any explicit date, such as 10/26/99, or it may be a relative date such as "1 week ago" or "tomorrow." The default value is "now," which is the current date. Refer to the clock man page for more details on relative dates. Note that the calendar does not automatically show the month for the specified date. If the currently displayed month is November 1999, for example, it will still be shown if you select 1/2/2000. If you then page forward to January 2000, then the 2nd will be selected.

14

show

Usage: pathName *show* ?date?
Description: Changes the currently displayed month to the value specified by the optional date argument. This argument may be an explicit date such as 10/26/99, or it may be a relative date such as "1 week ago" or "tomorrow." The default value is "now," which is the current date. Refer to the clock man page for more details on relative dates.

Components

The calendar [incr Widget] is composed of three Tk component widgets: two buttons, a canvas, and the outer hull frame.

Name	Class	Description
backward	Button	The button in the upper-left corner of the calendar used to turn the pages of the calendar backwards
forward	Button	The button in the upper-right corner of the calendar used to turn the pages of the calendar forwards
hull	Calendar	Outer frame around the calendar
page	Canvas	The canvas widget on which the calendar is drawn with a series of lines, rectangles, text, and windows

canvasprintbox

The canvasprintbox [incr Widget] is used to print the contents of a canvas widget to a printer or a file. The output is in PostScript format. The canvasprintbox has several features such as printing in either portrait or landscape mode, stretching canvas contents to fit the printed page, and even printing canvas contents across multiple pages if they are too large to fit on a single page. You import the contents of the canvas into the canvasprintbox with the public *setcanvas* method. The resulting imported image is called a "stamp" and is displayed as a thumbnail view of the original canvas. The stamp shows you how the printed output will appear according to the various configuration options. It's automatically updated as you modify options to configure output settings. You can also use the public *refresh* method to refresh the stamp if the original canvas widget is modified.

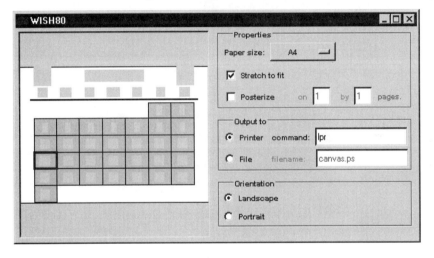

```
# Create the canvasprintbox.
iwidgets::canvasprintbox .cp -stretch 1
pack .cp

# Create a calendar.
iwidgets::calendar .cal -outline black
pack .cal

# Import the calendar into the canvasprintbox for printing later.
# Note that the text will not appear in the stamp.
update
.cp setcanvas [.cal component page]
pack forget .cal
```

Class Model

The canvasprintbox [incr Widget] inherits directly from itk::Widget and contains several other [incr Widgets]: two labeledframes, four entryfields, one radiobox, and one optionmenu.

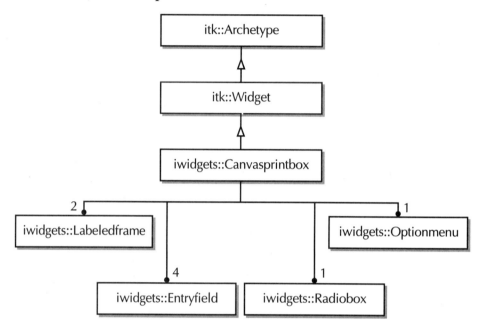

Configuration Options

Standard Options

Refer to the options man page for information on these standard options:

activebackground	activeborderwidth	activeforeground	background
borderwidth	cursor	disabledforeground	foreground
highlightcolor	highlightthickness	insertbackground	insertborderwidth
insertofftime	insertontime	insertwidth	selectbackground
selectborderwidth	selectcolor	selectforeground	

Associated Options

Refer to the associated [incr Widget] for information on each of these options:

Option Name	Associated With
popupcursor	optionmenu
textbackground	entryfield
textfont	entryfield

Inherited Options

Refer to Chapter 11 for information on this inherited option from the [incr Tk] Archetype base class.

Option Name	Inherited From
clientdata	itk::Archetype

Widget-Specific Options

-filename

Resource name: filename
Resource class: FileName
Description: Specifies the filename to which to write the PostScript output if the File radiobutton is selected. This option is tied to the contents of the filename entryfield; modifying one modifies the other.
Default value: canvas.ps

-hpagecnt

Resource name: hPageCnt
Resource class: PageCnt
Description: This option is used in conjunction with the Posterize checkbutton. It stores the number of pages to which to distribute the printed output horizontally. For example, if Posterize is selected and -hpagecnt is set to 3, then the canvas will be printed across three physical pages. The stamp is automatically updated when this option is modified. The number of pages to distribute the output vertically is determined by the -vpagecnt option.
Default value: 1

14

-labelfont

Resource name: labelFont
Resource class: Font
Description: Specifies the font to use for all text in the canvasprintbox except for the text inside the entryfields, which is controlled with the -textfont option
Default value: -adobe-helvetica-bold-r-normal-*-120-*-*-*-*-*-*

-orient

Resource name: orient
Resource class: Orient
Description: Specifies the orientation of the PostScript output to the printer. Valid values are landscape and portrait. This option reflects the currently selected radiobutton in the Orientation radiobox. Modifying this option selects the appropriate radiobutton and also orients the stamp accordingly.
Default value: landscape

-output

Resource name: output
Resource class: Output
Description: This option reflects the selection of either the Printer or File radiobutton. It determines where the PostScript output is sent. Modifying -output selects one of these radiobuttons, depending on the specified value, which must be either printer or file. The printer command or filename is retrieved from the corresponding entryfield component.
Default value: printer

-pagesize

Resource name: pageSize
Resource class: PageSize
Description: This option specifies the physical page size to use when sending output to a printer. Modifying -pagesize updates the optionmenu with the designated value (only in post-itcl3.0.1 releases), which must be one of A5, A4, A3, A2, A1, Legal, or Letter. The stamp is also sized accordingly.
Default value: A4

-posterize

Resource name: posterize
Resource class: Posterize
Description: Specifies whether posterizing the output is enabled or not. Valid values are 0 and 1. "Posterizing the output" means you can distribute it over multiple pages. This allows you to print canvas contents that are otherwise too large to fit on a single page. The resulting group of pages can then be pieced together like a puzzle to view the output. The number of pages is determined by the -hpagecnt and -vpagecnt options. You can also use -posterize with -stretch to blow up, or balloon, a section of a canvas. The stamp is automatically updated when this option is modified.
Default value: 0

-printcmd

Resource name: printCmd
Resource class: PrintCmd
Description: Specifies the command used to print the canvas contents when sending to a printer. Modifying this option automatically updates the command entryfield, but note that entering text into the command entryfield does not automatically update -printcmd.
Default value: lpr

-printregion

Resource name: printRegion
Resource class: PrintRegion
Description: A list of four coordinates that specifies the region of the canvas to print. If set to an empty string, the canvas's entire -scrollregion is printed. Modifying this option automatically updates the stamp.
Default value: {}

-stretch

Resource name: stretch
Resource class: Stretch
Description: Specifies whether or not the output should be stretched to fit the page. Valid values are 0 and 1. When stretched, the aspect ratio is retained, and the output will always stay within the page's boundaries. This option is tied to the "Stretch to fit" checkbutton. Note that selecting and deselecting

the checkbutton updates the stamp but does not update the -stretch option, and modifying -stretch updates the checkbutton but not the stamp. **Default value**: 0

-vpagecnt

Resource name: vPageCnt
Resource class: PageCnt
Description: This option is used in conjunction with the Posterize checkbutton. It stores the number of pages to which to distribute the printed output vertically. For example, if Posterize is selected and -vpagecnt is set to 2, then the canvas will be printed on two physical pages. The stamp is automatically updated when this option is modified. The number of pages to distribute the output horizontally is determined by the -hpagecnt option. **Default value**: 1

Public Methods

Associated Methods

None

Inherited Methods

Refer to Chapter 11 for information on each of these inherited methods.

Method Name	Inherited From
cget	itk::Archetype
component	itk::Archetype
config	itk::Archetype
configure	itk::Archetype

Widget-Specific Methods

getoutput

Usage: pathName *getoutput*
Description: Returns the value associated with the -filename or -printcmd option, depending on which radiobutton is selected. This value is the same as the contents of the corresponding entryfield.

print

Usage: pathName *print*
Description: Prints the contents of the canvas according to the values stored in each of the associated configuration options. A zero is returned if the printing failed, and a one is returned on success.

refresh

Usage: pathName *refresh*
Description: Refreshes the stamp. Use this method, for example, if the canvas has been modified to refresh the corresponding thumbnail view in the canvasprintbox.

setcanvas

Usage: pathName *setcanvas* canvas
Description: Imports the canvas widget specified by the canvas argument as a thumbnail image into the canvas component of the canvasprintbox. This thumbnail image is called the stamp. It shows you how the printed output will appear according to the output settings selected prior to output.

stop

Usage: pathName *stop*
Description: Stops the drawing of the stamp. Use this method if withdrawing the canvasprintbox to avoid extra processing when the screen is not being viewed.

Components

The canvasprintbox [incr Widget] is composed of numerous Tk widgets and [incr Widgets], as outlined in the following table.

Name	Class	Description
canvas	Canvas	The canvas area on the left side of the canvasprintbox in which the stamp is displayed
canvasframe	Frame	The frame that contains the canvas component

Name	Class	Description
fileef	Entryfield	The entryfield used for manually entering the filename
filerb	Radiobutton	The File radiobutton
hpcnt	Entryfield	The entryfield used for manually entering the number of horizontal pages to print when posterizing is enabled
hull	Canvasprintbox	The frame around the entire canvasprintbox
orientom	Radiobox	The radiobox used for output orientation
outputom	Labeledframe	Contains the two radiobuttons used for choosing output location: printer or file
pages	Label	The label widget to the left of the hpcnt and vpcnt components that simply reads, "pages"
paperom	Optionmenu	The "Paper size" optionmenu
postercb	Checkbutton	The Posterize checkbutton
printeref	Entryfield	The entryfield used for manually entering the printer command
printerrb	Radiobutton	The Printer radiobutton
propsframe	Labeledframe	The topmost labeledframe that contains the paper size, stretch to fit, and posterize options
stretchcb	Checkbutton	The "Stretch to fit" checkbutton
vpcnt	Entryfield	The entryfield used for manually entering the number of vertical pages to print when posterizing is enabled

canvasprintdialog

The canvasprintdialog [incr Widget] allows you to print the contents of a
canvas widget to a file or printer. A canvasprintdialog is basically just a dialog
window with a canvasprintbox [incr Widget]. You don't have to add buttons
to operate on the canvasprintbox since the dialogshell does this for you.

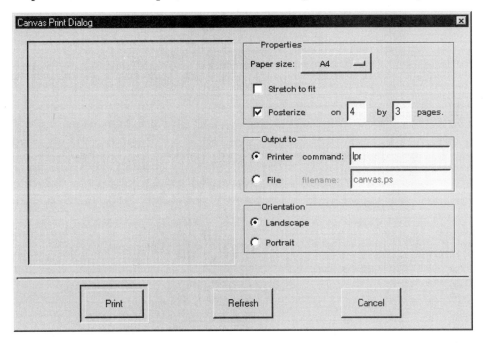

```
# Create the canvasprintdialog and tell it to draw itself.
iwidgets::canvasprintdialog .cpd -posterize 1 -hpagecnt 4 \
  -vpagecnt 3 -textbackground ghostwhite
.cpd activate
```

Class Model

The canvasprintdialog [incr Widget] inherits from iwidgets::Dialog and contains a canvasprintbox [incr Widget]. It also has a buttonbox through inheritance, which is shown in the class model for the dialogshell.

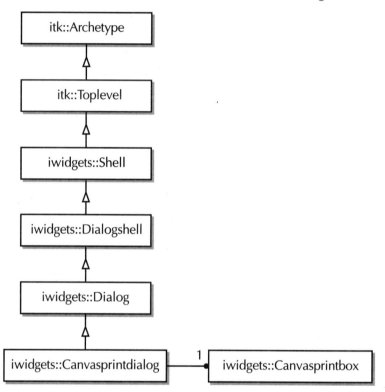

Configuration Options

Standard Options

Refer to the options man page for information on these standard options:

background	cursor	foreground	height

Associated Options

Refer to the associated [incr Widget] for information on each of these options:

Option Name	Associated With
filename	canvasprintbox
hpagecnt	canvasprintbox
orient	canvasprintbox
output	canvasprintbox
pagesize	canvasprintbox
posterize	canvasprintbox
printcmd	canvasprintbox
printregion	canvasprintbox
stretch	canvasprintbox
vpagecnt	canvasprintbox

Inherited Options

Refer to the [incr Widget] or [incr Tk] base class for information on each of these options. The [incr Tk] base classes are discussed in Chapter 11.

Option Name	Inherited From
buttonboxpadx	iwidgets::Dialogshell
buttonboxpady	iwidgets::Dialogshell
buttonboxpos	iwidgets::Dialogshell
clientdata	itk::Archetype
height	iwidgets::Shell
master	iwidgets::Shell
modality	iwidgets::Shell
padx	iwidgets::Dialogshell

14

Option Name	Inherited From
pady	iwidgets::Dialogshell
separator	iwidgets::Dialogshell
thickness	iwidgets::Dialogshell
width	iwidgets::Shell

Widget-Specific Options
None

Public Methods

Associated Methods

Refer to the associated [incr Widget] for information on each of these methods. The Canvasprintdialog class simply provides wrapper methods for these methods:

Method Name	Associated With
getoutput	canvasprintbox
print	canvasprintbox
refresh	canvasprintbox
setcanvas	canvasprintbox

Inherited Methods

Refer to the [incr Widget] or [incr Tk] base class for information on each of these methods. The [incr Tk] base classes are discussed in Chapter 11.

Method Name	Inherited From
activate	iwidgets::Shell
add	iwidgets::Dialogshell
buttonconfigure	iwidgets::Dialogshell
buttoncget	iwidgets::Dialogshell
cget	itk::Archetype

Method Name	Inherited From
center	iwidgets::Shell
childsite	iwidgets::Dialogshell
component	itk::Archetype
config	itk::Archetype
configure	itk::Archetype
deactivate	iwidgets::Shell
default	iwidgets::Dialogshell
delete	iwidgets::Dialogshell
hide	iwidgets::Dialogshell
index	iwidgets::Dialogshell
insert	iwidgets::Dialogshell
invoke	iwidgets::Dialogshell
show	iwidgets::Dialogshell

Widget-Specific Methods
None

Components

The canvasprintbox [incr Widget] is composed of a canvasprintbox and a buttonbox separated by a divider line. All components are packed inside the hull frame.

Name	Class	Description
cpb	Canvasprintbox	The canvasprintbox [incr Widget]
separator	Frame	The divider line between the canvasprintbox and the buttonbox
hull	Canvasprintdialog	The frame around the entire canvasprintdialog
bbox	Buttonbox	The buttonbox [incr Widget] at the bottom of the screen

14

checkbox

The checkbox [incr Widget] is used to group together multiple checkbuttons, similar to how a radiobox groups together multiple radiobuttons. The checkbox provides several public methods for manipulating checkbuttons; you can add, delete, insert, select, or deselect checkbuttons. You can also configure them through a variety of configuration options.

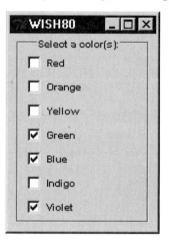

```
# Create the checkbox.
iwidgets::checkbox .cb -labeltext "Select a color(s):"
pack .cb -fill both -expand 1
wm geometry . 150x195

# Add checkbuttons.
.cb add red -text Red
.cb add orange -text Orange
.cb add yellow -text Yellow
.cb add green -text Green
.cb add blue -text Blue
.cb add indigo -text Indigo
.cb add violet -text Violet

# Select some.
.cb select 3; .cb select 4; .cb select end
```

Class Model

The checkbox [incr Widget] inherits from iwidgets::Labeledframe. It is one of only three [incr Widgets] that does not have either itk::Widget or itk::Toplevel in its inheritance hierarchy.

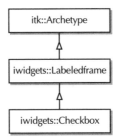

Configuration Options

Standard Options

Refer to the options man page for information on these standard options:

background	borderwidth	cursor	foreground	relief

Associated Options

None

Inherited Options

Refer to the [incr Widget] or [incr Tk] base class for information on each of these options. The [incr Tk] base classes are discussed in Chapter 11.

Option Name	Inherited From
clientdata	itk::Archetype
ipadx	iwidgets::Labeledframe
ipady	iwidgets::Labeledframe
labelbitmap	iwidgets::Labeledframe

Option Name	Inherited From
labelfont	iwidgets::Labeledframe
labelimage	iwidgets::Labeledframe
labelmargin	iwidgets::Labeledframe
labelpos	iwidgets::Labeledframe
labeltext	iwidgets::Labeledframe
labelvariable	iwidgets::Labeledframe

Widget-Specific Options

-command

Resource name: command
Resource class: Command
Description: Specifies a Tcl command to be evaluated when a change occurs in the current checkbox selection. Note that this only works in post-itcl3.0.1 releases.
Default value: {}

Public Methods

Associated Methods

None

Inherited Methods

Refer to the [incr Widget] or [incr Tk] base class for information on each of these methods. The [incr Tk] base classes are discussed in Chapter 11.

Method Name	Inherited From
cget	itk::Archetype
childsite	iwidgets::Labeledframe
component	itk::Archetype
config	itk::Archetype
configure	itk::Archetype

Widget-Specific Methods

add

Usage: pathName *add* tag ?arg arg ...?
Description: Adds a new checkbutton to the checkbox. The tag argument is the symbolic name to assign to the new checkbutton. This name can then be used with other methods such as *delete* and *component* to access the checkbutton. You may optionally specify any valid checkbutton configuration option and corresponding value following the tag argument to initialize the new checkbutton.

buttonconfigure

Usage: pathName *buttonconfigure* index ?arg arg ...?
Description: Use this method to modify a checkbutton's configuration option(s) or to print information about a single checkbutton option. The index argument can be either the symbolic name of the checkbutton specified when it was added or the numerical index of the checkbutton. For example, the topmost checkbutton for a checkbox with four checkbuttons has a numerical index of 0, and the bottommost has a numerical index of 3. Following index, you may optionally specify a single configuration option or pairs of configuration options and values. If you only specify the index argument, then all of that checkbutton's options are printed. If you specify a single option, then only that option's information is printed. If you specify one or more pairs of options and values, those options are configured with the designated values for the specified checkbutton.

delete

Usage: pathName *delete* index
Description: Deletes the checkbutton specified by the index argument. The checkbutton is destroyed, and the index values of the other checkbuttons are adjusted accordingly. See *buttonconfigure* for more information on the index argument.

deselect

Usage: pathName *deselect* index
Description: Deselects the checkbutton specified by the index argument. See *buttonconfigure* for more information on index.

14

flash

Usage: pathName *flash* index
Description: Flashes the checkbutton specified by the index argument.
See *buttonconfigure* for more information on index.

get

Usage: pathName *get* ?index?
Description: Returns the value of the checkbutton specified by the optional
index argument. If no argument is specified, then a list of all selected
checkbuttons is returned in increasing order by index. See *buttonconfigure* for
more information on index. The default value of index is an empty string.

index

Usage: pathName *index* index
Description: Returns the numerical index of the checkbutton corresponding
to the index argument. You can use this method to determine the numerical
index corresponding to a checkbutton's symbolic name. See *buttonconfigure* for
more information on the index argument.

insert

Usage: pathName *insert* index tag ?arg arg ...?
Description: Inserts a new checkbutton in the checkbox just before the
checkbutton specified by the index argument. See *buttonconfigure* for more
information on this argument. The tag argument is the symbolic name for
the new checkbutton. You can then optionally specify any number of valid
checkbutton configuration options to initialize the new checkbutton. This
method is similar to *add* except you have control over where the new
checkbutton is placed.

select

Usage: pathName *select* index
Description: Selects the checkbutton specified by the index argument
(post-itcl3.0.1 releases only). See *buttonconfigure* for more information on
index.

toggle

Usage: pathName *toggle* index
Description: Toggles the checkbutton specified by the index argument between selected and unselected. See *buttonconfigure* for more information on index.

Components

When a checkbox is first created, it contains hull, label, and childsite components, as outlined in the following table. As you add new checkbuttons to the checkbox, each one becomes a new component widget.

Name	Class	Description
childsite	Frame	The frame around the checkbuttons
hull	Checkbox	The frame around the entire checkbox
label	Label	The label that's positioned within the grooved relief of the hull frame

combobox

The combobox [incr Widget] is a specialized type of entryfield. There are actually two types of comboboxes. By default, an arrow button is provided next to the entryfield and is used to display a drop-down scrolledlistbox. The other type of combobox permanently displays the scrolledlistbox, and there is no arrow button. The type of combobox depends on the value of the -dropdown configuration option. Several methods are provided for you to manipulate the entries in the scrolledlistbox as well as the entryfield. A combobox is similar to an optionmenu, except you can manually edit the entries in a combobox. The combobox has other useful features such as autocompletion, which is determined by the -completion configuration option.

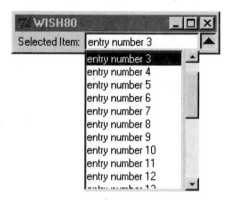

```
# Create the combobox.
iwidgets::combobox .cb -labeltext "Selected Item:"
pack .cb

# Insert some data into the scrolledlistbox.
for {set i 1} {$i <= 25} {incr i} {
  .cb insert list end "entry number $i"
}

# Select the third entry.
.cb selection set 2

# Display the dropdown scrolledlistbox.
update
.cb invoke
```

Class Model

The combobox [incr Widget] inherits from iwidgets::Entryfield. It also contains an instance of the scrolledlistbox [incr Widget].

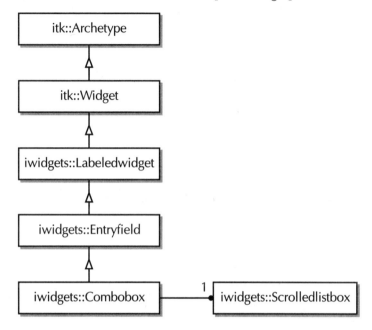

Configuration Options

Standard Options

Refer to the options man page for information on these standard options:

background	borderwidth	cursor	disabledforeground
exportselection	foreground	highlightcolor	highlightthickness
insertbackground	insertborderwidth	insertofftime	insertontime
insertwidth	justify	relief	selectbackground
selectborderwidth	selectforeground		

Associated Options

Refer to the associated [incr Widget] for information on each of these options:

Option Name	Associated With
hscrollmode	scrolledlistbox
textbackground	scrolledlistbox
textfont	scrolledlistbox
vscrollmode	scrolledlistbox

Inherited Options

Refer to the [incr Widget] or [incr Tk] base class for information on each of these options. The [incr Tk] base classes are discussed in Chapter 11.

Option Name	Inherited From
childsitepos	iwidgets::Entryfield
clientdata	itk::Archetype
command	iwidgets::Entryfield
fixed	iwidgets::Entryfield
focuscommand	iwidgets::Entryfield
invalid	iwidgets::Entryfield
labelbitmap	iwidgets::Labeledwidget
labelfont	iwidgets::Labeledwidget
labelimage	iwidgets::Labeledwidget
labelmargin	iwidgets::Labeledwidget
labelpos	iwidgets::Labeledwidget
labeltext	iwidgets::Labeledwidget
labelvariable	iwidgets::Labeledwidget
show	iwidgets::Entryfield
textbackground	iwidgets::Entryfield

Option Name	Inherited From
textfont	iwidgets::Entryfield
textvariable	iwidgets::Entryfield
validate	iwidgets::Entryfield
width	iwidgets::Entryfield

Widget-Specific Options

-arrowrelief

Resource name: arrowRelief
Resource class: Relief
Description: Specifies the relief to be used for the arrow button.
Default value: raised

-completion

Resource name: completion
Resource class: Completion
Description: A Boolean used to turn autocompletion on and off. If turned on, then the combobox attempts to autocomplete the text that is typed into the entryfield to match an entry that may exist in the listbox. For example, if an entry in the listbox reads "hello world" and is the only entry that begins with the letter h, then typing an h into the entryfield (if it's blank) will cause the text "hello world" to appear with all but the h highlighted. Then, if you type the letter e, all but the "he" will be highlighted. As soon as you type a letter that is not a match, the text is no longer highlighted.
Default value: true

-dropdown

Resource name: dropdown
Resource class: Dropdown
Description: A Boolean value that specifies the style to use for the combobox: drop-down or simple. A drop-down combobox has an arrow button used to pop up a scrollable listbox of items below the entryfield. A simple combobox does not have the arrow button and always shows the listbox.
Default value: true

14

-editable

Resource name: editable
Resource class: Editable
Description: A Boolean value that specifies whether input is allowed into the entryfield.
Default value: true

-grab

Resource name: grab
Resource class: Grab
Description: Specifies the grab level to be used for the combobox. Valid values are local and global. This option is used when the dropdown listbox is displayed.
Default value: local

-listheight

Resource name: listHeight
Resource class: Height
Description: Specifies the height in pixels of the scrolledlistbox component.
Default value: 150

-margin

Resource name: margin
Resource class: Margin
Description: Specifies the distance in pixels between the entryfield and the arrow button for the drop-down listbox.
Default value: 1

-popupcursor

Resource name: popupCursor
Resource class: Cursor
Description: Specifies the cursor shape to use over the drop-down scrolledlistbox. This option is only used when -dropdown is set to true.
Default value: arrow

-selectioncommand

Resource name: selectionCommand
Resource class: SelectionCommand
Description: Specifies a Tcl command to be evaluated when an item in the scrolledlistbox is selected. The drop-down listbox is removed (if -dropdown is set to true), the item is inserted into the entryfield, and then the -selectioncommand procedure is evaluated.
Default value: {}

-state

Resource name: state
Resource class: State
Description: Controls the state of the combobox. Valid values are normal and disabled. Disabling the combobox disallows entering text into the entryfield and opening the drop-down listbox. Note that this option only works correctly when -dropdown is true for itcl3.0.1.
Default value: normal

-unique

Resource name: unique
Resource class: Unique
Description: A Boolean value that determines whether or not duplicate entries are allowed in the listbox. Turning this option on allows duplicate entries to be inserted. If turned off, entering a duplicate entry causes that item to be selected.
Default value: true

Public Methods

Associated Methods

Refer to the associated [incr Widget] for information on each of these methods. The Combobox class simply provides wrappers for these methods:

Method Name	Associated With
curselection	scrolledlistbox
getcurselection	scrolledlistbox
justify	scrolledlistbox

14

Method Name	Associated With
selection	scrolledlistbox
size	scrolledlistbox
sort	scrolledlistbox
xview	scrolledlistbox
yview	scrolledlistbox

Inherited Methods

Refer to the [incr Widget] or [incr Tk] base class for information on each of these methods. The [incr Tk] base classes are discussed in Chapter 11.

Method Name	Inherited From
cget	itk::Archetype
childsite	iwidgets::Entryfield
component	itk::Archetype
config	itk::Archetype
configure	itk::Archetype
icursor	iwidgets::Entryfield
index	iwidgets::Entryfield
scan	iwidgets::Entryfield

Widget-Specific Methods

delete

Usage: pathName *delete* component index1 ?index2?
Description: Deletes items in the scrolledlistbox or text in the entryfield, depending on the value of the component argument. Valid values for component are entry and list. If entry is specified, then the text between

index1 and index2 in the entryfield is deleted. Otherwise, if list is specified, then the items between index1 and index2 in the scrolledlistbox are deleted. The index1 and index2 arguments should be numeric values corresponding to an indexed position in the entryfield or scrolledlistbox. The index2 argument is only optional when deleting items from the scrolledlistbox. It defaults to the empty string. If an entry in the scrolledlistbox is deleted that is currently displayed in the entryfield, it will be deleted from the entryfield.

get

Usage: pathName *get* ?index?
Description: Retrieves the contents of the entryfield unless the optional index argument is specified, which is an index into the scrolledlistbox.

insert

Usage: pathName *insert* component index args
Description: Inserts a new item into the scrolledlistbox or text into the entryfield, depending on the component argument. This argument must be either entry or list. The item or text is then inserted just before the element specified by the index argument. The value of args must be a single argument if inserting text into the entryfield. It may be variable length if inserting items into the scrolledlistbox. Each item in the latter case will become a separate entry in the scrolledlistbox.

invoke

Usage: pathName *invoke*
Description: Post or unpost the drop-down scrolledlistbox. If it is currently posted, then this method unposts it and vice versa.

selection

Usage: pathName *selection* option first ?last?
Description: Adjusts the selection within the listbox and updates the contents of the entryfield accordingly. The option argument must be anchor, clear, includes, or set. You can use set to select a listbox item and enter it in the entryfield, and you can use clear to deselect items and clear the entryfield.

14

Components

The combobox [incr Widget] is composed of a scrolledlistbox [incr Widget] and several other Tk widgets, as outlined in the following table.

Name	Class	Description
list	Scrolledlistbox	The scrolledlistbox displayed directly beneath the entryfield
popup	Toplevel	The top-level window created to display the scrolledlistbox if -dropdown is true
label	Label	The label component of the entryfield [incr Widget]
hull	Combobox	The frame around the combobox
entry	Entry	The entry component of the entryfield [incr Widget]
arrowBtn	Button	The arrow button used to display the scrolledlistbox when -dropdown is true

dateentry

The dateentry [incr Widget] combines the datefield and calendar [incr Widgets]. You can enter a date directly into the datefield with the keyboard, or you can press a button to display a calendar and then select a date with the mouse. When you select a date on the calendar, that date is entered into the datefield and the calendar is removed. You can open the calendar again at any time with the icon button.

```
# Create the dateentry.
iwidgets::dateentry .de -labeltext "Selected date:" \
  -outline black -weekendbackground grey60 \
  -weekdaybackground ghostwhite
pack .de

# Specify a particular date. Then you can manually click on the icon
# button to display the calendar as shown.
.de show 1/2/00
```

Class Model

The dateentry [incr Widget] inherits from iwidgets::Datefield. It also contains an instance of the calendar [incr Widget].

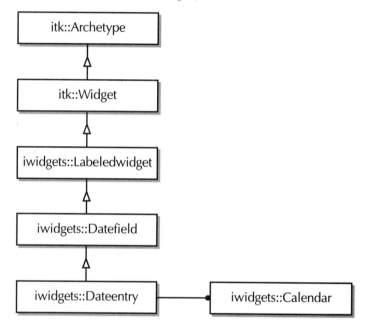

Configuration Options

Standard Options

Refer to the options man page for information on these standard options:

background	borderwidth	cursor	disabledforeground
exportselection	foreground	highlightcolor	highlightthickness
insertbackground	justify	relief	

Associated Options

Refer to the associated [incr Widget] for information on each of these options:

Option Name	Associated With
backwardimage	calendar
buttonforeground	calendar
currentdatefont	calendar
datefont	calendar
dayfont	calendar
days	calendar
forwardimage	calendar
height	calendar
outline	calendar
selectcolor	calendar
selectthickness	calendar
startday	calendar
titlefont	calendar
weekdaybackground	calendar
weekendbackground	calendar
width	calendar

Inherited Options

Refer to the [incr Widget] or [incr Tk] base class for information on each of these options. The [incr Tk] base classes are discussed in Chapter 11.

Option Name	Inherited From
childsitepos	iwidgets::Datefield
clientdata	itk::Archetype
command	iwidgets::Datefield
iq	iwidgets::Datefield
labelbitmap	iwidgets::Labeledwidget

14

Option Name	Inherited From
labelfont	iwidgets::Labeledwidget
labelimage	iwidgets::Labeledwidget
labelmargin	iwidgets::Labeledwidget
labelpos	iwidgets::Labeledwidget
labeltext	iwidgets::Labeledwidget
labelvariable	iwidgets::Labeledwidget
textbackground	iwidgets::Datefield
textfont	iwidgets::Datefield

Widget-Specific Options

-grab

Resource name: grab
Resource class: Grab
Description: Specifies the grab level to be used for the popup calendar [incr Widget]. Valid values are local and global. This option is only used when the calendar is displayed.
Default value: local

-icon

Resource name: icon
Resource class: Icon
Description: Specifies the image to use for the icon button next to the entry component. If one is not specified, then a default pixmap or bitmap is used.
Default value: {}

Public Methods

Associated Methods

Refer to the associated [incr Widget] for information on each of these methods. The Dateentry simply provides wrapper for these methods:

Method Name	Associated With
curselection	scrolledlistbox
getcurselection	scrolledlistbox
justify	scrolledlistbox
selection	scrolledlistbox
size	scrolledlistbox
sort	scrolledlistbox
xview	scrolledlistbox
yview	scrolledlistbox

Inherited Methods

Refer to the [incr Widget] or [incr Tk] base class for information on each inherited method. Note that the *childsite* method is defined in iwidgets::Datefield in post-itcl3.1.0 releases only. The [incr Tk] base classes are discussed in Chapter 11.

Method Name	Inherited From
cget	itk::Archetype
childsite	iwidgets::Datefield*
component	itk::Archetype
config	itk::Archetype
configure	itk::Archetype
get	iwidgets::Datefield
isvalid	iwidgets::Datefield
show	iwidgets::Datefield

Widget-Specific Methods

None

14

Components

The dateentry [incr Widget] is composed of two labels and an entry widget packed into the hull frame.

Name	Class	Description
label	Label	The label to the left of the entry component
iconbutton	Label	The icon button to the right of the entry component, used to open the calendar
hull	Dateentry	The frame around the dateentry
date	Entry	The entry area that displays the textual date

datefield

The datefield [incr Widget] is similar to an entryfield with an editable date string in the entry component. The default value is the current date, which is displayed as mm/dd/yyyy. You can edit the date directly in the entry widget or set it with the *show* method. When using the latter, you can even specify relative dates such as "3 weeks ago" or "tomorrow." Refer to the clock man page for more details on relative dates. The datefield also offers automatic date validation, depending on the -iq configuration option. By default, the datefield disallows entering invalid dates.

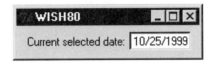

```
# Create the datefield.
iwidgets::datefield .df -labeltext "Current selected date:"
pack .df -padx 8 -pady 6

# Show the date 1 week from now.
.df show "1 week"
```

Class Model

The datefield [incr Widget] inherits from iwidgets::Labeledwidget. It does not interact with any other [incr Widgets] outside of its inheritance tree.

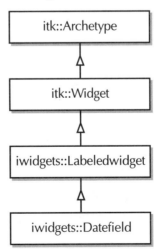

Configuration Options

Standard Options

Refer to the options man page for information on these standard options:

background	borderwidth	cursor	disabledforeground
exportselection	foreground	highlightcolor	highlightthickness
insertbackground	justify	relief	

Associated Options

None

Inherited Options

Refer to the [incr Widget] or [incr Tk] base class for information on each of these options. The [incr Tk] base classes are discussed in Chapter 11.

Option Name	Inherited From
clientdata	itk::Archetype
labelbitmap	iwidgets::Labeledwidget
labelfont	iwidgets::Labeledwidget
labelimage	iwidgets::Labeledwidget
labelmargin	iwidgets::Labeledwidget
labelpos	iwidgets::Labeledwidget
labeltext	iwidgets::Labeledwidget
labelvariable	iwidgets::Labeledwidget
state	iwidgets::Labeledwidget

Widget-Specific Options

-childsitepos

Resource Name: childSitePos
Resource Class: Position
Description: Specifies the positioning of the datefield's childsite frame. Valid values are n, s, e, and w. The childsite is typically only used by the dateentry [incr Widget], which places the calendar button in the childsite.

For a datefield object, the childsite is empty. You can add a widget to the childsite, such as a label or a button, by using the *childsite* method. See the documentation on this method for important details.
Default Value: e

-command

Resource name: command
Resource class: Command
Description: Specifies a Tcl command procedure to be evaluated when the RETURN key is pressed in the entry component.
Default value: {}

-iq

Resource name: iq
Resource class: Iq
Description: This option controls the "intelligence" of the datefield. Valid values are high, average, and low. If set to high, the datefield disallows setting invalid dates in the entry component, including leap years. For example, if the displayed date is 10/31/99, the datefield will automatically change the day to 30 if you change the month to 9 since there are only 30 days in September. If -iq is set to average, then the datefield will allow you to enter invalid days, such as 2/30/99. The months are still limited to 01-12, however. Setting -iq to low means there is no automatic date validation; you can enter a date of 99/99/99. It is assumed that if either average or low is used, the date will be validated at some future time via the public *isvalid* method.
Default value: high

-textbackground

Resource name: textBackground
Resource class: Background
Description: Specifies the background color of the entry component. The entry's -background option is renamed to -textbackground when it is added in the *constructor*.
Default value: Windows = SystemWindow, Unix = #d9d9d9

-textfont

Resource name: textFont
Resource class: Font
Description: Specifies the font to use for the text in the entry component. The entry's -font option is renamed to -textfont when it is added in the *constructor*.
Default value: Windows = {{MS Sans Serif} 8}, Unix = {Helvetica -12}

14

Public Methods

Associated Methods

None

Inherited Methods

Refer to Chapter 11 for information on each of these inherited methods.

Method Name	Inherited From
cget	itk::Archetype
component	itk::Archetype
config	itk::Archetype
configure	itk::Archetype

Widget-Specific Methods

childsite

Usage: pathName *childsite*
Description: Returns the Tk window pathname of the datefield's childsite frame. This frame is empty by default, but you can put a widget in it if desired and position it with the -childsitepos option. Make sure you use the **grid** command and not **pack** if you do this! Note also that this command only behaves properly in post-itcl3.1.0 releases.

get

Usage: pathName *get* ?format?
Description: Returns the contents of the entry component as either a date string or an integer clock value, depending on the value of the optional format argument. This argument may be either -string or -clicks, and it defaults to -string. Specifying -clicks returns the number of seconds corresponding to the designated date as calculated by the **clock scan** command.

isvalid

Usage: pathName *isvalid*
Description: Validates the contents of the entry component and returns either a one or a zero. If the date is valid, such as 09/21/1996, then a one is returned. A zero is returned for invalid dates such as 02/29/98.

show

Usage: pathName *show* ?date?
Description: Shows the date specified by the date argument in the entry component. The default value is the current date. You may specify a date string or an integer clock value. The date string may be a relative date such as tomorrow, yesterday, or "1 week ago." Refer to the clock man page for more details on relative dates.

Components

The datefield [incr Widget] simply consists of a label and an entry packed into the hull frame.

Name	Class	Description
label	Label	The label to the left (if -labelpos is set to w) of the entry component
hull	Datefield	The frame around the datefield
entry	Entry	The entry area that displays the textual date

dialog

The dialog [incr Widget] implements a standard dialog box with four buttons in a buttonbox component: OK, Apply, Cancel, and Help. The dialog provides a childsite frame that is used by derived classes to create different kinds of dialog boxes such as a fileselectiondialog and a promptdialog. You can also use the childsite to create other kinds of dialog boxes specific to the needs of your applications. All of the buttonbox public methods have corresponding public wrapper methods in the Dialog class, so you can modify the buttonbox directly through the dialog.

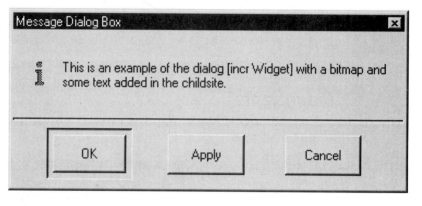

```
# Create the dialog.
iwidgets::dialog .d -title "Message Dialog Box"

# Hide the Help button.
.d hide Help

# Add an info bitmap and a message in the childsite frame.
set cs [.d childsite]
label $cs.info -bitmap info -foreground blue
message $cs.msg -justify left -width 300 -text "This is an\
   example of the dialog \[incr Widget\] with a bitmap and\
   some text added in the childsite."
pack $cs.info -padx 8 -side left
pack $cs.msg -pady 12 -side left

# Tell the dialog to draw itself in the middle of the screen.
.d center
update idletasks
after idle ".d activate"
```

Class Model

The dialog [incr Widget] inherits from iwidgets::Dialogshell and serves as the immediate base class for several [incr Widget] dialog boxes. It has a buttonbox component through inheritance, which is shown in the dialogshell class model.

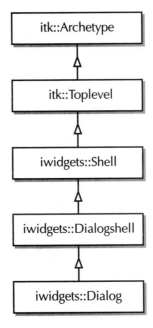

Configuration Options

Standard Options

Refer to the options man page for information on these standard options:

background	cursor	foreground	takefocus

Associated Options

None

Inherited Options

Refer to the [incr Widget] or [incr Tk] base class for information on each of these options. The [incr Tk] base classes are discussed in Chapter 11.

Option Name	Inherited From
buttonboxpadx	iwidgets::DialogShell
buttonboxpady	iwidgets::DialogShell
buttonboxpos	iwidgets::DialogShell
clientdata	itk::Archetype
height	iwidgets::Shell
master	iwidgets::Shell
modality	iwidgets::Shell
padx	iwidgets::DialogShell
pady	iwidgets::DialogShell
separator	iwidgets::DialogShell
thickness	iwidgets::DialogShell
title	iwidgets::Shell
width	iwidgets::Shell

Widget-Specific Options

None

Public Methods

Associated Methods

Refer to the associated [incr Widget] for information on each of these methods. The Dialog class simply provides wrappers for these methods:

Method Name	Associated With
add	buttonbox
buttoncget	buttonbox
buttonconfigure	buttonbox
default	buttonbox
delete	buttonbox
hide	buttonbox
index	buttonbox
insert	buttonbox
invoke	buttonbox
show	buttonbox

Inherited Methods

Refer to the [incr Widget] or [incr Tk] base class for information on each of these methods. The [incr Tk] base classes are discussed in Chapter 11.

Method Name	Inherited From
activate	iwidgets::Shell
cget	itk::Archetype
center	iwidgets::Shell
childsite	iwidgets::Dialogshell
component	itk::Archetype
config	itk::Archetype
configure	itk::Archetype
deactivate	iwidgets::Shell

Widget-Specific Methods

None

14

Components

The dialog [incr Widget] is composed of a childsite frame and a buttonbox [incr Widget] separated by a divider line. The childsite frame is non-public and not accessible via the *component* method. It is therefore not shown in the components table.

Name	Class	Description
bbox	Buttonbox	The buttonbox [incr Widget] at the bottom of the dialog box
hull	Dialog	The top-level window
separator	Frame	The divider line between the childsite and the buttonbox

dialogshell

The dialogshell [incr Widget] provides generic base class functionality for a dialog window. It has three main components: a childsite frame in which you can add messages or other widgets to create specialized dialog windows, a separator bar that is drawn between the childsite and the buttonbox, and a buttonbox in which you can add any number of buttons. When the dialogshell is initially created, both the childsite and the buttonbox are empty, so you have to fill in these areas. The dialogshell is used mainly as a base class for other [incr Widgets] such as the canvasprintdialog and fileselectiondialog. Usually, the type of dialog window you need is already available as a derived class, but you can build a new dialog box from scratch by creating a dialogshell and filling in the holes if necessary. The dialogshell provides appropriate methods for doing this.

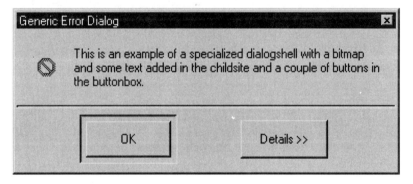

```
# Create the dialogshell.
set ds [iwidgets::dialogshell .ds -pady 12 \
  -title "Generic Error Dialog"]

# Add a couple of buttons.
$ds add ok -text OK -command "$ds deactivate"
$ds add details -text "Details >>" -command {
  # Display detailed error message.
}
$ds default ok

# Add a warning bitmap and a message in the childsite frame.
set cs [$ds childsite]
label $cs.err -bitmap error -foreground red
message $cs.msg -justify left -width 300 -text "This is an\
  example of a specialized dialogshell with a bitmap and\
  some text added in the childsite and a couple of buttons\
```

14

```
    in the buttonbox."
pack $cs.err -padx 8 -side left
pack $cs.msg -side left

# Tell the dialog to draw itself in the middle of the screen.
$ds center
update idletasks
after idle "$ds activate"
```

Class Model

The dialogshell [incr Widget] inherits from iwidgets::Shell and contains a
buttonbox [incr Widget].

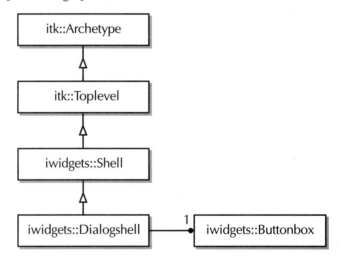

Configuration Options

Standard Options

Refer to the options man page for information on these standard options:

background	cursor	foreground	takefocus

Associated Options

None

Inherited Options

Refer to the [incr Widget] or [incr Tk] base class for information on each of these options. The [incr Tk] base classes are discussed in Chapter 11.

Option Name	Inherited From
clientdata	itk::Archetype
height	iwidgets::Shell
master	iwidgets::Shell
modality	iwidgets::Shell
title	iwidgets::Shell
width	iwidgets::Shell

Widget-Specific Options

-buttonboxpadx

Resource name: buttonBoxPadX
Resource class: Pad
Description: The buttonbox component's -padx option is renamed to -buttonboxpadx. This option specifies the number of pixels between the pushbutton group and the outer edge of the buttonbox hull frame in the x direction.
Default value: 5

-buttonboxpady

Resource name: buttonBoxPadY
Resource class: Pad
Description: The buttonbox component's -pady option is renamed to -buttonboxpady. This option specifies the number of pixels between the pushbutton group and the outer edge of the buttonbox hull frame in the y direction.
Default value: 5

-buttonboxpos

Resource name: buttonBoxPos
Resource class: Position
Description: Specifies the location of the buttonbox relative to the

14

childsite. Valid values are n, s, e, and w. Note that the separator is always between the buttonbox and the childsite, so if you configure this option to e or w, the separator is drawn vertically and the buttonbox is oriented vertically.
Default value: s

-padx

Resource name: padX
Resource class: Pad
Description: Specifies the number of pixels between the childsite and the outer edge of the hull frame in the x direction.
Default value: 10

-pady

Resource name: padY
Resource class: Pad
Description: Specifies the number of pixels between the childsite and the outer edge of the hull frame in the y direction.
Default value: 10

-separator

Resource name: separator
Resource class: Separator
Description: It may appear that this Boolean option determines whether or not the separator bar is drawn, but it actually just specifies whether the separator bar should have a sunken or flat relief. If this option is configured to a false value, then the separator bar is configured to have a flat relief. This means the frame is still mapped in the dialog box, so if you modify the -thickness option, the frame will still consume that space regardless of the value of -separator.
Default value: on

-thickness

Resource name: thickness
Resource class: Thickness
Description: Specifies the thickness of the separator bar. The frame's -height and -width options are configured to the specified value, and its -borderwidth option is configured to half that value.
Default value: 3

Public Methods

Associated Methods

Refer to the associated [incr Widget] for information on each of these methods. The Dialogshell class simply provides wrappers for these methods:

Method Name	Associated With
add	buttonbox
buttoncget	buttonbox
buttonconfigure	buttonbox
default	buttonbox
delete	buttonbox
hide	buttonbox
index	buttonbox
insert	buttonbox
invoke	buttonbox
show	buttonbox

Inherited Methods

Refer to the [incr Widget] or [incr Tk] base class for information on each of these methods. The [incr Tk] base classes are discussed in Chapter 11.

Method Name	Inherited From
activate	iwidgets::Shell
center	iwidgets::Shell
cget	itk::Archetype
component	itk::Archetype
config	itk::Archetype
configure	itk::Archetype
deactivate	iwidgets::Shell

14

Widget-Specific Methods

childsite

Usage: pathName *childsite*
Description: This is an accessor method that returns the Tk window pathname of the dialogshell's childsite frame. You can use this frame to specialize the dialogshell by adding application-specific widgets into the childsite, or you can make new generic dialog boxes such as informational or error dialog boxes.

Components

The dialogshell [incr Widget] consists of a buttonbox [incr Widget] and a childsite frame separated by a divider line. The childsite frame is non-public and is therefore not accessible via the *component* method and isn't shown in the components table.

Name	Class	Description
bbox	Buttonbox	The buttonbox [incr Widget] at the bottom of the dialog box
hull	Dialogshell	The top-level window
separator	Frame	The divider line between the childsite and the buttonbox

disjointlistbox

The disjointlistbox [incr Widget] provides a convenient way for selecting items in one listbox and moving them to another. The disjointlistbox provides two scrolledlistboxes and two buttons for doing this. The buttons can be placed between the scrolledlistboxes or beneath them. Configurable title labels are displayed above each scrolledlistbox, and the total item counts are displayed below each one. The disjointlistbox provides several configuration options and public methods for manipulating component widgets and modifying the data in the scrolledlistboxes.

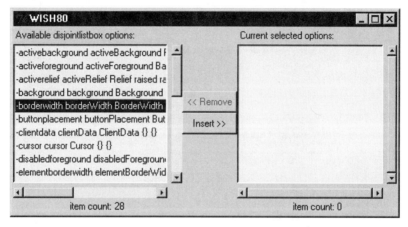

```
# Create the disjointlistbox with the buttons between the two
# scrolledlistboxes.
iwidgets::disjointlistbox .dl -buttonplacement center \
  -borderwidth 2 -textbackground ghostwhite \
  -lhslabeltext "Available disjointlistbox options:" \
  -rhslabeltext "Current selected options:"
pack .dl -fill both -expand 1
wm geometry . 475x225

# Move the labels to the northwest corner of the scrolledlistboxes.
.dl component lhs configure -labelpos nw
.dl component rhs configure -labelpos nw

# Add some data to the left hand side and select the 5th item.
.dl insertlhs [.dl configure]
.dl lhs selection set 4 4
```

14

Class Model

The disjointlistbox [incr Widget] inherits directly from itk::Widget and
contains two scrolledlistbox [incr Widgets].

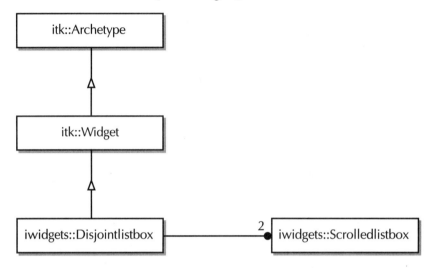

Configuration Options

Standard Options

Refer to the options man page for information on these standard options:

activebackground	activeforeground	background	borderwidth
cursor	disabledforeground	foreground	highlightcolor
highlightthickness	selectbackground	selectborderwidth	selectforeground

Associated Options

Refer to the associated Tk widget or [incr Widget] for information on each of
these options:

Option Name	Associated With
activerelief	Tk scrollbar widget
elementborderwidth	Tk scrollbar widget

Option Name	Associated With
hscrollmode	scrolledlistbox
jump	Tk scrollbar widget
selectmode	scrolledlistbox
textbackground	scrolledlistbox
textfont	scrolledlistbox
troughcolor	Tk scrollbar widget
vscrollmode	scrolledlistbox

Inherited Options

Refer to Chapter 11 for information on this inherited option from the [incr Tk] Archetype base class:

Option Name	Inherited From
clientdata	itk::Archetype

Widget-Specific Options

-buttonplacement

Resource name: buttonPlacement
Resource class: ButtonPlacement
Description: Specifies the location of the two button components. Valid values are center and bottom. Setting this option to center draws the buttons between the two scrolledlistboxes. Setting it to bottom draws the buttons below the scrolledlistboxes.
Default value: bottom

-labelfont

Resource name: labelFont
Resource class: Font
Description: Specifies the font to be used for all text except for text inside the scrolledlistboxes. This includes the labels above and below each scrolledlistbox as well as the buttons.
Default value: Windows = {{MS Sans Serif} 8}, Unix = {Helvetica -12 bold}

14

-lhsbuttonlabel

Resource name: lhsButtonLabel
Resource class: LabelText
Description: Specifies the text to display on the left button if
-buttonplacement is set to bottom. Otherwise, this option refers to the text
on the top button.
Default value: {Insert >>}

-lhslabeltext

Resource name: lhsLabelText
Resource class: LabelText
Description: Specifies the text to display for the label above the left
scrolledlistbox.
Default value: Available

-rhsbuttonlabel

Resource name: rhsButtonLabel
Resource class: LabelText
Description: Specifies the text to display on the right button if
-buttonplacement is set to bottom. Otherwise, this option refers to the text
on the bottom button.
Default value: {<< Remove}

-rhslabeltext

Resource name: rhsLabelText
Resource class: LabelText
Description: Specifies the text to display for the label above the right
scrolledlistbox.
Default value: Current

Public Methods

Associated Methods

None

Inherited Methods

Refer to Chapter 11 for information on each of these inherited methods:

Method Name	Inherited From
cget	itk::Archetype
component	itk::Archetype
config	itk::Archetype
configure	itk::Archetype

Widget-Specific Methods

clear

Usage: pathName *clear*
Description: Removes all items from both scrolledlistboxes and resets the item counts to zero.

getlhs

Usage: pathName *getlhs* ?first? ?last?
Description: Returns a list of items in the left scrolledlistbox between first and last, which are indices into the scrolledlistbox. The first argument defaults to zero, and last defaults to end.

getrhs

Usage: pathName *getrhs* ?first? ?last?
Description: Returns a list of items in the right scrolledlistbox between first and last, which are indices into the scrolledlistbox. The first argument defaults to zero, and last defaults to end.

insertlhs

Usage: pathName *insertlhs* items
Description: Inserts the specified list of items into the left scrolledlistbox. Items may not be duplicated.

insertrhs

Usage: pathName *insertrhs* items
Description: Inserts the specified list of items into the right scrolledlistbox. Items may not be duplicated.

lhs

Usage: pathName *lhs* args
Description: This method allows direct access to the left scrolledlistbox's public methods. The specified arguments are evaluated by this scrolledlistbox, so the arguments should make up a valid scrolledlistbox command.

rhs

Usage: pathName *rhs* args
Description: This method allows direct access to the right scrolledlistbox's public methods. The specified arguments are evaluated by this scrolledlistbox, so the arguments should make up a valid scrolledlistbox command.

setlhs

Usage: pathName *setlhs* items
Description: Replaces all items in the left scrolledlistbox with the new list of items specified by the items argument. The items are sorted before they are inserted.

setrhs

Usage: pathName *setrhs* items
Description: Replaces all items in the right scrolledlistbox with the new list of items specified by the items argument. The items are sorted before they are inserted.

Components

A disjointlistbox [incr Widget] is composed of two buttons, two labels, and two scrolledlistboxes. Each component is packed into the hull frame.

Name	Class	Description
hull	Disjointlistbox	The outermost frame around the disjointlistbox
lhs	Scrolledlistbox	The left scrolledlistbox
lhsbutton	Button	The button used to move items from the left scrolledlistbox to the right scrolledlistbox
lhsCount	Label	The items count label underneath the left scrolledlistbox
rhsbutton	Button	The button used to move items from the right scrolledlistbox to the left scrolledlistbox
rhsCount	Label	The items count label underneath the left scrolledlistbox
rhs	Scrolledlistbox	The right scrolledlistbox

entryfield

The entryfield is one of the most commonly used [incr Widgets]. It simply adds a text label to the left of an entry widget for labeling input areas in a screen. It also has a childsite in which you can add other text such as units for the entry widget. The entryfield has several configuration options and public methods used for controlling the input data. The -validate option is a robust option you can use to validate a wide variety of input, including numeric, hexadecimal, and alphanumeric text.

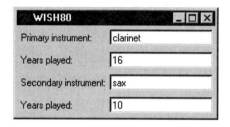

```
# Create some entryfields.
set primary [iwidgets::entryfield .pri \
  -labeltext "Primary instrument:" -validate alphabetic]
set priyears [iwidgets::entryfield .priyrs -validate numeric \
  -labeltext "Years played:"]
set secondary [iwidgets::entryfield .sec \
  -labeltext "Secondary instrument:" -validate alphabetic]
set secyears [iwidgets::entryfield .secyrs -validate numeric \
  -labeltext "Years played:"]
pack $primary $priyears $secondary $secyears -pady 4 -padx 2

# Line up the entryfields with this handy base class procedure.
iwidgets::Labeledwidget::alignlabels \
  $primary $priyears $secondary $secyears

# Add some data.
$primary insert 0 clarinet
$priyears insert 0 16
$secondary insert 0 sax
$secyears insert 0 10
```

Class Model

The entryfield [incr Widget] inherits from iwidgets::Labeledwidget. It does not interact with any other [incr Widgets] outside of its inheritance tree.

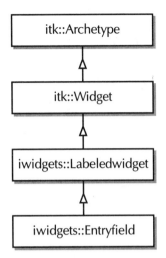

Configuration Options

Standard Options

Refer to the options man page for information on these standard options:

background	borderwidth	cursor	disabledforeground
exportselection	foreground	highlightcolor	highlightthickness
insertbackground	insertbackground	insertborderwidth	insertofftime
insertontime	insertwidth	justify	relief
selectbackground	selectborderwidth	selectforeground	textvariable

Associated Options

Refer to the associated widget for information on each of these options:

Option Name	Associated With
show	Tk entry widget
state	Tk entry widget
width	Tk entry widget

14

Inherited Options

Refer to the [incr Widget] or [incr Tk] base class for information on each of these options. The [incr Tk] base classes are discussed in Chapter 11.

Option Name	Inherited From
clientdata	itk::Archetype
labelbitmap	iwidgets::Labeledwidget
labelfont	iwidgets::Labeledwidget
labelimage	iwidgets::Labeledwidget
labelmargin	iwidgets::Labeledwidget
labelpos	iwidgets::Labeledwidget
labeltext	iwidgets::Labeledwidget
labelvariable	iwidgets::Labeledwidget

Widget-Specific Options

-childsitepos

Resource name: childSitePos
Resource class: Position
Description: Specifies the positioning of the entryfield's childsite frame. This frame is empty by default, but you can create a label inside of it to specify units of input, for example, and position the label to the right of the entry component with this option.
Default value: e

-command

Resource name: command
Resource class: Command
Description: Specifies a Tcl command to be evaluated when the RETURN key is pressed in the entry component.
Default value: {}

-fixed

Resource name: fixed
Resource class: Fixed
Description: Specifies the maximum number of characters you can type into the entry component. Note that this is independent of the entry component's width. The width may be 10 characters, but if -fixed is 2, you may only enter two characters. If -fixed is set to zero, then the number of input characters is unlimited.
Default value: 0

-focuscommand

Resource name: focusCommand
Resource class: Command
Description: Specifies a Tcl command to be evaluated when the entry component receives input focus, which occurs when it receives a <FocusIn> event.
Default value: {}

-invalid

Resource name: invalid
Resource class: Command
Description: Specifies a Tcl command to be evaluated if the entry component's contents fail validation. For example, this procedure would be invoked if you press an alpha character in an entryfield whose -validate option is set to integer.
Default value: bell

-textbackground

Resource name: textBackground
Resource class: Background
Description: Specifies the background color of the entry component. The entry's -background option is renamed to -textbackground when it is added in the *constructor*.
Default value: Windows = SystemWindow, Unix = #d9d9d9

14

-textfont

Resource name: textFont
Resource class: Font
Description: Specifies the font to be used for the text in the entry component. The entry's -font option is renamed to -textfont when it is added in the *constructor*.
Default value: Windows = {{MS Sans Serif} 8}, Unix = {Helvetica -12}

-validate

Resource name: validate
Resource class: Command
Description: Specifies a Tcl command to be evaluated each time you press a key on the keyboard when the entry component has input focus. Valid values are alphabetic, alphanumeric, hexadecimal, integer, real, and the empty string. An empty string disables validation. Use the other keywords for standard text validation. If you need more extensive validation, you can set -validate to the name of a Tcl command such as a procedure or class method. The command must return a Boolean value. If false is returned, then the -invalid option is evaluated. You may specify special substitution characters in the -validate command string to pass useful information into the validation procedure. These characters are outlined as follows:

◆ %W: Replaced with the Tk window pathname of the entryfield.

◆ %P: Replaced with the current contents of the entryfield including the last keystroke. This allows you to reject a keystroke before updating the contents.

◆ %S: Replaced with the current contents of the entryfield excluding the last keystroke.

◆ %c: Replaced with the last keystroke character.

Default value: {}

Public Methods

Associated Methods

Refer to the associated Tk widget for information on each of these methods:

Method Name	Associated With
delete	Tk entry widget
get	Tk entry widget
icursor	Tk entry widget
index	Tk entry widget
insert	Tk entry widget
scan	Tk entry widget
selection	Tk entry widget
xview	Tk entry widget

Inherited Methods

Refer to Chapter 11 for information on each of these inherited methods.

Method Name	Inherited From
cget	itk::Archetype
component	itk::Archetype
config	itk::Archetype
configure	itk::Archetype

Widget-Specific Methods

childsite

Usage: pathName *childsite*
Description: Returns the Tk window pathname of the entryfield's childsite frame. This frame is empty by default, but you can add other widgets to this frame if desired. For example, you might want to show text on both sides of the entry component. Use -labeltext for the left side, and you can create a label in the childsite to display text on the right side. By default, the childsite frame is to the right of the entry component. Its position is controlled with the -childsitepos option.

clear

Usage: pathName *clear*
Description: Deletes the entry component's contents and moves the input cursor to the first character position

Components

The entryfield [incr Widget] is composed of a label and an entry packed into the hull frame.

Name	Class	Description
label	Label	The label to the left (if -labelpos is set to w) of the entry component
hull	Entryfield	The frame around the entryfield
entry	Entry	The entry area used for input

extfileselectionbox

The extfileselectionbox [incr Widget] is useful for navigating throughout a directory structure and selecting a file. At the top of the extfileselectionbox is a combobox that you can use for filtering directory contents. Below this combobox are two scrolledlistboxes, one that displays directory names and one that displays filenames. They are displayed side by side in a panedwindow, each in its own pane. Below the scrolledlistboxes is another combobox that displays the current file selection. The extfileselectionbox is very similar to the fileselectionbox but extends its appearance by incorporating a panedwindow and replacing its entryfields with comboboxes.

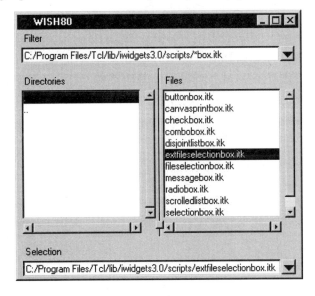

```
# Create the extfileselectionbox.
iwidgets::extfileselectionbox .efsb -mask "*box.itk" \
  -directory ${iwidgets::library}/scripts
pack .efsb -fill both -expand 1
```

14

Class Model

The extfileselectionbox [incr Widget] inherits directly from itk::Widget and contains several component [incr Widgets].

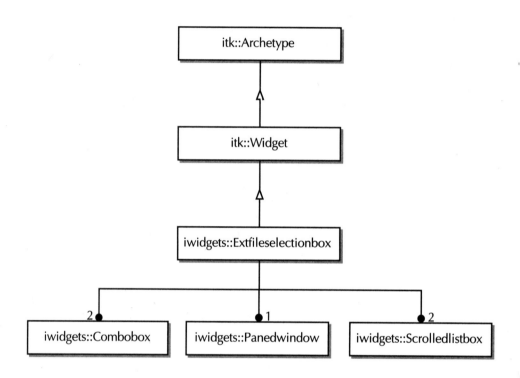

Configuration Options

Standard Options

Refer to the options man page for information on these standard options:

activebackground	background	borderwidth	cursor
foreground	highlightcolor	highlightthickness	insertbackground
insertborderwidth	insertofftime	insertontime	insertwidth
selectbackground	selectborderwidth	selectforeground	

Associated Options

Refer to the associated Tk widget or [incr Widget] for information on each of these options:

Option Name	Associated With
activerelief	Tk scrollbar widget
elementborderwidth	Tk scrollbar widget
jump	Tk scrollbar widget
labelfont	entryfield, scrolledlistbox
popupcursor	combobox
sashcursor	panedwindow
textbackground	entryfield, scrolledlistbox
textfont	entryfield, scrolledlistbox
troughcolor	Tk scrollbar widget

Inherited Options

Refer to Chapter 11 for information on this option inherited from the [incr Tk] Archetype base class:

Option Name	Inherited From
clientdata	itk::Archetype

Widget-Specific Options

-childsitepos

Resource name: childSitePos
Resource class: Position
Description: Specifies the location of the childsite frame. Valid values are n, s, e, w, top, and bottom.
Default value: s

-directory

Resource name: directory
Resource class: Directory

14

Description: Specifies the initial default directory. Specifying the empty string displays the contents of the current working directory, meaning the directory in which the command is invoked to create the extfileselectionbox.
Default value: {}

-dirsearchcommand

Resource name: dirSearchCommand
Resource class: Command
Description: Specifies a Tcl command to be evaluated to fill in the Directories scrolledlistbox. By default, only directories are listed in this scrolledlistbox, and they are sorted alphabetically. The extfileselectionbox automatically passes the current working directory and the filter mask to the designated procedure, so be sure to declare parameters for these two arguments if you use this option.
Default value: {}

-dirslabel

Resource name: dirsLabel
Resource class: Text
Description: Specifies the text to be displayed above the Directories scrolledlistbox. This option replaces this scrolledlistbox's -labeltext option.
Default value: Directories

-dirson

Resource name: dirsOn
Resource class: DirsOn
Description: A Boolean value that specifies whether the Directories scrolledlistbox should be displayed. If this option is set to a false value, then the Files scrolledlistbox stretches to fill the empty space.
Default value: true

-filesearchcommand

Resource name: fileSearchCommand
Resource class: Command
Description: Specifies a Tcl command to be evaluated to fill in the Files scrolledlistbox. By default, only regular files are listed in this scrolledlistbox, and they are sorted alphabetically. The extfileselectionbox automatically passes the current working directory and the filter mask to the designated procedure, so be sure to declare parameters for these two arguments if you use this option.
Default value: {}

-fileslabel

Resource name: filesLabel
Resource class: Text
Description: Specifies the text to be displayed above the Files scrolledlistbox. This option replaces this scrolledlistbox's -labeltext option.
Default value: Files

-fileson

Resource name: filesOn
Resource class: FilesOn
Description: A Boolean value that specifies whether the Files scrolledlistbox should be displayed. If this option is set to a false value, then the Directories scrolledlistbox stretches to fill the empty space.
Default value: true

-filetype

Resource name: fileType
Resource class: FileType
Description: Specifies type of files that can be displayed in the Files scrolledlistbox. Valid values are regular, directory, and any.
Default value: regular

-filtercommand

Resource name: filterCommand
Resource class: Command
Description: Specifies a Tcl command to be evaluated when the RETURN key is pressed in the entry component of the filter combobox.
Default value: {}

-filterlabel

Resource name: filterLabel
Resource class: Text
Description: Specifies the text to be printed above the topmost combobox. This option replaces this combobox's -labeltext option.
Default value: Filter

-filteron

Resource name: filterOn
Resource class: FilterOn

14

Description: A Boolean value that specifies whether the Filter combobox should be displayed. If this option is set to a false value, then the Directories and Files scrolledlistboxes will stretch to fill the empty space.
Default value: true

-height

Resource name: height
Resource class: Height
Description: Specifies the height in pixels of the extfileselectionbox.
Default value: 300

-invalid

Resource name: invalid
Resource class: Command
Description: Specifies an action to take when an invalid condition occurs, such as specifying an invalid directory in the Filter combobox.
Default value: bell

-mask

Resource name: mask
Resource class: Mask
Description: Specifies the file mask string used for displaying items in the Files scrolledlistbox. By default, this option is a wildcard; all files are displayed.
Default value: *

-nomatchstring

Resource name: noMatchString
Resource class: NoMatchString
Description: Specifies the string to be displayed in the Files scrolledlistbox if no regular files exist in the selected directory.
Default value: {}

-selectdircommand

Resource name: selectDirCommand
Resource class: Command

Description: Specifies a Tcl command to be evaluated when a directory is selected in the Directories scrolledlistbox.
Default value: {}

-selectfilecommand

Resource name: selectFileCommand
Resource class: Command
Description: Specifies a Tcl command to be evaluated when a file is selected in the Files scrolledlistbox.
Default value: {}

-selectioncommand

Resource name: selectionCommand
Resource class: Command
Description: Specifies a Tcl command to be evaluated when the RETURN key is pressed in the entry component of the selection combobox.
Default value: {}

-selectionlabel

Resource name: selectionLabel
Resource class: Text
Description: Specifies the text to be printed above the bottommost combobox. This option replaces this combobox's -labeltext option.
Default value: Selection

-selectionon

Resource name: selectionOn
Resource class: SelectionOn
Description: A Boolean value that specifies whether the Selection combobox should be displayed. If this option is set to a false value, then the Directories and Files scrolledlistboxes will stretch to fill the empty space.
Default value: true

-width

Resource name: width
Resource class: Width
Description: Specifies the width in pixels of the extfileselectionbox.
Default value: 350

14

Public Methods

Associated Methods

None

Inherited Methods

Refer to Chapter 11 for information on each of these inherited methods:

Method Name	Inherited From
cget	itk::Archetype
component	itk::Archetype
config	itk::Archetype
configure	itk::Archetype

Widget-Specific Methods

childsite

Usage: pathName *childsite*
Description: Returns the Tk window pathname of the childsite frame.

filter

Usage: pathName *filter*
Description: Filters the directory selected in the Directories scrolledlistbox according to the mask and populates the Files scrolledlistbox. This is equivalent to double-clicking on a directory name.

get

Usage: pathName *get*
Description: Returns the contents of the Selection combobox's entry component. The file selected in the Files scrolledlistbox is inserted into the Selection combobox.

Components

The extfileselectionbox [incr Widget] makes extensive use of composition and is composed of several different [incr Widgets], as outlined in the following table.

Name	Class	Description
dirs	Scrolledlistbox	The scrolledlistbox on the left that shows directory names
files	Scrolledlistbox	The scrolledlistbox on the right that shows filenames
filter	Combobox	The combobox at the top of the hull used for filtering
hull	Extfileselectionbox	The outer frame around the extfileselectionbox
listpane	Panedwindow	The panedwindow in which the scrolledlistboxes are displayed
selection	Combobox	The combobox at the bottom of the hull that shows the currently selected file

extfileselectiondialog

The extfileselectiondialog [incr Widget] allows you to navigate through a directory hierarchy and select a file. An extfileselectiondialog is essentially just a dialog window with an extfileselectionbox [incr Widget] in its childsite. You don't have to add buttons to control the window since the dialogshell does this for you.

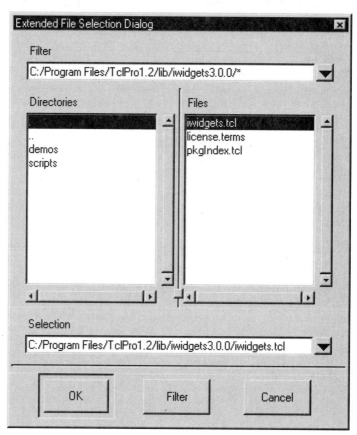

```
# Create the extfileselectiondialog. Note that this pathname may not
# exist on your system.
iwidgets::extfileselectiondialog .efsd \
  -directory "C:/Program Files/TclPro1.2/lib/iwidgets3.0.0" \
  -title "Extended File Selection Dialog"
```

```
# Tell it to draw itself in the middle of the screen.
update idletasks
.efsd center
after idle ".efsd activate"
```

Class Model

The extfileselectiondialog [incr Widget] inherits from iwidgets::Dialog and contains an extfileselectionbox [incr Widget]. It also has a buttonbox through inheritance, which is shown in the class model for the dialogshell.

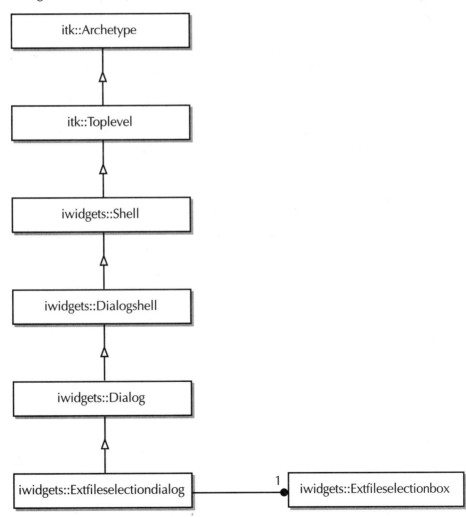

14

Configuration Options

Standard Options

Refer to the options man page for information on these standard options:

activebackground	background	borderwidth	cursor
foreground	highlightcolor	highlightthickness	insertbackground
insertborderwidth	insertofftime	insertontime	insertwidth
selectbackground	selectborderwidth	takefocus	

Associated Options

Refer to the associated Tk widget or [incr Widget] for information on each of these options:

Option Name	Associated With
activerelief	Tk scrollbar widget
childsitepos	extfileselectionbox
directory	extfileselectionbox
dirsearchcommand	extfileselectionbox
dirslabel	extfileselectionbox
dirson	extfileselectionbox
elementborderwidth	Tk scrollbar widget
filesearchcommand	extfileselectionbox
fileslabel	extfileselectionbox
fileson	extfileselectionbox
filetype	extfileselectionbox
filterlabel	extfileselectionbox
filteron	extfileselectionbox
height	extfileselectionbox
invalid	extfileselectionbox

Option Name	Associated With
jump	Tk scrollbar widget
labelfont	entryfield, scrolledlistbox
mask	extfileselectionbox
nomatchstring	extfileselectionbox
selectionlabel	extfileselectionbox
selectionon	extfileselectionbox
textbackground	entryfield, scrolledlistbox
textfont	entryfield, scrolledlistbox
troughcolor	Tk scrollbar widget
width	extfileselectionbox

Inherited Options

Refer to the [incr Widget] or [incr Tk] base class for information on each of these options. The [incr Tk] base classes are discussed in Chapter 11.

Option Name	Inherited From
buttonboxpadx	iwidgets::Dialogshell
buttonboxpady	iwidgets::Dialogshell
buttonboxpos	iwidgets::Dialogshell
clientdata	itk::Archetype
master	iwidgets::Shell
modality	iwidgets::Shell
padx	iwidgets::Dialogshell
pady	iwidgets::Dialogshell
separator	iwidgets::Dialogshell
thickness	iwidgets::Dialogshell
title	itk::Toplevel

14

Widget-Specific Options
None

Public Methods

Associated Methods

Refer to the associated [incr Widget] for information on each of these methods:

Method Name	Associated With
childsite	extfileselectionbox
filter	extfileselectionbox
get	extfileselectionbox

Inherited Methods

Refer to the [incr Widget] or [incr Tk] base class for information on each inherited method. The [incr Tk] base classes are discussed in Chapter 11.

Method Name	Inherited From
activate	iwidgets::Shell
add	iwidgets::Dialogshell
buttoncget	iwidgets::Dialogshell
buttonconfigure	iwidgets::Dialogshell
center	iwidgets::Shell
cget	itk::Archetype
component	itk::Archetype
config	itk::Archetype
configure	itk::Archetype
deactivate	iwidgets::Shell

Method Name	Inherited From
default	iwidgets::Dialogshell
delete	iwidgets::Dialogshell
hide	iwidgets::Dialogshell
index	iwidgets::Dialogshell
insert	iwidgets::Dialogshell
invoke	iwidgets::Dialogshell
show	iwidgets::Dialogshell

Widget-Specific Methods
None

Components

The extfileselectiondialog [incr Widget] is composed of an extfileselectionbox and a buttonbox separated by a divider line. All components are packed into the hull frame.

Name	Class	Description
fsb	Extfileselectionbox	The extfileselectionbox in the dialogshell's childsite
separator	Frame	The divider line between the extfileselectionbox and the buttonbox
hull	Extfileselectiondialog	The outer frame around the entire extfileselectiondialog
bbox	Buttonbox	The buttonbox at the bottom of the screen

14

feedback

The feedback [incr Widget] is useful for displaying the progress of a job or task with a known number of steps needed for completion. A status bar is provided to visually represent the percentage complete. This percentage is also displayed numerically with a label widget underneath the status bar and is updated each time the bar changes width. The status bar is a raised frame positioned in a sunken frame called a trough. Once the status bar fills the trough, the percentage complete is 100 percent. You instruct the status bar to increase its width in the trough with the public *step* method. You can control the number of steps it takes to fill the trough with the -steps configuration option. For example, if the -steps option is set to 50, then each step will increase the status bar by 2 percent. You will need to invoke *step* 50 times before the status bar reaches 100 percent in this case.

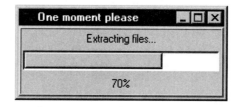

```
# Create the feedback.
iwidgets::feedback .fb -steps 50 -labeltext "Extracting files..." \
  -barcolor gray
wm geometry . 225x75
pack .fb -fill x

# Add a border by manipulating the hull.
.fb component hull configure -relief ridge -bd 3

# Increase the status bar to 70% complete.
update idletasks
.fb step 35
```

Class Model

The feedback [incr Widget] inherits from iwidgets::Labeledwidget. It does not interact with any other [incr Widgets] outside of its inheritance tree.

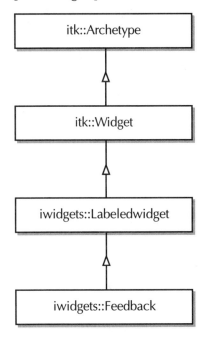

Configuration Options

Standard Options

Refer to the options man page for information on these standard options:

background	borderwidth	cursor	disabledforeground
font	foreground	highlightcolor	highlightthickness

Associated Options
None

Inherited Options
Refer to the [incr Widget] or [incr Tk] base class for information on each of these options. The [incr Tk] base classes are discussed in Chapter 11.

Option Name	Inherited From
clientdata	itk::Archetype
labelbitmap	iwidgets::Labeledwidget
labelfont	iwidgets::Labeledwidget
labelimage	iwidgets::Labeledwidget
labelmargin	iwidgets::Labeledwidget
labelpos	iwidgets::Labeledwidget
labeltext	iwidgets::Labeledwidget
labelvariable	iwidgets::Labeledwidget
state	iwidgets::Labeledwidget

Widget-Specific Options

-barcolor

Resource name: barColor
Resource class: BarColor
Description: Specifies the background color of the status bar, which is a Tk frame. This option replaces the frame's -background option.
Default value: blue

-barheight

Resource name: barHeight
Resource class: Height
Description: Specifies the height in pixels of the status bar, which is a Tk frame. This option replaces the frame's -height option.
Default value: 20

-steps

Resource name: steps
Resource class: Steps
Description: Specifies the total number of steps the status bar takes to fill in the trough.
Default value: 10

-troughcolor

Resource name: troughColor
Resource class: TroughColor
Description: Specifies the background color of the trough, which is a Tk frame. This option replaces the frame's -background option.
Default value: white

Public Methods

Associated Methods

None

Inherited Methods

Refer to the [incr Widget] or [incr Tk] base class for information on each inherited method. The [incr Tk] base classes are discussed in Chapter 11.

Method Name	Inherited From
cget	itk::Archetype
childsite	iwidgets::Labeledwidget
component	itk::Archetype
config	itk::Archetype
configure	itk::Archetype

Widget-Specific Methods

reset

Usage: pathName *reset*
Description: Resets the status bar to zero percent complete.

14

step

Usage: pathName *step* ?num?

Description: Increases the width of the status bar according to the number of specified steps. For example, if there are 25 steps in the feedback, then a single step will increase the status bar by 4 percent. The default is one step.

Components

The feedback [incr Widget] is composed of two frames and two labels packed into the hull frame.

Name	Class	Description
bar	Frame	The status bar (raised frame inside the trough)
hull	Feedback	The outer frame around the entire feedback
label	Label	The label that displays the text specified with the -labeltext option
percentage	Label	The text below the status bar that displays the percentage complete
trough	Frame	The sunken frame in which the status bar is displayed

fileselectionbox

The fileselectionbox [incr widget] is useful for navigating throughout a directory structure and selecting a file. At the top of the fileselectionbox is an entryfield that you can use for filtering directory contents. Below this entryfield are two scrolledlistboxes displayed side by side: one that displays directory names and one that displays file names. Below the scrolledlistboxes is another entryfield that displays the current file selection. The fileselectionbox is functionally equivalent to the extfileselectionbox, but a fileselectionbox does not have a panedwindow and it uses entryfields instead of comboboxes.

```
# Create the fileselectionbox. Note that this pathname may not
# exist on your system. This is the same code used in the
# extfileselectionbox example so you can see how similar the two
are.
iwidgets::fileselectionbox .fsb -mask "*box.itk" \
  -directory ${iwidgets::library}/scripts
pack .fsb -fill both -expand 1
```

Class Model

The fileselectionbox [incr Widget] inherits directly from itk::Widget and contains several component [incr Widgets].

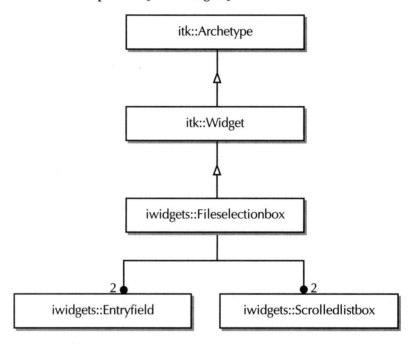

Configuration Options

Standard Options

Refer to the options man page for information on these standard options:

activebackground	background	borderwidth	cursor
foreground	highlightcolor	highlightthickness	insertbackground
insertborderwidth	insertofftime	insertontime	insertwidth
selectbackground	selectborderwidth	selectforeground	

Associated Options

Refer to the associated Tk widget or [incr Widget] for information on each of these options:

Option Name	Associated With
activerelief	Tk scrollbar widget
elementborderwidth	Tk scrollbar widget
jump	Tk scrollbar widget
labelfont	entryfield, scrolledlistbox
textbackground	entryfield, scrolledlistbox
textfont	entryfield, scrolledlistbox
troughcolor	Tk scrollbar widget

Inherited Options

Refer to Chapter 11 for information on this inherited option from the [incr Tk] Archetype base class:

Option Name	Inherited From
clientdata	itk::Archetype

Widget-Specific Options

-childsitepos

Resource name: childSitePos
Resource class: Position
Description: Specifies the location of the childsite frame. Valid values are n, s, e, w, top, and bottom.
Default value: s

-directory

Resource name: directory
Resource class: Directory

14

Description: Specifies the initial default directory. Specifying the empty string displays the contents of the current working directory, meaning the directory in which the command is invoked to create the fileselectionbox.
Default value: {}

-dirsearchcommand

Resource name: dirSearchCommand
Resource class: Command
Description: Specifies a Tcl command to be evaluated to fill in the Directories scrolledlistbox. By default, only directories are listed in this scrolledlistbox, and they are sorted alphabetically. The fileselectionbox automatically passes the current working directory and the filter mask to the designated procedure, so be sure to declare parameters for these two arguments if you use this option.
Default value: {}

-dirslabel

Resource name: dirsLabel
Resource class: Text
Description: Specifies the text to be displayed above the directories scrolledlistbox. This option replaces this scrolledlistbox's -labeltext option.
Default value: Directories

-dirson

Resource name: dirsOn
Resource class: DirsOn
Description: A Boolean value that specifies whether the directories scrolledlistbox should be displayed. If this option is set to a false value, then the Files scrolledlistbox stretches to fill the empty space.
Default value: true

-filesearchcommand

Resource name: fileSearchCommand
Resource class: Command
Description: Specifies a Tcl command to be evaluated to fill in the Files scrolledlistbox. By default, only regular files are listed in this scrolledlistbox, and they are sorted alphabetically. The fileselectionbox automatically passes the current working directory and the filter mask to the designated procedure, so be sure to declare parameters for these two arguments if you use this option.
Default value: {}

-fileslabel

Resource name: filesLabel
Resource class: Text
Description: Specifies the text to be displayed above the Files scrolledlistbox. This option replaces this scrolledlistbox's -labeltext option.
Default value: Files

-fileson

Resource name: filesOn
Resource class: FilesOn
Description: A Boolean value that specifies whether the Files scrolledlistbox should be displayed. If this option is set to a false value, then the Directories scrolledlistbox stretches to fill the empty space.
Default value: true

-filetype

Resource name: fileType
Resource class: FileType
Description: Specifies type of files that can be displayed in the Files scrolledlistbox. Valid values are regular, directory, and any.
Default value: regular

-filtercommand

Resource name: filterCommand
Resource class: Command
Description: Specifies a Tcl command to be evaluated when the RETURN key is pressed in the entry component of the Filter entryfield.
Default value: {}

-filterlabel

Resource name: filterLabel
Resource class: Text
Description: Specifies the text to be printed above the Filter entryfield. This option replaces this entryfield's -labeltext option.
Default value: Filter

-filteron

Resource name: filterOn
Resource class: FilterOn

14

Description: A Boolean value that specifies whether the filter entryfield should be displayed. If this option is set to a false value, then the Directories and Files scrolledlistboxes will stretch to fill the empty space.
Default value: true

-height

Resource name: height
Resource class: Height
Description: Specifies the height in pixels of the fileselectionbox.
Default value: 300

-invalid

Resource name: invalid
Resource class: Command
Description: Specifies an action to take when an invalid condition occurs, such as specifying an invalid directory in the filter entryfield.
Default value: bell

-mask

Resource name: mask
Resource class: Mask
Description: Specifies the file mask string used for displaying items in the files scrolledlistbox. By default, this option is a wildcard; all files are displayed.
Default value: *

-nomatchstring

Resource name: noMatchString
Resource class: NoMatchString
Description: Specifies the string to be displayed in the Files scrolledlistbox if no regular files exist in the selected directory.
Default value: {}

-selectdircommand

Resource name: selectDirCommand
Resource class: Command

Description: Specifies a Tcl command to be evaluated when a directory is selected in the Directories scrolledlistbox.
Default value: {}

-selectfilecommand

Resource name: selectFileCommand
Resource class: Command
Description: Specifies a Tcl command to be evaluated when a file is selected in the Files scrolledlistbox.
Default value: {}

-selectioncommand

Resource name: selectionCommand
Resource class: Command
Description: Specifies a Tcl command to be evaluated when the RETURN key is pressed in the entry component of the Selection entryfield.
Default value: {}

-selectionlabel

Resource name: selectionLabel
Resource class: Text
Description: Specifies the text to be printed above the Selection entryfield. This option replaces this entryfield's -labeltext option.
Default value: Selection

-selectionon

Resource name: selectionOn
Resource class: SelectionOn
Description: A Boolean value that specifies whether the selection entryfield should be displayed. If this option is set to a false value, then the Directories and Files scrolledlistboxes will stretch to fill the empty space.
Default value: true

-width

Resource name: width
Resource class: Width
Description: Specifies the width in pixels of the fileselectionbox.
Default value: 350

14

Public Methods

Associated Methods

None

Inherited Methods

Refer to Chapter 11 for information on each of these inherited methods:

Method Name	Inherited From
cget	itk::Archetype
component	itk::Archetype
config	itk::Archetype
configure	itk::Archetype

Widget-Specific Methods

childsite

Usage: pathName *childsite*
Description: Returns the Tk window pathname of the childsite frame.

filter

Usage: pathName *filter*
Description: Filters the directory selected in the Directories scrolledlistbox according to the mask and populates the Files scrolledlistbox. This is equivalent to double-clicking on a directory name.

get

Usage: pathName *get*
Description: Returns the contents of the Selection entryfield. The file selected in the Files scrolledlistbox is inserted into this entryfield.

Components

The fileselectionbox [incr Widget] is composed of two entryfields and two scrolledlistboxes packed into the hull frame.

Name	Class	Description
dirs	Scrolledlistbox	The scrolledlistbox on the left that shows directory names
files	Scrolledlistbox	The scrolledlistbox on the right that shows filenames
filter	Entryfield	The entryfield at the top of the hull used for filtering
hull	Fileselectionbox	The outer frame around the entire fileselectionbox
selection	Entryfield	The entryfield at the bottom of the hull that shows the currently selected file

fileselectiondialog

The fileselectiondialog [incr Widget] allows you to navigate through a
directory hierarchy and select a file. A fileselectiondialog is essentially just
a dialog window with a fileselectionbox [incr Widget] in its childsite. You
don't have to add buttons to control the window since the dialogshell does
this for you.

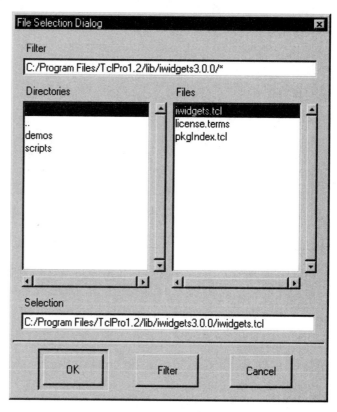

```
# Create the fileselectiondialog. Note that this pathname may not
# exist on your system. This is the same code used in the
# extfileselectiondialog example so you can see how similar the
# two are.
iwidgets::fileselectiondialog .fsd \
  -directory "C:/Program Files/TclPro1.2/lib/iwidgets3.0.0"

# Tell it to draw itself in the middle of the screen.
update idletasks
.fsd center
after idle ".fsd activate"
```

Class Model

The fileselectiondialog [incr Widget] inherits from iwidgets::Dialog and contains a fileselectionbox [incr Widget]. It also has a buttonbox through inheritance, which is shown in the class model for the dialogshell.

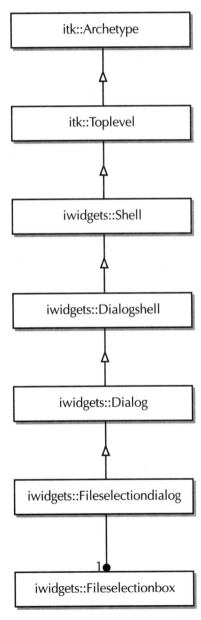

Configuration Options

Standard Options

Refer to the options man page for information on these standard options:

activebackground	background	borderwidth	cursor
foreground	highlightcolor	highlightthickness	insertbackground
insertborderwidth	insertofftime	insertontime	insertwidth
selectbackground	selectborderwidth	takefocus	

Associated Options

Refer to the associated Tk widget or [incr Widget] for information on each of these options:

Option Name	Associated With
activerelief	Tk scrollbar widget
childsitepos	fileselectionbox
directory	fileselectionbox
dirsearchcommand	fileselectionbox
dirslabel	fileselectionbox
dirson	fileselectionbox
elementborderwidth	Tk scrollbar widget
filesearchcommand	fileselectionbox
fileslabel	fileselectionbox
fileson	fileselectionbox
filetype	fileselectionbox
filterlabel	fileselectionbox
filteron	fileselectionbox
height	fileselectionbox
invalid	fileselectionbox

Option Name	Associated With
jump	Tk scrollbar widget
labelfont	entryfield, scrolledlistbox
mask	fileselectionbox
nomatchstring	fileselectionbox
selectionlabel	fileselectionbox
selectionon	fileselectionbox
textbackground	entryfield, scrolledlistbox
textfont	entryfield, scrolledlistbox
troughcolor	Tk scrollbar widget
width	fileselectionbox

Inherited Options

Refer to the [incr Widget] or [incr Tk] base class for information on each of these options. The [incr Tk] base classes are discussed in Chapter 11.

Option Name	Inherited From
buttonboxpadx	iwidgets::Dialogshell
buttonboxpady	iwidgets::Dialogshell
buttonboxpos	iwidgets::Dialogshell
clientdata	itk::Archetype
master	iwidgets::Shell
modality	iwidgets::Shell
padx	iwidgets::Dialogshell
pady	iwidgets::Dialogshell
separator	iwidgets::Dialogshell
thickness	iwidgets::Dialogshell
title	itk::Toplevel

14

Widget-Specific Options
None

Public Methods

Associated Methods
Refer to the associated [incr Widget] for information on each of these options:

Option Name	Associated With
childsite	fileselectionbox
filter	fileselectionbox
get	fileselectionbox

Inherited Methods
Refer to the [incr Widget] or [incr Tk] base class for information on each inherited method. The [incr Tk] base classes are discussed in Chapter 11.

Method Name	Inherited From
activate	iwidgets::Shell
add	iwidgets::Dialogshell
buttoncget	iwidgets::Dialogshell
buttonconfigure	iwidgets::Dialogshell
center	iwidgets::Shell
cget	itk::Archetype
component	itk::Archetype
config	itk::Archetype
configure	itk::Archetype
deactivate	iwidgets::Shell
default	iwidgets::Dialogshell

Method Name	Inherited From
delete	iwidgets::Dialogshell
hide	iwidgets::Dialogshell
index	iwidgets::Dialogshell
insert	iwidgets::Dialogshell
invoke	iwidgets::Dialogshell
show	iwidgets::Dialogshell

Widget-Specific Methods
None

Components

The fileselectiondialog [incr Widget] is composed of a fileselectionbox and a buttonbox separated by a divider line. All components are packed into the hull frame.

Name	Class	Description
fsb	Fileselectionbox	The fileselectionbox in the dialogshell's childsite
separator	Frame	The divider line between the fileselectionbox and the buttonbox
hull	Fileselectiondialog	The outer frame around the entire fileselectiondialog
bbox	Buttonbox	The buttonbox at the bottom of the screen

finddialog

The finddialog [incr Widget] is used as a search tool for scrolledtext [incr Widgets] or Tk text widgets. You can use the finddialog to search for simple text strings or for search patterns specified by a regular expression. An entryfield is provided at the top of the finddialog to specify this search pattern or string. Several checkbuttons are provided below the entryfield that provide a variety of functionality such as case sensitivity or searching backwards. To begin the search, press the Find button or the RETURN key. If a match is found, the text is highlighted. You can find the next match by again pressing Find or the RETURN key. To clear the highlighted text and the search pattern, press the Clear button.

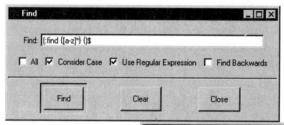

```
# Create a scrolledtext to associate with the finddialog and import
# a file into the text component. Note that the pathname may not
# exist on your system.
iwidgets::scrolledtext .st
.st import ${iwidgets::library}/scripts/finddialog.itk
pack .st -fill both -expand 1
wm title . "A scrolledtext \[incr Widget\] tied to the finddialog."
```

```
# Create the finddialog.
iwidgets::finddialog .fd -textwidget .st
.fd activate

# Find the implementation body of the find method. Turn on case
# sensitivity and use a regular expression since you may not know
# if there are any parameters. Note that the regexp doesn't take
# into consideration optional arguments.
.fd component case select
.fd component regexp select
.fd component pattern insert 0 "(:find {\[a-z\]*} {)$"
.fd find
```

Class Model

The finddialog [incr Widget] is a sibling class to iwidgets::Dialog, inheriting from iwidgets::Dialogshell. It contains an entryfield and a buttonbox.

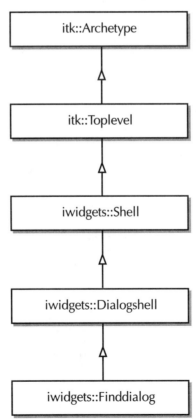

Configuration Options

Standard Options

Refer to the options man page for information on these standard options:

activebackground	activeforeground	background	borderwidth
cursor	disabledforeground	font	foreground
highlightcolor	highlightthickness	insertbackground	insertborderwidth
insertofftime	insertontime	insertwidth	selectbackground
selectborderwidth	selectforeground	takefocus	

Associated Options

Refer to the associated Tk widget or [incr Widget] for information on each of these options:

Option Name	Associated With
labelfont	entryfield
selectcolor	Tk checkbutton widget
textbackground	entryfield
textfont	entryfield

Inherited Options

Refer to the [incr Widget] or [incr Tk] base class for information on each of these options. The [incr Tk] base classes are discussed in Chapter 11.

Option Name	Inherited From
buttonboxpadx	iwidgets::Dialogshell
buttonboxpady	iwidgets::Dialogshell
buttonboxpos	iwidgets::Dialogshell
clientdata	itk::Archetype
height	iwidgets::Shell
master	iwidgets::Shell

Option Name	Inherited From
modality	iwidgets::Shell
padx	iwidgets::Shell
pady	iwidgets::Shell
separator	iwidgets::Dialogshell
thickness	iwidgets::Dialogshell
width	iwidgets::Shell
title	itk::Toplevel

Widget-Specific Options

-clearcommand

Resource name: clearCommand
Resource class: Command
Description: Specifies a Tcl command to be evaluated when the *clear* method is invoked, which happens when you press the Clear button. The specified command is meant to provide a convenient means of notification when the search string has been cleared. For example, you may want to disable a "Find Again" menu or perform some other similar task. Note that this option only works in post-itcl3.0.1 releases.
Default value: {}

-matchcommand

Resource name: matchCommand
Resource class: Command
Description: Specifies a Tcl command to be evaluated when the *find* method is invoked, which happens when you press the Find button. The command will only be evaluated if a search pattern is specified. The match point, which is the line number and initial character position of the search string, is automatically passed into the specified procedure as an argument, so make sure you declare a parameter to accept this argument in your procedure or method. If a match is not found for the search string, then the match point will be an empty string. Note that this option only works in post-itcl3.0.1 releases.
Default value: {}

14

-patternbackground

Resource name: patternBackground
Resource class: Background
Description: Specifies the background color of the text that matches the search pattern when it is found and highlighted in the text widget. Note that modifying this option does not change the color of the current highlighted text. The background color of the text is updated when the *next* match is found.
Default value: #707070

-patternforeground

Resource name: patternForeground
Resource class: Foreground
Description: Specifies the foreground color of the text that matches the search pattern when it is found and highlighted in the text widget. Note that modifying this option does not change the color of the current highlighted text. The color of the text is updated when the *next* match is found.
Default value: white

-searchbackground

Resource name: searchBackground
Resource class: Background
Description: Specifies the background color of the row in the text widget containing the text that matches the search pattern. Note that modifying this option does not change the color of the current highlighted row. The background color of the row is updated when the *next* match is found.
Default value: #c4c4c4

-searchforeground

Resource name: searchForeground
Resource class: Foreground
Description: Specifies the foreground color of the row in the text widget containing the text that matches the search pattern. Note that modifying this option does not change the color of the text in the current highlighted row. The color of the text is updated when the *next* match is found.
Default value: black

-textwidget

Resource name: textWidget
Resource class: TextWidget

Description: Specifies the Tk window pathname of a scrolledtext [incr Widget] or a Tk text widget to be associated with the finddialog.
Default value: {}

Public Methods

Associated Methods
None

Inherited Methods
Refer to the [incr Widget] or [incr Tk] base class for information on each inherited method. The [incr Tk] base classes are discussed in Chapter 11.

Method Name	Inherited From
activate	iwidgets::Shell
add	iwidgets::Dialogshell
buttoncget	iwidgets::Dialogshell
buttonconfigure	iwidgets::Dialogshell
center	iwidgets::Shell
cget	itk::Archetype
childsite	iwidgets::Dialogshell
component	itk::Archetype
config	itk::Archetype
configure	itk::Archetype
deactivate	iwidgets::Shell
default	iwidgets::Dialogshell
delete	iwidgets::Dialogshell
hide	iwidgets::Dialogshell
index	iwidgets::Dialogshell
insert	iwidgets::Dialogshell
invoke	iwidgets::Dialogshell
show	iwidgets::Dialogshell

14

Widget-Specific Methods

clear

Usage: pathName *clear*
Description: Clears the search pattern in the entryfield component and deselects the highlighted text resulting from a pattern match in the text widget. The command specified by the -clearcommand option is then evaluated. Invoking this method is equivalent to pressing the Clear button in the finddialog.

find

Usage: pathName *find*
Description: Searches in the text widget for the pattern specified in the entryfield component. The text widget is specified by the -textwidget option. If a matching string is found, it is highlighted according to the -patternbackground, -patternforeground, -searchbackground, and -searchforeground options. Invoking this method is equivalent to pressing the Find button in the finddialog.

Components

The finddialog [incr Widget] is composed of several Tk widgets and [incr Widgets], as outlined in the following table.

Name	Class	Description
all	Checkbutton	The leftmost checkbutton
backwards	Checkbutton	The rightmost checkbutton
bbox	Buttonbox	The buttonbox at the bottom of the finddialog
case	Checkbutton	The checkbutton second from the left
hull	Finddialog	The frame around the entire finddialog
pattern	Entryfield	The entryfield at the top of the finddialog used to specify a search pattern
regexp	Checkbutton	The checkbutton second from the right
separator	Frame	The divider line between the checkbuttons and the buttonbox

hierarchy

The hierarchy [incr Widget] is a hierarchical data viewer ideal for displaying directory file system trees. Different icons are used to represent directories and files called "nodes." These icons can be configured, but are automatically generated if unspecified. Directories, or branched nodes, can be expanded or collapsed. An indentation scheme is used to create a stairstep effect to make the directory structure easy to follow. A robust set of configuration options and public methods allow you to perform a wide variety of tasks and filtering on the hierarchy. For example, the -filter option allows you to display a more compact view of the hierarchy, showing branched nodes and selected nodes only.

The hierarchy contains a scrollable text widget in which the hierarchical structure is displayed, a label above the text widget that you can use to show the root node, and two menus: an item menu and a general menu. You have to manually add entries to either menu before it can be displayed. The item menu is displayed on a per-node basis when you right-click on a node. The general menu is displayed when you right-click anywhere else in the text widget other than on a node. You can add entries to these menus to perform various callback actions such as expanding or collapsing a branched node or selecting or deselecting a node.

```
# Define a default root directory. Note that this path may not exist
# on your system.
set root "C:/Program Files/Tcl/lib"
cd $root
wm withdraw .

proc ls {dir_} {
  global root
  if {$dir_ == ""} {
    set dir $root
  } else {
    set dir $dir_
  }
  if {![file isdirectory $dir]} {
    return
  }
  cd $dir
  set returnList ""
  foreach file [lsort [glob -nocomplain *]] {
    lappend returnList [list [file join $dir $file] $file]
  }
  return $returnList
}

# Create the hierarchy.
iwidgets::hierarchy .h -querycommand {ls %n} -visibleitems 45x20 \
  -labeltext $root -labelpos nw
pack .h -fill both -expand 1

# Expand a couple of directories.
update idletasks
.h expand $root/iwidgets3.0
.h expand $root/iwidgets3.0/demos

# Highlight the topmost expanded directory.
.h selection add $root/iwidgets3.0

# After everything's done, display the hierarchy.
after idle {wm deiconify .}
```

Class Model

The hierarchy [incr Widget] inherits from iwidgets::Scrolledwidget. It does not interact with any other [incr Widgets] outside of its inheritance tree.

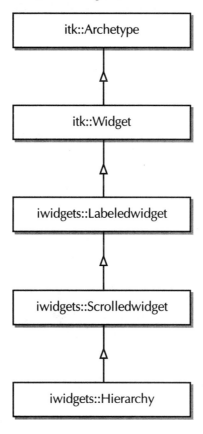

Configuration Options

Standard Options

Refer to the options man page for information on these standard options:

activebackground	activeforeground	background	borderwidth
disabledforeground	foreground	highlightcolor	highlightthickness
relief			

14

Associated Options

Refer to the associated Tk widget for information on these options:

Option Name	Associated With
activerelief	Tk scrollbar widget
elementborderwidth	Tk scrollbar widget
jump	Tk scrollbar widget
selectcolor	Tk menu widget
spacing1	Tk text widget
spacing2	Tk text widget
spacing3	Tk text widget
tabs	Tk text widget
troughcolor	Tk scrollbar widget

Inherited Options

Refer to the [incr Widget] or [incr Tk] base class for information on each of these options. The [incr Tk] base classes are discussed in Chapter 11.

Option Name	Inherited From
clientdata	itk::Archetype
hscrollmode	iwidgets::Scrolledwidget
labelbitmap	iwidgets::Labeledwidget
labelfont	iwidgets::Labeledwidget
labelimage	iwidgets::Labeledwidget
labelmargin	iwidgets::Labeledwidget
labelpos	iwidgets::Labeledwidget
labeltext	iwidgets::Labeledwidget
labelvariable	iwidgets::Labeledwidget
sbwidth	iwidgets::Scrolledwidget
scrollmargin	iwidgets::Scrolledwidget
vscrollmode	iwidgets::Scrolledwidget

Widget-Specific Options

-alwaysquery

Resource name: alwaysQuery
Resource class: AlwaysQuery
Description: A Boolean value that determines whether the command specified by the -querycommand option is evaluated each time the display is refreshed. If true, then a new query is made by evaluating -querycommand. Otherwise, the previous node list is used.
Default value: 0

-closedicon

Resource name: closedIcon
Resource class: Icon
Description: Specifies the Closed Folder icon to be used for collapsed branched nodes (directories) in the hierarchy. The hierarchy attempts to generate one for you if one is not specified.
Default value: {}

-expanded

Resource name: expanded
Resource class: Expanded
Description: A Boolean value that specifies whether the hierarchy should be completely expanded or not when it is drawn. For large hierarchies, be aware that this could take a while. It may be better to selectively expand nodes rather than expand all of them.
Default value: 0

-filter

Resource name: filter
Resource class: Filter
Description: A Boolean value that determines whether all nodes are displayed or a subset. If true, then only branch nodes (directories) are displayed plus selected nodes. A node is selected with the *selection* method. Note that marked nodes are not displayed in this case. Otherwise, if filtering is turned off, all nodes are displayed. The hierarchy is automatically updated when this option is modified.
Default value: 0

14

-font

Resource name: font
Resource class: Font
Description: Specifies the font to be used for all node names displayed in the hierarchy.
Default value: Windows = {{MS Sans Serif} 8}, Unix = {Helvetica -12 bold}

-height

Resource name: height
Resource class: Height
Description: Specifies the height in pixels of the hierarchy as a whole. The geometry of the hierarchy is typically handled by the -visibleitems option, but if -width and -height are nonzero, then they have precedence.
Default value: 0

-iconcommand

Resource name: iconCommand
Resource class: Command
Description: Specifies a Tcl command to be evaluated when you click on an icon in the hierarchy. If you include %n in this command, it is substituted with the name of the corresponding node. Similarly, %i is substituted with the name of the icon.
Default Value: {}

-markbackground

Resource name: markBackground
Resource class: Foreground
Description: Specifies the background color of the highlighted text when you mark a node with the *mark* method.
Default value: #a0a0a0

-markforeground

Resource name: markForeground
Resource class: Background
Description: Specifies the foreground color of the highlighted text when you mark a node with the *mark* method.
Default value: black

-menucursor

Resource name: menuCurcor
Resource class: Cursor
Description: Specifies the cursor shape for the pop-up item menu. This option replaces this menu's -cursor option.
Default value: arrow

-nodeicon

Resource name: nodeIcon
Resource class: Icon
Description: Specifies the icon to be used for nonbranched nodes (files) in the hierarchy. The hierarchy attempts to generate one for you if one is not specified.
Default value: black

-openicon

Resource name: openIcon
Resource class: Icon
Description: Specifies the Open Folder icon to be used for expanded branched nodes (directories) in the hierarchy. The hierarchy attempts to generate one for you if one is not specified.
Default value: {}

-querycommand

Resource name: queryCommand
Resource class: Command
Description: This is the option you use to build the hierarchy tree. It specifies a Tcl command to be evaluated for populating the hierarchy with nodes and querying the contents of each node. The name of the selected node can be passed into the procedure or method by specifying %n in the command.
Default value: {}

-selectbackground

Resource name: selectBackground
Resource class: Foreground
Description: Specifies the background color of the highlighted text when you select a node with the *selection* method.
Default value: Windows = SystemHighlight, Unix = #c3c3c3

14

-selectcommand

Resource name: selectCommand
Resource class: Command
Description: Specifies a Tcl command to be evaluated when you click on a node in the hierarchy to select it. If %n is included in the command, it is substituted with the node name. Similarly, %s is substituted with the node's current selection status: 1 for selected, 0 otherwise.
Default value: {}

-selectforeground

Resource name: selectForeground
Resource class: Background
Description: Specifies the foreground color of the highlighted text when you select a node with the *selection* method.
Default value: Windows = SystemHighlightText, Unix = black

-textbackground

Resource name: textBackground
Resource class: Background
Description: Specifies the background color of the text widget. This option replaces the text's -background option. Note that this does not affect the background color of the node icons.
Default value: Windows = SystemWindow, Unix = #d9d9d9

-textfont

Resource name: textFont
Resource class: Font
Description: Specifies the font to use for nonhierarchical text added to the text widget. To change the font for hierarchy nodes, use the -font option.
Default value: Windows = {{MS Sans Serif} 8}, Unix = {Courier -12}

-visibleitems

Resource name: visibleItems
Resource class: VisibleItems
Description: Specifies the width and height of the text widget in characters and lines. This option is typically used to control the hierarchy's geometry. If the -width and -height options are both zero, then -visibleitems is evaluated; otherwise, the designated width and height have precedence.
Default value: 80x24

-width

Resource name: width
Resource class: Width
Description: Specifies the width in pixels of the hierarchy as a whole. The geometry of the hierarchy is typically handled by the -visibleitems option, but if -width and -height are nonzero, then they have precedence.
Default value: 0

Public Methods
Associated Methods
Refer to the Tk text widget for information on each of these methods:

Method Name	Associated With
bbox	Tk text widget
compare	Tk text widget
delete	Tk text widget
dlineinfo	Tk text widget
dump	Tk text widget
get	Tk text widget
index	Tk text widget
insert	Tk text widget
scan	Tk text widget
search	Tk text widget
see	Tk text widget
tag	Tk text widget
window	Tk text widget
xview	Tk text widget
yview	Tk text widget

14

Inherited Methods

Refer to the [incr Widget] or [incr Tk] base class for information on each inherited method. The [incr Tk] base classes are discussed in Chapter 11.

Method Name	Inherited From
cget	itk::Archetype
childsite	iwidgets::Labeledwidget
component	itk::Archetype
config	itk::Archetype
configure	itk::Archetype

Widget-Specific Methods

clear

Usage: pathName *clear*
Description: Removes all items from the display.

collapse

Usage: pathName *collapse* node
Description: This method is the converse of *expand*. It collapses the hierarchy beneath a specified node. This may take a while for large hierarchies, so the cursor is changed to a watch until the node is collapsed.

current

Usage: pathName *current*
Description: Returns the node for which the item menu was most recently posted. This method is useful for the associated item menu code to determine the corresponding node.

draw

Usage: pathName *draw* ?when?
Description: Redraws the display according to the when argument, which may be either -now or -eventually. The default is -now, meaning the display is redrawn immediately. If -eventually is specified, the display is redrawn after any pending events in the event loop.

expand

Usage: pathName *expand* node
Description: This method is the converse of *collapse*. It expands the hierarchy beneath a specified node. This may take a while for large hierarchies, so the cursor is changed to a watch until this method completes.

mark

Usage: pathName *mark* op ?arg arg ...?
Description: Handles all marks for the hierarchy. A mark is a way of selecting certain nodes in the hierarchy. It's similar to the *selection* method except the default highlight color scheme is more of a "lowlight" than highlight. Also, marked nodes are not displayed when -filter is true. When you mark a node, it's highlighted and added to a list of marked nodes. You can add or remove new marks, or you can clear or retrieve all current marks. This depends on the op argument, which may be add, remove, clear, or get. Following op, you may specify a variable-length argument list containing node names.

prune

Usage: pathName *prune* node
Description: Removes the specified node from the hierarchy.

refresh

Usage: pathName *refresh* node
Description: Redraws the specified node if it is visible. No action is taken if the node is not currently visible.

selection

Usage: pathName *selection* op ?arg arg ...?
Description: Handles all selections for the hierarchy. This method is basically the same as the *mark* method except the default highlight color scheme is more contrasting. When you select a node, it's highlighted and added to a list of selected nodes. You can add or remove new selections, or you can clear or retrieve all current selections. This depends on the op argument, which may be add, remove, clear, or get. Following op, you may specify a variable-length argument list containing node names.

14

toggle

Usage: pathName *toggle* node
Description: This method just toggles the specified node's current state. If the node is currently expanded, it is collapsed. If it is currently collapsed, it is expanded.

Components

The hierarchy [incr Widget] is composed of several Tk widgets, as outlined in the following table. Each component is packed into the hull frame.

Name	Class	Description
bgMenu	Menu	The pop-up menu that is displayed if a node is not at the current (x,y) coordinates
clipper	Frame	The frame around the text widget
horizsb	Scrollbar	The horizontal scroll bar
hull	Hierarchy	The frame around the entire hierarchy
itemMenu	Menu	The pop-up menu that is displayed if a node is at the current (x,y) coordinates
list	Text	The text widget
label	Label	The label widget above the text component
vertsb	Scrollbar	The vertical scroll bar

hyperhelp

The hyperhelp [incr Widget] creates a top-level window with a pull-down menu that shows a list of topics. Each topic must be the name of an HTML-formatted file that resides in the directory specified by the -helpdir option. Additionally, the file should have the extension .html. The hyperhelp uses a scrolledhtml [incr Widget] to display the hypertext file. It also keeps a history list of links for quick backtracking.

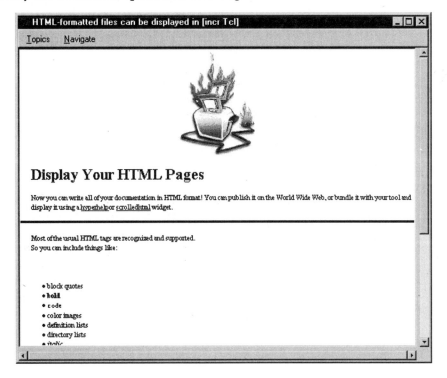

```
# Create the hyperhelp.
iwidgets::hyperhelp .hh \
  -title "HTML-formatted files can be displayed in \[incr Tcl\]" \
  -topics demo -helpdir [file join ${iwidgets::library} demos]

# Render the demo in the iwidgets3.0 demos directory.
.hh showtopic demo

# Center and display.
.hh center
update idletasks
.hh activate
```

Class Model

The hyperhelp [incr Widget] inherits directly from iwidgets::Shell. It contains one scrolledhtml.

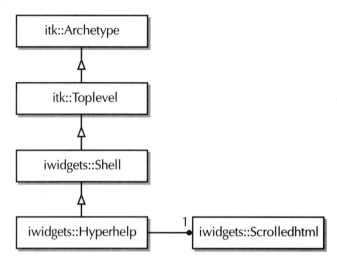

Configuration Options

Standard Options

Refer to the options man page for information on these standard options:

activebackground	activeforeground	background	borderwidth
cursor	foreground	highlightcolor	highlightthickness
relief	selectbackground	selectborderwidth	selectforeground
setgrid	takefocus		

Associated Options

Refer to the associated Tk widget or [incr Widget] for information on each of these options:

Option Name	Associated With
activerelief	Tk scrollbar widget
fixedfont	scrolledhtml
height	scrolledhtml
hscrollmode	scrolledhtml
link	scrolledhtml
linkhighlight	scrolledhtml
padx	scrolledhtml
pady	scrolledhtml
sbwidth	scrolledhtml
scrollmargin	scrolledhtml
textbg	scrolledhtml
unknownimage	scrolledhtml
visibleitems	scrolledhtml
vscrollmode	scrolledhtml
width	scrolledhtml
wrap	scrolledhtml

Inherited Options

Refer to the [incr Widget] or [incr Tk] base class for information on each of these options. The [incr Tk] base classes are discussed in Chapter 11.

Option Name	Inherited From
clientdata	itk::Archetype
master	iwidgets::Shell
modality	iwidgets::Shell
title	itk::Toplevel

14

Widget-Specific Options

-closecmd

Resource name: closeCmd
Resource class: CloseCmd
Description: Specifies a Tcl command to be evaluated when "Close" is selected from the menu.
Default value: {}

-helpdir

Resource name: helpDir
Resource class: Directory
Description: Specifies the directory location of help files.
Default value: .

-maxhistory

Resource name: maxHistory
Resource class: MaxHistory
Description: Specifies the maximum number of links that are stored in the history list.
Default value: 20

-topics

Resource name: topics
Resource class: Topics
Description: Specifies the menu entries to display under the "Topics" menubutton. For each entry, there must be a corresponding file with the extension .html, and it must be located in the directory specified by the -helpdir option.
Default value: {}

Public Methods

Associated Methods

None

Inherited Methods

Refer to the [incr Widget] or [incr Tk] base class for information on each inherited method. The [incr Tk] base classes are discussed in Chapter 11.

Method Name	Inherited From
activate	iwidgets::Shell
center	iwidgets::Shell
cget	itk::Archetype
childsite	iwidgets::Shell
component	itk::Archetype
config	itk::Archetype
configure	itk::Archetype
deactivate	iwidgets::Shell

Widget-Specific Methods

back

Usage: pathName *back*
Description: Shows the topic one back in the history list.

followlink

Usage: pathName *followlink* link
Description: Shows a new topic specified by the link argument. This method is the callback for clicking on a hypertext link.

forward

Usage: pathName *forward*
Description: Shows the topic one forward in the history list.

showtopic

Usage: pathName *showtopic* topic
Description: Renders the topic specified by the topic argument, which should be the name of an HTML-formatted file in the -helpdir directory. The file should have the extension .html.

14

updatefeedback

Usage: pathName *updatefeedback*
Description: Updates the feedback widget. This method is used for displaying the load status or rendering time of a new topic.

Components

The hyperhelp [incr Widget] is simply composed of a scrolledhtml [incr Widget] as shown in the following table. It is packed into the hull frame component.

Name	Class	Description
hull	Hyperhelp	The frame surrounding the entire hyperhelp
scrtxt	Scrolledhtml	The scrolledhtml where all HTML-formatted text is displayed

labeledframe

The labeledframe [incr Widget] combines a grooved frame and a childsite frame. It's not intended to be used as a general-purpose [incr Widget]; rather, it is intended to serve as a base class for other [incr Widgets]. In itcl3.x, the checkbox and radiobox inherit from the labeledframe. If you use the labeledframe, make sure you read the discussion about the childsite method later in this section.

```
# NOTE: It is not generally recommended to use the labeledframe
# as a general-purpose [incr Widget]. It is intended to be used
# as a base class for other [incr Widgets].

# Create the labeledframe.
iwidgets::labeledframe .lf -labelpos nw \
  -labeltext "\[incr Man\] by Michael Plaugher"
pack .lf -fill both -expand 1
wm geometry . 250x200

# Get the childsite and modify it so contained widgets will be
# visible.
set cs [.lf childsite]
$cs configure -background white
grid rowconfigure $cs 0 -weight 1
grid columnconfigure $cs 0 -weight 0

# Add a label in the childsite with the [incr Man] image. Note
# that this pathname will likely not exist on your system. You can
# get the [incr Man] image from www.tcltk.com/itcl/heroes.htm
label $cs.img -image [image create photo -file /tmp/iman2.gif] -bd 0
pack $cs.img -pady 14
```

14

Class Model

The labeledframe is the only [incr Widget] that does not inherit from either itk::Toplevel or itk::Widget. It inherits directly from itk::Archetype.

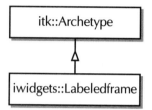

Configuration Options

Standard Options

Refer to the options man page for information on these standard options:

background	borderwidth	cursor	foreground	relief

Associated Options

None

Inherited Options

Refer to the Archetype [incr Tk] base class for information on this inherited option. This class is discussed in Chapter 11.

Option Name	Inherited From
clientdata	itk::Archetype

Widget-Specific Options

-ipadx

Resource name: iPadX
Resource class: IPad
Description: Specifies the width in pixels between the childsite and the hull border in the x direction.
Default value: 0

-ipady

Resource name: iPadY
Resource class: IPad
Description: Specifies the width in pixels between the childsite and the hull border in the y direction.
Default value: 0

-labelbitmap

Resource name: labelBitmap
Resource class: Bitmap
Description: Specifies a bitmap to use in place of the text in the grooved frame. This option replaces the label component's -bitmap option.
Default value: {}

-labelfont

Resource name: labelFont
Resource class: Font
Description: Specifies the font to use for the label component in the grooved frame. This option replaces the label component's -font option.
Default value: -Adobe-Helvetica-Bold-R-Normal-*-120-*-*-*-*-*

-labelimage

Resource name: labelImage
Resource class: Image
Description: Specifies an image to use in place of the text in the grooved frame. This option replaces the label component's -image option.
Default value: {}

-labelmargin

Resource name: labelMargin
Resource class: LabelMargin
Description: Specifies the number of pixels between the label and the most adjacent hull border. For example, if the -labelpos option is set to nw, the -labelmargin option specifies the number of pixels to the left of the label between the label and the hull border.
Default value: {}

14

-labelpos

Resource name: labelPos
Resource class: LabelPos
Description: Specifies the location of the label in the grooved frame.
Valid values are nw, n, ne, sw, s, se, en, e, es, wn, w, and ws.
Default value: n

-labeltext

Resource name: labelText
Resource class: Text
Description: Specifies the text to use for the label in the grooved frame.
Default value: {}

-labelvariable

Resource name: labelVariable
Resource class: Variable
Description: Specifies a variable to associate with the label in the grooved
frame. You can use this option to automatically update the label text with
the variable's value. This option replaces the label's -textvariable option.
Default value: {}

Public Methods

Associated Methods

None

Inherited Methods

Refer to the [incr Tk] base class for information on each inherited method.
The [incr Tk] base classes are discussed in Chapter 11.

Method Name	Inherited From
cgetr	itk::Archetype
component	itk::Archetype
config	itk::Archetype
configure	itk::Archetype

Widget-Specific Methods

childsite

Usage: pathName *childsite*
Description: Returns the Tk window pathname of the childsite frame. The labeledframe is not really meant to be used like an ordinary [incr Widget]. It's meant to serve as a generic base class to support the combination of a labeled grooved frame and a childsite. As a result, the childsite frame returned by the *childsite* method isn't very user friendly. You can't just start packing widgets into the childsite. You have to manually configure it with **grid** before any contained widgets will be displayed, and you have to use **grid** to insert widgets. The example code at the beginning of this section shows you how to do this, but due to the potential for error conditions, you should avoid instantiating and using a labeledframe as an ordinary [incr Widget].

Components

The labeledframe [incr Widget] is simply composed of a label and a childsite frame.

Name	Class	Description
childsite	Frame	The childsite frame inside the hull frame
hull	Labeledframe	The grooved frame around the childsite
label	Label	The label positioned in the grooved frame

labeledwidget

The labeledwidget [incr Widget] is a simple base class that combines a label and a childsite frame. It's similar to the labeledframe except the label component is contained inside the hull frame instead of being placed directly in its border. Several configuration options are provided to manipulate the label component, which may display text, a bitmap, or an image. The labeledwidget is not generally meant to be a general-purpose [incr Widget]; rather, it is meant to be a generic base class for many of the [incr Widgets]. Unlike the labeledframe, however, you can use the labeledwidget if you need to without any childsite restrictions. Simply obtain the childsite pathname via the public *childsite* method and pack new widgets into it.

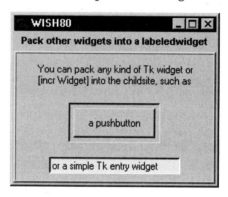

```
# Set the window size.
wm geometry . 285x195

# Create the labeledwidget.
iwidgets::labeledwidget .lw -labelpos n \
  -labeltext "Pack other widgets into a labeledwidget" \
  -labelfont -Adobe-Helvetica-Bold-R-Normal--*-140-*-*-*-*-*-*
pack .lw -fill both -expand 1

# Get the childsite and pack some example widgets into it.
set cs [.lw childsite]
$cs configure -relief ridge -bd 3
pack [label $cs.txt -text "You can pack any kind of Tk widget or\
  \[incr Widget\] into the childsite, such as" -wraplength 200\
  -justify left] -pady 8
pack [iwidgets::pushbutton $cs.pb -text "a pushbutton" \
  -defaultring 1] -pady 8
pack [entry $cs.e -background ghostwhite -width 25] -pady 8
$cs.e insert 0 "or a simple Tk entry widget"
```

Class Model

The labeledwidget [incr Widget] inherits directly from itk::Widget. It does not interact with any other [incr Widgets] outside of its inheritance tree.

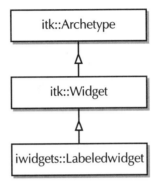

Configuration Options

Standard Options

Refer to the options man page for information on these standard options:

background	cursor	disabledforeground	foreground

Associated Options

None

Inherited Options

Refer to Chapter 11 for information on this inherited option from the [incr Tk] Archetype base class:

Option Name	Inherited From
clientdata	itk::Archetype

Widget-Specific Options

-labelbitmap

Resource name: labelBitmap
Resource class: Bitmap

14

Description: Specifies a bitmap to use in place of the text for the label component.
Default value: {}

-labelfont

Resource name: labelFont
Resource class: Font
Description: Specifies the font to use for the label component. This option replaces the label's -font option.
Default value: {{MS Sans Serif} 8}

-labelimage

Resource name: labelImage
Resource class: Image
Description: Specifies an image to use in place of the text for the label component.
Default value: {}

-labelmargin

Resource name: labelMargin
Resource class: LabelMargin
Description: Specifies the number of pixels between the label and the most adjacent hull border. For example, if the -labelpos option is set to nw, the -labelmargin option specifies the number of pixels to the left of the label between the label and the hull border.
Default value: 2

-labelpos

Resource name: labelPos
Resource class: LabelPos
Description: Specifies the location of the label component relative to the childsite. Valid values are nw, n, ne, sw, s, se, en, e, es, wn, w, and ws.
Default value: w

-labeltext

Resource name: labelText
Resource class: Text

Description: Specifies the text to use for the label component. Note that the text is only displayed when -labelbitmap is not defined.
Default value: {}

-labelvariable

Resource name: labelVariable
Resource class: Variable
Description: Specifies a variable to associate with the label component. You can use this option to automatically update the label text with the variable's value.
Default value: {}

-state

Resource name: state
Resource class: State
Description: Changes the foreground color of the label component. If this option is set to disabled, the foreground color is changed to the value of the -disabledforeground option. If this option is set to normal, the foreground color is set to the value of the -foreground option.
Default value: normal

Public Methods

Associated Methods

None

Inherited Methods

Refer to Chapter 11 for information on each of these inherited methods from the itk::Archetype base class:

Method Name	Inherited From
cget	itk::Archetype
component	itk::Archetype
config	itk::Archetype
configure	itk::Archetype

14

Widget-Specific Methods

childsite

Usage: pathName *childsite*
Description: Returns the Tk window pathname of the childsite frame. You can then use this pathname to pack new widgets into the childsite. This is how all labeledwidget's derived classes are created, such as the optionmenu, spinner, timefield, and scrolledframe to name a few.

Components

The labeledwidget [incr Widget] simply consists of a label and a childsite frame. The childsite is non-public and is therefore not shown in the following components table.

Name	Class	Description
hull	Labeledwidget	The frame around the entire labeledwidget
label	Label	The label widget that is positioned around the childsite frame according to -labelpos.

mainwindow

The mainwindow [incr Widget] can be used for a variety of interface applications such as text editors or network management. The mainwindow contains a menubar, two toolbars, a childsite, a messagedialog, and two labels used for help and status information. Each of the [incr Widget] components have associated public wrapper methods so that you can configure the mainwindow to suit your particular application. The only drawback to using a mainwindow is that you also need to know how to use whichever component [incr Widgets] you want to display. For example, if you want to display a menubar, you need to know how to use the menubar [incr Widget]. This is because the mainwindow does not define a bunch of individual wrapper methods for the menubar. It instead provides a single convenient *menubar* method that allows you to directly access the menubar's public methods. The same applies for each of the other [incr Widget] components.

Once you configure your mainwindow as desired, you can then use its *childsite* method to gain access to its childsite frame and then pack other widgets into the childsite. Examples include a scrolledtext for a text editor or a scrolledcanvas in which you could insert computer icons used for network management. The following screen snapshot shows a simple skeleton interface for a text editor. You can make this screen much more robust by adding several other toolbar and mousebar shortcut buttons.

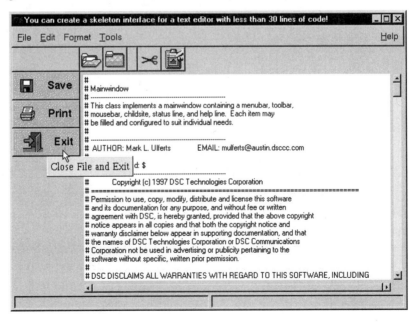

14

```
# Create the mainwindow.
iwidgets::mainwindow .mw -menubarfont {{MS Sans Serif} 10} \
   -title "You can create a skeleton interface for a text editor\
   with less than 30 lines of code!"

# This directory may not exist on your system.
set dir ${iwidgets::library}/demos/images

# Add some menu selections.
.mw menubar add menubutton file -text File -underline 0
.mw menubar add menubutton edit -text Edit -underline 0
.mw menubar add menubutton format -text Format -underline 2
.mw menubar add menubutton tools -text Tools -underline 0
.mw menubar add menubutton help -text Help -underline 0

# Add some toolbar items. (The 107 pixel width for the spacer1
# frame is the width of images used for the mousebar buttons plus
# some padding for the borderwidth.)
.mw toolbar add frame spacer1 -width 107 -relief raised -bd 2
.mw toolbar add button open -balloonstr "Open File" \
   -image [image create photo -file $dir/open.gif]
.mw toolbar add button close -balloonstr "Close File" \
   -image [image create photo -file $dir/close.gif]
.mw toolbar add frame spacer2 -width 16 -relief raised -bd 2
.mw toolbar add button cut -balloonstr "Cut Selection" \
   -image [image create photo -file $dir/cut.gif]
.mw toolbar add button paste -balloonstr "Paste Selection" \
   -image [image create photo -file $dir/paste.gif]

# Add some mousebar buttons.
.mw mousebar add button save -balloonstr "Save File" \
   -image [image create photo -file $dir/save.gif]
.mw mousebar add button print -balloonstr "Print File" \
   -image [image create photo -file $dir/print.gif]
.mw mousebar add button exit -balloonstr "Close File and Exit" \
   -image [image create photo -file $dir/exit.gif]

# Create a scrolledtext [incr Widget] and import the source code
# for the mainwindow.
set st [::iwidgets::scrolledtext [.mw childsite].st]
$st import $dir/../../scripts/mainwindow.itk
pack $st -fill both -expand 1
```

```
# Display the mainwindow in the middle of the screen after it's done
# building its components.
.mw center
after idle ".mw activate"
```

Class Model

The mainwindow [incr Widget] inherits from iwidgets::Shell and contains several component [incr Widgets].

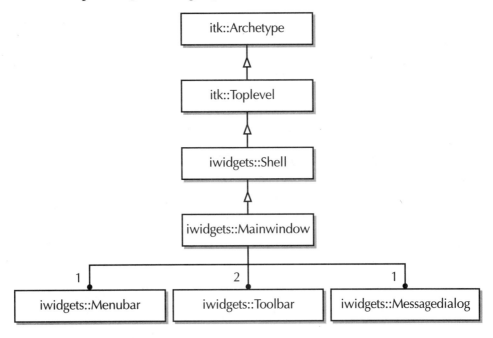

Configuration Options

Standard Options

Refer to the options man page for information on these standard options:

background	disabledforeground	cursor	font
foreground	highlightbackground	highlightcolor	highlightthickness
takefocus			

14

Associated Options

Refer to the associated [incr Widget] for information on each of these options:

Option Name	Associated With
balloonbackground	toolbar
balloondelay1	toolbar
balloondelay2	toolbar
balloonfont	toolbar
balloonforeground	toolbar

Inherited Options

Refer to the [incr Widget] or [incr Tk] base class for information on each of these options. The [incr Tk] base classes are discussed in Chapter 11.

Option Name	Inherited From
clientdata	itk::Archetype
height	iwidgets::Shell
master	iwidgets::Shell
modality	iwidgets::Shell
padx	iwidgets::Shell
pady	iwidgets::Shell
title	itk::Toplevel
width	iwidgets::Shell

Widget-Specific Options

-helpline

Resource name: helpLine
Resource class: HelpLine

Description: Boolean value that specifies whether or not to display the help component. Note that if you set -helpline to a false value, the status component stretches to fill the empty help area.
Default value: 1

-menubarbackground

Resource name: menuBarBackground
Resource class: Background
Description: Specifies the background color of the menubar component. This option replaces the menubar's -background option.
Default value: Windows = SystemButtonFace, Unix = #d9d9d9

-menubarfont

Resource name: menuBarFont
Resource class: Font
Description: Specifies the font to be used for the menubar component. This option replaces the menubar's -font option.
Default value: -Adobe-Helvetica-Bold-R-Normal-*-120-*-*-*-*-*

-menubarforeground

Resource name: menuBarForeground
Resource class: Foreground
Description: Specifies the foreground color of the menubar component. This option replaces the menubar's -foreground option.
Default value: black

-statusline

Resource name: statusLine
Resource class: StatusLine
Description: A Boolean value that specifies whether or not to display the status component. Note that if you set -statusline to a false value that the help component stretches to fill the empty status area.
Default value: 1

-toolbarbackground

Resource name: toolbarBackground
Resource class: Background
Description: Specifies the background color of the toolbar component. This option replaces the toolbar's -background option.
Default value: Windows = SystemButtonFace, Unix = #d9d9d9

-toolbarfont

Resource name: toolbarFont
Resource class: Font
Description: Specifies the font to be used for the toolbar component. This option replaces the toolbar's -font option.
Default value: -Adobe-Helvetica-Bold-R-Normal-*-120-*-*-*-*-*-*

-toolbarforeground

Resource name: toolbarForeground
Resource class: Foreground
Description: Specifies the foreground color of the toolbar component. This option replaces the toolbar's -foreground option.
Default value: #000000000000

Public Methods

Associated Methods

None

Inherited Methods

Refer to the [incr Widget] or [incr Tk] base class for information on each inherited method. The [incr Tk] base classes are discussed in Chapter 11.

Method Name	Inherited From
activate	iwidgets::Shell
center	iwidgets::Shell
cget	itk::Archetype
childsite	iwidgets::Shell
component	itk::Archetype

Method Name	Inherited From
config	itk::Archetype
configure	itk::Archetype
deactivate	iwidgets::Shell

Widget-Specific Methods

menubar

Usage: pathName *menubar* ?arg arg ...?
Description: This wrapper method allows you to directly access and modify the menubar component. You can specify any valid menubar command with its associated arguments as arguments to *menubar*. The example code at the beginning of this section uses the *menubar* method to add menubuttons to the menubar component.

mousebar

Usage: pathName *mousebar* ?arg arg ...?
Description: This wrapper method allows you to directly access and modify the mousebar component (this is the vertical toolbar). You can specify any valid toolbar command with its associated arguments as arguments to *mousebar*. The example code at the beginning of this section uses the *mousebar* method to add buttons to the mousebar component, complete with pop-up balloon windows.

msgd

Usage: pathName *msgd* ?arg arg ...?
Description: This wrapper method allows you to directly access and modify the msgd component. You can specify any valid messagedialog command with its associated arguments as arguments to *msgd*. You can use this method to display messages to the user. The messagedialog is deactivated by default, so you have to activate it in order to display it.

toolbar

Usage: pathName *toolbar* ?arg arg ...?
Description: This wrapper method allows you to directly access and modify the toolbar component (this is the horizontal toolbar). You can specify any valid toolbar command with its associated arguments as arguments to *toolbar*. The example code at the beginning of this section uses the *toolbar* method to add buttons to the toolbar component, complete with pop-up balloon windows.

14

Components

The mainwindow [incr Widget] makes extensive use of composition and is composed of several [incr Widgets], as outlined in the following table.

Name	Class	Description
help	Label	One of two sunken labels at the bottom of the screen. This one is used to show help information and is to the left of the status component when both are displayed.
hull	Mainwindow	The outer frame around the entire mainwindow.
menubar	Menubar	The menubar at the top of the screen.
mousebar	Toolbar	The vertical toolbar to the left of the childsite.
msgd	Messagedialog	The messagedialog [incr Widget]. This component is only displayed when activated.
status	Label	One of two sunken labels at the bottom of the screen. This one is used to show status information and is to the right of the help component when both are displayed.
toolbar	Toolbar	The horizontal toolbar just beneath the menubar component.

menubar

The menubar is one of the most popular [incr Widgets] because so many of today's applications are menu-driven. It provides a convenient way of creating menu hierarchies without having to build them through Tk, which can get complicated and hard to maintain. You can add new menubuttons and create corresponding menus with the *add* method, or you can use the -menubuttons option to create the entire menu hierarchy at once. Each menu may have one or more of several different menu entries, including commands, checkbuttons, radiobuttons, and separators for grouping related menu entries together. Once created, the menubar provides convenient access to each menu entry in the hierarchy with a menu pathname syntax. The menubar also lends itself to convenient help status bar areas in your application by defining a -helpvariable configuration option. This option can be used to print useful help information in a label or entry widget to help the users of your application better understand the functionality of each menu entry.

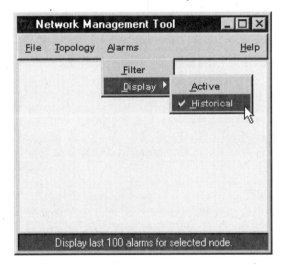

```
# Create the menubar and add a few menubuttons and menus with the
# -menubuttons configuration options. Note that this example is
# more of a guideline on how to create menus and different kinds
# of menu entries than something that's meant to be functional.
# It's intentionally lacking in consistency and functionality.
```

14

```
iwidgets::menubar .mb -activebackground grey40 \
  -activeforeground white \
  -helpvariable globalHelpVar -menubuttons {
    menubutton file -text File -underline 0 -menu {
      command save -label Save -underline 0
      command quit -label Exit -underline 1
    }
    menubutton top -text Topology -underline 0 -menu {
      cascade net -label Network -underline 0 -menu {
        command add -label "Add Node" -underline 0
        command rem -label "Remove Node" -underline 0
      }
      command status -label Status -underline 0
    }
    menubutton alarms -text Alarms -underline 0 -menu {
      command filter -label Filter -underline 0
      cascade display -label Display -underline 0 -menu {
        radiobutton curr -label Active -underline 0 \
          -helpstr "Display all active alarms for selected node."
        radiobutton hist -label Historical -selectcolor yellow \
          -activeforeground yellow -underline 0 \
          -helpstr "Display last 100 alarms for selected node."
      }
    }
  }

# Now add a help menubutton with the add method. Notice that a help
# menubutton is automatically packed on the right side.
.mb add menubutton help -text Help -underline 0

# Create a scrolledcanvas area in which a network topology could
# be drawn and managed with the menubar (quite simplified).
iwidgets::scrolledcanvas .sc -width 275 -height 185 \
  -hscrollmode dynamic -vscrollmode dynamic -textbackground ghostwhite

# Create a help status area.
label .help -relief sunken -bd 2 -bg grey40 -fg white \
  -textvariable globalHelpVar

pack .mb -fill x -expand 1
pack .sc -fill both -expand 1
pack .help -fill x -expand 1
```

Class Model

The menubar [incr Widget] inherits directly from itk::Widget. It does not interact with any other [incr Widgets] outside of its inheritance tree.

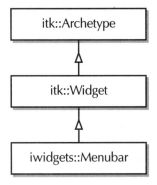

Configuration Options

Standard Options

Refer to the options man page for information on these standard options:

activebackground	activeborderwidth	activeforeground	anchor
background	borderwidth	cursor	disabledforeground
font	foreground	highlightbackground	highlightcolor
highlightthickness	justify	padx	pady
wraplength			

Associated Options

Refer to the associated Tk widget for information on these options:

Option Name	Associated With
height	Tk frame widget
width	Tk frame widget

14

Inherited Options

Refer to Chapter 11 for information on this inherited option from the [incr Tk] Archetype base class:

Option Name	Inherited From
clientdata	itk::Archetype

Widget-Specific Options

-helpvariable

Resource name: helpVariable
Resource class: HelpVariable
Description: Specifies a global variable to be updated whenever the cursor is over a menu entry. This global variable is set to the value of the current menu entry unless you have specified another value with the -helpstr option when you added the entry with the *add* method or the -menubuttons option. Using -helpvariable is useful for creating a help status bar, which is what the mainwindow [incr Widget] does. You can configure a label or entry widget's -textvariable option to the same variable name specified by -helpvariable. The label or entry will then be automatically updated to reflect the new menu entry name or the value of -helpstr if specified. You could use -helpstr, for example, to provide a description of the menu entry instead of its simple name—such as "Copy the selected text to the clipboard" instead of the menu entry name "Copy". When the cursor is moved away from the menu entry, the variable specified by -helpvariable is set to the blank string.
Default value: {}

-menubuttons

Resource name: menuButtons
Resource class: MenuButtons
Description: Use this option to populate the menubar with menubuttons and menus. This option is different than most [incr Widget] configuration options because you don't just specify a simple value. Instead, you specify a series of command fragments, each of which should return the Tk window pathname of a menubutton widget. Each menubutton as well as its associated menu widget then becomes a new menubar component. The menubutton component is the symbolic name of the menubutton, and the menu is this name followed by a -menu. Refer to the code at the beginning of this section to see an example of this, or refer to the menubutton man page.
Default value: {}

Public Methods

Associated Methods

None

Inherited Methods

Refer to Chapter 11 for information on each of these inherited methods from the itk::Archetype base class:

Method Name	Inherited From
cget	itk::Archetype
component	itk::Archetype
config	itk::Archetype
configure	itk::Archetype

Widget-Specific Methods

add

Usage: pathName *add* type path ?arg arg ...?
Description: Adds a new menubutton to the menubar or a new menu entry to an existing menu. What to add depends on the type argument, which has several valid values that are summarized as follows:

◆ menubutton: A new menubutton is added to the menubar, and two new components are added to the menubar's component list: the menubutton and its associated menu. The symbolic name of the menubutton in the component list is specified by the path argument. The symbolic name of the associated menu is the menubutton's symbolic name followed by "-menu". For example, adding a new menubutton called view results in the addition of a view component and a view-menu component. Any valid Tk menubutton configuration option may follow the path argument to initialize the new menubutton. Use its -menu option to configure the menu.

◆ cascade: A new cascade entry is created at the bottom of the menu specified by the path argument, and a new component is added to the menubar's component list, the cascade entry's associated menu. The component name is the symbolic name of the cascade entry followed by "-menu". For example, adding a new cascade entry called preferences

14

results in the addition of a preferences-menu component. The path argument must be of the form .menuName.cascadeName, where menuName is the symbolic name of the associated menu and cascadeName is the symbolic name for the cascade entry. (Note the preceding dot.) Any valid menu entry configuration option may follow the path argument to initialize the cascade entry. Refer to the table following this method description for available options. A -menu option is provided especially for cascade entries so that you can add menus underneath them.

◆ checkbutton: A new checkbutton entry is created at the bottom of the menu specified by the path argument. The path argument must be of the form .menuPath.name, where menuPath is the pathname of the associated menu and name is the symbolic name for the checkbutton entry. (Note the preceding dot.) Refer to the *path* method for details on menu pathnames. Any valid menu entry configuration option may follow the path argument to initialize the checkbutton entry, some of which are provided for checkbutton entries only. Refer to the table at the bottom of this method description for available options.

◆ command: A new command entry is created at the bottom of the menu specified by the path argument. The path argument must be of the form .menuPath.name, where menuPath is the pathname of the associated menu and name is the symbolic name for the command entry. (Note the preceding dot.) Refer to the *path* method for details on menu pathnames. Any valid menu entry configuration option may follow the path argument to initialize the command entry. Refer to the table at the bottom of this method description for available options.

◆ radiobutton: A new radiobutton entry is created at the bottom of the menu specified by the path argument. The path argument must be of the form .menuPath.name, where menuPath is the pathname of the associated menu and name is the symbolic name for the radiobutton entry. (Note the preceding dot.) Refer to the *path* method for details on menu pathnames. Any valid menu entry configuration option may follow the path argument to initialize the radiobutton entry, some of which are provided for radiobutton and checkbutton entries only. Refer to the table at the bottom of this method description for available options.

◆ separator: A new separator entry is created at the bottom of the menu specified by the path argument. The path argument must be of the form .menuPath.name, where menuPath is the pathname of the associated menu and name is the symbolic name for the separator entry. (Note the preceding dot.) Refer to the *path* method for details on menu pathnames. A separator has very few configuration options, and you can't select it or invoke it. It's simply drawn in a menu as a divider line to separate other menu entries.

Several restrictions apply to the symbolic name specified for a new menubutton or menu entry. You cannot use end, last, menu, or an integer as the name. Additionally, the name must begin with a lowercase letter since it is used as a Tk window pathname. The following table provides a list of the available menu entry configuration options. Some options are restricted to certain menu entry types as denoted by special characters in the table. These restrictions are explained following the table.

activebackground	activeforeground	accelerator	background
bitmap	columnbreak	command	font
foreground	hidemargin	image	**indicatoron
label	!menu	*offvalue	*onvalue
**selectcolor	**selectimage	state	underline
value	variable		

! Indicates this option is only available for cascade entries.
* Indicates this option is only available for checkbutton entries.
** Indicates this option is only available for checkbutton and radiobutton entries.

delete

Usage: pathName *delete* from ?to?
Description: Deletes a menubutton and its associated menu, a cascaded menu tree, a single menu entry, or a group of menus or menu entries. To delete a top-level menu, specify the menubutton's symbolic name as the from argument. The menubutton and its menu will be deleted and removed from the menubar's component list. To delete a cascade menu and its entry from its parent menu, specify the cascade entry's symbolic name as the from argument. The corresponding component is removed from the menubar's component list. To delete a single menu entry, specify its menu path as the from argument. The menu path should be of the form menuPath.name, where name is the symbolic name of the menu entry. Refer to the *path* method for details on menu pathnames. Finally, to delete a group of menus or menu entries, specify the to argument, which must be a valid symbolic name for menus or a menu pathname for menu entries. All menus/entries will be deleted inclusively. Note that both from and to must be of the same type, either menus or entries.

14

index

Usage: pathName *index* path
Description: Returns the numerical index of the menubutton or menu entry designated by the path argument. For menubuttons, the path argument is the symbolic name of the menubutton. For menu entries, the path argument should be of the form menuPath.name, where menuPath is the pathname of the associated menu and name is the symbolic name of the menu entry. Refer to the *path* method for details on menu pathnames. Menubuttons are indexed starting at zero, increasing from left to right. Menu entries are indexed starting at zero, increasing top to bottom. Note that separators also count as entries, so make sure to take this into consideration when using the *index* method. If the designated menubutton or menu entry does not exist, a -1 is returned.

insert

Usage: pathName *insert* before type path ?arg arg ...?
Description: Inserts a new menubutton into the menubar or a new menu entry into a menu before the menubutton or menu entry designated by the before argument. For menubuttons, the before argument must be the symbolic name of the menubutton. For menu entries, the before argument should be of the form menuPath.name, where menu path is the pathname of the menu and name is the symbolic name of the menu entry. The type, path, and optional arguments are the same as the *add* method's argument list (except the preceding dot for the menu path is optional for *insert*). Refer to *add* for further details.

invoke

Usage: pathName *invoke* path
Description: Evaluates the -command option of the designated menu entry. The path argument should be of the form menuPath.name, where menuPath is the pathname of the containing menu and name is the symbolic name of the menu entry.

menucget

Usage: pathName *menucget* componentMenu option
Description: Returns the value of the specified option for the specified component menubutton. The componentMenu argument is the symbolic

name for the menubutton component, which is specified when the menubutton is added to the menubar.

menuconfigure

Usage: pathName *menuconfigure* index ?option? ?arg arg ...?
Description: Use this method to modify a menubutton's configuration, to print a single option's information for a menubutton, or to print all of a menubutton's configuration options. The index argument is the numerical index of the menubutton or its symbolic name. If no arguments are specified following index, all of that menubutton's configuration options are printed. If one argument follows index, then it should be a valid menubutton configuration option; if so, its information is printed. If multiple arguments are specified after index, they must be in option/value pairs. You can do this to modify the menubutton's configuration.

path

Usage: pathName *path* ?mode? pattern
Description: Returns the menu pathname of a menu or menu entry that matches the pattern specified by the pattern argument and the search style specified by the mode argument. The mode argument defaults to -glob, but may be set to -regexp to specify more advanced search patterns. This method is useful for determining a menu pathname when you are using one of the other public methods that require this path as an argument. The pathname is dot-delimited like a Tk-window pathname, and it is also hierarchical, but it is not a full Tk window pathname. It's relative to the menubutton, which serves as the topmost component of the name. For example, the menu pathname for a Cut menu entry in an Edit menu would be .edit.cut. Be aware that only the last matching name is returned. For example, if you have Cut and Copy entries (in that order) in an Edit menu, specifying *e*c* as the search pattern will return the menu path of the Copy menu entry only, .edit.copy, since this entry is the last one that begins with the letter c.

type

Usage: pathName *type* path
Description: Returns the type according to the path argument. The type is one of cascade, checkbutton, command, menu, menubutton, radiobutton, or separator. The path argument should be the menu pathname of a menu or menu entry, or the symbolic name of a menubutton.

14

yposition

Usage: pathName *yposition* path

Description: Returns an integer representing the y-coordinate position of the topmost pixel in the menu entry specified by the path argument. The position is relative to the top of the menu entry's containing menu window. For example, if you open a menu, the y-coordinate for menu entry index 2 may be 30 pixels, which means the top of this menu entry is 30 pixels beneath the top of the menu window. This depends mostly on the font.

Components

When a menubar is first created, it only contains a hull and menubar component, as outlined in the following table. As you add new menubuttons to the menubar, each one becomes a new component widget along with its corresponding menu.

Name	Class	Description
hull	Menubar	The frame around the entire menubar
menubar	Frame	The frame that contains each of the menubutton components

messagebox

The messagebox [incr Widget] is used to display messages in a scrollable text area. Message types can be user defined so that different types, such as error messages or informational messages, can be displayed differently in the messagebox. Message types may be added, removed, or configured if they already exist. In addition to user-defined message types, the messagebox also provides file I/O with *save* and *export* methods. Also, a pop-up menu over the text area allows you to save the contents of the messagebox to a file, clear the contents, or search for a particular string in the messagebox with a finddialog [incr Widget].

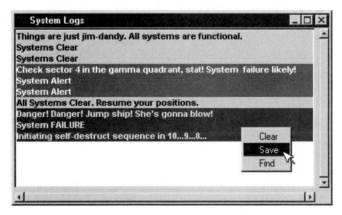

```
# Create the messagebox.
wm geometry . 410x220
wm title . "System Logs"
iwidgets::messagebox .mb -borderwidth 2
pack .mb -fill both -expand 1

# Create a couple of new message types.
set font -Adobe-Helvetica-Bold-R-Normal--*-140-*-*-*-*-*-*
.mb type add info -background grey75 -foreground black -font $font
.mb type add warning -background grey50 -foreground white -font
$font
.mb type add error -background red -foreground yellow -font $font

# Now add some messages.
.mb issue "Things are just jim-dandy. All systems are functional." \
  info
```

```
.mb issue "Systems Clear" info; .mb issue "Systems Clear" info
.mb issue "Check sector 4 in the gamma quadrant, stat! System \
  failure likely!" warning
.mb issue "System Alert" warning; .mb issue "System Alert" warning
.mb issue "All Systems Clear. Resume your positions." info
.mb issue "Danger! Danger! Jump ship! She's gonna blow!" error
.mb issue "System FAILURE" error
.mb issue "Initiating self-destruct sequence in 10...9...8..." error
```

Class Model

The messagebox [incr Widget] inherits directly from itk::Widget. It has a
scrolledtext [incr Widget] and an optional finddialog [incr Widget].

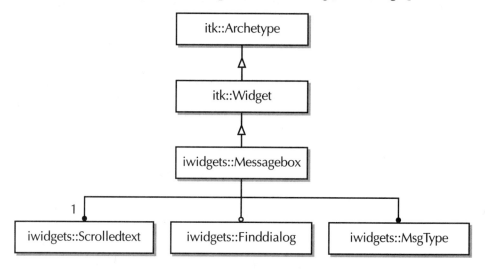

Configuration Options

Standard Options

Refer to the options man page for information on these standard options:

activebackground	activeforeground	background	borderwidth
cursor	exportselection	font	foreground
highlightcolor	highlightthickness	padx	pady
relief	troughcolor		

Associated Options

Refer to the associated Tk widget or [incr Widget] for information on each of these options:

Option Name	Associated With
activerelief	Tk scrollbar widget
elementborderwidth	Tk scrollbar widget
height	scrolledtext
hscrollmode	scrolledtext
jump	Tk scrollbar widget
labelbitmap	scrolledtext
labelfont	scrolledtext
labelimage	scrolledtext
labelmargin	scrolledtext
labelpos	scrolledtext
labeltext	scrolledtext
labelvariable	scrolledtext
sbwidth	scrolledtext
scrollmargin	scrolledtext
setgrid	scrolledtext
spacing1	scrolledtext
spacing2	scrolledtext
spacing3	scrolledtext
textbackground	scrolledtext
visibleitems	scrolledtext
vscrollmode	scrolledtext
width	scrolledtext

14

Inherited Options

Refer to Chapter 11 for information on this inherited option from the [incr Tk] Archetype base class:

Option Name	Inherited From
clientdata	itk::Archetype

Widget-Specific Options

-filename

Resource name: fileName
Resource class: FileName
Description: Specifies the value for the -initialfile option to pass to the **tk_getSaveFile** command when the Save option is selected from the pop-up menu. You can change the filename in the resulting dialog window. This option is just a convenient way to set a default value if it is unlikely to change.
Default value: {}

-maxlines

Resource name: maxLines
Resource class: MaxLines
Description: Specifies the maximum number of lines to display in the scrolledtext component. If the number of lines exceeds this option, enough lines are removed from the top of the scrolledtext to get the total number of lines just below the maximum value again. If you don't want the lines to be lost, you can save the scrolledtext contents to a file with the *save* method and then clear the contents with the *clear* method.
Default value: 1000

-savedir

Resource name: saveDir
Resource class: SaveDir
Description: Specifies the value for the -initialdir option to pass to the **tk_getSaveFile** command when the Save option is selected from the pop-up menu. You can change the directory name in the resulting dialog window. This option is just a convenient way to set a default value if it is unlikely to change.
Default value: The current working directory (the **pwd** command is used)

Public Methods

Associated Methods

None

Inherited Methods

Refer to Chapter 11 for information on each of these inherited methods from the itk::Archetype base class:

Method Name	Inherited From
cget	itk::Archetype
component	itk::Archetype
config	itk::Archetype
configure	itk::Archetype

Widget-Specific Methods

clear

Usage: pathName *clear*
Description: Clears the entire text area.

export

Usage: pathName *export* filename
Description: Copies the entire contents of the scrolledtext component into the file specified by the filename argument. Note that you are not warned if the filename already exists, so be careful when using this method because you will overwrite the file if it does exist.

find

Usage: pathName *find*
Description: The finddialog component is centered in the text area and activated. If this component does not already exist, *find* creates one and sets its -textwidget option to the scrolledtext component. You can then use the finddialog to search for strings in the messagebox.

14

issue

Usage: pathName *issue* string ?type?
Description: Posts the message specified by the string argument to the messagebox. The type argument may be used to post particular types of messages. See *type* for more details. If the specified type does not exist, an error is returned.

save

Usage: pathName *save*
Description: Use this method to save the contents of the messagebox to a file. A file selection box is displayed using the **tk_getSaveFile** command. The -filename and -savedir option values are passed to this command's -initialfile and -initialdir options, respectively, to initialize the resulting file selection dialog window.

type

Usage: pathName *type* op tag ?arg arg ...?
Description: Handles commands related to message types, which are actually instances of the iwidgets::MsgType [incr Tcl] class. This class is defined in the file containing the Messagedialog class definition. It's basically a configuration option container, defining five public variables: -background, -bell, -font, -foreground, and -show. Each new message type can then be configured to appear differently in the messagebox by setting these options. The op argument determines the action to take with the message type specified by the tag argument. These actions are outlined as follows:

◆ add: Adds a new message type (creates a new instance of iwidgets::MsgType). For example, you can define an error message type that will print messages with a boldface font, a red background, and a yellow foreground so that they stand out from other message types.

◆ cget: Returns the value of the specified option for the specified message type. This is basically a wrapper for the iwidgets::MsgType's *cget* method.

◆ configure: Configures a message type's option(s) or print information on one of the options. This is basically a wrapper for the iwidgets::MsgType's *configure* method.

◆ remove: Removes the specified message type (deletes the associated instance of iwidgets::MsgType).

The tag argument is a unique tag used to represent a new message type, and the optional arguments following tag should be one or more of the public variables defined in MsgType with associated values. Use the -bell option (a Boolean) to ring the system bell when certain message types are printed, and use the -show option (also a Boolean) to enable or disable certain message types. See the code at the beginning of this section for an example.

Components

When a messagebox is first created, it contains three components: hull, itemMenu, and text. Once you select the Find option from the itemMenu component, a new component called findd is added, which is of class type Finddialog. Since this component only exists under certain conditions, it is not listed in the following components table:

Name	Class	Description
hull	Messagebox	The frame around the entire messagebox.
itemMenu	Menu	The pop-up menu over the text area. Use this menu to save or clear the text area or to find a string.
text	Scrolledtext	The scrolledtext [incr Widget] that displays the text in the messagebox.

14

messagedialog

The messagedialog [incr Widget] is used to display generic text dialog windows. The messagedialog contains two labels you can use to display bitmaps or images next to a text message. Since messagedialog inherits from iwidgets::Dialog, it inherits a buttonbox component. You therefore don't have to add buttons or a separator bar since a base class does this for you. You do have access to the buttonbox through several public methods if you need to remove buttons or modify existing ones.

```
# Create the messagedialog.
iwidgets::messagedialog .md \
    -text "Burnin' down the house!\nLogo by John P. Davis\n\n\
    \[incr Widgets\] Made Possible By:\nMark Harrison\nAlfredo Jahn\n\
    Michael McLennan\nKris Raney\nBret Schumacher\nTako Schotanus\n\
    Bill Scott\nJohn Sigler\nJohn Tucker\nMark Ulferts\nSue Yockey" \
    -title "Give credit where credit is due: \[incr Widgets\]\
    Acknowledgements" -textpady 0

# Create an image to display next to the message.
set img [image create photo \
    -file ${iwidgets::library}/demos/iwidgets.gif]
.md configure -image $img
.md component image configure -relief ridge -bd 3
```

```
# Change the buttons a bit.
.md buttonconfigure 0 -text Great
.md buttonconfigure 1 -text Job
.md buttonconfigure 2 -text By
.md buttonconfigure 3 -text All
.md show 1;  .md show 3

# Center the messagedialog and activate it.
.md center
after idle ".md activate"
```

Class Model

The messagedialog [incr Widget] inherits from iwidgets::Dialog. It doesn't interact with any other [incr Widgets] directly, but it does have a buttonbox through inheritance, which is shown in the class model for the dialogshell.

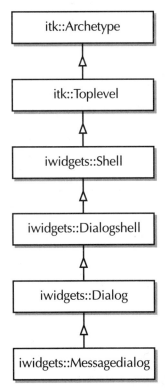

Configuration Options

Standard Options

Refer to the options man page for information on these standard options:

background	bitmap	cursor	font
foreground	image	takefocus	text

Associated Options

None

Inherited Options

Refer to the [incr Widget] or [incr Tk] base class for information on each of these options. The [incr Tk] base classes are discussed in Chapter 11.

Option Name	Inherited From
buttonboxpadx	iwidgets::Dialogshell
buttonboxpady	iwidgets::Dialogshell
buttonboxpos	iwidgets::Dialogshell
clientdata	itk::Archetype
height	iwidgets::Shell
master	iwidgets::Shell
modality	iwidgets::Shell
padx	iwidgets::Dialogshell
pady	iwidgets::Dialogshell
separator	iwidgets::Dialogshell
thickness	iwidgets::Dialogshell
title	itk::Toplevel
width	iwidgets::Shell

Widget-Specific Options

-imagepos

Resource name: imagePos
Resource class: Position
Description: Specifies the position of the image component relative to the message. Valid values are n, s, e, and w.
Default value: w

-textpadx

Resource name: textPadX
Resource class: Pad
Description: Specifies the distance in pixels between the text and any other component widget in the x direction.
Default value: 20

-textpady

Resource name: textPadY
Resource class: Pad
Description: Specifies the distance in pixels between the text and any other component widget in the y direction.
Default value: 20

Public Methods

Associated Methods

None

Inherited Methods

Refer to the [incr Widget] or [incr Tk] base class for information on each inherited method. The [incr Tk] base classes are discussed in Chapter 11.

Method Name	Inherited From
activate	iwidgets::Shell
add	iwidgets::Dialogshell
buttoncget	iwidgets::Dialogshell

14

Method Name	Inherited From
buttonconfigure	iwidgets::Dialogshell
center	iwidgets::Shell
cget	itk::Archetype
childsite	iwidgets::Dialogshell
component	itk::Archetype
config	itk::Archetype
configure	itk::Archetype
deactivate	iwidgets::Shell
default	iwidgets::Dialogshell
delete	iwidgets::Dialogshell
hide	iwidgets::Dialogshell
index	iwidgets::Dialogshell
insert	iwidgets::Dialogshell
invoke	iwidgets::Dialogshell
show	iwidgets::Dialogshell

Widget-Specific Methods
None

Components

The messagedialog [incr Widget] is composed of two labels and a buttonbox separated by a divider line, as outlined in the following table. Each of these is packed inside the hull frame component.

Name	Class	Description
bbox	Buttonbox	The buttonbox at the bottom of the screen
hull	Messagedialog	The frame surrounding the entire messagedialog
image	Label	A label widget used to display a photo or bitmap
message	Label	A label widget used to display the text message
separator	Frame	The divider line between the text message and the buttonbox

14

notebook

The notebook [incr Widget] implements a way to store pages in a virtual notebook. You can add pages to the notebook with the *add* method and then pack the desired widgets into the new page's childsite frame. Pages are displayed individually in the notebook's childsite frame. You can turn pages of the notebook by using the *prev, next, select,* or *view* methods. As each new page is displayed, the previous page is hidden. The notebook also provides a facility for scrolling through the notebook pages with its -scrollcommand option.

```
# Hide the root window until the notebook is ready.
wm withdraw .

# Create a scrollbar for scrolling through the notebook pages.
scrollbar .sb -orient horizontal -command ".nb view"

# Create the notebook.
iwidgets::notebook .nb -scrollcommand ".sb set" -height 200

# Create a radiobox for selecting pages in the notebook as an
# alternative to using the scrollbar.
iwidgets::radiobox .rb
.rb add page1 -text "Page 1"
.rb add page2 -text "Page 2"
.rb add page3 -text "Page 3"
pack .rb -fill x
update idletasks
foreach page "page1 page2 page3" {
```

```
    pack [.rb component $page] -side left -expand 1
}

# Create and fill in page 1. Note the pathname will likely not
# exist on your system.
set page1 [.nb add -label "Itcl Powered"]
frame $page1.f -relief ridge -bd 3
label $page1.f.img -relief ridge -bd 4 -image [image create photo \
  -file "C:/tmp/itclpwrd.gif"]
pack $page1.f.img -padx 16 -pady 16 -expand 1
pack $page1.f -fill both -expand 1

# Pages 2 and 3 are blank. You can add any kind of Tk widget or
# [incr Widget] to the page childsites stored in $page2 and $page3.
set page2 [.nb add -label blank2]
pack [label $page2.l -text "Welcome to page 2!"] -expand 1
set page3 [.nb add -label blank3]
pack [label $page3.l -text "Welcome to page 3!"] -expand 1

pack .nb -fill both -expand 1
pack .sb -fill x

# Configure the radiobox to select pages when the radiobuttons are
# selected, select the first radiobutton to select the first page,
# and draw the window.
.rb configure -command {.nb select [.rb index [.rb get]]}
.rb select 0; # This is equivalent to <.nb select "Itcl Powered">
wm deiconify .
```

Class Model

The notebook [incr Widget] inherits directly from itk::Widget. It contains zero or more page [incr Widgets]. For more information on pages, refer to the *add* method description.

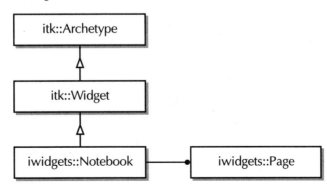

14

Configuration Options

Standard Options

The only standard option for a notebook is -cursor. Refer to the options man page for information on this option.

Associated Options

Refer to the associated Tk widget for information on each of these options:

Option Name	Associated With
height	Tk frame widget
width	Tk frame widget

Inherited Options

Refer to Chapter 11 for information on this inherited option from the [incr Tk] Archetype base class:

Option Name	Inherited From
clientdata	itk::Archetype

Widget-Specific Options

-auto

Resource name: auto
Resource class: Auto
Description: Boolean value that specifies whether or not the notebook will automatically pack and unpack pages as they are selected. If true, then selecting a page causes the previous page to be unpacked (via **pack forget**) and the new page to be packed. If false, then selecting a page does not appear to work since the page contents are unchanged.
Default value: true

-background

Resource name: background
Resource class: Background
Description: Specifies the background color to be used for all of the pages in the notebook.
Default value: #d9d9d9

-scrollcommand

Resource name: scrollCommand
Resource class: ScrollCommand
Description: This option is typically used in conjunction with the *view* method. You can use this option to provide a way to scroll through the notebook pages with a scroll bar. It is similar to the -xscrollcommand or -yscrollcommand options, which are available on some Tk widgets such as the canvas. To add this capability, create a scroll bar and configure the notebook's -scrollcommand to invoke the scroll bar's set command. Then configure the scroll bar's -command option to invoke the notebook's *view* method. You can see an example of this in the code at the beginning of this section.
Default value: {}

Public Methods

Associated Methods

None

Inherited Methods

Refer to the [incr Tk] base class for information on each inherited method. The [incr Tk] base classes are discussed in Chapter 11.

Method Name	Inherited From
cget	itk::Archetype
component	itk::Archetype
config	itk::Archetype
configure	itk::Archetype

Widget-Specific Methods

add

Usage: pathName *add* ?option value option value ...?
Description: Adds a new page to the notebook, initializing it with any specified pairs of option/value arguments. A notebook page is actually an instance of the iwidgets::Page class, which is defined in the file that defines the Notebook class definition. This class is encapsulated by the notebook and isn't really meant to be used other than in a notebook [incr Widget]. It inherits from itk::Widget and has the following valid configuration options:

14

-background, -clientdata, -command, -cursor, -disabledforeground, -height, -label, and -width. All options are self-explanatory, except perhaps -label. Use this option to associate a symbolic name with the page. You can then use this name later to view the page with the notebook's *select* method or to add new items to the page by retrieving the page's outer frame with the notebook's *childsite* method. Once a new Page object is created, it is added to a list of notebook pages for convenient selection.

childsite

Usage: pathName *childsite* ?index ?
Description: Returns a list of all page childsite frames if the index argument isn't specified. Otherwise, the childsite frame of the specified page is returned. The index argument may be a numerical value (the first page is index 0, the second is index 1, etc.), or it may be the symbolic name of the page if you specified its -label option during page addition.

delete

Usage: pathName *delete* from ?to?
Description: Deletes a single page specified by the from argument or a range of pages between the from and to arguments, inclusively, from the notebook. Both arguments may be either index values or symbolic names of pages. A page's symbolic name is specified by its -label option during page addition.

index

Usage: pathName *index* index
Description: Returns the numerical index of the page specified by the index argument. If not found, a -1 is returned.

insert

Usage: pathName *insert* index ?option value option value ...?
Description: Inserts a new page into the notebook just before the page specified by the index argument, which may be the symbolic name of the page or its numerical index. For information on the optional option/value pairs, refer to the *add* method description.

next

Usage: pathName *next*
Description: Selects the next page in the notebook. If you are currently viewing the last page, then the first page is displayed. Each page in the

notebook has a childsite frame in which its contents are stored. When a page is displayed, its childsite frame is packed into the notebook's childsite frame, and the previously selected page is unpacked. If your display is not updated when you change pages, make sure the notebook's -auto option is set to 1. This method returns the index of the next page or an error if the notebook is empty.

pageconfigure

Usage: pathName *index* index ?option value option value ...?
Description: Use this method to modify a page's configuration, to print a single option's information for a page, or to print all of a page's configuration options. The index argument is the numerical index of the page or its symbolic name. If no arguments are specified following index, all of that page's configuration options are printed. If one argument follows index, then it should be a valid page configuration option; if so, then its information is printed. If multiple arguments are specified after index, they must be in option/value pairs. You can do this to modify a page's configuration.

prev

Usage: pathName *prev*
Description: Selects the previous page in the notebook. If you are currently viewing the first page, then the last page is displayed. Each page in the notebook has a childsite frame in which its contents are stored. When a page is displayed, its childsite frame is packed into the notebook's childsite frame, and the previously selected page is unpacked. If your display is not updated, make sure the notebook's -auto option is set to 1. This method returns the index of the previous page or an error if the notebook is empty.

select

Usage: pathName *select* index
Description: Displays the page in the notebook specified by the index argument, which may be the page's numerical index or the symbolic name of the page. Each page in the notebook has a childsite frame in which its contents are stored. When a page is displayed, its childsite frame is packed into the notebook's childsite frame, and the previously selected page is unpacked. If your display is not updated, make sure the notebook's -auto option is set to 1. This method returns the index of the currently selected page or a -1 if there is no selection.

view

Usage: pathName *view* args
Description: This method is used in conjunction with the -scrollcommand option to provide the ability to scroll through the pages of the notebook with a scroll bar. When a notebook and a scroll bar are tied together, the scroll bar automatically passes data into the args argument for scrolling. The notebook then decides which page to display according to these arguments. An example of this facility is provided at the beginning of this section.

Components

A notebook [incr Widget] simply consists of a childsite frame and the hull frame, as outlined in the following table.

Name	Class	Description
cs	Frame	The notebook's childsite frame
hull	Notebook	The frame around the entire notebook

optionmenu

The optionmenu [incr Widget] is used as a general selection widget. It provides a menubutton that displays a pop-up menu with selectable entries when pressed. You can add items to this pop-up menu with the *insert* method. (Note that the -items option from version 2.2 is no longer present.) The optionmenu is automatically resized when new items are added, but you can explicitly set the width with the -width option. An item may be selected by clicking on the menubutton and then clicking on the desired menu entry in the pop-up menu. The optionmenu provides several public methods that allow you to perform a variety of operations such as sorting, inserting new items into the middle of the menu, and disabling individual menu entries. You should note that the optionmenu is not intended to show integral values.

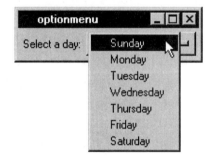

```
# Create the optionmenu.
iwidgets::optionmenu .op -labeltext "Select a day:"

# Insert a bunch of entries.
foreach day "Sun Mon Tues Wednes Thurs Fri Satur" {
  .op insert end ${day}day
}

wm title . optionmenu
pack .op
```

Class Model

The optionmenu [incr Widget] inherits from iwidgets::Labeledwidget. It does not interact with any other [incr Widgets] outside of its inheritance tree.

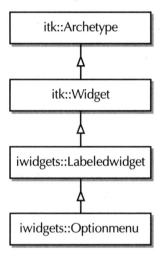

Configuration Options

Standard Options

Refer to the options man page for information on these standard options:

activebackground	activeborderwidth	activeforeground	background
borderwidth	cursor	disabledforeground	font
foreground	highlightcolor	highlightthickness	selectcolor

Associated Options

None

Inherited Options

Refer to the [incr Widget] or [incr Tk] base class for information on each of these options. The [incr Tk] base classes are discussed in Chapter 11.

Option Name	Inherited From
clientdata	itk::Archetype
labelbitmap	iwidgets::Labeledwidget
labelfont	iwidgets::Labeledwidget
labelimage	iwidgets::Labeledwidget
labelmargin	iwidgets::Labeledwidget
labelpos	iwidgets::Labeledwidget
labeltext	iwidgets::Labeledwidget
labelvariable	iwidgets::Labeledwidget

Widget-Specific Options

-clicktime

Resource name: clickTime
Resource class: ClickTime
Description: This option is used in conjunction with posting the pop-up menu. It's used to determine that a single mouse click has occurred. You should avoid modifying this option because it could affect how the single-click functionality behaves.
Default value: 150

-command

Resource name: command
Resource class: Command
Description: Specifies a Tcl command to be evaluated each time a new selection is made in the optionmenu.
Default value: {}

-cyclicon

Resource name: cyclicOn
Resource class: CyclicOn
Description: A Boolean value that specifies whether or not the right mouse button is enabled for cycling through the optionmenu selections. If true, then each right mouse click selects the next entry in the menu without

14

displaying the menu. If the last menu entry is currently selected, a right mouse click selects the first entry. Holding the SHIFT key while clicking the right mouse button cycles through the optionmenu in reverse order. Note that each time the right mouse button is clicked when -cyclicon is true, the optionmenu's -command option is evaluated.
Default value: true

-popupcursor

Resource name: popupCursor
Resource class: Cursor
Description: Specifies the cursor shape to use over the pop-up menu. This option replaces the popupMenu component's -cursor option. Note that this option may not work under Windows.
Default value: arrow

-state

Resource name: state
Resource class: State
Description: Specifies whether the optionmenu is enabled or disabled. Valid values are normal and disabled. If disabled, then the optionmenu foreground is changed to the value of the -disabledforeground option, and menu selection is disabled. The menubutton component's -state option is set to disabled, so both left and right mouse clicks are disabled.
Default value: normal

-width

Resource name: width
Resource class: Width
Description: Specifies the width in pixels of the optionmenu's menubutton component. The default behavior of the optionmenu is to resize the menubutton automatically when new items are added to the menu. If you configure the -width option, you override this behavior, which means entries too wide to fit in the menu will be clipped. Set this option back to zero to restore the default behavior.
Default value: 0

Public Methods

Associated Methods

None

Inherited Methods

Refer to the [incr Widget] or [incr Tk] base class for information on each inherited method. The [incr Tk] base classes are discussed in Chapter 11.

Method Name	Inherited From
cget	itk::Archetype
childsite	iwidgets::Labeledwidget
component	itk::Archetype
config	itk::Archetype
configure	itk::Archetype

Widget-Specific Methods

delete

Usage: pathName *delete* first ?last?
Description: Deletes an item in the pop-up menu specified by the first argument or a range of items between the first and last arguments, inclusively.

disable

Usage: pathName *disable* index
Description: Disables the menu entry specified by the index argument, which is a numerical value representing the position of the menu entry in the menu or the text as it appears in the menu. The topmost menu entry is index zero, and the index value increases from top to bottom. Disabling a menu entry means the user can no longer select that entry, but this does not affect the currently selected item. If you disable the entry that is currently selected, you should take the appropriate measures to perhaps disable the optionmenu or perform some other evasive action.

14

enable

Usage: pathName *enable* index
Description: Enables the menu entry specified by the index argument, which is a numerical value representing the position of the menu entry in the menu or the text as it appears in the menu. The topmost menu entry is index zero, and the index value increases from top to bottom. Enabling a menu entry means the user is able to select that entry.

get

Usage: pathName *get*
Description: Returns the currently selected item.

index

Usage: pathName *index* name
Description: Returns the numerical index of the name argument, which is either the name of the desired menu entry or an integer value. If the designated name does not exist, an error is returned.

insert

Usage: pathName *insert* index entry ?entry entry ...?
Description: Inserts one or more entries into the optionmenu, starting at the index indicated by the index argument. If you specify multiple arguments, each argument is inserted into the optionmenu.

popupMenu

Usage: pathName *popupMenu* args
Description: Allows direct access to the pop-up menu. The args argument should be a valid Tk menu command fragment. This command is evaluated against the pop-up menu, and the result of that evaluation is returned.

select

Usage: pathName *select* index
Description: Selects the menu entry corresponding to the index argument, which may be the name of the menu entry or its numerical index value

sort

Usage: pathName *sort* ?mode?
Description: Sorts the optionmenu's entries in either ascending or descending order as specified by the mode argument. Valid values are increasing, ascending (these are equivalent), decreasing, and descending (these are equivalent also). The default value is increasing. Note that sorting the entries does not affect the currently selected entry. The order in which the entries are displayed in the pop-up menu is all that is changed.

Components

The optionmenu [incr Widget] is composed of several Tk widgets, as outlined in the following table.

Name	Class	Description
hull	Optionmenu	The frame around the entire optionmenu
label	Label	The label widget that can be positioned at different locations around the optionmenu
menuBtn	Menubutton	The interface to the optionmenu's pop-up menu
popupMenu	Menu	The pop-up menu that is displayed when you click the menubutton

14

panedwindow

The panedwindow [incr Widget] implements a multipaned widget with individual panes that are separated by divider lines called separators. Each separator has a sash that can be used to drag the separator across the panedwindow to enlarge and shrink a pane. A sash is a small 3-D square that is attached to one end of each separator. Click on the sash to drag the separator across the panedwindow. Each pane contains a childsite frame, so you can pack any desired widget into a pane and group like widgets in separate panes. The user can then resize the panes as needed to view the desired data. Panes may be oriented vertically or horizontally.

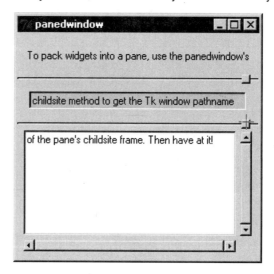

```
# Create the panedwindow.
iwidgets::panedwindow .pw

# Create three panes.
.pw add top
.pw add middle
.pw add bottom

# Create a Tk label widget in the top frame.
set topcs [.pw childsite top]
```

```
label $topcs.l \
  -text "To pack widgets into a pane, use the panedwindow's"
pack $topcs.l -expand 1

# Create an entryfield [incr Widget] in the middle frame.
set midcs [.pw childsite middle]
iwidgets::entryfield $midcs.ef -width 40 -textbackground #d9d9d9
$midcs.ef insert 0 "childsite method to get the Tk window pathname"
pack $midcs.ef -expand 1

# Create a scrolledtext [incr Widget] in the bottom frame.
set botcs [.pw childsite bottom]
iwidgets::scrolledtext $botcs.st -borderwidth 2
$botcs.st insert 1.0 "of the pane's childsite frame. Then have at it!"
pack $botcs.st -fill both -expand 1

wm title . panedwindow
wm geometry . 275x250

# Configure the amount of screen real estate each pane gets.
.pw fraction 20 20 60
pack .pw -fill both -expand 1
```

Class Model

The panedwindow [incr Widget] inherits directly from itk::Widget. It contains zero or more pane [incr Widgets]. For more information on panes, refer to the *add* method description.

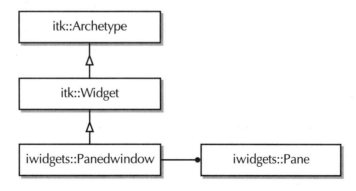

Configuration Options

Standard Options

Refer to the options man page for information on these standard options:

background	cursor

Associated Options

Refer to the associated Tk widget for information on each of these options:

Option Name	Associated With
height	Tk frame widget
width	Tk frame widget

Inherited Options

Refer to Chapter 11 for information on this inherited option from the [incr Tk]
Archetype base class:

Option Name	Inherited From
clientdata	itk::Archetype

Widget-Specific Options

-orient

Resource name: orient
Resource class: Orient
Description: Specifies the orientation of the panedwindow separators.
Valid values are vertical and horizontal.
Default value: horizontal

-sashborderwidth

Resource name: sashBorderWidth
Resource class: SashBorderWidth
Description: Specifies the 3-D border width in pixels of each
panedwindow sash.
Default value: 2

-sashcursor

Resource name: sashCursor
Resource class: SashCursor
Description: Specifies the cursor shape to be displayed when the cursor is over a sash.
Default value: crosshair

-sashheight

Resource name: sashHeight
Resource class: SashHeight
Description: Specifies the height in pixels of each sash in the panedwindow.
Default value: 10

-sashindent

Resource name: sashIndent
Resource class: SashIndent
Description: Specifies the distance in pixels to indent the sashes from the hull border. If the sashes are oriented horizontally, then a negative number positions them on the right side of the panedwindow, and a positive number positions them on the left side. If the sashes are oriented vertically, then a negative number positions them on the top of the panedwindow, and a positive number positions them on the bottom.
Default value: -10

-sashwidth

Resource name: sashWidth
Resource class: SashWidth
Description: Specifies the width in pixels of each sash in the panedwindow.
Default value: 10

-thickness

Resource name: thickness
Resource class: Thickness
Description: Specifies the thickness in pixels of the panedwindow separators.
Default value: 10

Public Methods

Associated Methods
None

Inherited Methods
Refer to the [incr Tk] base class for information on each inherited method. The [incr Tk] base classes are discussed in Chapter 11.

Method Name	Inherited From
cget	itk::Archetype
component	itk::Archetype
config	itk::Archetype
configure	itk::Archetype

Widget-Specific Methods

add

Usage: pathName *add* tag ?option value option value ...?
Description: Adds a new pane to the bottom or right side of the panedwindow, depending on the orientation of the separators. The tag argument specifies a symbolic name to be associated with the pane. A pane is actually an instance of the iwidgets::Pane class. It implements a childsite frame in which other widgets or [incr Widgets] may be packed. This class is implemented specifically for the panedwindow [incr Widget] and isn't meant to be used for any other purpose. It inherits from itk::Widget and has two valid configuration options: -margin and -minimum. The -margin option specifies the border distance between the pane and the pane's contents. The -minimum option specifies the minimum size for a pane. These options may be specified with the option/value argument pairs to the *add* method. Once a new Pane object is created, it becomes a new component widget of the panedwindow. Additionally, a new separator component is created to separate the new pane from other panes, and a new sash component is created that is used to drag the new separator. So, adding a new pane results in the addition of three new components to the panedwindow. Then, to add widgets to a pane, use the panedwindow's *childsite* method to retrieve the pane's childsite frame. You can then pack widgets into this frame.

childsite

Usage: pathName *childsite* ?index ?
Description: Returns a list of all pane childsite frames if the index argument isn't specified. Otherwise, the childsite frame of the specified pane is returned. The index argument may be a numerical value (the first pane—top for horizontal orientation, left for vertical orientation—is index 0, the second is index 1, etc.), or it may be the symbolic name of the pane as specified when the pane was added.

delete

Usage: pathName *delete* index
Description: Destroys the pane specified by the index, which may be the symbolic name of the pane or its numerical index value.

fraction

Usage: pathName *fraction* percentage1 percentage2 ?percentage percentage ...?
Description: Specifies the amount of panedwindow real estate each pane receives. Each argument should be a numerical value representing the desired visible percentage of each pane in the panedwindow. The number of arguments must be equal to the number of visible panes, and the total sum of argument values must be equal to 100.

hide

Usage: pathName *hide* index
Description: Removes the pane specified by the index argument from the panedwindow. The pane is not destroyed, just withdrawn until later. You can display it again with the *show* method, and it will be inserted back into its old location. For example, if you hide the middle pane of a three-paned panedwindow and then use *show* to redisplay it, it will be placed back in the middle.

index

Usage: pathName *index* name
Description: Returns the numerical index of the pane specified by the name argument, which would typically be the symbolic name of the pane. You may also specify the numerical index value of a pane.

insert

Usage: pathName *insert* index tag ?option value option value ...?
Description: Inserts a new pane with the symbolic name specified by the tag argument into the panedwindow just before the pane specified by the index argument, which may be the symbolic name of a pane or its numerical index. For information on the optional option/value pairs, refer to the *add* method description.

paneconfigure

Usage: pathName *paneconfigure* index ?option? ?value option value ...?
Description: Use this method to modify a pane's configuration, to print a single option's information for a pane, or to print all of a pane's configuration options. The index argument is the numerical index of the pane or its symbolic name. If no arguments are specified following index, all of that pane's configuration options are printed. If one argument follows index, then it should be a valid pane configuration option; if so, its information is printed. If multiple arguments are specified after index, they must be in option/value pairs. You can do this to modify a pane's configuration.

reset

Usage: pathName *reset*
Description: Redisplays the panes such that each visible pane occupies the same percentage as the others, i.e., if there are four panes, each pane will occupy 25 percent of the panedwindow. You can specify other percentages with the *fraction* method.

show

Usage: pathName *show* index
Description: Use this method to redisplay a hidden pane. The pane is drawn back into its original location. The index argument specifies the hidden pane's symbolic name or its numerical index value.

Components

When a panedwindow is first created, it only contains a hull component as shown in the following table. As you add new panes to the panedwindow, each one becomes a new component widget along with a new separator bar and sash.

Name	Class	Description
hull	Panedwindow	The frame around the entire panedwindow

promptdialog

The promptdialog [incr Widget] is a dialog window used to get information from the user. The promptdialog contains an entryfield in which the user enters the required information. Since promptdialog inherits from iwidgets::Dialog, it inherits a buttonbox component. You therefore don't have to add buttons or a separator bar since a base class does this for you. You do have access to the buttonbox through several public methods if you need to remove buttons or modify existing ones.

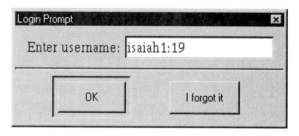

```
# Create the promptdialog.
iwidgets::promptdialog .pd -modality application \
  -labeltext "Enter username:" -labelpos w \
  -textfont 9x15bold -title "Login Prompt" \
  -labelfont 9x15bold

# Don't need the 'Apply' button.
.pd hide Apply
.pd buttonconfigure Cancel -text "I forgot it"

# Give focus to the input area.
focus [.pd component prompt component entry]

# Center the promptdialog and then display it.
.pd center
update idletasks
.pd activate
```

Class Model

The promptdialog [incr Widget] inherits from iwidgets::Dialog. It contains an entryfield and inherits a buttonbox, which is shown in the class model for the dialogshell.

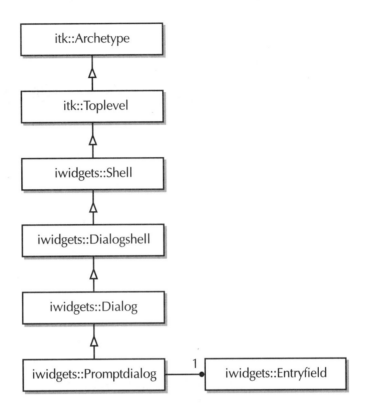

Configuration Options

Standard Options

Refer to the options man page for information on these standard options:

background	borderwidth	cursor	exportselection
foreground	highlightcolor	highlightthickness	insertbackground
insertborderwidth	insertofftime	insertontime	insertwidth
relief	selectbackground	selectborderwidth	selectforeground
takefocus			

Associated Options

Refer to the associated [incr Widget] for information on each of these options:

Option Name	Associated With
invalid	entryfield
labelfont	entryfield
labelpos	entryfield
labeltext	entryfield
show	entryfield
textbackground	entryfield
textfont	entryfield
validate	entryfield

Inherited Options

Refer to the [incr Widget] or [incr Tk] base class for information on each of these options. The [incr Tk] base classes are discussed in Chapter 11.

Option Name	Inherited From
buttonboxpadx	iwidgets::Dialogshell
buttonboxpady	iwidgets::Dialogshell
buttonboxpos	iwidgets::Dialogshell
clientdata	itk::Archetype
height	iwidgets::Shell
master	iwidgets::Shell
modality	iwidgets::Shell
padx	iwidgets::Dialogshell
pady	iwidgets::Dialogshell
separator	iwidgets::Dialogshell
thickness	iwidgets::Dialogshell
title	itk::Toplevel
width	iwidgets::Shell

Widget-Specific Options
None

Public Methods

Associated Methods
Refer to the associated [incr Widget] for information on each of these methods, which promptdialog provides as wrapper methods:

Method Name	Associated With
clear	entryfield
delete	entryfield
get	entryfield
icursor	entryfield
index	entryfield
insert	entryfield
scan	entryfield
selection	entryfield
xview	entryfield

Inherited Methods
Refer to the [incr Widget] or [incr Tk] base class for information on each inherited method. The [incr Tk] base classes are discussed in Chapter 11.

Method Name	Inherited From
activate	iwidgets::Shell
add	iwidgets::Dialogshell
buttoncget	iwidgets::Dialogshell
buttonconfigure	iwidgets::Dialogshell
center	iwidgets::Shell
cget	itk::Archetype
childsite	iwidgets::Dialogshell

14

Method Name	Inherited From
component	itk::Archetype
config	itk::Archetype
configure	itk::Archetype
deactivate	iwidgets::Shell
default	iwidgets::Dialogshell
hide	iwidgets::Dialogshell
invoke	iwidgets::Dialogshell
show	iwidgets::Dialogshell

Widget-Specific Methods
None

Components

The promptdialog [incr Widget] contains an entryfield and a buttonbox separated by a divider line, as outlined in the following table. Each of these is packed into the hull frame component.

Name	Class	Description
bbox	Buttonbox	The buttonbox at the bottom of the screen
hull	Promptdialog	The frame surrounding the entire promptdialog
prompt	Entryfield	An entryfield used to accept user input
separator	Frame	The divider line between the entryfield and the buttonbox

pushbutton

The pushbutton [incr Widget] is the simplest of [incr Widgets]. It simply contains a button component and a frame around the button that can be configured with a sunken relief to create the appearance of a default button. Having a default button means that you can press a hot key (typically the RETURN key or the SPACEBAR) anywhere in the screen to invoke that button. Default buttons are commonly used in dialog windows, and each of the [incr Widget] dialog windows uses the pushbutton for this purpose.

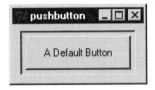

```
wm title . pushbutton
# Create the pushbutton.
iwidgets::pushbutton .pb -text "A Default Button" \
  -defaultring 1 -padx 15 -pady 6
pack .pb -padx 8 -pady 6
```

Class Model

The pushbutton [incr Widget] inherits directly from itk::Widget. It does not interact with any other [incr Widgets] outside of its inheritance tree.

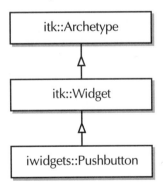

Configuration Options

Standard Options

Refer to the options man page for information on these standard options:

activebackground	activeforeground	background	bitmap
borderwidth	cursor	disabledforeground	font
foreground	highlightbackground	highlightcolor	highlightthickness
image	relief	takefocus	underline
wraplength			

Associated Options

Refer to the associated widget for information on each of these options:

Option Name	Associated With
command	Tk button widget
state	Tk button widget

Inherited Options

Refer to Chapter 11 for information on this inherited option from the [incr Tk] Archetype base class:

Option Name	Inherited From
clientdata	itk::Archetype

Widget-Specific Options

-defaultring

Resource name: defaultRing
Resource class: DefaultRing
Description: Boolean value that specifies whether or not the pushbutton should display the default ring, which is a sunken frame around the button component.
Default value: 0

-defaultringpad

Resource name: defaultRingPad
Resource class: Pad
Description: Specifies the size in pixels of the default padded ring around the button component.
Default value: 4

-height

Resource name: height
Resource class: Height
Description: Specifies the height in pixels of the pushbutton, which includes the area around the button used for displaying the padded ring. If the value is zero, the pushbutton automatically adjusts its size. Note that this option overwrites the -pady option.
Default value: 0

-padx

Resource name: padX
Resource class: Pad
Description: Specifies the distance between the text and the edge of the button component in the x direction. Note that the -width option overwrites this option.
Default value: 11

-pady

Resource name: padY
Resource class: Pad
Description: Specifies the distance between the text and the edge of the button component in the y direction. Note that the -height option overwrites this option.
Default value: 4

-width

Resource name: width
Resource class: Width
Description: Specifies the width in pixels of the pushbutton, which includes the area around the button used for displaying the padded ring. If the value is zero, the pushbutton automatically adjusts its size. Note that this option overwrites the -padx option.
Default value: 0

14

Public Methods

Associated Methods

Refer to the associated Tk widget for information on each of these methods:

Method Name	Associated With
flash	Tk button widget
invoke	Tk button widget

Inherited Methods

Refer to the [incr Tk] base class for information on each inherited method. The [incr Tk] base classes are discussed in Chapter 11.

Method Name	Inherited From
cget	itk::Archetype
component	itk::Archetype
config	itk::Archetype
configure	itk::Archetype

Widget-Specific Methods

None

Components

A pushbutton [incr Widget] simply consists of a button and a frame around the button, as outlined in the following table.

Name	Class	Description
hull	Pushbutton	The frame around the button component that is used as the default ring
pushbutton	Button	The button widget

radiobox

The radiobox [incr Widget] is used to group together multiple radiobuttons similar to how a checkbox groups together multiple checkbuttons. The radiobox provides several public methods for manipulating radiobuttons; you can add, delete, insert, select, or deselect radiobuttons. You can also configure them through a variety of configuration options.

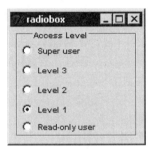

```
wm title . radiobox
wm geometry . 165x140

# Create the radiobox.
iwidgets::radiobox .rb -labeltext "Access Level"

# Add some radiobuttons
.rb add super -text "Super user"
.rb add three -text "Level 3"
.rb add two -text "Level 2"
.rb add one -text "Level 1"
.rb add ro -text "Read-only user"

# Select the second to lowest level.
.rb select one
pack .rb -fill both
```

Class Model

The radiobox [incr Widget] inherits from iwidgets::Labeledframe. It is one of only three [incr Widgets] that does not have either itk::Widget or itk::Toplevel in its inheritance hierarchy.

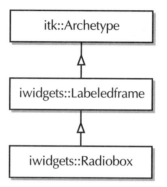

Configuration Options

Standard Options

Refer to the options man page for information on these standard options:

background	borderwidth	cursor	disabledforeground
foreground	relief	selectcolor	

Associated Options

None

Inherited Options

Refer to the [incr Widget] or [incr Tk] base class for information on each of these options. The [incr Tk] base classes are discussed in Chapter 11.

Option Name	Inherited From
clientdata	itk::Archetype
ipadx	iwidgets::Labeledframe
ipady	iwidgets::Labeledframe

Option Name	Inherited From
labelbitmap	iwidgets::Labeledframe
labelfont	iwidgets::Labeledframe
labelimage	iwidgets::Labeledframe
labelmargin	iwidgets::Labeledframe
labelpos	iwidgets::Labeledframe
labeltext	iwidgets::Labeledframe
labelvariable	iwidgets::Labeledframe

Widget-Specific Options

-command

Resource name: command
Resource class: Command
Description: Specifies a Tcl command to be evaluated when a change occurs in the current radiobox selection.
Default value: {}

Public Methods

Associated Methods

None

Inherited Methods

Refer to the [incr Tk] or [incr Widget] base class for information on each inherited method. The [incr Tk] base classes are discussed in Chapter 11.

Method Name	Inherited From
cget	itk::Archetype
childsite	iwidgets::Labeledframe
component	itk::Archetype
config	itk::Archetype
configure	itk::Archetype

14

Widget-Specific Methods

add

Usage: pathName *add* tag ?arg arg ...?
Description: Adds a new radiobutton to the radiobox with the symbolic name specified by the tag argument. This name can be used later with other methods such as *delete* and *component* to access the radiobutton. Any arguments following tag must be in option/value pairs and are used to initialize the new radiobutton. Each radiobutton becomes a new component of the radiobox.

buttonconfigure

Usage: pathName *buttonconfigure* index ?option value option value ...?
Description: Use this method to modify a radiobutton's configuration, to print a single option's information for a radiobutton, or to print all of a radiobutton's configuration options. The index argument is the numerical index of the radiobutton or its symbolic name. If no arguments are specified following index, all of that radiobutton's configuration options are printed. If one argument follows index, then it should be a valid radiobutton configuration option; if so, its information is printed. If multiple arguments are specified after index, they must be in option/value pairs. You can do this to modify a single radiobutton's configuration.

delete

Usage: pathName *delete* index
Description: Deletes the radiobutton specified by the index argument, which may be the symbolic name of the radiobutton or a numerical index value. The radiobutton is destroyed, and the index values of the other radiobuttons are adjusted accordingly.

deselect

Usage: pathName *deselect* index
Description: Deselects the radiobutton specified by the index argument, which may be the symbolic name of the radiobutton or a numerical index value

flash

Usage: pathName *flash* index
Description: Flashes the radiobutton specified by the index argument, which may be the symbolic name of the radiobutton or a numerical index value

get

Usage: pathName *get*
Description: Returns the symbolic name of the currently selected radiobutton.

index

Usage: pathName *index* index
Description: Returns the numerical index of the radiobutton specified by the index argument.

insert

Usage: pathName *insert* index tag ?arg arg ...?
Description: Inserts a new radiobutton in the radiobox just before the radiobutton specified by the index argument. The tag argument is the symbolic name for the new radiobutton. Any arguments following tag must be in option/value pairs and are used to initialize the new radiobutton. This method is similar to *add* except you have control over where the radiobutton is placed. Each new radiobutton inserted into the radiobox becomes a new component of the radiobox.

select

Usage: pathName *select* index
Description: Selects the radiobutton specified by the index argument.

Components

When a radiobox is first created, it contains hull, label, and childsite components, as outlined in the following table. As you add new radiobuttons to the radiobox, each one becomes a new component widget.

Name	Class	Description
childsite	Frame	The frame around the radiobuttons
hull	Radiobox	The frame around the entire radiobox
label	Label	The label that's positioned within the grooved relief of the hull frame

14

regexpfield

The regexpfield [incr Widget] provides a way to control user input by validating each input character in an entry widget against a specified regular expression string. A configuration option called -regexp is provided to configure this string. By default, all keypress events are allowed by the regular expression string ".*". You can tighten the reins by specifying a more restrictive string as your application necessitates. The regexpfield is similar to the entryfield and its -validate option, but the regexpfield's validation is much more robust through its use of regular expressions instead of the entryfield's finite set of validation capabilities.

```
wm title . regexpfield

# Create the regexpfield.
iwidgets::regexpfield .rf -labeltext "Enter text string:" \
  -fixed 14

# Set up a simple regular expression to control user input. The
# user must input an alpha character first, and if a numeric
# character is entered, no other characters are allowed.
.rf configure -regexp {^[a-zA-Z]+[0-9]?$}
pack .rf
```

Class Model

The regexpfield [incr Widget] inherits from iwidgets::Labeledwidget. It does not interact with any other [incr Widgets] outside of its inheritance tree.

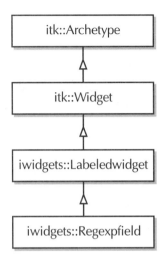

Configuration Options

Standard Options

Refer to the options man page for information on these standard options:

background	borderwidth	cursor	disabledforeground
exportselection	foreground	highlightcolor	highlightthickness
insertbackground	insertborderwidth	insertofftime	insertontime
insertwidth	justify	relief	selectbackground
selectborderwidth	selectforeground	textvariable	

Associated Options

Refer to the associated widget for information on each of these options:

Option Name	Associated With
show	Tk entry widget
state	Tk entry widget
width	Tk entry widget

Inherited Options

Refer to the [incr Widget] or [incr Tk] base class for information on each of these options. The [incr Tk] base classes are discussed in Chapter 11.

Option Name	Inherited From
clientdata	itk::Archetype
labelbitmap	iwidgets::Labeledwidget
labelfont	iwidgets::Labeledwidget
labelimage	iwidgets::Labeledwidget
labelmargin	iwidgets::Labeledwidget
labelpos	iwidgets::Labeledwidget
labeltext	iwidgets::Labeledwidget
labelvariable	iwidgets::Labeledwidget

Widget-Specific Options

-childsitepos

Resource name: childSitePos
Resource class: Position
Description: Specifies the positioning of the regexpfield's childsite frame. Valid values are n, s, e, and w. This frame is empty by default, but you can create a label inside of it to specify units of input, for example, and position the label to the right of the entry component with this option.
Default value: e

-command

Resource name: command
Resource class: Command
Description: Specifies a Tcl command to be evaluated when the RETURN key is pressed in the entry component.
Default value: {}

-fixed

Resource name: fixed
Resource class: Fixed

Description: Specifies the maximum number of characters you can type into the entry component. Note that this is independent of the entry component's width. The width may be 10 characters, but if -fixed is 2, you may only enter two characters. If -fixed is set to zero, then the number of input characters is unlimited.
Default value: 0

-focuscommand

Resource name: focusCommand
Resource class: Command
Description: Specifies a Tcl command to be evaluated when the entry component receives input focus, which occurs when it receives a <FocusIn> event.
Default value: {}

-invalid

Resource name: invalid
Resource class: Command
Description: Specifies a Tcl command to be evaluated if the entry component's contents fail validation. For example, this procedure would be invoked for each character that doesn't match the pattern specified by the -regexp option.
Default value: bell

-nocase

Resource name: nocase
Resource class: Nocase
Description: Specifies whether case should matter in the pattern match. Valid values are 0 and 1 only. If set to 1, case is ignored.
Default value: 0

-regexp

Resource name: regexp
Resource class: Regexp
Description: Specifies a regular expression to use when validating the entry component's contents. Each character typed into the entry is validated. If a character fails validation, the command specified by the -invalid option is evaluated.
Default value: .*

14

-textbackground

Resource name: textBackground
Resource class: Background
Description: Specifies the background color of the entry component. This option replaces the entry's -background option.
Default value: Windows = SystemWindow, Unix = #d9d9d9

-textfont

Resource name: textFont
Resource class: Font
Description: Specifies the font to be used for the text in the entry component. This option replaces the entry's -font option.
Default value: Windows = {{MS Sans Serif} 8}, Unix = {Helvetica =12}

Public Methods

Associated Methods

Refer to the associated widget for information on each of these methods:

Method Name	Associated With
delete	Tk entry widget
get	Tk entry widget
icursor	Tk entry widget
index	Tk entry widget
insert	Tk entry widget
scan	Tk entry widget
selection	Tk entry widget
xview	Tk entry widget

Inherited Methods

Refer to the [incr Tk] base class for information on each inherited method. The [incr Tk] base classes are discussed in Chapter 11.

Method Name	Inherited From
cget	itk::Archetype
component	itk::Archetype
config	itk::Archetype
configure	itk::Archetype

Widget-Specific Methods

clear

Usage: pathName *clear*
Description: Deletes the entry component's contents and moves the input cursor to the first character position.

childsite

Usage: pathName *childsite*
Description: Returns the Tk window pathname of the childsite frame.

Components

The regexpfield [incr Widget] is simply composed of a label and an entry, as outlined in the following table. Each of these is packed into the hull frame component.

Name	Class	Description
label	Label	The label to the left (if -labelpos is set to w) of the entry component
hull	Regexpfield	The frame around the entire regexpfield
entry	Entry	The entry widget used for input

scrolledcanvas

The scrolledcanvas [incr Widget] creates a scrollable canvas by attaching vertical and horizontal scroll bars to a canvas widget. The scrolledcanvas provides a variety of scroll bar management features such as turning them on and off as needed and even adjusting their sizes as needed. The -hscrollmode and -vscrollmode options can be used to turn the scroll bars on and off. The -autoresize option can be used to automatically adjust the scroll bars when a new item is added to the canvas or an existing item is deleted, moved, or resized. Additionally, the scrolledcanvas supports all Tk canvas commands and configuration options so that you can access the canvas component directly.

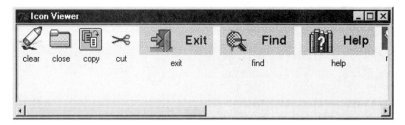

```
# Create the scrolledcanvas.
iwidgets::scrolledcanvas .sc -textbackground ghostwhite \
  -borderwidth 2 -width 520 -height 125 \
  -vscrollmode dynamic -hscrollmode dynamic

# Add a bunch of canvas images to create an icon viewer.
set dir ${iwidgets::library}/demos/images
set icons [glob $dir/*.gif]; # list of gif files
set xpad 10; set ypad 25    ; # x and y padding distances between items
set rightside 0             ; # x coord of right side of rightmost icon
set x 0                     ; # current x coordinate (center of icon)
set img 0                   ; # photo image number

foreach icon $icons {
  # Create the photo image with a unique number.
  image create photo gif$img -file $icon

  # Use the simple filename as the canvas tag.
  set tag [lindex [file split [file rootname $icon]] end]

  # Calculate the new (x,y) coordinates.
  set halfwidth [expr [image width gif$img] / 2]
```

```
set x [expr $halfwidth + $xpad + $rightside]
set y [expr ([image height gif$img] / 2) + $ypad]

# Create the image on the canvas and put its tagname beneath it.
.sc create image $x $y -image gif$img -tag $tag
.sc create text $x [expr [image height gif$img] + $ypad + 10] \
  -text $tag

# Get ready for the next iteration.
set rightside [expr $x + $halfwidth]
incr img
}

wm title . "Icon Viewer"
pack .sc -fill both -expand 1
```

Class Model

The scrolledcanvas [incr Widget] inherits from iwidgets::Scrolledwidget. It does not interact with any other [incr Widgets] outside of its inheritance tree.

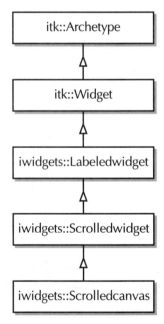

Configuration Options

Standard Options

Refer to the options man page for information on these standard options:

activebackground	background	borderwidth	cursor
disabledforeground	foreground	highlightcolor	highlightthickness
insertbackground	insertborderwidth	insertofftime	insertontime
insertwidth	relief	selectbackground	selectborderwidth
selectforeground	troughcolor		

Associated Options

Refer to the associated Tk widget for information on each of these options:

Option Name	Associated With
activerelief	Tk scrollbar widget
closeenough	Tk canvas widget
confine	Tk canvas widget
elementborderwidth	Tk scrollbar widget
jump	Tk scrollbar widget
scrollregion	Tk canvas widget
xscrollincrement	Tk canvas widget
yscrollincrement	Tk canvas widget

Inherited Options

Refer to the [incr Widget] or [incr Tk] base class for information on each of these options. The [incr Tk] base classes are discussed in Chapter 11.

Option Name	Inherited From
clientdata	itk::Archetype
height	iwidgets::Scrolledwidget
hscrollmode	iwidgets::Scrolledwidget

Option Name	Inherited From
labelbitmap	iwidgets::Labeledwidget
labelfont	iwidgets::Labeledwidget
labelimage	iwidgets::Labeledwidget
labelmargin	iwidgets::Labeledwidget
labelpos	iwidgets::Labeledwidget
labeltext	iwidgets::Labeledwidget
labelvariable	iwidgets::Labeledwidget
sbwidth	iwidgets::Scrolledwidget
scrollmargin	iwidgets::Scrolledwidget
state	iwidgets::Labeledwidget
vscrollmode	iwidgets::Scrolledwidget
width	iwidgets::Scrolledwidget

Widget-Specific Options

-automargin

Resource name: autoMargin
Resource class: AutoMargin
Description: Specifies the amount of space in pixels to reserve around all items in the canvas when doing autoresizing. The bounding box of all items is determined by the canvas component with the bbox command and the all tag, and the amount specified by -automargin is added as padding around the resulting bounding box values. This option is only applicable when autoresizing is enabled. See the -autoresize option for details.
Default value: 0

-autoresize

Resource Name: autoResize
Resource Class: AutoResize
Description: Boolean value that specifies whether or not to automatically adjust the scroll bars when new items are added to the canvas or existing items are deleted from the canvas. If true, then the scrolledcanvas adjusts the

14

scroll region of the canvas to try and make all items viewable. If all items cannot be viewed, then the scroll bars are adjusted accordingly.
Default Value: 1

-textbackground

Resource name: textBackground
Resource class: Background
Description: Specifies the background color for the canvas component.
Default value: Windows = SystemButtonFace, Unix = #d9d9d9

Methods

Associated Methods

Refer to the associated Tk widget man page for information on each of these methods, which scrolledcanvas provides as wrapper methods:

Method Name	Associated With
addtag	Tk canvas widget
bbox	Tk canvas widget
bind	Tk canvas widget
canvasx	Tk canvas widget
canvasy	Tk canvas widget
coords	Tk canvas widget
create	*Tk canvas widget
dchars	Tk canvas widget
delete	*Tk canvas widget
dtag	*Tk canvas widget
find	Tk canvas widget
focus	Tk canvas widget
gettags	Tk canvas widget

Method Name	Associated With
icursor	Tk canvas widget
index	Tk canvas widget
insert	Tk canvas widget
itemcget	Tk canvas widget
itemconfigure	*Tk canvas widget
lower	Tk canvas widget
move	*Tk canvas widget
postscript	Tk canvas widget
raise	Tk canvas widget
scale	Tk canvas widget
scan	Tk canvas widget
select	Tk canvas widget
type	Tk canvas widget
xview	Tk canvas widget
yview	Tk canvas widget

* Indicates this method is a wrapper method for the canvas command of the same name, but additionally the scroll bars are automatically adjusted if autoresizing is enabled.

Inherited Methods

Refer to Chapter 11 for information on each of these inherited methods from the itk::Archetype base class:

Method Name	Inherited From
cget	itk::Archetype
component	itk::Archetype
config	itk::Archetype
configure	itk::Archetype

14

Widget-Specific Methods

childsite

Usage: pathName *childsite*
Description: Returns the Tk window pathname of the childsite, which is actually the canvas component.

justify

Usage: pathName *justify* direction
Description: Justifies the canvas's scroll region according to the direction argument, which should be one of left, right, top, or bottom. If the canvas is not currently mapped (if the containing window is iconified, for example), this method does nothing.

Components

The scrolledcanvas [incr Widget] consists of several Tk widgets, as outlined in the following table.

Name		Description
canvas	Canvas	The canvas widget, also the childsite
clipper	Frame	The frame around the canvas that provides the relief
horizsb	Scrollbar	The horizontal scroll bar
hull	Scrolledcanvas	The frame around the entire scrolledcanvas
label	Label	The label widget that is positioned around the scrolledcanvas according to -labelpos
vertsb	Scrollbar	The vertical scroll bar

scrolledframe

The scrolledframe [incr Widget] implements a scrollable frame widget that allows you to create a window view of a region that might otherwise be too large to display onscreen. This is a very popular [incr Widget] since it allows you to save screen real estate by fitting more data into a single screen. The scrolledframe combines a childsite area with two scroll bars. You can pack any kind of Tk widget or [incr Widget] into the scrolledframe's childsite, which is accessible with the public *childsite* method. One nice feature of the scrolledframe is the ability to make the scroll bars turn on and off as needed. This is controlled with the -hscrollmode and -vscrollmode options. When set to dynamic, the scroll bars are only displayed if the contents of the childsite frame extend beyond the boundaries of the hull frame.

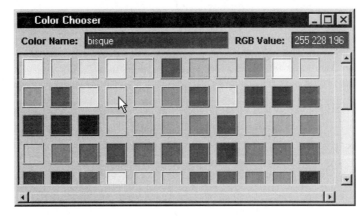

```
# Create the scrolledframe.
iwidgets::scrolledframe .sf -width 400 -height 175 \
  -borderwidth 2 -sbwidth 17

# Create a couple of entryfields to display the color name
# and RGB value.
iwidgets::entryfield .name -labeltext "Color Name: " -width 20 \
  -labelfont -Adobe-Helvetica-Bold-R-Normal--*-140-*-*-*-*-*-* \
  -textbackground grey40
iwidgets::entryfield .rgb -labeltext "RGB Value: " -width 3 \
  -labelfont -Adobe-Helvetica-Bold-R-Normal--*-140-*-*-*-*-*-* \
  -textbackground grey40
.name component entry configure -foreground white
.rgb component entry configure -foreground white
grid .name .rgb -sticky ew -padx 2 -pady 4
```

14

```
# Get the childsite from the scrolledframe, open the color
# definition file, and create colored squares in the childsite.
# Note that the path may not exist on your system. A similar
# file typically exists under /usr/openwin/lib on Unix systems.
set cs [.sf childsite]
set fid [open "C:/Program Files/exceed.95/user/rgb.txt" r]
set num 1; set row 1; set column 1
while {[gets $fid line] >= 0} {
  # Ignore anything that doesn't begin with a number.
  if {![regexp {^[0-9]} $line]} {
    continue
  }

  # Ignore this line if this color has already been displayed.
  set rgb [lrange $line 0 2]
  set name [lrange $line 3 end]
  if {[info exists used($rgb)]} {
    continue
  } else {
    set used($rgb) 1
  }

  # Create the squares 12 per row.
  if {[expr $column % 12] == 0} {
    incr row
    set column 1
  }

  # Create the colored square.
  frame $cs.$num -bg $name -relief ridge -bd 2 -width 25 -height 25
  grid $cs.$num -row $row -column $column -padx 4 -pady 4

  # Update the entryfields when the cursor enters and leaves frames.
  bind $cs.$num <Enter> "updateInfo [list $name $rgb 1]"
  bind $cs.$num <Leave> "updateInfo [list $name $rgb]"

  incr num; incr column

  # No need to show more than 10 rows in this example.
  if {$num == 120} {
    break
  }
}
```

```
close $fid

# Set the window title and pack the scrolledframe.
wm title . "Color Chooser"
grid .sf -columnspan 2 -sticky nsew

# This procedure updates the entryfields each time a <Enter> or
# <Leave> event is detected over one of the colored squares.
proc updateInfo {name_ rgb_ {enter_ 0}} {
  .name clear; .rgb clear
  if {!$enter_} {return}
  .name insert 0 $name_
  .rgb insert 0 $rgb_
}
```

Class Model

The scrolledframe [incr Widget] inherits from iwidgets::Scrolledwidget. It does not interact with any other [incr Widgets] outside of its inheritance tree.

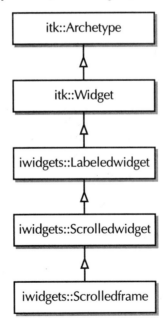

Configuration Options

Standard Options

Refer to the options man page for information on these standard options:

activebackground	background	borderwidth	cursor
disabledforeground	foreground	highlightcolor	highlightthickness
relief	troughcolor	insertofftime	insertontime

Associated Options

Refer to the associated Tk widget for information on each of these options:

Option Name	Associated With
activerelief	Tk scrollbar widget
elementborderwidth	Tk scrollbar widget
jump	Tk scrollbar widget

Inherited Options

Refer to the [incr Widget] or [incr Tk] base class for information on each of these options. The [incr Tk] base classes are discussed in Chapter 11.

Option Name	Inherited From
clientdata	itk::Archetype
height	iwidgets::Scrolledwidget
hscrollmode	iwidgets::Scrolledwidget
labelbitmap	iwidgets::Labeledwidget
labelfont	iwidgets::Labeledwidget
labelimage	iwidgets::Labeledwidget
labelmargin	iwidgets::Labeledwidget
labelpos	iwidgets::Labeledwidget

Option Name	Inherited From
labeltext	iwidgets::Labeledwidget
labelvariable	iwidgets::Labeledwidget
sbwidth	iwidgets::Scrolledwidget
scrollmargin	iwidgets::Scrolledwidget
vscrollmode	iwidgets::Scrolledwidget
width	iwidgets::Scrolledwidget

Widget-Specific Options
None

Public Methods

Associated Methods
Refer to the associated Tk widget man page for information on each of these methods, which scrolledframe provides as wrapper methods:

Method Name	Associated With
xview	Tk canvas widget
yview	Tk canvas widget

Inherited Methods
Refer to Chapter 11 for information on each of these inherited methods from the itk::Archetype base class:

Method Name	Inherited From
cget	itk::Archetype
component	itk::Archetype
config	itk::Archetype
configure	itk::Archetype

Widget-Specific Methods

childsite

Usage: pathName *childsite*
Description: Returns the Tk window pathname of the childsite, which is actually the frame widget inside the canvas component.

justify

Usage: pathName *justify* direction
Description: Justifies the canvas component's scroll region according to the direction argument, which should be one of left, right, top, or bottom. If the canvas is not currently mapped (if the containing window is iconified, for example), this method does nothing.

Components

The scrolledframe [incr Widget] consists of several Tk widgets, as outlined in the following table.

Name	Class	Description
canvas	Canvas	The canvas widget in which the childsite frame is packed
clipper	Frame	The frame around the canvas that provides the relief
horizsb	Scrollbar	The horizontal scroll bar
hull	Scrolledframe	The frame around the entire scrolledframe
label	Label	The label widget that is positioned around the scrolledframe according to -labelpos
vertsb	Scrollbar	The vertical scroll bar

scrolledhtml

The scrolledhtml [incr Widget] extends the functionality of the scrolledtext [incr Widget] through inheritance by supporting HTML-formatted documents. You can load HTML documents from a file with the *import* method or pass HTML-formatted text into the *render* method for displaying. The scrolledhtml is compliant with HTML version 3.2 with the following exceptions:

◆ Nothing that requires a connection to an HTTP server is supported.

◆ Some image alignments are unsupported because the Tk text widget does not support them.

◆ The <br> attributes that go with the image alignments are not implemented.

◆ Background images are unsupported since the Tk text widget doesn't support them.

◆ Automatic table and table cell sizing doesn't always work properly.

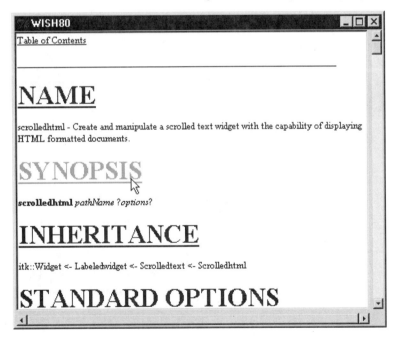

```
# Create the scrolledhtml.
iwidgets::scrolledhtml .sh -fontsize large -linkhighlight grey70 \
  -width 450 -height 350
pack .sh -fill both -expand 1

# Load the scrolledhtml HTML-formatted man page.
set dir ${iwidgets::library}/demos/html
.sh import $dir/scrolledhtml.n.html
```

Class Model

The scrolledhtml [incr Widget] inherits from iwidgets::Scrolledtext. It does not interact with any other [incr Widgets] outside of its inheritance tree.

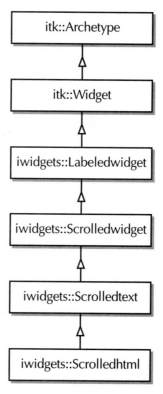

Configuration Options

Standard Options

Refer to the options man page for information on these standard options:

activebackground	background	borderwidth	cursor
disabledforeground	exportselection	foreground	highlightcolor
highlightthickness	insertbackground	insertborderwidth	insertofftime
insertontime	insertwidth	padx	pady
relief	selectbackground	selectborderwidth	selectforeground
setgrid	troughcolor		

Associated Options

Refer to the associated Tk widget for information on each of these options:

Option Name	Associated With
activerelief	Tk scrollbar widget
elementborderwidth	Tk scrollbar widget
jump	Tk scrollbar widget
spacing1	Tk text widget
spacing2	Tk text widget
spacing3	Tk text widget
state	Tk text widget
wrap	Tk text widget

Inherited Options

Refer to the [incr Widget] or [incr Tk] base class for information on each of these options. The [incr Tk] base classes are discussed in Chapter 11.

Option Name	Inherited From
clientdata	itk::Archetype
height	iwidgets::Scrolledtext

14

Option Name	Inherited From
hscrollmode	iwidgets::Scrolledwidget
labelbitmap	iwidgets::Labeledwidget
labelfont	iwidgets::Labeledwidget
labelimage	iwidgets::Labeledwidget
labelmargin	iwidgets::Labeledwidget
labelpos	iwidgets::Labeledwidget
labeltext	iwidgets::Labeledwidget
labelvariable	iwidgets::Labeledwidget
sbwidth	iwidgets::Scrolledwidget
scrollmargin	iwidgets::Scrolledwidget
textbackground	iwidgets::Scrolledtext
textfont	iwidgets::Scrolledtext
visibleitems	iwidgets::Scrolledtext
vscrollmode	iwidgets::Scrolledwidget
width	iwidgets::Scrolledtext

Widget-Specific Options

-alink

Resource name: alink
Resource class: ALink
Description: Specifies the foreground color (text color) for hypertext links when the cursor is over the link. This is the same as the -linkhighlight option. When the cursor is *not* over the link, the color specified by the -link option is used as the foreground color. Note that this option doesn't take effect unless the file is re-imported.
Default value: red

-feedback

Resource name: feedBack
Resource class: FeedBack

Description: Specifies a Tcl command to be evaluated when hypertext links are selected to give feedback on the current status. An argument representing the number of characters remaining is automatically passed to the designated command, so make sure to declare a parameter for this argument in the procedure or method.
Default value: {}

-fixedfont

Resource name: fixedFont
Resource class: FixedFont
Description: Specifies the name of the font to be used for fixed-width character text in the HTML document, such as <pre> ... </pre> and <tt> ... </tt>. (See -fontname for normal-width character text.) Valid values are courier, helvetica, symbol, and times.
Default value: courier

-fontname

Resource name: fontname
Resource class: FontName
Description: Specifies the name of the font to be used for normal-width character text in the HTML document. (See -fixedfont for fixed-width character text.) Valid values are courier, helvetica, symbol, and times.
Default value: times

-fontsize

Resource name: fontSize
Resource class: FontSize
Description: Specifies a general value for the font size. Valid values are small, medium, large, and huge.
Default value: medium

-link

Resource name: link
Resource class: Link
Description: Specifies the foreground color (text color) for hyperlink text when the cursor is not over the link. When the cursor *is* over the link, the color specified by the -linkhighlight option is used as the foreground color. Note that this option doesn't take effect unless the file is re-imported.
Default value: blue

14

-linkcommand

Resource name: linkCommand
Resource class: LinkCommand
Description: Specifies a Tcl command to be evaluated when a hypertext link is selected. The typical command would be to load HTML-formatted text from a file. If this option is not specified when you create a scrolledhtml, the *constructor* initializes it to invoke the *import* method with the -link option. See *import* for more details.
Default value: {}

-linkhighlight

Resource name: alink
Resource class: ALink
Description: Specifies the foreground color (text color) for hypertext links when the cursor is over the link. This is the same as the -alink option. When the cursor is *not* over the link, the color specified by the -link option is used as the foreground color. Note that this option doesn't take effect unless the file is re-imported.
Default value: red

-unknownimage

Resource name: unknownimage
Resource class: File
Description: Specifies the name of an image file to be displayed when an image specified by an img tag in the HTML document cannot be loaded.
Default value: {}

-update

Resource name: update
Resource class: Update
Description: Boolean value that indicates whether an HTML document should be updated during rendering. If false, the page will not be displayed until it is fully rendered. Note that if this is set to a false value then the -feedback option is not applicable.
Default value: 1

Public Methods

Associated Methods

None

Inherited Methods

Refer to the [incr Widget] or [incr Tk] base class for information on each inherited method. The [incr Tk] base classes are discussed in Chapter 11.

Method Name	Inherited From
bbox	iwidgets::Scrolledtext
cget	itk::Archetype
childsite	iwidgets::Scrolledtext
compare	iwidgets::Scrolledtext
component	itk::Archetype
config	itk::Archetype
configure	itk::Archetype
debug	iwidgets::Scrolledtext
delete	iwidgets::Scrolledtext
dlineinfo	iwidgets::Scrolledtext
export	iwidgets::Scrolledtext
get	iwidgets::Scrolledtext
index	iwidgets::Scrolledtext
insert	iwidgets::Scrolledtext
mark	iwidgets::Scrolledtext
scan	iwidgets::Scrolledtext
search	iwidgets::Scrolledtext
see	iwidgets::Scrolledtext
tag	iwidgets::Scrolledtext
window	iwidgets::Scrolledtext
xview	iwidgets::Scrolledtext
yview	iwidgets::Scrolledtext

Widget-Specific Methods

clear

Usage: pathName *clear*
Description: Deletes all text in the text area.

import

Usage: pathName *import* ?-link? filename ?#anchorname?
Description: Loads an HTML-formatted document from a file. If the -link argument is specified, the pathname of the file is assumed to be relative to the last loaded page (you can use the *pwd* method to determine this directory). Otherwise, it is assumed to be relative to the current working directory. If #anchorname is appended to the filename argument, the page is displayed starting at the anchor specified by anchorname. Otherwise, the page is displayed starting at the top of the document. If an anchor is specified without a filename, the current page is assumed.

pwd

Usage: pathName *pwd*
Description: Returns the directory name of the last page that was loaded.

render

Usage: pathName *render* text ?directory?
Description: Invokes the *clear* method to clear the text area and then displays the HTML-formatted text specified by the text argument. The optional directory argument is the base directory name to use for all links and images in the page. It defaults to the current working directory, ".".

title

Usage: pathName *title*
Description: Returns the title of the current page as specified by the <title> ... </title> field in the HTML document.

Components

The scrolledhtml [incr Widget] consists of several Tk widgets, as outlined in the following table.

Name	Class	Description
clipper	Frame	The frame around the text component that provides the relief
horizsb	Scrollbar	The horizontal scroll bar
hull	Scrolledhtml	The frame around the entire scrolledhtml
label	Label	The label widget that is positioned around the scrolledhtml according to -labelpos
text	Text	The text widget in which the HTML document is displayed
vertsb	Scrollbar	The vertical scroll bar

scrolledlistbox

The scrolledlistbox [incr Widget] is one of the most popular [incr Widgets] because scrollable listboxes are so commonly used in today's applications. The scrolledlistbox simply combines a listbox widget with horizontal and vertical scroll bars. All listbox commands and configuration options are provided for manipulating the listbox data. Additionally, the scrolledlistbox provides dynamic scroll bar support, which means you can configure the scrolledlistbox so that the scroll bars will come and go as needed. This is done with the -hscrollmode and -vscrollmode options. These options are set to static by default, but you can configure them to dynamic if desired.

```
# Create the scrolledlistbox.
iwidgets::scrolledlistbox .sl -textbackground ghostwhite \
  -labelpos nw -labeltext Composers: -selectmode extended \
  -labelfont -Adobe-Helvetica-Bold-R-Normal--*-140-*-*-*-*-*-* \
  -selectforeground blue -selectbackground grey70
pack .sl -fill both -expand 1

wm title . scrolledlistbox
wm geometry . 160x185

# Insert items into the listbox. Note that the -items option from
# iwidgets2.2 is no longer a valid option.
.sl insert 0 Bach Mozart Beethoven Chopin Liszt Brahms \
  Tchaikovsky Rachmaninoff Debussy Stravinsky Rodriguez Johnson

# Select some items.
.sl selection set 1; .sl selection set 3; .sl selection set 8
```

Class Model

The scrolledlistbox [incr Widget] inherits from iwidgets::Scrolledwidget. It does not interact with any other [incr Widgets] outside of its inheritance tree.

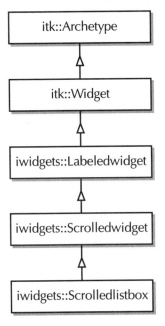

Configuration Options

Standard Options

Refer to the options man page for information on these standard options:

activebackground	background	borderwidth	cursor
disabledforeground	exportselection	foreground	highlightcolor
highlightthickness	relief	selectbackground	selectborderwidth
selectforeground	troughcolor		

Associated Options

Refer to the associated Tk widget for information on each of these options:

Option Name	Associated With
activerelief	Tk scrollbar widget
elementborderwidth	Tk scrollbar widget
jump	Tk scrollbar widget
selectmode	Tk listbox widget

Inherited Options

Refer to the [incr Widget] or [incr Tk] base class for information on each of these options. The [incr Tk] base classes are discussed in Chapter 11.

Option Name	Inherited From
clientdata	itk::Archetype
hscrollmode	iwidgets::Scrolledwidget
labelbitmap	iwidgets::Labeledwidget
labelfont	iwidgets::Labeledwidget
labelimage	iwidgets::Labeledwidget
labelmargin	iwidgets::Labeledwidget
labelpos	iwidgets::Labeledwidget
labeltext	iwidgets::Labeledwidget
labelvariable	iwidgets::Labeledwidget
sbwidth	iwidgets::Scrolledwidget
scrollmargin	iwidgets::Scrolledwidget
vscrollmode	iwidgets::Scrolledwidget

Widget-Specific Options

-dblclickcommand

Resource name: dblClickCommand
Resource class: Command
Description: Specifies a Tcl command to be evaluated when the user double-clicks on a listbox item. Note that -selectioncommand is also invoked when the -dblclickcommand is invoked. This is an intrinsic behavior of Tk, that double-click events also invoke two single-click events.
Default value: {}

-height

Resource name: height
Resource class: Height
Description: Specifies the height in pixels of the scrolledlistbox as an entire unit. If this option is set to zero along with -width, the -visibleitems option is used for sizing. Otherwise, -height and -width take precedence.
Default value: 0

-selectioncommand

Resource name: selectionCommand
Resource class: Command
Description: Specifies a Tcl command to be evaluated each time an item is selected in the scrolledlistbox. Note that this option is evaluated regardless of the value of the -selectmode option.
Default value: {}

-state

Resource name: state
Resource class: State
Description: Specifies the state of the scrolledlistbox. Valid values are disabled and normal. If disabled, scrolledlistbox item selection is disallowed.
Default value: normal

-textbackground

Resource name: textBackground
Resource class: Background

14

Description: Specifies the background color of the listbox component. This option replaces the listbox's -background option.
Default value: Windows = SystemButtonFace, Unix = #d9d9d9

-textfont

Resource name: textFont
Resource class: Font
Description: Specifies the font to be used inside the listbox component. This option replaces the listbox's -font option.
Default value: Windows = {{MS Sans Serif } 8}, Unix = {Helvetica -12 bold}

-visibleitems

Resource name: visibleItems
Resource class: VisibleItems
Description: Specifies the number of characters by lines to display in the listbox component. This option is only used if both -height and -width are set to zero. It only affects the size of the listbox component, as opposed to the behavior of -height and -width, which affect the scrolledlistbox geometry as a whole.
Default value: 20x10

-width

Resource name: width
Resource class: Height
Description: Specifies the width in pixels of the scrolledlistbox as an entire unit. If this option is set to zero along with -height, the -visibleitems option is used for sizing. Otherwise, -height and -width take precedence.
Default value: 0

Public Methods

Associated Methods

Refer to the associated Tk widget man page for information on each of these methods, which scrolledlistbox provides as wrapper methods:

Method Name	Associated With
activate	Tk listbox widget
bbox	Tk listbox widget

Method Name	Associated With
curselection	Tk listbox widget
delete	Tk listbox widget
get	Tk listbox widget
index	Tk listbox widget
insert	Tk listbox widget
nearest	Tk listbox widget
scan	Tk listbox widget
see	Tk listbox widget
selection	Tk listbox widget
size	Tk listbox widget
sort	Tk listbox widget
xview	Tk listbox widget
yview	Tk listbox widget

Inherited Methods

Refer to the [incr Widget] or [incr Tk] base class for information on each inherited method. The [incr Tk] base classes are discussed in Chapter 11.

Method Name	Inherited From
cget	itk::Archetype
childsite	iwidgets::Labeledwidget
component	itk::Archetype
config	itk::Archetype
configure	itk::Archetype

Widget-Specific Methods

clear

Usage: pathName *clear*
Description: Removes all items from the scrolledlistbox.

14

getcurselection

Usage: pathName *getcurselection*
Description: Returns a list of currently selected listbox items. Note that this is a list of the item names as opposed to the corresponding numerical index values of the items.

justify

Usage: pathName *justify* direction
Description: Justifies the contents of the scrolledlistbox via the scroll bars according to the direction argument, which must be one of left, right, top, or bottom.

selecteditemcount

Usage: pathName *selecteditemcount*
Description: Returns the number of items that are currently selected in the listbox. This is equivalent to using **llength** on the result of the *getcurselection* method.

Components

The scrolledlistbox [incr Widget] is composed of several Tk widgets, as outlined in the following table.

Name	Class	Description
horizsb	Scrollbar	The horizontal scroll bar
hull	Scrolledlistbox	The frame around the entire scrolledlistbox
label	Label	The label widget that is positioned around the scrolledlistbox according to -labelpos
listbox	Listbox	The listbox widget
vertsb	Scrollbar	The vertical scroll bar

scrolledtext

The scrolledtext [incr Widget] combines a text widget and horizontal and vertical scroll bars to create a scrollable text widget. This is useful for displaying large amounts of text that otherwise could not be shown in a single widget without implementing some sort of paging scheme or attaching scroll bars to a text widget manually. All text commands and configuration options are provided for manipulating the data in the text component. Additionally, the scrolledtext provides dynamic scroll bar support, which means you can configure the scrolledtext so that the scroll bars will come and go as needed. This is done with the -hscrollmode and -vscrollmode options. These options are set to static by default, but you can configure them to dynamic if desired. The scrolledtext also provides the ability to export the contents of the text component to a file as well as import a file into the text component at a specified index.

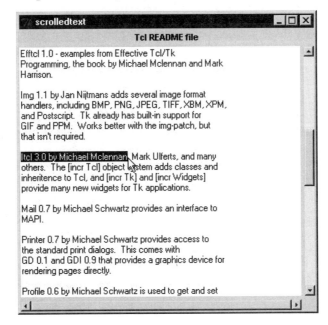

```
# Create the scrolledtext.
iwidgets::scrolledtext .st -labeltext "Tcl README file" \
   -labelfont -Adobe-Helvetica-Bold-R-Normal--*-140-*-*-*-*-*-* \
   -visibleitems 60x24
pack .st -fill both -expand 1

# Import the Tcl README file. Note this path may not exist
# on your system.
.st import "C:/Program Files/Tcl/readme.txt"
```

14

```
# Scroll down so that the [incr Tcl] info is visible.
update idletasks
.st see 43.0
```

Class Model

The scrolledtext [incr Widget] inherits from iwidgets::Scrolledwidget. It does not interact with any other [incr Widgets] outside of its inheritance tree.

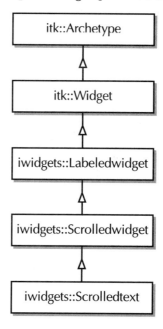

Configuration Options

Standard Options

Refer to the options man page for information on these standard options:

activebackground	background	borderwidth	cursor
disabledforeground	exportselection	foreground	highlightcolor
highlightthickness	insertbackground	insertborderwidth	insertofftime
insertontime	insertwidth	padx	pady
relief	selectbackground	selectborderwidth	selectforeground
setgrid	troughcolor		

Associated Options

Refer to the associated Tk widget for information on each of these options:

Option Name	Associated With
activerelief	Tk scrollbar widget
elementborderwidth	Tk scrollbar widget
jump	Tk scrollbar widget
spacing1	Tk text widget
spacing2	Tk text widget
spacing3	Tk text widget
state	Tk text widget
wrap	Tk text widget

Inherited Options

Refer to the [incr Widget] or [incr Tk] base class for information on each of these options. The [incr Tk] base classes are discussed in Chapter 11.

Option Name	Inherited From
clientdata	itk::Archetype
labelbitmap	iwidgets::Labeledwidget
labelfont	iwidgets::Labeledwidget
labelimage	iwidgets::Labeledwidget
labelmargin	iwidgets::Labeledwidget
labelpos	iwidgets::Labeledwidget
labeltext	iwidgets::Labeledwidget
labelvariable	iwidgets::Labeledwidget
sbwidth	iwidgets::Scrolledwidget
scrollmargin	iwidgets::Scrolledwidget
vscrollmode	iwidgets::Scrolledwidget

14

Widget-Specific Options

-height

Resource name: height
Resource class: Height
Description: Specifies the height in pixels of the scrolledtext as an entire unit. If this option is set to zero along with -width, the -visibleitems option is used for sizing. Otherwise, -height and -width take precedence.
Default value: 0

-textbackground

Resource name: textBackground
Resource class: Background
Description: Specifies the background color of the text component. This option replaces the text's -background option.
Default value: Windows = SystemWindow, Unix = #d9d9d9

-textfont

Resource name: textFont
Resource class: Font
Description: Specifies the font to be used inside the text component. This option replaces the text's -font option.
Default value: Windows = {{MS Sans Serif } 8}, Unix = {Courier -12}

-visibleitems

Resource name: visibleItems
Resource class: VisibleItems
Description: Specifies the number of characters by lines to display in the text component. This option is only used if both -height and -width are set to zero. It only affects the size of the text component, as opposed to the behavior of -height and -width, which affect the scrolledtext geometry as a whole.
Default value: 80x24

-width

Resource name: width
Resource class: Width

Description: Specifies the width in pixels of the scrolledtext as an entire unit. If this option is set to zero along with -height, the -visibleitems option is used for sizing. Otherwise, the -height and -width options take precedence.
Default value: 0

Public Methods

Associated Methods

Refer to the associated Tk widget man page for information on each of these methods, which scrolledlistbox provides as wrapper methods:

Method Name	Associated With
bbox	Tk text widget
compare	Tk text widget
debug	Tk text widget
delete	Tk text widget
dlineinfo	Tk text widget
get	Tk text widget
index	Tk text widget
insert	Tk text widget
mark	Tk text widget
scan	Tk text widget
search	Tk text widget
see	Tk text widget
tag	Tk text widget
window	Tk text widget
xview	Tk text widget
yview	Tk text widget

Inherited Methods

Refer to Chapter 11 for information on each of these inherited methods from the itk::Archetype base class:

Method Name	Inherited From
cget	itk::Archetype
component	itk::Archetype
config	itk::Archetype
configure	itk::Archetype

Widget-Specific Methods

childsite

Usage: pathName *childsite*
Description: Returns the Tk window pathname of the childsite, which is actually just the text component.

clear

Usage: pathName *clear*
Description: Deletes all text in the text component.

export

Usage: pathName *export* filename
Description: Saves the contents of the text component to the file specified by the filename argument. Be careful when using this method because you are not warned if the specified filename already exists. You could inadvertently overwrite a file as a result.

import

Usage: pathName *import* filename ?index?
Description: Loads text from the file specified by the filename argument and inserts it into the text component at the index specified by the optional index argument. The index defaults to "end".

Components

The scrolledtext [incr Widget] is composed of several Tk widgets, as outlined in the following table.

Name	Class	Description
clipper	Frame	The frame around the text component that provides the relief
horizsb	Scrollbar	The horizontal scroll bar
hull	Scrolledtext	The frame around the entire scrolledtext
label	Label	The label widget that is positioned around the scrolledtext according to -labelpos
text	Text	The text widget in which the text is displayed
vertsb	Scrollbar	The vertical scroll bar

selectionbox

The selectionbox [incr Widget] provides a scrolledlistbox of selectable items with an associated entryfield that contains the currently selected item. The entryfield is editable, so the user may also enter a value into it if the desired choice is not among the scrolledlistbox items. The selectionbox provides configurable labels for both components if you want to override the defaults. It also provides a childsite frame in which you can pack other widgets to interact with the selectionbox as your application may require.

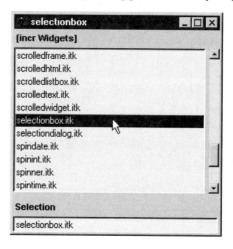

```
# Create the selectionbox.
wm title . selectionbox
iwidgets::selectionbox .sb -borderwidth 2 -height 250 \
  -labelfont -Adobe-Helvetica-Bold-R-Normal--*-140-*-*-*-*-* \
  -textbackground ghostwhite -itemslabel "\[incr Widgets\]"
pack .sb

# Glob the iwidgets in the scrolledlistbox.
cd ${iwidgets::library}/scripts
eval .sb insert items 0 [glob *.itk]
```

Class Model

The selectionbox [incr Widget] inherits directly from itk::Widget. It contains a scrolledlistbox and an entryfield.

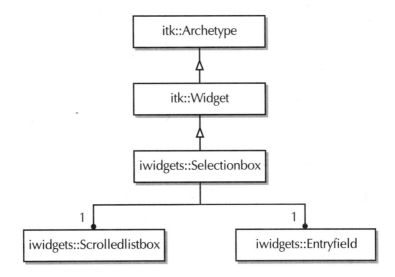

Configuration Options

Standard Options

Refer to the options man page for information on these standard options:

activebackground	background	borderwidth	cursor
exportselection	foreground	highlightcolor	highlightthickness
insertbackground	insertborderwidth	insertofftime	insertontime
insertwidth	selectbackground	selectborderwidth	selectforeground
troughcolor			

Associated Options

Refer to the associated Tk widget or [incr Widget] for information on each of these options:

Option Name	Associated With
activerelief	Tk scrollbar widget
dblclickcommand	scrolledlistbox
elementborderwidth	Tk scrollbar widget
jump	Tk scrollbar widget

Option Name	Associated With
labelfont	scrolledlistbox, entryfield
textbackground	scrolledlistbox, entryfield
textfont	scrolledlistbox, entryfield

Inherited Options

Refer to Chapter 11 for information on this inherited option from the [incr Tk] Archetype base class:

Option Name	Inherited From
clientdata	itk::Archetype

Widget-Specific Options

-childsitepos

Resource name: childSitePos
Resource class: Position
Description: Specifies the position of the childsite frame. Valid values are n, s, e, w, and center.
Default value: center

-height

Resource name: height
Resource class: Height
Description: Specifies the height of the hull frame. If this option is set to zero, the height is automatically adjusted according to the component widget dimensions.
Default value: 320 (pixels)

-itemscommand

Resource name: itemsCommand
Resource class: Command
Description: Specifies a Tcl command to be evaluated each time an item is selected in the scrolledlistbox component. This option replaces the scrolledlistbox's -selectioncommand option.
Default value: {}

-itemslabel

Resource name: itemsLabel
Resource class: Text
Description: Specifies the text to display for the scrolledlistbox's label component. This option replaces the scrolledlistbox's -labeltext option.
Default value: Items

-itemson

Resource name: itemsOn
Resource class: ItemsOn
Description: Boolean value that specifies whether the scrolledlistbox component should be displayed. If false, then the scrolledlistbox is removed from the screen. You can reinsert it by setting -itemson to true.
Default value: true

-margin

Resource name: margin
Resource class: Margin
Description: Specifies the distance between the scrolledlistbox and the entryfield.
Default value: 7 (pixels)

-selectioncommand

Resource name: selectionCommand
Resource class: Command
Description: Specifies a Tcl command to be evaluated each time the RETURN key is pressed in the entryfield. This option replaces the entryfield's -command option.
Default value: {}

-selectionlabel

Resource name: selectionLabel
Resource class: Text
Description: Specifies the text to display for the entryfield's label component. This option replaces the entryfield's -labeltext option.
Default value: Selection

14

-selectionon

Resource name: selectionOn
Resource class: SelectionOn
Description: Boolean value that specifies whether the entryfield component should be displayed. If false, then the entryfield is removed from the screen and the scrolledlistbox stretches to fill the empty space beneath it. You can reinsert it by setting -selectionon to true.
Default value: true

-width

Resource name: width
Resource class: Width
Description: Specifies the width of the hull frame. If this option is set to zero, the width is automatically adjusted according to the component widget dimensions.
Default value: 260 (pixels)

Public Methods

Associated Methods

Refer to the associated [incr Widget] for information on each of these methods, which selectionbox provides as wrapper methods:

Method Name	Associated With
curselection	scrolledlistbox
delete	scrolledlistbox
get	entryfield
index	scrolledlistbox
nearest	scrolledlistbox
scan	scrolledlistbox
selection	scrolledlistbox

Inherited Methods

Refer to the [incr Tk] base class for information on each inherited method. The [incr Tk] base classes are discussed in Chapter 11.

Method Name	Inherited From
cget	itk::Archetype
component	itk::Archetype
config	itk::Archetype
configure	itk::Archetype

Widget-Specific Methods

childsite

Usage: pathName *childsite*
Description: Returns the Tk window pathname of the childsite frame.

clear

Usage: pathName *clear* component
Description: Clears the contents of the component specified by the component argument. Valid values are selection and items.

insert

Usage: pathName *insert* component index string ?arg arg ...?
Description: Inserts a string into the scrolledlistbox or entryfield component, depending on the component argument, which must be either selection or items. The index argument determines the location in the component widget to insert the string. Refer to the Tk entry and listbox man pages for details on their insert methods.

selectitem

Usage: pathName *selectitem*
Description: Replaces the contents of the entryfield with the currently selected scrolledlistbox item. This method is useful if the entryfield has been manually edited and you want to quickly reconfigure it with the current selection.

14

Components

The selectionbox [incr Widget] is composed of an entryfield and a scrolledlistbox, as outlined in the following table. Each of these is packed in the hull frame component.

Name	Class	Description
hull	Selectionbox	The frame around the entire selectionbox
items	Scrolledlistbox	The scrolledlistbox [incr Widget] that is positioned above the entryfield
selection	Entryfield	The entryfield [incr Widget] that is positioned beneath the scrolledlistbox

selectiondialog

The selectiondialog [incr Widget] combines a dialog window with a selectionbox. The selectionbox is placed in the dialog's childsite, so you have a convenient interface already created for performing some action based on the selected item in the selectionbox. For example, you can create a man page viewer by displaying a list of [incr Widgets] in the scrolledlistbox and opening a scrolledhtml to display the HTML-formatted man page for the selected [incr Widget]. Since selectiondialog inherits from iwidgets::Dialog, it inherits a buttonbox component. Therefore, you don't have to add buttons or a separator bar since a base class does this for you. You do have access to the buttonbox through several public methods if you need to remove buttons or modify existing ones.

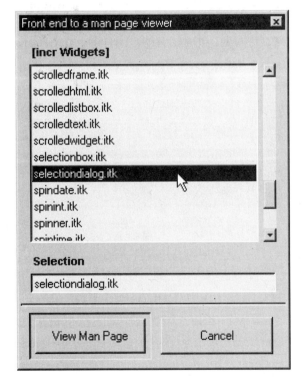

```
# Create the selectiondialog.
iwidgets::selectiondialog .sd -borderwidth 2 -height 325 \
    -width 265 -title "Front end to a man page viewer" \
    -itemslabel "\[incr Widgets\]" -textbackground ghostwhite \
    -labelfont -Adobe-Helvetica-Bold-R-Normal--*-140-*-*-*-*-*-*
```

14

```
# Get rid of the Apply button and modify the OK button. You can
# configure the OK button, for example, to create a scrolledhtml
# to display the HTML-formatted man page for the selected
# [incr Widget].
.sd hide Apply
.sd buttonconfigure OK -text "View Man Page"

# Glob the iwidgets in the scrolledlistbox.
cd ${iwidgets::library}/scripts
eval .sd insert items 0 [glob *.itk]

# When everything's done, display the dialog.
.sd center
update idletasks
.sd activate
```

Class Model

The selectiondialog [incr Widget] inherits from iwidgets::Dialog. It has a selectionbox locally and inherits a buttonbox from iwidgets::Dialogshell, which is shown in the class model for the dialogshell.

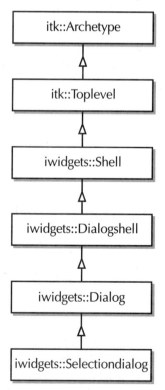

Configuration Options

Standard Options

Refer to the options man page for information on these standard options:

activebackground	background	borderwidth	cursor
exportselection	foreground	highlightcolor	highlightthickness
insertbackground	insertborderwidth	insertofftime	insertontime
insertwidth	selectbackground	selectborderwidth	selectforeground
takefocus	troughcolor		

Associated Options

Refer to the associated Tk widget or [incr Widget] for information on each of these options:

Option Name	Associated With
activerelief	Tk scrollbar widget
childsitepos	selectionbox
elementborderwidth	Tk scrollbar widget
itemscommand	selectionbox
itemslabel	selectionbox
itemson	selectionbox
jump	Tk scrollbar widget
labelfont	selectionbox
selectioncommand	selectionbox
selectionlabel	selectionbox
selectionon	selectionbox
textbackground	selectionbox
textfont	selectionbox

14

Inherited Options

Refer to the [incr Widget] or [incr Tk] base class for information on each of these options. The [incr Tk] base classes are discussed in Chapter 11.

Option Name	Inherited From
buttonboxpadx	iwidgets::Dialogshell
buttonboxpady	iwidgets::Dialogshell
buttonboxpos	iwidgets::Dialogshell
clientdata	itk::Archetype
height	iwidgets::Shell
master	iwidgets::Shell
modality	iwidgets::Shell
padx	iwidgets::Dialogshell
pady	iwidgets::Dialogshell
separator	iwidgets::Dialogshell
thickness	iwidgets::Dialogshell
title	itk::Toplevel
width	iwidgets::Shell

Widget-Specific Options

None

Public Methods

Associated Methods

Refer to the associated [incr Widget] for information on each of these methods, which selectiondialog provides as wrapper methods:

Method Name	Associated With
childsite	selectionbox
clear	selectionbox
curselection	selectionbox

Method Name	Associated With
delete	selectionbox
get	selectionbox
index	selectionbox
insert	selectionbox
nearest	selectionbox
scan	selectionbox
selection	selectionbox
selectitem	selectionbox
size	selectionbox

Inherited Methods

Refer to the [incr Widget] or [incr Tk] base class for information on each inherited method. The [incr Tk] base classes are discussed in Chapter 11.

Method Name	Inherited From
activate	iwidgets::Shell
add	iwidgets::Dialogshell
buttoncget	iwidgets::Dialogshell
buttonconfigure	iwidgets::Dialogshell
center	iwidgets::Shell
cget	itk::Archetype
component	itk::Archetype
config	itk::Archetype
configure	itk::Archetype
deactivate	iwidgets::Shell
default	iwidgets::Dialogshell
hide	iwidgets::Dialogshell
invoke	iwidgets::Dialogshell
show	iwidgets::Dialogshell

14

Widget-Specific Methods
None

Components

The selectiondialog [incr Widget] is composed of a selectionbox and a
buttonbox separated by a divider line. Each of these is packed in the hull
frame component.

Name	Class	Description
bbox	Buttonbox	The buttonbox at the bottom of the screen
hull	Selectiondialog	The frame surrounding the entire selectiondialog
selectionbox	Selectionbox	The selectionbox [incr Widget] in the dialog's childsite
separator	Frame	The divider line between the selectionbox and the buttonbox

shell

The shell [incr Widget] simply consists of a hull frame and a childsite. This [incr Widget] is the base class for all [incr Widget] dialog boxes as well as the mainwindow and hyperhelp. Its purpose is to provide common functionality and support for derived classes. Though you can create a shell and use it in your application, you most likely will never need to unless you're defining a new derived class. The shell defines several window management utilities such as window activation, deactivation, and modality.

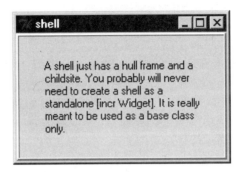

```
# Create the shell.
iwidgets::shell .sh -padx 20 -pady 20 -title shell -background bisque
.sh component hull configure -relief ridge -bd 3

# Create a message in the shell childsite.
set cs [.sh childsite]
message $cs.m -text "A shell just has a hull frame and a childsite.\
   You probably will never need to create a shell as a standalone\
   \[incr Widget\]. It is really meant to be used as a base class\
   only." -justify left -width 175 -background bisque
pack $cs.m

# Center and draw the shell window.
.sh center
update idletasks
.sh activate
```

Class Model

The shell [incr Widget] is the only class that inherits directly from itk::Toplevel. It serves as the base class [incr Widget] for all dialog windows as well as the mainwindow and hyperhelp.

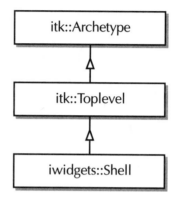

Configuration Options

Standard Options

Refer to the options man page for information on these standard options:

background	cursor	takefocus

Associated Options

None

Inherited Options

Refer to Chapter 11 for information on these inherited options from [incr Tk] base classes:

Option Name	Inherited From
clientdata	itk::Archetype
title	itk::Toplevel

Widget-Specific Options

-height

Resource name: height
Resource class: Height
Description: Specifies the height of the hull frame. If zero, then the hull is automatically adjusted according to the size needs of any child widgets.
Default value: 0

-master

Resource name: master
Resource class: Window
Description: Specifies the master window for the shell. The window manager is informed that the shell is a transient window whose master is specified by -master. This value defaults to the empty string for shells (meaning no master window) and to "." (the root window) for all dialog windows.
Default value: {}

-modality

Resource name: modality
Resource class: Modality
Description: Specifies the grab characteristic of the shell. Valid values are application, system, and none. A value of application means that no other toplevel windows in the application can receive input focus until the shell is deactivated. A value of system means that no other windows in the entire system can gain input focus, regardless of the application. A value of none performs no grabs.
Default value: none

-padx

Resource name: padX
Resource class: Pad
Description: Specifies the padding distance for the childsite in the x direction.
Default value: 0

14

-pady

Resource name: padY
Resource class: Pad
Description: Specifies the padding distance for the childsite in the
y direction.
Default value: 0

-width

Resource name: width
Resource class: Width
Description: Specifies the width of the hull frame. If zero, then the hull is
automatically adjusted according to the size needs of any child widgets.
Default value: 0

Public Methods

Associated Methods

None

Inherited Methods

Refer to the [incr Tk] base class for information on each inherited method.
The [incr Tk] base classes are discussed in Chapter 11.

Method Name	Inherited From
cget	itk::Archetype
component	itk::Archetype
config	itk::Archetype
configure	itk::Archetype

Widget-Specific Methods

activate

Usage: pathName *activate*
Description: Displays the shell window and then waits based on the value
of the -modality option.

center

Usage: pathName *center* ?widget?
Description: If the optional widget argument is specified, then the shell is positioned in the center of that widget. Otherwise, it's positioned in the center of the screen. Be aware that if you call *center* and immediately call *activate* that the shell may not be centered exactly. You should use the **update idletasks** command before activating the shell to make sure it is sized correctly so that the screen coordinates for centering are calculated correctly.

childsite

Usage: pathName *childsite*
Description: Returns the Tk window pathname of the childsite frame.

deactivate

Usage: pathName *deactivate* ?arg?
Description: Withdraws the shell window. The optional arg argument is saved and returned from the *activate* method if -modality is application or system.

Components

The shell [incr Widget] is only composed of the hull frame component as shown in the following table.

Name	Class	Description
hull	Shell	The frame around the entire shell

spindate

The spindate [incr Widget] implements a date selection widget with spinners. The spindate has three spinners: one for the day, one for the month, and one for the year. The months can be displayed as integers, abbreviated strings, or full month names. You can show specific dates in the spindate with the *show* method, or you can even show relative dates such as "1 week ago" or "tomorrow". You can also retrieve the current date in the spindate as a date string or an integer value as calculated by the **clock** command.

```
# Create the spindate.
iwidgets::spindate .spd -monthformat brief

# Show an explicit date.
.spd show 9/1/96

# Display the spindate.
wm geometry . 150x150
pack .spd -expand 1
grid [.spd component day] -pady 6; # -datemargin not working
```

Class Model

The spindate [incr Widget] inherits directly from itk::Widget. It contains two spinners and a spinint.

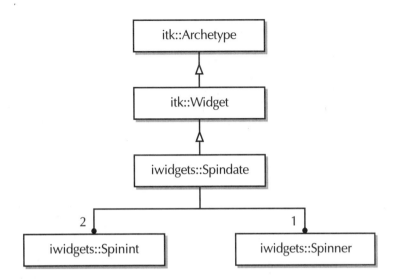

Configuration Options

Standard Options

Refer to the options man page for information on these standard options:

background	cursor	foreground	orient
relief	repeatdelay	repeatinterval	

Associated Options

Refer to the associated [incr Widget] for information on each of these options:

Option Name	Associated With
arroworient	spinint, spinner
labelfont	spinint, spinner
labelmargin	spinint, spinner
textbackground	spinint, spinner
textfont	spinint, spinner

Inherited Options

Refer to Chapter 11 for information on this inherited option from the [incr Tk] Archetype base class:

Option Name	Inherited From
clientdata	itk::Archetype

Widget-Specific Options

-datemargin

Resource name: dateMargin
Resource class: Margin
Description: Specifies the distance between each of the spinners. Note that this option only works correctly in post-itcl3.0.1 releases.
Default value: 1 (pixel)

-daylabel

Resource name: dayLabel
Resource class: Text
Description: Specifies the text to be displayed next to the day spinner. This option replaces the day spinner's -labeltext option.
Default value: Day

-dayon

Resource name: dayOn
Resource class: DayOn
Description: Boolean value that specifies whether or not to display the day spinner.
Default value: true

-daywidth

Resource name: dayWidth
Resource class: Width
Description: Specifies the width of the day spinner's entry component
Default value: 4 (characters)

-labelpos

Resource name: labelPos
Resource class: Position

Description: Specifies the location of each of the spinner's labels relative to its entry component. Valid values are n, s, e, and w.
Default value: w

-monthformat

Resource name: monthFormat
Resource class: MonthFormat
Description: Specifies the format of the month display. Valid values are brief, full, and integer. A value of brief causes the months to be displayed in abbreviated notation (Jan, Feb, Mar, etc.). A value of full causes the full names of the months to be displayed. A value of integer causes the integral value to be displayed (January = 1, February = 2, etc.).
Default value: integer

-monthlabel

Resource name: monthLabel
Resource class: Text
Description: Specifies the text to be displayed next to the month spinner. This option replaces the month spinner's -labeltext option.
Default value: Month

-monthon

Resource name: monthOn
Resource class: MonthOn
Description: Boolean value that specifies whether or not to display the month spinner.
Default value: true

-monthwidth

Resource name: monthWidth
Resource class: Width
Description: Specifies the width of the month spinner's entry component.
Default value: 4 (characters)

-yeardigits

Resource name: yearDigits
Resource class: YearDigits
Description: Specifies the number of digits to display in the year spinner. Valid values are 2 and 4.
Default value: 4

14

-yearlabel

Resource name: yearLabel
Resource class: Text
Description: Specifies the text to be displayed next to the year spinner. This option replaces the year spinner's -labeltext option.
Default value: Year

-yearon

Resource name: yearOn
Resource class: YearOn
Description: Boolean value that specifies whether or not to display the year spinner.
Default value: true

-yearwidth

Resource name: yearWidth
Resource class: Width
Description: Specifies the width of the year spinner's entry component.
Default value: 4 (characters)

Public Methods

Associated Methods

None

Inherited Methods

Refer to the [incr Tk] base class for information on each inherited method. The [incr Tk] base classes are discussed in Chapter 11.

Method Name	Inherited From
cget	itk::Archetype
component	itk::Archetype
config	itk::Archetype
configure	itk::Archetype

Widget-Specific Methods

get

Usage: pathName *get* ?format?
Description: Returns the current date contained in the spindate according to the format argument, which may be either -string or -clicks. If -string is specified (this is the default value), the content of each of the spinners is returned as a list in one of two formats: "day month year" or "month/day/year". If -monthformat is set to integer, the latter format is used; otherwise, the former is used. If -clicks is specified, the **clock** command is used to return an integer value representing the specified date. See the clock man page for more information on this value.

show

Usage: pathName *show* date
Description: Configures the spindate to display the date specified by the date argument. This may be an explicit date such as 5/20/1975 or a relative date like "next week". See the clock man page for more details on date formatting and relative dates.

Components

The spindate [incr Widget] is composed of two spinints and one spinner, as outlined in the following table. Each of these is packed into the hull frame component.

Name	Class	Description
day	Spinint	The day spinner
hull	Spindate	The frame surrounding the entire spindate
month	Spinner	The month spinner
year	Spinint	The year spinner

spinint

The spinint [incr Widget] implements an integer spinner widget. It provides an entry widget that displays the current integer value and up and down arrows to increase and decrease the value, respectively. It also provides a label widget that can be positioned around the spinint as well as a childsite frame. The spinint provides a -range option that allows the user to specify minimum and maximum values that are displayed. When either boundary value is reached, the spinint can be configured to automatically wrap with its -wrap option. The user may also specify the amount by which the integer value is modified when the up and down arrows are pressed.

```
# Create the spinint.
iwidgets::spinint .sp -labeltext "Enter desired volume: " \
  -width 5 -range "-10 100"
pack .sp -pady 12 -padx 12
wm title . spinint

# This is a trick you can use to specify units next to a spinner.
set lcs [winfo parent [.sp childsite]]
label $lcs.db -text dB
grid $lcs.db -row 0 -column 2

# Clear the entry and start at 28dB.
.sp clear
.sp insert 0 28
```

Class Model

The spinint [incr Widget] inherits from iwidgets::Spinner. It does not interact with any other [incr Widget] outside of its inheritance tree.

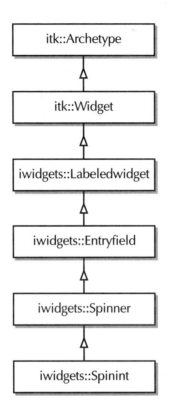

Configuration Options

Standard Options

Refer to the options man page for information on these standard options:

background	borderwidth	cursor	disabledforeground
exportselection	foreground	highlightcolor	highlightthickness
insertbackground	insertborderwidth	insertofftime	insertontime
insertwidth	justify	relief	repeatdelay
repeatinterval	selectbackground	selectborderwidth	selectforeground

14

Associated Options
None

Inherited Options
Refer to the [incr Widget] or [incr Tk] base class for information on each of these options. The [incr Tk] base classes are discussed in Chapter 11.

Option Name	Inherited From
arroworient	iwidgets::Spinner
childsitepos	iwidgets::Entryfield
clientdata	itk::Archetype
command	iwidgets::Entryfield
decrement	iwidgets::Spinner
fixed	iwidgets::Entryfield
focuscommand	iwidgets::Entryfield
increment	iwidgets::Spinner
invalid	iwidgets::Entryfield
labelbitmap	iwidgets::Labeledwidget
labelfont	iwidgets::Labeledwidget
labelimage	iwidgets::Labeledwidget
labelmargin	iwidgets::Labeledwidget
labelpos	iwidgets::Labeledwidget
labeltext	iwidgets::Labeledwidget
labelvariable	iwidgets::Labeledwidget
show	iwidgets::Entryfield
state	iwidgets::Entryfield
textbackground	iwidgets::Entryfield
textfont	iwidgets::Entryfield
textvariable	iwidgets::Entryfield
validate	iwidgets::Entryfield
width	iwidgets::Entryfield

Widget-Specific Options

-range

Resource name: range
Resource class: Range
Description: Specifies the minimum and maximum values of the spinint.
The format of this option should be a list with two values, the first
representing the minimum value.
Default value: {}

-step

Resource name: step
Resource class: Step
Description: Specifies the integer value with which to increment and
decrement the spinint when the up and down arrows are pressed.
Default value: 1

-wrap

Resource name: wrap
Resource class: Wrap
Description: A Boolean value that specifies whether the spinint should
wrap if it reaches a boundary value. For example, if the maximum value is 10
and the minimum value is 5, then the spinint will wrap from 10 to 5 if the
up arrow is pressed and -wrap is true.
Default value: true

Public Methods

Associated Methods

None

Inherited Methods

Refer to the [incr Widget] or [incr Tk] base class for information on each of
these methods. The [incr Tk] base classes are discussed in Chapter 11.

Method Name	Inherited From
cget	itk::Archetype
childsite	iwidgets::Entryfield
clear	iwidgets::Entryfield

14

Method Name	Inherited From
component	itk::Archetype
config	itk::Archetype
configure	itk::Archetype
delete	iwidgets::Entryfield
get	iwidgets::Entryfield
icursor	iwidgets::Entryfield
index	iwidgets::Entryfield
insert	iwidgets::Entryfield
scan	iwidgets::Entryfield
selection	iwidgets::Entryfield
xview	iwidgets::Entryfield

Widget-Specific Methods

down

Usage: pathName *down*
Description: Decrement the spinint value by the amount specified by the
-step option. This method is invoked each time the down arrow is pressed.
Note that invoking this method does not evaluate the command specified
by the -decrement option.

up

Usage: pathName *up*
Description: Increment the spinint value by the amount specified by the
-step option. This method is invoked each time the up arrow is pressed. Note
that invoking this method does not evaluate the command specified by the
-increment option.

Components

The spinint [incr Widget] is composed of two canvases, an entry, and a label, as outlined in the following table. Each of these is packed into the hull frame component.

Name	Class	Description
downarrow	Canvas	The down arrow button
entry	Entry	The entry widget in which the spinint value is displayed
hull	Spinint	The frame around the entire spinint
label	Label	The label widget positioned around the spinint according to the -labelpos option
uparrow	Canvas	The up arrow button

spinner

The spinner [incr Widget] implements a generic spinner widget. It is generally meant to be used as a base class with derived classes providing specialized functionality, such as the spinint. The spinner provides an entry widget and up and down arrows for modifying its contents. It also provides a label that can be positioned around the spinner as well as a childsite frame in which the up and down arrows are packed. In order to create a working spinner, you have to manually implement commands to be evaluated when the up and down arrows are pressed. The -decrement and -increment options are used to specify these commands.

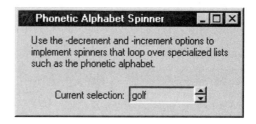

```
wm title . "Phonetic Alphabet Spinner"

# Initialize a list for the spinner to loop over.
set alphabet "alpha bravo charlie delta echo foxtrot golf hotel\
  india juliett kilo lima mike november oscar papa quebec romeo\
  sierra tango uniform victor whiskey xray yankee zulu"
set index 6

# Description of spinner.
message .m -text "Use the -decrement and -increment options to\
  implement spinners that loop over specialized lists such as\
  the phonetic alphabet." -width 250
pack .m -padx 8 -pady 4

# Create the spinner.
iwidgets::spinner .sp -labeltext "Current selection:" -width 12 \
  -decrement {spin .sp backward} -increment {spin .sp} \
  -textbackground bisque
.sp insert 0 [lindex $alphabet $index]
pack .sp -pady 12

# Spin the alphabet character forward or backward as specified
# by the direction_ argument.
proc spin {spinner_ {direction_ forward}} {
  global index alphabet
  if {$direction_ == "forward"} {
```

```
    incr index
} elseif {$direction_ == "backward"} {
    incr index -1
} else {
    error "Bad argument: \"$direction_\". Should be backward or\
        forward."
}

# Check boundary conditions.
if {$index == [llength $alphabet]} {
    set index 0
} elseif {$index == -1} {
    set index [expr [llength $alphabet] - 1]
}

# Out with the old and in with the new!
.sp clear
.sp insert 0 [lindex $alphabet $index]
}
```

Class Model

The spinner [incr Widget] inherits from iwidgets::Entryfield. It does not interact with any other [incr Widgets] outside of its inheritance tree.

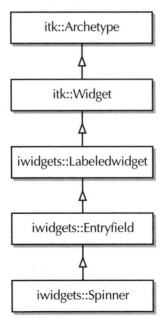

14

Configuration Options

Standard Options

Refer to the options man page for information on these standard options:

background	borderwidth	cursor	disabledforeground
exportselection	foreground	highlightcolor	highlightthickness
insertbackground	insertborderwidth	insertofftime	insertontime
insertwidth	justify	relief	repeatdelay
repeatinterval	selectbackground	selectborderwidth	selectforeground

Associated Options

None

Inherited Options

Refer to the [incr Widget] or [incr Tk] base class for information on each of these options. The [incr Tk] base classes are discussed in Chapter 11.

Option Name	Inherited From
childsitepos	iwidgets::Entryfield
clientdata	itk::Archetype
command	iwidgets::Entryfield
fixed	iwidgets::Entryfield
focuscommand	iwidgets::Entryfield
invalid	iwidgets::Entryfield
labelbitmap	iwidgets::Labeledwidget
labelfont	iwidgets::Labeledwidget
labelimage	iwidgets::Labeledwidget
labelmargin	iwidgets::Labeledwidget
labelpos	iwidgets::Labeledwidget
labeltext	iwidgets::Labeledwidget

Option Name	Inherited From
labelvariable	iwidgets::Labeledwidget
show	iwidgets::Entryfield
state	iwidgets::Entryfield
textbackground	iwidgets::Entryfield
textfont	iwidgets::Entryfield
textvariable	iwidgets::Entryfield
validate	iwidgets::Entryfield
width	iwidgets::Entryfield

Widget-Specific Options

-arroworient

Resource name: arrowOrient
Resource class: Orient
Description: Specifies the orientation of the arrows. Valid values are vertical and horizontal. Note that this doesn't modify the direction in which the arrows point; rather, it determines whether the buttons themselves are positioned vertically or horizontally.
Default value: vertical

-decrement

Resource name: decrement
Resource class: Command
Description: Specifies a Tcl command to be evaluated when the down arrow is pressed.
Default value: {}

-increment

Resource name: increment
Resource class: Command
Description: Specifies a Tcl command to be evaluated when the up arrow is pressed.
Default value: {}

14

Public Methods

Associated Methods

None

Inherited Methods

Refer to the [incr Widget] or [incr Tk] base class for information on each of these methods. The [incr Tk] base classes are discussed in Chapter 11.

Method Name	Inherited From
cget	itk::Archetype
childsite	iwidgets::Entryfield
clear	iwidgets::Entryfield
component	itk::Archetype
config	itk::Archetype
configure	itk::Archetype
delete	iwidgets::Entryfield
get	iwidgets::Entryfield
icursor	iwidgets::Entryfield
index	iwidgets::Entryfield
insert	iwidgets::Entryfield
scan	iwidgets::Entryfield
selection	iwidgets::Entryfield
xview	iwidgets::Entryfield

Widget-Specific Methods

down

Usage: pathName *down*
Description: This method is meant to be a "pure virtual" method, meaning it should be implemented by a derived class. Invoking this method is a no-op. Note that it does not evaluate the command specified by the -decrement option. This method is meant to handle the down arrow button press event and decrement the entry value.

up

Usage: pathName *up*
Description: This method is meant to be a "pure virtual" method, meaning it should be implemented by a derived class. Invoking this method is a no-op. Note that it does not evaluate the command specified by the -increment option. This method is meant to handle the up arrow button press event and increment the entry value.

Components

The spinner [incr Widget] is composed of two canvases, an entry, and a label, as outlined in the following table. Each of these is packed into the hull frame component.

Name	Class	Description
downarrow	Canvas	The down arrow button
entry	Entry	The entry widget in which the spinner value is displayed
hull	Spinner	The frame around the entire spinner
label	Label	The label widget positioned around the spinner according to the -labelpos option
uparrow	Canvas	The up arrow button

14

spintime

The spintime [incr Widget] implements a time selection widget with spinners. The spintime has three spinners: one for the hour, one for the minute, and one for the second. You can show specific times in the spintime with the *show* method, or you can even show relative times such as "3 hours ago". You can also retrieve the current time in the spintime as a time string or an integer value as calculated by the **clock** command.

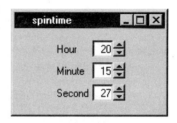

```
# Create the spintime.
iwidgets::spintime .st -timemargin 6

# Show the current time.
.st show

wm title . spintime
wm geometry . 175x95
pack .st -expand 1
```

Class Model

The spintime [incr Widget] inherits directly from itk::Widget. It contains three spinints.

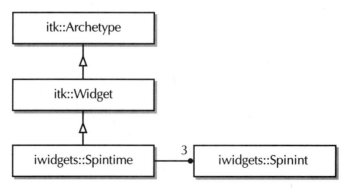

Configuration Options

Standard Options

Refer to the options man page for information on these standard options:

background	cursor	foreground	orient
relief	repeatdelay	repeatinterval	

Associated Options

Refer to the associated [incr Widget] for information on each of these options:

Option Name	Associated With
arroworient	spinint
labelfont	spinint
labelmargin	spinint
textbackground	spinint
textfont	spinint

Inherited Options

Refer to Chapter 11 for information on this inherited option from the [incr Tk] Archetype base class.

Option Name	Inherited From
clientdata	itk::Archetype

Widget-Specific Options

-hourlabel

Resource name: hourLabel
Resource class: Text
Description: Specifies the text to be displayed next to the hour spinint. This option replaces the hour spinint's -labeltext option.
Default value: Hour

14

-houron

Resource name: hourOn
Resource class: HourOn
Description: Boolean value that specifies whether or not to display the hour spinint.
Default value: true

-hourwidth

Resource name: hourWidth
Resource class: Width
Description: Specifies the width of the hour spinint's entry component.
Default value: 3 (characters)

-labelpos

Resource name: labelPos
Resource class: Position
Description: Specifies the location of each of the spinner's labels relative to its entry component. Valid values are n, s, e, and w.
Default value: w

-militaryon

Resource name: militaryOn
Resource class: MilitaryOn
Description: Boolean value that specifies whether to display a 24-hour clock or a 12-hour clock.
Default value: true

-minutelabel

Resource name: minuteLabel
Resource class: Text
Description: Specifies the text to be displayed next to the minute spinint. This option replaces the minute spinint's -labeltext option.
Default value: Minute

-minuteon

Resource name: minuteOn
Resource class: MinuteOn

Description: Boolean value that specifies whether or not to display the minute spinint.
Default value: true

-minutewidth

Resource name: minuteWidth
Resource class: Width
Description: Specifies the width of the minute spinint's entry component.
Default value: 3 (characters)

-secondlabel

Resource name: secondLabel
Resource class: Text
Description: Specifies the text to be displayed next to the second spinint. This option replaces the second spinint's -labeltext option.
Default value: Year

-secondon

Resource name: secondOn
Resource class: SecondOn
Description: Boolean value that specifies whether or not to display the second spinint.
Default value: true

-secondwidth

Resource name: secondWidth
Resource class: Width
Description: Specifies the width of the second spinint's entry component.
Default value: 3 (characters)

-timemargin

Resource name: timeMargin
Resource class: Margin
Description: Specifies the distance between each of the spinints.
Default value: 1 (pixel)

Public Methods

Associated Methods

None

Inherited Methods

Refer to the [incr Tk] base class for information on each inherited method. The [incr Tk] base classes are discussed in Chapter 11.

Method Name	Inherited From
cget	itk::Archetype
component	itk::Archetype
config	itk::Archetype
configure	itk::Archetype

Widget-Specific Methods

get

Usage: pathName *get* ?format?
Description: Returns the current time contained in the spintime according to the format argument, which may be either -string or -clicks. If -string is specified (this is the default value), the content of each of the spinners is returned as a list in the format hour:minute:second. If -clicks is specified, the **clock** command is used to return an integer value representing the specified time. See the clock man page for more information on this value.

show

Usage: pathName *show* time
Description: Configures the spintime to display the time specified by the time argument. This may be an explicit time such as 23:09:47 or a relative time like "6 hours ago". Even though relative times are supported, they aren't that useful with spintime. A spindate would be more appropriate for relative times. See the clock man page for more details on time formatting and valid relative time strings.

Components

The spintime [incr Widget] is composed of multiple spinint [incr Widgets], as outlined in the following table. Each of the spinints is packed into the hull frame component.

Name	Class	Description
hour	Spinint	The hour spinint
hull	Spintime	The frame surrounding the entire spintime
minute	Spinint	The minute spinint
second	Spinint	The second spinint

tabnotebook

The tabnotebook [incr Widget] is a widget that contains a set of notebook pages, each of which has an associated tab with which the page can be selected. The tabnotebook is empty until you add new pages and tabs to it with the *add* or *insert* methods. A robust set of configuration options then allows you to create a wide variety of tabnotebook appearances. You can manipulate several of the pixel spacings in and around the tabs, you can configure the tabnotebook to display its tabs at different locations around the notebook, and you can change the color schemes of the tabs and notebook pages. Once the notebook pages and tabs have been added, you can get the childsite of each page via the *childsite* method and pack any kind of Tk widget or [incr Widget] into the page. This provides a convenient separation of concerns by being able to group like items in separate notebook pages, easily accessible with that page's tab selector.

The notebook and tabset [incr Widgets] make the tabnotebook possible. The notebook can be a stand-alone widget and is therefore discussed earlier in this chapter in its own section. Several tabnotebook public methods and options are actually wrappers for the notebook component. The tabset, on the other hand, is really designed to be a component of the tabnotebook and not a stand-alone widget. It therefore does not have its own section in this chapter. For more information on the tabset, you should refer to its man page.

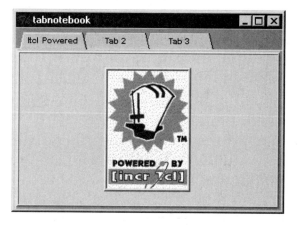

```
wm title . tabnotebook

# Create the tabnotebook.
iwidgets::tabnotebook .tb -tabpos n -width 325 -height 215 \
  -backdrop grey65
```

```
# Create and fill in the page for tab 1. Note the pathname will
# likely not exist on your system.
set tab1 [.tb add -label "Itcl Powered"]
frame $tab1.f -relief ridge -bd 3
label $tab1.f.img -relief ridge -bd 4 -image [image create photo \
  -file "C:/tmp/itclpwrd.gif"]
pack $tab1.f.img -padx 16 -pady 16 -expand 1
pack $tab1.f -fill both -expand 1

# Pages 2 and 3 are blank. You can add any kind of Tk widget or
# [incr Widget] to the page childsites stored in $tab2 and $tab3.
set tab2 [.tb add -label "Tab 2"]
pack [label $tab2.l -text "Welcome to tab 2!"] -expand 1
set tab3 [.tb add -label "Tab 3"]
pack [label $tab3.l -text "Welcome to tab 3!"] -expand 1

pack .tb -fill both -expand 1
.tb select 0
```

Class Model

The tabnotebook [incr Widget] inherits directly from itk::Widget. It contains
zero or more notebook [incr Widgets] as well as zero or more tabset
[incr Widgets].

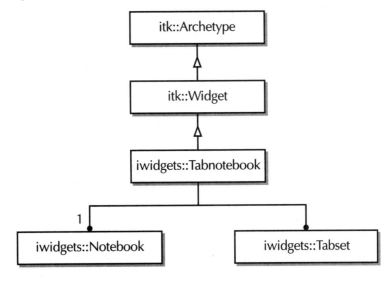

14

Configuration Options

Standard Options

Refer to the options man page for information on these standard options:

borderwidth	cursor	disabledforeground	font
foreground			

Associated Options

Refer to the associated [incr Widget] for information on each of these options:

Option Name	Associated With
auto	notebook
scrollcommand	notebook

Inherited Options

Refer to Chapter 11 for information on this inherited option from the [incr Tk] Archetype base class:

Option Name	Inherited From
clientdata	itk::Archetype

Widget-Specific Options

-angle

Resource name: angle
Resource class: Angle
Description: Specifies the slope angle from the inner edge to the outer edge of each tab. Setting this value to zero results in square tabs. Valid values are in the range 0 to 45, inclusive. This option is only valid if the -tabpos option is n or s.
Default value: 15

-backdrop

Resource name: backDrop
Resource class: BackDrop

Description: Specifies the background color to be used for the area behind the tabs.
Default value: #d9d9d9

-background

Resource name: background
Resource class: Background
Description: Specifies the background color of both the currently selected tab and the notebook page.
Default value: #d9d9d9

-bevelamount

Resource name: bevelAmount
Resource class: BevelAmount
Description: Specifies the pixel size of each tab's corners. Setting this option to zero means the tabs have no corners.
Default value: 0

-equaltabs

Resource name: equalTabs
Resource class: EqualTabs
Description: Boolean value that specifies whether or not to force all tabs to be equally sized. If configured as a false value, then tabs are sized according to the text that's displayed in them.
Default value: true

-gap

Resource name: gap
Resource class: Gap
Description: Specifies the amount of space in pixels to insert between each tab. The value overlap is also supported, which causes the tabs to appear overlapped in the tabnotebook.
Default value: overlap

-height

Resource name: height
Resource class: Height
Description: Specifies the overall height of the tabnotebook.
Default value: 150 (pixels)

-margin

Resource name: margin
Resource class: Margin
Description: Specifies the distance between the outer edge of each tab and the hull frame.
Default value: 4 (pixels)

-padx

Resource name: padX
Resource class: PadX
Description: Specifies the padding distance to use for each tab's text label in the x direction. This creates extra space in the tab, so the larger the number, the wider the tabs become.
Default value: 4 (pixels)

-pady

Resource name: padY
Resource class: PadY
Description: Specifies the padding distance to use for each tab's text label in the y direction. This creates extra space in the tab, so the larger the number, the taller the tabs become.
Default value: 4 (pixels)

-raiseselect

Resource name: raiseSelect
Resource class: RaiseSelect
Description: Boolean value that specifies whether to raise selected tabs. This makes the selected tab appear taller than the others.
Default value: false

-start

Resource name: start
Resource class: Start
Description: Specifies the amount of space between the first tab and the hull frame. For tabnotebooks whose -tabpos is set to n, for example, this option specifies the amount of space to the left of the leftmost tab. If -tabpos is set to w, it's the amount of space above the uppermost tab.
Default value: 4 (pixels)

-state

Resource name: state
Resource class: State
Description: Specifies the state of the tabs in the tabnotebook. Valid values are normal and disabled. Setting this option to disabled disallows selection of any tabs. It does not, however, disallow operating on widgets within the currently selected tab. So, be aware that you must take appropriate action to disable all of the currently selected page's internal widgets if trying to disable the entire tabnotebook.
Default value: normal

-tabbackground

Resource name: tabBackground
Resource class: TabBackground
Description: Specifies the background color to be used for all tabs that are currently unselected.
Default value: #d9d9d9

-tabborders

Resource name: tabBorders
Resource class: TabBorders
Description: Boolean value that specifies whether an outline border is drawn around each of the unselected tabs. The selected tab always has a border.
Default value: true

-tabforeground

Resource name: tabForeground
Resource class: TabForeground
Description: Specifies the foreground color (text color) to be used for all tabs that are currently unselected.
Default value: black

-tabpos

Resource name: tabPos
Resource class: TabPos
Description: Specifies the location of the tabs relative to the notebook pages. Valid values are n, s, e, and w.
Default value: s

14

-width

Resource name: width
Resource class: Width
Description: Specifies the overall width of the tabnotebook.
Default value: 300 (pixels)

Public Methods

Associated Methods

Refer to the associated [incr Widget] for information on these methods:

Method Name	Associated With
childsite	notebook
delete	notebook, tabset
index	notebook
insert	notebook, tabset
next	notebook, tabset
pageconfigure	notebook
prev	notebook, tabset
select	notebook, tabset
view	notebook

Inherited Methods

Refer to the [incr Tk] base class for information on each inherited method.
The [incr Tk] base classes are discussed in Chapter 11.

Method Name	Inherited From
cget	itk::Archetype
component	itk::Archetype
config	itk::Archetype
configure	itk::Archetype

Widget-Specific Methods

None. All public methods are wrappers for notebook and/or tabset public methods of the same name. The notebook is documented earlier in this chapter. Since the tabset is really only meant to be a part of a tabnotebook, it does not have a section in this chapter. You can refer to the tabset man page if necessary.

Components

The tabnotebook [incr Widget] is composed of a Tk canvas widget and two [incr Widgets]: a notebook and a tabset. Each of these is packed into the hull frame component.

Name	Class	Description
canvas	Canvas	The canvas containing the notebook component.
hull	Tabnotebook	The frame around the entire tabnotebook.
notebook	Notebook	Widgets displayed in the tabnotebook are actually packed in the notebook component.
tabset	Tabset	The set of tabs attached to the notebook.

timeentry

The timeentry [incr Widget] is basically the same as the timefield except it adds a watch that the user can use to set the time with the mouse instead of having to use the keyboard only. An icon is provided next to the entry widget that opens a pop-up window when clicked. This pop-up contains a watch and a button for closing the window. The modality of the pop-up can be configured as a local or global grab with timeentry's -grab option. The hands of the watch can be moved to the desired time, and when the window is closed the text entry is updated with the selected time. All of the watch's configuration options are available for direct access to the watch. Further, timeentry provides several public methods such as *show* to show a specific time or a relative time, *get* to retrieve the current selected time, and *isvalid* to validate the specified time.

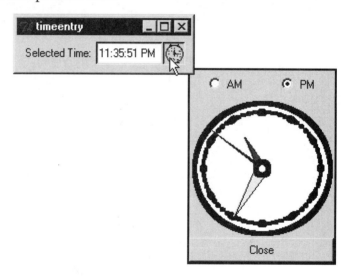

```
wm title . timeentry
iwidgets::timeentry .te -labeltext "Selected Time:"
pack .te -pady 6 -padx 6
```

Class Model

The timeentry [incr Widget] inherits from iwidgets::Timefield. It contains an optional watch.

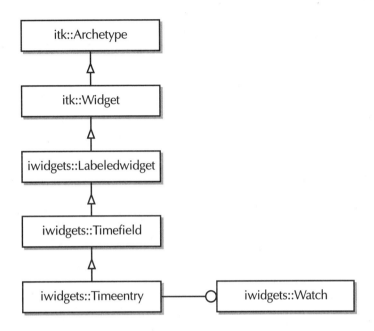

Configuration Options

Standard Options

Refer to the options man page for information on these standard options:

background	borderwidth	cursor	disabledforeground
exportselection	foreground	highlightcolor	highlightthickness
insertbackground	justify	relief	

Associated Options

Refer to the associated [incr Widget] for information on each of these options:

Option Name	Associated With
clockcolor	watch
clockstipple	watch
hourcolor	watch

14

Option Name	Associated With
hourradius	watch
minutecolor	watch
minuteradius	watch
pivotcolor	watch
pivotradius	watch
secondcolor	watch
secondradius	watch
tickcolor	watch

Inherited Options

Refer to the [incr Widget] or [incr Tk] base class for information on each of these options. The [incr Tk] base classes are discussed in Chapter 11.

Option Name	Inherited From
childsitepos	iwidgets::Timefield
clientdata	itk::Archetype
command	iwidgets::Timefield
format	iwidgets::Timefield
iq	iwidgets::Timefield
labelbitmap	iwidgets::Labeledwidget
labelfont	iwidgets::Labeledwidget
labelimage	iwidgets::Labeledwidget
labelmargin	iwidgets::Labeledwidget
labelpos	iwidgets::Labeledwidget
labeltext	iwidgets::Labeledwidget
labelvariable	iwidgets::Labeledwidget
seconds	iwidgets::Timefield
textbackground	iwidgets::Timefield
textfont	iwidgets::Timefield

Widget-Specific Options

-closetext

Resource name: closeText
Resource class: Text
Description: Specifies the text for the button underneath the pop-up watch.
Default value: Close

-grab

Resource name: grab
Resource class: Grab
Description: Specifies the grab level to perform when displaying the pop-up watch. Valid values are local and global.
Default value: global

-icon

Resource name: icon
Resource class: Icon
Description: Specifies the image to be used for the icon next to the entry component in the timeentry. Clicking on this icon creates the pop-up watch window. If no image is specified, a default clock bitmap is created.
Default value: {}

-state

Resource name: state
Resource class: State
Description: Specifies the current state of the timeentry. Valid values are normal and disabled. If disabled, opening the watch pop-up window is disallowed, but note that you can still type into the entry.
Default value: normal

-watchheight

Resource name: watchHeight
Resource class: Height
Description: Specifies the height of the watch in the pop-up window.
Default value: 175 (pixels)

-watchwidth

Resource name: watchWidth
Resource class: Width
Description: Specifies the width of the watch in the pop-up window.
Default value: 155 (pixels)

Public Methods

Associated Methods

None

Inherited Methods

Refer to the [incr Widget] or [incr Tk] base class for information on each of these methods. The [incr Tk] base classes are discussed in Chapter 11.

Method Name	Inherited From
cget	itk::Archetype
childsite	iwidgets::Labeledwidget
component	itk::Archetype
config	itk::Archetype
configure	itk::Archetype
get	iwidgets::Timefield
isvalid	iwidgets::Timefield
show	iwidgets::Timefield

Widget-Specific Methods

None

Components

The timeentry contains several components, as outlined in the following table. When the pop-up watch window is displayed, two additional components are added: watch and close. Since these components aren't persistent, they are not shown in the components table. The watch component is the watch [incr Widget], and the close component is the button at the bottom of the pop-up window. When the window is closed, these two components are destroyed. They are re-created each time the pop-up is reopened.

Name	Class	Description
hull	Timeentry	The frame around the entire timeentry
iconButton	Label	The clock icon next to the entry widget
label	Label	The label widget that is positioned around the timeentry according to -labelpos
time	Entry	The entry widget that displays the textual time

timefield

The timefield [incr Widget] is similar to an entryfield with an editable time string in the entry component. The default value is the current time, which is displayed as hour:minute:second. You can edit the time directly in the entry widget or set it with the *show* method. When using the latter, you can even specify relative times such as "6 hours ago". Refer to the clock man page for more details on relative times. The timefield also offers automatic time validation depending on the -iq configuration option. By default, the timefield disallows entering invalid times.

```
wm title . timefield

# Create the timefield.
iwidgets::timefield .tf -labeltext "Current selected time:" \
  -format military
pack .tf -padx 8 -pady 6

# Show the time 7 hours ago.
.tf show "7 hours ago"
```

Class Model

The timefield [incr Widget] inherits from iwidgets::Labeledwidget. It does not interact with any other [incr Widgets] outside of its inheritance tree.

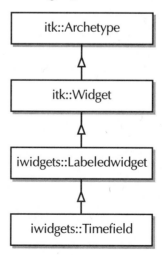

Configuration Options

Standard Options

Refer to the options man page for information on these standard options:

background	borderwidth	cursor	disabledforeground
exportselection	foreground	highlightcolor	highlightthickness
insertbackground	justify	relief	

Associated Options

None

Inherited Options

Refer to the [incr Widget] or [incr Tk] base class for information on each of these options. The [incr Tk] base classes are discussed in Chapter 11.

Option Name	Inherited From
clientdata	itk::Archetype
labelbitmap	iwidgets::Labeledwidget
labelfont	iwidgets::Labeledwidget
labelimage	iwidgets::Labeledwidget
labelmargin	iwidgets::Labeledwidget
labelpos	iwidgets::Labeledwidget
labeltext	iwidgets::Labeledwidget
labelvariable	iwidgets::Labeledwidget
state	iwidgets::Labeledwidget

Widget-Specific Options

-childsitepos

Resource name: childSitePos
Resource class: Position
Description: Specifies the positioning of the timefield's childsite frame. Valid values are n, s, e, and w. The childsite is typically only used by the

14

timeentry [incr Widget], which places the clock image in the childsite. For a timefield object, the childsite is empty. You can add a widget to the childsite such as a label or a button by using the *childsite* method. See the documentation on this method for important details.
Default value: e

-command

Resource name: command
Resource class: Command
Description: Specifies a Tcl command to be evaluated when the RETURN key is pressed in the entry component.
Default value: {}

-format

Resource name: format
Resource class: Format
Description: Specifies whether the time is displayed as military time (24-hour clock) or with a standard 12-hour clock. Valid options are military or civilian.
Default value: civilian

-iq

Resource name: iq
Resource class: Iq
Description: This option controls the "intelligence" of the timefield. Valid values are high and low. If set to high, the timefield disallows setting invalid times in the entry component. For example, if you enter the number 8 as the first number in the hours field, timefield automatically changes the hours to read 08 since an 8 as the first digit is invalid. Setting -iq to low means there is no automatic time validation; you can enter a time of 88:88:88. It is assumed in this case that the time will be manually validated at some future point via the public *isvalid* method.
Default value: high

-textbackground

Resource name: textBackground
Resource class: Background
Description: Specifies the background color of the entry component. This option replaces the entry's -background option.
Default value: Windows = SystemWindow, Unix = #d9d9d9

-textfont

Resource name: textFont
Resource class: Font
Description: Specifies the font to use for the text in the entry component. This option replaces the entry's -font option.
Default value: Windows = {{MS Sans Serif} 8}, Unix = {Helvetica -12}

Public Methods

Associated Methods

None

Inherited Methods

Refer to the [incr Widget] or [incr Tk] base class for information on each of these methods. The [incr Tk] base classes are discussed in Chapter 11.

Method Name	Inherited From
cget	itk::Archetype
childsite	iwidgets::Labeledwidget
component	itk::Archetype
config	itk::Archetype
configure	itk::Archetype

Widget-Specific Methods

get

Usage: pathName *get* ?format?
Description: Returns the contents of the entry component as either a time string or an integer clock value, depending on the value of the optional format argument. This argument may be either -string or -clicks, and it defaults to -string. Specifying -clicks returns the number of seconds corresponding to the designated time as calculated by the **clock scan** command.

isvalid

Usage: pathName *isvalid*
Description: Validates the contents of the entry component and returns either a one or a zero. If the time is valid, such as 07:38:52, then a one is returned. A zero is returned for invalid dates such as 07:38:62.

show

Usage: pathName *show* ?time?
Description: Shows the time specified by the time argument in the entry component. The default value is the current time. You may specify a time string or an integer clock value. The time string may be a relative time such as "3 hours ago". Refer to the clock man page for more details on relative times.

Components

The timefield [incr Widget] is simply composed of a label and an entry, as outlined in the following table. Each of these is packed into the hull frame component.

Name	Class	Description
label	Label	The label that is positioned around the timefield according to -labelpos; defaults to w (left side)
hull	Timefield	The frame around the timefield
time	Entry	The entry area that displays the textual time

toolbar

The toolbar [incr Widget] arranges a group of widgets into either a row or a column. This is typically done beneath menu bars to give quick and convenient shortcuts to menubar options in an application. Instead of navigating through a series of cascading menus, for example, the user may be able to click on a single button in the toolbar to invoke the same command. Any kind of widgets may be placed into a toolbar, but command-oriented widgets such as buttons are most frequently used.

```
wm title . toolbar

# Create the toolbar.
iwidgets::toolbar .tb

# Add some text editing buttons.
set dir ${iwidgets::library}/demos/images
.tb add button copy -balloonstr "Copy to clipboard" \
  -image [image create photo -file $dir/copy.gif]
.tb add button paste -balloonstr "Paste from clipboard" \
  -image [image create photo -file $dir/paste.gif]
.tb add button cut -balloonstr "Cut selected text" \
  -image [image create photo -file $dir/cut.gif]
.tb add button erase -balloonstr "Erase selected text" \
  -image [image create photo -file $dir/clear.gif]

pack .tb -padx 18 -pady 12
```

Class Model

The toolbar [incr Widget] inherits directly from itk::Widget. It does not interact with any other [incr Widgets] outside of its inheritance tree.

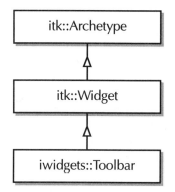

Configuration Options

Standard Options

Refer to the options man page for information on these standard options:

activebackground	activeforeground	background	cursor
disabledforeground	font	foreground	highlightbackground
highlightcolor	highlightthickness	orient	selectbackground
selectborderwidth	selectforeground	troughcolor	

Associated Options

None

Inherited Options

Refer to Chapter 11 for information on this inherited option from the [incr Tk] Archetype base class:

Option Name	Inherited From
clientdata	itk::Archetype

Widget-Specific Options

-balloonbackground

Resource name: balloonBackground
Resource class: BalloonBackground

Description: Specifies the background color for the pop-up balloon help window.
Default value: yellow

-balloondelay1

Resource name: balloonDelay1
Resource class: BalloonDelay1
Description: Specifies the number of milliseconds to wait while the cursor is over one of the toolbar buttons before a balloon pop-up help window is initially displayed. If a balloon pop-up is already displayed, then see the -balloondelay2 option. Moving the cursor off the button cancels the timer event.
Default value: 1000

-balloondelay2

Resource name: balloonDelay2
Resource class: BalloonDelay2
Description: This option is similar to -balloondelay except it is used for *continuing* to display balloon pop-up windows instead of the initial display. For example, when you move the cursor over a toolbar for the first time, -balloondelay1 is used. Then, if you move the cursor to the button directly next to the current button, instead of waiting the entire default 1,000 milliseconds, the new balloon pop-up is displayed in $1/5^{th}$ that time (if the default value is used). This is to avoid having to wait the full second for each button in the toolbar if the cursor never leaves the toolbar. You can quickly browse each button's balloon pop-up window in the toolbar as a result.
Default value: 200

-balloonfont

Resource name: balloonFont
Resource class: BalloonFont
Description: Specifies the font to be used for the balloon pop-up windows.
Default value: 6x10

-balloonforeground

Resource name: balloonForeground
Resource class: BalloonForeground
Description: Specifies the foreground color (text color) for the balloon pop-up windows.
Default value: black

14

-helpvariable

Resource name: helpVariable
Resource class: HelpVariable
Description: Specifies a global variable to be updated whenever the mouse is in motion over a toolbar widget. This global variable is set to the value of the widget's -helpstr option. Using -helpvariable is useful for creating a help status bar, which is what the mainwindow [incr Widget] does. You can configure a label or entry widget's -textvariable option to the same variable name specified by -helpvariable. The label or entry will then be automatically updated to reflect the value of the current widget's -helpstr option. You could use -helpstr, for example, to provide a description of the toolbar widget such as "Cut the selected text" for a button that shows a pair of scissors. When the cursor is moved away from the menu entry, the variable specified by -helpvariable is set to the empty string.
Default value: {}

-state

Resource name: state
Resource class: State
Description: Specifies the select state of the toolbar. Valid values are normal and disabled. If disabled, then the toolbar buttons are grayed out and do not respond to input events such as a mouse click. The button motion event is still active, so you can see the balloon pop-up windows and any associated text in a help status bar, if provided, even if the toolbar is disabled.
Default value: normal

Public Methods

Associated Methods

None

Inherited Methods

Refer to Chapter 11 for information on each of these inherited methods from the itk::Archetype base class:

Method Name	Inherited From
cget	itk::Archetype
component	itk::Archetype
config	itk::Archetype
configure	itk::Archetype

Widget-Specific Methods

add

Usage: pathName *add* type name ?arg arg ...?
Description: Adds a new widget to the toolbar. The widget type is specified by the type argument, and its symbolic name is specified by the name argument. Any arguments after this should be valid option/value pairs for that widget. The toolbar additionally supports the -helpstr and -balloonstr options for component toolbar widgets. The -helpstr option can be used to print a brief description of the widget in a help status bar. The -balloonstr option is printed to the balloon pop-up window when displayed over that widget.

delete

Usage: pathName *delete* index1 ?index2?
Description: Deletes all widgets in the toolbar between index1 and index2, inclusively. The arguments may be either symbolic widget names or numerical index values.

index

Usage: pathName *index* name
Description: Returns the numerical index value of the toolbar widget specified by the name argument. You can also specify a numerical index value as name. If the index is not found, a -1 is returned.

insert

Usage: pathName *insert* before type name ?arg arg ...?
Description: Inserts a new widget into the toolbar before the widget specified by the before argument, which may either be a numerical index

14

value or the symbolic name of the widget. The type, name, and optional arguments are the same as the *add* method's argument list. Refer to *add* for further details.

itemcget

Usage: pathName *itemcget* widget option
Description: Returns the value of the specified option for the specified component toolbar widget. The widget argument is the symbolic name for the toolbar widget, which is specified when the widget is added with the *add* or *insert* method.

itemconfigure

Usage: pathName *itemconfigure* name ?option? ?arg arg ...?
Description: Use this method to modify a toolbar widget's configuration, to print a single option's information for a toolbar widget, or to print all of a toolbar widget's configuration data. The name argument is either the numerical index of the widget or its symbolic name. If no arguments are specified following name, all of that widget's configuration options are printed. If one argument follows name, then it should be a valid option for that particular widget type; if so, then its information is printed. If multiple arguments are specified after name, they must be in option/value pairs. You can do this to modify a single toolbar widget's configuration.

Components

When a toolbar is first created, it only contains a hull component as shown in the following table. As you add new widgets to the toolbar, each one becomes a new component.

Name	Class	Description
hull	Toolbar	The frame around the entire toolbar

watch

The watch [incr Widget] implements a clock drawn on a canvas widget. The watch provides numerous configuration options for modifying its appearance, such as the sizes and colors of its hands. The watch provides an hour, minute, and second hand, each of which is movable. This allows the user to select a time by using the mouse instead of the keyboard. Once selected, the selected time can be retrieved with the *get* method. The watch also provides two radiobuttons for determining whether the specified time is A.M. or P.M.

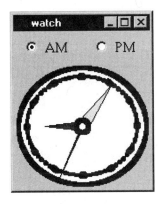

```
wm title . watch
iwidgets::watch .ironman -labelfont 6x10 -hourradius .6
.ironman show 09:06:34
pack .ironman
```

Class Model

The watch [incr Widget] inherits directly from itk::Widget. It does not interact with any other [incr Widgets] outside of its inheritance tree.

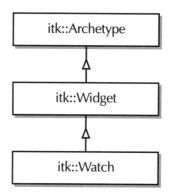

Configuration Options

Standard Options

Refer to the options man page for information on these standard options:

activebackground	activeforeground	background	cursor
disabledforeground	foreground	highlightcolor	highlightthickness
insertbackground	insertborderwidth	insertofftime	insertontime
selectbackground	selectborderwidth	selectforeground	

Associated Options

Refer to the associated Tk widget for information on this option:

Option Name	Associated With
selectcolor	radiobutton

Inherited Options

Refer to Chapter 11 for information on this inherited option from the [incr Tk] Archetype base class:

Option Name	Inherited From
clientdata	itk::Archetype

Widget-Specific Options

-clockcolor

Resource name: clockColor
Resource class: Color
Description: Specifies the background color for the watch.
Default value: white

-clockstipple

Resource name: clockStipple
Resource class: ClockStipple
Description: Specifies the stipple pattern to be used for the watch background color.
Default value: {}

-height

Resource name: height
Resource class: Height
Description: Specifies the height of the watch.
Default value: 175 (pixels)

-hourcolor

Resource name: hourColor
Resource class: Color
Description: Specifies the fill color to use for the hour hand on the watch.
Default value: red

-hourradius

Resource name: hourRadius
Resource class: Radius
Description: Specifies the length of the hour hand relative to the radius of the watch. This value is a percentage.
Default value: .50

-labelfont

Resource name: labelFont
Resource class: Font
Description: Specifies the font to be used for the A.M. and P.M. radiobuttons.
Default value: -*-Courier-Medium-R-Normal-*-120-*-*-*-*-*-*

14

-minutecolor

Resource name: minuteColor
Resource class: Color
Description: Specifies the fill color to be used for the minute hand on the watch.
Default value: yellow

-minuteradius

Resource name: minuteRadius
Resource class: Radius
Description: Specifies the length of the minute hand relative to the radius of the watch. This value is a percentage.
Default value: .80

-pivotcolor

Resource name: pivotColor
Resource class: Color
Description: Specifies the fill color to be used for the pivot point in the center of the watch.
Default value: white

-secondcolor

Resource name: secondColor
Resource class: Color
Description: Specifies the fill color to be used for the second hand on the watch.
Default value: yellow

-secondradius

Resource name: secondRadius
Resource class: Radius
Description: Specifies the length of the second hand relative to the radius of the watch. This value is a percentage.
Default value: .90

-showampm

Resource name: showAmPm
Resource class: ShowAmPm
Description: Boolean value that specifies whether to display the A.M. and P.M. radiobuttons. If configured as a false value, then the radiobuttons are withdrawn, not destroyed.
Default value: true

-state

Resource name: state
Resource class: State
Description: Specifies the state of the watch. Valid values are normal and disabled. If disabled, all input events are disallowed.
Default value: normal

-tickcolor

Resource name: tickColor
Resource class: Color
Description: Specifies the fill color of the tick marks around the perimeter of the watch. Note that this option only works in post-itcl3.0.1 releases.
Default value: black

-width

Resource name: width
Resource class: Width
Description: Specifies the width of the watch.
Default value: 155 (pixels)

Public Methods
Associated Methods
None

Inherited Methods

Refer to Chapter 11 for information on each of these inherited methods from the itk::Archetype base class:

Method Name	Inherited From
cget	itk::Archetype
component	itk::Archetype
config	itk::Archetype
configure	itk::Archetype

Widget-Specific Methods

get

Usage: pathName *get* ?format?
Description: Returns the current time shown on the watch according to the format argument, which may be either -string or -clicks. If -string is specified (this is the default value), then the time is returned as "hour:minute:second AM/PM". If -clicks is specified, then the **clock** command is used to return an integer value representing the specified time. See the clock man page for more information on this value.

show

Usage: pathName *show* time
Description: Configures the watch to display the time specified by the time argument. This may be an explicit time such as 23:09:47 or a relative time like "1 hour ago". See the clock man page for more details on time formatting and valid relative time strings.

watch

Usage: pathName *watch* args
Description: Evaluates the specified arguments against the canvas component. You can use this method to directly access the watch by accessing the actual canvas tags that represent it.

Components

The watch [incr Widget] is composed of two radiobuttons, a canvas, and a frame, as outlined in the following table. Each of these is packed into the hull frame component.

Name	Class	Description
am	Radiobutton	The A.M. radiobutton
canvas	Canvas	The canvas in which the actual watch figure is drawn
frame	Frame	The frame around the A.M. and P.M. radiobuttons
hull	Watch	The frame around the entire watch
pm	Radiobutton	The P.M. radiobutton

Index

defining base classes allowing for, 257–258
defining derived classes for, 258–260
limitations on [incr Tcl], 263–265
naming ambiguities, 262–263
purpose of, 252–253
testing code for, 260–261
See also inheritance

N

names
ambiguities in and multiple inheritance,
262–263
auto-generated object, 115, 120–121
avoiding conflicts for object, 15–18
avoiding using fully qualified command,
313–314
conventions for mega-widgets, 335, 336
declaring identical method names in inheritance
tree, 60–62
of files containing namespaces, 315–316
fully qualified, 313–314, 316–317
registering object, 119–120
namespace command
accessing private class methods with, 56
as Tcl command, 308
namespace current command, 316–317, 318
namespace eval command, 309
namespace export command, 312
namespace import command, 312, 313–314
namespace qualifiers
declaring identical method names in inheritance
tree, 60–62
preceding commands, 5, 9
with *this* variable, 80–81
namespace resolution. *See* namespaces
namespaces, 308–328
about, 308–314
access control for, 311–314
as classes, 308
encapsulation by, 310–311
usage of, 309–310
automatically loading packages, 315
creating for class definitions, 110
creating packages, 321–328
implementing namespace and loading
packages, 321–324
setting up package, 324–328
leaving objects undeleted in, 205–206
moving between namespaces, 314–321

object visibility, 314–318
variable visibility, 318–321
portability of packages, 308, 328
resolving
accessing overloaded base class methods
by, 244–246
building tables for methods and variables
in class definition, 114
with ServerSocket objects, 174
with *this* variable, 81
verifying class name is unique in, 106, 107–108
See also packages
naming, omitting reserved characters from class names,
109–110
network-oriented application, 236–237
Node objects, 324
notebook [incr Widget], 572–578
class model, 573
components, 578
configuration options, 574–575
public methods, 575–578

O

object creation, 115–120
object lifetime, 205–212
creating temporary objects, 206–207
implementing alternative definition for Trace
using local command, 208–212
leaving objects undeleted in namespace,
205–206
object visibility, 314–318
Object-Oriented Analysis and Design with Applications
(Booch), 253
object-oriented programming. *See* OOP
objects
auto-generated names for, 120–121
creating, 12–18
adding new components to class
definitions, 14–15
copies with copy constructors, 135–136
naming conflicts, 15–18
role of constructors in, 12–13
temporary, 206–207
deconstructor errors and, 131–132
deleting, 20–22
getting started with, 4–8
registering with other objects using *this* variable,
86–89
relationship to classes, 7–8